JAVA LANGUAGE
API SUPERBIBLE

Dan Groner, K.C. Hopson,
Harish Prabandham, Todd Sundsted

BWPQ

**WAITE
GROUP
PRESS™**

A Division of
Sams Publishing

Corte Madera, CA

PUBLISHER: Mitchell Waite
ASSOCIATE PUBLISHER: Charles Drucker
ACQUISITIONS MANAGER: Jill Pisoni
ACQUISITIONS EDITOR: Joanne Miller

EDITORIAL DIRECTOR: John Crudo
PROJECT EDITOR: Lisa Goldstein
CONTENT EDITOR: Frank Pittelli
TECHNICAL REVIEWERS: Glenn Twiggs, Bob Besaha, Ethan Henry
COPY EDITORS: Merilee Eggleston

PRODUCTION DIRECTOR: Julianne Ososke
PRODUCTION MANAGER: Cecile Kaufman
PRODUCTION EDITOR: Mark Nigara
SENIOR DESIGNER: Sestina Quarequio
DESIGNER: Karen Johnston
PRODUCTION: Mona Brown, Charlotte Clapp, Cheryl Dietsch, Mike Henry, Carl Pierce, Mark Walchle
ILLUSTRATIONS: Larry Wilson
COVER IMAGE: ©Steven Hunt/Image Bank

© 1996 by The Waite Group, Inc.
Published by Waite Group Press™, 200 Tamal Plaza, Corte Madera, CA 94925

Waite Group Press is a division of Sams Publishing.

Printed in the United States of America
96 97 98 99 • 10 9 8 7 6 5 4 3 2 1

Library of Congress Cataloging-in-Publication Data
Java language API superbible: the comprehensive reference to the Java programming language:
everything you need to know about the standard language, input/output,
and debugging classes / Daniel Groner..[et al..]
p.   cm.
Includes index.
ISBN (invalid) 1-57169-038-7
1. Java (Computer program language)
I. Groner, Daniel, 1959–
QA76.73.J38J37   1996
005.13'3--dc20

                                                        96-27012

                                                        CIP

Dedications

To Mom, Dad, and Susan.

—Dan Groner

To my wonderful wife, Ann.

—K.C. Hopson

To my parents for the support and encouragement in
every phase of my life.

—Harish Prabandham

To Tracy, Samantha, and Katherine.

—Todd Sundsted

Message from the
Publisher

WELCOME TO OUR NERVOUS SYSTEM

Some people say that the World Wide Web is a graphical extension of the information superhighway, just a network of humans and machines sending each other long lists of the equivalent of digital junk mail.

I think it is much more than that. To me, the Web is nothing less than the nervous system of the entire planet—not just a collection of computer brains connected together, but more like a billion silicon neurons entangled and recirculating electro-chemical signals of information and data, each contributing to the birth of another CPU and another Web site.

Think of each person's hard disk connected at once to every other hard disk on earth, driven by human navigators searching like Columbus for the New World. Seen this way, the Web is more of a super entity, a growing, living thing, controlled by the universal human will to expand, to be more. Yet, unlike a purposeful business plan with rigid rules, the Web expands in a nonlinear, unpredictable, creative way that echoes natural evolution.

We created our Web site not just to extend the reach of our computer book products but to be part of this synaptic neural network, to experience, like a nerve in the body, the flow of ideas, and then to pass those ideas up the food chain of the mind. Your mind. Even more, we wanted to pump some of our own creative juices into this rich wine of technology.

TASTE OUR DIGITAL WINE

And so we ask you to taste our wine by visiting the body of our business. Begin by understanding the metaphor we have created for our Web site—a universal learning center, situated in outer space in the form of a space station. A place where you can journey to study any topic from the convenience of your own screen. Right now we are focusing on computer topics, but the stars are the limit on the Web.

If you are interested in discussing this Web site or finding out more about the Waite Group, please send me e-mail with your comments and I will be happy to respond. Being a programmer myself, I love to talk about technology and find out what our readers are looking for.

Sincerely,

Mitchell Waite

Mitchell Waite, C.E.O. and Publisher

200 Tamal Plaza
Corte Madera CA 94925
415-924-2575
415-924-2576 fax

Internet email:
support@waite.com

Website:
http://www.waite.com/waite

CREATING THE HIGHEST QUALITY COMPUTER BOOKS IN THE INDUSTRY

Waite Group Press
Waite Group New Media

Come Visit
WAITE.COM
Waite Group Press
World Wide Web Site

Now find all the latest information on Waite Group books at our new Web site, **http://www.waite.com/waite.** You'll find an online catalog where you can examine and order any title, review upcoming books, and send email to our authors and editors. Our FTP site has all you need to update your book: the latest program listings, errata sheets, most recent versions of Fractint, POV Ray, Polyray, DMorph, and all the programs featured in our books. So download, talk to us, ask questions, on **http://www.waite.com/waite.**

The New Arrivals Room has all our new books listed by month. Just click for a description, Index, Table of Contents, and links to authors.

The Backlist Room has all our books listed alphabetically.

The People Room is where you'll interact with Waite Group employees.

Links to Cyberspace get you in touch with other computer book publishers and other interesting Web sites.

The FTP site contains all program listings, errata sheets, etc.

The Order Room is where you can order any of our books online.

The Subject Room contains typical book pages which show description, Index, Table of Contents, and links to authors.

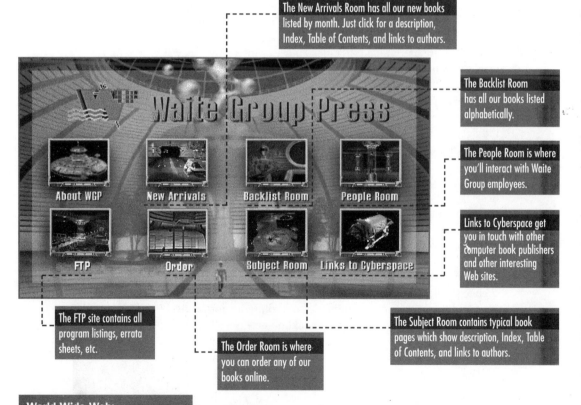

World Wide Web:

COME SURF OUR TURF—THE WAITE GROUP WEB

http://www.waite.com/waite
Gopher: gopher.waite.com
FTP: ftp.waite.com

About the Authors

Daniel Groner develops financial software that focuses on analytical libraries and applications, as well as optimization models. He has also developed models and applications for production and distribution planning. He received his B.S. and M. Eng. in Operations Research from Cornell University, and an M.B.A. in Finance from the University of Chicago. Dan can be reached at TheGroners@worldnet.att.net.

K.C. Hopson is President of Geist Software and Services, Inc., an independent consultant firm in the Baltimore/Washington D.C. metro area. However, K.C. thrives in cyberspace and enjoys using it to work anywhere in the world. He specializes in distributed computing solutions and has deep experience in GUI programming (especially Windows), relational databases, and client/server. K.C. was a lead architect of the software used in Bell Atlantic's Stargazer interactive television system. He writes regularly about Java for *Internet Advisor* and is co-author of the book *Developing Professional Java Applets*. K.C. has a B.S. in Applied Mathematics from University of California, Irvine and a Masters in Computer Science from University of Maryland, Baltimore County. In his spare time, K.C. enjoys his family, studies history, and indulges in music and literature. He can be reached at chopson@universe.digex.net or visit his home page at http://www.universe.digex.net/~chopson.

Harish Prabandham is a software developer with three years experience in design and development of multimedia systems, compilers, and distributed object-oriented systems. His current interests include Componentware, Java, and other Internet-related technologies. He received his M.S. in Computer Science in India in 1993. Readers are welcome to contact him via e-mail at harish@finex.com.

Todd Sundsted is an engineer at Southern Company Services and an Internet and Web technologies educator and consultant for companies interested in implementing Internet based applications. Todd is also a columnist for *JavaWorld,* an online magazine. You can reach him at tsund@quicklink.net.

Table of Contents

Contents

Contents

Contents

Contents

Introduction

Right now you are probably asking yourself, "Do I really need a 1,000-page book on Java?"

This is a good question, especially if you rarely get through a Tom Clancy novel, or if you don't like carrying things approaching your own weight.

Why a SuperBible?

One of Java's strengths is that the language covers so much. This is a departure from the C language, where a bare minimum of capabilities is defined. This minimalism was a boon for compiler writers, but has proven to be a barrier for those of us developing complex, multiplatform applications. Other languages, like C++, started minimally and have been growing over time. But Java's initial substantial, standardized capabilities has been instrumental in its becoming *the* Internet and multiplatform language.

It is precisely Java's breadth that makes a comprehensive guide so valuable for both the applet and application developer. This book, along with the companion volume, *Java Networking and AWT API SuperBible*, covers *every* method and variable in *every* Java package, as of version 1 of the language. In particular, this volume covers the Java language and the java.lang and java.io packages, as well as the sun.debug package. The enclosed CD contains chapters that cover the java.util package.

As broad as Java is today, it is also just a starting point. Database access, multimedia features, extensions for commerce—these are already proposed or being considered. Whatever forms these may take, they will be rooted in the fundamentals of Java and its core classes. You will be better prepared for these new features by having an in-depth understanding of the language and java.lang package.

Audience

This book assumes you know a programming language like C, and are familiar with object-oriented concepts. If you already know an object-oriented language, like C++, Objective-C, or Smalltalk, you'll be able to get up to speed that much faster. Even if you already know Java, this book provides you with a complete, quick reference to the lang, io, util, and debug packages.

How This Book Is Organized

The opening chapters of the book give you a tour of Java and details on the syntax of the Java language. The rest of the book describes particular Java classes, and provides detailed reference sections covering the APIs. These chapters are organized into four parts: basic classes, execution classes, I/O, and debugging.

Part I: Overview of Java

Chapter 1, Welcome to Java, surveys the language, its capabilities, and the various standard class libraries ("packages," in Java terms). Chapter 2, The Java Language, details each facet of the language, including primitives, statements, classes, arrays, packages, error handling, and synchronization.

Part II: Basic Classes

In this second section, the core Java classes are covered. Chapter 3, Global Classes, describes the Object class, which every other Java class is based on. The Class class and the Runnable interface are also detailed.

Chapter 4, Numbers, covers the classes that represent numbers (Number, Double, Float, Integer, and Long), and the mathematical operations provided by the Math class. In Chapter 5, Boolean and Character Classes, details of the class analogs to these Java primitives are presented. Chapter 6, Classes String and StringBuffer, describes these Java classes for representing character sequences.

Part III: Execution Classes

In this part, the rest of the classes in the java.lang package are covered. These classes relate to the running of Java applets and applications. Chapter 7, System Classes, details the System, Runtime, and Process classes. In Chapter 8, Thread and ThreadGroup, the classes and interfaces that facilitate multithreaded programs are covered. Java's error handling facilities are described in Chapter 9, Exceptions. The highly dynamic facilities in Java are discussed in Chapter 10, ClassLoader and SecurityManager.

Part IV: Java I/O

The input/output facilities in Java are covered in this part. Chapter 11, Basic I/O, covers those classes involved in standard input and output. Files in Java are described in Chapter 12, File I/O. The remaining I/O classes, including those dealing with bytearray, buffered, sequential, and linenumber streams, are in Chapter 13, Additional I/O.

Part V: Java Debugging Tools

This last part covers the sun.debug package, which augments the primary Java packages. Chapter 14, Java Debugging Model, describes the debugging-related classes that mirror Java types.

Appendixes

Convenient references for Java classes and exceptions are provided in Appendix A, Class and Interface Inheritance Diagrams, and Appendix B, Exception Cross-Reference. Appendix C, Writing Native Methods in C/C++, details the steps for calling other functions written in other languages, such as C, from Java. Appendix D, Glossary, is an alphabetical list of definitions for terms used in this book. Finally, Appendix E, Using the Enclosed CD-ROM, gives an overview of what's on the CD.

On the CD: Java Utility Classes

There were a lot of other things that we wanted to include in this book, but we just couldn't bind that many pages. Instead, included on the CD is Java Utilities, which is taken from the *Java Networking and AWT API SuperBible*. These chapters document the java.util classes, including collections (Dictionary, Hashtable, Vector, Stack, Enumerations, BitSet), Java's date class, and the Observable-Observer pair. The format of these chapters is the same as those in this book.

About the Projects

One of the unique aspects of this book is that woven into each chapter is a substantive project. This serves two purposes. First, it provides a way to bring together the concepts presented in the chapter. Second, you get code that you may find useful, either as a model or as is. (Note that all project code is printed in the book, as well as included on the CD.) In a language as new as Java, where certain functionality is not yet available, this can be especially helpful.

For example, Chapter 4, Numbers, includes a class for formatting numbers. To most programmers, this might sound academic, but indeed, Java has no built-in facility for this. Chapter 6, Classes String and StringBuffer, includes a pair of classes for parsing a mathematical expression. Chapter 7, System Classes, illustrates how to launch a child Java process from a parent, and communicate between the two. (The ability to establish communication between a parent and a child should never be underestimated!) File I/O is illustrated in Chapter 12, File I/O, in a project that implements a simple yet functional database.

Examples

In addition to each chapter's project, there is sample code provided with each method's reference entry. Certain examples may need some helper code in order to run. Generally, you can surround any provided code fragments with

```
class test {
    public static void main(String args[]) {

    // place code fragment below here

    }
}
```

One Lump or Two?

Well, you didn't expect to get this far without a Java pun, right? You will see a variety of programming styles in this book, representing the variety of authors. This is intentional, to help highlight the different ways Java allows you to approach problems.

Whether you read this book from front to back, or employ it as a reference, we hope it helps you unleash Java's power, whatever your needs may be. We're sure Java has set the stage for some great things to come—we wish you luck in being part of them.

About the CD-ROM

The CD-ROM included with this book contains the source code for many examples and all of the projects in the book. It also contains the Java Developer's Kit (JDK) tools, and chapters that cover the Java utility package classes (java.util), from the *Java Networking and AWT SuperBible*. These bonus chapters are provided in Acrobat format; an Acrobat reader is also provided on the CD. The organization of these files is explained in Appendix E, Using the Enclosed CD-ROM.

You can copy the chapter files to your hard disk, or use them directly from your CD. There is no "setup" program provided with the chapter files—you can copy these files as you would any others, using operating system commands or a file manager. For installation instructions pertaining to the JDK and the Acrobat reader, see information contained in those directories.

Assistance

If you have difficulty with the CD, technical assistance can be obtained from the Waite Group Press through these channels:

Phone: (415) 924-8102
E-mail: support@waite.com
Mail: 200 Tamal Plaza, Suite 101
         Corte Madera, CA 94925

PART I

OVERVIEW OF JAVA

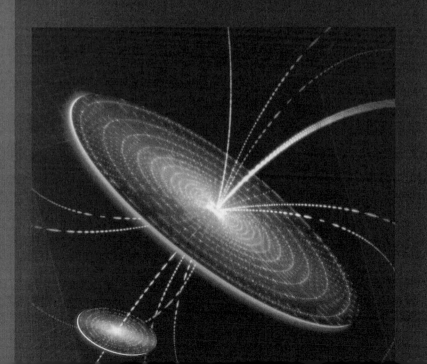

1

WELCOME TO JAVA

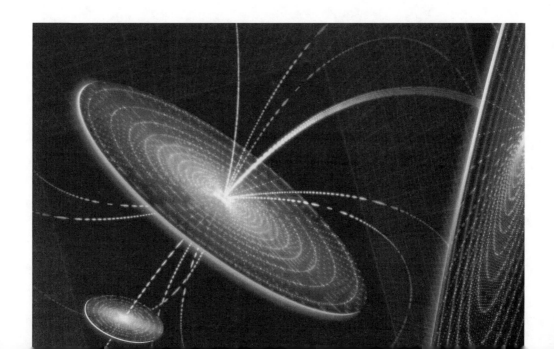

1

WELCOME TO JAVA

Java is a portable, secure, object-oriented language that is suitable for software development projects of all sizes. Sun Microsystems developed Java and released it, along with a World Wide Web browser named HotJava that was implemented entirely in Java, in the late spring of 1995. Since then, the Java programming language has been the focus of an incredible amount of attention—from developers, software companies, and from the media. At this point in time, Java stands a good chance of becoming *the* language for creating applications that span the Internet. Only time will tell whether or not it lives up to these expectations.

When the Java developers created the language, they drew their inspiration from a number of existing languages. Java's syntax is reminiscent of C and C++. Its class library combines ideas from the class libraries of Smalltalk and Objective-C. The language supports exceptions, as does Ada and the current incarnation of C++. Even garbage collection, a common feature of interactive languages such as LISP and Smalltalk, is present in Java.

However, do not let this list of features fool you into thinking that the developers of Java took the "kitchen sink" approach to designing a new programming language. In fact, Java is syntactically very clean, and very easy to learn. Java took the best parts from a number of programming languages, while ignoring their less useful and more complex aspects.

As can be seen from the classic Hello, World program shown in Listing 1-1, a Java program need not be complicated. This program is a Java *application*—a stand-alone program invoked directly from the command line. For many, Java is better known for *applets*. An applet is a Java program that is executed within a Web browser. Listing 1-2 presents the Java source code for a Hello, World applet. Figure 1-1 is a screenshot of this applet in action.

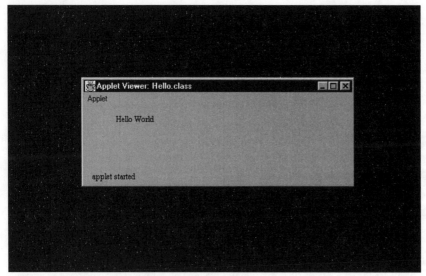

Figure 1-1   The Hello, World applet in action

Listing 1-1 A Hello, World application

```
public class Hello
{
    public static void main(String [] args)
    {
        System.out.println("Hello World");
    }
}
```

Listing 1-2 A Hello, World applet

```
import java.applet.Applet;
import java.awt.Graphics;

public class HelloApplet extends Applet
{
    public void init()
    {
        resize(150, 25);
    }
    public void paint(Graphics g)
    {
        g.drawString("Hello World", 50, 25);
    }
}
```

The History of Java

Even though the Java programming language is now thought of primarily in connection with the World Wide Web, its origin actually predates the Web.

Java began life as the programming language Oak. Oak was developed by members of the Green project, a group formed in the early '90s to create products for the smart consumer electronics market. The team decided that existing programming languages were not well suited for use in consumer electronics, so they created a new programming language. Oak included several features necessary for use in consumer electronics—features such as portability, simplicity, and robustness.

The smart consumer electronics market did not materialize as quickly as expected, so in 1993 members of the Green project (now known as FirstPerson, Inc.) began to explore another emerging market—the *set-top box* market. Oak was well suited for use in set-top boxes, since it produced code that was small and platform independent—more importantly, it included security features not found in any other language. Unfortunately, the set-top box market also failed to materialize as desired. The designers of Oak were left with a language and nothing to use it for.

What Is a Set-Top Box?

A set-top box is the brains of a system that turns a home television set into an interactive gateway to the world. Similar to but more powerful than the current generation of cable television boxes, a set-top box provides the user with access to services such as on-demand television programming, online shopping, and even the Internet.

During this time, the World Wide Web reached critical mass. Only a year earlier, Mosaic, the first graphical Web browser, hit the streets, and people all over the world began to take a look at the Internet and the World Wide Web. Members of the original project team realized that Oak provided the features necessary to create a very powerful, platform-independent, fully extensible browser for the World Wide Web. Java, though constructed for another purpose entirely, turned out to be a perfect match for the Web.

Surprisingly enough, the thinking has now come almost full circle, and Java is once again being considered for use in a variety of applications, including consumer electronics.

The Object-Oriented Features of Java

Java is an object-oriented programming language. Object-oriented programming languages possess the following four major characteristics:

- Objects
- Encapsulation

- Inheritance and specialization
- Polymorphism

Objects

The object-oriented paradigm encourages programmers to view the world as a collection of objects with well-defined attributes and behaviors. Object-oriented programming languages allow programmers to formally define these objects, and to define their interactions. In order for a language to be an object-oriented programming language, it must first possess a well-defined notion of an object.

The Java programming language is a class-based object-oriented language—every object is an instance of a class. A class definition specifies the attributes and behaviors of the objects that belong to that class. Objects are created by *instantiating* a class with the *new* operator, as illustrated in Listing 1-3.

Listing 1-3 Instantiation

```
Point p = new Point();

SystemValue sv = new SystemValue(p);
```

Encapsulation

As mentioned above, all objects have attributes and behaviors. Attributes describe an object. Behaviors define how an object interacts with other objects. In an object-oriented programming language, the values of these attributes and the definition of these behaviors must be part of the object—they are encapsulated within the object.

To help you understand what this means from a programmer's standpoint, consider an application that manipulates Widgets. Widgets have two attributes—their identifier and their color. They also have two behaviors. One behavior, when invoked, returns the Widget's color. The other behavior, when invoked, prints a message about the Widget's color to the screen.

In an application that models Widgets, the attributes and behaviors may be stored in any number of locations. The information may be stored as part of the program logic—perhaps in a *switch* statement. For an example of this type of organization, consider the code in Listing 1-4 in which the attributes and behaviors of a Widget object are distributed throughout the application.

Listing 1-4 Distributed Widget attributes and behaviors

```
procedure get_color(widget_id)
   switch (widget_id)
      case 1
         return blue
      case 2
         return red


      .
      .
      .


procedure do_print(widget_id)
   switch (widget_id)
      case 1
         print "blue widget selected..."
      case 2
         print "red widget selected..."
```

Object-oriented programming languages, however, encourage the programmer to capture all of the behavior and attributes of an object within the object itself, as in the code in Listing 1-5.

Listing 1-5 Encapsulated Widget attributes and behaviors

```
object RedWidget
   data id = 1
   data color = red
   procedure get_color() { return color }
   procedure do_print() { print color + " widget selected..." }

object BlueWidget
   data id = 2
   data color = blue
   procedure get_color() { return color }
   procedure do_print() { print color + " widget selected..." }
```

Objects in Java are instances of a class. An object's attributes and behaviors are part of the class definition. Attributes correspond to the class's instance variables. Behaviors correspond to the class's methods. The values in the instance variables of an object of a particular class may differ from those of another object of that class, but both share the same methods. Figure 1-2 illustrates this fact. Listing 1-6 contains the Java language implementation of a Widget class. A red Widget object and a blue Widget object, corresponding to the objects described earlier, could be created by instantiating this class.

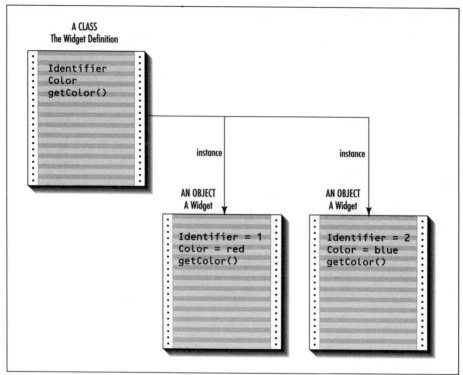

Figure 1-2 Classes and objects

Listing 1-6 Class Widget

```
class Widget
{
   int nId;
   String strColor;

   public Widget(int n, String str)
   {
      nId = n;
      strColor = str;
   }

   public String getColor()
   {
      return strColor;
   }

   public void doPrint()
   {
      System.out.println(strColor + " widget selected...");
   }
}
```

Inheritance and Specialization

A programmer may define a new object by elaborating upon the definition of an existing object. The new object inherits all of the attributes and behaviors of the original object. Additional attributes and behaviors may be added to, but not deleted from, the new object's definition. New objects are said to be "derived from" the original object.

Figure 1-3 depicts two objects. The Employee object defines the attributes and behaviors of an imaginary employee. This Employee object has a name, a Social Security number, and a function within the organization. The behavior goToLunch() sends the Employee object to the cafeteria for something to eat. The behavior goHome() sends the Employee object home. The Vice President object defines the attributes and behaviors of an imaginary vice president. The Vice President object also has a name, a Social Security number, and a function designation. In addition, a Vice President object has an expense account number. The behavior goToLunch() sends the Vice President object to the executive dining room rather than the cafeteria. The behavior goHome() sends the Vice President object home.

A brief examination of the two objects described above reveals that the Vice President object has all of the attributes of the Employee object. The Vice President object also has all of the behaviors of the Employee object (although its destination for lunch is different). It is therefore possible to define the Vice President object in terms of the Employee object. The definition of the Vice President object is said to "inherit from" the definition of the Employee object. The behavior goToLunch() must be redefined in the Vice President object. In addition, the expense account number attribute must be added to the Vice President object's definition since it is not present in the Employee object. A Vice President object is now a special type of Employee object. Figure 1-4 illustrates this arrangement.

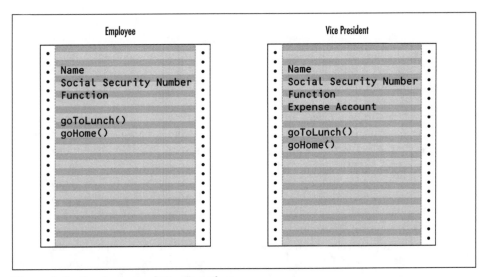

Figure 1-3 Employees and Vice Presidents

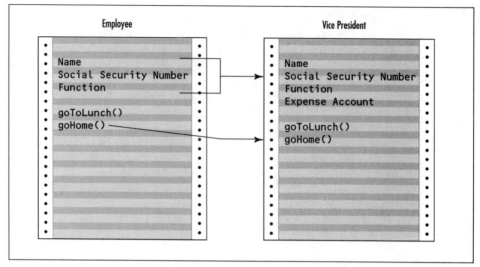

Figure 1-4 A Vice President as a special type of employee

In Java, a programmer defines a new class of objects by "extending" the definition of an existing class of objects. The new class inherits all of the instance variables and methods of the original class. The operation of any of the original methods can be changed simply by redefining that method in the new class. Additional instance variables and methods can be added to the new class as necessary. Instance variables and methods from the original class cannot be deleted in the new class, because the new class must provide the same functionality that was present in the original class.

Polymorphism

Since a programmer cannot delete attributes and behaviors when extending an object, a newly derived object may be used as if it were the original object; none of the necessary functionality is missing (although it may have been redefined). A procedure that invokes a behavior of the original object will also invoke the same behavior of the newly defined object without any modification.

Figure 1-5 illustrates a Send-To-Lunch machine. This machine takes a group of Employee objects and sends them off to lunch by invoking their goToLunch() method. If a Vice President object is added to this group, the Send-To-Lunch machine will send every object to the correct location for lunch—Employee objects to the cafeteria and the Vice President object to the executive dining room. The Send-To-Lunch machine works correctly without knowing anything more about the objects in the group than that they are all Employee objects (or are derived from an Employee object) and have a method named goToLunch().

The Vice President object can be used wherever the Employee object is valid. However, the reverse is not true. The original object cannot be used wherever the new object is required. If you don't understand why, try renting a car on your vice president's expense account.

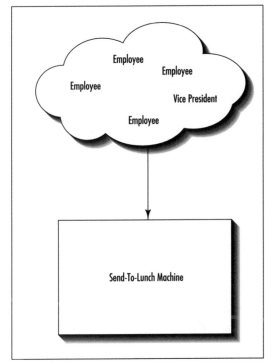

Figure 1-5 The Send-To-Lunch machine

Polymorphism in Java is achieved via references. A reference is a variable that "refers to" an object. A reference declaration specifies the class of objects that a reference refers to. A reference thus declared may refer to any object of that class or of any class derived from it. Listing 1-7 illustrates polymorphism in action. The method testBase() accepts objects created from class Derived because such objects are guaranteed to provide the same functionality as objects created from class Base. The method testDerived() will not accept objects created from class Base, however, because such objects may not provide all of the instance variables and methods available in objects created from class Derived.

Listing 1-7 References

```
class Base { }
class Derived extends Base { }

    .
    .
    .

class Test
{
```

continued on next page

continued from previous page

```
Base base;
Derived derived;

void testBase(Base b) ...
void testDerived(Derived d) ...

Test()
{
   base = new Base();
   derived = new Derived();

   testBase(base);          // this is okay
   testBase(derived);       // this is okay

   testDerived(derived);    // this is okay
   testDerived(base);       // this is not
```

.
.

Three More Features of Java

In addition to objects, the Java programming language provides several features designed to ease the task of developing modern software. This section covers three of those features—threads, automatic memory management, and exceptions. Security and portability, two additional features of importance, are covered at the end of the chapter, in conjunction with the World Wide Web.

Threads

Modern applications typically need to do more than one operation at a time. A typical interactive, network application might need to send and receive information over a network, get data from the user, and process both—all at the same time. Java supports the development of such applications by providing threads.

A thread is a flow of execution through an application. A thread may operate independently of any other thread in an application. Or multiple threads may work together. The important point is that threads may execute concurrently.

The Java class library is thread safe. A thread safe class library protects the threads in an application from inadvertently interfering with each other when they both use the classes and methods in the library.

Automatic Memory Management and Garbage Collection

Java removes the burden of memory management from the shoulders of the programmer. Languages such as C and C++ require the programmer to explicitly allocate and deallocate much of the memory used by a program. In order to do this, the programmer must keep track of what memory is currently being referenced and what memory is no longer needed. Experience has shown that this task is not as simple as it sounds, yet it is critically important to get it right. If unused memory is not freed, an application will eventually reach a point where it is unable to request enough memory from the operating system to continue execution. If memory is freed more than once, the memory allocation system can become corrupted.

Java provides the *new* operator to allocate memory, in the form of objects, from the operating system. Objects no longer referenced in a program are reclaimed automatically by the garbage collector. The garbage collector runs independently of the main program (as a separate thread) and automatically frees any memory that is not being used. This task is totally transparent to the programmer.

Exceptions

Exceptions interrupt the normal processing flow in a Java program to report exceptional conditions that have occurred at a lower level in the program to a handler at a higher level. Exceptions allow a programmer to handle unusual or unexpected conditions without having to clutter the flow of program code with endless error checks. The result is program code that is easier to read and more robust (programmers often forget to explicitly check for error conditions). In addition, all handling of exceptional conditions can be deferred and dealt with at a single point in the code.

The Structure of a Java Program

The two Hello, World examples presented at the beginning of this chapter are not very ambitious demonstrations of Java programming. Real programs define more than one class and are often spread across multiple source files. They also make use of predefined classes from class libraries, such as the one supplied with the Java Developer's Kit (JDK). Class libraries are typically organized into packages. Before you begin your first program, it is important that you understand how Java uses classes, files, and packages.

The Class Definition

The class definition is the principal building block of a Java program. Unlike object-oriented languages such as C++, Java demands that you define all variables and procedures within the context of a class definition.

Java classes are defined within source files. These source files must end with the .java extension. Unlike languages like C and C++, which allow you to split class definitions between a header file (that typically defines the interface) and a source file (that typically contains the implementation), the Java programming language uses only source files. Furthermore, the Java compiler requires a class to be completely defined within a single source file. The class definition may not be spread throughout several source files, as is possible in C++ (native methods are an exception to this rule—refer to Appendix C, Writing Native Methods in C/C++, if you would like to learn more about native methods).

Although a class definition must be contained completely within a single source file, a source file may contain more than one class definition. Figure 1-6 illustrates this arrangement. A typical source file will contain one primary class definition and the definitions of zero or more helper classes. The helper classes assist the primary class in performing its duties.

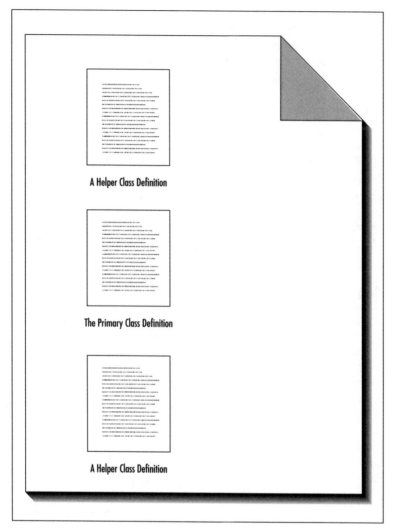

Figure 1-6   Classes and source files

The Package

A package is a convenient mechanism for organizing classes. All of the classes defined in a single source file belong to the same package. The package to which the classes belong may be specified in the source file explicitly. If a source file does not explicitly specify a package, its classes all belong to the default package. Several source files may define classes that belong to the same package. Figure 1-7 shows how the classes from multiple source files are grouped together as a single package. Packages are often organized so that they can be used in more than one program. They play the same role that libraries play in other languages.

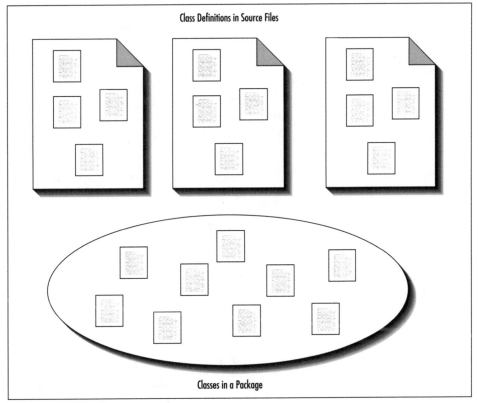

Figure 1-7 Classes and packages

The Java Developer's Kit

Unless you already own a third-party Java development environment, you must obtain and install a copy of the JDK before you can compile your first Java program. The JDK was developed by Sun Microsystems and is distributed free of charge.

Obtaining a Copy

The JDK for Windows95/NT, Solaris, and Macintosh systems are included on the CD-ROM that comes with this book. You can also download the JDK from Sun's Web pages at http://www.javasoft.com/. There you will find instructions that explain how to do so.

Installation Under Windows NT/95

The JDK for Windows NT and Windows 95 is distributed as a self-extracting archive. The following instructions assume you are installing the JDK from within the DOS command line shell.

First, copy the archive to the directory in which you wish to install the JDK. If you plan to install it in the top-level directory of the C drive, copy the file there. Then enter the following at the command prompt:

```
JDK-1_0_2-win32-x86
```

The installation program will create the directory C:\JAVA and install all of the JDK files inside. The executables for the compiler and interpreter (JAVAC.EXE and JAVA.EXE) can be found in the directory C:\JAVA\BIN. To add this directory to your path, enter the following at the command prompt:

```
path %PATH%;C:\JAVA\BIN
```

If you would like your path set every time you boot your computer, you should add this command to your AUTOEXEC.BAT file.

You have now successfully installed the JDK. You are now ready to write, compile, and run your first Java program.

Installation on Solaris

The JDK for Solaris is distributed as a compressed tar file. The following instructions assume you are installing the JDK from within a command line shell.

First, copy the archive to the directory in which you wish to install the JDK. If you plan to install the JDK off the root directory, copy the file there. Then enter the following at the command prompt:

```
gunzip -c JDK-1_0_2-solaris2-sparc.tar.Z | tar xvf -
```

This command will create the directory /java and install all of the JDK files inside. The executables for the compiler and interpreter (javac and java) can be found in the directory /java/bin. You must add this directory to your path. If you use the C shell, enter the following at the command prompt:

```
setenv PATH $PATH\:/java/bin
```

If you use the Korn shell or the Bourne shell, enter the following instead:

```
PATH=$PATH:/java/bin
export PATH
```

If you would like your path set correctly every time you log in, you should add this command to your .cshrc or .profile file.

You have now successfully installed the JDK. You are ready to write, compile, and run your first Java program.

A Java Programming Primer

Java is a compiled language. This section of the chapter covers those issues related to writing, compiling, and running Java programs.

> ## Is Java Interpreted or Compiled?
> There is a lot of confusion surrounding this question. Just as in C and C++, code written in Java must be explicitly compiled from source code form into simpler machinelike instructions. Since the machine on which these instructions execute hasn't been built yet, you can't execute these instructions directly. You must make do with interpreting the machine code in a program (the virtual machine) that mimics the functionality of the nonexistent machine. Therefore, Java has features of both compiled and interpreted languages.

Editing

Java source files are simple text files. You can create them and edit them with any text editor. The JDK does not supply a text editor, but most operating systems provide one or more tools for editing text. Under Windows 95, the Notepad accessory will do the trick. From the DOS command line, use the edit command. Popular editors for Solaris include vi and emacs.

Compiling and Running

The Java compiler is named javac. Javac translates the textual description of Java language classes in a Java source file into the executable byte codes in one or more Java class files. Every source file must be compiled into a class file and must be free of errors before the interpreter will execute it.

To compile a Java language source file named A.java, enter the following at either the DOS or UNIX command prompt:

```
javac A.java
```

If a program consists of multiple source files, they can either be compiled separately or together. To compile three Java language source files named A.java, B.java, and C.java at the same time, enter the following at the command prompt:

```
javac A.java B.java C.java
```

If the source file contained no errors, the compiler will create a class file for each class definition in the source file. The class files will be created in the current directory, unless a *package* statement was included in the source file.

The code contained in a class file can be executed by the Java interpreter. To execute the code in the class file A.class, enter the command

```
java A
```

This command causes the interpreter to load the A.class class file. After it loads the data in the class file it tries to invoke the method

```
public static void main(String [] args)
```

The runtime system will issue an error message if this method does not exist in class A, and execution will terminate. The java command expects, as an argument, the name of the class, not the name of the class file. Thus the following command is incorrect:

```
java A.class
```

Java and the World Wide Web

Java's most visible domain is the World Wide Web. It is its acceptance here that has really spurred its remarkable growth. This section is therefore devoted to a discussion of Java's role in the story of the World Wide Web.

The World Wide Web

Consider the bird's-eye view of a portion of the World Wide Web presented in Figure 1-8. The World Wide Web is the name given to a loose collection of servers and clients (or browsers) whose preferred method of communication is via the underlying Internet. Servers that understand HTTP (HyperText Transfer Protocol) serve up HTML (HyperText Markup Language) documents to browsers across the Web. These servers and browsers run on a heterogeneous collection of computers.

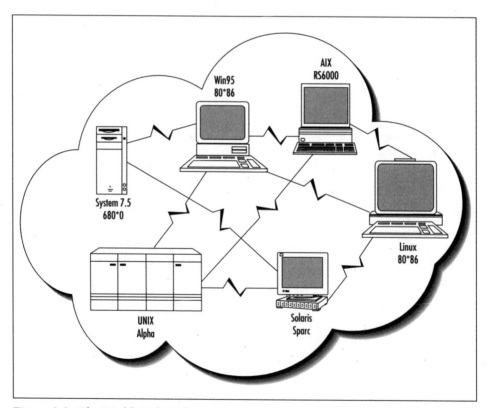

Figure 1-8 The World Wide Web

Executable Content

The Java programming language brings to the World Wide Web the ability to distribute executable content. Until the advent of the Java programming language, browsers were handicapped in two important ways. They were capable of displaying only static information, and they were limited to handling only predefined types of content. These limitations were the result of the World Wide Web's origin as a hypertext document distribution system.

The designers of browsers repeatedly solved these problems by extending the basic HTML definition. But neither problem could be solved permanently, and neither could be solved without the distribution of new versions of the improved browsers. A more general solution was necessary. Unfortunately, the only truly general solution involved distributing programs (executable content), and this created two big problems—portability and security.

Portability

Executable content, in order to be portable, must run on every available browser (or at least the majority of them). Given the number of different machines, operating systems, and browsers, this is not a trivial problem. The Java developers solved the portability problem by creating a language that is compiled into a portable intermediate representation (called byte code) rather than native machine code. The byte code is interpreted by a virtual machine, which is nothing more than a program executing on a real machine. As long as an interpreter has been written for a particular platform, any and all Java distributed via the World Wide Web will run on that machine.

Security

In this age of viruses, Trojan horses, and worms, the security problem is easy to understand. Surfing the Web involves visits to perhaps hundreds of Web pages. These pages may have executable content (in the form of applets) embedded within them. These applets execute on your machine. Since you didn't write, compile, and install every bit of that code, you cannot be sure what it is doing.

Up until now, the spread of viruses and their ilk have been controlled somewhat by limited distribution. The victim must consciously choose to download a piece of infected software. The nature of the World Wide Web, with its hypertext links and automatic transfer of embedded content, changes that model dramatically.

The Java programming language and its class library were designed from the ground up with security in mind. Security is enforced first at the level of the Java language interpreter. The interpreter verifies that byte code received from any source doesn't break any of the safety rules. Furthermore, the class library prevents applets from accessing important system resources, such as the file system. Together, these two layers provide a thick blanket of defense against attacks from malicious (or poorly designed) applets.

The Welcome to Java Project: A Fibonacci Sequence Generator

Project Overview

The project developed in this chapter calculates the members of the Fibonacci sequence. The Fibonacci sequence is a sequence of numbers with the following characteristic: Each number in the sequence is the sum of the two preceding numbers in the sequence. Figure 1-9 illustrates the method by which successive numbers are calculated. The first two numbers in the sequence are, by definition, one. The third number in the sequence is the sum of the first two numbers. The fourth number is the sum of the second and third numbers. The fifth number is the sum of the third and fourth numbers, and so on.

Calculation of the Fibonacci sequence lends itself to an iterative solution; however, this project calculates the sequence recursively. A recursive solution was selected because it better demonstrates certain features of the Java programming language—features that otherwise might not have been used. In addition, this project demonstrates how to compile and execute a Java application.

Building the Project

The following series of steps describe the project.

1. Listing 1-8 defines the FibonacciNumber class. An instance of this class represents a position in the Fibonacci sequence. Instances of this class contain three pieces of data: the number associated with this position in the Fibonacci sequence, and references to the preceding two positions in the sequence. An instance of this class calculates the number at its position in the sequence by first creating an instance of FibonacciNumber for each of the preceding two positions in the sequence and then adding their numbers. The instances of FibonacciNumber

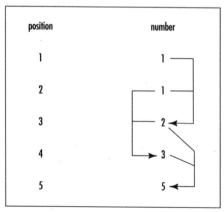

Figure 1-9　The Fibonacci sequence

corresponding to the preceding two positions in the sequence each calculate their numbers in a similar manner. This solution is recursive rather than iterative. The method valueOf() returns the number corresponding to a particular position in the Fibonacci sequence. The method toString() returns the string representation of the numbers in the sequence up to and including this position.

Listing 1-8 FibonacciNumber.java

```java
public class FibonacciNumber
{
    int nValue;
    FibonacciNumber fib1;
    FibonacciNumber fib2;

    public FibonacciNumber(int n)
    {
        if (n < 0)
            throw new IllegalArgumentException(String.valueOf(n));

        if (n == 0) nValue = 1;

        else if (n == 1)
        {
            fib1 = new FibonacciNumber(n - 1);
            nValue = fib1.valueOf();
        }

        else
        {
            fib1 = new FibonacciNumber(n - 1);
            fib2 = new FibonacciNumber(n - 2);
            nValue = fib1.valueOf() + fib2.valueOf();
        }
    }

    public int valueOf()
    {
        return nValue;
    }

    public String toString()
    {
        StringBuffer str = new StringBuffer();
        if (fib1 != null) str.append(fib1.toString() + " ");
        str.append(String.valueOf(nValue));
        return str.toString();
    }
}
```

2. Listing 1-9 defines the interface class. This class is the entry point for the program. When the program is run, the String array *args* will contain any values specified on the command line. The method Integer.parseInt() takes the string representation of an integer and converts it to a value of type int. This value specifies the position in the Fibonacci sequence of the FibonacciNumber object about to be created. The method System.out.println() prints the string representation of the value specified in its parameter list to the screen.

Listing 1-9 Main.java

```
public class Main
{
    public static void main(String [] args)
    {
        for (int i = 0; i < args.length; i++)
        {
            FibonacciNumber fib =
                new FibonacciNumber(Integer.parseInt(args[i]));
            System.out.println(args[i] + " = " + fib.toString());
        }
    }
}
```

3. Using the Java compiler, compile each of the files created in steps 1 and 2. Both files may be compiled at the same time with the command

```
javac Main.java FibonacciNumber.java
```

4. The compiler will create two class files in the current directory. The class files will be named Main.class and FibonacciNumber.class. Run the program by entering the following command at the command prompt:

```
java Main 5 11
```

5. The program should run and the print the following two lines:

```
5 = 1 1 2 3 5 8
11 = 1 1 2 3 5 8 13 21 34 55 89 144
```

6. Congratulations, you have written, compiled, and run your first Java program!

2

THE JAVA LANGUAGE

2

THE JAVA LANGUAGE

This chapter describes the Java language, as of version 1.0. Included here are details of the Java syntax needed to write applications and applets; excluded are the aspects of particular classes, which are covered in later chapters. The reader is assumed to have some exposure to C, and to C++ or another object-oriented language. The full details of the language are given in Sun's "The Java Language Specification," which is available from their Java Web site (http://www.javasoft.com).

This chapter has several sections. In the first section, some basics of Java programs are described. The second section details primitive types, such as int and float, and operations on these. Next, control flow statements are described, then classes and methods, which are the fundamental parts of a Java program. Following classes and methods, arrays are introduced. Considerations about expressions with classes and arrays are next, then program structure is described, in particular, "packages." Java's error handling facility, exceptions, is reviewed in the next section, followed by tools for multithreaded programs. The last section touches on the standard classes available in the current Java release. The details of these classes are covered in the rest of this book.

About the Project

Some of the code examples in the following sections are based on the project at the end of the chapter. Briefly, this is a code-breaking game, in which you try to guess the color sequence of a hidden code. After each guess, the game gives you clues as to how close you are by telling you how many colors are in the right place, and how many are correct colors in the wrong place. For example, if the hidden code was

```
red     blue    green   yellow
```

and your guess was

```
white   green   red
```

you would receive a clue of (1, 2), since one color is right (green), and two colors are right but in the wrong place (blue and red). Through a sequence of guesses and clues, it is possible to correctly guess the hidden code. The object of the game is to determine the hidden code in as few guesses as possible.

Basics

Java programs are written in the Unicode character set, which is a superset of ASCII. Unicode uses 16 bits to represent characters (ASCII uses 8), which allows for multilingual coverage. In most situations, though, you will still be writing programs using plain old ASCII characters.

Comments

Java continues the C++ tradition of adding another comment style. In addition to supporting C-style comments (/* comment here */), and C++-style comments (// comment from here to line end), Java introduces an extra asterisk to C-style comments in order to be picked up by automated documentation tools:

```
/** This is a Java auto-doc comment */
```

The javadoc program included in the Java Developer's Kit (JDK) generates HTML documentation based on the double-asterisk type comment.

Names and Keywords

Java programs include *names* to identify certain program items. (These items—packages, classes, interfaces, methods, variables, and statement labels—will be described in later sections.) Valid names are composed of an "unlimited" number of Unicode letters and digits, and must begin with a letter. Names cannot be Java keywords.

Java Keywords
Java keywords include those that are used in version 1 of the language, and those that are reserved for use in future versions. The keywords used in version 1 are

abstract boolean break byte case catch char class continue default do double else extends final finally float for generic if implements import instanceof int interface long native new null package private protected public return short static super switch synchronized this throw throws transient try void volatile while

In addition to these, the keywords reserved for future use are

byvalue cast const future generic goto inner operator outer rest var

---

Primitives

Although Java is object-oriented, it defines several nonobject, primitive data types, which are similar to, but not exactly like, the primitives available in C. These include the integral types (byte, short, int, long), floating-point types (float, double), a character type (char), and a logical type (boolean). Primitive types may appear as literals (e.g., 1.23), as variables (e.g., a variable named *sumtotal*), or as expressions (e.g., a + b).

Unlike C, Java specifies the size of each primitive and the resulting range of values. The language-defined sizes are one element to facilitate program portability. Also unlike C, Java does not have a choice of "signed" and "unsigned" versions of these types. The arithmetic primitives are signed, and the char primitive is implicitly unsigned. Table 2-1 summarizes the Java primitives, including their sizes and maximum values.

Table 2-1 Java primitives

Group	Subgroup	Type	Bit Size	Maximum	
Arithmetic	Integral	byte	8	255	
		short	16	32,768	
		int	32	2,147,483,647	
		long	64	9.2e18	(approx.)
	Floating point	float	32	3.4e38	(approx.)
		double	64	1.8e308	(approx.)
Nonarithmetic	Character	char	16	N/A	
	Logical	boolean	1	N/A	

Integral Literals

Java integers can be expressed in decimal, hexadecimal, or octal, and are distinguished by their beginning characters. Decimal literals start with a nonzero digit (1–9), and can have additional digits following. Hexadecimal numbers begin with 0x or 0X, and have additional hex digits (0–9, a-f, A-F) following. Octal literals begin with 0, which can be followed by octal digits (0–7). A preceding "-" can be used for negative values; technically this is not part of the literal, but is applied as a unary operator. A suffix of "L" (upper- or lowercase) can be added to indicate the value is a Java long, otherwise it is taken as an int. Table 2-2 shows some examples of integer literals.

Table 2-2 Example integer literals

Literal Type	Example
Decimal	100
Hexadecimal	0x51
Octal	0124

Floating-Point Literals

A floating point has several potential parts: a whole number, a decimal point, a fractional part, an exponent, and a type suffix. The whole-number part consists of a sequence of digits, as does the fractional part; at least one of these must be present. The exponent is indicated by an e or E, followed by a positive or negative integer. A floating-point literal is considered a double unless a type suffix of f or F is added; in this case, the literal is a float. Some example literals are shown in Table 2-3.

Table 2-3 Example floating-point literals

Literal Type	Examples	
Double	1.234	1.234e+56
Float	1.234f	1.234e5f

Boolean Literals

There are two boolean literals: *true* and *false*. Since boolean is a built-in type, these do not correspond to any particular arithmetic values (e.g., zero and one).

Character Literals

A character literal is a character (or escape sequence) in single quotes, much like in C. The escape sequences are '\b' (backspace), '\t' (tab), '\n' (linefeed), '\f' (form feed), '\r' (carriage return), '\"' (double quote), '\'' (single quote), and '\\' (backslash). Also, Unicode characters can be represented by a backslash followed by an octal value.

String Literals

String literals are any number of characters enclosed in double quotes. The escape sequences described above can be included. String literals are closely related to the String class (see Chapter 6, Classes String and StringBuffer). Although String is not a primitive type, it has a language-defined operator, +, which is used for concatenation. This gives it the appearance in certain cases of being a primitive. Some of the examples in this chapter use the String type.

Operators

As shown in Table 2-4, Java's primitive operators can be grouped according to which primitives they take as operators, as well as what functions they perform.

Table 2-4 Primitive operators

Group	Function	Operators
Arithmetic	Comparison	==, !=, <, <=, >, >=
	Unary	+, -
	Algebraic	+, -, *, /, %
	Postfix	++, --
Boolean	Relational	==, !=
	Logical	!, &, |, ^, &&, ||
Integral	Shift	<<, >>, >>>
	Bitwise	~, &, |, ^
String	Concatenation	+

The arithmetic operators take one or two integral (byte, short, int, long) or floating-point (float, double) types. The comparison operators take on the usual meanings: equality (==), inequality (!=), less than (<), less than or equal to (<=), greater than (>), and greater than or equal to (>=). The unary and algebraic operators also provide the usual functions. The remainder operator (%) results in the remainder of the division of its arguments. The postfix operators work as in C, incrementing or decrementing the argument by one; these can also be used as prefixes.

The boolean operators include the relational (==, !=) and the logical: not (!), and (&), inclusive or (|), exclusive or (^). There are also the "short-circuit" operators: and (&&), as well as or (||). For these arguments, the right-hand side is evaluated only if needed.

Several operators work with integral types. The shift operators, << and >>, shift the left-hand argument's bits to the left or right by the distance given by the right-hand argument. The shift distance is less than 32 if the first argument is an int, or less than 64 if it is a long. The unsigned right shift, >>>, works the same as >> if the first argument is positive. Otherwise, the result of n >>> s is (n>>s) + (2<<(k-s-1)), where k is 32 if n is an int, or 64 for n a long.

There is a single String operator, +, which is used to concatenate two strings. If only one argument is a String literal (or a String), then the other argument will be converted to a string. This allows for expressions like

```
"The result is: " + (1+2)
```

Note that in the above expression, the first plus sign performs concatenation, while the second plus sign is for addition.

In addition to the assignment operator (=), there are compound operators of the form

```
a <op>= b
```

where <op> is one of (*, /, %, +, -, <<, >>, >>>, &, ^, |). The compound expression is equivalent to

```
a = a <op> b
```

Primitive Type Conversion

Primitives may undergo a change of type in three ways: by arithmetic promotion, by assignment conversion, and by explicit casting.

arithmetic promotion

In order to carry out primitive binary operations, Java may convert one or both arguments to a larger type. The rules are as follows:

- If an operand is a double, the other is converted to double.
- Otherwise, if one operand is a float, the other is converted to float.
- Otherwise, if one operand is a long, the other is converted to long.
- Otherwise, both operands are converted to int.

Booleans cannot be converted to or from arithmetic types; a char can be converted to or from any numeric type.

assignment conversion

In an assignment statement, if a variable type differs from the right-side expression, a conversion may take place, or a compile-time error may occur. A conversion takes place if the magnitude of the result can be preserved in the receiving variable. Java refers to this as a "widening" conversion. As you might expect, the opposite is a narrowing conversion, where the magnitude of the result may not be preserved. A compile-time error will result if a narrowing conversion is implied by the assignment. (You can suppress this error with an explicit cast, described below.) Some widening conversions may cause rounding to occur, for example, when converting from a long to a float. Figure 2-1 characterizes the conversion between each pair of primitives.

explicit casts

The most flexible conversion is the explicit cast. Unlike assignment conversions, a cast can perform a narrowing conversion. Java allows this, since with an explicit cast you are essentially stating your intentions. As in C, casts are specified by enclosing a type in parentheses, for example:

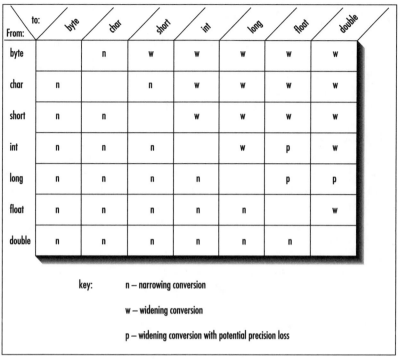

Figure 2-1 Primitive conversions

```
long getalong = 1234567890;
int squeezethisin = (int) getalong;
```

Here, the cast to an int is needed, since the compiler won't allow a long to be assigned directly to an int. Any primitive type can be cast to any other, except for booleans, which can't be cast to anything else. To convert booleans to arithmetic values, the expressions in Table 2-5 can be used (the "?" operator is presented in the next section).

Table 2-5 Converting to and from booleans

From	To	Expression	Where
arithmetic	boolean	((a) != 0)	a is an arithmetic expression
boolean	arithmetic	((b) ? 1 : 0)	b is a boolean expression

Statements and Control Flow

In this section, *statements* are described with detail on those that control program flow. The selection statements, *if* and *switch*, choose between alternatives. Iteration statements, *while*, *do*, and *for*, control loops. The jump statements transfer control; these are *break*, *continue*, and *return*. All of these work similarly to C. Note that Java doesn't have a *goto* statement (although *goto* is a reserved word).

Statements and Blocks

Most statements in Java are *expression* statements, which are followed by a semicolon. These are assignment statements (e.g., a = 1), increment and decrement statements (e.g., i++), method calls (see the section Classes and Methods), or allocation expressions. Statements can also be *blocks*, which are enclosed in braces ({ }), and may contain variable declarations and/or other statements.

The if Statement

The *if* statement, and the optional *else* clause, model choices. Here is an example, which shows a three-way decision, using *if*, *else if*, and *else*:

```
double min = 0.;
boolean same = false;
if (a < b)
    min = a;
else if (a > b)
    min = b;
else {
    min = a;
    same = true;
}
```

The conditional operator, ?, can be used in place of certain *if-else* constructs. As in C, it evaluates a boolean expression and returns one of two expressions.

```
min m = (a < b) ? a : b;
```

The switch Statement

The *switch* statement provides an alternative to *if-else* when the expression to test can take on one of several integral values. Potential values are identified in a *case* label; a *default* label covers all other cases. Usually, control is interrupted by a *break* or *return* statement right before the next *case* statement (otherwise the program flows through to the next label). Here is an example:

```
// convert an integer to a color name
String type = "";
switch (n) {
    case 0:
        type = "none";
        break;
    case 1:
```

```
    type = "red";
    break;
case 2:
    type = "green";
    break;
case 3:
    type = "blue";
    break;
case 4:
    type = "white";
    break;
case 5:
    type = "yellow";
    break;
case 6:
    type = "black";
    break;
default:
    type = "?";
}
```

The while Statement

The *while* statement provides the simplest iteration statement. The body is executed until the controlling expression is false. Unlike C, the expression must be a boolean (C allows any expression type). For example, the main loop in this chapter's project is essentially

```
// play until number correct is equal to number of pegs in code
int correct = 0;
while (correct < PEGS) {
    // get guess
    // count # correct
    // give hint
}
```

The do Statement

The *do* statement functions similarly to *while*, except the test to continue looping is executed at the bottom of the statement. This ensures at least one pass through the body of the *do*. The preceding loop could be restated as

```
// play until number correct is equal to number of pegs in code
int correct = 0;
do {
    // get guess
    // count # correct
    // give hint
} while (correct < PEGS);
```

The for **Statement**

The *for* statement provides a compact representation of certain *while* loops. Loops that use *while* as follows:

```
Initialization
while ( TestExpression ) {
    Statement(s)
    Increment;
}
```

can be more concisely represented by a *for* loop:

```
for ( Initialization; TestExpression; Increment )
    Statement(s)
```

The TestExpression and Increment are optional. Unlike C, the initialization clause can't be a comma-separated list of expressions.

Classes and Methods

Every program in Java has one or more classes. This is one difference from C++, in which a valid program may have no classes. A Java class defines a set of *variables* (which hold data) and/or *methods* (which define actions). Very often the class models something, where the variables maintain the state of the thing, and the methods provide ways of interacting with it. Java refers to a class's variables and methods as its *fields*.

A class is introduced by the *class* keyword, has an *identifier*, and has opening and closing braces to delimit its contents. Here is a simple Java class that minimally models a single peg from the code-breaking game:

```
class Peg {
    int color;
    void setColor(int c) { color = c;}
    int  getColor() { return color;}
}
```

Peg is defined to have one variable (*color*, an int), and two methods, one that can set color, and one that can get its value. The setColor() method does not return anything (it is declared *void*), and takes an integer parameter. The getColor() method does not take any parameters, and returns an int. Once defined, the Peg class can be used as a variable, similar to primitives, for example:

```
Peg p;
```

Here, the variable *p* stores an *instance* of a peg; *p* is also called an *object*. Essentially, classes are structures that can have functions in addition to variables.

Unlike structures, class contents may be hidden from other classes. In fact, the default is to make variables and methods unknown to other types of objects, unless classes are in the same *package*, or are related through *inheritance* (packages and inheritance are described later in this chapter). To override this privacy, the keyword *public* declares a method or variable available to all other objects. The example below declares both of Peg's methods public, but keeps its data private.

In the previous example, each Peg has its own variable for color. You can also define class variables that are shared by all instances of the class. These are *static* variables. Often, static variables represent constants, and their values are not intended to change after initialization. These are *final* variables. Any variable can be declared static, final, static and final, or neither. Although Java does not have C enums, a set of static final variables is often used to model a fixed set of choices. Below, the Peg class is enhanced to contain names for colors, as well as to distinguish public fields.

```
class Peg {
   int color;
   public void setColor(int c) { color = c;}
   public int  getColor() { return color;}

   // define names for colors
   public static final int none   = 0;
   public static final int red    = 1;
   public static final int green  = 2;
   public static final int blue   = 3;
   public static final int white  = 4;
   public static final int yellow = 5;
   public static final int black  = 6;
}
```

Methods

Methods are represented by a *signature*, which is based on the method's name, its parameters, and its return type. A return type of *void* indicates that nothing is returned from the method. A method that has the same name as the class name is a *constructor*, so-named because it constructs new instances of a particular class. Constructors have no return value; their return type is implicitly a reference to an instance of the class. Here is an example constructor for Peg:

```
Peg() { color = Peg.none; }
```

Unlike other methods, constructors are used in concert with the *new* keyword in order to allocate memory. Often this is done when a variable is declared, in order to *instantiate* an object and assign the variable a reference for that object. For example:

```
Peg p = new Peg();
```

Unlike C++, there is no "destructor" to reclaim memory. Instead, Java provides a *garbage collector* to automatically deallocate the memory when it is detected to be no longer needed. Beyond this, additional steps can be taken by a class when an instance is no longer needed by defining a method called finalize(), which takes no arguments and returns void. The finalize() method is usually written to free nonmemory resources that certain classes may have.

Static Methods

As with variables, methods may be declared static. A static method can only access static variables; it also can't call any nonstatic methods. Static methods are usually defined to manipulate static variables, or to provide "stand-alone" functionality that is not dependent on any instance of the class. Static methods are invoked directly, without the need to create on object of the given class. To call a static method, the name of the class, plus a period, is used as a prefix to the method name, for example:

```
double y = Math.sin(x);
```

Overloaded Methods

Unlike variables, methods may share names. In this case, the parameter lists must differ. As in C++, sharing names between methods is called *overloading*. The return types may differ between methods having the same name. Overloading the constructor is also allowed.

At compile time, if need be, Java decides which of the overloaded methods should be called. For each call to an overloaded set of methods, it selects those methods with the same number of parameters as the method call. Then, each argument in the method call is checked to see if it can be assigned to the corresponding parameter in the method definition.

If only one method meets these rules, then it is the one selected by the compiler. If no methods meet the rules, then it is a compile-time error. If several methods meet these rules, then the most "specific" method is chosen. The most specific method is the one whose parameters can be cast (by an assignment conversion—see the section Primitive Type Conversion, earlier in this chapter) from the other (less-specific) methods. If this determination is not possible, then the compiler considers this an ambiguity, and a compile-time error results.

Native Methods

Java allows methods to be written in a language other than Java. These are referred to as "native" methods. (Oddly, these methods might be thought of as "non-native" to Java.) Typically, they are written in C or assembly language. Native methods are indicated by the *native* keyword, and contain only a semicolon after the declaration. The details of writing native methods are included in Appendix C, Writing Native Methods in C/C++. Here is an example declaration:

```
native public static double abs(double d);
```

Class Inheritance

One of the most powerful features of an object-oriented language is to add features to an existing class, without modifying the class directly. This reusability is achieved through *inheritance*. Java provides this with the keyword *extends*, which can be included in the class declaration. For example:

```
public class Bird {
   public boolean flies() { return true;  }
   public boolean swims() { return false; }
   public boolean walks() { return true;  }
}

public class Cardinal extends Bird {
   public String color() { return "red"; }
}
```

This defines a new class (Cardinal), which is based on another class (Bird). In addition to inheriting all nonprivate variables and nonconstructor methods defined in Bird, the Cardinal class implements the method color(). The Java terms that describe inheritance relationships are defined in Table 2-6.

Table 2-6 Java inheritance relationships

Relationship	Definition
A is a *superclass* of C	C extends A; or C extends a class that is a subclass of A; or C is A.
C is a *subclass* of A	A is a superclass of C.
A is an *immediate superclass* of B	B's class declaration includes "extends A."
B is an *immediate subclass* of A	B's class declaration includes "extends A."
C is a *proper superclass* of A	A is a superclass of C, and A is not C.
A is a *proper subclass* of C	A is a subclass of C, and A is not C.

In the above example, color() isn't defined by Bird, but it is possible to do so. In this case, Cardinal's definition would *override* the one provided by Bird. Further, Bird can declare a color() method, but not implement its body. This is an *abstract* method.

```
public abstract class Bird {
   public abstract String color();
}

public class Cardinal extends Bird {
   public String color() { return "red"; }
}
```

Abstract methods provide a consistent way to achieve certain functionality. A class that contains any abstract methods is itself called abstract, and must be declared so as shown above. Abstract classes cannot be constructed with *new*. For example, using the latest definition of Bird, the following is illegal:

```
Bird bird = new Bird();
```

However, variables based on abstract classes can be declared, and they can refer to valid instances of their subclasses. The following is an example of a variable containing a more specialized object:

```
Bird bird = new Cardinal();
```

The opposite of an abstract class is a *final* class. Where abstract classes must have subclasses in order to be useful, final classes cannot have subclasses. Several of Java's standard classes are declared final. A class is declared final by placing the keyword *final* before the *class* keyword in the class definition. Methods may also be declared as final. In this case, the class can have subclasses, but the final methods cannot be overridden.

If the *extends* clause is omitted from the class declaration, then the class is an immediate subclass of Java's Object class (Object is described in Chapter 3, Global Classes). Object serves as a common superclass to every other Java class.

If a class has no constructors defined, then Java generates one. It takes no arguments, and calls the immediate superclass's no-argument constructor. Also, it initializes all instance variables. If the superclass hasn't a no-argument constructor, then a compile-time error results.

Keywords this *and* super

In an instance (nonstatic) method, there is a special variable, *this*, that refers to the current instance. The *this* variable may be used as an argument to another method. It can also be used to call a constructor from within another constructor. In this case, the syntax is: this(arguments).

Similar to *this*, there is *super*, which refers to the variables and methods of the immediate superclass. The *super* variable is useful for accessing methods or variables in the parent that are overridden or hidden in the class. *Super* may be used from within a constructor to call a parent's constructor. In the absence of any explicit constructor call, Java will make a call from a class's constructor to the parent's no-argument constructor (i.e., super();).

Interfaces: Inheriting Form, Not Function

In addition to inheriting from a superclass, a class may *implement* one or more *interfaces*. An interface is like a class in which all methods are abstract. More specifically, an interface declares a set of methods and/or variables, but not their implementation. Interfaces may not be declared final, native, static, or synchronized. By not defining any method's implementation, a class's support for multiple interfaces is conceptually easier than dealing with multiple inheritance. Here is an example of an interface:

```
public interface Flier {
    public double wingspan();
}
```

The Cardinal class might be augmented as follows:

```
public class Cardinal extends Bird implements Flier {
    public String color() { return "red"; }
    public double wingspan() { return 1.2; }
}
```

In addition to being implemented by classes, interfaces can be used in variable declarations. In this case, the variable refers to an instance of a class that implements (either directly or via inheritance) that interface. This is similar to declaring variables with the type of an abstract class. For example, a variable of type Flier can be declared as follows:

```
public class Nest {
   Flier tweetie;
   // ...
}
```

Arrays

Like primitives, arrays are special types defined by the language. Arrays contain a number of variables. These variables are called *components*. The array is of a given type, and all the components of the array are of this same type. The particular type can be any valid Java type.

Arrays are declared including brackets after the type and before or after the array name. Here are two array declarations:

```
int[] asetofints;
String args[];
```

In the above declarations, no memory is allocated. This can be done, as with objects, at declaration time or later:

```
int[] asetofints = new int[10];
String args[];
args = new String[10];
```

Arrays can be allocated space and initialized all at once:

```
int[] prime = {1, 3, 5, 7, 11, 13, 17, 19};
```

The elements of an array are accessed by the array name followed by a bracketed int. In order to find the number of allocated entries in an array, the array's *length* variable is used:

```
int[] squares = {1, 4, 9, 16, 25};
for (int i=0; i<squares.length; i++)
   System.out.println(squares[i] + " " + Math.sqrt(squares[i]));
```

Since the components can be any Java type, this includes array types. This is how multidimensional arrays are achieved. Here is an example of a two-dimensional array:

```
long[][] twoDnumbers;
```

Despite their special features, arrays function as objects with a superclass of Object. Any of Object's methods can be called by an array. Arrays can be cast to Objects, so variables of type Object can have arrays assigned to them. Also, array memory is managed by garbage collection, as is done for objects.

Reference Expressions

Objects and arrays are considered *reference* types in Java. This is because object and array variables hold a reference (pointer) to the actual data. Contrast this with primitives, which hold the actual data directly. Because of this difference, operations and conversions work differently for objects and arrays. This section covers certain special considerations for the reference types.

Assignment

For primitives, an assignment makes a copy of the data. Subsequent operations on the receiving variable have no effect on the right-hand side of the assignment. This is often referred to as a deep copy. But for reference types, an assignment makes a copy only of the reference (pointer) to the data. This is in effect a shallow copy. Consider the following:

```
int[] a1 = {1, 2, 3};
int[] a2 = a1;
a1[0] = -1;
```

In this example, both a1 and a2 refer (point) to the same set of data. Changing the first element to -1 affects both variables.

In situations where you need to have distinct copies of the same initial data, the Object.clone() method can provide a deeper copy. The above example can be rewritten as follows:

```
int[] a1 = {1, 2, 3};
int[] a2 = (int[]) a1.clone();
a1[0] = -1;
```

In this case, the last statement has no effect on a2, since it has received a separate copy of the data via the clone() method.

Comparison

Similar to assignment, reference types have a different behavior than primitives for comparisons (==, !=). Primitive comparisons check the value of the expressions against each other, promoting types if needed. Reference expressions are compared by checking to see if the pointers are the same. Here is a specific example:

```
String s1 = new String("tobecompared");
String s2 = new String("tobecompared");
boolean test = (s1 == s2);
```

In this case, the value of test is false, since s1 and s2 refer to different memory locations (which happen to have the same character sequence). For this reason, Object defines an equals() method, which classes may elect to override. In the case of the String class, equals() is defined to compare the sequence of characters so in the revised fragment, the variable test will be true.

```
String s1 = new String("tobecompared");
String s2 = new String("tobecompared");
boolean test = s1.equals(s2);
```

The `instanceof` Operator

One operator can only be applied to reference types: *instanceof*. It provides a means of checking a type at runtime. The result is true if the first argument is the type or subclass of the second argument. Here is an example:

```
if (argument instanceof String)
    argument = "something or other";
```

Conversions

Recall that earlier in this chapter, there was a distinction between assignment conversions and casts. Reference types have their own rules for these conversions. Figure 2-2 shows what assignments are valid in the statement s = t, where s is an object of class S, and t is an object of class T.

S is: \ T is:	class, not final	final class	interface
class, not final	T must be a subclass of S	T must be a subclass of S	compile-time error
final class	Compile time error	T must be same class as S	compile-time error
interface	T must implement S	T must implement S	T must be subinterface of S

Figure 2-2   Compiler tests for Object assignments

Using the notation of the previous figure, if T is an array with components of type B, then S must be Object, or S must have components that are the same primitive type, or a reference type that B can be assigned to.

For certain explicit casts, the compiler may be able to prove them incorrect. If this is the case, a compile-time error results. Otherwise, the validity is checked at runtime. Figure 2-3 shows the rules for class casting.

S is: \ T is:	class, not final	final class	interface
class, not final	T must be a subclass of S, or vice versa	T must be a subclass of S	correct at compile time
final class	S must be a subclass of T	T must be same class as S	S must implement T
interface	correct at compile time	T must implement S	correct at compile time

Figure 2-3 Compiler tests for class casting

Concerning arrays, the rules for casting are the same as for assignment conversions, except that an Object may be able to be explicitly cast to an array. The runtime validity will depend on whether the object actually holds a reference to the array of the left-hand side's type.

Reference Default

For objects and arrays that are not initialized at declaration time, the variable is assigned a special value, *null*. The meaning of null is that the variable does not yet refer to anything.

Program Structure

Java classes and interfaces are grouped into related sets called *packages*. Packages are used for controlling access to methods and variables. They also help to manage name-spaces. Facilities for accessing packages are used instead of using header files and *#include* statements in C and C++. In fact, since Java has none of the other # statements of C, it has no corresponding macro preprocessor.

Compilation Units

Before describing packages, a *compilation unit* needs to be defined. This is the contents of a file that would be compiled by the Java compiler. A compilation unit can have no, one, or several classes defined in it. If more than one class is present, then no more than one can be declared public.

Packages

Each Java package consists of any number of compilation units. A compilation unit places itself into a package by the *package* statement. If there is no *package* statement present in the compilation unit, then it is placed in a default unnamed package in the current directory (at compile time).

Packages have hierarchical names that generally correspond to subdirectory names. The package names are delimited with periods. The standard Java packages begin with "java.". Here are some example packages:

```
java.lang
sun.debug
smason.tools
```

Packages control access to class fields. As described previously, *private* fields are only known to the class. *Public* fields are available to any class. *Protected* fields are available to those classes in the same package as the declaring class, and to the subclasses of that class. If the field isn't qualified as private, public, or protected, then it is available only to classes in the same package as the declaring class.

An *import* statement can be used in order to refer to classes by abbreviated names. The *import* can include a fully qualified class name from a package, for example:

```
import java.util.Hashtable;
```

This allows the name Hashtable to be used in the compilation unit. All classes in a package can be imported using an asterisk, for example:

```
import java.io.*;
```

Each compilation unit implicitly imports java.lang, so that Object, String, and other java.lang classes can be referred to simply by their class names.

Exceptions

In Java, handling problems at runtime is typically done by throwing and catching *exceptions*. Exception is a standard class, which is subclassed to represent specific exceptions. Java keywords related to exception handling are *try*, *throw*, *throws*, *catch*, and *finally*.

The *throw* statement is used in methods when an exceptional condition occurs. A method declaration should contain the *throws* clause for those exceptions that the method does not handle itself:

```
class Divider {
   public static double divide(double a, double b)
     throws ArithmeticException
   {
      if (b == 0.)
         throw new ArithmeticException();
      return a / b;
   }
}
```

Here, if the second parameter is zero, control is returned to the caller via the *throw* statement. The chain of callers is searched until a suitable *catch* statement is found. The *catch* always has an introductory *try* statement:

```
class driver {
   public static void main(String [] args) {
      try {
         double d = Divider.divide(1, 0);
      } catch (ArithmeticException ae) {
         System.out.println(ae);
      } finally {
         System.out.println("Done attempting divide");
      }
   }
}
```

As shown above, there is also a *finally* clause; which is optional. A *finally* clause is always executed, whether or not an exception has occurred.

Synchronization

Java supports multiple threads executing in one process. This gives rise to special facilities to effectively manage multithreading. These include the ability to synchronize a block or an entire method.

The *synchronized* keyword is used in a method's declaration to indicate that the method should obtain a lock before executing. This lock will limit access to the object (or to the class, if the method is static) until the method completes.

Synchronized can also be used to qualify a block of code. In this case, *synchronized* takes a reference to an object or array. The statement waits for the lock associated with the object to be free, acquires the lock, executes the statement, and then releases the lock. The form of the *synchronized* statement is

```
synchronized ( expression )
   statement
```

Variables can have a special indication with respect to synchronization. The *volatile* keyword is used to declare variables that are modified asynchronously. For a volatile variable, the compiler arranges their access in a consistent way.

Standard Classes

The Java language specification defines several packages of standard classes. This breaks from the usual programming language evolution, where library and class library components become standards later in the life cycle of the language (for example, the Standard Template Library in C++).

Most of this book details the standard classes available. Table 2-7 lists the Java packages, and examples of their classes.

Table 2-7 Standard Java packages

Package	Description	Example Classes
java.applet	Browser application framework	Applet
java.awt	Windowing toolkit	Window, Button, Menu
java.io	Input/output	InputStream, OutputStream
java.lang	Basic language classes	Object, Exception, String, Double
java.net	Network classes	ftp, http, telnet
java.util	Utility classes	Vector, Hashtable, BitSet, Date

The Java Language Project: A Code-Breaking Game

Project Overview

This chapter's project implements a code-breaking game, described at the beginning of the chapter. In order to keep the project simple, the interface to the game is simple terminal input/output, instead of a graphical interface that usually accompanies games. Adding such an interface would be an interesting exercise, once you are familiar with a Java windowing package, such as awt. The game is structured so that its logic is largely separate from the I/O.

The game is made up of several classes. A Peg class describes one part of the code. The Code class is made up of several pegs, and contains methods to randomly generate a hidden code and compare how close two codes are. The Game class keeps track of the hidden code and the sequence of code guesses. A GameException class is used to communicate errors specific to the game. Lastly, a Play class coordinates the input and output of the game.

Playing the Game

After compiling the source, the game is started by typing

```
java Play
```

The game prompts you for a code guess, which you enter as an ordered list of four colors. The valid colors are red, green, blue, yellow, white, and black. For example, you could enter this guess:

```
red red green blue
```

The game then responds with the number of colors that are in the right place, followed by the number of colors that are correct, but in the wrong place. For example:

```
reply: 1, 1
```

This would indicate that one color is in the right place, another color is in the wrong place, and the two remaining entries are the wrong colors. You can continue guessing until you get the response

```
reply: 4, 0
```

This indicates that you've guessed the code. If your patience is running out, you can see the hidden code by entering "quit" as your guess.

Building the Project

1. The first file presented is the simplest. The GameException class is defined to help handle exceptions that may arise while the game is played. Most of the standard exceptions defined in Java take this form: they extend Exception by simply defining constructors. Enter the following code (Listing 2-1) into a file named GameException.java, and compile it with javac GameException.java.

Listing 2-1 GameException.java

```java
// Used for game-specific problems

public
class GameException extends Exception {

    public GameException() {
    super();
    }

    public GameException(String s) {
    super(s);
    }
}
```

2. The Peg class represents a single part of a multipeg code. This class wraps a single variable, which represents the color of the peg. The constructors and setColor() methods are overloaded to allow setting the peg color by integer or by string. Certain integers are given symbolic names via public, static, final variables. Two methods inherited from Object, toString() and isEquals(), are overridden to provide more useful functions. Note that the GameException (defined in step 1) is thrown when an unknown color is detected.

Enter the following code (Listing 2-2) into a file named Peg.java, and compile it with javac Peg.java.

Listing 2-2 Peg.java

```java
// represent a single part of the code (peg)

import GameException;

class Peg {

   // default constructor sets the peg to no color
   public Peg() {
     _color = none;
   }

   // initialize a peg to given color
   public Peg(int c) throws GameException {
      setColor(c);
   }

   // initialize a peg to named color
   public Peg(String s) throws GameException {
      setColor(s);
   }

   // make sure color indentifier is valid
   void checkColor(int c) throws GameException {
      if (c < 0 || c > max_color) {
         throw new GameException("Peg color value (" + c + ") out of range");
      }
      return;
   }

   // return the color identifier
   public int color() {
      return _color;
   }

   // set the color
   public void setColor(int c) throws GameException {
      checkColor(c);
      _color = c;
   };
```

continued on next page

continued from previous page

```
// set color given a name
public void setColor(String s) throws GameException {
    for (int i=0; i<max_color; i++) {
        if (s.equals(_names[i])) {
            _color = i;
            return;
        }
    }
    throw new GameException("Peg color (" + s + ") not known");
}

// determine if two pegs have the same color
public boolean isEqual(Peg p)
{
    return (_color == p.color());
}

// return name of peg color (overrides Object definition)
public String toString() {
    return _names[_color];
}


// this is the only instance data -- the peg's color
int _color;

// for converting from ints to color strings
final static String _names[] = {"none", "red", "green", "blue",
                    "white", "yellow", "black",
                    "turquoise", "pink" };

// define static names for colors
// might want to allow for more colors, and/or have game control max-valid
public final static int none      = 0;
public final static int red       = 1;
public final static int green     = 2;
public final static int blue      = 3;
public final static int white     = 4;
public final static int yellow    = 5;
public final static int black     = 6;
public final static int turquoise = 7;
public final static int pink      = 8;
public final static int max_color = 8;
}
```

3. The Code class keeps a collection of Pegs and defines related methods, such as generating a random code. The class shows the use of arrays and certain built-in Java classes (StringTokenizer, Random). Enter the following code (Listing 2-3) into a file named Code.java, and compile it with javac Code.java.

Listing 2-3 Code.java

```java
// a code is an ordered collection of Pegs

import GameException;
import Peg;
import java.util.Random;
import java.util.StringTokenizer;

class Code {

    // construct a code of size n, with non-colored pegs
    public Code(int n) {
        _pegs = new Peg[n];
        for (int i=0; i<n; i++) {
            _pegs[i] = new Peg();
        }
    }

    // construct a code from an array of pegs
    public Code(Peg p[]) {
        _pegs = p;
    }

    // construct a code by parsing a string of colors
    public Code(String s) throws GameException {
        fromString(s);
    }

    // return the ith peg in the code
    public Peg peg(int i) throws GameException {
        checkBound(i);
        return _pegs[i];
    }

    // set the ith position of code to given peg
    public void setPeg(int i, Peg p) throws GameException {
        checkBound(i);
        _pegs[i] = p;
    }

    // return the length (number of pegs) in the code
    public int length() {
        return _pegs.length;
    }

    // validate the requested index
    void checkBound(int i) throws GameException {
        if (i < 0 || i > _pegs.length)
            throw new GameException("Index for code position out of bounds");
        return;
    }
```

continued on next page

continued from previous page

```
// check that lengths of this and another code are the same
void checkLength(int len) throws GameException {
    if (len != _pegs.length)
        throw new GameException("Codes to compare are different lengths");
    return;
}

// generate a code
public void generate(int max) throws GameException {
    Random r = new Random();
    for (int i=0; i<_pegs.length; i++) {
        int c = (int) (r.nextFloat() * max) + 1;
        _pegs[i] = new Peg(c);
    }
}

// determine hint array; 1st item is # of exact matches
//   2nd item is # of right colors in wrong places
public int[] hint(Code c) throws GameException {
    int i;
    int len = c.length();
    checkBound(len);

    int result[] = new int[2];
    result[0] = result[1] = 0;

    int match[] = new int[len];
    for (i=0; i<len; i++) {
        match[i] = -1;
    }

    // find exact matches
    for (i=0; i<len; i++) {
        if (peg(i).isEqual(c.peg(i))) {
            result[0]++;
            match[i] = i;
        }
    }

    // find and count near matches
    for (i=0; i<len; i++) {
        if (match[i] == -1) {
            for (int j=0; j<len; j++) {
                if (!inlist(j, match) && peg(i).isEqual(c.peg(j))) {
                    result[1]++;
                    match[i] = j;
                    break;
                }
            }
        }
    }

    return result;
}

// see if element is in list
static boolean inlist(int a, int[] list) {
    for (int i=0; i<list.length; i++)
```

```
        if (a == list[i])
            return true;
    return false;
}

// display code as a string (ordered list of color names)
public String toString() {
    String string = "";
    for (int i=0; i<_pegs.length; i++)
        string = string + " " + _pegs[i].toString();
    return string;
}

// allows simple number or color input
public void fromString(String s) throws GameException {
    StringTokenizer t = new StringTokenizer(s);
    int n = t.countTokens();
    _pegs = new Peg[n];
    for (int i=0; i<n; i++) {
        String token = t.nextToken();
        _pegs[i] = new Peg(token);
    }
    return;
}

// the data is an array of Pegs
Peg _pegs[];
}
```

4. The Game class uses the previously defined classes to track the play of the game. Note that one of its constructors calls the other Game constructor using the *this* keyword. As is useful in classes that collect other classes, Game's toString() method invokes the toString() method of the contained data. Enter the following code (Listing 2-4) into a file named Game.java, and compile it with javac Game.java.

Listing 2-4 Game.java

```
// Game keeps track of the hidden code and guesses so far

class Game {

    public final int MAXGUESS = 20;

    // construct a new game, with given number of pegs and valid colors
    public Game(int pegs, int colors) throws GameException {
        _pegs = pegs;
        _colors = colors;
        _guess = new Code[MAXGUESS];
        _guesses = 0;
        _secret = new Code(_pegs);
        _secret.generate(_colors);
```

continued on next page

continued from previous page

```
   }

   // default game has 4 pegs, and 6 possible colors
   public Game() throws GameException {
      this(4, 6);
   }

   // representation of all the guesses so far
   public String toString() {
      String string = "";
      for (int i=0; i<_guesses; i++)
         string = string + "\n" + _guess[i].toString();
      return string;
   }

   // accept the next guess
   public void nextGuess(Code code) throws GameException
   {
      check_length();
      _guess[_guesses++] = code;
   }

   // make sure we haven't hit the max number of guesses
   public void check_length() throws GameException {
      if (_guesses == MAXGUESS )
         throw new GameException("Too many guesses");
   }

   // validate request for a given guess
   public void check_index(int i) throws GameException {
      if (i >= _guesses || i < 0)
         throw new GameException("index out of range");
   }

   // return the ith code guess
   public Code guess(int i) throws GameException
    { check_index(i); return _guess[i]; }

   // the hidden code
   public Code secret() {
      return _secret;
   }

   // return the number of pegs in the code
   public int pegs() {
      return _pegs;
   }

   // return the number of valid colors to draw from
   public int colors() {
      return _colors;
   }

   // return the number of guesses made so far
   public int guesses() {
      return _guesses;
   }
```

```
// these are the guesses made so far
Code _guess[];

// this is the secret code
Code _secret;

// this is the number of pegs in the code
int  _pegs;

// this is the number of feasible colors for any peg
int  _colors;

// this is the actual number of code guesses made
int  _guesses;
}
```

5. The Play class orchestrates the play of the game. The classes defined so far have lacked any I/O; the class defined below is the sole input and output gateway between the player and the program. This separation between logic and interface would allow a different class, perhaps based on the awt package, to provide a full-screen interface that could still use the Peg, Code, and Game classes unchanged. Enter the following code (Listing 2-5) into a file named Play.java, and compile it with javac Play.java.

Listing 2-5 Play.java

```
// test program to play code-breaker by a simple terminal interface

import Game;
import GameException;
import java.io.*;

class Play {

    public static void main(String args[]) throws IOException {

        // The hint is the response to a guess; 1st entry is # colors correct,
        //    2nd is # colors near (right color, wrong place)
        int hint[] = new int[2];
        hint[0] = 0;

        // these could be parameterized (for example @ the cmd line)
        int PEGS = 4;
        int COLORS = 6;

        Game game; // this stores the secret code and all the guesses
        Code secret; // this is the secret code

        // setup game, store secret code
        try {
            game = new Game(PEGS, COLORS);
            secret = game.secret();
        }
```

continued on next page

continued from previous page

```java
        // can't recover if hit an error
        catch (GameException e) {
            System.out.println(e);
            return;
        }

        // play until guessed, quit, or max guesses
        for (int i=0; hint[0] < PEGS && i < game.MAXGUESS; i++) {

            // read a guess from terminal
            System.out.println("Guess? ");
            String line =  "";
            char c;
            while ( (c = (char)System.in.read()) != '\n')
                line = line + c;

            // nothing entered is ok
        if (line.length() == 0) {
                continue;
            }

            // reveal the code if player gives up
            if (line.equals("quit")) {
                System.out.println("hidden code: " + game.secret());
                return;
            }

            // parse and store guess
            try {
                Code guess = new Code(line);
                game.nextGuess(guess);

                // formulate and show hint
                hint = secret.hint(guess);
                System.out.println("Reply: " + hint[0] + "," + hint[1]);
            }
            // catch unknown color, wrong # of pegs;
            //   recover by ignoring input, get another guess
            catch (GameException e) {
                System.out.println(e);
                System.out.println("guess again");
            }
        } // end for

    } // end main

}
```

PART II
BASIC CLASSES

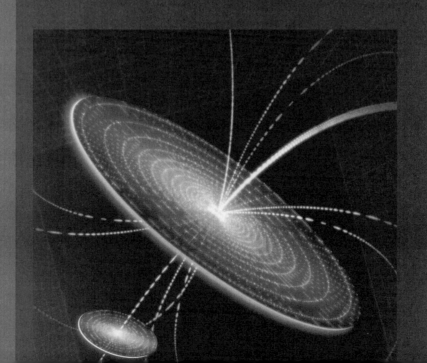

3

GLOBAL CLASSES

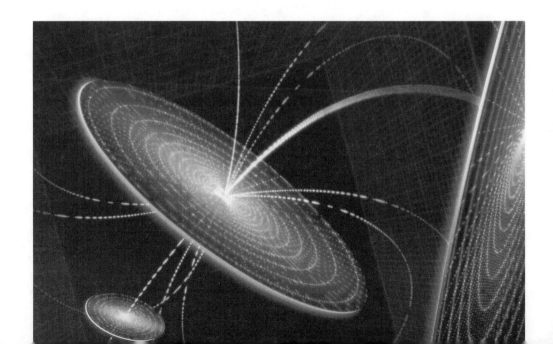

3

GLOBAL CLASSES

This chapter covers those classes and interfaces that relate to all Java classes, including the Object class, the Class class, and the Cloneable interface. All Java classes inherit from the Object class. The Class class can be used to find out class information about any Java object. The Cloneable interface is implemented by classes that can make copies of their objects. Table 3-1 shows the classes and interface covered in this chapter, and Figure 3-1 shows their inheritance relationships.

Table 3-1 The global classes

Class	Description
Object	A generic class from which all other classes are derived.
Class	Information on a particular class (e.g., parent, interfaces).
Cloneable	An interface that indicates clone() is implemented for the class.

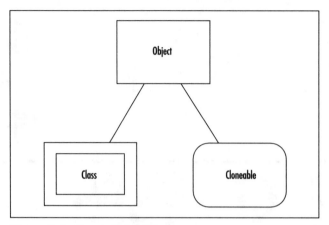

Figure 3-1 Class relationships

The Object Class

Every Java class is derived, directly or indirectly, from the Object class (except for Object itself, which has no parent). Inheritance, which allows a class to extend its parent class, is described in Chapter 2, The Java Language. Every public and protected Object method is available to every class. Some of these methods are declared final by Object, and so their behavior will be the same for all classes. The other public Object methods can be overridden. In this case the method is always available, but may behave differently in different classes. For example, finalize() doesn't do anything by default, but may be given behavior by a descendant class. Conversely, clone() has a behavior defined by Object, but can be overridden to do nothing.

> **Java Parents**
> Object is the only class in Java that has no parent. Every other class must have a parent, and Object is their ultimate ancestor. Think of Object as the "Adam" of the class hierarchy.

Objects Everywhere

The Object class is pervasive, in ways that aren't always apparent. Listing 3-1 provides a look at a Hello, World program in Java:

Listing 3-1 Hello, World

```
class Hello {
   public static void main(String[] args) {
      System.out.println("Hello, World");
   }
}
```

At first glance, there seems to be no sign of the Object class, but in fact there are several uses of it. First, since the Hello class declaration omits the *extends* clause, it implicitly inherits from Object. In other words, Hello is a type of Object. The arguments to main, declared as String[] args, are in fact an array of Objects, since String inherits from Object. The System class, used in line 3, also inherits from Object. Its *out* member is of type PrintStream, which inherits indirectly from Object. In addition to accepting a String as an argument, the println() method is overloaded to accept an Object, in which case it invokes the toString() method to convert the object to a printable representation.

As can be seen from this example, Objects are pervasive. As the parent to every class, every one of Object's public methods is available to every Java object. Also, Object may be the declared type for any method argument, allowing a method to accept arguments of any reference type. Lastly, variables may be declared as Object.

Object Methods

Object's methods fall into the following categories: comparison, information, life cycle, and synchronization. Table 3-2 shows the methods arranged by these categories. The comparison methods are equals() and hashCode(). Methods that provide information are toString(), which provides a String representation of an object, and getClass(), which returns a Class description of the class. The Class class is described later in this chapter. Life cycle methods include clone(), which "gives birth" to a new instance, and finalize(), which defines additional steps to take when an object is no longer needed. Lastly, synchronization methods are notify(), notifyAll(), and wait(). These provide "stop and go" capabilities to threads and Runnable classes. The Thread class is presented in Chapter 8, Thread and ThreadGroup.

Table 3-2 Object methods, by category

Category	Methods
Comparison	equals, hashCode
Information	toString, getClass
Life cycle	clone, finalize
Synchronization	notify, notifyAll, wait

Of Object's methods, only wait() is overloaded. Its various signatures allow a thread to wait until a timeout, or until notified. Most other methods take no arguments, except equals(), which takes one argument. Object has no static methods or public data. Its only constructor takes no arguments.

Object's Methods: Leave It or Take It

Certain Object methods are final, so their behavior will be the same for every class. These are the thread-related methods, as well as getClass(). This leaves a few methods that can be overridden: clone(), equals(), finalize(), hashCode(), and toString().

Overriding Object's Methods

When writing a class, you need to decide which of Object's methods (if any) to override. For equals(), this comes down to the distinction between comparing references and comparing values. Object defines equals() to compare the *references* between two instances to see if they are the same. This is the definition of the == operator. But in several cases, a preferred definition would be to test to see if the *values* of two instances are the same. The String class implements this behavior by testing to see if the two variables have the same sequence of characters. Other Java classes that override equals() in this manner are Date and BitSet. The equals() method is used in the standard collection classes, Hashtable and Vector, when searching for a contained value.

Incomparable Comparisons

Some classes define equals() to compare references, some classes compare values, and classes could be defined that compare certain elements by references and others by value. The == operator always gives you reference comparisons. For equals(), you need to know which class(es) you're comparing to know how the comparison is done.

The default behavior of clone() is to generate a bitwise copy of the object. That is, all primitive data values and all current object references are copied into a new memory space. Classes may elect to make a "deeper" copy, that is, make a distinct copy of any or all contained objects in the class, by overriding the clone() method. In this case, the class should include an *implements Cloneable* in its class declaration. If a class does not support cloning, then a CloneNotSupportedException is thrown when clone() is called.

The toString() method is redefined in many of Java's classes in order to create a more meaningful String representation of an object. The PrintStream.print() method invokes toString() in order to write out an object. This makes toString() quite useful for debugging. If the information generated by toString() is complete, then the String can be used to pass an object's state between processes, or to save and restore a persistent copy of the object.

The Object finalize() method is interesting in that it does nothing. Its purpose is to provide classes with a standard way to clean up after themselves when they are no longer being referenced. The Java garbage collector takes care of freeing memory, but a class may need to free other resources. As an example, the finalize() method is redefined in the FileInputStream class, in order to free its file handle when it is no longer needed.

Java Utility Classes and Objects

The classes in the java.utils package demonstrate an interesting use of objects. The Dictionary, Hashtable, Stack, and Vector classes provide generic ways to collect a set of objects. What makes them generic is that their methods and private data use Object as a means of specifying and storing data. In practice, programs generally provide more specific data (for example, Strings). The collection classes allow this, since subclasses can be used where their superclass is specified. This works since Java uses references (pointers) when passing and assigning objects.

Order, Please

As described above, Object provides the equals() method to compare two objects to see if they are the same. Classes may provide their own implementation of "sameness." The equals() method is a straightforward way to search for an object, or to avoid duplicates in a collection. What if you want to see if one object is less than another? For example, you might want to maintain a sorted list. The first problem is that not all classes may have a sensible notion of "less than." This is why Object does not have a method to do this (what would Object's own definition of this be?).

For classes that do have a reasonable definition of "less than," there is no common way to compare values. While String has a compareTo() method, the Double class has no comparison methods (other than equals()). One solution to this would be to define an interface (e.g., Comparable) that has one method (e.g., isLessThan()). Then simple classes could be defined that implement Comparable and inherit or contain the classes of interest, such as String or Double. With this, a SortedVector class could be defined that contained Comparables. This approach is taken in Chapter 5's project.

The Java Language and Objects

The Java language defines several items that relate to the Object class. Special Java components—interfaces, exceptions, and errors—all inherit from Object. Like Objects, arrays are also reference types, and Java allows them to behave nearly like Objects. Object methods can be invoked on an array, and arrays can be passed to, or returned from, methods where the return type is Object. Listing 3-2 shows this use of arrays as Objects.

Listing 3-2 Arrays as Objects

```
public String[] array_clone(String[] s) {
// clone() is an Object method which returns an Object
// note cast from Object to String[] on return value
   return (String[]) s.clone();
}
```

Arrays and Objects
Arrays can be thought of as Objects that have some convenience items, like brackets for element access, instead of get and set methods. Using Object.getClass() and Class.getSuperclass(), you can determine that any array's parent is the Object class. Based on this, it might appear that arrays are implemented as special classes.

A Class About Classes

Java provides a class that can describe any object's class. This is the Class class (excuse the stutter!). The Class class provides a capability similar to C++'s RTTI (runtime type information). Class provides a way to query an object's type. It is a metaclass—a class about other classes.

One use of Class is to provide runtime type constraints. For example, you may want to ensure that a collection holds the same kind of things, for example, only numbers. The Java collection utilities, like Vector, allow any kind of object to be included. A subclass of Vector could override all methods that add elements by prescreening for the object's type. This technique is used in the project at the end of this chapter, to define a type-consistent linked list.

Since Class is an informational class, its instance methods are primarily accessors, and take no arguments. There is one static method, forName(), which is used to generate a Class instance from a String. Methods can be grouped into those that identify the class (forName(), getName(), toString()), those that provide class information (getInterfaces(), getSuperclass(), isInterface()), and those related to generating an object (getClassLoader(), newInstance()). Table 3-3 shows the Class methods, by category.

Table 3-3 Class methods, by category

Category	Methods
Generate	getClassLoader, newInstance
Identify	forName, getName, toString
Information	getInterfaces, getSuperclass, isInterface

The Java *instanceof* comparison operator also provides runtime type identification. It tests to see if a variable or expression can represent an object of a particular type. It returns true if the expression is a class or subclass of the given type. Since the given type must be specified at compile time, use of the Class may be required for more dynamic situations. Listing 3-3 shows an example use of *instanceof*.

Listing 3-3 Use of the `instanceof` *operator*

```
// insert object into list if it is a Number (or subclass of Number)
public boolean addIfNumber(Object d) {
    if (d instanceof Number) {
        addItem(d);
        return true;
    }
    else {
        return false;
    }
}
```

Class vs. Object

Since Class and Object both relate to every Java class, they are sometimes confused. Every Java class (except Object) *inherits* from Object, while every class can be *characterized* via a Class. From this it follows that Class inherits from Object, and Objects can be characterized by a Class. Additionally, each class has a method to get to the other. Object.getClass() returns a Class description of an object. And Class.newInstance() generates an object from a Class instance. Lastly, while Object's role is to provide a base class from which others are derived, the Class class is final—no other classes can be extended from it.

About the Project

This chapter's project is a linked list, which makes use of the Object and Class classes. The project is an example of a collection class, that is, a class that collects items. Java provides certain collections in the java.utils package, notably Vector, which is a resizable array. Vectors handle several cases well, but are not particularly suited for insertions, since elements need to be moved in order to make room. The list doesn't have this problem, since elements are not moved to make room for a new item.

The project also illustrates the concept of "type safety." Java's Vector class allows Objects to be inserted, which means any instance of any class can be included. So, there is nothing in Vector that prevents you from inadvertently creating a collection of Numbers, Strings, and Threads. The classes in this project offer a solution to this problem. The List class, like Vector, allows any kind of object to be inserted. A second class, TypedList, is a collection that lets you constrain what type(s) of objects can be inserted. This constraint is imposed using features of the Class class, which allows runtime type querying.

Object and Class Method Summaries

The Java Object and Class classes are described in detail in the following sections. A short description of each method is in Table 3-4. Detailed reference sections for java.lang.Object and java.lang.Class follow.

Table 3-4 Summary of Object and Class methods

Class	Method	Description
Object	clone	Returns a copy of the object
	equals	Tests to see if objects refer to the same thing
	finalize	Action to perform right before garbage collection
	getClass	Returns a Class descriptor for an object
	hashCode	Generates a hash code
	notify	Notifies a waiting thread
	notifyAll	Notifies all waiting threads
	toString	Returns a String representation of the object
	wait	Puts a thread into wait until time elapsed or notified
Class	forName	Returns a Class instance, given the name of a class
	getClassLoader	Returns the class's ClassLoader, if any (see Chapter 10)
	getInterfaces	Returns all interfaces implemented by the class
	getName	Gets name of the class
	getSuperclass	Gets a Class instance of the parent class
	isInterface	Indicates if a Class describes an interface
	newInstance	Generates an instance of the class specified
	toString	Gets a String representation

The java.lang.Object Class

The public methods for the Java Object class are detailed below. Since Object has no parent, it inherits no methods. There is no public data associated with Object.

OBJECT

Description	Object is the root of the Java class hierarchy. Its methods are common to all Java classes.
Syntax	public class **Object**
Package	java.lang
Import	java.lang.Object
Constructors	public **Object()**
Parameters	None.
Comments	Objects are useful from a class designer's point of view, since all classes inherit directly or indirectly from Object. They are also useful for writing generic methods that may apply to any class. An example of this is the java.util.Vector class, which can be used to form a collection of any Objects.
Example	In this example, an object is created.

```
Object obj = new Object();
```

Methods

CLONE

Class Name	Object
Description	Returns a copy of the object.
Syntax	protected Object **clone()**
Parameters	None.
Returns	The return type is Object. A clone of the object is returned.
Exceptions	If the object can't be cloned, a CloneNotSupportedException is thrown.
See Also	Cloneable
Comments	For Objects, the copying is bitwise. For classes that override the clone() method, the copying may be different. For example, the class may elect to make a "deeper" copy by cloning the underlying data, not just the pointers to it. The Cloneable interface is implemented by classes that support clone().
Example	In this example, a trivial class is defined that implements a deep copy for its clone() method.

```
class CloneAround implements Cloneable {
   int j;
   public CloneAround(int i) {j = i;}
   protected Object clone() {
      CloneAround twin = new CloneAround(j);
      return (Object) twin;
   }
}
```

EQUALS

Class Name	Object
Description	Compares two objects.
Syntax	public boolean **equals**(Object *object*)
Parameters	
Object *object*	A second object to compare.
Returns	The return type is boolean. The value true is returned if the objects are the same, false otherwise.
Exceptions	None.
Comments	The Object class implements this method by comparing the two instances to see if they are identical. This is the same as the Java equality operator (==), when used for objects. Classes overriding this method may choose to compare the instances to see if they are equal by value. For example, the String class does this by comparing the two strings to see if they have the same sequence of characters.
	The Vector class uses the equals() method, to see if an instance is contained in a collection. Example overriding methods can be found in String, Date, and BitSet.
See Also	String, Date, BitSet
Example	In this example, two Strings are compared to see if they are equal.

```
String s = "Hello";
String t = "Goodbye";
boolean doubletalk = s.equals(t);
```

FINALIZE

Class Name	Object
Description	Action to perform right before garbage collection normally occurs for this object.
Syntax	protected void **finalize**()
Parameters	None.
Returns	None.
Exceptions	None.
Comments	The Object class defines finalize() as an empty method (it does nothing). Classes may provide an override method where resources (other than memory) might need to be freed. For example, the file-related classes FileInputStream and FileOutputStream override finalize() in order to close the stream. In other cases, finalize() could be used to decrease a global counter or remove an entry from a list. The finalize() method can resurrect

the instance. In this case, the Java runtime system will not reclaim the instance's storage.

See Also	FileInputStream, FileOutputStream
Example	In this example, a hypothetical resource is freed in a hypothetical class.

```
public void finalize() {
   release(resource); // a method which frees a resource
}
```

GETCLASS

Class Name	Object
Description	Returns a Class descriptor for this object.
Syntax	public final Class **getClass**()
Parameters	None.
Returns	The return type is Class, in which information about the class of the instance is returned.
Exceptions	None.
See Also	Class
Comments	This method provides a Class instance, which can be queried for information about the class. See the java.lang.Class section later in this chapter for more information about what information is available.
Example	In this example, the class descriptor is accessed for the Object class.

```
Object o = new Object();
Class c = o.getClass();
```

HASHCODE

Class Name	Object
Description	Generates an integer hash code.
Syntax	public int **hashCode**()
Parameters	None.
Returns	The return type is int. It is a number that can be used as a key in hash tables.
Exceptions	None.
See Also	Hashtable, String, Date, BitSet
Comments	This method is used by the Hashtable class. A few methods provide overriding methods, including String, Date, and BitSet.
Example	The hash code of a string is returned and assigned to a variable.

```
String s = "Hello";
int hashcode = s.hashCode();
```

NOTIFY

Class Name	Object
Description	Notifies a thread. The notify() method is generally used with multiple threads.
Syntax	public final void **notify()**
Parameters	None.
Returns	None.
Exceptions	None.
See Also	Thread, ThreadGroup
Example	See Chapter 8, Thread and ThreadGroup, for example usage.

NOTIFYALL

Class Name	Object
Description	Notifies all threads.
Syntax	public final void **notifyAll()**
Parameters	None.
Returns	None.
Exceptions	None.
See Also	Thread, ThreadGroup
Comment	The notifyAll() method is generally used to coordinate threads.
Example	For examples and more detail on Threads, see Chapter 8, Thread and ThreadGroup.

TOSTRING

Class Name	Object
Description	Returns a string representation of the object.
Syntax	public String **toString()**
Parameters	None.
Returns	The return type is String. It contains a string representing the instance.
Exceptions	None.
See Also	String
Comments	Object provides a very generic implementation of this method, by returning the name of the class and a number that appears to be a memory address. It is recommended that classes override this method with something more useful. Some interesting overrides are in the numeric wrapper classes (like Double and Integer). The toString() method is used by the

concatenation operator (+, when used with objects). It is also used by certain I/O methods, such as PrintStream's print() and println().

Example   In this example, a string representation of a simple object instance is created.

```
Object o = new Object();
String s = o.toString();
```

WAIT

Class Name	Object
Description	Causes thread to wait for an amount of time, or until notified.
Syntax	public final void **wait**()
	public final void **wait**(long *millisec*)
	public final void **wait**(long *millisec*, int *nanosec*)
Parameters	
long *millisec*	Time to wait, in milliseconds (a thousandth of a second).
int *nanosec*	Additional time to wait, in nanoseconds (less than one million).
Returns	None.
Exceptions	If the wait is interrupted, an InterruptedException will be thrown. An IllegalMonitorStateException is thrown if the current thread does not own the Object's monitor.
See Also	Thread, ThreadGroup
Comments	Only synchronized methods can call wait().
Example	For examples and more detail see Chapter 8, Thread and ThreadGroup.

The java.lang.Class Class

The public methods for the Java Class class are detailed below. Class inherits methods from Object. No other classes inherit from Class—it is declared final. There is no public data associated with Class.

CLASS

Description	Class provides runtime information on the type of an object (its class).
Syntax	public final class **Class** extends Object
Package	java.lang
Import	java.lang.Class
Constructors	None.
Parameters	None.

Comments	There is no constructor for Class. Instead, a Class instance is created from calling Object.getClass(), or from certain methods of this class: forName(), getInterfaces(), and getSuperclass().
Example	This example gets the Class descriptor for a String.

```
String s = "Hello";
Class c = s.getClass();
```

Methods

FORNAME

Class Name	Class
Description	Returns a Class instance, given the name of a class.
Syntax	public static Class **forName**(String *name*)
Parameters	
String *name*	The name of the class, fully qualified (e.g., "java.lang.String").
Returns	The return type is Class. It describes the class that was requested in the parameter.
Exceptions	A ClassNotFoundException results if the string parameter is not a class name.
See Also	String
Comments	This is the sole static method for the Class class.
Example	This example generates a Class descriptor for the String class.

```
Class c = null;
try {
 c = Class.forName("java.lang.String");
} catch (ClassNotFoundException  e)
   ;
```

GETCLASSLOADER

Class Name	Class
Description	Returns the ClassLoader for this class, if one is defined.
Syntax	public ClassLoader **getClassLoader**()
Parameters	None.
Returns	The return type is ClassLoader. null is returned if this class has no associated class loader.
Exceptions	None.
See Also	ClassLoader

Comments   Most classes don't have a tailored ClassLoader. Examples of those that do are Toolkit, URL, and URLConnection. ClassLoader is described in Chapter 10, ClassLoader and SecurityManager.

Example   This example gets the class loader for a URL.

```
class test {
   static public void main(String args[]) {
      if (args.length == 0) return;
      try {
         URL u = new URL(args[0]);
         ClassLoader c = u.getClass().getClassLoader();
      }
      catch (MalformedURLException e)
         ;
   }
}
```

GETINTERFACES

Class Name   Class

Description   Gets the descriptions of all interfaces implemented by the class.

Syntax   public Class[] **getInterfaces**()

Parameters   None.

Returns   The return type is a Class array. Each entry in the array describes an interface implemented by the class. An array of length 0 is returned if no interfaces are implemented.

Exceptions   None.

Example   This example prints the interfaces supported for the requested class.

```
class showinterfaces {
   public static void main(String args[]) {
      if (args.length == 0) return; // requires an argument
      Class c = null;
      try {
         c = Class.forName(args[0]);  // attempt to generate a Class
      } catch (ClassNotFoundException e) {
         System.out.println("unknown class");
         return;
      }
      // get interfaces supported by class and print
      Class[] interfaces = c.getInterfaces();
      if (interfaces.length == 0) {
         System.out.println("No interfaces are implemented by class");
         return;
      }
      for (int i=0; i<interfaces.length; i++)
         System.out.println(interfaces[i].getName());
   }
}
```

GETNAME

Class Name	Class
Description	Gets the name of the class.
Syntax	public String **getName**()
Parameters	None.
Returns	The return type is String. It is the fully qualified class name of the Class.
Exceptions	None.
See Also	String
Comments	This method is an inverse method of Class.forName(). Where forName() returns a Class for a given string, getName() returns a String for a given Class.
Example	This example prints the name of the parent class, for a requested class.

```java
class showparent {
   public static void main(String args[]) {
      if (args.length == 0) { // requires an argument
         System.out.println("usage: java showparent <classname>");
         return;
      }
      Class c = null;
      try {
         c = Class.forName(args[0]); // attempt to generate a Class
      } catch (ClassNotFoundException e) {
         System.out.println("unknown class");
         return;
      }
      // get parent, show name
      Class parent = c.getSuperclass();
      if (parent == null) {
         System.out.println("no parent");
         return;
      }
      System.out.println(parent.getName());
   }
}
```

GETSUPERCLASS

Class Name	Class
Description	Provides information on the parent class of this class.
Syntax	public Class **getSuperclass**()
Parameters	None.
Returns	The return type is Class. It describes the parent of the class.
Exceptions	None.
Comments	For the Object class, null is returned. This method is interesting in that it is both a method of Class, and also returns an instance of Class. There is no method for finding the subclasses of a class.

Example   This example shows the ancestors of the class.

```
class showparents {
   public static void main(String args[]) {
      if (args.length == 0) return; // requires an argument
      Class c = null;
      try {
         c = Class.forName(args[0]);  // attempt to generate a Class
      } catch (ClassNotFoundException e) {
         System.out.println("unknown class");
         return;
      }
      // recursively get parents and print
      Class parent = c.getSuperclass();
      if (parent == null) {
         System.out.println("no parent");
         return;
      }
      while (parent != null) {
         System.out.println(parent.getName());
         parent = parent.getSuperclass();
      }
   }
}
```

ISINTERFACE

Class Name	Class
Description	Indicates if a Class describes an interface.
Syntax	public boolean **isInterface**()
Parameters	None.
Returns	The return type is boolean. It is true if the particular Class is an interface.
Exceptions	None.
Example	This example tests to see if a class is an interface.

```
class checkinterface {
   public static void main(String args[]) {
      if (args.length == 0) return; // requires an argument
      Class c = null;
      try {
         c = Class.forName(args[0]);  // attempt to generate a Class
      } catch (ClassNotFoundException e) {
         System.out.println("unknown class");
         return;
      }
      // see if this is an interface
      boolean isinterface = c.isInterface();
      if (isinterface)
         System.out.println(c + " is an interface");
      else
         System.out.println(c + " is not an interface");
   }
}
```

NEWINSTANCE

Class Name	Class
Description	Generates an instance of the class specified in the Class instance.
Syntax	public Object **newInstance**()
Parameters	None.
Returns	Although the return type is Object, the object returned is actually of the specific type requested. It is a default constructed instance of the type indicated by the Class instance.
Exceptions	None.
Comments	The instance returned is constructed similarly to the default constructor of the class. There is no analogous method for returning objects from constructors with parameters.
Example	This example generates a String instance from the Class instance.

```
String s = "Hello";
Class c = s.getClass();
String t = (String) c.newInstance(); // note cast required
```

TOSTRING

Class Name	Class
Description	Returns a string representation of the Class instance.
Syntax	public String **toString**()
Parameters	None.
Returns	The return type is String. It is a description of the Class.
Exceptions	None.
See Also	String
Comments	The result is similar to that returned by getName. This method includes the qualifier "Class:" or "Interface:" in its returned string.
Example	This example shows the toString() result from a String class.

```
String s = "Hello";
String class_string = s.getClass().toString();
System.out.println(class_string);
```

The java.lang.Cloneable Interface

This section provides a reference for the java.lang.Cloneable interface. Cloneable inherits from Object, and defines no methods. Classes that implement Cloneable define the clone() method, which is inherited from Object.

CLONEABLE

Description	An interface that, when implemented, indicates that a useful clone() method is provided.
Syntax	public interface **Cloneable** extends Object
Package	java.lang
Import	java.lang.Object
Comments	Although Cloneable doesn't define any methods, classes implementing Cloneable should define a useful clone() method.
Example	In this example, a trivial class is shown that implements the Cloneable interface and defines clone().

```
class tearsofaclone implements Cloneable {
   int j;
   public tearsofaclone(int i) {j = i;}
   protected Object clone() {
      tearsofaclone twin = new tearsofaclone(j);
      return (Object) twin;
   }
}
```

The Global Classes Project: A Type-Safe Linked List

Project Overview

This chapter's project is a linked list, which makes use of the Object and Class classes. The project is an example of a collection class, that is, a class that collects items. Java provides certain collections in the java.utils package, notably Vector, which is a resizable array. Vectors handle several cases well, but are not well suited for insertions, since elements need to be moved in order to make room.

A linked list solves this problem, since adjacent elements don't need to occupy adjacent memory locations. Instead, each element has a link to its neighbor. In this project, a doubly linked list is implemented (named the List class). Each element has a link to its neighbors both ahead and behind it. This makes for easy insertion and removal at the head or tail of the list (since only links need to be adjusted). For this reason, doubly linked lists are well-suited for implementing FIFO (first-in, first-out) queues, where all additions are at one end, and all removals are at the other. This is in contrast to a stack, in which entries are added and removed from the same side (LIFO, or last-in, first-out). Stacks are generally implemented as vectors.

Since the List class is very similar to Java's Vector class, where possible, most of List's methods are named identically to Vector methods. This allows for switching from a Vector to a List just by changing a declaration statement. Also, the List implemented here can be constructed from a Vector. This allows for changing from one to the other at runtime.

One of the misconceptions of Java is that it has no pointers. Since lists have links that are typically modeled by using pointers, this shortcoming would make lists difficult to do in Java. While Java does not have an explicit pointer type, it implicitly has pointers, since it passes and assigns arrays and objects by reference. The List class demonstrates how links between items in the list are established, by simply using Java's assignment by reference.

Safety First

The List class also illustrates the concept of type safety. The java.util.Vector class allows Objects to be inserted, which means any instance of any class can be included. This is good news and bad news. On the one hand, a single Vector class can be used to model a heterogeneous collection. On the other hand, there is nothing in Vector that prevents you from inadvertently creating a collection of Numbers, Strings, and Threads.

The classes in this project offer a solution to this problem. The List class, like Vector, allows any kind of object to be inserted. A second class, TypedList, is a collection that lets you constrain what type(s) of objects can be inserted. This constraint is imposed using features of the Class class, which allows runtime type querying. The TypedList inherits from the List class, and simply overrides the insertion methods in order to check to see if the inserted object is "OK." If it is, the object is passed up to the List class to do the usual insertion. This arrangement lets the TypedList class focus on its added feature, type checking, and defer all other aspects back to its parent.

Lastly, note that TypedList can have as strict or relaxed type checking as you need. For example, if you need a collection of Numbers that may contain Doubles or Integers, you can constrain the list to allow in Numbers, since Doubles and Integers *are* Numbers. The type checking looks up the hierarchy to see that the candidate element is (or is an ancestor of) the allowed type. In one extreme case, if you constrain the allowed types to be Objects, then the TypedList behaves exactly like the simple List (although with additional overhead of checking each inserted object). In the spirit of paying only for what you need, both List and TypedList are offered here, to allow a choice between fast and careful.

The classes in the project are shown in Table 3-5.

Table 3-5 Project classes

Class	File	Description
List	List.java	A doubly linked list
List0	List0.java	A minimal doubly linked list
listest0	listest0.java	A sample driver that exercises the lists
ListItem	ListItem.java	An element in the list (including links to neighbors)
TypedList	TypedList.java	A type-safe doubly linked list
TypedList0	TypedList0.java	A minimal type-safe doubly linked list

Building the Project

1. Enter the following code (Listing 3-4) into a file named ListItem.java, and compile it with javac. ListItem represents one leaf (data plus pointers) of the linked list.

Listing 3-4 ListItem.java

```java
// ListItem is a leaf (entry) of a doubly linked list
// it contains data (type Object), a reference to the next leaf, and
//  a reference to the prior leaf
// defined here are the data elements and set and get methods on each
// as well as a constructor

class ListItem {

    // the heart of the leaf (data)
    Object _data;

    // reference to the next leaf
    ListItem _link_next;

    // reference to the prior leaf
    ListItem _link_prior;

    // only constructor - requires data and both links specified
    // can use null on any item if appropriate or not yet known
    public ListItem(Object data, ListItem link_next, ListItem link_prior)
    {
        _data = data;
        _link_next = link_next;
        _link_prior = link_prior;
    }

    // return the data of the leaf
    public Object data() { return _data; }

    // return reference to the next leaf
    public ListItem link_next() { return _link_next; }

    // return reference to the prior leaf
    public ListItem link_prior() { return _link_prior; }

    // set data of leaf
    public void set_data(Object o) {_data = o;}

    // set reference to next leaf
    public void set_link_next(ListItem link) { _link_next = link; }

    // set reference to prior leaf
    public void set_link_prior(ListItem link) { _link_prior = link; }
}
```

2. Enter the following code (Listing 3-5) into a file named List0.java, and compile it with javac. List0 implements a subset of a list's typical functionality. A superset of the list presented here can be found on the CD, in List.java. The methods included here are clone(), size(), contains(), indexOf(), addElement(), insertElementAt(), prependElement(), removeAllElements(), and toString(). List.java augments these by also defining array(), isEmpty(), firstElement(), lastElement(), elementAt(), lastIndexOf(), removeFirstElement(), removeLastElement(), removeElementAt(), copyInto(), and toStringReverse().

Listing 3-5 List0.java

```
// implement a doubly-link list of any type of Object
// subset of functionality that is in List.java

import ListItem;
import java.util.Vector;

public class List0 implements Cloneable {

    // reference to the start of the list, or null if empty list
    ListItem _head;

    // reference to the end of the list, or null if empty list
    ListItem _tail;

    // number of items in the list (for efficiency)
    int _count;

    // default constructor an empty list
    public List0()
    {
        removeAllElements();
    }

    // convenience constructor - a list from an array
    public List0(Object anArray[]) {
        removeAllElements();
        int length = anArray.length;

        for (int i=0; i<length; i++)
            addElement(anArray[i]);
    }

    // create a new linked list
    public synchronized Object clone() {
        List0 result = new List0();
        ListItem item = _head;
        for (int i=0; i<_count; i++) {
            result.addElement(item.data());
            item = item.link_next();
        }
        return result;
    }

    // return number of entries in list
```

```
public int size()
{
   return _count;
}

// return true if an element is contained in the list
public boolean contains(Object elem) {
   return indexOf(elem) >= 0;
}

// return the index of a particular element, or -1 if not found
public int indexOf(Object elem) {
   return indexOf(elem, 0);
}

// return the index of a particular element, looking from a starting index
//  -1 if not found
public synchronized int indexOf(Object elem, int start)
{
   if (elem == null || start >= _count)
      return -1;

   // fast forward
   ListItem item = _head;
   int i;
   for (i=0; i<start; i++)
      item = item.link_next();

   for (; item != null; i++) {
      if (elem.equals(item.data()))
         return i;
      item = item.link_next();
   }
   return -1;
}

// an element to end of list
public synchronized void addElement(Object obj)
{
   ListItem newitem = new ListItem(obj, null, _tail);
   if (_tail != null)
      _tail.set_link_next(newitem);
   _tail = newitem;
   if (_head == null)
      _head = newitem;
   _count++;
}

// place an element at the start of the list
public synchronized void prependElement(Object obj)
{
   ListItem new_entry = new ListItem(obj, _head, null);
   if (_head != null)
      _head.set_link_prior(new_entry);
   _head = new_entry;
   if (_tail == null)
```

continued on next page

continued from previous page

```
        _tail = new_entry;
    _count++;
}

// put an element at a particular location
// return false if the location is negative or too large
//   this should probably throw an exception instead
public synchronized boolean insertElementAt(Object obj, int index)
{
    // handle prepend and append as simpler cases
    if (index == 0) {
        prependElement(obj);
        return true;
    }
    if (index == _count) {
        addElement(obj);
        return true;
    }

    // off end of list no good, could throw exception
    if (index < 0 || index > _count) {
        return false;
    }

    // find location and adjust pointers
    ListItem item = _head.link_next();
    int i = 1;
    while (item != null) {
        if (index == i) {
            ListItem before = item.link_prior();
            ListItem new_entry = new ListItem(obj, item, before);
            item.set_link_prior(new_entry);
            before.set_link_next(new_entry);
            _count++;
            return true;
        }
        item = item.link_next();
        i++;
    }
    // shouldn't get here, but just in case
    return false;
}

// reset list to empty
//   presumably this will fire the garbage collector on the dropped elements
public synchronized void removeAllElements()
{
    _head = null;
    _tail = null;
    _count = 0;
}

// String rep of list, by chaining together String rep of elements
public synchronized String toString()
{
    String result = "";
    ListItem item = _head;
    while (item != null) {
```

```
        Object obj = item.data();
        result = result + obj.toString() + "\n";
        item = item.link_next();
    }
    return result;
}

}
```

3. Enter the following code (Listing 3-6) into a file named TypedList0.java, and compile it with javac. TypedList0 augments the List0 class (shown above) by defining constructors and insertion methods that check an element's type before inserting it into the list. The CD also contains TypedList.java, which defines TypedList to inherit from the more full-featured List.

Listing 3-6 *TypedList0.java*

```java
// Augment the List class to constrain allowable types in the list
// In addition to constructors and type-checking methods,
// all element insertion methods in List are overridden

import List0;

class TypedList0 extends List0 {

    // maintain the acceptable class
    Class _class;

    // construct an empty list, with particular type
    public TypedList0(Class allowed_class)
    {
        super();
        _class = allowed_class;
    }

    // methods to check for valid type and complain

    public synchronized void checkType(Object obj)
    {
        for (Class c = obj.getClass(); c != null; c = c.getSuperclass()) {
            if (c.equals(_class))
                return;
        }
        typeComplaint(obj);
    }

    void typeComplaint(Object obj)
    {
        throw new IllegalArgumentException(
                "Can't add object of type " +
                obj.getClass().getName()   +
                " to TypedList of type "    +
                _class.getName());
    }
```

continued on next page

continued from previous page

```
    // intercept all methods that add items to list, to check their type

    // add item to end of list
    public synchronized void addElement(Object obj)
    {
        checkType(obj);
        super.addElement(obj);
    }

    // insert item at a particular place in the list
    public synchronized boolean insertElementAt(Object obj, int index)
    {
        checkType(obj);
        return super.insertElementAt(obj, index);
    }

    // put item at start of list
    public synchronized void prependElement(Object obj)
    {
        checkType(obj);
        super.prependElement(obj);
    }
}
```

4. Enter the following code (Listing 3-7) into a file named listest0.java, and compile it with javac. This is driver to test the list and the type-safe list.

Listing 3-7 listest0.java

```
// test a doubly linked list, as well as the strongly typed variant

import TypedList0;

class listest0 {
    static public void main(String[] args)
        throws IllegalArgumentException, ClassNotFoundException
    {

        // add and remove strings and numbers from a List
        List0 list = new List0();
        list.addElement("Hello");
        list.addElement("Goodbye");

        // since this list isn't typed, any objects are allowed
        list.addElement(new Integer(999));

        list.insertElementAt("Pre Item", 0);
        System.out.println(list);
        System.out.println("Size=" + list.size());

        list.insertElementAt("1", 1);
        list.insertElementAt("3", 3);
        System.out.println(list);

        list.removeAllElements();

        // make a list from a string array
```

```
String s[] = {"one", "two", "three"};
List0 list2 = new List0(s);
System.out.println(list2);

System.out.println(""+list2.indexOf("three"));
System.out.println(""+list2.contains("four"));

// make a list from a clone
List0 clone = (List0) list2.clone();
System.out.println(clone);

// make a typed list of numbers
TypedList0 typed_list =
    new TypedList0(Class.forName("java.lang.Number"));

// ok to add a more specialized type (e.g., Integer)
typed_list.addElement(new Integer(1));

// not ok to add a more general type (e.g., Object)
// so an exception will be thrown here
typed_list.addElement(new Object());

return;
    }
}
```

Running the Program

At a command prompt, run the program with

```
java listest0
```

Note that the program is designed to generate an exception as a result of the last operation, which attempts to add a invalid object to a typed list.

4

NUMBERS

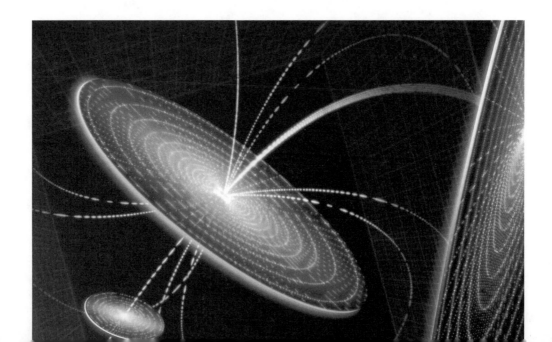

4

NUMBERS

In Chapter 2, The Java Language, the primitive arithmetic types, byte, short, int, long, float, and double, were described. Java defines four classes, Integer, Long, Float, and Double, that extend the Number class and provide object representations of most of these primitives. This allows programmers to treat numbers as objects. (Boolean and Character are class representations of boolean and character primitives, and are covered in Chapter 5, Boolean and Character Classes.) The Number classes also provide several useful methods, mostly for converting between different types of numbers, or between numbers and Strings. Constants in these classes include the maximum and minimum values that numeric primitives can take.

Java's Math class provides a family of methods for operating on numbers. Included are methods for trigonometry, exponentials, rounding, random numbers, and comparisons. Also, approximations for the mathematical constants e and pi are defined in the Math class. The classes covered in this chapter, and their inheritance relationships, are shown in Figure 4-1.

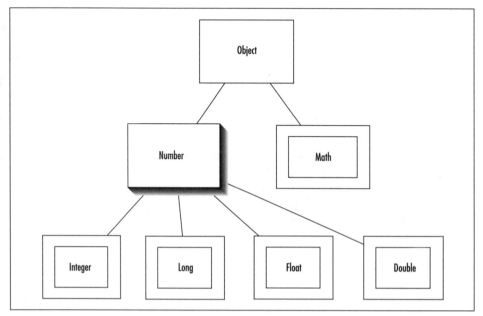

Figure 4-1 Number and Math classes

The Number Classes

Java's primitives, int, long, float, and double, have corresponding classes, Integer, Long, Float, and Double. These are "wrapper" classes, so-called because a primitive variable is contained inside of a class. Listing 4-1 shows a skeletal example of a Double wrapper. These classes are provided in order to use primitives where objects are required, such as method parameters, return values, or variables. Examples of such usage are in Java's collection classes, Vector, Hashtable, Stack, and Dictionary. These allow insertion and searching of Objects. Since primitives aren't Objects, they can't be used with the standard collections. Instead, you can use the Number classes to build collections of numbers. Note that Integer, Float, Double, and Long are final classes, so no classes can extend them.

Listing 4-1 The essentials of the Double class

```
public final class Double extends Number {

    // The value of the Double
    private double value;

    // Construct double wrapper for specified double primitive
    public Double(double d) {
        value = d;
    }
```

```
// return the double primitive
public double doubleValue() {
   return value;
}

// other constants and methods not shown
}
```

Why Primitives?

Having seen why there is a need for number classes, you might ask the reverse question: why primitives? In a pure object-oriented language, there would be no primitives — everything would be an object. In Java, this is not the case. Certain number types have both a language-defined primitive type and a class analog. Since Java does not allow operator overloading, primitives allow for streamlined arithmetic expressions like a = b + c, instead of an object-based expression like a = b.add(c). Primitives are also likely to be more efficient than objects in most operations. Lastly, Java borrows heavily from the C language, including its support for primitive types and operations.

Number Methods

The number methods can be grouped into several categories: casting, converting, comparing, describing, and properties. These are shown in Table 4-1.

Table 4-1 Number classes methods, by category

Class	Category	Methods
Double	Casting	doubleValue, floatValue, intValue, longValue
	Conversion	doubleToLongBits, longBitsToDouble, toString, valueOf
	Comparison	equals, hashCode
	Description	isInfinite, isNaN
Float	Casting	doubleValue, floatValue, intValue, longValue
	Conversion	floatToIntBits, intBitsToFloat, toString, valueOf
	Comparison	equals, hashCode
	Description	isInfinite, isNaN
Integer	Casting	doubleValue, floatValue, intValue, longValue
	Comparison	equals, hashCode
	Conversion	parseInt, toString, valueOf
	Properties	getInteger
Long	Casting	doubleValue, floatValue, intValue, longValue
	Comparison	equals, hashCode
	Conversion	parseLong, toString, valueOf
	Properties	getLong
Number	Casting	doubleValue, floatValue, intValue, longValue

> ### Inherited Methods
> Since Number's children inherit indirectly from their "grandparent," Object, all of Object's methods are available to these classes. Three of Object's methods are overridden (redefined) by Double, Float, Integer, and Long: equals(), hashCode(), and toString(). The other Object methods inherited are clone(), finalize(), getClass(), notify(), notifyAll(), and wait().

Of the comparison methods, equals() tests to see if two objects have the same type and contained value. This is different from the Object definition, which compares the instances to see if they are the same. The hashCode() method is provided to generate an integer code used in hash tables.

Casting and conversion methods include toString(), which generates a String representation of a number. The primitive contained in an object can be extracted with doubleValue(), floatValue(), intValue(), and longValue(). These methods will cast the value, if needed, to the requested type. The valueOf(), parseInt(), and parseLong() methods convert from a string (e.g., "123") to a number. The bit pattern of floating primitives can be transferred to and from the similarly sized integral type. These methods are doubleToLongBits(), longBitsToDouble(), floatToIntBits(), and intBitsToFloat().

The Double and Float classes allow testing for special values by isNaN() and isInfinite(). The methods getInteger() and getLong() are provided as a convenience for inquiring about a property. For more information about properties, see System, described in Chapter 7, System Classes.

Number Constants

Each of the Number classes defines the range of valid primitive values in the constants MAX_VALUE and MIN_VALUE. Additionally, Double and Float define special values: NEGATIVE_INFINITY, POSITIVE_INFINITY, and NaN (Not a Number). While MAX_VALUE is a definite value that is the largest a type can hold, POSITIVE_INFINITY is a special value that is larger than any other value, including MAX_VALUE. These constants are shown in Table 4-2.

Table 4-2 Number classes constants

Class	Constants
Double	MAX_VALUE, MIN_VALUE, NEGATIVE_INFINITY, NaN, POSITIVE_INFINITY
Float	MAX_VALUE, MIN_VALUE, NEGATIVE_INFINITY, NaN, POSITIVE_INFINITY
Integer	MAX_VALUE, MIN_VALUE
Long	MAX_VALUE, MIN_VALUE

When Is a Number Not a Number?

The results of certain mathematical expressions aren't valid. For example, there is no way to take the square root of a negative number. In Java, as in some other languages, a special value called NaN (Not a Number) is returned to represent the result of the invalid calculation. Java takes this approach as opposed to throwing exceptions. The check for NaN can be made through Double.isNaN() and Float.isNaN(). Here are some cases that return NaN:

Operations with NaN:

a * NaN;   a / NaN;   a % NaN;   a + NaN;   a - NaN

Operations with Inf:

Inf * 0;   Inf - NegInf;   Inf / Inf;   Inf % a

Operations with 0:

0 / 0;   a % 0

The Number Classes Method Summaries

This section provides a reference for the Number-related classes. Table 4-3 lists these classes. Following this, each class is described in detail.

Table 4-3 The Number classes

Class	Description
Double	A class corresponding to the double primitive
Float	A class corresponding to the float primitive
Integer	A class corresponding to the int primitive
Long	A class corresponding to the long primitive
Number	An abstract parent class for the above four classes

The java.lang.Double Class

This section provides a reference for the java.lang.Double class. The constants are shown in Table 4-4. In Table 4-5, a short description of each method is given. Following these tables are sections that describe each method and constant in detail.

Table 4-4 Summary of Double constants

Constant	Description
MAX_VALUE	The maximum allowable double value
MIN_VALUE	The minimum allowable positive double value

continued on next page

continued from previous page

Constant	Description
NaN	Special value of Not a Number
NEGATIVE_INFINITY	Negative infinity (smaller than any possible double)
POSITIVE_INFINITY	Positive infinity (larger than any possible double)

Table 4-5 Summary of Double methods

Method	Description
doubleToLongBits	Converts a double to long bits
doubleValue	Returns the primitive double value of the object
equals	Tests to see if an object is equal to this Double instance
floatValue	Returns the value of the object, as a float
hashCode	Returns a hash code
intValue	Returns the value of the object, as an int
isInfinite	Checks to see if the value is a Java infinity
isNaN	Checks to see if the value is a Java Not a Number
longBitsToDouble	Copies the bit pattern from a long to a double
longValue	Returns the value of the object, as a long
toString	Converts the Double to a String
valueOf	Converts a String to a Double

DOUBLE

Description	A class representation of a double, and constants and methods related to double.
Syntax	public class **Double** extends Number
Package	java.lang
Import	java.lang.Double (not required)
Constructors	public **Double**(double *value*) public **Double**(String *str*)
Parameters	
double *value*	A primitive double to use as the wrapped value.
String *str*	A string to parse to a double.
Exceptions	A NumberFormatException is thrown if the String does not contain a valid double.

Example   In this example, Doubles are constructed using both forms of the constructor.

```
Double d1 = new Double(100.);
Double d2 = new Double("100.");
```

Constants

MAX_VALUE

Class Name	Double
Description	The maximum value that a Java double can store.
Syntax	public final static double **MAX_VALUE**
See Also	MIN_VALUE
Comments	The value is 1.79769313486231570e+308.
Example	In this example, a variable is initialized with MAX_VALUE.

```
double result = Double.MAX_VALUE;
```

MIN_VALUE

Class Name	Double
Description	The minimum positive value that a Java double can store.
Syntax	public final static double **MIN_VALUE**
See Also	MAX_VALUE
Comments	The value is 4.94065645841246544e-324.
Example	In this example, a variable is initialized with MIN_VALUE.

```
double result = Double.MIN_VALUE;
```

NaN

Class Name	Double
Description	A double representation of Not a Number.
Syntax	public final static double **NaN**
See Also	isNaN()
Comments	NaN is returned when the mathematical expression can't be evaluated. Examples, such as 0./0., are shown earlier in this chapter.
Example	A method that throws an exception, instead of generating a NaN on invalid divides, is defined below.

```
public static double checkdivide(double a, double b) throws Exception {
    if (Double.isNaN(a) || Double.isNaN(b))
        throw new Exception("Invalid Division");
    return a / b;
}
```

NEGATIVE_INFINITY

Class Name	Double
Description	A double representation of negative infinity.
Syntax	public final static double **NEGATIVE_INFINITY**
See Also	POSITIVE_INFINITY
Comments	The value is generated by -1.0 / 0.0. A negative infinity results when any negative number is divided by zero.
Example	In this example, a variable is initialized to negative infinity.

```
double result = Double.NEGATIVE_INFINITY;
```

POSITIVE_INFINITY

Class Name	Double
Description	A double representation of positive infinity.
Syntax	public final static double **POSITIVE_INFINITY**
See Also	NEGATIVE_INFINITY
Comments	The value is generated by 1.0 / 0.0. A positive infinity results when any positive number is divided by zero.
Example	In this example, a variable is initialized to positive infinity.

```
double result = Double.POSITIVE_INFINITY;
```

Methods

DOUBLETOLONGBITS

Class Name	Double
Description	Converts a double to long bits.
Syntax	public static long **doubleToLongBits**(double *value*)
Parameters	
double *value*	The value to convert.
Returns	The return type is long. Its value is the number represented as a set of bits.
Exceptions	None.

See Also	longBitsToDouble()
Comments	This transfers the double's bit pattern to a long. To convert the value to a rounded long value, use longValue(). This method is used by Double.equals()—the doubles being compared are converted to longs, and then compared (this is probably more efficient that a simple comparison of doubles). It is also used in DataOutputStream and RandomAccessFile for writing doubles.
Example	In this example, two numbers are compared using their long bits representation.

```
double a = 5.;
double b = 5.;
long la = Double.doubleToLongBits(a);
long lb = Double.doubleToLongBits(b);
boolean compare = (la == lb);
```

DOUBLEVALUE

Class Name	Double
Description	Returns the primitive double value of the object.
Syntax	public double **doubleValue()**
Parameters	None.
Returns	The return type is double. It is the value of the double contained in the Double object.
Exceptions	None.
Example	This example, constructs a Double, then extracts its value.

```
Double a = new Double(5.);
double d = a.doubleValue();
```

EQUALS

Class Name	Double
Description	Tests to see if an object is equal to this Double instance.
Syntax	public boolean **equals**(Object *obj*)
Parameters	
Object *obj*	Object to compare.
Returns	The return type is boolean. It returns true if the parameter is a Double, and the values are the same. If the parameter is another type of Number with the same value, equals() returns false.
Exceptions	None.

Comments

Double overrides the definition provided by Object, which compares references instead of values. The Double.doubleToLongBits() method is used to compare the doubles as represented by their long bit equivalents.

Example

In this example, two distinct doubles with the same value are compared.

```
Double a = new Double(5.);
Double b = new Double(5.);
boolean c = a.equals(b);
```

FLOATVALUE

Class Name	Double
Description	Returns the value of the object, as a float.
Syntax	public float **floatValue**()
Parameters	None.
Returns	The return type is float. It is the value contained in the Double object, cast to a float.
Exceptions	None.
Comments	The conversion is performed by a simple cast. If the value is too large to fit into a float, an infinity will result. Rounding may also occur.
Example	A value too large for a float is converted below.

```
Double a = new Double(Double.MAX_VALUE);
float f = a.floatValue();
```

HASHCODE

Class Name	Double
Description	Returns a hash code.
Syntax	public int **hashCode**()
Parameters	None.
Returns	The return type is int. It is a hash code for the object.
Exceptions	None.
See Also	Hashcode
Example	A hash code is generated below.

```
Double a = new Double(5.);
int hash = a.hashCode();
```

INTVALUE

Class Name	Double
Description	Returns the value of the object, as an int.
Syntax	public int **intValue**()
Parameters	None.
Returns	The return type is int. It is the value contained in the Double object, cast to an int.
Exceptions	None.
Comments	The value is truncated to an integral value. If the value's magnitude is too large to fit into an int, then the largest or smallest int will result. If the value is NaN, a zero will result. No exceptions are thrown.
Example	In this example, a Double is constructed, and its value, cast to an integer, is extracted.

```
Double a = new Double(5.9);
int i = a.intValue();
```

ISINFINITE

Class Name	Double
Description	Checks to see if the value is a Java infinity.
Syntax	public boolean **isInfinite**() public static boolean **isInfinite**(double *d*)
Parameters	
double *d*	A value to check.
Returns	The return type is boolean. It is true if the value represents a Java infinity.
Exceptions	None.
Comments	This method has two variants: a static method, and an instance method. true is returned if the value is Double.POSITIVE_INFINITY or Double.NEGATIVE_INFINITY.
Example	This example confirms that the two infinities test true.

```
double posinf = Double.POSITIVE_INFINITY;
double neginf = Double.NEGATIVE_INFINITY;
System.out.println("Positive Infinity test: " + Double.isInfinite(posinf));
System.out.println("Negative Infinity test: " + Double.isInfinite(neginf));
```

isNaN

Class Name	Double
Description	Checks to see if the value is a Java Not a Number.
Syntax	public boolean **isNaN**()
	public static boolean **isNaN**(double *d*)
Parameters	
double *d*	A value to check.
Returns	The return type is boolean. It is true if the value represents a Java NaN.
Exceptions	None.
Comments	This method has two variants: a static method and an instance method. isNaN() should be used instead of the equality operator, since == always returns false if either operand is a NaN.
Example	This example checks to see that a division is valid, using isNaN().

```
public static double checkdivide2(double a, double b) {
   double result = a / b;
   if (Double.isNaN(result) || Double.isInfinite(result))
      throw new Exception("Divide result is NaN or Infinite");
   return result;
}
```

LONGBITSTODOUBLE

Class Name	Double
Description	Copies the bit pattern from a long to a double.
Syntax	public static double **longBitsToDouble**(long *value*)
Parameters	
long *value*	The long to convert.
Returns	The return type is double. It is the set of bits from the parameter.
Exceptions	None.
See Also	doubleToLongBits()
Comments	This method is used in DataInputStream and RandomAccessFile for reading doubles.
Example	In this example, a long is converted, first by bits, and then by value.

```
long bits = 0;
double d = Double.longBitsToDouble(bits);
double d2 = (double) bits;
```

LONGVALUE

Class Name	Double
Description	Returns the value of the object, as a long.
Syntax	public long **longValue**()
Parameters	None.
Returns	The return type is long. It is the value contained in the Double object, cast to a long.
Exceptions	None.
Comments	The value is truncated to an integral value. If the value's magnitude is too large to fit into a long, then the largest or smallest long will result. If the value is NaN, a zero will result. No exceptions are thrown.
Example	This example checks the conversion of NaN to long.

```
Double a = new Double(Double.NaN);
long zilch = a.longValue();
```

TOSTRING

Class Name	Double
Description	Converts the Double to a String.
Syntax	public String **toString**()
	public static String **toString**(double *d*)
Parameters	
double *d*	A double to convert to a String.
Returns	The return type is String. It is a string representation of the number.
Exceptions	None.
Comments	The instance method overrides the implementation in Object.toString(). No particular formatting can be specified.
Example	In this example, both types of toString() methods are used to convert a number to a String.

```
Double a = new Double(5.);
String s = a.toString();
String s2 = Double.toString(5.);
```

VALUEOF

Class Name	Double
Description	Converts a String to a Double.
Syntax	public static Double **valueOf**(String s)
Parameters	
String s	A String to parse and convert.
Returns	The return type is Double. It is a Double representation of the number stored in the string.
Exceptions	If the value can't be converted, a NumberFormatException is thrown.
See Also	toString()
Example	In this example, a sample set of Strings are converted to Doubles.

```
String [] strings = {"1", "10", "100", "1000", "Mom"};
int length = strings.length;
Double d[] = new Double[length];
for (int i=0; i<length; i++) {
   try {
      d[i] = Double.valueOf(strings[i]);
   } catch (NumberFormatException e) {
      System.out.println("Invalid Number: " + strings[i]);
   }
}
```

The java.lang.Float Class

This section provides a reference for the java.lang.Float class. The constants are shown in Table 4-6. In Table 4-7 a short description of each method is given. Following these tables are sections that describe each constant and method in detail.

Table 4-6 Summary of Float constants

Constant	Description
MAX_VALUE	The maximum allowable float value
MIN_VALUE	The minimum allowable positive float value
NaN	Special value of Not a Number
NEGATIVE_INFINITY	Negative infinity
POSITIVE_INFINITY	Positive infinity

Table 4-7 Summary of Float methods

Method	Description
doubleValue	Returns the value of the object, as a double
equals	Tests to see if an object is equal to this Float instance
floatToIntBits	Converts a float to int bits
floatValue	Returns the primitive value of the object
hashCode	Returns a hash code
intBitsToFloat	Copies the bit pattern from an int to a float
intValue	Returns the value of the object, as an int
isInfinite	Checks to see if the value is a Java infinity
isNaN	Checks to see if the value is a Java Not a Number
longValue	Returns the value of the object, as a long
toString	Converts the Float to a String
valueOf	Converts a String to a Float

FLOAT

Description	A class representation of a float, and constants and methods related to float.
Syntax	public class **Float** extends Number
Package	java.lang
Import	java.lang.Float (not required)
Constructors	public **Float**(float *value*) public **Float**(double *dvalue*) public **Float**(String *str*)
Parameters	
float *value*	A primitive float to use as the wrapped value.
double *dvalue*	A double to use as the wrapped value.
String *str*	A string to parse to a float.
Exceptions	A NumberFormatException is thrown if the String does not contain a valid float.
Example	In this example, floats are constructed using both forms of the constructor.

```
Float d1 = new Float(100);
Float d2 = new Float("100");
```

Constants

MAX_VALUE

Class Name	Float
Description	The maximum value that a Java float can store.
Syntax	public static float **MAX_VALUE**
See Also	MIN_VALUE
Comments	The value is approximately 3.4e38.
Example	In this example, a variable is initialized with MAX_VALUE.

```
float result = Float.MAX_VALUE;
```

MIN_VALUE

Class Name	Float
Description	The minimum positive value that a Java float can store.
Syntax	public static float **MIN_VALUE**
See Also	MAX_VALUE
Comments	The value is approximately 1.4e-45.
Example	In this example, a variable is initialized with MIN_VALUE.

```
float result = Float.MIN_VALUE;
```

NaN

Class Name	Float
Description	A float representation of Not a Number.
Syntax	public static float **NaN**
See Also	isNaN()
Comments	NaN is returned when the mathematical expression can't be evaluated. Examples, such as 0./0., are described earlier in this chapter.
Example	A method that throws an exception, instead of generating a NaN on invalid divides, is defined below.

```
public static float checkdivide(float a, float b) throws Exception {
   if (Float.isNaN(a) || Float.isNaN(b))
      throw new Exception("Invalid Division");
   return a / b;
}
```

NEGATIVE_INFINITY

Class Name	Float
Description	A float representation of negative infinity.
Syntax	public static float **NEGATIVE_INFINITY**
See Also	POSITIVE_INFINITY
Comments	The value is generated by -1.0 / 0.0.
Example	This example initializes a variable to negative infinity.

```
float result = Float.NEGATIVE_INFINITY;
```

POSITIVE_INFINITY

Class Name	Float
Description	A float representation of positive infinity.
Syntax	public static float **POSITIVE_INFINITY**
See Also	NEGATIVE_INFINITY
Comments	The value is generated by 1.0 / 0.0.
Example	This example initializes a variable to positive infinity.

```
float result = Float.POSITIVE_INFINITY;
```

Methods

DOUBLEVALUE

Class Name	Float
Description	Returns the primitive value of the object, as a double.
Syntax	public double **doubleValue**()
Parameters	None.
Returns	The return type is double. It is the value of the object, cast to a double.
Exceptions	None.
Example	This example constructs a Float, then extracts its value.

```
Float a = new Float(5.);
double d = a.doubleValue();
```

EQUALS

Class Name	Float
Description	Tests to see if an object is equal to this Float instance.
Syntax	public boolean **equals**(Object *obj*)
Parameters	
Object *obj*	Object to compare.
Returns	The return type is boolean. It returns true if the parameter is a Float and the values are the same.
Exceptions	None.
Comments	Float overrides the definition provided by Object, which compares references instead of values. The floatToIntBits() method is used to compare the floats as represented by their int bit equivalents.
Example	In this example, two distinct floats with the same value are compared.

```
Float a = new Float(5);
Float b = new Float(5);
boolean c = a.equals(b);
```

FLOATTOINTBITS

Class Name	Float
Description	Converts a float to int bits.
Syntax	public static int **floatToIntBits**(float *value*)
Parameters	
float *value*	The value to convert.
Returns	The return type is int. Its value is the number represented as a set of bits.
Exceptions	None.
See Also	intBitsToFloat()
Comments	This transfers the float's bit pattern to an int. This method is used by Float.equals()—the floats being compared are converted to ints, and then compared. It is also used in DataOutputStream and RandomAccessFile for writing floats. To convert a Float to a rounded int value, use intValue().
Example	In this example, two numbers are compared using their int bits representation.

```
float a = 5.f;
float b = 5.f;
int ia = Float.floatToIntBits(a);
int ib = Float.floatToIntBits(b);
boolean compare = (ia == ib);
```

FLOATVALUE

Class Name	Float
Description	Returns the value of the object, as a float.
Syntax	public float **floatValue**()
Parameters	None.
Returns	The return type is float. It is the value contained in the Float object.
Exceptions	None.
Example	This example constructs a Float, then extracts its value.

```
Float a = new Float(Float.MAX_VALUE);
float f = a.floatValue();
```

HASHCODE

Class Name	Float
Description	Returns a hash code.
Syntax	public int **hashCode**()
Parameters	None.
Returns	The return type is int. It is a hash code for the object.
Exceptions	None.
See Also	Hashcode
Example	A hash code is generated below.

```
Float a = new Float(5);
int hash = a.hashCode();
```

INTBITSTOFLOAT

Class Name	Float
Description	Copies the bit pattern from an int to a float.
Syntax	public static float **intBitsToFloat**(int *value*)
Parameters	
int *value*	The int to convert.
Returns	The return type is float. It is formed from the set of bits in the parameter.
Exceptions	None.
See Also	floatToIntBits()
Comments	This method is used in DataInputStream and RandomAccessFile for reading floats.

Example   In this example, an int is converted, first by bits, and then by value.

```
int bits = 0;
float d = Float.intBitsToFloat(bits);
float d2 = (float) bits;
```

INTVALUE

Class Name	Float
Description	Returns the value of the object, as an int.
Syntax	public int **intValue**()
Parameters	None.
Returns	The return type is int. It is the value contained in the Float object, cast to an int.
Exceptions	None.
Comments	The value is truncated to an integral value. If the value's magnitude is too large to fit into an int, then the largest or smallest int will result. If the value is NaN, a zero will result. No exceptions are thrown.
Example	In this example, a Float is constructed and its value, cast to an integer, is extracted.

```
Float a = new Float(5.9);
int i = a.intValue();
```

ISINFINITE

Class Name	Float
Description	Checks to see if the value is a Java infinity.
Syntax	public boolean **isInfinite**() public static boolean **isInfinite**(float *d*)
Parameters	
float *d*	A value to check.
Returns	The return type is boolean. It is true if the value represents a Java infinity.
Exceptions	None.
Comments	This method has two variants: a static method, and an instance method. true is returned if the value is Float.POSITIVE_INFINITY or Float.NEGATIVE_INFINITY.
Example	This example confirms that the two infinities test true.

```
float posinf = Float.POSITIVE_INFINITY;
float neginf = Float.NEGATIVE_INFINITY;
System.out.println("Positive Infinity test: " + Float.isInfinite(posinf));
System.out.println("Negative Infinity test: " + Float.isInfinite(neginf));
```

ISNaN

Class Name	Float
Description	Checks to see if the value is a Java Not a Number.
Syntax	public boolean **isNaN**()
	public static boolean **isNaN**(float *d*)
Parameters	
float *d*	A value to check.
Returns	The return type is boolean. It is true if the value represents a Java NaN.
Exceptions	None.
Comments	This method has two variants: a static method and an instance method. isNaN() should be used instead of the equality operator, since == always returns false if either operand is a NaN.
Example	This example checks to see that a division is valid, using isNaN().

```
public static float checkdivide2(float a, float b) {
   float result = a / b;
   if (Float.isNaN(result) || Float.isInfinite(result))
      throw new Exception("Divide result is NaN or Infinite");
   return result;
}
```

LONGVALUE

Class Name	Float
Description	Returns the value of the object, as a long.
Syntax	public long **longValue**()
Parameters	None.
Returns	The return type is long. It is the value contained in the Float object, cast to a long.
Exceptions	None.
Comments	The value is truncated to an integral value. If the value's magnitude is too large to fit into a long, then the largest or smallest long will result. If the value is NaN, a zero will result. No exceptions are thrown.
Example	This example checks the conversion of NaN to long.

```
Float a = new Float(Float.NaN);
long zilch = a.longValue();
```

TOSTRING

Class Name	Float
Description	Converts the Float to a String.
Syntax	public String **toString**()
	public static String **toString**(float *d*)
Parameters	
float *d*	A float to convert to a String.
Returns	The return type is String. It is a string representation of the number.
Exceptions	None.
Comments	The instance method overrides the implementation in Object.toString(). No particular formatting can be specified.
Example	In this example, both types of toString() methods are used to convert a number to a String.

```
Float a = new Float(5);
String s = a.toString();
String s2 = Float.toString(5);
```

VALUEOF

Class Name	Float
Description	Converts a String to a Float.
Syntax	public static Float **valueOf**(String *s*)
Parameters	
String *s*	String to convert to a float
Returns	The return type is Float. It is a Float representation of the number stored in the string.
Exceptions	If the value can't be converted, a NumberFormatException is thrown.
See Also	toString()
Example	In this example, a sample set of Strings are converted to floats.

```
String [] strings = {"1", "10", "100", "1000", "Dad"};
Float d[] = new Float[5];
for (int i=0; i<strings.length; i++) {
   try {
      d[i] = Float.valueOf(strings[i]);
   } catch (NumberFormatException e) {
       System.out.println("Invalid Number: " + strings[i]);
   }
}
```

The java.lang.Integer Class

This section provides a reference for the java.lang.Integer class. The constants are shown in Table 4-8. In Table 4-9 a short description of each method is given. Following these tables are sections that describe each method and constant in detail.

Table 4-8 Summary of Integer constants

Constant	Description
MAX_VALUE	The maximum allowable int value
MIN_VALUE	The minimum allowable int value

Table 4-9 Summary of Integer methods

Method	Description
doubleValue	Returns the value of the object as a double
equals	Tests to see if an object is equal to this Integer instance
floatValue	Returns the value of the object, as a float
getInteger	Returns a system property
hashCode	Returns a hash code
intValue	Returns the primitive value of the object
longValue	Returns the value of the object, as a long
parseInt	Converts a String to an int
toString	Converts the Integer to a String
valueOf	Converts a String to an Integer

INTEGER

Description	A class representation of an int, and constants and methods related to int.
Syntax	public class **Integer** extends Number
Package	java.lang
Import	java.lang.Integer (not required)
Constructors	public **Integer**(int *value*)
	public **Integer**(String *str*)
Parameters	
int *value*	A primitive int to use as the wrapped value.
String *str*	A string to parse to an int.

Exceptions	A NumberFormatException is thrown if the String does not contain a valid integer.
Example	In this example, integers are constructed using both forms of the constructor.

```
Integer i = new Integer(100);
Integer i2 = new Integer("100");
```

Constants

MAX_VALUE

Class Name	Integer
Description	The maximum value that a Java int can store.
Syntax	public static int **MAX_VALUE**
See Also	MIN_VALUE
Comments	The value is 2,147,483,647 (2^{31}-1).
Example	In this example, a variable is initialized with MAX_VALUE.

```
int result = Integer.MAX_VALUE;
```

MIN_VALUE

Class Name	Integer
Description	The minimum value that a Java int can store.
Syntax	public final static double **MIN_VALUE**
See Also	MAX_VALUE
Comments	The value is -2,147,483,648 (-2^{31}).
Example	In this example, a variable is initialized with MIN_VALUE.

```
int result = Integer.MIN_VALUE;
```

Methods

DOUBLEVALUE

Class Name	Integer
Description	Returns the primitive value of the object as a double.
Syntax	public double **doubleValue**()
Parameters	None.

Returns	The return type is double. It is the value contained in the Integer object, cast to a double. No precision is lost.
Exceptions	None.
Example	This example constructs an Integer, then extracts its value as a double.

```
Integer a = new Integer(5);
double d = a.doubleValue();
```

EQUALS

Class Name	Integer
Description	Tests to see if an object is equal to this Integer instance.
Syntax	public boolean **equals**(Object *obj*)
Parameters	
Object *obj*	Object to compare.
Returns	The return type is boolean. It returns true if the parameter is an Integer and the contained values are the same.
Exceptions	None.
Comments	Integer overrides the definition provided by Object, which compares references instead of values.
Example	In this example, two distinct integers with the same value are compared.

```
Integer a = new Integer(5);
Integer b = new Integer(5);
boolean c = a.equals(b);
```

FLOATVALUE

Class Name	Integer
Description	Returns the value of the object, as a float.
Syntax	public float **floatValue**()
Parameters	None.
Returns	The return type is float. It is the value contained in the Integer object, cast to a float.
Exceptions	None.
Comments	The conversion is performed by a cast. Some precision may be lost in the conversion if the value's magnitude is larger than 16,777,216.
Example	A value is converted below.

```
Integer a = new Integer(Integer.MAX_VALUE);
float f = a.floatValue();
```

GETINTEGER

Class Name	Integer
Description	Get the value of an integer property.
Syntax	public static Integer **getInteger**(String *prop*)
	public static Integer **getInteger**(String *prop*, int *defint*)
	public static Integer **getInteger**(String *prop*, Integer *defInt*)
Parameters	
String *prop*	The name of the property.
int *defint*	Value to return if property doesn't exist.
Integer *defInt*	Value to return if property doesn't exist.
Returns	The return type is Integer. It is the value of the property, if it exists.
Exceptions	None.
See Also	System
Comments	If the property doesn't exist, or isn't an integer property, then the second parameter's value is returned. If the second parameter isn't provided, then 0 is returned. The function parses hexadecimal and octal property values.
Example	A hypothetical property is retrieved.

```
Integer property = Integer.getInteger("SomeIntProperty");
```

HASHCODE

Class Name	Integer
Description	Returns a hash code.
Syntax	public int **hashCode**()
Parameters	None.
Returns	The return type is int. It is a hash code for the object.
Exceptions	None.
Comments	The hash code is used in java.util.Hashcode. It is simply the value of the Integer.
Example	A hash code is generated below.

```
Integer a = new Integer(5);
int give_me_five = a.hashCode();
```

INTVALUE

Class Name	Integer
Description	Returns the value of the object.
Syntax	public int **intValue**()

Parameters	None.
Returns	The return type is int. It is the value contained in the Integer object.
Exceptions	None.
Comments	This is the contained value of the Integer.
Example	In this example, an Integer is constructed and its value is extracted.

```
Integer a = new Integer(5);
int i = a.intValue();
```

LONGVALUE

Class Name	Integer
Description	Returns the value of the object, as a long.
Syntax	public long longValue()
Parameters	None.
Returns	The return type is long. It is the value contained in the Integer object, cast to a long.
Exceptions	None.
Example	This example checks the conversion of an Integer to long.

```
Integer a = new Integer(Integer.MAX_VALUE);
long value = a.longValue();
```

PARSEINT

Class Name	Integer
Description	Converts a String to an int.
Syntax	public static int **parseInt**(String *str*) public static int **parseInt**(String *str*, int *radix*)
Parameter	
String *str*	A String representation of a number.
int *radix*	The radix (base) to use for conversion (between 2 and 36).
Returns	The return type is int. It is an int representation of the number stored in the string.
Exceptions	If the value can't be converted, a NumberFormatException is thrown.
Comments	This is similar to the valueOf() method, which returns an Integer. If the radix is omitted, 10 is assumed.
Example	In this example, a sample set of Strings are converted to ints, using various radices.

```
String [] strings = {"1", "10", "100", "1000", "Adam"};
int radi[] = {10, 10, 2, 16, 10);
```

continued on next page

continued from previous page

```
int d[] = new int[5];
for (int i=0; i<strings.length; i++) {
   try {
      d[i] = Integer.parseInt(strings[i], radi[i]);
   } catch (NumberFormatException e) {
      System.out.println("Invalid Number: " + strings[i]);
   }
}
```

TOSTRING

Class Name	Integer
Description	Converts the Integer to a String.
Syntax	public String **toString**()
	public static String **toString**(int *n*)
	public static String **toString**(int *n*, int *radix*)
Parameters	
int *n*	An integer to convert to a String.
int *radix*	The radix (base) to use for conversion (between 2 and 36).
Returns	The return type is String. It is a string representation of the number.
Exceptions	None.
Comments	The instance method overrides the implementation in Object.toString(). No particular formatting can be specified. If the radix is not specified, 10 is assumed.
Example	In this example, each type of toString() method is used to convert a number to a String.

```
Integer a = new Integer(5);
String s1 = a.toString();
String s2 = Integer.toString(5);
String s3 = Integer.toString(5, 10);
```

VALUEOF

Class Name	Integer
Description	Converts a String to an Integer.
Syntax	public static Integer **valueOf**(String *str*)
	public static Integer **valueOf**(String *str*,int *radix*)
Parameters	
String *str*	The String to convert.
int *radix*	The radix (base) to use for conversion (between 2 and 36).

Returns	The return type is Integer. It is an Integer representation of the number stored in the string.
Exceptions	If the value can't be converted, a NumberFormatException is thrown.
See Also	toString(), parseInt()
Example	In this example, a sample set of Strings are converted to integers.

```
String [] strings = {"1", "10", "100", "1000", "Stef"};
Integer d[] = new Integer[5];
for (int i=0; i<strings.length; i++) {
   try {
      d[i] = Integer.valueOf(strings[i]);
   } catch (NumberFormatException e) {
       System.out.println("Invalid Number: " + strings[i]);
   }
}
```

The java.lang.Long Class

This section provides a reference for the java.lang.Long class. The constants are shown in Table 4-10. In Table 4-11 a short description of each method is given. Following these tables are sections that describe each constant and method in detail.

Table 4-10 Summary of Long constants

Constant	Description
MAX_VALUE	The maximum allowable long value
MIN_VALUE	The minimum allowable long value

Table 4-11 Summary of Long methods

Method	Description
doubleValue	Returns the value of the object as a double
equals	Tests to see if an object is equal to this Long instance
floatValue	Returns the value of the object, as a float
getLong	Returns a system property
hashCode	Returns a hash code
intValue	Returns the value of the object as an int
longValue	Returns the primitive value of the object
parseLong	Converts a String to a long
toString	Converts the Long to a String
valueOf	Converts a String to a Long

LONG

Description	A class representation of a long, and constants and methods related to long.
Syntax	public class **Long** extends Number
Package	java.lang
Import	java.lang.Long (not required)
Constructors	public **Long**(long *value*) public **Long**(String *str*)
Parameters	
long *value*	A primitive long to use as the wrapped value.
String *str*	A string to parse to a long.
Exceptions	A NumberFormatException is thrown if the String does not contain a valid long.
Example	In this example, Longs are constructed using both forms of the constructor.

```
Long i = new Long(100);
Long i2 = new Long("100");
```

Constants

MAX_VALUE

Class Name	Long
Description	The maximum value that a Java long can store.
Syntax	public static long **MAX_VALUE**
See Also	MIN_VALUE
Comments	The value is $(2^{63}-1)$, which is approximately 9.2×10^{18}.
Example	In this example, a variable is initialized with MAX_VALUE.

```
long result = Long.MAX_VALUE;
```

MIN_VALUE

Class Name	Long
Description	The minimum value that a Java long can store.
Syntax	public final static double **MIN_VALUE**
See Also	MAX_VALUE

Comments	The value is (-2^{63}) , which is approximately -9.2 x 10^{18}.
Example	In this example, a variable is initialized with MIN_VALUE.

```
long result = Long.MIN_VALUE;
```

Methods

DOUBLEVALUE

Class Name	Long
Description	Returns the primitive value of the object as a double.
Syntax	public double **doubleValue**()
Parameters	None.
Returns	The return type is double. It is the value contained in the Long object, cast to a double.
Exceptions	None.
Comments	Rounding may occur if the long has more significant digits than a double can hold.
Example	This example constructs a Long, then extracts its value as a double.

```
Long a = new Long(Long.MAX_VALUE);
double d = a.doubleValue();
```

EQUALS

Class Name	Long
Description	Tests to see if an object is equal to this Long instance.
Syntax	public boolean **equals**(Object *obj*)
Parameters	
Object *obj*	Object to compare.
Returns	The return type is boolean. It returns true if the parameter is a Long and the contained values are the same.
Exceptions	None.
Comments	Long overrides the definition provided by Object, which compares references instead of values.
Example	In this example, two distinct longs with the same value are compared.

```
Long a = new Long(5);
Long b = new Long(5);
boolean c = a.equals(b);
```

FLOATVALUE

Class Name	Long
Description	Returns the value of the object, as a float.
Syntax	public float **floatValue**()
Parameters	None.
Returns	The return type is float. It is the value contained in the Long object, cast to a float.
Exceptions	None.
Comments	Rounding may occur if the long has more significant digits than a float can hold.
Example	A value is converted below.

```
Long a = new Long(Long.MAX_VALUE);
float f = a.floatValue();
```

GETLONG

Class Name	Long
Description	Get a system property.
Syntax	public static Long **getLong**(String *prop*)
	public static Long **getLong**(String *prop*, long *deflong*)
	public static Long **getLong**(String *prop*, Long *defLong*)
Parameters	
String *prop*	The name of the property.
long *deflong*	Value to return if property doesn't exist.
Long *defLong*	Value to return if property doesn't exist.
Returns	The return type is Long. It is the value of the property, if it exists.
Exceptions	None.
See Also	System
Comments	If the property doesn't exist, then the second parameter's value is returned. If the second parameter isn't provided, then 0 is returned. The function parses hexadecimal and octal property values.
Example	This example gets a hypothetical long property.

```
Long property = Long.getLong("SomeLongProperty");
```

HASHCODE

Class Name	Long
Description	Returns a hash code.
Syntax	public int **hashCode**()
Parameters	None.
Returns	The return type is int. It is a hash code for the object.
Exceptions	None.
Comments	The hash code is used in java.util.Hashcode. It is the value of the Long, cast to an int.
Example	A hash code is generated here:

```
Long a = new Long(5);
int hash = a.hashCode();
```

INTVALUE

Class Name	Long
Description	Returns the value of the object, cast to an int.
Syntax	public int **intValue**()
Parameters	None.
Returns	The return type is int. It is the value contained in the Long object, cast to an int.
Exceptions	None.
Comments	If the magnitude is too large, then Integer.MIN_VALUE or Integer.MAX_VALUE is returned.
Example	In this example, a Long is constructed and its int value is extracted.

```
Long a = new Long(5);
int i = a.intValue();
```

LONGVALUE

Class Name	Long
Description	Returns the value of the object.
Syntax	public long **longValue**()
Parameters	None.
Returns	The return type is long. It is the value contained in the Long object.

Exceptions	None.
Example	This example constructs a Long, then extracts its primitive value.

```
Long a = new Long(5);
long value = a.longValue();
```

PARSELONG

Description	Converts a String to a long.
Syntax	public static long **parseLong**(String *str*)
	public static long **parseLong**(String *str*, int *radix*)
Parameters	
String *str*	A String representation of a number.
int *radix*	The radix (base) to use for conversion (between 2 and 36).
Returns	The return type is long. It is a long representation of the number stored in the string.
Exceptions	If the value can't be converted, a NumberFormatException is thrown.
Comments	This is similar to the valueOf() method, which returns a Long. If the radix is omitted, 10 is assumed.
Example	In this example, a sample set of Strings is converted to longs, using various radices.

```
String [] strings = {"1", "10", "100", "1000", "Susan"};
int radi[] = {10, 10, 2, 16, 10};
long d[] = long[5];
for (int i=0; i<strings.length; i++) {
   try {
      d[i] = Long.parseLong(strings[i], radi[i]);
   } catch (NumberFormatException e) {
        System.out.println("Invalid Number: " + strings[i]);
   }
}
```

TOSTRING

Class Name	Long
Description	Converts the Long to a String.
Syntax	public String **toString**()
	public static String **toString**(long *n*)
	public static String **toString**(long *n*, int *radix*)
Parameters	
long *n*	A long to convert to a String.
int *radix*	The radix (base) to use for conversion (between 2 and 36).

Returns	The return type is String. It is a string representation of the number.
Exceptions	None.
Comments	The instance method overrides the implementation in Object.toString(). No particular formatting can be specified. If the radix is not specified, 10 is assumed.
Example	In this example, each type of toString() method is used to convert a number to a String.

```
Long a = new Long(5);
String s1 = a.toString();
String s2 = Long.toString(5);
String s3 = Long.toString(5, 10);
```

VALUEOF

Class Name	Long
Description	Converts a String to a Long.
Syntax	public static Long **valueOf**(String *str*)
	public static Long **valueOf**(String *str*, int *radix*)
Parameters	
String *str*	The String to convert.
int *radix*	The radix (base) to use for conversion (between 2 and 36).
Returns	The return type is Long. It is a Long representation of the number stored in the string.
Exceptions	If the value can't be converted, a NumberFormatException is thrown.
See Also	toString(), parseLong()
Example	In this example, a sample set of Strings are converted to Longs.

```
String [] strings = {"1", "10", "100", "1000", "Rebecca"};
Long d[] = new Long[5];
for (int i=0; i<strings.length; i++) {
   try {
      d[i] = Long.valueOf(strings[i]);
   } catch (NumberFormatException e) {
       System.out.println("Invalid Number: " + strings[i]);
   }
}
```

The java.lang.Number Class

This section provides a reference for the java.lang.Number class. In Table 4-12 a short description of each method is given. In addition to these methods, Number inherits all of Object's methods (Chapter 3, Global Classes, details Object's methods). Following these tables are sections that describe each method in detail. Since Number is an abstract class, examples are not given in this reference section. For examples, see the corresponding reference sections in the Double, Float, Integer, and Long classes.

Table 4-12 Summary of Number methods

Method	Description
doubleValue	Returns the object's value, as a double
floatValue	Returns the object's value, as a float
intValue	Returns the object's value, as an int
longValue	Returns the object's value, as a long

NUMBER

Description	Parent class to primitive number wrapper classes.
Syntax	public abstract class **Number** extends Object
Package	java.lang
Import	java.lang.Number (not required)
Constructors	None.
Parameters	None.
Example	See the Double, Float, Integer, and Long classes, earlier in this chapter.

Methods

DOUBLEVALUE

Class Name	Number
Description	Returns the value of the object, as a double.
Syntax	public abstract double **doubleValue**()
Parameters	None.
Returns	The return type is double. It is the value contained in the object, cast to a double if needed. Some precision may be lost.
Exceptions	None.

FLOATVALUE

Class Name	Number
Description	Returns the value of the object, as a float.
Syntax	public abstract float **floatValue**()
Parameters	None.

Returns	The return type is float. It is the value contained in object, cast to a float if needed.
Exceptions	None.
Comments	Precision may be lost. If the magnitude is too large to fit into a float, the maximum or minimum float value will result.

INTVALUE

Class Name	Number
Description	Returns the value of the object, as an int.
Syntax	public abstract int **intValue**()
Parameters	None.
Returns	The return type is int. It is the value contained in the object, converted if needed to an int.
Exceptions	None.
Comments	The value may be rounded. If the magnitude is too large to fit into an int, the maximum or minimum int value will result.

LONGVALUE

Class Name	Number
Description	Returns the value of the object, as a long.
Syntax	public abstract long **longValue**()
Parameters	None.
Returns	The return type is long. It is the value contained in the object, converted to a long if needed.
Exceptions	None.
Comments	If the magnitude is too large to fit into a long, the maximum or minimum long will result.

The Math Class

The Math class provides a set of constants and static methods for basic math functions. This includes trigonometric functions, exponential functions, methods for different types of rounding, random number generation, and methods for comparing two numbers. The methods and constants available are arranged by category in Table 4-13.

Table 4-13 Math methods and constants, by category

Category	Constants and Methods
Adjustment	abs, ceil, floor, rint, round
Comparison	max, min
Exponentials	E, exp, log, pow, sqrt
Random numbers	random
Remainder	IEEEremainder
Trigonometric	PI, acos, asin, atan, atan2, cos, sin, tan

There is no constructor for the Math class, and all methods are static. Math is used as a qualifier when referring to the constants and methods in the class, as shown in Listing 4-2.

Listing 4-2 Math as a qualifier

```
double larger = Math.max(a, b);
double cosine = Math.cos(Math.PI);
```

All methods take one or two numeric parameters, except Math.random(), which takes no parameters. Every method returns a numeric result, usually of the same type as the parameter type(s). Most methods take doubles as their parameters. One method, abs(), can also take an int, long, float, or double. The comparison methods, max() and min(), take two parameters of the same type, which are either ints, longs, floats, or doubles.

Most of the methods in the Math class are "native" methods (implemented in another language, such as C). This was likely chosen for efficiency, and to reuse existing math libraries. The native methods have no practical effect on the use of the class, but the actual code that implements the methods is not provided with the Java Developer's Kit.

Certain pairs of methods define functions that are inverses of each other. For example, if a() is an inverse method of b(), then a(b(x)) returns x (for a valid x). Table 4-14 shows the inverse methods in the Math class.

Table 4-14 Inverse methods in the Math class

Method	Inverse Method
exp	log
cos	acos
sin	asin
tan	atan

The java.lang.Math Class

This section provides a reference for the java.lang.Math class. The constants are shown in Table 4-15. In Table 4-16 a short description of each method is given. Following these tables are sections that describe each method and constant in detail.

Table 4-15 Summary of Math constants

Constant	Description
E	The mathematical constant e
PI	The mathematical constant Π (pi)

Table 4-16 Summary of Math methods

Method	Description
IEEEremainder	Calculates the remainder resulting from dividing two numbers
abs	Returns the absolute value of a number
acos	Calculates the arc cosine
asin	Calculates the arc sine
atan	Calculates the arc tangent
atan2	Converts rectangular coordinates to polar coordinates
ceil	Calculates the smallest integer greater or equal to x
cos	Calculates the cosine of an angle
exp	Computes e^x
floor	Calculates the largest integer less than or equal to x
log	Computes the natural log
max	Returns the larger of two values
min	Returns the smaller of two values
pow	Calculates x raised to the power y
random	Generates a pseudo-random number
rint	Returns a rounded value as a double
round	Returns a rounded value
sin	Calculates the sine of an angle
sqrt	Calculates the square root of a number
tan	Calculates the tangent of an angle

MATH

Description	A class providing mathematical functions.
Syntax	public class **Math** extends Object
Package	java.lang
Import	java.lang.Math (not required)
Constructors	None.
Parameters	None.
Example	Take the absolute value of a number.

```
double v = Math.abs(-1.0);
```

Constants

E

Class Name	Math
Description	The mathematical constant e. It is the double representation of the number whose natural log is equal to 1.
Syntax	public final static double **E**
Comments	Since E is an irrational number, the value is necessarily rounded. In Java it is 2.7182818284590452354.
Example	In this example, E is used in the log function.

```
double lonliest_number = Math.log(Math.E);
```

PI

Class Name	Math
Description	The mathematical constant pi. It is the double representation of the ratio of a circle's circumference to its radius.
Syntax	public final static double **PI**
Comments	Since PI is an irrational number, the value is necessarily rounded. Several of the trigonometric functions take parameters as a multiple of pi.
Example	In this example, PI is used as an argument to the sin() function.

```
double nearzilch = Math.sin(Math.PI);
```

Methods

IEEEREMAINDER

Class Name	Math
Description	Calculates the remainder resulting from dividing two numbers, using the IEEE 754 standard.
Syntax	public static double **IEEEremainder**(double *numer*, double *denom*)
Parameters	
double *numer*	The numerator of the division.
double *denom*	The denominator of the division.
Returns	The return type is double. Its value is the remainder of the first parameter divided by the second.
Exceptions	None.
Comments	Java also defines the % operator for remainder (see Chapter 2, The Java Language). The % operator uses truncating division, whereas IEEEremainder uses rounding division.
Example	In this example, the remainder of two numbers is calculated.

```
double a = 5.;
double b = 9.;
double remround = Math.IEEEremainder(a, b);
double remtrunc = a % b;
```

ABS

Class Name	Math
Description	Returns the absolute value of a number.
Syntax	public static int **abs**(int *x*)
	public static long **abs**(long *x*)
	public static float **abs**(float *x*)
	public static double **abs**(double *x*)
Parameters	
x	The value to take the absolute value of.
Returns	The return type matches the parameter type. Its value is the absolute value, that is, a positive number with the same magnitude as the parameter.
Exceptions	None.

Comments	If the parameter is positive, then the return value is the same as the para-meter. If different input and output types are desired, cast can be used.
Example	This example takes the absolute value of a number.

```
double v = Math.abs(-1.0);
```

ACOS

Class Name	Math
Description	Calculates the trigonometric arc cosine.
Syntax	public static double **acos**(double x)
Parameters	
double x	The value to compute the arc cosine of.
Returns	The return type is double. Its value is the arc cosine of x, expressed in radians. It ranges from 0 through pi (0 to 180 degrees).
Exceptions	None.
See Also	asin(), atan(), atan2(), cos(), sin(), tan(), PI
Comments	0 is returned for all values outside (-1, 1). This function is the inverse of the cosine function. For example, the value of x would be returned from acos(cos(x)).
Example	This example computes a table of arc cosines.

```
for (double x=-1.25; x <= 1.25; x += .25) {
   System.out.println(x + " " + Math.acos(x));
}
```

ASIN

Class Name	Math
Description	Calculates the trigonometric arc sine.
Syntax	public static double **asin**(double x)
Parameters	
double x	The value to compute the arc sine of.
Returns	The return type is double. Its value is the arc sine of x, expressed in radians. It ranges from -pi/2 through pi/2 (-90 to 90 degrees).
Exceptions	None.
See Also	acos(), atan(), atan2(), cos(), sin(), tan(), PI
Comments	0 is returned for all values outside (-1, 1). This function is the inverse of the sine function. For example, the value of x would be returned from asin(sin(x)).

Example   This example computes a table of arc sines.

```
for (double x=-1.25; x <= 1.25; x += .25) {
   System.out.println(x + " " + Math.asin(x));
}
```

ATAN

Class Name	Math
Description	Calculates the trigonometric arc tangent.
Syntax	public static double **atan**(double x)
Parameters	
double x	The value to compute the arc tangent of.
Returns	The return type is double. Its value is the arc tangent of x, expressed in radians. It ranges from -pi/2 through pi/2 (-90 to 90 degrees).
Exceptions	None.
See Also	acos(), asin(), atan2(), cos(), sin(), tan(), PI
Comments	This function is the inverse of the tangent function. For example, the value of x would be returned from atan(tan(x)).
Example	This example computes an arc tangent.

```
double result = Math.atan(1.);
```

ATAN2

Class Name	Math
Description	Converts rectangular coordinates to polar coordinates.
Syntax	public static double **atan2**(double y, double x)
Parameters	
double y	The y coordinate of the rectangular pair.
double x	The x coordinate of the rectangular pair.
Returns	The return type is double. Its value is the angle determined by the arc from (0,0) to (x, y), in the range -pi to pi (-180 to 180 degrees).
Exceptions	None.
Comments	This method computes the "phase theta" by computing an arc tangent of y/x. If x is 0, then for non-negative y the result is 0, and for negative y the result is pi.
Example	This example computes the arc tangent of a unit vector.

```
double share_dessert = Math.atan2(1, 0);  // Pi/2
```

CEIL

Class Name	Math
Description	ceil(x) calculates the smallest integer greater than or equal to x.
Syntax	public static double **ceil**(double x)
Parameters	
double x	The value to take the ceil of.
Returns	The return type is double. Its value is the smallest integer greater than or equal to the parameter (the ceiling).
Exceptions	None.
See Also	floor()
Comments	This function rounds up the value. For integers, this function returns the value of the parameter. For noninteger negative numbers, the result will be larger, but the magnitude is smaller. For example, ceil(-1.5) is -1.
Example	This example takes the ceiling of several values.

```
for (double x=-1.5; x<=1.5; x+=.5) {
   System.out.println(x + " " + Math.ceil(x));
```

COS

Class Name	Math
Description	Calculates the cosine of an angle.
Syntax	public static double **cos**(double x)
Parameters	
double x	The angle to take the cosine of, in radians, as a multiple of pi.
Returns	The return type is double. Its value is the cosine of x.
Exceptions	None.
See Also	acos(), asin(), atan(), atan2(), sin(), tan(), PI
Example	This example takes the cosine of 180 degrees.

```
double result = Math.cos(Math.PI);
```

EXP

Class Name	Math
Description	Computes e^x.
Syntax	public static double **exp**(double x)
Parameters	
double x	The power to raise e to.

Returns	The return type is double. Its value is the exponential, e, raised to the specified power.
Exceptions	None.
See Also	E, log()
Example	This example computes e^0.

```
double all_for = Math.exp(0);
```

FLOOR

Class Name	Math
Description	floor(x) calculates the largest integer less than or equal to x.
Syntax	public static double **floor**(double *x*)
Parameters	
double *x*	The value to take the floor of.
Returns	The return type is double. Its value is the largest integer greater than or equal to the parameter.
Exceptions	None.
See Also	ceil()
Comments	This function rounds down the value. For integers, this function returns the value of the parameter. For noninteger negative numbers, the result will be smaller, but the magnitude is larger. For example, floor(-1.5) is -2.
Example	This example takes the floor of several values.

```
for (double x=-1.5; x<=1.5; x+=.5) {
   System.out.println(x + " " + Math.floor(x));
```

LOG

Class Name	Math
Description	Computes the natural log of x.
Syntax	public static double **log**(double *x*)
Parameters	
double *x*	The value to take the log of.
Returns	The return type is double. Its value is the natural log of x. If x<0, then NaN results.
Exceptions	None.
Comments	This is the inverse function of exp(). This function is base e (not base 10). The value for e is represented in Java as Math.E. A base 10 log is not provided by Math; it can be calculated by: 1/Math.log(10)*Math.log(x).

Example   Calculate the natural log of e.

```
double theonly = Math.log(Math.E);
```

MAX

Class Name	Math
Description	Returns the larger of two values.
Syntax	public static int **max**(int *x1*, int *x2*)
	public static long **max**(long *x1*, long *x2*)
	public static float **max**(float *x1*, float *x2*)
	public static double **max**(double *x1*, double *x2*)
Parameters	
x1	First value to be compared.
x2	Second value to be compared.
Returns	The return type matches the type of the parameters. The larger of the two values is returned.
Exceptions	None.
See Also	min()
Comments	Although inputs and outputs to max() must be of the same type, Java will promote one of the parameters to be consistent with the other, if needed. See Chapter 2, The Java Language, for the rules on how Java chooses from overloaded methods.
Example	This example finds the largest value in an array.

```
double a[] = {0., Math.E, Math.PI};
double result = a[0];
for (int i=1; i<a.length; i++)
   result = Math.max(result, a[i]);
System.out.println("largest = " + result);
```

MIN

Class Name	Math
Description	Returns the smaller of two values.
Syntax	public static int **min**(int *x1*, int *x2*)
	public static long **min**(long *x1*, long *x2*)
	public static float **min**(float *x1*, float *x2*)
	public static double **min**(double *x1*, double *x2*)
Parameters	
x1	First value to be compared.
x2	Second value to be compared.

Returns	The return type matches the type of the parameters. The smaller of the two values is returned.
Exceptions	None.
See Also	max()
Comments	Although inputs and outputs to min() must be of the same type, Java will promote one parameter to be consistent with the other, if needed. See Chapter 2, The Java Language, for the rules on how Java chooses from overloaded methods.
Example	This example finds the smallest value in an array.

```
double a[] = {0., Math.E, Math.PI};
double result = a[0];
for (int i=1; i<a.length; i++)
   result = Math.min(result, a[i]);
System.out.println("smallest = " + result);
```

POW

Class Name	Math
Description	Calculates x raised to the power y.
Syntax	public static double **pow**(double *x*, double *y*)
Parameters	
double *x*	The value that is raised to the power y.
double *y*	The power that x is raised to.
Returns	The return type is double. The return value is x^y.
Exceptions	None.
Comments	If x is zero and y isn't positive, Double.POSITIVE_INFINITY results. If x is zero or negative, and y isn't a whole number, Double.NaN results. (Note: the comments in the source code indicate that an exception is thrown in these cases.)
Example	This example generates a two-dimensional power table.

```
for (int i=0; i<5; i++) {
   for (int j=0; j<5; j++)
      System.out.print(Math.pow(i, j) + " ");
   System.out.println();
}
```

RANDOM

Class Name	Math
Description	Generates a pseudo-random number.
Syntax	public static synchronized double **random**()

Parameters	None.
Returns	The return type is double. Its value is a pseudo-random number between 0 and 1.
Exceptions	None.
See Also	random(), Random.nextDouble() (The Random class is covered in Volume 2, *Java Networking and AWT API SuperBible*.)
Comments	The numbers are generated as a function of the system clock, and their behavior isn't purely random (but is a good approximation). As shown in the example below, the results from random() can be scaled. Transformations can also be used to create samplings from statistical distributions, like the Normal distribution.
Example	This example simulates the roll of two dice.

```
int dice1 = (int) (Math.random() * 6 + 1); // scale from 1 to 6
int dice2 = (int) (Math.random() * 6 + 1);
```

RINT

Class Name	Math
Description	Returns a rounded value as a double.
Syntax	public static double **rint**(double *x*)
Parameters	
double *x*	The value to round.
Returns	The return type is double. The return value is the rounded value of the parameter.
Exceptions	None.
Comments	Note that the return value is double, while a similiar function, round(), returns either an int or a long.
See Also	round()
Example	This example rounds a few sample values.

```
for (double d = -1.5; d <= 1.5; d+=.1) {
 double result = Math.rint(d);
  System.out.println(d+ " " + result);
}
```

ROUND

Class Name	Math
Description	Returns a rounded value.

Syntax	public static int **round**(float *x*) public static long **round**(double *x*)
Parameters	
x	The value to round.
Returns	The return type is either int or long, depending on the parameter type. The return value is computed by adding .5, then finding the largest integer less than or equal to this value (via floor()).
Exceptions	None.
Comments	Since floats and doubles cover numbers larger in magnitude than ints and longs, results are not correct for very large or very negative numbers. In this case, one of Integer.MAX_VALUE, Integer.MIN_VALUE, Long.MAX_VALUE, or Long.MIN_VALUE is returned.
Example	Round a number.

```
double d = 3.5;
long result = Math.round(d);
```

SIN

Class Name	Math
Description	Calculates the sine of an angle.
Syntax	public static double **sin**(double *x*)
Parameters	
double *x*	The angle to take the sine of, in radians, as a multiple of pi.
Returns	The return type is double. Its value is the sine of x.
Exceptions	None.
See Also	acos(), asin(), atan(), atan2(), cos(), tan(), PI
Example	Find the sine of pi.

```
double or = Math.sin(Math.PI);
```

SQRT

Class Name	Math
Description	Calculates the square root of a number.
Syntax	public static double **sqrt**(double *x*)
Parameters	
double *x*	The value to take the square root of.
Returns	The return type is double. Its value is $x^{1/2}$. If x<0, NaN results.

Exceptions	None.
Comments	sqrt(x) is equivalent to pow(x, .5).
Example	This example prints the square roots of some numbers.

```
double squares[] = {0, 1, 4, 9, 25};
for (int i=0; i <squares.length; i++) {
   double square_root = Math.sqrt(squares[i]);
   System.out.println(squares[i] + " " + square_root);
}
```

TAN

Class Name	Math
Description	Calculates the tangent of an angle.
Syntax	public static double **tan**(double *x*)
Parameters	
double *x*	The angle to take the tangent of, in radians, as a multiple of pi.
Returns	The return type is double. Its value is the tangent of x.
Exceptions	None.
See Also	acos(), asin(), atan(), atan2(), cos(), sin(), PI
Example	This example takes the tangent of 45 degrees.

```
double result = Math.tan(Math.PI / 4.);
```

The Numbers Project: Formatted Numbers

Project Overview

This chapter's project augments the Number classes by providing a way to print formatted numbers. This is useful, since Java has no class or methods for doing this. Specifically, a new class, NumberFormat, is defined. This class allows you to set various printing styles, including length, decimal places, and, optionally, dollar sign, commas, percent sign, and parentheses for negatives. These options can be set via methods, or with a constructor via a String.

Once the format is described, numbers can be formatted with the NumberFormat.toString(double) method. All of the Java arithmetic types can be used as an argument, but large longs will lose precision. One extension to this class would be to add a toString(long) method in order to handle this case. Another useful addition would allow scientific formatting (e.g., 1.234E+10); the implementation of NumberFormat presented here only supports fixed decimal formatting (e.g., 12340000000.000). The NumberFormat methods are summarized in Table 4-17. The String shorthand components for setting a NumberFormat are shown in Table 4-18. Example shorthands are shown in Table 4-19.

Table 4-17 Summary of NumberFormat methods

Method	Description
NumberFormat	Constructs a format with the following defaults: 6 decimals, no decorations
NumberFormat(String)	Constructs a format with characteristics described in the String argument
setComma	Toggles comma inclusion
setComma(boolean)	Includes or excludes commas
setDollar	Toggles dollar sign inclusion
setDollar(boolean)	Includes or excludes dollar sign
setParens	Toggles parenthesis inclusion for negatives
setParens(boolean)	Includes or excludes parentheses for negatives
setPercent	Toggles percent sign inclusion
setPercent(boolean)	Includes percent sign and multiplies by 100, or excludes percent sign
toString	Shows current NumberFormat, as a String
toString(double)	Converts the double to a string, given the current formatting

Table 4-18 String descriptions of NumberFormat

String	Description
$	Includes a dollar sign
(	Includes parentheses for negatives, instead of a minus sign
,	Includes commas every 3 places
%	Multiplies value by 100, and includes a percent sign
l.d	Sets length to l, decimal places to d

Table 4-19 Example formats and resulting formatted numbers

Format	Number	Formatted Number
"10.3"	-1234.56	" -1234.560"
".1"	-1234.56	"1234.6"
"($,.2"	-1234.56	"($1,234.56)
"%.0"	.99	"99%"

Building the Project

1. Enter the following code (Listing 4-3) into a file named NumberFormat.java, and compile it with javac NumberFormat.java.

Listing 4-3 NumberFormat.java

```java
/* The NumberFormat class describes a format for printing numbers,
 *  and a method to print a number in that format.
 *
 * For example,
 *
 * NumberFormat nf = new NumberFormat("$,10.2");
 * System.out.println(nf.toString(1234.56));
 *
 * will produce as output:
 *
 *   $1,234.56
 */


class NumberFormat {

    int     _length;  // the length of the formatted number, 0 is size-to-fit
    int     _decimals; // # of decimal places to include
    boolean _comma;    // true if commas are included
    boolean _dollar;   // true if a dollar sign is included
    boolean _parens;   // true if parens are included for negative, instead of "-"
    boolean _percent;  // true if add "%" sign, and multiply for 100

    // the default constructor
    // 2 decimals, no decorations
    public NumberFormat() {
        defaults();
    }

    /* The String constructor allows options set, instead of thru methods.
     * The string passed indicates length and decimals (a.b), and turn
     * on decorations by including any of: , ( % $
     * For example,
     *
     *   NumberFormat nf =  NumberFormat("$,5.2");
     *
     * is equivalent to:
     *
     *   NumberFormat nf = new NumberFormat();
     *   nf.setDollar(true);
     *   nf.setComma(true);
     *   nf.setLength(5);
     *   nf.setComma(2);
     */
    public NumberFormat(String s) {
        // set defaults before parsing argument
        defaults();

        // parse the string
        // turn on decorations
        if (s.indexOf(',') != -1)
            _comma = true;
        if (s.indexOf('(') != -1)
            _parens = true;
        if (s.indexOf('%') != -1)
            _percent = true;
```

```
   if (s.indexOf('$') != -1)
      _dollar = true;

   // parse a.b (length and decimals)
   int pd = s.indexOf('.');
   if (pd == -1)
      return;

   String len = "";
   for (int i=pd-1; i>=0; i--) {
      char c = s.charAt(i);
      if (Character.isDigit(c))
         len = c + len;
      else
         break;
   }
   _length = Integer.parseInt(len);

   String dec = "";
   for (int i=pd+1; i<s.length(); i++) {
      char c = s.charAt(i);
      if (Character.isDigit(c))
         dec = dec + c;
      else
         break;
   }
   _decimals = Integer.parseInt(dec);
}

// set defaults: 2 decimals, no decorations
void defaults() {
   _length = 0;
   _decimals = 2;
   _comma = false;
   _dollar = false;
   _parens = false;
   _percent = false;
}

// set the length
public void setLength(int i) {
   _length = i;
}

// set # of decimal places
public void setDecimals(int i) {
   _decimals = i;
}

// turn commas on or off
public void setComma(boolean b) {
   _comma = b;
}

// toggle commas
public void setComma() {
   _comma = ! _comma;
}
```

continued on next page

continued from previous page

```java
// turn dollar on or off
public void setDollar(boolean b) {
   _dollar = b;
}

// toggle dollar
public void setDollar() {
   _dollar = !_dollar;
}

// turn parentheses on or off
public void setParens(boolean b) {
   _parens = b;
}

// toggle parentheses
public void setParens() {
   _parens = !_parens;
}

// turn pecentage on or off
public void setPercent(boolean b) {
   _percent = b;
}

// toggle percentage
public void setPercent() {
   _percent = !_percent;
}

// display format description
public String toString() {
   String s = "";
   if (_parens) s = s + "(";
   if (_dollar) s = s + "$";
   if (_comma) s = s + ",";
   s = s + _length + "." + _decimals;
   if (_percent) s = s + "%";
   return s;
}

// display a double based on formatting
// could generalize to take the various primitives and / or wrapper numbers
public String toString(double d) {
   String s = "";
   int i;

   // handle negative and opening parenthesis
   boolean negative = false;
   if (d < 0.) {
      d = -d;
      if (_parens) {
         s = "(";
         negative = true;
      }
      else
         s = "-";
   }
```

```
   // add $
   if (_dollar)
      s = s + "$";

   // scale if percent format
   if (_percent)
      d = d * 100.;

   // find the number of integral places
   int power = power(d);

   // build the integral part
   for (i=power-1; i>=0; i--) {
      double order = Math.pow(10, i);
      int digit = (int) (d / order);
      s = s + digit;
      d = d - digit * order;
      if ( _comma && (i%3) == 0 && i>0)
         s = s + ",";
   }

   // place leading 0 if needed
   if (power <= 0)
      s = s + '0';

   // insert decimal, if needed
   if (_decimals > 0)
      s = s + ".";

   // round remaining fraction to the requested number of digits
   d = Math.round(d * Math.pow(10, _decimals));

   // build the fractional part
   for (i=_decimals-1; i>=0; i--) {
      double order = Math.pow(10, i);
      int digit = (int) (d / order);
      s = s + digit;
      d = d - digit * order;
   }

   // add trailing characters
   if (_percent)
      s = s + "%";
   if (negative)
      s += ")";

   // fill to requested length
   if (_length > 0)
      s = pad(s);
   return s;
}

// right size the result
String pad(String s) {
   int w = s.length();
   // just right size
   if (w == _length)
      return s;
```

continued on next page

continued from previous page

```
// overflow
if (w > _length) {
    s = "*";
    for (int i=1; i<_length; i++)
        s = s + "*";
    return s;
}
// prepad
for (int i=0; i<(_length - w); i++)
    s = " " + s;
return s;
}

// cache 1 / ln(10) for the log10() function
static double inverse_log10;
static {
    inverse_log10 = 1. / Math.log(10.);
}

// base 10 log (not a standard math function)
double log10(double x) {
    return inverse_log10 * Math.log(x);
}

// find number of places in the integral part of a number
int power(double d) {
    return (int) Math.ceil(log10(d));
  }
}
```

2. Enter the following code (Listing 4-4) into a file named Formatest.java, and compile it with javac Formatest.java. This class contains a main() for interactive testing of the NumberFormat class.

Listing 4-4 Formatest.java

```
// Interactive driver to test NumberFormat class

// Allows entry of a new number
// or single characters to control format , $ % (
// or :d where d is number of decimals
// or #l where l is the length

import NumberFormat;
import java.io.*;

class Formatest {

    public static void main(String args[]) {

        showHelp();

        double d = 0;
        NumberFormat nf = new NumberFormat();
```

```
while(true) {
   // read next line from terminal
   String line = Formatest.getln();
   line = line.trim().toLowerCase();

   // if "quit", then exit
   if (line.equals("quit"))
      break;

   // if empty line
   else if (line.length() == 0)
      continue;

   // toggle comma display
   else if (line.equals(","))
      nf.setComma();

   // toggle dollar display
   else if (line.equals("$"))
      nf.setDollar();

   // toggle percent display
   else if (line.equals("%"))
      nf.setPercent();

   // toggle parens
   else if (line.equals("("))
      nf.setParens();

   // get help
   else if (line.equals("?")) {
      showHelp();
      continue;
   }

   // set decimal places
   else if (line.charAt(0) == ':') {
      if (line.length() == 1) {
         System.out.println("must include number of decimals");
         continue;
      }
      String s = line.substring(1);
      try {
         Integer i = Integer.valueOf(s);
         nf.setDecimals(i.intValue());
      } catch (NumberFormatException e) {
         System.out.println("invalid number of decimals");
         continue;
      }
   }

   // set width
   else if (line.charAt(0) == '#') {
      if (line.length() == 1) {
         System.out.println("must include number for length");
         continue;
      }
```

continued on next page

continued from previous page

```
            String s = line.substring(1);
            try {
                Integer i = Integer.valueOf(s);
                nf.setLength(i.intValue());
            } catch (NumberFormatException e) {
                System.out.println("invalid number for length");
                continue;
            }
        }

        // otherwise, assume it's a new number (complain if it isn't)
        else {
            try {
                Double dbl = Double.valueOf(line);
                d = dbl.doubleValue();
            } catch (NumberFormatException e) {
                System.out.println("Invalid command or number");
                continue;
            }
        }

        // show the current number, formatted, and the format descriptor
        System.out.println(nf.toString(d) + "      " + nf);

    }
}

// print a help msg
static void showHelp() {
    System.out.print(
        "Valid commands are:\n" +
        "  <number>  set number displayed\n" +
        "  #n        set length to n places\n" +
        "  :n        set to n decimal places\n" +
        "  ,         toggle comma inclusion\n" +
        "  $         toggle dollar inclusion\n" +
        "  (         toggle parens for negative numbers\n" +
        "  %         toggle percentage\n" +
        "  ?         display help (this message)\n" +
        "  quit      quit\n"
    );
}

// read next line from terminal
static String getln() {

    int c = 0;
    String line = "";
    while (true) {
        try {
            c = System.in.read();
        } catch (IOException e) {
        }
        // read until newline
        if (c == '\n')
            break;
```

```
        line = line + (char)c;
    }
    return line;
}

}
```

Running the Program

At a command prompt, type

```
java Formatest
```

The program allows you to enter a number, or indicate a change to the current format. At startup, there is a working number of 100, and the current format is a default NumberFormat. You can request help by typing a "?".

5

BOOLEAN AND CHARACTER CLASSES

5

BOOLEAN AND CHARACTER CLASSES

Like the Number family of classes, Boolean and Character are "wrapper" classes for the boolean and char primitive types. They are provided in order to allow the use of primitives where objects are required. For example, Objects may be required as method parameters or return types, or as variable types. The Boolean and Character classes also provide several methods for converting, adjusting, or characterizing booleans and chars. Boolean and Character are final classes, so no classes may extend them. These classes are shown in Table 5-1. The primitive classes and their inheritance relationships are shown in Figure 5-1.

Table 5-1 The Boolean and Character classes

Class	Description
Boolean	A class encapsulating the primitive Java boolean data type
Character	A class encapsulating the primitive Java character data type

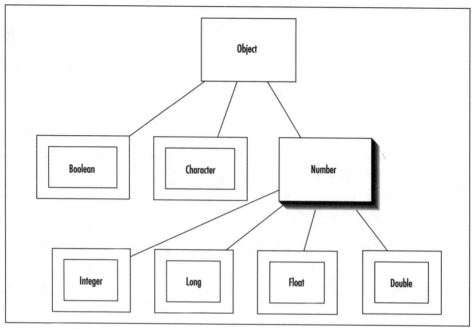

Figure 5-1 Java's primitive classes

Methods

The methods for Boolean and Character can be grouped into several categories: comparison, conversion, adjustment, characterization, and properties. These are shown in Table 5-2.

Table 5-2 Boolean and Character methods, by category

Class	Category	Methods
Boolean	Comparison	equals, hashCode
	Conversion	booleanValue, toString, valueOf
	Properties	getBoolean
Character	Adjustment	toLowerCase, toUpperCase
	Characterization	isDigit, isLowerCase, isSpace, isUpperCase
	Comparison	equals, hashCode
	Conversion	charValue, digit, forDigit, toString

Boolean and Character have the same comparison methods. The equals() method tests to see if two objects have the same type and contained value. This is different from the default Object definition, which compares the references to see if they are the same. The hashCode() method is provided to generate an integer code useful in hash tables.

Conversion methods include toString(), which is available in both classes for generating a String representation. The primitive contained in an object can be extracted with either booleanValue() or charValue(). Boolean provides valueOf() to convert from a string (e.g., "true", "false") to a boolean. Character provides digit() and forDigit() to convert between characters and integers.

Character provides several static methods to adjust or characterize a character. The methods toLowerCase() and toUpperCase() generate a char from the parameter, which itself is left unchanged. A character can be characterized by the following methods, which all return a bool: isDigit(), isLowerCase(), isUpperCase(), and isSpace(). The isSpace() method returns true if the character is a "whitespace" character, which includes space, tab, form feed, newline, and return.

The Boolean method getBoolean() is provided as a convenience for inquiring about a property. For more information about properties, see System, described in Chapter 7, System Classes.

Inherited Methods

Boolean and Character inherit from Object, and are in the same package (java.lang). Because of this, all of Object's public and protected methods are available to Booleans and Characters. Three of Object's methods are overridden (redefined) by Boolean and Character: equals(), hashCode(), and toString(). The other Object methods inherited are clone(), finalize(), getClass(), notify(), notifyAll(), and wait().

Constants

Boolean and Character provide a convenient place for certain constants. These are summarized in Table 5-3. Boolean offers TRUE and FALSE, which are class analogs to the language constants true and false. MIN_VALUE and MAX_VALUE provide the lower and upper bounds to valid chars.

Character has two constants: MIN_RADIX and MAX_RADIX. These indicate the valid range that a radix can take on. The radix is the base to use when converting between characters and integers.

Common Radix Values

Java supports all (integral) radices between 2 and 36 for converting between characters and integers. The more common ones are 2 (binary), 8 (octal), 10 (decimal), and 16 (hex).

Table 5-3 Summary of Boolean and Character constants

Class	Constant	Description
Boolean	FALSE	An instance of false, as a Boolean object
	MAX_VALUE	The largest valid Character value
	MIN_VALUE	The smallest valid Character value
	TRUE	An instance of true, as a Boolean object
Character	MAX_RADIX	Maximum base for converting numbers to or from strings
	MIN_RADIX	Minimum base for converting numbers to or from strings

Yes, We Have No Exceptions

There are no exceptions thrown by the Boolean and Character classes. Instead, methods handle invalid arguments by returning special values. This is arguably at odds with the exception error handling model. For Boolean, conversions from Strings to booleans will return false if the String contains something other than "true" or "false" (ignoring case distinctions). For Character.digit(), any nondigit character parameter results in a return value of -1 (the normal return values range from 0 to one less than the radix). If the radix is invalid (less than 2 or more than 36), Character.forDigit() returns the null character ('\0', not to be confused with the character '0').

About the Project

This chapter's project implements a sorted list, and demonstrates its use with the Character class. Sorting in Java in a generic way isn't straightforward, since Object provides no way to test to see if one object is less than another. The project demonstrates how to extend a "final" class through wrapping, how to override Object methods, and how to define and use an interface to mix in new functionality—in this case, sortability.

Boolean and Character Method Summaries

Boolean and Character are described in detail in the following sections. A short description of each method is in Table 5-4.

Table 5-4 Summary of Boolean and Character methods

Class	Method	Description
Boolean	booleanValue	Returns the object's value as a primitive boolean
	equals	Tests to see if two boolean values are the same
	getBoolean	Determines if property value is true
	hashCode	Provides a hash code for use with Hashtable

Class	Method	Description
	toString	Provides a string representation of a boolean
	valueOf	Converts a string to a boolean
Character	charValue	Returns the primitive character of the instance
	digit	Converts a character to an integer
	equals	Compares two characters
	forDigit	Converts an integer to a character, given a radix
	hashCode	Returns a hash code for this instance
	isDigit	Tests to see if the character is a digit
	isLowerCase	Tests to see if the character is lowercase
	isSpace	Tests to see if the character is whitespace
	isUpperCase	Tests to see if the character is uppercase
	toLowerCase	Returns the character in lowercase
	toString	Generates a String representation of the character
	toUpperCase	Converts a character to uppercase

The java.lang.Boolean Class

The public methods for the Java Boolean class are detailed below. In addition to these, Boolean inherits certain methods from Object: clone(), finalize(), getClass(), notify(), notifyAll(), and wait(). Three others, equals(), hashCode(), and toString(), are declared in Object, but overridden by Boolean.

BOOLEAN

Description	Boolean provides a class representation of the boolean primitive data type, as well as methods for comparing and converting booleans.
Syntax	public final class **Boolean** extends Object
Package	java.lang
Import	java.lang.Boolean
Constructors	public **Boolean**(boolean *bool*) public **Boolean**(String *string*)
Parameters	
boolean *bool*	A boolean value
String *string*	A String, whose lowercase value is either "true" or "false." If the string is neither of these, then the value is set to false.
Comments	Once the value is established for a Boolean, it can only be changed by another new Boolean() statement, or from a method that returns a Boolean. If the string argument is not "true" or "false" (ignoring case), then the contained value is set to false.

Example   In this example, a Boolean variable is declared and set to true by the String constructor. It is then printed out.

```
Boolean b = new Boolean("true");
System.out.println(b);
```

Constants

FALSE

Class Name	Boolean
Description	A constant class representation of the boolean value false. This constant can be used instead of constructing new instances of Boolean.
Syntax	public final static Boolean **FALSE**
See Also	**TRUE**
Example	In this example, the FALSE constant is used to initialize a Boolean.

```
Boolean a = Boolean.FALSE;
```

MAX_VALUE

Class Name	Boolean
Description	The largest valid Character value.
Syntax	public final static char **MAX_VALUE**
See Also	**MIN_VALUE**
Comments	The value is \uffff. A more natural location would seem to be in the Character class.
Example	In this example, the maximum character value is accessed.

```
char max = Boolean.MAX_VALUE;
```

MIN_VALUE

Class Name	Boolean
Description	The smallest valid Character value.
Syntax	public final static char **MIN_VALUE**
See Also	**MAX_VALUE**
Comments	The value is \u0000. A more natural location would seem to be in the Character class.
Example	In this example, the minimum character value is accessed.

```
char min = Boolean.MIN_VALUE;
```

TRUE

Class Name	Boolean
Description	A constant class representation of the boolean value true.
Syntax	public final static Boolean **TRUE**
See Also	**FALSE**
Comments	This constant can be used instead of constructing new instances of Boolean.
Example	In this example, the TRUE constant is used to initialize a Boolean.

```
Boolean a = Boolean.TRUE;
```

Methods

BOOLEANVALUE

Class Name	Boolean
Description	Returns the object's value as a primitive boolean.
Syntax	public boolean **booleanValue**()
Parameters	None.
Returns	The return type is boolean. The underlying value of the Boolean is returned.
Exceptions	None.
Example	This example shows the creation of a Boolean variable, and the use of booleanValue() for extracting its primitive boolean.

```
Boolean a = Boolean.TRUE;
boolean b = a.booleanValue();
```

EQUALS

Class Name	Boolean
Description	Tests to see if two Boolean values are the same.
Syntax	public boolean **equals**(Object *obj*)
Parameters	
Object *obj*	The value to compare against.
Returns	The return type is boolean. True is returned if the parameter is of type Boolean and both values are true, or if both values are false.
Exceptions	None.
Comments	No type conversion is performed. For example, passing in a string whose value is "true" or "false" will always return false.

Example   In this example, two Booleans are constructed and compared.

```
Boolean a = Boolean.TRUE;
Boolean b = new Boolean(true);
boolean result = a.equals(b);
```

GETBOOLEAN

Class Name	Boolean
Description	Determines if a particular property value is true.
Syntax	public static boolean **getBoolean**(String *prop*)
Parameters	
String *prop*	The name of the property to check.
Returns	The return type is boolean. True is returned if the property exists and its value is "true."
Exceptions	None.
See Also	System
Comments	For more information on properties, see the System.getProperty() method in Chapter 7, System Classes.
Example	In this example, a hypothetical property is checked to see if its value is true.

```
String s = "SomeProperty";
boolean offmyproperty = Boolean.getBoolean(s);
```

HASHCODE

Class Name	Boolean
Description	Provides a hash code for use with Hashtable, or with other methods requiring hashing.
Syntax	public int **hashCode**()
Parameters	None.
Returns	The return type is int. It is a hash code value.
Exceptions	None.
See Also	Hashtable
Comments	Hash codes are used in the Hashtable class, although it is unusual to store a collection of Booleans in a hash table.
Example	In this example, the hash codes for both Booleans are printed.

```
Boolean b = Boolean.TRUE;
int hashcode = b.hashCode();
```

```
System.out.println (b + " " + hashcode);
b = Boolean.FALSE;
hashcode = b.hashCode();
System.out.println (b + " " + hashcode);
```

TOSTRING

Class Name	Boolean
Description	Provides a string representation of a boolean.
Syntax	public String **toString**()
Parameters	None.
Returns	The return type is String. It is either "true" or "false."
Exceptions	None.
See Also	String
Example	In this example, the String representations of Boolean are printed.

```
Boolean t = Boolean.TRUE;
Boolean f = Boolean.FALSE;
String tomyword = t.toString();
String patently = f.toString();
System.out.println("Boolean.TRUE: " + tomyword);
System.out.println(" Boolean.FALSE: " + patently);
```

VALUEOF

Class Name	Boolean
Description	Converts a string to a Boolean.
Syntax	public static Boolean **valueOf**(String *string*)
Parameters	
String *string*	The string to translate to a Boolean.
Returns	The return type is Boolean. It corresponds to the string argument.
Exceptions	None.
Comments	If the string, when converted to lowercase, is "true," then the result is a Boolean with value true. All other strings generate a false Boolean. This is essentially the inverse of the toString() method.
Example	Selected Strings are converted to booleans.

```
Boolean b1 = Boolean.valueOf("true");
Boolean b2 = Boolean.valueOf("TrUe");
Boolean b3 = Boolean.valueOf("FALSE");
Boolean b4 = Boolean.valueOf("D. None of the above");
```

The java.lang.Character Class

The public methods for the Java Character class are detailed below. In addition to these, Character inherits certain methods from Object: clone(), finalize(), getClass(), notify(), notifyAll(), and wait(). Three others, equals(), hashCode(), and toString(), are declared in Object, but overridden by Character.

CHARACTER

Description	The Character class provides an object representation for the char primitive data type, as well as several character-related constants and methods. Java characters are 2 bytes wide, in order to represent the Unicode character set.
Syntax	public final class **Character** extends Object
Package	java.lang
Import	java.lang.Character
Constructors	public **Character**(char *ch*)
Parameters	
char *ch*	A character to use as the value of the newly constructed Character.
Example	In this example, a Character is constructed.

```
Character c = new Character('a');
```

Constants

MAX_RADIX

Class Name	Character
Description	Maximum base for converting numbers to or from strings.
Syntax	public static final int MAX_RADIX = 36
Example	Print the maximum radix.

```
System.out.println("Max Radix = " + Character.MAX_RADIX);
```

MIN_RADIX

Class Name	Character
Description	Minimum base for converting numbers to or from strings.
Syntax	public static final int MIN_RADIX = 2
Example	Print the minimum radix.

```
System.out.println("Min Radix = " + Character.MIN_RADIX);
```

Methods

CHARVALUE

Class Name	Character
Description	Returns the primitive character of the instance.
Syntax	public char **charValue**()
Parameters	None.
Returns	The return type is char. It is the primitive char contained in the class instance.
Exceptions	None.
Example	In this example, a character is constructed, and its primitive value is extracted.

```
Character c = new Character('a');
char same = c.charValue();
```

DIGIT

Class Name	Character
Description	Converts a character to an integer.
Syntax	public static int **digit**(char *ch*, int *radix*)
Parameters	
char *ch*	The character to convert.
int *radix*	The base to use for conversion.
Returns	The return type is int. It is the integer value of the character, given the radix specified. If the digit is invalid for the radix, or if the radix is invalid, -1 is returned.
Exceptions	None.
Example	In this example, valid and invalid characters are converted to a digit.

```
char nine = '9';
int  digit = Character.digit(nine, 10); // base 10
char fox = 'F';
int  fifteen = Character.digit(fox, 16); // hex
char question = '?';
int  badigit = Character.digit(question, 10); // returns -1
```

EQUALS

Class Name	Character
Description	Compares an object to the Character.

Syntax	public boolean **equals**(Object *obj*)
Parameters	
Object *obj*	An Object to compare against the Character instance.
Returns	The return type is boolean. It returns true if the parameter is a Character and the contained characters are the same.
Exceptions	None.
Example	In this example, two Characters with the same value are favorably compared.

```
Character a = new Character('a');
Character b = new Character('a');
boolean same = b.equals(a);
```

FORDIGIT

Class Name	Character
Description	Converts an integer to a character, the given radix.
Syntax	public static char **forDigit**(int *digit*, int *radix*)
Parameters	
int *digit*	The digit to convert.
int *radix*	The base to use for conversion.
Returns	The return type is char. It is the character corresponding to the first parameter, given the base specified in the second parameter.
Exceptions	None.
Comments	If the digit isn't consistent with the given radix, the character '\0' results.
Example	In this example, valid digits for each radix are displayed as characters.

```
for (int radix = 2; radix <= 36; radix++) {
   for (int digit = 0; digit < radix; digit++) {
      char cdigit = Character.forDigit(digit, radix);
      System.out.print(cdigit);
   }
   System.out.println();
}
```

HASHCODE

Class Name	Character
Description	Returns a hash code for the Character instance.
Syntax	public int **hashCode**()
Parameters	None.
Returns	The return type is int. It is a hash code for the Character.

Exceptions	None.
See Also	Hashtable
Example	This example displays hash codes for the lowercase alphabet.

```
for (char c = 'a'; c <= 'z'; c++) {
    Character ch = new Character(c);
    int hashcode = ch.hashCode();
    System.out.println(ch + " " + hashcode);
}
```

isDigit

Class Name	Character
Description	Tests to see if the character is a digit.
Syntax	public static boolean **isDigit**(char *ch*)
Parameters	
char *ch*	A character to test.
Returns	The return type is boolean. It returns true if the character is a digit ('0', '1', ... '9').
Exceptions	None.
Comments	The assumed radix is 10.
Example	This example shows a more general function to test to see if a character is a digit, under any valid radix.

```
boolean isDigitWithRadix(char ch, int radix) {
    int digit = Character.digit(ch, radix);
    return (digit != -1);
}
```

isLowerCase

Class Name	Character
Description	Tests to see if the character is lowercase.
Syntax	public static boolean **isLowerCase**(char *ch*)
Parameters	
char *ch*	A character to test.
Returns	The return type is boolean. It returns true if the character is lowercase.
Exceptions	None.
Example	This example tests to see if a character is lowercase.

```
char c = 'a';
boolean test = Character.isLowerCase(c);
```

ISSPACE

Class Name	Character
Description	Tests to see if the character is whitespace.
Syntax	public static boolean **isSpace**(char *ch*)
Parameters	
char *ch*	A character to test.
Returns	The return type is boolean. It returns true if the character is whitespace.
Exceptions	None.
Comments	Java considers the following characters to be whitespace: blank, tab, form feed, newline, and carriage return. Table 5-5 shows their various representations.
Example	This example verifies the whitespace characters.

```
char whitespace[] = {' ', '\t', '\n', '\f', '\r'};
String name[] = {"blank", "tab", "newline", "formfeed", "return"};
for (int i=0; i<whitespace.length; i++) {
   boolean test = Character.isSpace(whitespace[i]);
   System.out.println(name[i] + " " + test);
}
```

Table 5-5 Java whitespace characters

Character	Escape	Unicode	Abbreviation
blank		\u0020	
carriage return	\r	\u000d	CR
form feed	\f	\u000c	FF
newline	\n	\u000a	LF
tab	\t	\u0009	HT

ISUPPERCASE

Class Name	Character
Description	Tests to see if the character is uppercase.
Syntax	public static boolean **isUpperCase**(char *ch*)
Parameters	
char *ch*	A character to test.
Returns	The return type is boolean. It returns true if the character is uppercase.
Exceptions	None.

Example   This example tests to see if a character is uppercase.

```
char c = 'A';
boolean test = Character.isUpperCase(c);
```

toLowerCase

Class Name	Character
Description	Returns the character in lowercase.
Syntax	public static char **toLowerCase**(char *ch*)
Parameters	
char *ch*	A character to convert.
Returns	The return type is char. It returns the character as lowercase.
Exceptions	None.
Example	This example generates a lowercase character.

```
char biga = 'A';
char littlea = Character.toLowerCase(biga);
```

toString

Class Name	Character
Description	Generates a String representation of the Character.
Syntax	public String **toString**()
Parameters	None.
Returns	The return type is String. It is a one-character String.
Exceptions	None.
See Also	String
Example	This example generates a string from a Character.

```
Character u = new Character('U');
String youup = u.toString();
```

toUpperCase

Class Name	Character
Description	Converts a character to uppercase.
Syntax	public static char **toUpperCase**(char *ch*)
Parameters	
char *ch*	A character to convert.

Returns	The return type is char. It is the character in uppercase.
Exceptions	None.
Example	This example generates an uppercase character from one that is lowercase.

```
char littlea = 'a';
char biga = Character.toUpperCase(littlea);
```

The Character and Boolean Project: A Sorted List

Project Overview

This chapter's project implements a generic sorted list. A sortable character is defined and used to test the list. The project demonstrates a few techniques:

- Extending a "final" class through wrapping
- Overriding Object methods
- Defining and using an interface to mix in new functionality
- Implementing a collection class that automatically resizes itself

As described in Chapter 3, Global Classes, all classes have a consistent method, equals(), for equality tests. But there is no common way to test to see if one object is less than another. This is a prerequisite for maintaining a sorted list. In this project, a Sortable interface is defined, which contains one method, lessThan(). Classes that implement this method can then be used for ordered comparisons. As described in Chapter 2, The Java Language, Java interfaces define, but do not implement, a set of methods. The actual workings of these methods are filled in by classes that *implement* the interface.

To maintain a sorted list of characters, the Character class would be a useful starting point. But since it is declared final, you cannot extend it in order to implement the Sortable interface. Instead, you can wrap the Character class by making it the sole data member of a new class, SortableCharacter. This new class implements Sortable, and passes certain methods it inherits from Object through to the contained Character.

The class that maintains the sorted list is SortedVector. It is a collection of Sortables, implemented as an array that grows itself, as needed. An ignoreDuplicates() method is provided to screen out duplicates, if desired. SortedVector isn't full-featured—for example, it doesn't have a method for removing objects or for searching for a particular object. You can consider adding these and other missing features.

The project demonstrates SortedVector's use by parsing a String into SortableCharacters and adding them to a SortedVector. Any other class that can be ordered (for example, String), can also be wrapped and stored by SortedVector.

Building the Project

1. Enter the following code (Listing 5-1) into a file named Sortable.java. This defines a Sortable interface. Compile it with javac Sortable.java.

Listing 5-1 Sortable.java

```
// The Sortable interface defines a way to compare objects in order to sort

public interface Sortable {

    public abstract boolean lessThan(Object o);

}
```

2. Enter the following code (Listing 5-2) into a file named SortableCharacter.java. This defines a SortableCharacter, which contains a Character, and augments it by implementing the Sortable interface. Compile it with javac SortableCharacter.java.

Listing 5-2 SortableCharacter.java

```
import Sortable;

// Wrap a Character, adding a lessThan method (implementing Sortable)
// Defines constructors, also methods inherited from Object

class SortableCharacter implements Sortable {

    // the wrapped Character:
    Character _char;

    // Allow constructing from a Character or a char

    SortableCharacter(Character c)
    {
        _char = c;
    }

    SortableCharacter(char c)
    {
        _char = new Character(c);
    }

    // return a Character
    Character getCharacter() {
        return _char;
    }

    // return a char
    char charValue() {
        return _char.charValue();
    }

    // implement the lone Sortable function
    public boolean lessThan(Object o)
    {
        if (o instanceof SortableCharacter) {
            SortableCharacter param = (SortableCharacter) o;
```

continued on next page

continued from previous page

```
        char c1 = getCharacter().charValue();
        char c2 = param.getCharacter().charValue();
        return (c1 < c2);
    }
    // may be better to throw an exception
    return false;
}

// Object's methods - pass thru to Character

public int hashCode() {
    return _char.hashCode();
}

// we can't pass thru to Character since this method is protected
protected Object clone() {
    char c = _char.charValue();
    return new SortableCharacter(c);
}

public boolean equals(Object o) {
    SortableCharacter c = (SortableCharacter) o;
    return _char.equals(c.getCharacter());
}

public String toString() {
    return _char.toString();
}
}
```

3. Enter the following code (Listing 5-3) into a file named SortedVector.java. This
defines a SortedVector class, which implements a growable array that maintains
Sortables in order. Compile it with javac SortedVector.java.

Listing 5-3 SortedVector.java

```
// SortedVector maintains a sorted list
// elements must implement the Sortable interface
// will grow itself as needed (assuming system memory is available
// can include or exclude duplicates in the vector

import Sortable;

class SortedVector {

    // the number of elements in the collection
    int _length;

    // the number of slots allocated
    int _capacity;

    // true if duplicates discarded
    boolean _unique;
```

```
// the array of elements
Sortable[] _array;

// default constructor sets empty collection with small initial capacity
// duplicates allowed by default
public SortedVector()
{
    _length = 0;            // empty to begin with
    _capacity = 10;         // size for 10 to start
    _array = new Sortable[10];  // allocate memory for elements
    _unique = false;        // allow duplicates
}

// return the number of elements currently in the collection
public int length() {
    return _length;
}

// set the policy to screen out duplicates; by default duplicates allowed
public void preventDuplicates() {
    _unique = true;
}

// return element at requested index
public Sortable elementAt(int index) throws ArrayIndexOutOfBoundsException
{
    if (index < 0 || index >= _length) {
        String msg =
           "SortedVector: length is " + _length + "; requested is " + index;
        throw new ArrayIndexOutOfBoundsException(msg);
    }
    return _array[index];
}

// add an element to the vector
public boolean insert(Sortable s)
{
    int i;
    for (i=0; i<_length; i++) {
        if (s.lessThan(_array[i]))
            break;
    }

    // screen for duplicates, if policy
    if (i > 0 && _unique) {
        if (s.equals(_array[i-1]))
            return false;
    }

    return insertAt(s, i);
}

// insert an element at a specific place
// take care of growing array and moving elements over, if need be
// this is private, so that the list insertion is controlled to be sorted
boolean insertAt(Sortable s, int index)
```

continued on next page

continued from previous page

```
{
    // if the array is at capacity, then grow
    if (_length == _capacity)
        grow();

    // if not appending, then move things over
    if (index < _length)
        moveAt(index);

    // lay in the element
    _array[index] = s;

    // augment the length
    _length++;

    return true;
}

// shift everything over 1, starting at parameter
// this opens up a space for an insertion
void moveAt(int index)
{
    // there is a lower level function that is more efficient
    for (int i=_length; i>index; i--)
        _array[i] = _array[i-1];
}

// resize the array by doubling its capacity and copying
//   previously stored elements into new larger array
// the garbage collector will take care of the old array
void grow()
{
    int new_capacity = _capacity * 2;
    if (new_capacity <= 0)
        new_capacity = 10;
    Sortable newarray[] = new Sortable[new_capacity];
    for (int i=0; i<_length; i++)
        newarray[i] = _array[i];
    _array = newarray;
}

// build a string out of string representation of each element
// seperated by spaces
public String toString()
{
    String s = "";
    for (int i=0; i<_length; i++)
        s = s + " " + _array[i].toString();
    return s;
}
}
```

4. Enter the following code (Listing 5-4) into a file named sortest.java. This defines a driver for testing the SortedVector using the SortedCharacter class. Compile it with javac sortest.java.

Listing 5-4 sortest.java

```java
// Test SortedVector and SortableCharacter
// reports all the unique letters, in alphabetic order, of the argument

import SortedVector;
import SortableCharacter;

class sortest {

    // takes one argument - a string to parse into the sorted vector
    public static void main(String args[]) {

        // make sure argument was provided
        if (args.length == 0) {
            System.out.println("Syntax: sortest <string>");
            return;
        }

        // instantiate an empty vector
        SortedVector vector = new SortedVector();

        // only keep distinct entries
        vector.preventDuplicates();

        // Take apart the first argument character by character, add to vector
        String s = args[0];
        for (int i=0; i<s.length(); i++) {
            SortableCharacter sc = new SortableCharacter(s.charAt(i));
            vector.insert(sc);
        }

        // see what we ended up with
        System.out.println(vector);
    }
}
```

Running the Program

At a command prompt, type

```
java sortest <string>
```

The program will output the unique letters of the string, in alphabetic order.

6

CLASSES STRING AND STRINGBUFFER

6

CLASSES STRING AND STRINGBUFFER

String processing is the bread and butter of computer programming. If you think of user interface design (particularly graphical user interface design) as a course of foie gras, and networking as a plate of spaghetti, you will better understand this analogy. String processing is part of nearly every meal we prepare, and even though it might be somewhat plain, it is, as you shall see, quite filling.

Given the ubiquitous nature of string processing, you might expect the Java class library to provide a string class. In fact, it provides two string classes. This chapter describes in detail these two classes—the String class and the StringBuffer class. It also illustrates the role both play in even the simplest programs.

Figure 6-1 depicts the inheritance relationship between classes String and StringBuffer and class Object. Both class String and class StringBuffer are final and cannot be subclassed.

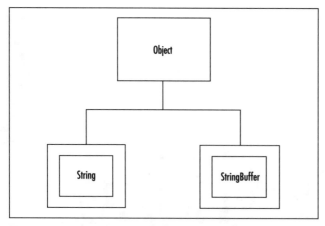

Figure 6-1 Class String and class StringBuffer

An Introduction to Strings

Figure 6-2 illustrates the conceptual representation of a string. A string is simply an arbitrary sequence of characters. The Java programming language allows any character to be placed anywhere within a string. Even the null character, which indicates the end of a string in languages such as C and C++, is valid anywhere within a Java language string. Each character in a string occupies a distinct position. The positions are numbered from zero (the position of the first character) to one less than the total number of characters in the string (the position of the last character).

String processing consists of using a small set of operations on such a sequence of characters. These operations include

- Creating strings

- Taking strings apart

- Putting strings together

- Searching strings for characters and sequences of characters

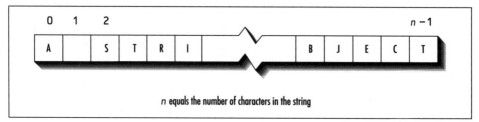

Figure 6-2 The conceptual representation of a string

- Accessing the characters that make up strings

- Copying strings

- Inserting characters into strings

- Replacing parts of strings

- Transforming strings into other data types

- Transforming other data types into strings

The string classes in the Java class library provide methods for performing these operations. Each method is covered in detail in the reference section of this chapter.

The String and StringBuffer Classes

Listing 6-1 shows a short Java program that makes use of both the String class and the StringBuffer class. Even though the program in Listing 6-1 mentions only one of the two classes, both classes are present. And even though the class String is mentioned only once, the String class itself is used extensively. The compiler allows the programmer to hide much of the detail associated with common string operations behind a bit of syntactic trickery. The next section describes these transformations in detail.

Listing 6-1 Hello.java

```
public class Hello
{
    public static void main(String [] args)
    {
        if (args.length > 1)
        {
            System.out.println("Hello " + args[0] + "...");
        }
    }
}
```

The Compiler and the String Classes

As you learned in Chapter 1, Welcome to Java, compilation turns a Java language source file into one or more class files. Compilation is often referred to as translation, because the compiler translates information in one domain (the Java source file) into a different representation of the same information in another domain (the Java class file). Figure 6-3 represents this process of translation.

During compilation, the Java compiler translates certain features of the language into operations on Java classes. The classes that may be used in such a manner by the compiler are found in the package java.lang and are often called language support classes. Class String and class StringBuffer are language support classes.

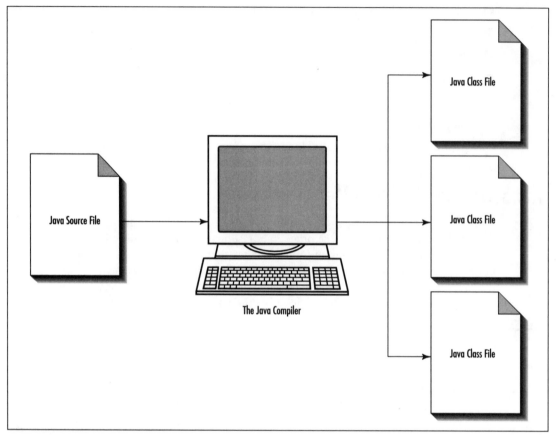

Figure 6-3 The compilation/translation process

Here is an example of how the compiler uses class String.

A string literal is a sequence of characters surrounded by quotation marks. An example of a string literal is the phrase "error in file open sequence". When the Java compiler encounters a string literal in a Java language source file, it creates an instance of a String object to hold it.

Thus, the statement

```
System.out.println("Hello ");
```

becomes, after translation, the following statement:

```
System.out.println(new String(<hello>));
```

In the line of code above, the symbol `<hello>` represents the sequence of characters found in the string literal "Hello".

At runtime, the characters that make up the string literal "Hello" are passed as a parameter to the constructor for the String class. The constructor returns a newly created instance of class String. This String instance is then passed as a parameter to *System.out.println()*, which prints the String object to the console.

Here is an example of how the compiler uses class String and class StringBuffer together.

When the compiler encounters the string concatenation operator (represented by the symbol +) between two strings, it translates the expression into a series of append() operations. For example, the statement

```
String str = "Hello" + string;
```

is translated into the following statement:

```
String str =
    new StringBuffer().append(new String(<hello>))
                      .append(string)
                      .toString();
```

Once again, the symbol *<hello>* represents the sequence of characters found in the string literal "Hello".

At runtime, the program above creates an empty StringBuffer object. A StringBuffer is a string that provides methods for appending and inserting character data. After creating the StringBuffer object, the characters that make up the string literal "Hello" are passed as a parameter to the constructor for the String class. The characters in the newly created String object are then appended onto the end of the StringBuffer object. The characters in the String object *string* are appended onto that. Finally, all of the characters in the StringBuffer object are converted into a String object with a call to the toString() method of the StringBuffer object.

If the program in Listing 6-1 were written as it looked after translation, it would look a lot like the program in Listing 6-2. If you compare the programs in Listing 6-1 and Listing 6-2, you will probably agree that the former is far more readable.

Listing 6-2 The Hello.java program

```
public class Hello
{
    public static void main(String [] args)
    {
        if (args.length == 1)
        {
            System.out.println(new StringBuffer()
                .append(new String(<hello>)).append(args[0])
                .append(new String(<...>)).toString());
        }
    }
}
```

Why Are There Two Classes?

The Java class library provides two string classes, not just one. However, each inhabits a niche that is not well suited for the other.

The String class implements static strings. The contents of these strings, once defined, cannot be changed under normal circumstances. An instance of the String class always contains the same sequence of characters. Because the compiler knows this fact about String objects, it can optimize how String objects are used. For example, since a String object is immutable, its internal data may be shared with other String objects—even String objects in different threads.

On the other hand, the StringBuffer class implements dynamic strings. Methods for appending, inserting, and changing the internal character data, missing from the String class, are present in this class. These characteristics, however, prevent StringBuffer objects from sharing their internal data. This information must be copied every time the StringBuffer is copied. Therefore, duplicating StringBuffer objects typically takes longer than duplicating String objects.

About the Project

Imagine that you are a programmer, and that XYZ Software, the well-known creator of educational software for children, has hired you to create AlgeGraph. AlgeGraph is to be an educational tool capable of turning a complicated function of up to two parameters into a three-dimensional plot of the function's value as the two parameters vary.

XYZ Software has decided the application will be written in the Java programming language. You have already studied the problem and have divided the work to be done into three main tasks:

- The application must read a textual function description and translate it into an internal (computationally oriented) representation.

- The application must use the internal representation to generate the data to be visualized.

- The application must graphically display the generated data.

This chapter doesn't include the necessary information for you to complete the final task. However, by using the two classes about to be described in detail, you can finish the first two tasks.

String and StringBuffer Class Summaries

Table 6-1 briefly describes class String and class StringBuffer.

Table 6-1 The String and StringBuffer classes

Class	Description
String	The class of objects used to represent immutable strings
StringBuffer	The class of objects used to represent mutable strings

The java.lang.String Class

An instance of the Java programming language String class represents an immutable sequence of characters. The String class definition provides methods for common string operations. Table 6-2 summarizes the methods provided by this class.

Table 6-2 Summary of String methods

Method	Description
charAt	Returns the character at the specified position within the String.
compareTo	Lexically compares the String to the String specified in the parameter list.
concat	Creates a new String that is composed of the String specified in the parameter list concatenated onto the end of the original String.
copyValueOf	Creates a new String containing the string representation of the parameter specified in the parameter list.
endsWith	Determines whether or not the String ends with the String specified in the parameter list.
equals	Compares the String to the String specified in the parameter list.
equalsIgnoreCase	Compares the String to the String specified in the parameter list. Case is not significant.
getBytes	Copies characters from the String into the byte array specified in the parameter list.
getChars	Copies characters from the String into the character array specified in the parameter list.
hashcode	Returns the hash code for the String.
indexOf	Returns the position within the String of the first occurrence of the character or String specified in the parameter list.
intern	Returns a String from the internal String table with the same sequence of characters as the String.
lastIndexOf	Returns the position within the String of the last occurrence of the character or String specified in the parameter list.
length	Returns the number of characters in the String.
regionMatches	Determines whether or not the String specified in the parameter list is found somewhere within the String.
replace	Creates a new String in which all occurrences of one character have been replaced by another.
startsWith	Determines whether or not the String begins with the String specified in the parameter list.
substring	Returns a substring of the String.
toCharArray	Copies the characters in the String into a newly allocated character array.
toLowerCase	Creates a new String in which all of the uppercase characters have been replaced by their lowercase equivalent.
toString	Returns the String.
toUpperCase	Creates a new String in which all of the lowercase characters have been replaced by their uppercase equivalent.
trim	Creates a new String from which all of the leading and trailing whitespace has been removed.
valueOf	Creates a new String containing the string representation of the parameter specified in the parameter list.

STRING

Description	The String class represents an immutable sequence of characters.
Syntax	public final class **String** extends Object

Package	java.lang
Import	java.lang.String
Constructors	public **String**()
	public **String**(String *str*)
	public **String**(StringBuffer *strbuf*)
	public **String**(char [] *rgc*)
	public **String**(char [] *rgc*, int *nOffset*, int *nCount*)
	public **String**(byte [] *rgb*, int *nHigh*)
	public **String**(byte [] *rgb*, int *nHigh*, int *nOffset*, int *nCount*)

Parameters

String *str*	A String.
StringBuffer *strbuf*	A StringBuffer.
char [] *rgc*	A reference to a character array.
int *nOffset*	The position within the array at which to begin copying.
int *nCount*	The number of elements (characters or bytes) to copy from the array beginning at the specified offset.
byte [] *rgb*	A reference to a byte array.
int *nHigh*	An integer containing the high-order byte necessary to create a 2-byte Unicode character.
Exceptions	If a constructor requires a range be specified (with *nOffset* and *nCount*), it will throw a StringIndexOutOfBoundsException if the range is invalid.
Comments	If a String object is to be created from a byte array, each character in the string will be formed from a byte from the byte array and the value of the parameter *nHigh*. The byte becomes the low-order byte of each 2-byte Unicode character. The value of the parameter *nHigh* becomes the high-order byte.
Example	The following example demonstrates the creation of several String objects from a variety of sources.

```
void main()
{
   byte [] rgb = { 1, 2, 3};
   char [] rgc = { 'a', 'b', 'c', 'd' };

   String str = "one two three";
   StringBuffer strbuf = new StringBuffer("hello world");

   String str1 = new String();
   String str2 = new String(str);
   String str3 = new String(strbuf);
   String str4 = new String(rgc, 1, 2);
   String str5 = new String(rgb, 0);
}
```

Methods

CHARAT

Class Name	String
Description	This method provides direct access to the characters that make up a String object. With this method, the characters in a String object can be read either sequentially or randomly.
Syntax	public char **charAt**(int *nIndex*)
Parameters	
int *nIndex*	The position of the desired character in the String. This parameter must specify a value between zero and one less than the length of the String, inclusive.
Returns	The character at the indicated position within the String.
Exceptions	If the parameter *nIndex* is outside the specified range, this method will throw a StringIndexOutOfBoundsException.
Example	The following example prints each String in the input String array backwards.

```
void main(String [] rgstr)
{
   for (int i = 0; i < rgstr.length; i++)
   {
      for (int j = rgstr[i].length(); j > 0; j--)
      {
         System.out.print(rgstr[i].charAt(j - 1));
      }
      System.out.println();
   }
}
```

COMPARETO

Class Name	String
Description	This method lexically compares this String to the String specified in the parameter list. The lexical ordering of strings is an ordering based on the ordering of the characters that make them up (see Figure 6-4). You are probably most familiar with the lexical ordering that occurs when you alphabetize a list of English words (much as you might do when constructing a dictionary). Since, when constructing a dictionary, the word "bat" comes before "cactus," and "dog" comes after "do," you say that "bat" is less than "cactus" and "dog" is greater than "do."
Syntax	public int **compareTo**(String *str*)

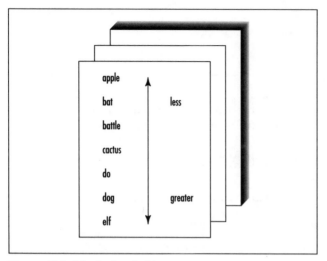

Figure 6-4 A lexical ordering

Parameters

String *str*   The String to which to compare this String.

Returns   An integer value that depends on the ordering of the two Strings. If this String is represented by *this* and the String to be compared to is represented by *str*, then the following holds (*n* is some integer—the class definition only specifies the sign of *n*, not its magnitude):

if *this* < *str*, then return -*n*

if *this* = *str*, then return 0

if *this* > *str*, then return +*n*

Exceptions   None.

Comments   The lexical comparison of strings is a common string operation. It is the string equivalent of the numeric comparison operations <, >, and ==. It is an important component of algorithms that operate on collections of String objects, such as sorting algorithms.

Example   The following example uses this method to compare two strings specified on the command line.

```
class Main
{
    public static void main(String [] rgstr)
    {
        if (rgstr.length == 2)
        {
            int i = rgstr[0].compareTo(rgstr[1]);

            if (i < 0)
            {
                System.out.println(rgstr[0] + " < " + rgstr[1]);
            }
```

```
         else if (i == 0)
         {
            System.out.println(rgstr[0] + " == " + rgstr[1]);
         }
         else if (i > 0)
         {
            System.out.println(rgstr[0] + " > " + rgstr[1]);
         }
      }
   }
}
```

CONCAT

Class Name	String
Description	This method creates a new String that is composed of the characters in this String immediately followed by the characters in the String specified in the parameter list. Neither String is itself transformed by this operation.
Syntax	public String **concat**(String *str*)
Parameters	
String *str*	The String to concatenate with this String.
Returns	The String formed by copying the characters in the two original Strings.
Exceptions	None.
Example	The following example concatenates all of the strings specified on the command line and prints the result.

```
class Main
{
   public static void main(String [] rgstr)
   {
      String str = new String();

      for (int i = 0; i < rgstr.length; i++)
      {
         str = str.concat(rgstr[i]).concat(" ");
      }

      System.out.println(str);
   }
}
```

COPYVALUEOF

Class Name	String
Description	This method allocates and returns a String containing the same sequence of characters as the character array specified in the parameter list (or a subset thereof). It differs from the valueOf() method because it is guaranteed to copy the characters into a newly allocated internal character array,

rather than simply setting the internal character array reference to point to the character array in the parameter list.

Syntax	public static String **copyValueOf**(char [] *rgc*)
	public static String **copyValueOf**(char [] *rgc*, int *nOffset*, int *nCount*)
Parameters	
char [] *rgc*	A reference to a character array.
int *nOffset*	The position within the character array at which to begin copying.
int *nCount*	The number of characters to copy from the character array beginning at the specified offset.
Returns	A String.
Exceptions	None.
See Also	valueOf()
Example	The following example demonstrates how to create a String from a character array. The new String will contain the characters "bc".

```
class Main
{
    static char [] rgc = { 'a', 'b', 'c' };

    public static void main(String [] rgstr)
    {
        String str = String.copyValueOf(rgc, 1, 2);
    }
}
```

ENDSWITH

Class Name	String
Description	This method determines whether or not this String ends with the same sequence of characters as the String specified in the parameter list.
Syntax	public boolean **endsWith**(String *str*)
Parameters	
String *str*	A String.
Returns	The boolean value true if this String ends with the String in the parameter list, and the boolean value false otherwise.
Exceptions	None.
See Also	regionMatches(), startsWith()
Example	The following example uses this method to determine which String objects in the String array *rgstr* end with the string "ism".

```
void main(String [] rgstr)
{
    for (int i = 0; i < rgstr.length; i++)
    {
        if (rgstr[i].endsWith("ism"))
        {
```

```
        System.out.println(rgstr[i]);
    }
  }
}
```

EQUALS

Class Name	String
Description	This method compares this String to the String specified in the parameter list. It tests for equivalence (both Strings consist of the same sequence of characters), not equality (both Strings are actually the same object).
Syntax	public boolean **equals**(Object *str*)
Parameters	
Object *str*	An Object.
Returns	The boolean value true if this String contains the same characters as the String specified in the parameter list, and false otherwise. If the supplied parameter is not a String object, this method returns false.
Exceptions	None.
See Also	equalsIgnoreCase()
Comments	Testing strings for equivalence is a common string operation. It is the string equivalent of the numeric equality operation ==. It is an important component of algorithms that operate on collections of strings.
Example	The following example uses this method to compare every String object in the String array *rgstr* with the string "hello".

```
void main(String [] rgstr)
{
   for (int i = 0; i < rgstr.length; i++)
   {
      if (!rgstr[i].equals("hello"))
      {
         System.out.println(rgstr[i]);
      }
   }
}
```

EQUALSIGNORECASE

Class Name	String
Description	This method compares this String to the String specified in the parameter list. It tests for equivalence (both Strings consist of the same sequence of characters), not equality (both Strings are actually the same object). The case of the two Strings is not significant.
Syntax	public boolean **equalsIgnoreCase**(String *str*)

Parameters

String *str*   A String.

Returns   The boolean value true if this String contains the same characters as the String in the parameter list, and false otherwise.

Exceptions   None.

See Also   equals()

Comments   Testing strings for equivalence is a common string operation. It is the string equivalent of the numeric equality operation ==. It is an important component of algorithms that operate on collections of strings. This method currently knows how to map only the first 256 characters of the Unicode character set from upper- to lowercase.

Example   The following example uses this method to compare every String object in the String array *rgstr* with the string "hello". Since case is unimportant, the strings "Hello", "HELLO", and "HeLLo" also match.

```
void main(String [] rgstr)
{
   for (int i = 0; i < rgstr.length; i++)
   {
      if (!rgstr[i].equalsIgnoreCase("hello"))
      {
         System.out.println(rgstr[i]);
      }
   }
}
```

GETBYTES

Class Name   String

Description   This method copies characters from this String into the byte array specified in the parameter list. Each character in the source array will be truncated to byte size.

Syntax   public void **getBytes**(int *nSrcBegin*, int *nSrcEnd*, byte [] *rgbDst*, int *nDstBegin*)

Parameters

int *nSrcBegin*   The position within this String at which to begin copying.

int *nSrcEnd*   The position within this String of the last character to be copied.

byte [] *rgbDst*   The byte array that serves as the destination. The byte array must have already been created and it must be large enough to hold all of the characters from the String.

int *nDstBegin*   The position within the destination byte array at which to begin copying bytes.

Returns   None.

Exceptions	If the destination array *rgbDst* is not large enough, this method will throw an ArrayIndexOutOfBoundsException.
See Also	getChars()
Example	The following example uses this method to copy the characters from the String objects in the String array *rgstr* into a byte array.

```
void main(String [] rgstr)
{
   int n = 0;

   byte [] rgb = new byte [1000];

   for (int i = 0; i < rgstr.length; i++)
   {
      rgstr[i].getBytes(0, rgstr[i].length() - 1, rgb, n);
      n += rgstr[i].length();
   }

   System.out.println(new String(rgb, 0));
}
```

GETCHARS

Class Name	String
Description	This method copies characters from this String into the character array specified in the parameter list.
Syntax	public void **getChars**(int *nSrcBegin*, int *nSrcEnd*, char [] *rgcDst*, int *nDstBegin*)
Parameters	
int *nSrcBegin*	The position within this String at which to begin copying.
int *nSrcEnd*	The position within this String of the last character to be copied.
char [] *rgcDst*	The character array that serves as the destination. The character array must have already been created and it must be large enough to hold all of the characters from the String.
int *nDstBegin*	The position within the destination character array at which to begin copying characters.
Returns	None.
Exceptions	If the destination array *rgcDst* is not large enough, this method will throw an ArrayIndexOutOfBoundsException.
See Also	getBytes(), toCharArray()
Example	The following example uses this method to copy the characters from the String objects in the String array *rgstr* into a character array.

```
void main(String [] rgstr)
{
   for (int i = 0; i < rgstr.length; i++)
```

continued on next page

continued from previous page

```
{
    char [] rgc = new char [rgstr[i].length()];

    rgstr[i].getChars(0, rgstr[i].length() - 1, rgc, 0);

    for (int j = rgc.length; j > 0; j++)
    {
        System.out.print(rgc[j - 1]);
    }
    System.out.println("");
}
}
```

HASHCODE

Class Name	String
Description	This method redefines the method of the same name in the Object class. The String class generates a hash code based on the character values in the String object. The hash codes of two Strings may be the same even if the Strings are not equivalent. This method is usually used in conjunction with the Hashtable class. The Hashtable class provides a convenient mechanism for searching a large amount of information quickly.
Syntax	public int **hashcode**()
Parameters	None.
Returns	An integer based entirely on the character values in the String object.
Exceptions	None.
Example	The following example uses this method to print the hash code for each String object in the String array *rgstr*.

```
void main(String [] rgstr)
{
    for (int i = 0; i < rgstr.length; i++)
    {
        System.out.println("the hashcode of " + rgstr[i] +
                           " is " + rgstr[i].hashcode());
    }
}
```

INDEXOF

Class Name	String
Description	This method returns the position of the first occurrence of the String or character specified in the parameter list.

Syntax	public int **indexOf**(String *str*)
	public int **indexOf**(int *c*)
	public int **indexOf**(String *str*, int *nFrom*)
	public int **indexOf**(int *c*, int *nFrom*)
Parameters	
String *str*	The String to search for.
int *c*	The character to search for. The value is passed as an integer but is automatically converted to a character before the search is performed.
int *nFrom*	The position within the String from which to search.
Returns	An integer representing the position of the String or character. If it is not in the String, this method returns the value -1.
Exceptions	None.
See Also	lastIndexOf()
Example	The following example uses this method to locate the first occurrence of a space character in each String object in the String array *rgstr*.

```
void main(String [] rgstr)
{
    for (int i = 0; i < rgstr.length; i++)
    {
        System.out.println(rgstr[i].indexOf(' '));
    }
}
```

INTERN

Class Name	String
Description	The String class internally maintains a table of unique Strings. This method returns the String in this table that has the same character sequence as this String. If such a String does not exist, then this String is added to the table.
Syntax	public String **intern**()
Parameters	None.
Returns	A String from the internal String table.
Exceptions	None.
Comments	When two equivalent Strings are interned, the resulting String references returned will contain the same value. These two Strings are thus equal as well as equivalent. In other words, they will reference the same chunk of memory and the "==" operator will yield true.
Example	The following example uses this method to add String objects to the internal String table and to fetch them again for comparison with String objects passed down in the String array *rgstr*.

```
class Intern
{
   static String strLet, strWhile, strFor;

   static
   {
      strLet = "let".intern();      // put these keywords into
      strWhile = "while".intern(); // the internal String table
      strFor = "for".intern();
   }

   public static void main(String [] rgstr)
   {
      for (int i = 0; i < rgstr.length; i++)
      {
         String str = rgstr[i].intern();

         if (str == strLet)
            System.out.println("keyword: let");
         else if (str == strWhile)
            System.out.println("keyword: while");
         else if (str == strFor)
            System.out.println("keyword: for");
      }
   }
}
```

LASTINDEXOF

Class Name	String
Description	This method returns the position of the last occurrence of the String or character specified in the parameter list.
Syntax	public int **lastIndexOf**(String *str*)
	public int **lastIndexOf**(int *c*)
	public int **lastIndexOf**(String *str*, int *nFrom*)
	public int **lastIndexOf**(int *c*, int *nFrom*)
Parameters	
String *str*	The String to search for.
int *c*	The character to search for. The value is passed as an integer but is automatically converted to a character before the search is performed.
int *nFrom*	The position within the String from which to search.
Returns	An integer representing the position of the String or character. If it is not in the String, this method returns the value -1.
Exceptions	None.
See Also	indexOf()
Example	The following example uses this method to locate the last occurrence of a space character in each String object in the String array *rgstr*.

```
void main(String [] rgstr)
{
    for (int i = 0; i < rgstr.length; i++)
    {
        System.out.println(rgstr[i].lastIndexOf(' '));
    }
}
```

LENGTH

Class Name	String
Description	This method returns the number of characters in the String.
Syntax	public int length()
Parameters	None.
Returns	An integer whose value is equal to the number of characters in the String.
Exceptions	None.
Comments	This method is commonly used in the conditional part of a control statement to prevent reading or writing past the end of the internal character buffer of the String. It might also be used to get the number of characters in the String for informational purposes, as in the example below.
Example	The following example prints out the length of each String object in the String array *rgstr*.

```
void main(String [] rgstr)
{
    for (int i = 0; i < rgstr.length; i++)
    {
        System.out.println(rgstr[i] + ": " + rgstr[i].length());
    }
}
```

REGIONMATCHES

Class Name	String
Description	This method determines whether or not the String specified in the parameter list is found somewhere within this String. Case may or may not be important for this comparison.
Syntax	public boolean **regionMatches**(int *nOffset*, String *str*, int *nStrOffset*, int *nLength*)
	public boolean **regionMatches**(boolean *fCase*, int *nOffset*, String *str*, int *nStrOffset*, int *nLength*)
Parameters	
int *nOffset*	The position within this String at which to begin searching.
String *str*	The String for which to search.

int *nStrOffset*	The position within String *str* at which to begin the comparison.
int *nLength*	The number of successive characters from String *str* that must be present in this String.
boolean *fCase*	The value true if case should be ignored while making the comparison, false otherwise.
Returns	Returns true if the regions match, and false otherwise.
Exceptions	None.
See Also	endsWith(), startsWith()
Comments	This method currently knows how to map only the first 256 characters of the Unicode character set from upper- to lowercase.
Example	The following example uses this method to count the number of times the first String object occurs within the second String object.

```
void main(String str1, String str2)
{
   int c = 0;
   int n = 0;

   while (n < str2.length())
   {
      if (str2.regionMatches(n, str1, 0, str1.length() - 1))
      {
         c++;
      }
   }
}
```

REPLACE

Class Name	String
Description	This method creates a new String in which all occurrences of one character have been replaced by another. The original String is not modified.
Syntax	public String **replace**(char *cOld*, char *cNew*)
Parameters	
char *cOld*	The character to replace.
char *cNew*	The character to replace character *cOld* with.
Returns	A String.
Exceptions	None.
Example	The following example uses this method to replace every occurrence of the blank space character in a String object with the dash.

```
void main(String [] rgstr)
{
   for (int i = 0; i < rgstr.length; i++)
   {
```

```
    System.out.println(rgstr[i].replace(' ', '-'));
  }
}
```

STARTSWITH

Class Name	String
Description	This method determines whether or not this String begins with the same sequence of characters as the String specified in the parameter list.
Syntax	public boolean **startsWith**(String *str*)
	public boolean **startsWith**(String *str*, int *nOffset*)
Parameters	
String *str*	A String.
int *nOffset*	The position in String *str* at which to begin the comparison.
Returns	The boolean value true if this String starts with the String in the parameter list, and the boolean value false otherwise.
Exceptions	None.
See Also	endsWith(), regionMatches()
Example	The following example uses this method to determine which String objects in the String array *rgstr* start with the String "let ".

```
void main(String [] rgstr)
{
  for (int i = 0; i < rgstr.length; i++)
  {
    if (rgstr[i].startsWith("let "))
    {
      System.out.println(rgstr[i]);
    }
  }
}
```

SUBSTRING

Class Name	String
Description	This method returns a substring of this String.
Syntax	public String **substring**(int *nBeginning*)
	public String **substring**(int *nBeginning*, int *nEnding*)
Parameters	
int *nBeginning*	The position within the String from which to begin copying.
int *nEnding*	The position within the String at which to finish copying.
Returns	A new String composed of the characters from *nBeginning* to the end of this String, or to *nEnding* (inclusive) if specified.

Exceptions   If the range (specified by *nBeginning* and *nEnding*) is invalid, this method
will throw a StringIndexOutOfBoundsException.

Example   The following example prints out the characters in each String object in
the String array *rgstr* following the first word. A word in this example is a
sequence of characters delineated by a space.

```
void main(String [] rgstr)
{
   for (int i = 0; i < rgstr.length; i++)
   {
      int c = rgstr[i].indexOf(' ');

      if (c > -1)
      {
         System.out.println(rgstr[i].substring(c + 1));
      }
      else
      {
         System.out.println(rgstr[i]);
      }
   }
}
```

toCharArray

Class Name   String

Description   This method copies the characters in the String into a newly allocated
character array.

Syntax   public char [] **toCharArray**()

Parameters   None.

Returns   A character array containing the characters that make up this String.

Exceptions   None.

See Also   getChars()

Example   The following example uses this method to write each String object in the
String array *rgstr* into a character array before writing the character array
to the output stream.

```
void process(String [] rgstr, OutputStream os)
{
   for (int i = 0; i < rgstr.length; i++)
   {
      char [] rgc = rgstr.toCharArray();

      os.write(rgc);
   }
}
```

toLowerCase

Class Name	String
Description	This method allocates and returns a String in which all of the uppercase characters from the original String have been replaced with their lowercase equivalent.
Syntax	public String **toLowerCase()**
Parameters	None.
Returns	A String.
Exceptions	None.
See Also	Character.toLowerCase(), String.toUpperCase()
Comments	This method currently knows how to map only the first 256 characters of the Unicode character set from upper- to lowercase.
Example	The following example uses this method to convert all of the String objects in the String array *rgstr* to lowercase.

```
void main(String [] rgstr)
{
    for (int i = 0; i < rgstr.length; i++)
    {
        System.out.println(rgstr[i].toLowerCase());
    }
}
```

toString

Class Name	String
Description	This method literally returns itself. This method redefines the method of the same name in class Object. Typically it will be called for a String that is being referenced as an Object.
Syntax	public string **toString()**
Parameters	None.
Returns	A String.
Exceptions	None.
Example	This example uses this method to obtain a reference to the original String object even though the original String object is being referenced as an instance of class Object.

```
void main()
{
    Object obj = new String("hello");

    String str = obj.toString();
}
```

toUpperCase

Class Name	String
Description	This method allocates and returns a String in which all of the lowercase characters from the original String have been replaced with their uppercase equivalent.
Syntax	public String **toUpperCase**()
Parameters	None.
Returns	A String.
Exceptions	None.
See Also	Character.toUpperCase(), String.toLowerCase()
Comments	This method currently knows how to map only the first 256 characters of the Unicode character set from lower- to uppercase.
Example	The following example uses this method to convert all of the String objects in the String array *rgstr* to uppercase.

```
void main(String [] rgstr)
{
   for (int i = 0; i < rgstr.length; i++)
   {
      System.out.println(rgstr[i].toUpperCase());
   }
}
```

TRIM

Class Name	String
Description	This method allocates and returns a String from which all of the leading and trailing whitespace has been removed. Whitespace consists of all characters numerically less than or equal to the space character (0x20).
Syntax	public String **trim**()
Parameters	None.
Returns	A String.
Exceptions	None.
Example	The following example removes the leading and trailing whitespace from each String object in the String array *rgstr* and prints the result.

```
void main(String [] rgstr)
{
   for (int i = 0; i < rgstr.length; i++)
   {
      System.out.println('<' + rgstr[i].trim() + '>');
   }
}
```

VALUEOf

Class Name	String
Description	This method allocates and returns a String containing the character representation of the parameter specified in the parameter list.
Syntax	public static String **valueOf**(Object *obj*)
	public static String **valueOf**(boolean *bool*)
	public static String **valueOf**(char *c*)
	public static String **valueOf**(char [] *rgc*)
	public static String **valueOf**(char [] *rgc*, int *nOffset*, int *nCount*)
	public static String **valueOf**(int *i*)
	public static String **valueOf**(long *l*)
	public static String **valueOf**(float *f*)
	public static String **valueOf**(double *d*)
Parameters	
Object *obj*	An Object.
boolean *bool*	A boolean value.
char *c*	A character.
char [] *rgc*	A reference to a character array.
int *nOffset*	The position within the character array at which to begin copying.
int *nCount*	The number of characters to copy from the character array beginning at the specified offset.
int *i*	An int.
long *l*	A long.
float *f*	A float.
double *d*	A double.
Returns	A String.
Exceptions	None.
See Also	copyValueOf()
Comments	If an Object is passed to this method, this method calls that Object's toString() method and returns the result.
Example	The following example uses these methods to create a String object containing the string representation of the parameters specified in the parameter list.

```
String process(Object obj, char [] rgc, int i)
{
   String str = String.valueOf(obj) + " " +
                String.valueOf(rgc) + " " +
                String.valueOf(i);
   return str;

}
```

The java.lang.StringBuffer Class

An instance of the Java programming language StringBuffer class represents a mutable sequence of characters. The StringBuffer class definition provides methods for common string operations. Table 6-3 summarizes the methods provided by this class.

Table 6-3 Summary of StringBuffer methods

Method	Description
append	Appends the string representation of the parameter specified in the parameter list to the StringBuffer
capacity	Returns the character storage capacity of the StringBuffer
charAt	Returns the character at the specified position within the StringBuffer
ensureCapacity	Sets the size of the character storage buffer
getChars	Copies characters from the StringBuffer into the character array specified in the parameter list
insert	Inserts the string representation of the parameter specified in the parameter list into the StringBuffer
length	Returns the number of characters in the StringBuffer
setCharAt	Changes a character in the StringBuffer
setLength	Sets the length of the StringBuffer
toString	Returns a String containing the contents of the StringBuffer

STRINGBUFFER

Description	The StringBuffer class represents a mutable sequence of characters.
Syntax	public final class **StringBuffer** extends Object
Package	java.lang
Import	java.lang.StringBuffer
Constructors	public **StringBuffer**()
	public **StringBuffer**(int *nSize*)
	public **StringBuffer**(String *str*)
Parameters	
int *nSize*	The desired initial storage capacity. If the initial storage capacity is eventually exceeded, the StringBuffer will automatically allocate additional storage.
String *str*	A String.
Comments	You should use the first constructor if you are not creating a StringBuffer from an existing String and do not know or cannot guess (or just don't care to calculate) the approximate final size of the StringBuffer. If you know or can guess the final number of characters that will be stored in the StringBuffer, it is a good idea to use the second constructor. Doing so will

allow you to avoid the costly reallocations that will otherwise occur when the internal buffer's storage capacity is exceeded. Very often you will have a String that you would like to modify. Since Strings are immutable, you must use the third constructor to create a StringBuffer from the String. You may then modify a copy of the character information that was in the original String. The new character information can then be retrieved as a String using the toString() method.

Example   The following example demonstrates the creation of several StringBuffer objects.

```
void main()
{
   String str = "one two three";

   StringBuffer strbuf1 = new StringBuffer();
   StringBuffer strbuf2 = new StringBuffer(100);
   StringBuffer strbuf3 = new StringBuffer(str);
}
```

Methods

APPEND

Class Name	StringBuffer
Description	This method appends the string representation of the parameter specified in the parameter list to the contents of the StringBuffer.
Syntax	public synchronized StringBuffer **append**(Object *obj*)
	public synchronized StringBuffer **append**(String *str*)
	public synchronized StringBuffer **append**(char [] *rgc*)
	public synchronized StringBuffer **append**(char [] *rgc*, int *nOffset*, int *nCount*)
	public synchronized StringBuffer **append**(boolean *bool*)
	public synchronized StringBuffer **append**(char *c*)
	public synchronized StringBuffer **append**(int *i*)
	public synchronized StringBuffer **append**(long *l*)
	public synchronized StringBuffer **append**(float *f*)
	public synchronized StringBuffer **append**(double *d*)
Parameters	
Object *obj*	An Object.
String *str*	A String.
char [] *rgc*	A reference to a character array.
int *nOffset*	The position within the character array at which to begin copying.

int *nCount*	The number of characters to copy from the character array beginning at the specified offset.
boolean *bool*	A boolean value.
char *c*	A character.
int *i*	An int.
long *l*	A long.
float *f*	A float.
double *d*	A double.
Returns	The StringBuffer itself. This method does not allocate a new StringBuffer.
Exceptions	None.
See Also	insert()
Comments	A parameter is first transformed into a String and then the characters in the String are appended to the contents of the StringBuffer. If an Object is passed to this method, this method calls that Object's toString() method and appends the result.
Example	The following example uses these methods to create a StringBuffer object containing the string representation of the parameters specified in the parameter list.

```
StringBuffer process(Object obj, char [] rgc, int i)
{
    StringBuffer strbuf = new StringBuffer();

    strbuf.append(obj).append(" ")
                .append(rgc).append(" ")
                .append(i);
    return strbuf;
}
```

CAPACITY

Class Name	StringBuffer
Description	This method returns the character storage capacity of the StringBuffer. The storage capacity is the number of characters that may be stored in the StringBuffer before the StringBuffer must be resized.
Syntax	public int **capacity**()
Parameters	None.
Returns	The size of the internal buffer used for storing character data.
Exceptions	None.
See Also	ensureCapacity()
Comments	This method, in conjunction with the method ensureCapacity(), can be used to guarantee that a StringBuffer is optimally sized. Since both

methods are thread safe, this operation could even be performed in a separate thread.

Example   The following example uses the methods length() and capacity() to print out a summary of the usage of the internal storage buffer.

```
void stats(StringBuffer strbuf)
{
   int len = strbuf.length();
   int cap = strbuf.capacity();

   System.out.println("Length = " + len);
   System.out.println("Capacity = " + cap);
   System.out.println("Usage = " +
                      ((float)len / (float)cap) * 100.0 +
                      "%");
}
```

CHARAT

Class Name	StringBuffer
Description	This method provides direct access to the characters that make up a StringBuffer object. With this method, the characters in a StringBuffer object can be read either sequentially or randomly.
Syntax	public synchronized char **charAt**(int *nIndex*)
Parameters	
int *nIndex*	The position of the desired character in the StringBuffer. This parameter must specify a value between zero and one less than the length of the StringBuffer, inclusive.
Returns	The character at the indicated position within the StringBuffer.
Exceptions	If the parameter *nIndex* is outside the specified range, this method will throw a StringIndexOutOfBoundsException.
See Also	setCharAt()
Example	The following example prints each StringBuffer in the input StringBuffer array backwards.

```
void reverse(StringBuffer [] rgstrbuf)
{
   for (int i = 0; i < rgstrbuf.length; i++)
   {
      for (int j = rgstrbuf[i].length(); j > 0; j--)
      {
         System.out.print(rgstrbuf[i].charAt(j - 1));
      }
      System.out.println();
   }
}
```

ENSURECAPACITY

Class Name	StringBuffer
Description	This method checks the size of the character storage buffer and ensures that it is at least of a minimum size. If the character storage buffer is too small, it will be resized.
Syntax	public synchronized void **ensureCapacity**(int *nMinimum*)
Parameters	
int *nMinimum*	The minimum acceptable size of the internal buffer used for storing character data.
Returns	None.
Exceptions	None.
See Also	capacity()
Comments	This method, in conjunction with the method capacity(), can be used to guarantee that a StringBuffer is optimally sized. Since both methods are thread safe, this operation could even be performed in a separate thread.
Example	The following example shows a method that can be used to ensure that a StringBuffer has a certain percentage of its character storage capacity free.

```
void ensure(StringBuffer strbuf, double d)
{
   double free;
   int len, cap;

   if (d < 0.0 || d > 100.0) throw new RuntimeException();

   len = strbuf.length();
   cap = strbuf.capacity();

   free = 100.0 - (float)len / (float)cap * 100.0;

   if (free < d) strbuf.ensureCapacity(cap * 2);
}
```

GETCHARS

Class Name	StringBuffer
Description	This method copies characters from this StringBuffer into the character array specified in the parameter list.
Syntax	public synchronized void **getChars**(int *nSrcBegin*, int *nSrcEnd*, char [] *rgcDst*, int *nDstBegin*)
Parameters	
int *nSrcBegin*	The position within this StringBuffer at which to begin copying.
int *nSrcEnd*	The position within this StringBuffer of the last character to be copied.

char [] *rgcDst*	The character array that serves as the destination. The character array must have already been created and it must be large enough to hold all of the characters from the StringBuffer.
int *nDstBegin*	The position within the destination character array at which to begin copying characters.
Returns	None.
Exceptions	If the destination array *rgcDst* is not large enough, this method will throw a StringIndexOutOfBoundsException.
Example	The following example uses this method to copy the StringBuffer objects in the StringBuffer array *rgstr* into character arrays before printing the characters in reverse order.

```
void process(StringBuffer [] rgstr)
{
   for (int i = 0; i < rgstr.length; i++)
   {
      char [] rgc = new char [rgstr[i].length()];

      rgstr[i].getChars(0, rgstr[i].length() - 1, rgc, 0);

      for (int j = rgc.length; j > 0; j--)
      {
         System.out.print(rgc[j - 1]);
      }
      System.out.println("");
   }
}
```

INSERT

Class Name	StringBuffer
Description	This method inserts the string representation of the parameter specified in the parameter list into the contents of the StringBuffer.
Syntax	public synchronized StringBuffer **insert**(int *nOffset*, Object *obj*)
	public synchronized StringBuffer **insert**(int *nOffset*, String *str*)
	public synchronized StringBuffer **insert**(int *nOffset*, char [] *rgc*)
	public synchronized StringBuffer **insert**(int *nOffset*, boolean *bool*)
	public synchronized StringBuffer **insert**(int *nOffset*, char *c*)
	public synchronized StringBuffer **insert**(int *nOffset*, int *i*)
	public synchronized StringBuffer **insert**(int *nOffset*, long *l*)
	public synchronized StringBuffer **insert**(int *nOffset*, float *f*)
	public synchronized StringBuffer **insert**(int *nOffset*, double *d*)
Parameters	
int *nOffset*	The position within the contents of the StringBuffer at which to begin inserting characters.

Object *obj*	An Object.
String *str*	A String.
char [] *rgc*	A reference to a character array.
boolean *bool*	A boolean value.
char *c*	A character.
int *i*	An int.
long *l*	A long.
float *f*	A float.
double *d*	A double.
Returns	The StringBuffer itself. This method does not allocate and return a new StringBuffer.
Exceptions	If the parameter *nOffset* specifies an invalid position, this method will throw a StringIndexOutOfBoundsException.
See Also	append()
Comments	A parameter is first transformed into a String and then the characters in the String are inserted into the StringBuffer. If an Object is passed to this method, this method calls that Object's toString() method and inserts the result.
Example	The following example uses these methods to create a StringBuffer object containing the string representation of the parameters specified in the parameter list in the reverse order from which they were specified.

```
StringBuffer process(Object obj, char [] rgc, int i)
{
    StringBuffer strbuf = new StringBuffer();

    strbuf.insert(0, obj).insert(0, " ")
                 .insert(0, rgc).insert(0, " ")
                 .insert(i);
    return strbuf;
}
```

LENGTH

Class Name	StringBuffer
Description	This method returns the number of characters in the StringBuffer.
Syntax	public int **length**()
Parameters	None.
Returns	An integer whose value is equal to the number of characters in the StringBuffer.
Exceptions	None.
See Also	setLength()

Comments	This method is commonly used in the conditional part of a control statement to prevent reading or writing past the end of the internal character buffer of the String. It might also be used to get the number of characters in the String for informational purposes, as in the example below.
Example	The following example defines a method that takes as a parameter a StringBuffer and prints its length and its contents on the console.

```
void printBuffer(StringBuffer strbuf)
{
    System.out.println(strbuf.length() + ": " + strbuf);
}
```

SETCHARAT

Class Name	StringBuffer
Description	This method replaces the character at the specified position within the StringBuffer with the character indicated in the parameter list.
Syntax	public synchronized void **setCharAt**(int *nIndex*, char *c*)
Parameters	
int *nIndex*	The position within the StringBuffer at which to change the character.
char *c*	The character with which to replace the one at the specified position.
Returns	None.
Exceptions	If the position *nIndex* specifies an invalid position, this method will throw a StringIndexOutOfBoundsException.
See Also	charAt()
Example	The following example defines a method that performs a function similar to the replace() method from the class String. It replaces all occurrences of one character with another character in the StringBuffer specified in the parameter list.

```
void replace(StringBuffer strbuf, char cOld, char cNew)
{
    for (int i; i < strbuf.length(); i++)
    {
        if (strbuf.charAt(i) == cOld) strbuf.setCharAt(i, cNew);
    }
}
```

SETLENGTH

Class Name	StringBuffer
Description	This method changes the number of characters stored in the StringBuffer.
Syntax	public synchronized void **setLength**(int *nNewLength*)

Parameters

int *nNewLength*   The new length of the StringBuffer. Additional storage will be allocated if the specified length exceeds the current capacity of the internal buffer.

Returns   None.

Exceptions   If the parameter *nNewLength* is less than zero, this method will throw a StringIndexOutOfBoundsException.

See Also   length()

Comments   If the length of the StringBuffer is reduced, characters are truncated off the end of the StringBuffer. If the length is increased, characters are added. Characters that are added have the value 0. This method is useful in situations where a string must be constrained to be a certain length, often to satisfy formatting requirements.

Example   The following example defines a method that uses the setLength() method to print the information in the String array parameter in a fixed width column.

```
void printColumn(String [] rgStr)
{
    for (int i = 0; i < rgStr.length; i++)
    {
        StringBuffer strbuf = new StringBuffer(rgStr[i]);

        strbuf.setLength(10);

        System.out.println("| " + strbuf + " |");
    }
}
```

TOSTRING

Class Name   StringBuffer

Description   This method creates a new String containing the same sequence of characters as the StringBuffer.

Syntax   public String **toString**()

Parameters   None.

Returns   A String containing the same sequence of characters as the StringBuffer.

Exceptions   None.

Comments   A programmer will often use a StringBuffer to create an arbitrary sequence of characters and then create a String from the StringBuffer in order to pass the new String to other methods for further processing.

Example   The following example defines a method that takes as its only parameter an Object array. It uses a StringBuffer internally to format the data and then returns it to the caller as a String.

```
String convert(Object [] rgObj)
{
   StringBuffer strbuf = new StringBuffer();

   for (int i = 0; i < rgObj.length; i++)
   {
      strbuf.append(i);
      strbuf.append(": ");
      strbuf.append(obj.getClass.toString());
      strbuf.append(" = ");
      strbuf.append(obj);
      strbuf.append('\n');
   }

   return strbuf.toString();
}
```

The String and StringBuffer Project: AlgeGraph

Project Overview

This section of the chapter provides additional information about the project as well as complete source code. You may wish to review the description of the application presented earlier in the chapter before reading on.

Using AlgeGraph

In order to use AlgeGraph, the user must describe the function to be visualized using a very simple language that is best introduced by example. Assume the user wishes to visualize the following function:

```
z = cos(x) * cos(y)
```

The user must first break this function into a sequence of steps, each consisting of no more than one arithmetic operation. Assume the user breaks the function above apart as follows:

```
tx = cos(x)
ty = cos(y)
z = tx * ty
```

The user must then rewrite each step using the following template as a guide:

```
let [identifier] = [operation] ( [value] [, value] .... )
```

From the three steps above, the user would obtain the following three lines:

```
let tx = cos(x)
let ty = cos(y)
let z = product(tx, ty)
```

In order to evaluate these three lines, the user must first start the AlgeGraph program by typing the command

```
java Alge
```

Next, the user must enter the following:

```
let tx = cos(x)
let ty = cos(y)
let z = product(tx, ty)
end
```

The last line must contain the *end* statement. The program will parse the input and evaluate the resulting function as the coordinates represented by x and y change. The program's output is a table of the z values. Figure 6-5 contains a screenshot of the program's output, given the function above.

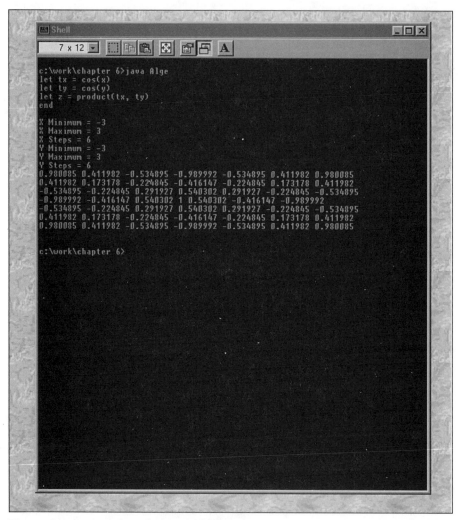

Figure 6-5 A screenshot of AlgeGraph's output

How AlgeGraph Works

The program builds a treelike data structure representing the function to be evaluated. Figure 6-6 presents the tree for the function given in the previous section. Each fork (node) in a tree represents an arithmetic operation. An operation has zero or more arguments, each represented by a line stretching downward from the node.

A tree is evaluated by evaluating the topmost node. A node calculates its value by first retrieving the value of each of its subnodes and then performing the specified arithmetic operation on these values. Each subnode calculates its value in a similar manner. The evaluation of a tree is therefore inherently recursive.

Every node has a name. Figure 6-7 presents the tree from Figure 6-6 modified so that each node is associated with its name. Names are typically arbitrary strings of characters; however, some names (in particular, "x", "y", and "z") have special meaning. The nodes named "x" and "y" store the values of the x and y coordinates during evaluation. In addition, it is from the node named "z" that the value of the tree is retrieved after evaluation.

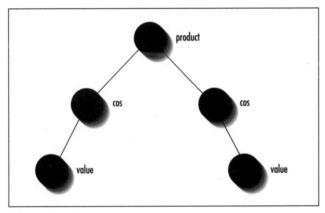

Figure 6-6 Tree representation

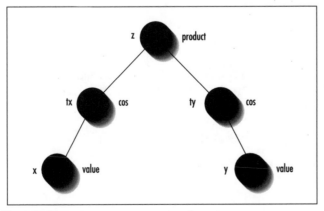

Figure 6-7 Tree representation with node names

Building the Project

1. The file Alge.java contains the code necessary to initialize the system, read and parse the input data, and display the results. It defines one class—class Alge. Class Alge is public but is not meant to be instantiated (thus the private constructor).

```java
import java.io.DataInputStream;
import java.util.Hashtable;
import java.util.Vector;

public class Alge
{
    private Alge() { }
```

2. The method named main() is this application's entry point. The variable *htSymbolTable* stores the mapping between nodes and their symbolic names. The variables *dXMin*, *dXMax*, *dYMin*, and *dYMax* define the boundaries of the plane over which the function will be evaluated. The variables *nXSteps* and *nYSteps* define the number of sections in which to divide the plane. The variables *x* and *y* store the x and y coordinate values during evaluation. The vector *vecInputLines* stores each line of program input. The variable *p* stores a reference to the Parser object.

```java
public static void main(String [] args)
{
    Hashtable htSymbolTable = new Hashtable();

    double dXMin = -3.0, dXMax = 3.0;
    double dYMin = -3.0, dYMax = 3.0;

    int nXSteps = 6, nYSteps = 6;

    op_value x = new op_value(0.0);
    op_value y = new op_value(0.0);

    htSymbolTable.put("x", x);
    htSymbolTable.put("y", y);

    Vector vecInputLines = new Vector();

    Parser p = new Parser();
```

3. The following loop reads all of the lines from standard input and adds them to the vector *vecInputLines*. The loop terminates when the string "end" is encountered.

```java
while (true)
{
    String str = null;
    DataInputStream dis = new DataInputStream(System.in);

    try
```

```
   {
      str = dis.readLine();
   }
   catch (Exception e)
   {
      System.out.println(e);
      System.exit(-1);
   }

   if (str == null || str.equals("end")) break;

   vecInputLines.addElement(str);
}

System.out.println();
```

4. The parse() method parses each line of input and builds a piece of the tree representing the function to be evaluated. The variable *nErr* holds a count of the number of lines containing errors. If the parser encountered any errors, the program exits.

```
int nErr = 0;

for (int i = 0; i < vecInputLines.size(); i++)
{
   String str = (String)vecInputLines.elementAt(i);

   if (p.parse(str, htSymbolTable) == false)
      nErr++;
}

if (nErr > 0)
{
   System.out.println("There was/were " + nErr + " error/s.");
   System.exit(-1);
}
```

5. After every line has been parsed and the tree has been built, the program looks for the node with the name "z". This node should be the topmost node of the tree and must exist. Evaluation is carried out inside of a nested loop. New values for x and y are calculated and node z is evaluated (via its apply() method). The result is printed.

```
opx z = (opx)htSymbolTable.get("z");

if (z == null)
{
   System.out.println("Definition of 'z' required.");
   System.exit(-1);
}

System.out.println("X Minimum = " + dXMin);
System.out.println("X Maximum = " + dXMax);
System.out.println("X Steps = " + nXSteps);
System.out.println("Y Minimum = " + dYMin);
```

continued on next page

continued from previous page

```java
        System.out.println("Y Maximum = " + dYMax);
        System.out.println("Y Steps = " + nYSteps);

        double dX = dXMin;
        double dY = dYMin;

        while (dX <= dXMax)
        {
            while (dY <= dYMax)
            {
                x.set(dX);    // set the new x coordinate
                y.set(dY);    // set the new y coordinate

                dY += (dYMax - dYMin) / nYSteps;

                System.out.print(z.apply() + " ");
            }

            dY = dYMin;
            dX += (dXMax - dXMin) / nXSteps;

            System.out.println();
        }
        System.out.println();
    }
}
```

6. The file FLib.java contains code for the available operators.

```java
import java.util.Hashtable;
```

7. The opx class is the class from which all operators are derived. An operator is an encapsulated function that operates on zero or more operands. Every operand is also an operator. The array variable *rgopx* contains a reference to an operator's operands. An operand is specified via the set() method. The set() method requires a reference to an operator and an index into the operand array. An operator is evaluated via its apply() method.

```java
abstract class opx
{
    protected opx [] rgopx;

    opx(int n)
    {
        rgopx = new opx [n];
    }

    int argc()
    {
        return rgopx.length;
    }

    void set(opx op, int i)
    {
```

```
      rgopx[i] = op;
   }

   abstract double apply();
}
```

8. The following class defines an operator that simply stores a value. The value is returned via the apply() method. This operator requires no operands.

```
class op_value extends opx
{
   private double rValue;

   op_value()
   {
      this(0.0);
   }

   op_value(double rValue)
   {
      super(0);

      this.rValue = rValue;
   }

   double set(double rValue)
   {
      return this.rValue = rValue;
   }

   double apply()
   {
      return this.rValue;
   }
}
```

9. The following class defines an operator that calculates the absolute value of its operand. Most of this class's functionality is implemented by its parent class (class opx).

```
class op_abs extends opx
{
   op_abs()
   {
      super(1);
   }

   double apply()
   {
      return Math.abs(rgopx[0].apply());
   }
}
```

10. The following class defines an operator that negates the value of its operand. Most of this class's functionality is implemented by its parent class (class opx).

```
class op_neg extends opx
{
    op_neg()
    {
        super(1);
    }

    double apply()
    {
        return -rgopx[0].apply();
    }
}
```

11. The following class defines an operator that calculates the trigonometric sine of the value of its operand. Most of this class's functionality is implemented by its parent class (class opx).

```
class op_sin extends opx
{
    op_sin()
    {
        super(1);
    }

    double apply()
    {
        return Math.sin(rgopx[0].apply());
    }
}
```

12. The following class defines an operator that calculates the trigonometric cosine of the value of its operand. Most of this class's functionality is implemented by its parent class (class opx).

```
class op_cos extends opx
{
    op_cos()
    {
        super(1);
    }

    double apply()
    {
        return Math.cos(rgopx[0].apply());
    }
}
```

13. The following class defines an operator that calculates the minimum of the values of its operands. Most of this class's functionality is implemented by its parent class (class opx).

```
class op_min extends opx
{
    op_min()
    {
```

```
      super(2);
   }

   double apply()
   {
      return Math.min(rgopx[0].apply(), rgopx[1].apply());
   }
}
```

14. The following class defines an operator that calculates the product of the values of its operands. Most of this class's functionality is implemented by its parent class (class opx).

```
class op_product extends opx
{
   op_product()
   {
      super(2);
   }

   double apply()
   {
      return rgopx[0].apply() * rgopx[1].apply();
   }
}
```

15. The following class associates each of the classes defined above with a unique name. The code below uses the forName() method to obtain the Class object corresponding to the named class. The Class object is then associated with a name and stored in a hash table.

```
final public class FLib
{
   static Hashtable ht = new Hashtable();

   static
   {
      try
      {
         ht.put("abs", Class.forName("op_abs"));
         ht.put("neg", Class.forName("op_neg"));
         ht.put("min", Class.forName("op_min"));
         ht.put("sin", Class.forName("op_sin"));
         ht.put("cos", Class.forName("op_cos"));
         ht.put("product", Class.forName("op_product"));
      }
      catch (ClassNotFoundException e)
      {
         e.printStackTrace();
         System.exit(-1);
      }
   }

   private FLib() { }
```

16. Once a class has been associated with a name, the following method can instantiate that class given only its name. An instance of the named class is created via a call to the newInstance() method of the associated Class object.

```
static opx generate(String str)
{
    opx o = null;

    try
    {
        Class cls = (Class)ht.get(str);
        if (cls != null) o = (opx)cls.newInstance();
    }
    catch (Exception e)
    {
        e.printStackTrace();
        System.exit(-1);
    }

    return o;
}
```

17. The file Scanner.java contains the code for the scanner. The scanner breaks a line of text into smaller pieces, each of which represents a meaningful unit of information. The scanner operates by applying a set of match criteria (called actions) to the string being scanned. These actions identify meaningful pieces of the string, which are then returned. All actions are derived from the class ScannerAction. Each subclass must define a method named apply() that performs the identification action. The line to be scanned is passed down in the variable *str*. The piece of the input string the action identifies is returned in the variable *strbuf*.

```
abstract class ScannerAction
{
    abstract void apply(String str, StringBuffer strbuf);
}
```

18. The following class identifies a string composed of successive occurrences of the character *c*. The matching portion of the input line will be ignored by the scanner.

```
class IgnoreAction extends ScannerAction
{
    private char c;

    IgnoreAction(char c) { this.c = c; }

    void apply(String str, StringBuffer strbuf)
    {
        int i = 0;
        while (i < str.length() && str.charAt(i) == c)
        {
            strbuf.append(c);
            i++;
```

```
      }
   }
}
```

19. The following class identifies a string composed of characters from the string *str*. The matching portion of the input line is called an identifier (which is typically a variable or operator name).

```
class IdentifierAction extends ScannerAction
{
   private String str;

   IdentifierAction(String str) { this.str = str; }

   void apply(String str, StringBuffer strbuf)
   {
      int i = 0;
      while (i < str.length() && this.str.indexOf(str.charAt(i)) > -1)
      {
         strbuf.append(str.charAt(i));
         i++;
      }
   }
}
```

20. The following class identifies a floating-point number.

```
class FloatAction extends ScannerAction
{
   void apply(String str, StringBuffer strbuf)
   {
      boolean f = false;

      StringBuffer strbufTemp = new StringBuffer();

      int i = 0;

      if (str.charAt(i) == '-' || str.charAt(i) == '+')
      {
         strbufTemp.append(str.charAt(i++));
      }
      while (i < str.length() &&
             "0123456789".indexOf(str.charAt(i)) > -1)
      {
         f = true;
         strbufTemp.append(str.charAt(i));
         i++;
      }
      if (i < str.length () && str.charAt(i) == '.')
      {
         strbufTemp.append(str.charAt(i++));
      }
      while (i < str.length() &&
             "0123456789".indexOf(str.charAt(i)) > -1)
      {
         strbufTemp.append(str.charAt(i));
```

continued on next page

continued from previous page

```
            i++;
      }

      if (f) strbuf.append(strbufTemp);
   }
}
```

21. The following class identifies the keyword specified by the variable *str*. A keyword is a specific sequence of characters (such as the word "let").

```
class KeywordAction extends ScannerAction
{
   private String str;

   KeywordAction(String str) { this.str = str; }

   void apply(String str, StringBuffer strbuf)
   {
      if (str.startsWith(this.str))
      {
         strbuf.append(this.str);
      }
   }
}
```

22. Each string identified by one of the actions described above is represented by an instance of the Token class. An instance of the Token class consists of a reference to the scanner action that identified the piece of text (*act*), the matching text (*str*), and the position of the piece of text in the overall text (*n*).

```
class Token
{
   ScannerAction act;
   String str;
   int n;
}
```

23. A new Scanner object is created from the string containing the text to be scanned (*str*) and an array of scanner actions to be applied to the string (*rgact*). The variable *tok* contains a reference to a Token object. The variable *n* contains the current position in the string being scanned.

```
class Scanner
{
   private String str;
   private ScannerAction [] rgact;
   private Token tok;
   private int n;

   /**
    * Create a new Scanner.
    */
   Scanner(String str, ScannerAction [] rgact)
   {
```

```
        this.str = str;
        this.rgact = rgact;
        this.tok = null;
        this.n = 0;
}
```

24. An instance of the Scanner class breaks a string into a series of instances of the
Token class. It does this by applying each scanner action to the currently
unscanned portion of the input string. Of the scanner actions that match, the one
that matches the longest piece of the input string is selected and a new Token
object is created. If no actions match, the current character is returned as a Token
object.

```
Token nextToken()
{
    int n = this.n;
    ScannerAction act = null;
    StringBuffer strbuf = new StringBuffer();

    if (tok != null)
    {
        Token tok = this.tok;
        this.tok = null;
        return tok;
    }

    while (this.n < str.length())
    {
        n = this.n;

        for (int i = 0; i < rgact.length; i++)
        {
            StringBuffer strbufTemp = new StringBuffer();

            rgact[i].apply(str.substring(n), strbufTemp);

            if (strbufTemp.length() > strbuf.length())
            {
                strbuf = strbufTemp;
                act = rgact[i];
            }
        }

        if (act == null) strbuf.append(str.charAt(n));

        this.n += strbuf.length();

        if (! (act instanceof IgnoreAction))
            break;

        strbuf = new StringBuffer();
        act = null;
    }

    Token tok = new Token();
```

continued on next page

continued from previous page

```
        tok.act = act;
        tok.str = strbuf.toString();
        tok.n = n;

        return tok;
    }
```

25. The following method pushes a Token object back into the scanner. It will be returned on the next call to the nextToken() method.

```
void pushToken(Token tok)
{
    this.tok = tok;
}
}
```

26. The StringParseException is thrown whenever the parser encounters a grammatical construction it does not understand.

```
class StringParseException extends Exception
{
    StringParseException() { super(); }
    StringParseException(String str) { super(str); }
}
```

27. The file Parser.java contains the code for the parser. The parser takes the sequence of Token objects generated by the scanner and verifies that they occur as specified by the grammar the parser was designed to parse. Briefly, the grammar for the AlgeGraph parser states the following:

- A line must begin with the keyword *let*.

- It must be followed by an identifier (the name to assign to the following operation).

- The identifier must be followed by the symbol "=".

- This symbol must be followed by another identifier (the name of the operator to apply) and the symbol "(".

- The parameter list that follows must contain zero or more values separated by the symbol ",".

- The final symbol must be ")".

The variable *scan* contains a reference to the Scanner object this Parser object is using. The variable *sym* contains a reference to the Hashtable object that maps operators to their textual names. The variable *str* contains the String to parse. The variable *tok* contains a reference to the last Token object returned from the scanner. The variable *o* contains a reference to the operator currently being constructed.

```
class Parser
{
    private Scanner scan;
    private Hashtable sym;
    private String str;
    private Token tok;
    private opx o;
```

28. The following code defines the scanner actions this Parser object uses when parsing a line.

```
static private ScannerAction LET;
static private ScannerAction IDENTIFIER;
static private ScannerAction IGNORE_SP;
static private ScannerAction FLOAT;

static
{
    LET = new KeywordAction("let");
    IDENTIFIER = new IdentifierAction("abcdefghijklmnopqrstuvwxyz");
    IGNORE_SP = new IgnoreAction(' ');
    FLOAT = new FloatAction();
}

static private ScannerAction [] rgact =
    { LET, IDENTIFIER, FLOAT, IGNORE_SP };
```

29. This is the entry point for the parser. It initializes the parser and begins the parse. It handles error conditions and issues diagnostic messages.

```
boolean parse(String str, Hashtable sym)
{
    this.str = str;
    this.sym = sym;
    this.scan = new Scanner(str, rgact);

    try
    {
        parse();
    }
    catch (StringParseException e)
    {
        issueDiagnostic(e.getMessage());
        return false;
    }
    catch (ArrayIndexOutOfBoundsException e)
    {
        issueDiagnostic("too many arguments");
        return false;
    }

    return true;
}
```

30. This method implements the grammar production:

```
LINE := 'let' IDENT '=' EXPR
```

This says that a line is made up of the keyword *let* followed by an identifier, the character "=", and an expression.

```java
void parse() throws StringParseException
{
    tok = scan.nextToken();
    expect(LET, "unknown keyword");

    tok = scan.nextToken();
    expect(IDENTIFIER, "missing required identifier");

    if (sym.get(tok.str) != null)
        throw new StringParseException("identifier redefinition");

    String str = tok.str;

    tok = scan.nextToken();
    expect("=", "missing assignment operator");

    parse_expression();

    sym.put(str, o);

    tok = scan.nextToken();
    expect("", "error at end of line");
}
```

31. This method implements the grammar production:

```
VALUE := IDENT | FLOAT
```

This says that a value is either an identifier or a floating-point number.

```java
void parse_value() throws StringParseException
{
    opx o = null;

    tok = scan.nextToken();

    if (tok.act == IDENTIFIER)
    {
        o = (opx)sym.get(tok.str);

        if (o == null)
            throw new StringParseException("unknown identifier");
    }
    else if (tok.act == FLOAT)
    {
        o = new op_value(Double.valueOf(tok.str).doubleValue());
    }
    else
    {
        throw new StringParseException("identifier or float required");
```

```
        }

        this.o = o;
    }
```

32. This method implements the grammar production:

```
EXPR := IDENT PARAMS
```

This says that an expression is an identifier followed by a parameter list.

```
void parse_expression() throws StringParseException
{
    opx o = null;

    tok = scan.nextToken();
    expect(IDENTIFIER, "missing function name");

    o = (opx)FLib.generate(tok.str);

    if (o == null) throw new StringParseException("unknown function");

    parse_parameters(o);

    this.o = o;
}
```

33. This method implements the grammar production:

```
PARAMS := '(' VALUE ( ',' VALUE )* ')'
```

This says that a parameter list consists of the character "(", followed by one or more values separated by the character ",", followed by the character ")".

```
void parse_parameters(opx o) throws StringParseException
{
    tok = scan.nextToken();
    expect("(", "syntax error");

    int i = 0;
    tok = scan.nextToken();
    while (!tok.str.equals(")"))
    {
        if (i == 0) scan.pushToken(tok);

        if (i > 0) expect(",", "syntax error");

        parse_value();

        o.set(this.o, i++);

        tok = scan.nextToken();
    }

    if (i < o.argc()) throw new StringParseException("too few arguments");
}
```

34. These methods examine the contents of the last Token object and verify that it contains the expected information at this point in the parse.

```
void expect(ScannerAction act, String strErrorMsg) throws
    StringParseException
{
    if (act == tok.act) return;
    throw new StringParseException(strErrorMsg);
}

void expect(String str, String strErrorMsg) throws
    StringParseException
{
    if (str.equals(tok.str)) return;
    throw new StringParseException(strErrorMsg);
}
```

35. This method issues an error message describing the error that occurred and the position in the line at which it occurred.

```
void issueDiagnostic(String str)
{
    System.out.println("Error: " + str);
    System.out.println("Occured In Line: " + this.str);
    System.out.print("                ");
    for (int i = 0; i < tok.n; i++) System.out.print(" ");
    System.out.println("^");
}
}
```

PART III
EXECUTION
CLASSES

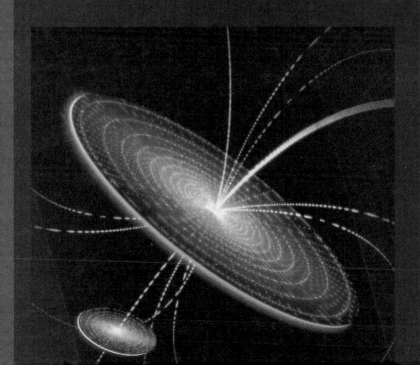

7

SYSTEM CLASSES

7

SYSTEM CLASSES

Most applications, even those that are very simple, require access to a variety of system-level resources. Perhaps the clearest example of the use of such resources is the writing of some text to standard output. Such an activity, although simple, requires system-level resources, because the action needs access to a low-level device, namely the output console. A converse operation, the reading of characters from the keyboard, also requires access to system resources. The Java System class is constructed to provide *platform independent* access to these basic resource operations, as well as other useful system-level functionality.

If access to *platform specific* features is desired, a programmer can directly interface with the runtime environment through the Runtime class. This class provides a couple of important features not available through the System class, including the ability to spawn a new subprocess. However, it does so at the price of compromising the portability of the program, thus taking away one of Java's most important features. The capabilities of the System and Runtime classes, their relationship to each other, and when to use one or the other is the topic of this chapter.

System Class

The System class provides a platform independent way to interact with the resources of the runtime environment. It provides easy access to the most widely used system resources—the standard input and output streams. However, the System class also provides access to other important resources. System properties are used to keep track of environmental definitions such as the user name or the current version of Java that is running. The dynamic loading of libraries is used for bringing in "native methods"—programs that are not written in Java. The garbage collector is Java's mechanism for removing objects from memory that are no longer needed, hence freeing up more memory for other objects. Finally, the system Security Manager provides and enforces access rules that control how system resources can be used. The System class provides a way to interface with all of these resources, thus giving the programmer yet another way to increase the power of his or her application.

All the variables and methods of the System class are static. Since the class does need to be instantiated, System methods and variables can be accessed in one simple step.

Standard Input and Output Streams

The System class provides access to the three standard streams that are used to interact with the user: standard input, output, and error. These are implemented as variables in the System class with the names *in*, *out*, and *err*, respectively. The *System.out* and *System.err* variables are treated as instances of the PrintStream class, which is constructed especially for printing string messages. Conversely, the *System.in* variable is instantiated as an InputStream object. The InputStream class is designed for reading a stream of bytes. However, as will be shown briefly, it can also be used to construct a custom stream object that is well suited for reading in lines of String input.

The standard output and error streams are typically written to the same device, which is usually a terminal window or system console. Since they are both instances of the same class, they both function in the same manner. Thus, the following two calls write out the same messages.

```
// Print out a fictitious numeric error code
// to standard output
System.out.println("The error code is " + myErr);

// Print out a fictitious numeric error code
// to standard error
System.err.println("The error code is " + myErr);
```

On many platforms, the default behavior would be to write both strings to the same device. In this situation it would not be possible if the stream was standard output or error. However, redirection and other techniques can be used to differentiate the streams.

The println() method is used to write out a String followed by a carriage return. However, the previous two calls could give functionally similar behavior by calling the print() method in the following fashion:

```
System.err.print("The error code is " + myErr+ "\n");
```

The "\n" at the end of the string is a special code used to designate that a newline character should be added. The println() method automatically adds this code at the end of each message, whereas it needs to be added manually to the print() method for the same results. Java uses various two-character codes to indicate special characters such as tabs ("\t") and newlines; these codes are similar to those used in C.

The other important method of PrintStream is write(), which is used for non-ASCII data such as binary streams. See Chapter 11, Basic I/O, for a description of PrintStream and for more details of how the standard error and output variables can work.

The primary method of the InputStream class is read(). Unlike PrintStream, this does not naturally work with String characters, but works on byte streams. The following code reads in a single byte from standard input.

```
byte b = System.in.read();
```

The read() method returns a -1 when there are no more characters to be read.

A simpler way to manage input is through the use of the DataInputStream. This class provides a general set of methods for reading streams of certain data types, one of which is type String. An instance of the DataInputStream class can be constructed with an input stream object as a parameter. This means that the *System.in* variable can be used to construct a DataInputStream as follows:

```
// Build from standard input...
    DataInputStream in = new DataInputStream(System.in);
```

The readLine() method can then be used to read in a String of input that has been followed by a newline or other special characters:

```
// Read from the DataInputStream
String s = in.readLine();
```

Most methods prefixed by read() need to catch IOException objects that may be thrown. See Chapters 11-13 for more information on how to use the input stream classes that are relevant to the *System.in* variable.

System Properties

In most traditional programming environments, there is some kind of mechanism for setting and retrieving general system and program information. In environments such as UNIX and MS-DOS, *environment variables* are used to carry such data. Environment variables may contain such information as the user name, paths to find executables, or a home directory.

Java has a similar need to manage environment information. Since it is abstracted away from a specific underlying operating platform, however, the information to be managed is different. Furthermore, since Java is an object-oriented environment, the mechanism for conveying this information needs to be packaged in an object-oriented manner. Java provides such a mechanism through its Properties class, which is a hash table of String keys and String values. The System Properties object extends this class by containing general system data.

The System Properties object has some basic information that will appear on all platforms. Table 7-1 details some of the properties that should be available anywhere Java is running. Various methods can be used to get this information. The getProperties() method returns a reference to the System Properties object. Since the Properties table is a subclass of the Hashtable class (found in the java.util package), the table can be manipulated through the get() and put() operations. The getProperty() method can be used to retrieve an individual element in the table that matches a String key. The setProperties() method replaces the System Properties table with a new Properties object. The following code shows how to create a temporary copy of the System Properties table, make changes to the copy, and then write back the changes by replacing the table.

```
// Create a copy of the System's property list...
    Properties p = new Properties(System.getProperties());
    p.list(System.out);
    // Set the user's name...
    // This method is actually part of
    // the hashtable class...
    p.put("user.name","Casey Hopson");
    // Now set this properties list to the
    // System properties...
    System.setProperties(p);
```

Table 7-1 Values found in the Java System Properties object

Property	Description
file.separator	File separator in path (such as \ in Windows)
java.class.path	Path to classes
java.class.version	Version number of API
java.home	Installation directory
java.vendor	String describing Java vendor (probably Sun Microsystems)
java.vendor.url	URL of Java vendor
java.version	Java version number
line.separator	Line separator (such as \n)
os.arch	Operating system architecture
os.name	Operating system
os.version	Operating system version
path.separator	Path separator (such as : in UNIX or ; in Windows)
user.dir	Current working directory
user.home	User home directory
user.name	User name

Garbage Collection

Like most modern object-oriented languages, Java frees the programmer from having to run new methods and delete others to create and destroy objects, respectively. Instead, it uses a technique called garbage collection to remove any objects that are not being referenced by other objects. With garbage collection, the programmer does not have to explicitly delete any object; instead, the collector removes the unreferenced objects and hence frees up memory. The garbage collector is run automatically by Java as a separate thread. It is called explicitly when there is not enough memory to fulfill a request to create a new object. However, a programmer may want to run the garbage collector explicitly after a large set of objects (like a linked list) is no longer being used. It may also be good to run the collector during idle periods. The System.gc() method is used to explicitly run the garbage collector.

Another operation related to garbage collection is finalization. The finalize() method is used as a way of cleaning up an object before it is destroyed; this cleanup may include such things as removing references to other objects. The finalize() method can be invoked manually or may be called by the garbage collector when the object is about to be destroyed. The garbage collector will only call an object's finalize() method if all references to it have been removed, making the object ready to be deleted. The runFinalization() method calls the finalize() method of any objects pending finalization; that is, objects to which there are no more references. However, it may not actually always call an object's finalize() method. The garbage collector is actually a more reliable way to make sure that finalize() is invoked.

Other Methods

The System class provides a series of other important methods. They are related to subjects that are too extensive to address in this section of the book, but they are introduced for the sake of completeness. The getSecurityManager() and setSecurityManager() methods are used to get and set information related to the Security Manager object. This object regulates all kinds of operations a program can perform, ranging from I/O to network access to System properties and object modification. It can prohibit an operation such as writing a file to the client's hard disk. Most browsers supporting Java come equipped with a Security Manager. These can be queried with the getSecurityManager() method. However, a security violation will probably occur if there is an attempt to replace the Security Manager with the setSecurityManager() method. This method is best used for stand-alone programs and browser internal operations.

The Load() and LoadLibrary() methods are used for loading libraries that contain native methods. See Appendix C, Writing Native Methods in C/C++, for a full description of how to use native methods.

The Runtime

The Runtime class gives the programmer direct access to the runtime environment in which the Java virtual machine is executing. Supported operations on the runtime include the ability to launch a subprocess, getting information about and managing system memory, loading dynamic libraries, and exiting the runtime environment. Many of the methods needed to perform these operations are provided by the System class, which is usually the preferred way to interact with the runtime. The reasons for this preference are important.

The System class is structured to provide a platform independent interface to the runtime environment. On the other hand, the Runtime class provides a direct interface to platform specific features. This can be seen in the exec() method, which is used to launch a subprocess. The subprocess can be another Java program or another secure program. A secure non-Java program could be written in such a way that takes advantage of platform specific features. In this case, however, portability is compromised. Another portability problem occurs in the exec() methods that take a String array of environment variables as an input parameter. These variables are formatted in a platform specific manner. Hence, this code may not be portable either. Finally, the exec() method is subject to security constraints. Many browsers will not allow the exec() operation because it compromises security—it is a way of running non-Java code on a client machine. Such a program could take malicious advantage of system resources, because it is not subject to the built-in security of the Java language.

While the exec() method has platform specific characteristics, other Runtime methods do not. Many methods can be mapped directly upward to the System class. For such methods as those used for garbage collection or loading dynamic libraries, the System class does little more than call the corresponding method in the Runtime. The use of these methods via the Runtime class does not compromise portability, since they are written in a platform independent manner. However, it is good programming practice to use the System class whenever possible.

Runtime and the Process Class

The Runtime exec() methods are noteworthy because they offer unique access to instances of the Process class. Process objects, which are what is returned by exec() methods, can be used to manage the standard input and output of the newly created subprocess. The Process class's getInputStream(), getOutputStream(), and getErrorStream() methods can be used to redirect the subprocess standard streams in a way dictated by the parent process. The Process object can also be used to destroy the process, or wait for it to complete.

About the Project

The chapter project provides an illustration of an interrelated Java program and subprocess. The parent program launches another Java program as a subprocess via the Runtime exec() method. The parent reads the standard output from the child via the instance of the Process class produced by the call to the exec() method. This output is then redirected to standard output using the System class's *out* variable.

Summaries of System Classes and Methods

Table 7-2 summarizes the system classes discussed in this chapter. Table 7-3 provides an overview of the methods of these classes.

Table 7-2 The System classes

Class	Description
System	Provides a portable interface to system-level functionality
Runtime	Represents a platform dependent interface to the underlying runtime environment
Process	Used to manage elements of a subprocess

Table7-3 System classes methods, by category

Class	Category	Methods/Variables
System	Stream variables	err, in, out
	Memory management	gc, runFinalization
	Task management	exit, load, loadLibrary
	Security Manager	getSecurityManager, setSecurityManager
	System properties	getProperties, getProperty, setProperties
	Utilities	arraycopy, currentTimeMillis
Runtime	Task management	exec, exit, load, loadLibrary(), getRuntime
	Memory management	gc, runFinalization, freeMemory, totalMemory
	Stream management	getLocalizedInputStream, getLocalizedOutputStream
	System traces	traceInstructions, traceMethodCalls
Process	Process management	destroy, exitValue, waitFor
	Stream management	getErrorStream, getInputStream, getOutputStream

The java.lang.System Class

The System class provides a platform independent way to interact with the runtime environment. It provides access to critical system resources such as the standard input and output streams, which are defined as public variables. The System.out.println() method call is frequently used to write a String out to standard output. Since the System class cannot be instantiated, these streams are readily available to the programmer without a need to create a special object.

The System class also provides a list of Properties for the current program session. The System Properties correspond to traditional environment variables. However, System abstracts away from the platform specific workings of environment variables by providing a portable class to manipulate these variables. The getProperty(), getProperties(), and setProperties() methods can be used to read and write the System properties.

The System class also provides methods for other useful operations such as running the garbage collector, getting the current time, and copying blocks of an array. It also allows the loading of dynamic libraries and access to the Security Manager. However, the performance of these latter operations are subject to the security restraints of the runtime environment, such as those found in the native browser. Tables 7-4 and 7-5 summarize the methods and variables provided by this class, respectively.

Table 7-4 Summary of System methods

Method	Description
arraycopy	Copies elements of a source to a destination array
currentTimeMillis	Returns the current time in milliseconds
exit	Causes an exit from the Java virtual machine
gc	Causes the garbage collector to run
getenv	Obsolete
getProperties	Gets the system properties object
getProperty	Gets the String value of the specified system property
getSecurityManager	Returns a reference to the system SecurityManager
load	Loads a dynamic library
loadLibrary	Loads a dynamic library
runFinalization	Runs finalization methods on objects needing it
setProperties	Sets the System properties table
setSecurityManger	Sets the SecurityManager of the system

Table 7-5 Summary of System variables

Variable	Description
err	Standard Error
in	Standard Input
out	Standard Output

SYSTEM

Description	The System class is used to interface with system-level features. The class's support for standard input and output streams is one of its most useful features. It also provides methods for accessing the Security Manager, loading dynamic libraries, and managing system properties. Since all of the methods and variables of the System class are static, the class need not be instantiated.
Syntax	public final class **System** extends Object
Package	java.lang
Import	java.lang.System
Constructors	No public constructors.
Parameters	None.

See Also   Object, PrintStream, InputStream, SecurityManager

Example   This example prints something to standard output.

```
System.out.println("This is a message.");
```

Variables

ERR

Class Name	System
Description	Represents the standard error stream. Standard error is typically where programs write error messages. Its display medium is often the same as standard output, such as a system console. However, it can be differentiated from standard output by redirecting standard error to a separate file. The file can then be surveyed for any useful information. Mostly useful for diagnosing problems, standard error is used to provide a separate stream of data for printable output that indicates abnormal behavior. Use the *System.err* variable to print a String to standard error.
Syntax	public static PrintStream **err**
See Also	in, out, PrintStream
Example	This example tries an operation and prints a message to standard error if a problem occurs.

```
try {  // Call custom method
 myMethod(data1,data2);
}
catch (Exception e) {
 // Print the message to standard error
 System.err.println("My Method failed. Message = " + e.getMessage());
}
```

IN

Class Name	System
Description	Represents the standard input stream. The standard input stream reads in a stream of characters. This input could be the terminal/keyboard, or a file if redirection is used. This stream functions similarly to the C language getchar() function, which—in most environments—waits for a carriage return before making the data available to the program. Use the *System.in* variable to read data from standard input.
Syntax	public static InputStream **in**
See Also	err, out, InputStream

Example   This example reads in a character from standard input and checks to see if it is a digit or not. It prints a good character to standard output, a bad one to standard error. The InputStream read() method requires that the IOException be caught.

```
try {
            char ch = (char) System.in.read();
            if (Character.isDigit(ch))
                    System.out.println("Character " +
ch + " is a digit");
            else
                    System.err.println("Character " +
ch + " is not a digit");
}
      catch (IOException e) {
            System.err.println("Error reading from
standard input");
      }
```

OUT

Class Name   System

Description   Represents the standard output stream. Standard output is where character output from a program is usually written. This is typically the terminal, although standard output could be redirected to a file. The *System.out* variable can be used to write character messages to standard output.

Syntax   public static PrintStream **out**

See Also   in, err, PrintStream

Example   This example uses the System currentTimeMillis() method to print out the current GMT time in milliseconds.

```
System.out.println("GMT current time in milliseconds is " +
            System.currentTimeMillis());
```

Methods

ARRAYCOPY

Class Name   System

Description   This method copies elements from the source array to a destination array. The copy begins at the specified positions of the source and destination arrays and continues until the number of elements specified by the length parameter is reached. The method assumes that the memory of the destination array has already been allocated. If the destination array is not sized large enough to receive the number of elements specified by *length*, an exception is thrown.

Syntax	public static void arraycopy(Object *src*, int *src_pos*, Object *dest*, int *dest_pos*, int *length*)
Parameters	
Object *src*	The source array to start copying.
int *src_pos*	Where to start copying from the source array.
Object *dest*	The destination array of the copy.
int *dest_pos*	Where to start copying to the destination array.
int *length*	The number of elements to copy.
Returns	None.
Exceptions	This method throws an ArrayIndexOutOfBoundsException if during the copy an illegal array index is used. An ArrayStoreException is thrown if the destination array is receiving an object from the source array that is not of the correct type. See the example of the ArrayStoreException in Chapter 9, Exceptions, to see a case where the ArrayStoreException is thrown when arraycopy() is used.
See Also	ArrayStoreException
Example	This example copies the last five elements of an integer array to the beginning of another integer array. Since arrays are first class Objects, integer arrays can be used as the Object parameters in this method.

```
// Create the source array
    int a[] = new int[15];
    // Copy numbers into the array...
    for (int i = 0; i < a.length; ++i)
       a[i] = i;
    // Create the destination array...
    int b[] = new int[10];
    // Copy the last 5 elements of the source array
    // to the first five slots of the destination array
    System.arraycopy(a,10,b,0,5);
    // Print out the first five elements of b to make
    // sure all looks good...
    for (int i = 0; i < 5; ++i)
       System.out.println(b[i]);
```

CURRENTTIMEMILLIS

Class Name	System
Description	The currentTimeMillis() method can be used to get the current time in milliseconds. This time is based on Greenwich Mean Time, with a reference date of 00:00:00 UTC, January 1, 1970. Since this time variable is based on a signed 64-bit integer, programmers do not need to worry about integer overflow until the year 292280995.
Syntax	public static long currentTimeMillis()
Parameters	None.

Returns	None.
Exceptions	None.
See Also	java.util.Date
Example	This example prints the current time in milliseconds to standard output.

```
System.out.println("GMT current time in milliseconds is " +
            System.currentTimeMillis());
```

EXIT

Class Name	System
Description	This method is used to cause a program to exit from the Java virtual machine with the exit code specified in the status parameter. Since this method does not return, it is important to perform any cleanup operations before exit() is called.
Syntax	public static void exit(int *status*)
Parameters	
int *status*	The exit code.
Returns	None.
Exceptions	When this method is used in a browser such as Netscape Navigator, a SecurityException is thrown. This is because other applets also need the virtual machine to run.
See Also	Runtime.exit()
Example	This code fragment leaves the virtual machine with a status code of 0.

```
System.exit(0);
```

GC

Class Name	System
Description	This method causes the garbage collector to run so that available memory may be increased. Like most modern object-oriented languages, Java frees the programmer from having to run new methods and delete others to create and destroy objects, respectively. Instead, it uses a technique called garbage collection to remove any objects that are not being referenced by other objects. With garbage collection, the programmer does not have to explicitly delete any object; instead, the collector removes the unreferenced objects and hence frees up memory. The garbage collector is run automatically by Java as a separate thread. It is called explicitly when there is not enough memory to fulfill a request to create a new object. However, a programmer may want to run the garbage collector explicitly after a large set of objects (like a linked list) is no longer being used. It may also be

good to run the collector during idle periods. The System.gc() method is used to explicitly run the garbage collector.

Syntax	public static void gc()
Parameters	None.
Returns	None.
Exceptions	None.
See Also	Runtime.gc()
Example	The following example shows a situation where you might want to run the garbage collector.

```
//    Create a large set of object lists... .
//    Do work on the lists
//    Remove references to the objects
//    Get the program ready for more work by
// calling the garbage collector...
System.gc();
```

GETENV

Class Name	System
Description	Obsolete. This method was the traditional way of getting a value associated with an environment variable. However, it has been superseded in Java by the use of the Properties class. See the getProperty(), getProperties(), and setProperties() methods for how to use the new type of environment variables.
Syntax	public static String getenv(String *env*)
Parameters	
String *env*	The key of the environment variable to find.
Returns	The String representing the value corresponding to the key.
Exceptions	None.
See Also	java.util.Properties, getProperty(), getProperties(), setProperties()

GETPROPERTIES

Class Name	System
Description	This method retrieves the System Properties object. The System Properties object is an object that represents the environment in which a Java program is running. The Properties class is a hash table of String keys and String values and replaces the traditional getenv() and setenv() techniques that C programmers use to get the program's environment. The getProperties() method returns a reference to the System Properties object.

The object can then be queried for property values. The getProperty() and setProperties() methods of the System class can be used to retrieve and set the values of this Properties object, as can direct calls to the object. There is a guaranteed set of properties that are part of the System Properties object. See Table 7-1 for a complete listing of these properties.

Syntax	public static Properties getProperties()
Parameters	None.
Returns	None.
Exceptions	None.
See Also	java.util.Properties, getProperty(), setProperties()
Example	This example gets the System Properties object and sends a listing of its keys and values to standard output.

```
// Get the system's properties objects
Properties p = System.getProperties();
// Print to standard output
//   the entire list of properties
// and their corresponding values...
p.list(System.out);
```

GETPROPERTY

Class Name	System
Description	This method gets the String value of the specified System property corresponding to the key value. The System Properties object is an object that represents the environment in which a Java program is running. The Properties object is a hash table of String keys and String values and replaces the traditional getenv() and setenv() techniques that C programmers use to get the program's environment. The getProperty() method returns the String value of a property associated with the specified key. If the key is not found, a null String is returned. There is a guaranteed set of properties that are part of the System Properties object. See the overview of this section for a complete listing of these properties.
Syntax	public static String getProperty(String *key*)
	public static String getProperty(String *key*, String *def*)
Parameters	
String *key*	The key value of the property to find.
String *def*	The value to use if the key is not found.
Returns	The String value associated with the property. A null String is returned if the property key is not found.
Exceptions	None.

See Also   java.util.Properties,
getProperties(), setProperties()

Example   This example prints out some information about the Java version and vendor. It also tries to get information about a nonexistent property. A null String is returned in this case.

```
// Print out information
// about the Java version and vendor
System.out.println("Java Version Number: " +
          System.getProperty("java.version"));
System.out.println("Java Vendor: " +
          System.getProperty("java.vendor"));
System.out.println("Java Vendor URL: " +
          System.getProperty("java.vendor.url"));
// Print out a non-existent System method
// This call will return a Null string.
System.out.println("Property not found: " +
          System.getProperty("My property"));
// Checks to see if Home Page is part of
// System properties.  If not then return a
// default value
System.out.println("Home Page: " +
      System.getProperty("Home Page",
          "http://www.waite.com/waite/"));
```

GETSECURITYMANAGER

Class Name   System

Description   This method returns a reference to the system Security Manager. One of the key features of Java is the attention the environment pays to security issues. Security is generally related to rules of access. There are tight regulations regarding I/O operations, network access, system properties, and Object modification. The getSecurityManager() method returns a reference to the system Security Manager. This object can then be queried for various access rights.

Syntax   public static SecurityManager getSecurityManager()

Parameters   None.

Returns   A reference to the system Security Manager.

Exceptions   None.

See Also   SecurityManager, SecurityException

Example   This example gets a reference to the system Security Manager and then queries it to see if it has access to the System class's properties table.

```
// Get the System security manager
    SecurityManager m = System.getSecurityManager();
    // See if we have access to the System properties...
    try {
      m.checkPropertiesAccess();
```

continued on next page

continued from previous page
```
        System.out.println("ACCESS to System
properties ALLOWED!");
     }
     // Security exception error = no access
     catch (SecurityException e) {
         System.out.println("NO ACCESS to System properties!");
     }
     // Catch any other execeptions
     catch (Exception e) {
         System.out.println("Other Exception in
security test: " +
                 e.getMessage());
     }
```

LOAD

Class Name	System
Description	This method loads a dynamic library using a complete path name. Dynamic libraries contain native methods, which are routines written in a language other than Java. The load() method looks for a dynamic library using a full path. Appendix C, Writing Native Methods in C/C++, contains a full description of native methods.
Syntax	public static void load(String *filename*)
Parameters	
String *filename*	The library to load with full path.
Returns	None.
Exceptions	This method throws an UnsatisfiedLinkError if the library is not found.
See Also	loadLibrary()
Example	This code fragment loads a dynamic library using a full path.

```
System.load("/java/lib/MyClass.so");
```

LOADLIBRARY

Class Name	System
Description	This method loads a dynamic library from the current or library directory. Dynamic libraries contain native methods, which are routines written in a language other than Java. The loadLibrary() method looks in a library or current directory to load the file specified. Appendix C contains a full description of native methods.
Syntax	public static void loadLibrary(String *filename*)
Parameters	
String *filename*	The library to load with full path.

Returns	None.
Exceptions	This method throws an UnsatisfiedLinkError if the library is not found.
See Also	load()
Example	This code fragment loads a dynamic library from the current or library directories.

```
System.load("MyClass.so");
```

RUNFINALIZATION

Class Name	System
Description	This method runs the finalization methods of any objects that are no longer referenced by any other objects. The runFinalization() method is meant to be used as a way of cleaning up an object before it is destroyed. A typical use of finalize() is to remove references to other objects. The finalize() method can be invoked manually or is often, but not reliably, called by the garbage collector. The garbage collector will only call an object's finalize() method if all references to it have been removed, making it ready to be deleted. The runFinalization() method calls the finalize() method of any objects pending finalization; that is, objects to which there are no more references. However, it may not actually always call an object's finalize() method; the garbage collector is actually a more reliable technique.
Syntax	public static void runFinalization()
Parameters	None.
Returns	None.
Exceptions	None.
See Also	gc()
Example	This example starts with a simple class whose only method is finalize().

```
// Class used to demonstrate finalization...
class MyClass  {
   public void finalize() {
      System.out.println("Finalize method called!");
   }
};
```

The class is next instantiated.

```
// Create finalization class...
MyClass m;
m = new MyClass();
```

Later, the reference to the class is removed.

```
m = null;
```

Finally, the System class's finalization method is invoked. This *may* cause the String in the MyClass finalize() method to be displayed to standard output.

```
System.runFinalization();
```

SETPROPERTIES

Class Name	System
Description	This method sets the System properties table to the specified Properties object. The System Properties object is an object that represents the environment in which a Java program is running. Properties is a subclass of the Hashtable class, consisting of String keys and String values. This class replaces the traditional getenv() and setenv() techniques that C programmers use to get the program's environment. The setProperties() method is used to replace the System's properties table with a new Properties object. The current System properties can be retrieved through the getProperties() method. Since the Properties class is a Hashtable, values can be modified with the put() method. A duplicate of the Properties table can also be made using the alternate Properties constructor as shown in the example. In this case, the copied Properties table can be modified using the put() method, and then written back to the System object with setProperties().
Syntax	public static void setProperties(Properties *props*)
Parameters	
Properties *prop*	The Properties object to replace the existing System Properties table.
Returns	None.
Exceptions	None.
See Also	java.util.Properties, getProperty(), getProperties()
Example	This example makes a copy of the System properties object using an alternate constructor. It then changes the "user name" key with the put() method. The new table is then written back to the System with the setProperties() method.

```
// Create a copy of the System's property list...
     Properties p = new Properties(System.getProperties());
     p.list(System.out);
     // Set the user's name...
     // This method is actually part of
     // the hashtable class...
     p.put("user.name","Joe Programmer");
     // Now set this properties list to the
     // System properties...
     System.setProperties(p);
```

SETSECURITYMANAGER

Class Name	System
Description	This method sets the Security Manager of the system. One of the key features of Java is the attention the language pays to security issues. Security is generally related to rules of access. There are tight regulations regarding I/O operations, network access, system properties, and Object modification. The setSecurityManager() method is used to set the Security Manager of the system. However, the System SecurityManager can only be set once, and attempts to do so again will result in a SecurityException object being thrown. Since browsers will generally have their own SecurityManager objects already running, this method is generally called only by stand-alone applications.
Syntax	public static void setSecurityManager(SecurityManager s)
Parameters	
SecurityManager s	The new SecurityManager.
Returns	None.
Exceptions	SecurityException
See Also	SecurityManager, SecurityException
Example	This code fragment tries to assign a SecurityManager object to the System. An exception is thrown if the System already has a SecurityManager.

```
try {
        // Try to set a new security manager
        System.setSecurityManager(mySecurityManager);
}
catch (Exception e) {
        System.out.println("Security Exception: " + e.getMessage());
}
```

The java.lang.Runtime Class

The Runtime class allows the programmer direct access to the runtime environment in which the Java virtual machine is executing. Supported operations on the runtime include the ability to launch a subprocess, getting information about and managing system memory, loading dynamic libraries, and exiting the runtime environment. Many of the methods to perform these operations are provided by the System class, which is usually the preferred way to interact with the runtime. The reasons for this preference are important.

The System class is structured to provide a platform independent interface to the runtime environment. On the other hand, the Runtime class provides a direct interface to platform specific features. For example, the exec() method has platform specific characteristics, such as its use of environment variables. Many other Runtime methods can be mapped directly upward to the System class. For such methods as those used for garbage collection or loading dynamic libraries, the System class does little more than call the corresponding method in the Runtime. The use of these methods via the Runtime class does not compromise portability, since they are written in a platform independent manner. However, it is good programming practice to use the System class whenever possible.

It should be mentioned that the exec() and other Runtime methods are subject to security constraints. Many browsers will not allow the exec() operation because it compromises security—it is a way of running non-Java code on a client machine. Such a program could take malicious advantage of system resources, because it is not subject to the built-in security of the Java language. The methods of the Runtime class are shown in Table 7-6.

Table 7-6 Summary of Runtime methods

Method	Description
exec	Starts a subprocess
exit	Causes an exit from the Java virtual machine
freeMemory	Returns an estimate of the amount of system memory
gc	Causes the garbage collector to run
getLocalizedInputStream	Translates an input stream in a local format to Unicode
getLocalizedOutputStream	Translates an output stream from Unicode to a local format
getRuntime	Returns a reference to the runtime
load	Loads a dynamic library
loadLibrary	Loads a dynamic library
runFinalization	Runs finalization methods on objects needing it
totalMemory	Returns the total amount of system memory
traceInstructions	Turns the trace on or off
traceMethodCalls	Turns the trace memory on or off

RUNTIME

Description   This class represents a platform dependent interface to the underlying runtime environment. This allows direct access to system resources. Although the System class is typically used to address these resources, the Runtime class allows access to features not available to the System class, such as executing system commands. In fact, many of the methods of the System class end up invoking Runtime class methods. Like the System class, the Runtime class cannot be instantiated. The getRuntime() method returns a reference to the runtime environment.

Syntax	public class **Runtime** extends Object
Package	java.lang
Import	java.lang.Runtime
Constructors	No public constructors.
Parameters	None.
See Also	Object, Process, System
Example	This code fragment uses a reference to the runtime to print an estimate of the amount of free system memory remaining.

```
System.out.println("Free memory: " +
        Runtime.getRuntime().freeMemory());
```

Methods

EXEC (STRING CMD)

Class Name	Runtime
Description	This method executes a system command. The command to be executed can be a Java application or another secure program. The parameter String can include command line arguments in addition to the actual program to be executed. The method returns a reference to a Process object that can be used to manage the standard input and output streams of the executed command. See the Process class for how this works.
Syntax	public Process exec(String *cmd*) throws IOException
Parameters	
String *cmd*	The system command to be executed.
Returns	A Process object that can be used to manage the standard input, output, and error of the newly created process.
Exceptions	This method throws an IOException if there is a problem executing the system command. The method may reject the command request for security reasons.
See Also	Process
Example	The following call launches the Java compiler, which builds the class contained in the file ExecTest.java.

```
try {
        // Get a reference to the Runtime environment and
        // then launch the command to compile a file
        Runtime.getRuntime().exec("javac ExecTest.java");
}
catch (IOException e) {
        System.out.println("Exec error " + e.getMessage() );
}
```

EXEC

Class Name	Runtime
Description	This method executes a system command. The command that is to be executed can be a Java application or another secure program. This method takes as input a String array, where the first element (*cmdarray[0]*) is the command to be executed. The remaining elements in the array specify the arguments that the command will use. The exec() method returns a reference to a Process object that can be used to manage the standard input and output streams of the executed command. See the Process class for how this works.
Syntax	public Process **exec**(String *cmdarray[]*) throws IOException
Parameters	
String *cmdarray[]*	A String array where the command to be executed is in the first element, with its arguments in the remaining elements of the array.
Returns	A Process object that can be used to manage the standard input, output, and error of the newly created process.
Exceptions	This method throws an IOException if there is a problem executing the system command. The method may reject the command request for security reasons.
See Also	Process
Example	This example calls the exec() method with a String command array. The first element of the String array states that the command to be executed is the Java compiler. The second element is the command argument, which is the file to be compiled. This example is functionally the same as the previous example.

```
// Creates the String command to be executed
String cmd[] = new String[2];
cmd[0] = "javac";
cmd[1] = "ExecTest.java";
try {
        // Get a reference to the Runtime environment and
        // then launch the command to compile a file
        Runtime.getRuntime().exec(cmd);
}
catch (IOException e) {
        System.out.println("Exec error " + e.getMessage() );
}
```

EXEC

Class Name	Runtime
Description	This method executes a system command, with a String array representing the program's environment. The command specified in the String parame-

ter can be a Java application or another secure program. The environment array consists of Strings that each consist of an environment variable and corresponding value. How an environment String is composed is *platform dependent*. For the Windows 95 environment, the String is of the format "variable = value". This illustrates how the Runtime class can be used in a nonportable manner. The exec() method returns a reference to a Process object that can be used to manage the standard input and output streams of the executed command. See the Process class for how this works.

Syntax   public Process exec(String *cmd*,String *envp[]*) throws IOException

Parameters

String *cmd*   The system command to be executed.

String *envp[]*   A String array composed of Strings that contain an environment variable and its corresponding value.

Returns   A Process object that can be used to manage the standard input, output, and error of the newly created process.

Exceptions   This method throws an IOException if there is a problem executing the system command. The method may reject the command request for security reasons.

See Also   Process

Example   This example calls a Windows 95 program called "test", passing it an environment variable called *EnvVar*. A C program can get the value ("100") attached to the environment variable through the function call getenv().

```
try {
    // Create the environment to be passed
    // to the program.
    String envp[] = new String[2];
        envp[0] = "EnvVar=100";  // The env variable
    // Get a reference to the Runtime environment and
        // then launch the program called "test" which
    // uses the environment variable
        Runtime.getRuntime().exec("test",envp);
}
catch (IOException e) {
        System.out.println("Exec error " + e.getMessage() );
}
```

EXEC

Class Name   Runtime

Description   This method executes a system command, with a String array representing the program's environment. The first String array specifies the command to be executed and its corresponding arguments. The first element (*cmd[0]*) is the command to be run. The remaining elements in the array specify the arguments that the command will use. The environment array consists of Strings that each consist of an environment variable and corresponding value. How an environment String is composed is platform dependent. For the Windows 95 environment, the String is of the format "variable = value." This illustrates how the Runtime class can be used in a nonportable manner. The exec() method returns a reference to a Process object that can be used to manage the standard input and output streams of the executed command. See the Process class for how this works.

Syntax

public Process exec(String *cmd[]*, String *envp[]*) throws IOException

Parameters

String *cmd[]*
A String array where the command to be executed is in the first element with its arguments in the remaining elements of the array.

String *envp[]*
A String array composed of Strings that contain an environment variable and its corresponding value.

Returns
A Process object that can be used to manage the standard input, output, and error of the newly created process.

Exceptions
This method throws an IOException if there is a problem executing the system command. The method may reject the command request for security reasons.

See Also
Process

Example
To illustrate this method, a sample program written in the C language takes arguments and an environment variable and writes them to a file called "data." Listing 7-1 provides the code of the C program.

```
try {
     // Create the environment to be passed
     // to the program.
       String envp[] = new String[2];
       envp[0] = "EnvVar=100";  // The env variable
       // Create the command array
       String cmds[] = new String[3];
       cmds[0] = "test";
       cmds[1] = "argument1";
       cmds[2] = "argument2";
       // Get a reference to the Runtime environment and
       // then launch the program called "test" which
     // uses the environment variable and arguments
       Runtime.getRuntime().exec(cmds,envp);
   }
   catch (IOException e) {
      System.out.println("Exec error " + e.getMessage() );
   }


The output from the produced data file is

Arg 0: test
Arg 1: argument1
Arg 2: argument2

EnvVar = 100
```

Listing 7-1 C program illustrating use of arguments and environment variables

```c
#include <stdio.h>
#include <stdlib.h>

main(int argc, char *argv[]) {
  FILE *fp;
  int i;
  // Open a file to write the arguments
  // and environment
  fp = fopen("data", "w");
  for (i = 0; i < argc; ++i) {
   fprintf(fp, "Arg %d: %s\n", i, argv[i]);
  }
  // Print out the environment variable...
  fprintf(fp,"\nEnvVar = %s\n", getenv("EnvVar"));
  fclose(fp);
}
```

EXIT

Class Name	Runtime
Description	This method is used to cause a program to exit from the Java virtual machine with the exit code specified in the status parameter. Since this method does not return, it is important to perform any cleanup operations before exit() is called. For portability considerations, the System exit() method should be used instead of the Runtime method.
Syntax	public void exit(int *status*)
Parameters	
Int *status*	The exit code
Returns	None.
Exceptions	None.
See Also	System.exit()
Comments	When this method is used in a browser such as Netscape Navigator, a security exception is thrown. This is because other applets also need the virtual machine to run.
Example	This code fragment leaves the virtual machine with a status code of 0.

```
Runtime.getRuntime().exit(0);
```

FREEMEMORY

Class Name	Runtime
Description	This method returns an estimate of the amount of system memory that is available. However, this number is only an estimate and so should not be

used as an exact figure. The garbage collector can be invoked with the gc() method if more memory is needed.

Syntax	public long freeMemory()
Parameters	None.
Returns	The total amount of available system memory.
Exceptions	None.
See Also	gc(), totalMemory()
Example	This code fragment prints to standard output an estimate of the amount of free system memory remaining.

```
System.out.println("Free memory: " +
        Runtime.getRuntime().freeMemory());
```

GC

Class Name	Runtime
Description	This method causes the garbage collector to run so that available memory may be increased. Like most modern object-oriented languages, Java frees the programmer from having to run new methods and delete others to create and destroy objects, respectively. Instead it uses a technique called garbage collection to remove any objects that are not being referenced by other objects. With garbage collection, the programmer does not have to explicitly delete any object; instead, the collector removes the unreferenced objects and hence frees up memory. The garbage collector is run automatically by Java as a separate thread. It is called explicitly when there is not enough memory to fulfill a request to create a new object. However, a programmer may want to run the garbage collector explicitly after a large set of objects (like a linked list) is no longer being used. It may also be good to run the collector during idle periods. The gc() method is used to explicitly run the garbage collector. For portability considerations, the System gc() method should be used instead of the Runtime method.
Syntax	public void gc()
Parameters	None.
Returns	None.
Exceptions	None.
See Also	System.gc()
Example	This example illustrates a situation where you might want to run the garbage collector.

```
//   Create a large set of object lists... .
//   Do work on the lists...
//   Remove references to the objects
//   Get the program ready for more work by
```

```
// calling the garbage collector...
Runtime.getRuntime().gc();
```

GETLOCALIZEDINPUTSTREAM

Class Name	Runtime
Description	This method translates an input stream in a local format to a stream in Unicode format. Characters in Java are not represented in the traditional 8-bit ASCII character set, but are in the Unicode 16-bit character set. This is important for the support of international character sets. When an input stream is being read in using a local format, the getLocalizedInputStream() method can be invoked to automatically translate the stream to a Unicode input stream.
Syntax	public InputStream getLocalizedInputStream(InputStream *in*)
Parameters	
InputStream *in*	The local input stream.
Returns	An input stream with input translated to Unicode.
Exceptions	None.
See Also	getLocalizedOutputStream(), InputStream
Example	This code takes standard input as the local stream and invokes the getLocalizedInputStream() to create a Unicode input stream.

```
InputStream input =
         Runtime.getRuntime().getLocalizedInputStream(System.in);
```

GETLOCALIZEDOUTPUTSTREAM

Class Name	Runtime
Description	This method translates an output stream in Unicode format to a stream in local format. Characters in Java are not represented in the traditional 8-bit ASCII character set, but are in the Unicode 16-bit character set. This is important for the support of international character sets. When an output stream is being written out in Unicode format, the getLocalizedOutputStream() method can be invoked to automatically translate the stream to a stream in the local format.
Syntax	public OutputStream getLocalizedOutputStream(OutputStream *out*)
Parameters	
OutputStream *out*	The Unicode output stream.
Returns	An output stream with output translated to the local format.
Exceptions	None.
See Also	getLocalizedInputStream(), OutputStream

Example   This code takes standard output as the Unicode stream and invokes the
                            getLocalizedOutputStream() to create a locally formatted output stream.

```
OutputStream output =
        Runtime.getRuntime().getLocalizedOutputStream(System.out);
```

GetRuntime

Class Name	Runtime
Description	This method returns a reference to the runtime. Since the Runtime class cannot be instantiated, it needs a reference for it to be used. The getRuntime() method provides a reference to the runtime environment class. Runtime methods can then be invoked with this reference.
Syntax	public static Runtime getRuntime()
Parameters	None.
Returns	A reference to the runtime.
Exceptions	None.
See Also	Runtime
Example	This code fragment uses a reference to the runtime to print an estimate of the amount of free system memory remaining.

```
System.out.println("Free memory: " +
        Runtime.getRuntime().freeMemory());
```

LOAD

Class Name	Runtime
Description	This method loads a dynamic library using a complete path name. Dynamic libraries contain native methods, which are routines written in languages other than Java. The load() method looks for a dynamic library using a full path. Appendix C, Writing Native Methods in C/C++, contains a full description of native methods.
Syntax	public synchronized void load(String *filename*)
Parameters	
String *filename*	The library to load with full path.
Returns	None.
Exceptions	This method throws an UnsatisfiedLinkError if the library is not found.
See Also	loadLibrary()
Example	This code fragment loads a dynamic library using a full path.

```
Runtime.getRuntime().load("/java/lib/MyClass.so");
```

LOADLIBRARY

Class Name	Runtime
Description	This method loads a dynamic library from the current or library directory. Dynamic libraries contain native methods, which are routines written in languages other than Java. The loadLibrary() method looks in a library or current directory to load the file specified. Appendix C, Writing Native Methods in C/C++, contains a full description of native methods.
Syntax	public synchronized void loadLibrary(String *filename*)
Parameters	
String *filename*	The library to load with full path.
Returns	None.
Exceptions	This method throws an UnsatisfiedLinkError if the library is not found.
See Also	load()
Example	This code fragment loads a dynamic library from the current or library directories.

```
Runtime.getRuntime().load("MyClass.so");
```

RUNFINALIZATION

Class Name	Runtime
Description	This method runs the finalization methods of any objects that are no longer referenced by any other objects. The runFinalization() method is meant to be used as a way of cleaning up an object before it is destroyed. A typical finalize() activity is to remove references to other objects. The finalize() method can be invoked manually or is often, but not reliably, called by the garbage collector. The garbage collector will only call an object's finalize() method if all references to it have been removed and it is ready to be deleted. The runFinalization() method calls the finalize() method of any objects pending finalization; that is, objects to which there are no more references. However, it may not actually call an object's finalize() method as would be expected. The garbage collector, on the other hand, performs finalization in a more predictable manner.
Syntax	public void runFinalization()
Parameters	None.
Returns	None.
Exceptions	None.
See Also	gc()
Example	This example starts with a simple class whose only method is finalize().

```
// Class used to demonstrate finalization...
class MyClass {
   public void finalize() {
      System.out.println("Finalize method called!");
   }
};
```

The class is next instantiated.

```
// Create finalization class...
MyClass m;
m = new MyClass();
```

Later, the reference to the class is removed.

```
m = null;
```

Finally, the Runtime's finalization method is invoked. This *may* cause the String in the MyClass finalize() method to be displayed to standard output.

```
Runtime.getRuntime().runFinalization();
```

TOTALMEMORY

Class Name	Runtime
Description	This method returns the total amount of system memory.
Syntax	public long totalMemory()
Parameters	None.
Returns	The amount of system memory.
Exceptions	None.
See Also	freeMemory()
Example	This code fragment prints to standard output the amount of system memory.

```
System.out.println("Total memory = " +
         Runtime.getRuntime().totalMemory());
```

TRACEINSTRUCTIONS

Class Name	Runtime
Description	This method enables or disables the tracing of instructions.
Syntax	public void traceInstructions(boolean *on*)
Parameters	
boolean *on*	Turns the trace on or off.
Returns	None.
Exceptions	None.

See Also	traceMethodCalls()
Example	This example turns on instruction tracing.

```
Runtime.getRuntime().traceInstructions(true);
```

TRACEMETHODCALLS

Class Name	Runtime
Description	This method enables or disables the tracing methods.
Syntax	public void traceMethodCalls(boolean *on*)
Parameters	
boolean *on*	Turns the trace on or off.
Returns	None.
Exceptions	None.
See Also	traceInstructions()
Example	This example turns on the tracing of method calls.

```
Runtime.getRuntime().traceMethodCalls(true);
```

The java.lang.Process Class

When the exec() methods of the Runtime class are called, a class instance of the Process class is returned. This Process object can then be used to manage various aspects of the running of the subprocess. This includes

- Managing the standard input, output, and error streams of the process
- Terminating the process
- Waiting for the subprocess to finish running
- Getting its exit code

In general, the Process class functions as the parent of the child subprocess. However, it is not necessary to use the Process object for the subprocess to function properly. If the exec() method is called and the returned Process object is ignored, the subprocess will continue to execute. In most cases, the subprocess will run independently of how the Process object is referenced.

It should be noted that the Process class is abstract. Its actual implementations are platform specific. Consequently, the "Process objects" you get are actually objects of a subclass of Process. For this reason, phrases like "instances of the Process class" are not absolutely correct—the Process class is abstract. However, a style based on phrases like the above is easier to read, so if you understand that this actually refers to a subclass of Process, the style should not be a problem. The methods of the Process class are shown in Table 7-7.

Table 7-7 Summary of Process methods

Method	Description
destroy	Terminates the subprocess
exitValue	Gets the exit value of a process that has completed running
getErrorStream	Returns an InputStream connected to the standard error stream of the subprocess
getInputStream	Returns an InputStream connected to the standard output stream of the subprocess
getOutputStream	Returns an InputStream connected to the standard input stream of the subprocess
waitFor	Waits for a subprocess to finish running

PROCESS

Description	Subclasses of this abstract class can be used to manage a subprocess launched by the exec() method of the Runtime class. A Process subclass instance is returned by the exec() methods of the Runtime class. Process subclasses can be used to manage the standard input and output streams of the newly created subprocess. It can also be used to gracefully terminate the subprocess. Process is an abstract class and has no constructor. It is generally only used in conjunction with the exec() method.
Syntax	public abstract class **Process** extends Object
Package	java.lang
Import	java.lang.Process
Constructors	Abstract class. No public constructors.
Parameters	None.
See Also	Object, Runtime
Example	This code launches a Java program and redirects its standard input to the calling code via the getOutputStream() method. When the subprocess reads in from standard input (such as *System.in*), it will get the String written out by this code. The example creates a PrintStream object using the subprocess OutputStream as the constructor. That way it is easy to write Strings (instead of bytes) to the child process.

```
// Launch a test Java program...
Process p = Runtime.getRuntime().exec("java ExecTest");
// Get the standard input stream of the process...
// and create a print stream from it...
PrintStream in = new PrintStream(p.getOutputStream());
// Write to standard input of the subprocess
in.println("Send this string to the subprocess");
```

Methods

DESTROY

Class Name	Process
Description	This method kills the subprocess associated with this class. The waitFor() method can be used to wait for the subprocess to be completely dead.
Syntax	abstract public void destroy()
Parameters	None.
Returns	None.
Exceptions	None.
See Also	waitFor(), exitValue(), Runtime
Example	This example starts another Java program and then destroys it after a delay.

```
try {
        // Launch a test Java program...
        Process p = Runtime.getRuntime().exec("java ExecTest");
    //   do something
    // Kill it!
    p.destroy();
}
// Handle any exceptions caused by the process...
catch (IOException e) {
        // Just print out the error...
        System.out.println(e.getMessage());
}
```

EXITVALUE

Class Name	Process
Description	This method is used to get the exit code of a subprocess that has finished executing. The exitValue() method can only be called when the subprocess is no longer running, otherwise an IllegalThreadStateException object will be thrown.
Syntax	abstract public int **exitValue()**
Parameters	None.
Returns	The value of the exit code of the terminated subprocess.
Exceptions	This method throws an IllegalThreadStateException object if the process is still running.
See Also	Runtime
Example	This example starts another Java program, waits for it to finish, and then prints out its error code.

```
try {
        // Launch a test Java program...
        Process p = Runtime.getRuntime().exec("java ExecTest");
        System.out.println("Created the process!");
        // Wait for the process to complete...
        try {
            p.waitFor();
        }
        // This is thrown if the wait fails...
        catch (InterruptedException e) {
            System.out.println("Subprocess interrupted");
        }
        // Get the exit code...
        try {
            System.out.println("ExitValue is: " + p.exitValue());
        }
        // Thrown if process is not done, although it will
        // be if we got here...
        catch (IllegalThreadStateException e) {
            System.out.println("Subprocess in illegal state");
        }
}
// Handle any exceptions caused by the process...
catch (IOException e) {
        // Just print out the error...
        System.out.println(e.getMessage());
}
```

GETERRORSTREAM

Class Name	Process
Description	This method is used to redirect the standard error stream of the sub-process. The error stream becomes an InputStream of this process, which can be read in through the read() method. The buffer from the error stream is unbuffered and can be converted into a String format for additional operations such as printing to the terminal.
Syntax	abstract public InputStream getErrorStream()
Parameters	None.
Returns	An InputStream connected to the standard error stream of the subprocess.
Exceptions	None.
See Also	Runtime, InputStream
Example	This code launches a Java program that may write out to standard error using the System.err.println() method. The example code will try to catch this output by connecting to the error stream with the getErrorStream() method. It then reads from the stream. The program will wait until something is printed to standard error or the subprocess terminates. The code will print out the input stream redirected from standard error if it is produced. Otherwise, a blank line will be printed out.

```
try {
        // Launch a test Java program...
        Process p = Runtime.getRuntime().exec("java ExecTest");
   // Get the standard Error stream of the process...
        InputStream err = p.getErrorStream();
        // Try to read any standard error from the
        // process. Will block until done or if the
        // process terminates...
        try {
           byte b[] = new byte[80];
     err.read(b);
     // Convert the stream to a string and print it...
           System.out.println(new String(b,0));
        }
        // Catch any exception thrown by the read operation...
        catch(IOException e) {
           System.out.println("Nothing read from
standard error");
        }
}
// Handle any exceptions caused by the process...
catch (IOException e) {
        // Just print out the error...
        System.out.println(e.getMessage());
}
```

GETINPUTSTREAM

Class Name	Process
Description	This method is used to redirect the standard output stream of the sub-process. The output stream becomes an InputStream of this process, which can be read in through the read() method. The stream from the output is buffered and can be converted into a String format for additional operations such as printing to the terminal.
Syntax	abstract public InputStream getInputStream()
Parameters	None.
Returns	An InputStream connected to the standard output stream of the sub-process.
Exceptions	None.
See Also	Runtime, InputStream
Example	This code launches a Java program that may write to standard output using the System.out.println() method. The example code will try to catch this output by connecting to the output stream with the getInputStream() method. It then reads from the stream. The program will wait until something is printed to standard output or the subprocess terminates. The code will print out the input stream redirected from standard output if it is produced. Otherwise, a blank line will be printed out.

```
try {
        // Launch a test Java program...
        Process p = Runtime.getRuntime().exec("java ExecTest");
   // Get the standard Error stream of the process...
        InputStream out = p.getInputStream();
        // Try to read any standard output from the
        // process. Will block until done or if the
        // process terminates...
        try {
          byte b[] = new byte[80];
     err.read(b);
     // Convert the stream to a string and print it...
        System.out.println(new String(b,0));
        }
        // Catch any exception thrown by the read operation...
        catch(IOException e) {
          System.out.println("Nothing read from
standard output");
        }
}
// Handle any exceptions caused by the process...
catch (IOException e) {
        // Just print out the error...
        System.out.println(e.getMessage());
}
```

GETOUTPUTSTREAM

Class Name	Process
Description	This method is used to redirect the standard input stream of the sub-process. Whenever the subprocess reads in data from standard input via the *System.in* variable, it will actually be getting the data from this OutputStream. The OutputStream is buffered so the code writing to this stream will not wait for the subprocess to read from it.
Syntax	abstract public OutputStream getOutputStream()
Parameters	None.
Returns	An OutputStream connected to the standard input stream of the sub-process.
Exceptions	None.
See Also	Runtime, OutputStream
Example	This code launches a Java program and redirects its standard input to the calling code via the getOutputStream() method. When the subprocess reads in from standard input (such as *System.in*), it will get the String written out by this code. The example creates a PrintStream object using the subprocess OutputStream as the constructor. That way it is easy to write Strings (instead of bytes) to the child process.

```
// Launch a test Java program...
Process p = Runtime.getRuntime().exec("java ExecTest");
// Get the standard input stream of the process...
```

```
// and create a print stream from it...
PrintStream in = new PrintStream(p.getOutputStream());
// Write to standard input of the subprocess
in.println("Send this string to the subprocess");
```

WAITFOR

Class Name	Process
Description	The waitFor() method is used to wait for the running of a subprocess to be completed. If the process is still running, the method will block the calling thread until the subprocess is finished. If the subprocess is already complete, the method will return immediately. In either case, the waitFor() method will return the exit value of the subprocess.
Syntax	abstract public int waitFor() throws InterruptedException
Parameters	None.
Returns	The value of the exit code of the terminated subprocess.
Exceptions	This method throws an InterruptedException object if this thread has been interrupted by another thread.
See Also	Runtime
Example	This example starts another Java program, waits for it to finish, and then prints out its exit code.

```
try {
        // Launch a test Java program...
        Process p = Runtime.getRuntime().exec("java ExecTest");
        System.out.println("Created the process!");
        // Wait for the process to complete...
    // print out its exit code when done...
        try {
System.out.println("Exit code: " + p.waitFor());
        }
        // This is thrown if the wait fails...
        catch (InterruptedException e) {
            System.out.println("Subprocess interrupted");
        }
}
// Handle any exceptions caused by the process...
catch (IOException e) {
        // Just print out the error...
        System.out.println(e.getMessage());
}
```

The System Classes Project: Running a Subprocess in Java

Project Overview

The following project provides an illustration of an interrelated Java program and subprocess. The parent program launches another Java program as a subprocess via the

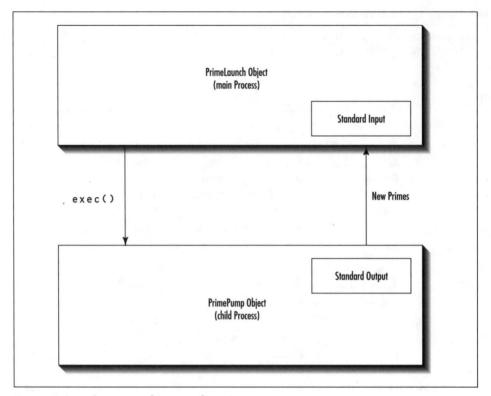

Figure 7-1 Architecture of System classes project

Runtime exec() method. The parent reads the standard output from the child via the instance of the Process class produced by the call to the exec() method. This output is then redirected to standard output using the System class's *out* variable. Figure 7-1 shows the general architecture of the project.

Building the Project

1. Create the file PrimePump.java and add the following code. This class produces primes up to a given value. The primes are printed to standard output. After the maximum prime is reached, the program outputs the String "Done!" and exits.

```
// Imports the class the program needs...
import java.lang.*;
import java.io.*;

// Does little more than produce prime numbers ad infinitum...
public class PrimePump {
    // Produce primes forever and print to standard out...
    public static void main(String args[]) {
        // Convert max # from arguments
        int maxNum = Integer.parseInt(args[0]);
        int i,currentNumber,stop;
```

```
      boolean isPrime = false;
      // Print primes up to maximum number...
for (currentNumber = 2; currentNumber < maxNum ;    ++currentNumber) {
          // See if it is prime...
          isPrime = true;
          stop = (currentNumber / 2) + 1;
      for (i = 2; i < stop; ++i) {
        if ((currentNumber % i) == 0) {
          isPrime = false;
          break;
        }
      }  // end outer
          // If its a prime, then print to standard out...
          if (isPrime)
              System.out.println(currentNumber);
  } // end big for loop...
      System.out.println("Done!");
    }
}
```

2. Create the file PrimeLaunch.java and add the following code. This class starts the PrimePump class as a separate process using the Runtime exec() method. It opens up a stream to the PrimePump's standard output with the Process class getInputStream() method. The class then reads in lines of output from PrimePump and formats them for display on standard output. When a String that equals "Done!" is found, the program quits.

```
import java.lang.*;
import java.io.*;


// Create a process that produces Primes which are
// redirected to this program.  PrimeLaunch in turn
// prints the primes to Standard out.  When a "Done!"
// string is found the program quits reading and leaves...
public class PrimeLaunch  {
   // Create the subprocess, read output from it
   // until it is complete...
   public static void main(String args[]) {
      // Create the PrimePump subprocess...
      try {
         // Set up command array for process...
         String cmdArray[] = new String[3];
         cmdArray[0] = "java";
         cmdArray[1] = "PrimePump";
         cmdArray[2] = "100"; // Max # of times pump should count
         // Create the process...
         Process childPr = Runtime.getRuntime().exec(cmdArray);
         // Take in the output from process...
         DataInputStream childIn =
             new DataInputStream(childPr.getInputStream());
         String s; // The latest prime number...
         // Print the primes until we see
         // the finished flag...
         for (int i = 0; ; ++i) {
             // Get input string...
```

continued on next page

continued from previous page

```
            try {
                s = childIn.readLine();
            }
            // Quit if read error...
            catch (IOException e) {
                break;
            }
            // Quit if we are done...
            if (s.equals("Done!"))
                break;
            // Print out the latest results...
            System.out.println("Prime # " + i + " = " + s);
        }
    }
    // Quit out if error with subprocess...
    catch (IOException e) {
        System.out.println("Error: " + e.getMessage());
        System.exit(0);
    }
  }
}
```

How It Works

This example illustrates how the Process and Runtime classes interact. The exec()
method of the Runtime class returns an instance of the Process class that can be used
to manipulate the standard input and output streams of the subprocess. In this example, the Process object, called childPr, gets the subprocess output stream through the
getInputStream(). By doing this, the stream becomes the standard output for the subprocess. It can then read in newline delimited Strings through the readLine() method
of the DataInputStream class. The PrimeLaunch class uses DataInputStream instead of
InputStream because the former is better for managing Strings. The line

```
DataInputStream childIn =
        new DataInputStream(childPr.getInputStream());
```

takes the standard output of the child process and converts it into an input stream that
works with data types such as Strings.

As mentioned elsewhere in this chapter, the exec() method will face security restrictions when called from an applet. This is because the invocation of non-Java code that
the exec() method allows compromises security. It is a way of running malicious programs, such as those written in the C programming language. Programs written in C
have much wider access to operating system resources than Java does, and so can be
much more dangerous (sometimes by mistake!). Consequently, browsers will often
prevent the exec() method from being carried out, since it could launch such potentially malicious applications.

8

THREAD AND THREADGROUP

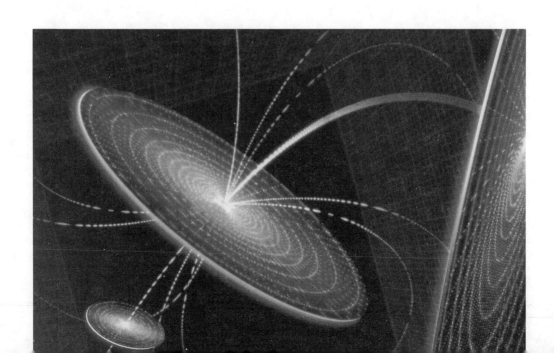

8

THREAD AND THREADGROUP

One of the most important features of Java is its support for multithreading. Many programmers (particularly PC developers) are used to creating applications that are single threaded, allowing only one chain of execution to run through a program. While this might be adequate for simple applications, this limitation has a severe performance and usability impact on more advanced programs. GUI applications, for example, are generally driven by user-initiated events such as mouse clicks and keystrokes. When the user is not interacting with the application in a single-threaded GUI program, nothing happens. A multithreaded program, on the other hand, can do work in the "background"—such as spell checking a document—while the user decides what to do next.

For network applications, single-threaded applications are particularly cumbersome. When the user is reading a document or making a decision, a multithreaded program can be downloading graphical images, raw data, or getting the next document. With this approach, the user will not have to spend most of his or her time waiting for information to arrive from the network. On the other hand, single-threaded network applications typically have the order of click-and-wait, click-and-wait, click-and-wait, and so on, with no hope of improvement.

The creators of Java understood how important multithreading would be for distributed network programming and advanced object-oriented development. They built constructs into the language that aid in the development of multithreaded programs. The most important of these constructs is the *synchronized* keyword, which helps coordinate activities of related threads. The developers of Java also created a set of classes that provide the foundations for building threaded classes. These core thread classes are the focus of this chapter. Figure 8-1 shows the hierarchy of the classes and interfaces discussed in this chapter.

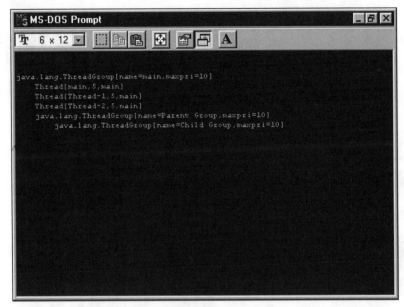

Figure 8-1 Thread classes and interfaces

Basics of the Thread Class

A thread is a single sequential flow of execution operating within a process. A process can have one or more threads. Sophisticated object-oriented languages, such as Java or Smalltalk, provide mechanisms for letting users develop multiple threaded classes within an application. A threaded class is a class with its own sequential flow of a control.

Most threaded classes will be written as extensions of the Thread class. This class provides a suite of methods that allows the programmer to create, run, and change the state of a threaded object. The most important method in the Thread class is run(), which is where all the threaded activity occurs. The run() method generally has three parts: any startup activity, such as variable initialization; some kind of central looping or sequential behavior, such as preloading graphics or performing a calculation; and exit activities.

For example, suppose you wanted a Thread class to monitor some kind of activity. You would structure the class as follows:

```
class MonitorThread extends Thread {
    public void run() {
        // Initialize stuff...
        // Main Monitor Loop
    }
}
```

The start() method is used to initiate Thread execution. Its main activity is to cause the run() method to be invoked. The method assumes that the Thread class has already been created. The following is applet code that can be used to create and start an instance of MonitorThread:

```
public class MonitorApp extends java.applet.Applet  {
        public void init() {
        MonitorThread th;
        th = new MonitorThread();
            th.start();
            //...
        }
    }
```

Another method, stop(), can be used to terminate a Thread. The simplest form of the method takes no parameters and immediately causes the Thread to "die" by making the Thread exit its run() method. The Thread object, however, still exists—it just is not "active." An active Thread is one that has been started but not stopped. An inactive Thread's methods can still be invoked, however. For example, you may want to query a Thread that has been stopped about the state that it was in when its run() method was terminated.

Thread Constructors and the Runnable Interface

Another way to create a threaded class is to implement the Runnable interface, which provides a protocol for writing threaded objects. Since Runnable is an interface, a class must be created to implement the interface. Writing a class that implements Runnable is usually done in cases where the developer does not want to subclass Thread. The Runnable interface consists of only one method, run(). Like the Thread class, the run() method is where the threaded execution of the object occurs. However, using the Runnable interface to implement a threaded object is often better than subclassing Thread, because it allows you to separate the design of your class from the fact that it runs as a Thread. For example, the Applet class has a large set of features. However, it is not a subclass of Thread. If you want it to run as a thread, then you need to create a subclass of Applet that implements the Runnable interface. That way you inherit the behavior of the Applet, yet can run it as a thread.

The Runnable interface is illustrated with a variation of the MonitorThread class just discussed. The class could be structured as follows:

```
class MonitorThread implements Runnable {
    public void run() {
        // Initialize stuff...
        // Main Monitor Loop
    }
}
```

The following code could be used to create and invoke a MonitorThread object:

```
MonitorThread t = new MonitorThread();  // Construct the object
new Thread(t).start();  // Starts the thread
```

The second line is one of several Thread constructors. In this case, the constructor creates a new Thread, which invokes the run() method of the Runnable parameter when the start() method is called.

Perhaps the most frequently used Thread constructor will be the one that takes no parameters, which was illustrated in the previous section. Other constructors allow the user to give the Thread a String name or add it to a ThreadGroup (discussed later). Combinations of naming, adding to groups, and using Runnable targets are also available.

Changing the State of a Thread

The generally stated purpose of multithreading is to allow multiple sequences of execution to run at the same time. However, defining multithreading this way is not completely technically correct. Threads do not actually execute simultaneously; rather, they function by sharing slices of processing time. The Java thread scheduler is responsible for determining when a thread should run and how much time a thread should receive. The priority of a thread determines how much of this time the thread will get relative to other threads. The higher the priority, the more processing time a thread gets; the lower the priority, the less processing time the thread will be allocated, and so will take longer to complete execution.

The Thread class defines three public constants that indicate important priority values:

■ MAX_PRIORITY   Set to the value 10, this indicates the maximum priority value.

■ MIN_PRIORITY   Set to 1, this represents the minimum priority bound.

■ NORM_PRIORITY   This is the default value, set to 5.

It is wise to use the maximum and minimum priority values with some restraint, as they may result in unexpected performance (the Threads taking too much or too little processing time).

The current priority value of a Thread can be retrieved via the getPriority() method. The setPriority() method establishes a new Thread priority. Priority values are further constrained by the maximum priority value of the ThreadGroup in which a Thread belongs, a topic that will be discussed later.

Another feature of Threads that can be useful is the ability to temporarily halt and, conversely, continue a Thread's sequence of execution. The resume(), suspend(), and sleep() methods act on threads in the manner indicated by their names. There are also methods that let a Thread work cooperatively with other threads. The yield() method lets the currently executing Thread surrender its current processing cycle to some other Thread. A Thread that needs to wait for another Thread to cease execution ("die") can wait for this to happen by employing the join() method. It is good practice to use join() when killing Threads right before exiting an application. Otherwise, the program might seem to "hang" in an unexpected manner. The following example starts a Thread, stops it, and waits for it to die:

```
// Create and start the thread...
    MyThread t = new MyThread();
    t.start();
    //    Do something
    // Stop the thread...
    t.stop();
    // Wait for it to die...
    try {
        t.join();
    }
    catch (InterruptedException e) { }
    //    It's dead. Continue...
```

Threads and Synchronization

Having looked at the previous examples, it may seem that writing a threaded object is not particularly difficult. This is misleading, however. Multithreaded programming becomes more difficult when objects need to share data. The problem is one of concurrency. Recall that threads function by time slicing. This means that a thread in the middle of executing a method may have its slice of time interrupted by another thread. A problem arises if one thread is altering data while another thread is accessing the same data. In this situation, it is possible that the information can be left in an incorrect state. This situation is called the producer/consumer problem: one thread is producing information while another is consuming it.

Listing 8-1 shows the class definition of a first-in first-out (FIFO) list. An item is added to the list through the add() method. The front item in the list is returned (and removed from the list) via the remove() method. A simple accessor class called FIFOItem stores an Object and the next item in the list. Listing 8-2 provides the code for the FIFOThread that loops and prints out the String reference of the first item in a FIFO. This thread can be said to *consume* FIFO items. The FIFOThread sleeps if the list is empty. Listing 8-3 displays an applet that creates a FIFO, adds some elements to it, and starts a thread that displays any items in the FIFO. You can add (*produce*) more elements to the FIFO by clicking on the mouse.

Listing 8-1 Classes used to implement FIFO list

```
// Implement a first-in first-out queue...
class FIFO {
    // FIFOItem is a simple accessor class that stores data and
    // then next FIFOItem...
    FIFOItem first;
    FIFOItem last;
    // Initialize the queue...
    public FIFO() {
```

continued on next page

continued from previous page

```
        first = null;
        last = null;
    }
    // Add an item to the queue...
    public void add(Object o) {
        // Add item to the end of the list...
        FIFOItem f = new FIFOItem(o,null);
        // See if it should be added to the beginning or end of the list...
        if (first == null)
            first = f;
        else
            last.setNext(f);
        // Make the last object point to this..
        last = f;
    }
    // Remove the first item from the queue...
    public Object remove() throws IllegalArgumentException {
        if (first == null)
            throw new IllegalArgumentException();
        // Assign the new first item...
        FIFOItem f = first;
        first = f.getNext();
        return f.getData();
    }
}
```

Listing 8-2 FIFO thread that reads (consumes) items from FIFO and displays them

```
// Reads item from FIFO...
class FIFOThread extends Thread {
    FIFO f;
    // Constructors adds FIFO to thread...
    public FIFOThread(FIFO f) {
        this.f = f;
    }
    // Loop and spit out elements in FIFO...
    public void run() {
        Object o;
        while (true) {
            // Print out item from FIFO if exists...
            try {
                o = f.remove();
                System.out.println("Found object: " + o);
            }
            // Sleep some if FIFO is empty...
            catch (IllegalArgumentException e) {
                try {
                    sleep(250);
                }
                catch (InterruptedException ex) { }
            }
        }
    }
}
```

Listing 8-3 FIFO applet that produces items on the FIFO

```
public class FIFOTest extends Applet  {
    FIFO f;
    int counter = 4;
    public void init() {
        f = new FIFO();
        f.add("First");
        f.add("Second");
        f.add("Third");
        // Start the thread...
        FIFOThread t = new FIFOThread(f);
        t.start();
    }

    // When user clicks on mouse add elements to the FIFO...
    public boolean mouseDown(Event ev, int x, int y) {
        // Increment counter...
        f.add(Integer.toString(counter++));
return true;
    };
}
```

In this applet, there are two threads using the same FIFO object. The applet is producing items, while the thread consumes them. However, a problem can occur if the applet is calling the FIFO add() method at the same time the FIFOThread is calling remove(). Consider the following code sequence when there is only one item in the FIFO:

```
add():          if (first == null)  // False!
remove():       FIFOItem f = first;
remove():       first = f.getNext();  // First now is null!
add();          last.setNext(f);  // Will never be called!
```

In the first line, the add() method checks to see if the *first* item variable is null. In this case, it is not. Consequently, the method will invoke the fourth line (setNext()) of the code. However, the method is interrupted by a call to remove(). The remove() code consequently changes the *first* variable. When add() resumes execution, however, the *last* variable that is modified will never be called because nothing will point to it. This is because the add() method was interrupted before it was finished. If it was allowed to run through before being interrupted, there would be no problem, because the *first* variable assignment in the remove() method would point to the new item.

Java provides a way around this synchronization problem by introducing the lock construct. Each object or class has a single lock associated with it. This lock can be used to synchronize operations such as producer/consumer. The *synchronized* keyword is used to guarantee that the execution of a method or block of code cannot be achieved unless the lock of the object in question has been attained. The lock is released when the execution of the method or block is complete. At this point, other methods can aquire the lock and execute the code.

If the *synchronized* keyword is introduced to the add() and remove() methods of the FIFO class, the producer/consumer problem goes away.

```
public synchronized void add(Object o)
public synchronized Object remove()
```

This fixes the problem, because a synchronized method cannot be interrupted by another call to synchronized code in the same object until the method is complete. Consequently, the add() method cannot be interleaved by calls to the remove() method.

In addition to methods, blocks of code can be synchronized by specifying any object to be used as the lock—that is, any segment of code can be synchronized with another, using the lock associated with any object. The following illustrates the syntax for doing this:

```
Boolean baton;
baton =  new Boolean(false);
//
// Thread #1
synchronized(baton) {  // Get lock of baton
    // do work...
baton = Boolean.TRUE;
    } // Release baton lock
    // Thread #2
    synchronized(baton) {  // Get lock of baton
if (baton == Boolean.TRUE)
    // .. do something...
else
    // ... do something different...
    } // Release baton lock
```

In this situation, one thread is responsible for setting the baton Boolean object to true. The other Thread uses the state of the baton object to determine its mode of processing.

An additonal way to synchronize behavior is through the wait(), notify(), and notifyAll() methods of an object. These methods are available to every object, since they are defined as part of the base Object class. They can only be called from within synchronized methods or synchronized code and are used to inform one thread using an Object that another thread has done something to the state of the object. For example, a thread may need an object variable to be in a certain state. It calls the wait() method to pause until another thread changes the object. When, and if, another thread makes the change, it lets the first thread know of this change by invoking the notify() method. This "wakes up" the first thread, which can then look at the state of the object. The wait() and notify() methods can only be called from within the thread that currently has the lock of a synchronized Object. If it is called from anywhere else, an IllegalMonitorStateException is thrown.

Other Thread Techniques

There are a couple of subtle things about Threads that are useful to know. A static Thread method, called currentThread(), exists so that information about Threads can be obtained without specifically constructing a Thread. This way you can get a reference to the currently executing Thread so that methods, like sleep(), can be applied to it. For example, the following code could be executed to get the reference to the current Thread so that it can be made to sleep half a second.

```
Thread t = Thread.currentThread();
try {
t.sleep(500);
}
catch (InterruptedException e) { }
```

Another useful operation is to get the current ThreadGroup by invoking the getThreadGroup() method on this reference.

It is also possible to write a Thread that runs independently of other Threads, providing a service that is needed by a variety of objects within the application. Such a Thread is called a *daemon* Thread. A good example of a daemon is a background Thread that loads files from the local file system and network, something that is found often in Web browsers. Daemon Threads are typically used as general providers of services that are needed throughout an application.

The Thread class provides a couple of methods that can be used to convert a Thread into a daemon. The setDaemon() method designates the Thread as a daemon. This needs to be called before the Thread is started. Otherwise, an IllegalThreadStateException object will be thrown. The isDaemon() method can be used to determine if the Thread is a daemon.

Since a daemon is an independent Thread, it is not necessarily destroyed when the Thread that created it goes away. However, since Java does not exit an application when there are Threads running, doesn't the existence of daemons prevent Java from ever exiting the program? Not really, since Java distinguishes between *user* Threads and daemon Threads. When user Threads (the default) are active, Java does not quit the application. However, when only daemon Threads are running, Java terminates the daemons and leaves the program.

Thread Groups

ThreadGroups contain a set of Threads or other ThreadGroups. By default, every Thread belongs to a ThreadGroup. This allows operations over a set of Threads to occur in a synchronized manner. For example, the ThreadGroup stop() method is applied to every active Thread in a ThreadGroup. This spares the developer from having to manually invoke the stop() method for every Thread in the group.

ThreadGroups are organized in a hierarchical manner. The top-level ThreadGroup is responsible for the main Thread of execution for an applet. This ThreadGroup is the parent of all other ThreadGroups that are created for the applet. Because of this hierarchical structure, ThreadGroup methods are often recursive. That is, an invoked ThreadGroup method may be also applied to the child ThreadGroups. For example, the stop() method not only stops all Threads in a ThreadGroup, but also stops all Threads in its child ThreadGroups. The enumerate() method, which lists Threads or groups within a ThreadGroup, has an optional parameter that lets the programmer decide whether or not child groups should be inspected.

ThreadGroups are also used to control access relationships. Specifically, a ThreadGroup that is a child of another ThreadGroup cannot modify the parent ThreadGroup. However, the parent ThreadGroup can apply a method across all its children. This access control is exemplified by the recursive nature of ThreadGroup methods like enumerate() and stop().

ThreadGroups and Constructors

ThreadGroups have String names. A new ThreadGroup can be constructed with the following call:

```
ThreadGroup myThreadGroup = new ThreadGroup("My Thread Group");
```

The parameter String becomes the name of the group. Since this constructor has no ThreadGroup parameter, the system assigns this new group to the ThreadGroup of the currently executing Thread. For example, if this group was created from the main Applet class of a program, the parent of the new group would be the top-level ThreadGroup.

To assign a specific ThreadGroup parent, the group could be constructed as follows:

```
ThreadGroup myThreadGroup = new ThreadGroup(grpParent,"My ThreadGroup");
```

In this code, *grpParent* is another ThreadGroup.

Assigning a Thread to a ThreadGroup is done in a similar fashion. If a Thread's constructor does not specify a ThreadGroup, it is automatically assigned to the ThreadGroup of the currently executing Thread. On the other hand, there are three Thread constructors that can be used to assign a new Thread to a specific group. For example,

```
AThreadClass myThread = new AThreadClass(myThreadGroup,"My Thread");
```

assigns the new Thread to the ThreadGroup constructed in the previous examples.

Thread Death and the Stop Method

The stop() method with no parameters is the most widely used method to terminate a Thread. It forces the Thread to leave its run() method and so conclude its processing sequence. The internals on how stop() works are illuminating. The stop() method throws a ThreadDeath object at the Thread. ThreadDeath is not an Exception object (which is already caught frequently by Thread classes), but a type of Error. The ThreadDeath Error is a Thread specific way of saying that the user has issued the stop() method. In general, it is not necessary to catch ThreadDeath, unless some special cleanup process needs to occur. If ThreadDeath is caught by the Thread, then it needs to be rethrown so that the Thread will die.

This example shows a Thread that catches ThreadDeath. It performs some cleanup, and then rethrows the ThreadDeath object.

```
class DeathCatcherThread extends Thread {
    public void run() {
```

```
        try {
            // Loop forever...
            while (true) {
// Do something...
}
        }
        catch (ThreadDeath death) {    // Catch ThreadDeath...
            // ... Do some extraordinary cleanup here...
            throw death;   // Rethrow ThreadDeath object...
        }
    }
}
```

Another form of the stop() method takes a Throwable object as its parameter. This allows the user to define his or her own Error class to manage the shutdown of a class's run() method. This would be implemented in a manner very similar to the DeathCatcherThread example just discussed. It is illuminating to note that, for a Thread *t*, a call to

```
t.stop();
```

is equivalent to

```
t.stop(new ThreadDeath());
```

About the Project

The project for this chapter takes requests for numeric calculations and performs these calculations as separate Threads. The user submits the calculations in a series of batches. The program uses a subclass of ThreadGroup to manage these batch submissions. The status of the batches can be requested at any time, even while the calculations are still going on. Some features of the Threads and ThreadGroups can be altered, such as their priority.

Thread and Associated Interface Method Summaries

Table 8-1 summarizes the classes and interfaces necessary for developing custom Thread and related objects in Java. The methods for each class/interface, by category, are listed in Table 8-2. The following sections describe each method in more detail.

Table 8-1 The Thread and related objects classes/interfaces

Class/Interface	Description
Runnable	An interface that can be used to implement threadable classes
Thread	A class for creating and controlling threads of execution
ThreadGroup	A class for writing groups that contain Threads and ThreadGroups
ThreadDeath	An Error subclass that is thrown when a Thread is stopped

Table 8-2 Thread and related objects methods, by category

Class/Interface	Category	Methods
Runnable	Thread execution	run
Thread	Thread execution	destroy, resume, run, start, stop, suspend, yield
	Thread states	currentThread, interrupt, interrupted, isAlive, isInterrupted, join, sleep
	Thread information	getName, setName, toString
	ThreadGroup information	activeCount, checkAccess, enumerate, getThreadGroup
	Priority	getPriority, setPriority
	Daemons	isDaemon, setDaemon
	Debugging	countStackFrames, dumpStack
ThreadGroup	Thread execution	destroy, resume, stop, suspend, uncaughtException
	Enumerating members	activeCount, activeGroupCount, enumerate, list
	General information	checkAccess, getName, getParent, parentOf, toString
	Priority	getMaxPriority, setMaxPriority
	Daemons	isDaemon, setDaemon

The java.lang.Runnable Interface

Table 8-3 summarizes the Runnable Interface, of which the only method is run().

Table 8-3 Summary of Runnable methods

Method	Description
run	Method where threaded activity occurs

RUNNABLE

Description   The Runnable interface provides a way of writing a threaded class without subclassing the Thread class. This interface is critical for cases where your class needs to subclass another class but also needs to run as a thread. Since the Runnable interface's only method is run(), it can be used in these situations instead of a subclassed Thread. Runnable classes are instantiated as a thread by using the Thread constructor. The Runnable run() method is then invoked by calling the Thread's start()

method. The methods of Thread can then be invoked to change the threaded behavior of the Runnable object, such as its priority.

Syntax	public interface **Runnable** extends Object
Package	java.lang
Import	java.lang.Runnable
Constructors	None.
Parameters	None.
See Also	Thread
Example	See the example for the run() method below.

Methods

RUN

Interface Name	Runnable
Description	The method where all threaded activity occurs. The run() method is invoked via the start() method and continues until the method terminates naturally or is killed by the stop() method.
Syntax	public abstract void run()
Parameters	None.
Returns	None.
Exceptions	None.
See Also	Thread
Example	Here is the structure of a typical class that implements Runnable:

```
class MyRunnable implements Runnable {
// Run until terminated by stop()...
public void run() {
while(true) {
    // ... do something...
}
}
}
```

To start the class as a thread you could call

```
new Thread(new MyRunnable()).start();
```

The java.lang.Thread Class

Table 8-4 summarizes the many methods of the Thread class. Table 8-5 lists the constants.

Table 8-4 Summary of Thread methods

Method	Description
activeCount	Returns the number of active Threads in the ThreadGroup of the current Thread
checkAccess	Checks to see if the current Thread can modify this Thread
countStackFrames	Returns the number of stack frames taken by the suspended Thread
currentThread	Returns a reference to the currently executing Thread object
destroy	Used as a last resort to destroy a Thread
dumpStack	Used for debugging, prints the stack trace of the currently executing Thread object
enumerate	Copies, into the provided array, a reference to every active Thread in this Thread's ThreadGroup
getName	Returns this Thread's name
getPriority	Returns this Thread's current priority
getThreadGroup	Returns a reference of the ThreadGroup in which this Thread belongs
interrupt	Sends an interrupt to a Thread
interrupted	Queries whether this Thread has been interrupted
isAlive	Returns information as to whether a Thread is active (has been started but not stopped)
isDaemon	Returns information as to whether or not this is a daemon or user Thread
isInterrupted	Returns information as to whether another Thread has been interrupted
join	Waits indefinitely or for a specified time for this Thread to die
	Waits for the specified time for this Thread to die
	Waits for more precise time for this Thread to die
resume	Resumes execution of the Thread after it has been suspended
run	Method where threaded activity occurs
setDaemon	Designates whether this is a daemon or user Thread
setName	Sets the name of the Thread
setPriority	Sets the priority of the Thread
sleep	Causes the Thread to cease executing for the specified time
start	Starts threaded execution by causing the Thread's run() method to be called
stop	Stop the threaded processing of a Thread
suspend	Suspends the execution of an active Thread
toString	Returns String representation of the Thread
yield	Yields the execution time of this Thread to the next scheduled Thread

Table 8-5 Summary of Thread Constants

Constant	Description
MAX_PRIORITY	Maximum priority of a Thread
MIN_PRIORITY	Minumum priority of a Thread
NORM_PRIORITY	Normal (default) priority of a Thread

THREAD

Description	Developers can create custom threaded classes by writing extensions of the Thread class. This class provides a suite of methods that allows the programmer to create, run, and change the state of a threaded object. The most important method in the Thread class is run(), which is where all the threaded activity occurs. Threads can be stopped, interrupted, and alternately suspended and resumed. Each Thread has a priority, indicating how much processing time a Thread should have relative to other Threads. Thread constructors allow the user to give the Thread a String name or add it to a ThreadGroup. Constructors that combine thread naming, adding to groups, and using Runnable targets are also available.
Syntax	public class **Thread** implements Runnable
Package	java.lang
Import	java.lang.Thread
Constructors	See Constructors section below.
Parameters	See Constructors section below.
See Also	Runnable
Example	Here is the general structure of how to create, run and stop a thread.

```
// Construct a thread with a ...
MyThread t = new MyThread();
t.start();   // Start the thread
// Do something..
t.stop();  // Stop the thread...
```

Constants

MAX_PRIORITY

Class Name	Thread
Description	A Thread can be given more or less processing time by increasing or decreasing its priority. The constant MAX_PRIORITY represents the maximum priority of a Thread. This maximum value is set to 10. The priority of a Thread can be set to MAX_PRIORITY through the setPriority() method. An IllegalArgumentException will be raised if the priority value is set to a value greater than MAX_PRIORITY. Setting the priority to maximum should be done with the understanding that there may be some undesired consequences. In particular, other Threads may not receive the processing time they need when another Thread is running at MAX_PRIORITY.
Syntax	public final static int MAX_PRIORITY
See Also	MIN_PRIORITY, NORM_PRIORITY

Example　　　　　This example prints out the value of the MAX_PRIORITY variable. It uses a custom Thread called myThread, which is structured as follows:

```
// This Thread class loops forever, updating the counter class values.
public class MyThread extends Thread {
// The body of the Thread...
    public void run() {
        // ... do threaded processing here...
    }
}
```

The following prints out the maximum priority:

```
// Use own custom Thread
MyThread th;
th = new MyThread();
// Print out the maximum priority value
System.out.println("Maximum Priority  = " + th.MAX_PRIORITY);
```

MIN_PRIORITY

Class Name	Thread
Description	The minimum priority that a thread can be given is set through the variable MIN_PRIORITY. This value is set to 1. The priority of a Thread can be set to MIN_PRIORITY through the setPriority() method.
Syntax	public final static int MIN_PRIORITY
See Also	MAX_PRIORITY, NORM_PRIORITY
Comments	An IllegalArgumentException will be raised if the priority value is set to a value less than MIN_PRIORITY. Setting the priority to MIN_PRIORITY should be done with the understanding that there may be some undesired consequences. In particular, the Thread may receive too little processing time to manage its tasks in a desirable amount of time.
Example	The following sets the priority of a custom Thread (defined in the MAX_PRIORITY variable discussion) to the lowest priority. It uses getPriority() to display that it has been set to MIN_PRIORITY.

```
MyThread th;
th = new MyThread();
th.setPriority(th.MIN_PRIORITY);
th.start();
System.out.println("The Priority of the thread is " + th.getPriority());
```

NORM_PRIORITY

Class Name	Thread
Description	A newly created thread is set to the default priority value indicated by the variable NORM_PRIORITY. This value is set to 5 and is in the middle of the lower and upper priority bounds MIN_PRIORITY and MAX_PRI-

ORITY, which are set to values of 1 and 10, respectively. The priority can be modified after object instantiation by calling the setPriority() method.

Syntax   public final static int NORM_PRIORITY

See Also   MIN_PRIORITY, MAX_PRIORITY

Comments   The default value can be affected by the MAX_PRIORITY value of the parent ThreadGroup. If this value is less than 5, a new thread may have a default priority that differs from NORM_PRIORITY.

Example   This example resets the priority of a Thread to NORM_PRIORITY if its value is greater than the default value. The custom Thread class, MyThread, is defined in the MAX_PRIORITY variable discussion.

```
MyThread th;
th = new MyThread();
th.start();
// ... do something...
// If a priority is greater than a normal priority, reset to normal value
if (th.getPriority() > th.NORM_PRIORITY)
  th.setPriority(th.NORM_PRIORITY);
System.out.println("The new priority is set to " + th.getPriority());
```

Constructors

The constructors are listed here due to the interrelationship with the Runnable interface and the ThreadGroup Class. Detailed knowledge of these constructors will lead to a deeper appreciation for how Threads work in the Java environment.

THREAD

Class Name   Thread

Description   Constructs a new Thread. Since there are no parameters for this constructor, the new Thread object is given a system-assigned name. The ThreadGroup to which it is assigned is that of the calling Thread. After the Thread is constructed, its run() method must be called to execute the Thread. This method needs to be overridden by the programmer if the class is to perform as a threaded task.

Syntax   public Thread()

Parameters   None.

Example   The following code illustrates the body of a simple Thread and a stand-alone applet that launches it. The class, SimpleThread, is derived from the Thread class, and uses its simple constructor (since it is not overridden). The print message at the end of this code displays the system-assigned name and ThreadGroup.

```
// Our simple thread class
class SimpleThread extends Thread {
    // The run method needs to be overridden!
```

continued on next page

continued from previous page

```
public void run() {
    // Loop until stopped...
while(true) {
    // Do something...
}
}
}

// Stand-alone program that calls the simple thread
public class TestApp {
    SimpleThread th;
     public static void main(String args[]) {
        // Use the simple constructor
        th = new SimpleThread();
        // Start the thread.  Ends up invoking the run method
        th.start();
        System.out.println("System assigned name: " + th.getName());
        System.out.println("System assigned ThreadGroup: " +
            th.getThreadGroup().getName());
    // ...
    }
}
```

THREAD(RUNNABLE TARGET)

Class Name	Thread
Description	This constructor takes a class that implements the Runnable interface as its target. Calling the Thread's start() method applies the run() method of the target, and so executes the class as a thread. This approach is the primary technique that is used to execute a Runnable-based class in a thread. Classes implementing the Runnable interface are typically used in cases where the developer does not want to subclass the Thread class, as when only the run() method will be overridden. The Thread's name and ThreadGroup are automatically assigned when this constructor is used. Calling the Thread's stop() method will terminate the Runnable's run() method processing.
Syntax	public Thread(Runnable *target*)
Parameters	
Runnable *target*	A class that implements the Runnable interface whose run() method is to be applied.
Example	This example shows two different ways of constructing and starting a Runnable Thread. First, a simple class, MyRunnable, is written to implement the Runnable interface. The class features a customized stop() method that is used to indicate when to leave the run() method.

```
// A simple class to implement the runnable interface
class MyRunnable implements Runnable {
    boolean done = false;  // Flag to control when to stop
```

```
    public void run() {
        while(done == false) {
            // Do something...
        } // end while
        // Done set to true, leave run method...
    }
    // Custom stop.  Kick out of run by checking a boolean flag...
    public void stop() {
        done = true;
    }
}
```

The following code shows one way to instantiate the Runnable class and execute its run() method:

```
MyRunnable r;
Thread th;
r = new MyRunnable();  // Instantiate the runnable class
th = new Thread(r);    // Assign it to a thread
  th.start();  // Start MyRunnable's run method...
```

A couple of steps can be removed to simplify this code, provided you do not need the Thread reference at a later time:

```
MyRunnable r;
r = new MyRunnable();  // Instantiate the runnable class
new Thread(r).start();
```

The Thread object does not need to be assigned to a variable because its methods may not be needed, since MyRunnable has its own stop() method, the Thread is system assigned to the current Thread's ThreadGroup, and active Threads are not garbage collected.

To stop the run() method, the MyRunnable class's stop() method can be called. Recall that this method is *not* an override of the Thread's stop() method, but a method completely specific to MyRunnable. It could just as easily be called something else.

```
    // Use the MyRunnable specific method
// to terminate the run() method...
    r.stop();
```

THREAD(THREADGROUP GROUP, RUNNABLE TARGET)

Class Name	Thread
Description	The two parameters of this constructor serve different purposes. The ThreadGroup parameter is used to indicate that the Thread is to be created as part of the specified group. The ThreadGroup class is a container of Threads and can be used as a high-level control of multiple Threads. For example, the suspend() method of ThreadGroup can be used to suspend all active Threads in the group. Classes implementing the Runnable interface are typically used in cases where the developer does not want to subclass the Thread class, as when only the run() method will be

overridden. The Runnable target's run() method is applied when the
Thread's start() method is called.

Syntax   public Thread(ThreadGroup *group*, Runnable *target*)

Parameters

ThreadGroup *group*   The ThreadGroup to which the Thread is to belong.

Runnable *target*   A class that implements the Runnable interface whose run() method is to
                        be applied.

Example   The MyRunnable class in this example is structured the same as its
                        namesake in the example for the constructor Thread(Runnable *target*).

```
      // Create the Runnable class and Thread Group
      MyRunnable r;
      ThreadGroup t;
      t = new ThreadGroup("MyThreadGroup");
      r = new MyRunnable();
      // Create the thread and start the runnable
      // The constructor makes the MyRunnable object
// part of "MyThreadGroup"
      new Thread(t,r).start();
      // ... Do something...
      // Print the active threads in the ThreadGroup
      System.out.println("TestGroup active count = " +
t.activeCount());
      // Kill the run method of the MyRunnable class
      r.stop();
```

THREAD(STRING NAME)

Class Name   Thread

Description   Constructs a new Thread assigned with the name provided in the para-
                        meter. Otherwise, the constructor functions the same as the simple
                        constructor Thread(), discussed earlier.

Syntax   public Thread(String *name*)

Parameters

String *name*   The name assigned to the Thread.

Example   This example shows how to create a Thread with a custom name
                        assigned to it.

```
    MyThread t;
    // Construct a thread with a user defined name...
    t = new MyThread("MyThread #1");
    t.start();   // Start the thread
    // Do something..
t.stop();  // Stop the thread...
```

THREAD(THREADGROUP GROUP, STRING NAME)

Class Name	Thread
Description	Constructs a Thread that has the specified name and is placed in the specified ThreadGroup. The ThreadGroup class is a container of Threads and can be used as a high-level control of multiple Threads. This ThreadGroup, for example, can be used to simultaneously reprioritize, resume, suspend, or stop a group of Threads.
Syntax	public Thread(ThreadGroup *group*, String *name*)
Parameters	
ThreadGroup *group*	The ThreadGroup to which the Thread is to belong.
String *name*	The name assigned to the Thread.
Example	This applet constructs two Threads (of class MyThread) as part of the same ThreadGroup. MyThread does nothing more than loop and print out its name (assigned in the constructor). The ThreadGroup object is used to enumerate its Threads into an array. This array is processed to start and stop the Threads.

```
import java.lang.*;
// Custom Thread that does nothing but print asterisks
class MyThread extends Thread {
    // ...
    // This is the constructor for ThreadGroups
    public MyThread(ThreadGroup grp, String name) {
        super(grp,name);
    }
    // Threaded processing goes here...
    public void run() {
        int i = 0;
        // Loop until stopped...
        while(true) {
            // Occasionally print out the name...
            if (++i > 10000) {
                        System.out.println("*");
                i = 0;
            }
        } // end while
    }
}

// The applet that creates two instances of MyThread which both belong to a
// local ThreadGroup.
public class TestApp extends java.applet.Applet {
    ThreadGroup grp;
        public void init() {
        // Create the thread group and add threads...
        grp = new ThreadGroup("My Thread Group");
```

continued on next page

continued from previous page

```
        new MyThread(grp,"MyThread #1");
        new MyThread(grp,"MyThread #2");
        // Create an array for enumerating the group...
        Thread th_array[];
        th_array = new Thread[grp.activeCount()];
        // Start both threads in the group by enumerating the group...
        int count = grp.enumerate(th_array);
        for (int i = 0; i < count; ++i)  {
                System.out.println("Start thread " +
th_array[i].getName());
th_array[i].start();
        }
        // ...
        // Do something...
        // ...
        // Kill the threads...
        for (int i = 0; i < count; ++i) {
                System.out.println("Stop thread " +
th_array[i].getName());
                th_array[i].stop();
        }
// ...
    }
}
```

THREAD(RUNNABLE TARGET, STRING NAME)

Class Name	Thread
Description	This constructor takes a class that implements the Runnable interface as its target, giving the Thread the specified name. Calling the Thread's start() method applies the run() method of the target, and so executes the class as a Thread. Classes implementing the Runnable interface are typically used in cases where the developer does not want to subclass the Thread class. Calling the Thread's stop() method will terminate the Runnable's run() method. The ThreadGroup of the Thread is that of the Thread in which it was created.
Syntax	public Thread(Runnable *target*, String *name*)
Parameters	
Runnable *target*	A class that implements the Runnable interface whose run() method is to be applied.
String *name*	The name assigned to the Thread.
Example	This example creates a Thread with an instance of MyRunnable as its target and a user defined string as its name. MyRunnable was defined in the example of the constructor Thread(Runnable *target*) discussed earlier.

```
        MyRunnable r;
        r = new MyRunnable();  // Instantiate the runnable class
        // Construct the thread (giving it a name) and start the
// runnable...
        new Thread(r,"Runnable Thread").start();
```

THREAD(THREADGROUP GROUP, RUNNABLE TARGET, STRING NAME)

Class Name	Thread
Description	This constructor ties all the elements of the other Thread constructors into a single call. It places the Thread into a ThreadGroup that can be used to manage multiple Threads. The constructor also takes as a parameter a class that implements the Runnable interface as its target. Calling the Thread's start() method applies the run() method of the target, and so executes the class as a threaded object. Calling the stop() method of the Thread or its ThreadGroup will terminate the Runnable's run() method. The last parameter gives the Thread the specified name.
Syntax	public Thread(ThreadGroup *group*, Runnable *target*, String *name*)
Parameters	
ThreadGroup *group*	The ThreadGroup to which the Thread is to belong.
Runnable *target*	A class that implements the Runnable interface whose run() method is to be applied.
String *name*	The name assigned to the Thread.
Example	This example executes a couple of Threads that launch Runnable targets (myRunnable). The Threads are assigned user names and are placed in a ThreadGroup. The ThreadGroup is used to kill both Threads at once by calling its stop() method.

```
    // Create the thread group and add Threads with Runnable targets
    ThreadGroup grp = new ThreadGroup("My Thread Group");
    new Thread(grp,new MyRunnable(),"MyRunnable #1");
    new Thread(grp,new MyRunnable(),"MyRunnable #2");
    // Start both threads in the group by enumerating the group...
    Thread th_array[];
    th_array = new Thread[grp.activeCount()];
    int count = grp.enumerate(th_array);
    for (int i = 0; i < count; ++i)  {
            System.out.println("Start thread " +
th_array[i].getName());
            th_array[i].start();
    }
    // ...
    // Do something....
    // ...
    // Kill the threads...
    grp.stop();
```

Methods

ACTIVECOUNT

Class Name	Thread
Description	Returns the number of active Threads in the ThreadGroup of the currently executing Thread object. An active Thread is one that has been started but not stopped.
Syntax	public static int activeCount()
Parameters	None.
Returns	The number of active Threads of the currently executing Thread's ThreadGroup.
Exceptions	None.
See Also	ThreadGroup
Example	This example launches a Thread object, TestThread, which prints its active count. A ThreadGroup object, TestGroup, then launches TestThread as part of its group. Counterintuitively, the stand-alone Thread displays "2" as its active count, whereas the Thread in the group displays "1". This is because the stand-alone Thread is in the ThreadGroup of the top-level Thread—hence the value 2.

```
import java.lang.*;

// A Thread that prints its active count at the start of the run() method..
class TestThread extends Thread {
    // Pass the constructors through to its superclass...
    public TestThread(ThreadGroup tg, String thread_name) {
        super(tg,thread_name);
    }
    public TestThread() {
        super();
    }
    // Start theaded processing by printing out
// the activeCount of its group...
    public void run() {
        System.out.println("TestThread ActiveCount: " + activeCount());
        // Do something...
    }
}

// A customized ThreadGroup that creates and starts a Thread that prints out its active
count...
class TestGroup extends ThreadGroup {
    public TestGroup(String name) {
        super(name);
        TestThread th;
        th = new TestThread(this,"TestThread");
th.start();
// Do something...
    }
```

```
}

// A stand-alone program for printing out active counts...
public class TestApp  {
    // Entry point of stand-alone program..
     public static void main(String args[]) {
    // The active count that is printed out by this Thread is two...
        TestThread th = new TestThread();
        th.start();
        // ... .
        // The active count in this Thread will be one...
        TestGroup t = new TestGroup("TestGroup");
    }

}
```

CHECKACCESS

Class Name	Thread
Description	Checks to see if the current Thread can modify this Thread. When a Thread is created it is assigned either manually or automatically to a ThreadGroup. ThreadGroups are used, among other things, to control access to a Thread. This prevents Threads that do not have proper access from modifying or accessing each other. For example, if ThreadGroup A contains ThreadGroup B, then a Thread in A can access a Thread in B.
Syntax	public void checkAccess()
Parameters	None.
Returns	None.
Exceptions	A SecurityException is raised if the current Thread is not allowed to access this Thread.
See Also	ThreadGroup
Example	This example illustrates a simple access relationship. A stand-alone application creates a ThreadGroup with a single Thread. It checks to see if it has access to this Thread and prints the result. It in fact has access because the top-level ThreadGroup *contains* the ThreadGroup with the Thread. Consequently, it can access and modify those Threads. In this case, it both starts and stops the Thread.

```
public class TestApp  {
    public static void main(String args[]) {
        // Create the ThreadGroup and add Thread...
        ThreadGroup grp = new ThreadGroup("My Thread Group");
        MyThread th = new MyThread(grp);
        // Start the thread. We can because we have access!
        th.start();
        // Print if if we have access to it...
        String access;
        try {    // This will work!
```

continued on next page

continued from previous page

```
      th.checkAccess();
        access = new String("allowed");
    }
    catch (SecurityException se) {
        access = new String("forbidden");
    }
    System.out.println("Access is " + access);  // allowed!
    // Do something...
    // ...
    // Kill the thread...
    th.stop();
    System.out.println("Done!");
  }
}
```

countStackFrames

Class Name	Thread
Description	Returns the number of stack frames being used by the suspended Thread. If the Thread is not suspended when this method is called, an exception is thrown. This method is used mainly for debugging purposes.
Syntax	public int countStackFrames()
Parameters	None.
Returns	The number of stack frames taken by the suspended Thread.
Exceptions	Throws an IllegalThreadStateException if the Thread is not suspended.
See Also	dumpStack()
Example	A custom Thread is defined as follows:

```
// Sample Thread with multiple stack frames
class MyThread extends Thread {
// Threaded processing goes here...
    public void run() {
        runit();  // Force stack frames to be at least two...
    }
// This is where the actual work will be done..
    void runit() {
        while(true) {
            // do something...
        }  // end while
    }
}
```

Since the active Thread will always be in the runit() method, the number of stack frames taken by a MyThread object will always be at least two. This is the output reflected by the following actions on the Thread:

```
// Create and start the Thread...
MyThread t;
t.start();
```

```
    // ...
    // Suspend the Thread to get the stack frame count... .
    t.suspend();
    System.out.println("The number of stack frames = " +
t. countStackFrames());
    // ...
    // Resume the  Thread...
    t.resume();
```

CURRENTTHREAD

Class Name	Thread
Description	References the currently executing Thread object. This may not be the same as the Thread that is referenced.
Syntax	public static Thread currentThread()
Parameters	None.
Returns	A reference to the currently executing Thread object.
Exceptions	None.
See Also	Any Thread method.
Example	The following code gets the reference to the current Thread so that it can be made to sleep half a second:

```
    Thread t = Thread.currentThread();
try {
t.sleep(500);
}
catch (InterruptedException e) { }
```

DESTROY

Class Name	Thread
Description	Used as a last resort to destroy a Thread. Usually stop() is used to terminate a Thread, but if there is some errant behavior, it might be desirable to use the stronger destroy() to kill the Thread. The destroy() method is a graceless version of stop() and has the problem that any monitors (such as a synchronized object) that are locked are not unlocked. This means that the program can enter into a deadlocked state if another Thread is waiting on the locked monitor. Consequently, destroy() should be used with great discretion.
Syntax	public void destroy()
Parameters	None.
Returns	None.
Exceptions	None.
See Also	stop(), ThreadDeath

Comments	At the time of this writing (Java Developer's Kit (JDK) 1.0), destroy() had not been implemented. Calling the method results in a NoSuchMethodError.
Example	This example calls destroy(), handling the NoSuchMethodError that results from the method's not being implemented yet. It exits the program when the error is caught.

```
      MyThread t;
      t = new MyThread();
      t.start();
      //... .
System.out.println("Destroy the thread!");
      try {
          t.destroy();
      }
          catch (NoSuchMethodError e) {
     System.out.println("Caught destroy error!");
          System.exit(0);
      }
```

DUMPSTACK

Class Name	Thread
Description	This is used to print the stack trace of the currently executing Thread object. This trace is similar to the one that appears in standard error when an unhandled exception occurs. The dumpStack() method is useful for debugging problems, such as unusual exceptions.
Syntax	public static void dumpStack()
Parameters	None.
Returns	None.
Exceptions	None.
See Also	countStackFrames()
Example	In a custom Thread object, this example dumps the stack when an unusual exception occurs.

```
// Sample Thread that dumps the stack if there is an error
class MyThread extends Thread {
    // Threaded processing goes here...
        public void run() {
            // ...
// At some point MyMethod will be called directly
// or indirectly...
        }
        // Some internal method that dumps the stack when an internal
        // exception occurs...
        private myMethod(void) {
            // ...
            // Try something that may cause internal exception...
     try {
                // ... normal code...
```

```
        }
catch (MyException e) {
// ... dump information about the exception...
// Dump the stack for more debug info...
dumpStack();
}
            // ...
        }
}
```

ENUMERATE

Class Name	Thread
Description	Copies a reference to every active Thread in this Thread's ThreadGroup into the provided array. The programmer can then iterate through the array and execute methods of the individual Threads. The method activeCount() can be employed to ascertain the size of the array.
Syntax	public static int enumerate (Thread *list[]*)
Parameters	
Thread *list[]*	The array into which the Thread references are to be copied.
Returns	The number of references placed into the array.
Exceptions	None.
See Also	ThreadGroup
Example	This prints out information about the active Threads in a thread's ThreadGroup.

```
// This code is within an internal method of a Thread class.
Thread thArray[];
thArray = new Thread[activeCount()];
int count = enumerate(thArray);
System.out.println("# Threads enumerated: " + count);
for (int i = 0; i < count; ++i) {
    System.out.println("Thread " + i + " Name: " + th_Array[i].getName() +
        " Priority: " + thArray[i].getPriority());
}
```

GETNAME

Class Name	Thread
Description	Returns a Thread's name. The name can be set by the programmer through any of a number of constructors. If these constructors are not used, then Java automatically assigns a name. The Thread can be renamed via the setName() method.
Syntax	public final String getName()
Parameters	None.

Returns	The Thread's name.
Exceptions	None.
See Also	setName()
Example	The following code stores the name of the Thread in a String variable and displays it.

```
// Define a custom Thread
class TestThread extends Thread {
    // Threaded processing goes here...
    public void run() {
        String s = getName();
System.out.println("Thread Name: " + s);
// Do work...
    }
}
```

GETPRIORITY

Class Name	Thread
Description	Returns the Thread's current priority. Threads function by sharing slices of processing time. A Thread can be given more or less processing time by increasing or decreasing its priority. Two Thread constants, MIN_PRIORITY and MAX_PRIORITY, set the lower and upper bounds of the acceptable priority values; these are set to 1 and 10, respectively. The default is NORM_PRIORITY, set to 5.
Syntax	public final int getPriority()
Parameters	None.
Returns	The Thread's priority value. It will be in the range MIN_PRIORITY to MAX_PRIORITY, inclusive.
Exceptions	None.
See Also	setPriority()
Example	The following code prints out a Thread's priority as well as the values of the Thread priority constants (typically 1, 5, and 10, respectively). The custom Thread, MyThread, is defined in the section on Thread variables.

```
        // Create and start the custom Thread..
        MyThread th;
        th = new MyThread();
        th.start();
        // Print out priority information.
        // This will output 5 (Normal Priority)
        System.out.println("Thread Priority: " + th.getPriority());
        // This will output 1, 5, and 10, respectively.
        System.out.println("Constant Priorities.  Min = " +
th.MIN_PRIORITY
+ " Normal = " + th.NORM_PRIORITY + " Max = " + th.MAX_PRIORITY);
```

GETTHREADGROUP

Class Name	Thread
Description	Returns the ThreadGroup in which a Thread belongs. ThreadGroups contain Threads and other ThreadGroups. All user Threads belong to a ThreadGroup. The primary application Thread belongs to the top-level ThreadGroup (the ancestor of all other ThreadGroups). The ThreadGroup returned from this method can have its methods executed to retrieve other information, such as the name of the ThreadGroup.
Syntax	public final ThreadGroup getThreadGroup()
Parameters	None.
Returns	A reference to the Thread's ThreadGroup.
Exceptions	None.
See Also	Constructors
Example	This applet prints the name of the ThreadGroup in which the Applet Thread belongs. It uses the static currentThread() method to get a reference to the top-level Thread.

```
// Test applet that prints out the name of the top-level ThreadGroup
public class TestApp extends java.applet.Applet  {
    public void init() {
        // Use static currentThread methods to get the
        // primary Thread.  Then print the name of its ThreadGroup..
        System.out.println("Top-level ThreadGroup: " +
            Thread.currentThread().getThreadGroup().getName());
        // ...
    }
}
```

INTERRUPT

Class Name	Thread
Description	This method is used to send an interrupt to a Thread.
Syntax	public void interrupt()
Parameters	None.
Returns	None.
Exceptions	None.
Comments	At the time of this writing (JDK 1.0), interrupt() had not been implemented. Calling the method results in a NoSuchMethodError.
Example	This example calls interrupt(), handling the NoSuchMethodError that results from the method's not being implemented yet.

```
// Create and start the Thread
TestThread t;
t = new TestThread();
t.start();
//... .
// Interrupt is not implemented so an Error is thrown..
try {
    t. interrupt();
}
catch (NoSuchMethodError e) {
    System.out.println("Interrupt not implemented.");
}
```

INTERRUPTED

Class Name	Thread
Description	This method queries whether a Thread has been interrupted.
Syntax	public static boolean interrupted()
Parameters	None.
Returns	Boolean true if the Thread has been interrupted.
Exceptions	None.
Comments	At the time of this writing (JDK 1.0), interrupted() had not been implemented. Calling the method results in a NoSuchMethodError.
Example	This example calls interrupted(), handling the NoSuchMethodError that results from the method's not being implemented yet.

```
// Create and start the Thread
TestThread t;
t = new TestThread();
t.start();
//... .
// Interrupted is not implemented so an Error is thrown..
try {
    System.out.println("The thread interrupted state is " +
t.interrupted());
}
catch (NoSuchMethodError e) {
    System.out.println("Interrupted not implemented.");
}
```

ISALIVE

Class Name	Thread
Description	This method is used to determine whether a Thread is active. An active Thread is one that has been started but not stopped. The thread can stop by terminating naturally (exiting its run() method) or having the stop() method applied to it.
Syntax	public final boolean isAlive()

Parameters	None.
Returns	Boolean true if the Thread is alive. False means it is not active.
Exceptions	None.
See Also	start(), run(), stop()
Example	This example uses isAlive() to tell whether a Thread is active. If it is, then the Thread is stopped. Before the program proceeds to other work, the join() method is called to wait for the Thread to die.

```
      // Create and start a custom Thread...
      MyThread t;
      t = new MyThread();
      t.start();
      // do something...
      // Now see if the Thread is alive. If so, then kill it...
      if (t.isAlive())
t.stop();
      //Wait for thread to die...
      try {
          t.join();
      }
      catch (InterruptedException e) {
// Just exit if Thread can't be killed...
          System.exit(0);
      }
      System.out.println("It's dead, Jim");
      // ... do more work...
```

ISDAEMON

Class Name	Thread
Description	This method returns information as to whether or not a Thread is a daemon. Daemon Threads are systemwide Threads whose services can be made available to objects throughout an application. A classic daemon is a print spooler. Threads that are not daemons are user Threads. The isDaemon() method returns the daemon flag of a Thread. This flag is a boolean indicating whether the Thread is a user or daemon Thread. A true value indicates that it is a Daemon thread.
Syntax	public final boolean isDaemon()
Parameters	None.
Returns	Boolean true if the Thread is a daemon. False means it is a user Thread.
Exceptions	None.
See Also	setDaemon()
Example	In this example, the KillIfNotADaemon() method checks to see whether or not the Thread is a daemon. If it is not a daemon, then the Thread is killed. If it is to be killed, the method waits until it is dead by employing the join() method.

```
// Kill this thread if it is not a daemon..
void KillIfNotADaemon(Thread thr) {
    // Is it a daemon?
    if (thr.isDaemon() == false) {
        System.out.println("Not a daemon. Kill it!");
        // Yes, kill it!
        thr.stop();
        // Wait until it is dead...
        try {
            thr.join();
            System.out.println("Thread stopped");
        }
        catch () { }
    }
    else
        System.out.println("It's a daemon. Leave alone...");
}
```

ISINTERRUPTED

Class Name	Thread
Description	This method queries as to whether another Thread has been interrupted.
Syntax	public boolean isInterrupted()
Parameters	None.
Returns	Boolean true if another Thread has been interrupted.
Exceptions	None.
Comments	At the time of this writing (JDK 1.0), isInterrupted() had not been implemented. Calling the method results in a NoSuchMethodError.
Example	This example calls interrupted(), handling the NoSuchMethodError that results from the method's not being implemented yet.

```
        // Create and start a Thread...
        TestThread t;
        t = new TestThread();
        t.start();
        // Since isInterrupted is not implemented,
// an error will be thrown..
        //... .
        try {
 System.out.println("Another Thread has been interrupted is " +
t.isInterrupted());
        }
        catch (NoSuchMethodError e) {
            System.out.println("isInterrupted not implemented.");
        }
```

JOIN

Class Name	Thread
Description	Join() makes the calling Object wait indefinitely for a Thread to "die." A Thread is dead when its run() method has concluded or the Thread's stop() method has been invoked. Although a Thread is dead, it is still a valid object. This means that methods can still be invoked on the object, such as querying for data. If some Thread processing needs to be completed before a thread dies, it would be useful to employ the join() method to wait for the Thread to conclude. In general, it is always useful to use join() when a Thread is stopped, because Threads often do not terminate as quickly as one might expect. The time parameter states how many milliseconds the calling Object should wait before the Thread dies. It may be desirable to put in a time parameter if it is possible that the Thread could take an indefinite amount of time to finish processing (it acts like it is "hung"). If the time specified in the parameter expires, then the Object continues processing regardless of what happened to the Thread. Note that one millisecond is 10^{-3} of a second, whereas a nanosecond is 10^{-9} of a second.
Syntax	public final void join() throws InterruptedException
	public final void join(long *milliseconds*) throws InterruptedException
	public final void join(long *milliseconds*, int *nanoseconds*) throws InterruptedException
Parameters	
long *milliseconds*	The number of milliseconds to wait for a Thread to die.
int *nanoseconds*	The number of nanoseconds to wait in addition to the milliseconds.
Returns	None.
Exceptions	An InterruptedException is thrown if the Thread has been interrupted by another Thread. This exception must be caught.
See Also	stop()
Example	The following code outline illustrates a Thread (WorkThread) that performs some work and does not leave until its Boolean member doneBaton is set to false. It then makes some final calculations, cleans up, and "dies" by the leaving the run() method. The parent object, JoinApp, illustrates the join() method by stopping the Thread and waiting for it to conclude.
	The code also illustrates use of Java's synchronized modifier. In this case, the flag for telling the Thread to conclude (the Boolean doneBaton) is

locked with the *synchronized* keyword. This prevents the WorkThread
and JoinApp objects from accessing the baton object at the same time.

```java
import java.lang.*;
// Custom Thread that has Boolean modifier (doneBaton) that indicates when a Thread should
// terminate...
class WorkThread extends Thread {
public Boolean doneBaton;  // Indicates if Thread should keep running...
    int calcValue;  // Calculated value that is produced in the Thread...
    // Constructor: Set up the baton...
    public WorkThread() {
        super();    // Call superclass constructor...
        doneBaton = new Boolean(false);   // Set baton to false...
    }
    // Execute threaded code here...
    public void run() {
        // Internal flag is set to true when baton is set to true..
        boolean stoploop = false;
        while(stoploop == false) {
            // DO SOME CALCULATIONS
            // modify CalcValue...
            // ...
            // Wait for the lock...
            synchronized(doneBaton) {
                // Quit if some other object has set baton to True...
                if (doneBaton.equals(Boolean.TRUE))
                    stoploop = true;
            }
        }  // end while
        // Leave run...
        // Clean up...
        // After we leave here the thread is "dead"
    }
    // Return what was calculated by the Thread...
public int getCalculatedValue() {
return calcValue;  // The calculated value..
}
}

// Stand-alone application starts custom calculation Thread
public class JoinApp  {
    public static void main(String args[]) {
        // Create and start the custom Thread...
        WorkThread th;
        th = new WorkThread();
        th.start();
        // Do something here...
        // ...
        // Now kill the thread. Wait for the lock...
        synchronized(th.doneBaton) {
          th.doneBaton = Boolean.TRUE;
        }
        // Wait till its dead...
        try {
            th.join();
            System.out.println("Thread stopped");
        }
        catch (InterruptedException e) {     }
```

```
        // Do something with the results of the Thread
        th.getCalculatedValue();
    }

}
```

This example illustrates this version of the join() method by stopping a custom Thread and waiting a half second for it to die. A Thread can be terminated by other methods besides stop(). It could have an internal flag that is set to tell it to finish processing (see join() method). In this example, MyThread loops until its done flag is set to true; this is accomplished through its public method finishProcessing(). Since the MyThread's exit cleanup might take a while, the calling Object calls join() with the millisecond parameter.

```
// A custom Thread that is terminated via its own finishProcessing method...
// It has some cleanup that needs to be done after it is done processing - this
// may take a while...
class MyThread extends Thread {
    boolean done = false;      // Process until this is set to true...
    // Threaded processing goes here...
    public void run() {
        // Delay...
        while(done == false) {
            // ... Do something...
        } // end while
        // Clean up code that might take a while..
        // ....
    }
    // This is called by the external object to stop the run method
    public void finishProcessing() {
        done = true;
    }
}
```

Here is the calling Object code.

```
// Create and start the thread...
        MyThread t = new MyThread();
        t.start();
        // ... Do something...
        // Stop the thread through its custom stop..
        t.finishProcessing();
        // Wait half a second for it to die...
        long timeToWait = 500;  // Half a second...
        try {
            t.join(timeToWait);
        }
        catch (InterruptedException e) { }
        // ... It's dead. Continue...
```

This example shows a calling Object that waits one and a half milliseconds for a Thread to die.

```
// Wait 1 and a half milliseconds for a thread to die...
try {
    t.join(1,500000);
```

continued on next page

continued from previous page

```
    }
    catch (InterruptedException e) {    // Error...
        System.out.println("Interrupted thread exception");
        System.exit(0);
    }
```

RESUME

Class Name	Thread
Description	This method resumes the execution of a Thread after its processing has temporarily been halted through the suspend() method. If the suspend() method has not been called previously (the Thread is still running), no action will be taken with no exception raised.
Syntax	public final void resume()
Parameters	None.
Returns	None.
Exceptions	None.
See Also	suspend()
Example	This code shows how the resume() and suspend() methods can be used to toggle a custom Thread's processing state:

```
  // Toggle the running of a Thread between being suspended and resumed
  // On Parameter says what state to put it - true means resume
// Returns true if thread is resumed, false if not running or suspended
  boolean toggleThreadState(Thread thr, boolean on) {
      // Check if thread is alive, if not then leave...
      if (thr.isAlive() == false) {
          System.out.println("Thread is not alive!");
          return false;
      }
      // Suspend the thread...
      if (on == false) {
          System.out.println("Suspend running thread");
          thr.suspend();
          return false;
      }
      else {  // Resume the thread...
          System.out.println("Resume thread");
          thr.resume();
          return true;
      }
  }
```

RUN

Class Name	Thread
Description	The method where all threaded activity occurs. This method needs to be overridden by the programmer if any work is to happen. The run() method is invoked via the start() method and continues until the method terminates naturally or is killed by the stop() method. It can also catch the ThreadDeath object or other thrown objects to determine when and how to terminate; see the stop() methods for details.
Syntax	public void run()
Parameters	None.
Returns	None.
Exceptions	None.
See Also	start(), stop()
Example	Here is the structure of a typical Thread class:

```
class MyThread extends Thread {
// Run until terminated by stop()...
public void run() {
while(true) {
    // ... do something...
}
}
}
```

To instantiate and start the Thread you could call

```
MyThread t = new MyThread();
t.start();
```

SETDAEMON

Class Name	Thread
Description	The setDaemon() method is used to designate whether a Thread is to be a daemon or user Thread. Daemon Threads are systemwide Threads whose services can be made available to objects throughout an application. A classic daemon is a print spooler. Threads that are not daemons are user threads. Since the default value of a Thread is user, this method only needs to be called if a daemon Thread is desired. The setDaemon() method needs to be called before a Thread is activated, otherwise an exception will occur.
Syntax	public final void setDaemon(boolean *on*)

Parameters

boolean *on*   Set to true if the Thread is to be a daemon. A false value indicates that it
                             should be a user Thread.

Returns   None.

Exceptions   An IllegalThreadStateException is thrown if this method is called after a
                             Thread has been started.

See Also   isDaemon()

Example   This code takes a user defined Thread and launches it as a daemon.

```
// Create the object...
MyDaemon th;
th = new MyDaemon();
// Set the Thread as a daemon...
th.setDaemon(true);
// Start the thread...
th.start();
```

SETNAME

Class Name   Thread

Description   Sets the name of a Thread. Java automatically assigns a default name if a
                             name is not set in the Thread's constructor. The setName() method can
                             be used to assign a new name.

Syntax   public final void setName(String *name*)

Parameters

String *name*   The new name of the thread.

Returns   None.

Exceptions   None.

See Also   getName()

Example   Here is some code that creates a thread, displays its Java-created name,
                             changes its name to a user defined name, displays the name, and then
                             reverts back to the original name.

```
th = new NameThread();
String orgName = th.getName();
System.out.println("Original Thread name: " + th.getName());
// Start the thread
th.start();
th.setName("My Thread #1");
System.out.println("New Thread name: " + th.getName());
th.setName(orgName);
System.out.println("Back to old Thread name: " + th.getName());
```

SETPRIORITY

Class Name	Thread
Description	This method sets the priority of a Thread. A Thread can be given more or less processing time by increasing or decreasing its priority. The setPriority() method sets the priority within the range MIN_PRIORITY and MAX_PRIORITY, inclusive, which are public Thread integer constants. The minimum priority is set to 1, and the high value is set to 10.
Syntax	public final void setPriority(int *pr*)
Parameters	
int *pr*	The new priority value needs to be in the range MIN_PRIORITY to MAX_PRIORITY, inclusive; otherwise, an exception will be thrown. The range is also subject to the maximum priority value of the Thread's ThreadGroup.
Returns	None.
Exceptions	An IllegalArgumentException object is thrown if the priority value is invalid.
See Also	getPriority()
Example	Here is a method that sets the priority of a Thread, trapping the exception.

```
boolean SetPriority(Thread th,int pty) {
    boolean ret = true;
    try {
        th.setPriority(pty);
    }
    catch (IllegalArgumentException e) {
        System.out.println("Set Priority error...");
        ret = false;
    }
    return ret;  // Returns true if success, else error
}
```

SLEEP

Class Name	Thread
Description	This method causes the Thread to sleep for a certain number of milliseconds. Periodically, it may be necessary to suspend a Thread's activities for a period of time. Sometimes this amount may be very short, long enough to give processing time to another Thread. The delay may also be a necessary part of the internal timing of the Thread, such as how it displays something. The sleep() method causes the currently executing Thread to sleep for a specified amount of time.

Syntax	public static void sleep(long *milliseconds*) throws InterruptedException
	public static void sleep(long *milliseconds*, int *nanoseconds*) throws InterruptedException

Parameters

long *milliseconds*	The number of milliseconds to wait for the Thread to sleep.
int *nanoseconds*	The number of nanoseconds to wait in addition to the milliseconds.

Returns   None.

Exceptions   An InterruptedException object is thrown if the Thread has been interrupted by another Thread.

Example   This example consists of a Thread that does little more than emit asterisks after sleeping a specified amount of time. The default delay is 1000 milliseconds (one second). However, a constructor is provided to set a custom delay.

```
// A class that emits asterisks to standard output...
class SleepStarThread extends Thread {
    long sleepTime = 1000; // Default - sleep a second between emissions...
    // Constructor that just uses default sleep time.....
    public SleepStarThread() { }
    // Employ user-defined timing..
    public SleepStarThread(long delay) {
        sleepTime = delay;
    }
    // The threaded processing  loops and emit asterisks...
    public void run() {
        // Loop until stopped...
        while(true) {
            // Sleep a bit before throwing out a star...
            try {
                // Sleep some custom number of milliseconds
                sleep(sleepTime);
        // Sleep one and a half milliseconds
Thread.currentThread().sleep(1,500000);
            }
            catch (InterruptedException e) {     }
            // Emit an asterisk
            System.out.println("*");
        } // end while
    }
}
```

To construct and start the Thread to sleep half a second between asterisk emissions, use the following:

```
SleepStarThread t = new SleepStarThread(500);
t.start();
```

START

Class Name	Thread
Description	This method will cause the run() method to be called, causing threaded sequential execution to begin. After the start() method begins the Thread, control returns immediately to the calling Thread.
Syntax	public synchronized void start()
Parameters	None.
Returns	None.
Exceptions	An IllegalThreadStateException is thrown if the thread has already been started.
See Also	run(), stop()
Example	This following code illustrates a custom start() method, which calls its superclass start() method to activate the run() method. It will usually not be the case that the start() method will need to be overridden (initialization can occur in the constructor), but it is done here for illustrative purposes.
	The start() method called by the applet traps the exception caused by the Thread that has already been started.

```
// A Thread that has a custom start method..
class StartTestThread extends Thread {
    int data;    // Internal data...
    // This custom start() invokes the run method after
// initalizing the data...
    public synchronized void start() {
        data = 100;
        super.start();  // Cause the run method to be invoked...
    }
    // Threaded processing  Do something with the
// data initialized in start
    public void run() {
        System.out.println("Data = " + data);
        // ...
    }
}

// An Applet that creates and starts the custom Thread...
public class StartTestApp extends java.applet.Applet  {
    public void init() {
        // ...
        // Instantiate and start the Thread..
        StartTestThread th;
        th = new StartTestThread();
```

continued on next page

continued from previous page

```
        try {
            th.start();
        }
        // Catch a double start exception (even though
// it won't happen here...)
        catch (IllegalThreadStateException e) {
            System.out.println("Thread already started...");
        }
        // ...
    }
}
```

STOP

Class Name	Thread
Description	This is the most widely used method to stop a Thread. It forces the Thread to leave its run() method and so conclude its processing sequence. The internals on how stop() works are illuminating. The stop() method throws a ThreadDeath object at the Thread. ThreadDeath is not an Exception object (which is already caught frequently by Thread classes), but a type of Error. The ThreadDeath Error is a Thread specific way of saying that the user has issued the stop() method. In general, it is not necessary to catch ThreadDeath, unless some special cleanup process needs to occur. If ThreadDeath is caught by the Thread, then it needs to be rethrown so that the Thread will die. No error will be passed to a top-level error handler if this is not handled properly.
Syntax	public synchronized void stop()
Parameters	None.
Returns	None.
Exceptions	None.
See Also	ThreadDeath
Example	This example shows a Thread that catches ThreadDeath. It performs some cleanup, and then rethrows the ThreadDeath object.

```
// A custom Thread that custom catches ThreadDeath errors
class DeathCatcherThread extends Thread {
    // Threaded processing continues until ThreadDeath
    public void run() {
        try {
            // Loop forever...
            while (true) {
// Do something...
}
        }
        catch (ThreadDeath death) {   // Catch ThreadDeath...
            //   Do some extraordinary cleanup here...
            throw death;   // Rethrow ThreadDeath object...
```

```
            }
        }
    }
```

Here is how the calling Object executes (no pun intended) DeathCatcherThread:

```
// Create and start the thread...
DeathCatcherThread t = new DeathCatcherThread();
t.start();
//   do something...
// Stop the thread.  Note the simplicity of the call...
t.stop();
// continue...
```

STOP(THROWABLE O)

Class Name	Thread
Description	This version of the stop() method is an alternative approach to terminating a Thread (as opposed to the stop() method with no parameters). This method lets the user define a custom Throwable object to be caught when a Thread is to be stopped. The stop() method with no parameters throws a ThreadDeath object at the Thread. ThreadDeath is not an Exception object (which is already caught frequently by Thread classes), but a type of Error. The ThreadDeath Error is a Thread specific way of saying that the user has issued the stop() method. While the use of this technique to stop a Thread is not encouraged, it may be necessary if some unusual exception handling is required.
Syntax	public final synchronized void stop(Throwable o)
Parameters	
Throwable o	The Throwable object that is to be thrown at the Thread.
Returns	None.
Exceptions	None.
See Also	ThreadDeath
Example	The first part of this example defines a simple Error class that is a custom Error object for the Thread class that is described next.

```
// Custom Error class simply builds on the Error class...
class CustomThreadDeathError extends Error {}
```

The CustomDeathCatcherThread class is a custom Thread class that catches CustomThreadDeathError to terminate its run() method.

```
// A Thread class with a custom way of stopping a Thread...
class CustomDeathCatcherThread extends Thread {
    // Threaded processing until custom error is thrown (or ThreadDeath)...
    public void run() {
        try {
            // Loop forever...
```

continued on next page

continued from previous page

```
            while (true) {
// Do something...
}
        }
        catch (CustomThreadDeathError death) {    // Catch custom error...
            // ... Do some extraordinary cleanup here...
            // Throw ThreadDeath to really die...
            throw new ThreadDeath();
        }
    }
}
```

To process this class, the following code needs to be executed:

```
// Create and start the thread...
CustomDeathCatcherThread t = new CustomDeathCatcherThread();
t.start();
// ... Do something...
// Kill the Thread, using the custom Throwable object...
t.stop(new CustomThreadDeathError());
```

The default version of stop() calls this version of stop(). Technically,

```
t.stop(new ThreadDeath());
```

is the same as

```
t.stop();
```

where t is a Thread object.

SUSPEND

Class Name	Thread
Description	This method suspends the execution of a Thread. The Thread's processing can be continued by calling the resume() method. No action will be taken (and no exception is raised) if the Thread is already suspended.
Syntax	public final void suspend()
Parameters	None.
Returns	None.
Exceptions	None.
See Also	resume()
Example	This code shows how the resume() and suspend() methods can be used to toggle a custom Thread's processing state.

```
// Toggle the running of a thread between being suspended and resumed
// On Parameter says what state to put it - true means resume
// Returns true if thread is resumed, false if not running
// or suspended
    boolean toggleThreadState(Thread thr, boolean on) {
        // Check if thread is alive, if not then leave...
        if (thr.isAlive() == false) {
```

```
        System.out.println("Thread is not alive!");
        return false;
    }
    // Suspend the thread...
    if (on == false) {
        System.out.println("Suspend running thread");
        thr.suspend();
        return false;
    }
    else {  // Resume the thread...
        System.out.println("Resume thread");
        thr.resume();
        return true;
    }
}
```

TOSTRING

Class Name	Thread
Description	This method is used to return information about a Thread in a formatted string. The information includes the name of the Thread, its priority, and its ThreadGroup.
Syntax	public String toString()
Parameters	None.
Returns	A String with the name, priority, and ThreadGroup of a Thread.
Exceptions	None.
See Also	String
Example	This example creates a custom Thread, setting its name and priority. The code uses the toString() method to display information about the Thread.

```
MyThread t = new MyThread("My Custom Name");
t.start();
// Set its priority
t.setPriority(4);
// Display info about it
System.out.println(t.toString());
```

YIELD

Class Name	Thread
Description	This method is used to yield the CPU time of the currently executing Thread so that another Thread may be given CPU time. Threads function by sharing slices of CPU time. Java's scheduling algorithm determines how this time is to be divided. Sometimes there is a point in a Thread's sequential processing where it is desirable to give up CPU time to another process. Yielding is a way of letting the next scheduled running Thread be executed.

Syntax	public static void yield()
Parameters	None.
Returns	None.
Exceptions	None.
See Also	sleep()
Example	This code shows how a Thread might be structured to yield time to another Thread.

```
public void run() {
      // Loop forever...
      while (true) {
// Do some intensive processing
yield();   // Let some other Thread run
// More intensive processing
}
   }
```

The java.lang.ThreadGroup Class

Table 8-5 summarizes the methods of ThreadGroup.

Table 8-5 Summary of ThreadGroup methods

Method	Description
activeCount	Returns number of active Threads in this ThreadGroup
activeGroupCount	Returns number of ThreadGroups in this ThreadGroup
checkAccess	Checks to see whether the current Thread is allowed to modify this ThreadGroup
destroy	Marks a ThreadGroup as destroyed so no new Threads can be added to it
enumerate	Copies, into the provided array, a reference to every active Thread or ThreadGroup in this ThreadGroup
getMaxPriority	Returns the maximum priority of any Thread belonging to this ThreadGroup
getName	Returns the name of this ThreadGroup
getParent	Returns the parent of this ThreadGroup
isDaemon	Returns information as to whether or not this ThreadGroup is a daemon
list	Used for debugging, prints information about the Threads and ThreadGroups in this ThreadGroup
parentOf	Returns information as to whether or not this ThreadGroup is a parent of or equal to the parameter ThreadGroup
resume	Resumes all Threads in a ThreadGroup that have been suspended
setDaemon	Sets the daemon state of a ThreadGroup
setMaxPriority	Sets the maximum priority of any Thread belonging to this ThreadGroup
stop	Stops the execution of all Threads in the ThreadGroup
suspend	Suspends the execution of all Threads in the ThreadGroup
toString	Returns the String representation of the ThreadGroup
uncaughtException	Allows the ThreadGroup to catch an exception that is thrown when one of the Threads in the group has entered an uncaught exception state

THREADGROUP

Description   ThreadGroups contain a set of Threads or other ThreadGroups. They are used to provide a group-level control over the operations of Threads. A ThreadGroup method such as suspend(), resume(), or stop() is applied to every active Thread in a ThreadGroup. This makes it easier to have a high-level control over the synchronization of Threads. For example, a background ThreadGroup responsible for formatting images can have all of its Threads suspended and then resumed at once, freeing the programmer from having to manually invoke these methods on each of the Threads. Every Thread in an application belongs to a ThreadGroup. Because of its hierarchical structure, ThreadGroup methods are often nested. That is, an invoked ThreadGroup method may be also applied to the child ThreadGroups. For example, the stop() method not only stops all Threads in a ThreadGroup, but also terminates all Threads in its child ThreadGroups. The enumerate() method, which lists Threads or groups within a ThreadGroup, has an optional parameter that lets the programmer decide whether or not child groups should be inspected. The hierarchical relationship also extends to ThreadGroup access methods; child groups have restricted access to ancestor groups.

Syntax   public class **ThreadGroup** extends Object

Package   java.lang

Import   java.lang.ThreadGroup

Constructors   See Constructors section below.

Parameters   See Constructors section below.

See Also   Thread

Example   The following code shows a ThreadGroup contained within another ThreadGroup. The use of enumerate in this case is set to not recurse into this child ThreadGroup.

```
    // Set up a parent and child ThreadGroup...
ThreadGroup grpParent = new ThreadGroup("Parent Group");
ThreadGroup grpChild = new ThreadGroup(grpParent,"Child Group");
    // ... . Add Threads to the ThreadGroup
    // Create and size array to get enumerated info...
    Thread thArray[];
    thArray = new Thread[grpParent.activeCount()];
    // Set recurse flag to false
    boolean recurse = false;
    // Walk through the group, displaying the name and
    //  priority of each Thread...
    int count = grpParent.enumerate(thArray,recurse);
    System.out.println("# Threads enumerated: " + count);
    for (int i = 0; i < count; ++i) {
System.out.println("Thread " + i + " Name: " +
thArray[i].getName() + "
Priority: " + thArray[i].getPriority());
    }
```

ThreadGroup(String name)

Class Name	ThreadGroup
Description	Constructs a new ThreadGroup assigned with the name provided in the parameter. Since ThreadGroups can contain other ThreadGroups and are nested within a hierarchy of ThreadGroups, this group will need a ThreadGroup parent. In this constructor, the ThreadGroup will be assigned to the ThreadGroup of the current Thread.
Syntax	public **ThreadGroup**(String *name*)
Parameters	
String *name*	The name assigned to the ThreadGroup.
Returns	None.
Example	This example constructs two Threads (of class MyThread) as part of the same ThreadGroup. The ThreadGroup object is used to enumerate its Threads into an array. This array is walked through (via the enumerate() method) to start and stop the Threads.

```
// Create the thread group and add threads...
ThreadGroup grp = new ThreadGroup("My Thread Group");
new MyThread(grp,"MyThread #1");
new MyThread(grp,"MyThread #2");
// Create an array for enumerating the group...
Thread th_array[];
th_array = new Thread[grp.activeCount()];
// Start both threads in the group by enumerating the group...
int count = grp.enumerate(th_array);
for (int i = 0; i < count; ++i)  {
        System.out.println("Start thread " + th_array[i].getName());
th_array[i].start();
     }
// ...
// Do something...
// ...
// Kill the threads...
for (int i = 0; i < count; ++i) {
        System.out.println("Stop thread " +
th_array[i].getName());
        th_array[i].stop();
     }
```

ThreadGroup(ThreadGroup parent, String name)

Class Name	ThreadGroup
Description	Constructs a new ThreadGroup assigned with the name provided in the parameter. Since ThreadGroups can contain other ThreadGroups, this method allows the new ThreadGroup to be specified as a child of a parent ThreadGroup. This hierarchical structure of ThreadGroups is important, since methods applied to a parent ThreadGroup (such as

stop() or setMaxPriority()) are recursively assigned to the child ThreadGroups and their corresponding Threads.

Syntax public **ThreadGroup**(ThreadGroup *parent*, String *name*)

Parameters

ThreadGroup parent The parent ThreadGroup to which the ThreadGroup is assigned.

String name The name assigned to the ThreadGroup.

Returns None.

Example This example creates a parent ThreadGroup to which a child ThreadGroup is assigned. These each contain one Thread. The parent ThreadGroup setMaxPriority() call is used to recursively set the maximum priority of all the Threads. Likewise, the stop() method of the Parent ThreadGroup is used to recursively stop all the Threads.

```
    // Create the parent ThreadGroup
    ThreadGroup grpParent = new ThreadGroup("Parent Group");
    // Add a child to it...
    ThreadGroup grp = new ThreadGroup(grpParent,"Child Group");
    // Recursively set the maximum priority to all Threads...
    grpParent.setMaxPriority(4);
    // Assign a Thread to the parent ThreadGroup
    MyThread t = new MyThread(grpParent,"In Parent ThreadGroup");
    // Assign a Thread to the child ThreadGroup
    MyThread t2 = new MyThread(grp,"In Child ThreadGroup");
    //    start the Threads
    //    do something
    // Recursively stop all the Threads in the Parent
// ThreadGroup and its children...
    grpParent.stop();
```

Methods

ACTIVECOUNT

Class Name ThreadGroup

Description Recursively returns an estimate of the number of active Threads in the ThreadGroup. An active Thread is one that has been started, but not stopped. Since ThreadGroups can contain other ThreadGroups, the figure returned also includes any Threads contained in child ThreadGroups of this ThreadGroup.

Syntax public synchronized int **activeCount()**

Parameters None.

Returns The number of active Threads in the ThreadGroup.

Exceptions None.

See Also activeGroupCount()

Example This stand-alone program fragment illustrates the nested quality of ThreadGroups. The program creates a parent ThreadGroup to which a child ThreadGroup is assigned. These child Threadgroups each contain one Thread. After the Threads are started, the ThreadGroups are queried for the number of active Threads. Also queried is the top-level ThreadGroup, which contains both of these groups; the static currrentThread() method is used to get information about this ThreadGroup. The top-level ThreadGroup always has one Thread running, namely the main program Thread. Because of the nested relationships of these programs, the activeCount() output of the printouts is 3 for the top-level ThreadGroup, 2 for the parent ThreadGroup, and 1 for the child ThreadGroup.

```
// Stand-alone application to display active counts of Threadgroups...
public class TestApp  {
    public static void main(String args[]) {
        // Create the parent ThreadGroup
        ThreadGroup  grpParent = new ThreadGroup("Parent Group");
        // Add a child to it...
        ThreadGroup  grp = new ThreadGroup(grpParent,"Child Group");
        // Recursively set the maximum priority to all Threads...
        grpParent.setMaxPriority(4);
        // Assign a Thread to the parent ThreadGroup
        MyThread t = new MyThread(grpParent,"In Parent ThreadGroup");
        // Assign a Thread to the child ThreadGroup
        MyThread t2 = new MyThread(grp,"In Child ThreadGroup");
        // Start the Threads
        t.start();
        t2.start();
        // Show the number of active Threads
        // Use static currentThread() methodto get the active
// count in the top-level ThreadGroup
        System.out.println("# of active Threads in Top-level
ThreadGroup = "
            + Thread.currentThread().getThreadGroup().activeCount());
        System.out.println("# of active Threads in parent ThreadGroup = "
            + grpParent.activeCount());
        System.out.println("# of active Threads in child ThreadGroup = "
            + grp.activeCount());
        // ... .
    }
}
```

ACTIVEGROUPCOUNT

Class Name	ThreadGroup
Description	Recursively returns an estimate of the number of ThreadGroups in this ThreadGroup. Since ThreadGroups can contain other ThreadGroups, the figure returned also includes any ThreadGroups contained in the child ThreadGroups of this ThreadGroup.
Syntax	public synchronized int activeGroupCount ()

Parameters	None.
Returns	The number of ThreadGroups in the ThreadGroup.
Exceptions	None.
See Also	activeCount()
Comments	In the JDK 1.0, it is not clear why this method is called "active." The number of ThreadGroups returned is not impacted by the amount of active Threads in the group. The example illustrates this.
Example	This example shows the issue raised in the Comment above by creating a Parent ThreadGroup with a child ThreadGroup that has an active Thread, and a child with no Thread. Surprisingly, the output from the print out for the number of "active" ThreadGroups in the parent is 2. The value of 1 would be expected, since there is nothing really "active" about the ThreadGroup grpNoThread. As expected, the child ThreadGroup returns a value of 0, since it contains no other ThreadGroups.

```
        // Create the parent ThreadGroup
        ThreadGroup grpParent = new ThreadGroup("Parent Group");
        // Add a child to it...
        ThreadGroup grp = new ThreadGroup(grpParent,"Child Group");
        ThreadGroup grpNoThread = new ThreadGroup(grpParent,
"No Thread Group");
        // Recursively set the maximum priority to all Threads...
        grpParent.setMaxPriority(4);
        // Assign a Thread to the parent ThreadGroup
        MyThread t = new MyThread(grpParent,"In Parent ThreadGroup");
        // Assign a Thread to the child ThreadGroup
        MyThread t2 = new MyThread(grp,"In Child ThreadGroup");
 // Start the threads...
        t.start();
        t2.start();
System.out.println("# of active Groups in parent ThreadGroup = "
            + grpParent.activeGroupCount());
        System.out.println("# of active Groups in child ThreadGroup = "
            + grp.activeGroupCount());
```

CHECKACCESS

Class Name	ThreadGroup
Description	This method checks to see whether the current Thread is allowed to modify a ThreadGroup. ThreadGroups are used, among other things, to control access to and from a Thread. This prevents Threads that do not have proper access from modifying other ThreadGroups. For example, if ThreadGroup A contains ThreadGroup B, then a Thread in A can access ThreadGroup B. Access from group B to group A is restricted, however. A SecurityException is raised if modification of this ThreadGroup is forbidden.
Syntax	public void **checkAccess**()
Parameters	None.

Returns	None.
Exceptions	A SecurityException is thrown if the current Thread is not allowed to modify this ThreadGroup.
See Also	SecurityException
Example	This example Thread class does little more than loop and check for access to a ThreadGroup when a value is set through the setTestGroupAccess() method. The Thread performs one access test, prints the result, resets the ThreadGroup flag (to prevent another test), and then waits for another test request.

```java
// Example Thread that checks access to a ThreadGroup
class CheckAccessThread extends Thread {
    ThreadGroup testGroup;
    // Constructor that adds it to a ThreadGroup
    public CheckAccessThread(ThreadGroup grp,String name) {
        super(grp,name);
    }
    // Add a group to be tested...
    public void setTestGroupAccess(ThreadGroup grp) {
        testGroup = grp;
    }
    // Loop and check access to a current thread...
    public void run() {
            // Loop until stopped, running access tests...
            while(true) {
                // See if we have access to the test ThreadGroup...
                if (testGroup != null) {
                    String access;
                    try { // Exception means access is forbidden
                        testGroup.checkAccess();
                        access = new String("allowed");
                    }
                    catch (SecurityException se) {
                        access = new String("forbidden");
                    }
System.out.println("Access to group "
+ testGroup.getName()      + " is "
+ access);
                    // Reset for next test...
                    testGroup = null;
                }
                try {   // Sleep a while for the next test
                    sleep(50);
                }
                catch (InterruptedException e) {     }
            } // end while
    }
}
```

DESTROY

Class Name	ThreadGroup
Description	This method marks a ThreadGroup as destroyed. This means that the group can no longer have Threads added to it. It is not permitted to destroy a ThreadGroup that currently has one or more active Threads; doing so will result in an IllegalThreadStateException being raised.
Syntax	public final synchronized void **destroy()**
Parameters	None.
Returns	None.
Exceptions	An IllegalThreadStateException is thrown if the ThreadGroup has an active Thread belonging to it.
See Also	stop()
Example	This example shows when it is and is not legal to destroy a ThreadGroup. After creating a ThreadGroup with an active Thread, the program attempts to destroy the group. Since it has an active Thread, the attempt fails. The code then stops the Thread and tries to destroy the group again, this time with success. It then tries to add a Thread to the ThreadGroup. This fails, however, because the ThreadGroup has been destroyed.

```
// Create the parent ThreadGroup
    ThreadGroup grpParent = new ThreadGroup("Parent Group");
    // Assign a Thread to the parent ThreadGroup
    MyThread t = new MyThread(grpParent,"In Parent ThreadGroup");
    // Start the thread...
    t.start();
    // ... do something...
    // Destroy the ThreadGroup with running Thread
    // This will fail!
    try {
        grpParent.destroy();
    }
    catch (IllegalThreadStateException e) {
System.out.println("Cannot destroy ThreadGroup
with running Thread...");
    }
    // ...

    // Stop the Thread first. Then destroy...
    t.stop();
    // Wait for the Thread to die
    try {
        t.join();
    }
    catch (InterruptedException e) { }
    // This will succeed now!
    grpParent.destroy();
    // ... .

    // This will fail now!
    new MyThread(grpParent,"Will Not Work");
```

ENUMERATE

Class Name	ThreadGroup
Description	Copies, into the provided array, a reference to every active Thread or ThreadGroup in this ThreadGroup. The programmer can then iterate the array and execute methods of the individual Threads or ThreadGroups. The array must be large enough to hold all references; this size can be determined with activeCount() for Threads and activeGroupCount() for enumerating ThreadGroups. The boolean parameter is used to control whether or not the enumeration should recurse into child ThreadGroups. If the boolean is set to true, then all Threads in the contained ThreadGroup hierarchy are placed into the output array. Otherwise, the method only looks at this ThreadGroup.
Syntax	public static int **enumerate** (Thread *list[]*)
	public static int **enumerate** (Thread *list[]*, boolean *recurse*)
	public static int **enumerate** (ThreadGroup *list[]*)
	public static int **enumerate** (ThreadGroup *list[]*, boolean *recurse*)
Parameters	
Thread *list[]*	The array into which the Thread references are to be copied.
ThreadGroup *list[]*	The array into which the ThreadGroup references are to be copied.
boolean *recurse*	True if the method should recurse into contained ThreadGroups, false if it should only look at this ThreadGroup.
Returns	The number of references placed into the array.
Exceptions	None.
See Also	list()
Example	This prints out information about the active Threads in a ThreadGroup:

```
ThreadGroup grpParent = new ThreadGroup("Parent Group");
   //  .  Add Threads to the ThreadGroup

    // Create and size array to get enumerated info
    Thread thArray[];
    thArray = new Thread[grpParent.activeCount()];
    // Walk through the group, displaying the name and
    //  priority of each Thread
    int count = grpParent.enumerate(thArray);
    System.out.println("# Threads enumerated: " + count);
    for (int i = 0; i < count; ++i) {
System.out.println("Thread " + i +
" Name: " + thArray[i].getName() +
" Priority: " + thArray[i].getPriority());
    }
```

The following code shows a ThreadGroup contained within another ThreadGroup. The use of enumerate() in this case is set to not recurse into this child ThreadGroup.

```
    // Set up a parent and child ThreadGroup...
ThreadGroup grpParent = new ThreadGroup("Parent Group");
```

```
ThreadGroup grpChild = new ThreadGroup(grpParent,"Child Group");
    // . Add Threads to the ThreadGroup...

    // Create and size array to get enumerated info...
    Thread thArray[];
    thArray = new Thread[grpParent.activeCount()];
    // Set recurse flag to false
    boolean recurse = false;
    // Walk through the group, displaying the name and
    //  priority of each Thread...
    int count = grpParent.enumerate(thArray,recurse);
    System.out.println("# Threads enumerated: " + count);
    for (int i = 0; i < count; ++i) {
System.out.println("Thread " + i + " Name: "
+ thArray[i].getName() +
" Priority: " + thArray[i].getPriority());
    }
```

This prints out information about the active ThreadGroups in a ThreadGroup.

```
    // Create the parent ThreadGroup
    ThreadGroup grpParent = new ThreadGroup("Parent Group");
    //   add ThreadGroups and Threads...

    // Create the reference array...
    ThreadGroup thgrpArray[];
    thgrpArray = new ThreadGroup[grpParent.activeGroupCount()];
    // Enumerate the parent ThreadGroup, displaying each ThreadGroup's
    // name and active Thread count...
    int count = grpParent.enumerate(thgrpArray);
    System.out.println("# Thread Groups enumerated: " + count);
    for (int i = 0; i < count; ++i) {
System.out.println("Thread Group" + i +
" Name: " + thgrpArray[i].getName() +
" # of Active Threads = " + thgrpArray[i].activeCount());
    }
```

The following code shows a ThreadGroup contained within another ThreadGroup. The use of enumerate() in this case is set to not recurse into this child ThreadGroup.

```
    // Create the parent and child ThreadGroups...
ThreadGroup grpParent = new ThreadGroup("Parent Group");
ThreadGroup grpChild = new ThreadGroup(grpParent,"Child Group");
    // ... . Add Threads to the ThreadGroup...

    // Create the reference array...
    ThreadGroup thgrpArray[];
    thgrpArray = new ThreadGroup[grpParent.activeGroupCount()];
    // Enumerate the parent ThreadGroup, displaying each ThreadGroup's
    // name and active Thread count...
    // Set recurse flag to false
    boolean recurse = false;
    int count = grpParent.enumerate(thgrpArray,recurse);
    System.out.println("# Thread Groups enumerated: " + count);
    for (int i = 0; i < count; ++i) {
System.out.println("Thread Group" + i +
" Name: " + thgrpArray[i].getName() +
" # of Active Threads = " + thgrpArray[i].activeCount());
    }
```

GETMAXPRIORITY

Class Name	ThreadGroup
Description	This method returns the maximum priority of any Thread belonging to this ThreadGroup. Threads function by sharing slices of processing time. A Thread can be given more or less processing time by increasing or decreasing its priority. ThreadGroups can be used to set a maximum priority for any Threads that are contained in the group. This maximum priority is set recursively for any ThreadGroups contained in the group. Any Threads in these subgroups that attempt to change their priority will have their priority level restricted to a value at or below this maximum value. The highest value the ThreadGroup maximum priority can be set at is the MAX_PRIORITY constant of a Thread (see discussion of Thread priorities under Changing the State of a Thread, earlier in this chapter), which is 10. Likewise, the lowest maximum priority is the Thread's MIN_PRIORITY constant, which is set to 1.
Syntax	public final int **getMaxPriority()**
Parameters	None.
Returns	The ThreadGroup's maximum priority value. It will be in the range of the Thread constant values of MIN_PRIORITY to MAX_PRIORITY, inclusive (which are set to 1 and 10, respectively).
Exceptions	None.
See Also	setMaxPriority()
Example	This example creates a parent ThreadGroup with a child ThreadGroup, each of which has a Thread. The maximum priority of the parent is set to 4 through the setMaxPriority() method. This maximum priority is recursively applied to the child ThreadGroup and the corresponding Threads. The getMaxPriority() method used in the print commands reflects this change.

```
    // Create the ThreadGroups
    ThreadGroup grpParent = new ThreadGroup("Parent Group");
    ThreadGroup grpChild = new ThreadGroup(grpParent,"Child Group");
    // Set the max priority of the parent.
// This is recursively applied to the child.
grpParent.setMaxPriority(4);
    // Assign a Thread to the parent ThreadGroup
    MyThread t = new MyThread(grpParent,"In Parent ThreadGroup");
    MyThread t2 = new MyThread(grpChild,"In Child ThreadGroup");
    // Start the thread...
    t.start();
    t2.start();
    // Print out the various priority values...
System.out.println("Max Priority for Parent = " +
grpParent.getMaxPriority());
    System.out.println("Max Priority for Child = " +
```

```
grpChild.getMaxPriority());
        System.out.println("Thread 1 priority = " + t.getPriority());
        System.out.println("Thread 2 priority = " + t2.getPriority());
```

GETNAME

Class Name	ThreadGroup
Description	The getName() method returns the name of this ThreadGroup. ThreadGroups must be assigned a name in their constructor.
Syntax	public final String **getName()**
Parameters	None.
Returns	A String representing the name of this ThreadGroup.
Exceptions	None.
See Also	See the Constructors section.
Example	This code fragment prints the name of the ThreadGroup. In this case the name that is output is "My ThreadGroup".

```
ThreadGroup grp = new ThreadGroup("My ThreadGroup");
System.out.println("The name of the ThreadGroup is " + grp.getName());
```

GETPARENT

Class Name	ThreadGroup
Description	This method returns the parent of this ThreadGroup. Since ThreadGroups can contain other ThreadGroups, and are nested within a hierarchy, ThreadGroups will always have a parent, except for the top-level ThreadGroup (to which all groups belong). One of the ThreadGroup constructors sets the parent of a new ThreadGroup. In the other constructor, the parent is automatically set to the ThreadGroup of the current Thread.
Syntax	public final ThreadGroup **getParent()**
Parameters	None.
Returns	The parent ThreadGroup of this ThreadGroup.
Exceptions	None.
See Also	See the Constructors section.
Example	This applet code prints the parent-child relationships of related ThreadGroups. The parent of the grpParent ThreadGroup is the top-level ThreadGroup. Its system-assigned name is "applet- ParentTestApp".

```
public class ParentTestApp extends java.applet.Applet   {
public void init() {
    // Create a Parent ThreadGroup with a Child...
```

continued on next page

continued from previous page

```
ThreadGroup grpParent = new ThreadGroup("The Parent");
ThreadGroup grpChild = new ThreadGroup(grpParent,"The Child");
// Print out their name relationships
System.out.println("The parent of " + grpParent.getName() +
            " is " + grpParent.getParent().getName());
System.out.println("The parent of " + grpChild.getName() +
        " is " + grpChild.getParent().getName());
// ...
    }
}
```

ISDAEMON

Class Name	ThreadGroup
Description	Returns information as to whether or not the ThreadGroup is a daemon. Daemon ThreadGroups provide services that are available throughout an application. This means that some of the ThreadGroup access restrictions are relaxed if it is a daemon. The ThreadGroup is destroyed when the last Thread or ThreadGroup in the group is terminated. The flag that is returned by the isDaemon() method is a boolean indicating whether the ThreadGroup is a daemon. A true value indicates that it is a daemon. Otherwise, it is not.
Syntax	public final boolean **isDaemon()**
Parameters	None.
Returns	Boolean true if the ThreadGroup is a daemon. False means it is not.
Exceptions	None.
See Also	setDaemon()
Example	This example queries a ThreadGroup's services if it is a daemon.

```
MyThreadGroup grp = new ThreadGroup("Daemon ThreadGroup");
    // ...
    if (grp.isDaemon() )
        // ... query its services...
```

LIST

Class Name	ThreadGroup
Description	To be used only for debugging, this method recursively descends through a ThreadGroup, printing to the standard system output each ThreadGroup and Thread that is contained in the group. The output is formatted in an outline style, with nested relationships being indicated by nested tabbing. For ThreadGroups, that information is the name of the group and its priority. For Threads, the output is the Thread name, its priority, and the name of its ThreadGroup.

Syntax	public synchronized void **list()**
Parameters	None.
Returns	None.
Exceptions	None.
See Also	See the Constructors section.
Example	In this example, a parent-child ThreadGroup relationship is created in a stand-alone application. The parent and child each have a Thread. Using the static currentThread() method, all of the ThreadGroups and Threads in the current application are sent to the standard output by applying the list method to the top-level ThreadGroup.

```
// A stand-alone application that uses the list method to illustrate
// parent-child ThreadGroup relationships...
public class ListTestApp  {
    public static void main(String args[]) {
        // Create the parent ThreadGroup
        ThreadGroup grpParent = new ThreadGroup("Parent Group");
        ThreadGroup grpChild = new ThreadGroup(grpParent,"Child Group");

        // Assign Threads to the ThreadGroups
        MyThread t = new MyThread(grpParent,"In Parent ThreadGroup");
        MyThread t2 = new MyThread(grpChild,"In Child ThreadGroup");

        // Print all of the ThreadGroups and Threads in the application
        // from the top-level ThreadGroup.
        Thread.currentThread().getThreadGroup().list();
        // ...
    }
}
```

PARENTOf

Class Name	ThreadGroup
Description	The parentOf() method returns information as to whether this ThreadGroup is a parent of or equal to the ThreadGroup provided in the parameter. Since ThreadGroups are nested in a hierarchical relationship, and actions of a parent ThreadGroup affect the child ThreadGroups, this relationship is important.
Syntax	public final boolean **parentOf**(ThreadGroup *grp*)
Parameters	
ThreadGroup *grp*	The ThreadGroup to be tested as to whether it is a child of or equal to this ThreadGroup.
Returns	A boolean indicating whether or not this ThreadGroup is a parent of or equal to the ThreadGroup provided in the parameter. A true value means that it is a parent of or equal to the parameter ThreadGroup; otherwise, it is neither.

Exceptions	None.
See Also	See the Constructors section.
Example	This example creates parent and child ThreadGroups and prints to standard output their parentOf relationships. The first output ("Parent is parentOf Child is") returns true, the other returns false.

```
// Create the parent and child ThreadGroups
ThreadGroup grpParent = new ThreadGroup("Parent Group");
ThreadGroup grpChild = new ThreadGroup(grpParent,"Child Group");

// This prints out true...
System.out.println("Parent is parentOf Child is " +
grpParent.parentOf(grpChild));
// This prints out false...
System.out.println("Child is parentOf Parent is " +
grpChild.parentOf(grpParent));
```

RESUME

Class Name	ThreadGroup
Description	This method resumes the execution of all Threads in a ThreadGroup that have had their processing temporarily halted through the suspend() method (issued by the Thread or an appropriate ThreadGroup). The resume() method is recursively applied to any child subgroups and their corresponding Threads. After this method is complete, all Threads in this ThreadGroup and its subgroups will be in an active processing state.
Syntax	public final synchronized void **resume()**
Parameters	None.
Returns	None.
Exceptions	None.
See Also	suspend()
Example	This code creates two ThreadGroups, with the child group contained in the parent. Each has an active Thread. After a while, both Threads are suspended through the issuance of the suspend() method from the parent ThreadGroup. After another delay, their processing is resumed through the execution of the like-named method of the parent ThreadGroup.

```
// Create the parent and child ThreadGroups
    ThreadGroup grpParent = new ThreadGroup("Parent Group");
ThreadGroup grpChild = new ThreadGroup(grpParent,"Child Group");
```

```
    // Assign a Thread to each ThreadGroup
    MyThread t = new MyThread(grpParent,"In Parent ThreadGroup");
    MyThread t2 = new MyThread(grpChild,"In Child ThreadGroup");

    // Start the threads...
    t.start();
    t2.start();

    // ... Do something...

    // Suspend all the threads...
    grpParent.suspend();

    // ... Do more work...

    // Resume all the threads...
    grpParent.resume();
```

SETDAEMON

Class Name	ThreadGroup
Description	Sets the ThreadGroup daemon state. Daemon ThreadGroups provide services that are available throughout an application. This means that some of the ThreadGroup access restrictions are relaxed if it is a daemon. The ThreadGroup is destroyed when the last Thread or ThreadGroup in the group is terminated. This should be called before any Threads are started in the group, since Threads need to know their daemon state before they are run.
Syntax	public final void **setDaemon** (boolean *on*)
Parameters	
boolean *on*	Set to true if the ThreadGroup is to be a daemon.
Returns	None.
Exceptions	None.
See Also	isDaemon()
Example	This code creates a ThreadGroup. It is set as a daemon, then threads are added and started.

```
    // Create the group, set it as a daemon...
MyThreadGroup grp = new ThreadGroup("Daemon ThreadGroup");
grp.setDaemon(true);
// Add and start the Threads...
    new MyThread(grp,"Daemon #1").start();
    new MyThread(grp,"Daemon #2").start();
```

SETMAXPRIORITY

Class Name	ThreadGroup
Description	This method sets the maximum priority of any Thread belonging to this ThreadGroup. Threads function by sharing slices of processing time. A Thread can be given more or less processing time by increasing or decreasing its priority. ThreadGroups can be used to set a maximum priority for any Threads that are contained in the group. This maximum priority is set recursively for any ThreadGroups contained in the group. Any Threads in these subgroups that attempt to change their priority will have their priority level restricted to a value at or below this maximum value. The highest value to which the ThreadGroup maximum priority can be set is the MAX_PRIORITY constant of a Thread (see discussion of Thread priorities under Changing the State of a Thread, earlier in this chapter), which is 10. Likewise, the lowest maximum priority is the Thread's MIN_PRIORITY constant, which is set to 1.
Syntax	public final synchronized void **setMaxPriority** (int *pri*)
Parameters	
int *pri*	The new priority value needs to be in the range of the Thread constant values of MIN_PRIORITY to MAX_PRIORITY (which are set to 1 and 10, respectively).
Returns	None.
Exceptions	None.
See Also	getMaxPriority()
Example	This example creates a parent ThreadGroup with a child ThreadGroup, each of which has a Thread. The maximum priority of the parent is set to 4 through the setMaxPriority() method. This maximum priority is recursively applied to the child ThreadGroup and the corresponding Threads. The getMaxPriority() method used in the print commands reflects this change.

```
    // Create the ThreadGroups
    ThreadGroup grpParent = new ThreadGroup("Parent Group");
    ThreadGroup grpChild = new ThreadGroup(grpParent,"Child Group");
    // Set the max priority of the parent.
// This is recursively applied to the child.
grpParent.setMaxPriority(4);
    // Assign a Thread to the parent ThreadGroup
    MyThread t = new MyThread(grpParent,"In Parent ThreadGroup");
    MyThread t2 = new MyThread(grpChild,"In Child ThreadGroup");
    // Start the Thread...
    t.start();
    t2.start();
```

```
// Try to change the thread values and show their restrictions
t.setPriority(6);
t2.setPriority(7);
// The new priorities should be set at 4
System.out.println("Thread 1 priority = " + t.getPriority());
System.out.println("Thread 2 priority = " + t2.getPriority());
```

STOP

Class Name	ThreadGroup
Description	This method stops the execution of all Threads in a ThreadGroup. The stop() method is recursively applied to any child subgroups and their corresponding Threads. After this method is complete, all Threads in this ThreadGroup and its subgroups should be dead.
Syntax	public final synchronized void stop()
Parameters	None.
Returns	None.
Exceptions	None.
See Also	Thread
Example	This code creates two ThreadGroups, with the child group contained in the parent. Each has an active Thread. After a while, both Threads are terminated through the issuance of the parent ThreadGroup stop() method.

```
// Create the parent and child ThreadGroups
    ThreadGroup grpParent = new ThreadGroup("Parent Group");
ThreadGroup grpChild = new ThreadGroup(grpParent,"Child Group");

    // Assign a Thread to each ThreadGroup
    MyThread t = new MyThread(grpParent,"In Parent ThreadGroup");
    MyThread t2 = new MyThread(grpChild,"In Child ThreadGroup");

    // Start the threads...
    t.start();
    t2.start();

    // ... Do something...

    // Stop all the threads...
    grpParent.stop();
```

SUSPEND

Class Name	ThreadGroup
Description	This method suspends the execution of all Threads in a ThreadGroup. The suspend() method is recursively applied to any child subgroups and their corresponding Threads. After this method is complete, all Threads in this ThreadGroup and its subgroups will be in a suspended state.
Syntax	public final synchronized void **suspend()**
Parameters	None.
Returns	None.
Exceptions	None.
See Also	resume()
Example	This code creates two ThreadGroups, with the child group contained in the Parent. Each has an active Thread. After a while, both Threads are suspended through the issuance of the suspend() method from the parent ThreadGroup. After another delay, their processing is resumed through the execution of the like-named method of the parent ThreadGroup.

```
// Create the parent and child ThreadGroups
   ThreadGroup grpParent = new ThreadGroup("Parent Group");
ThreadGroup grpChild = new ThreadGroup(grpParent,"Child Group");

   // Assign a Thread to each ThreadGroup
   MyThread t = new MyThread(grpParent,"In Parent ThreadGroup");
   MyThread t2 = new MyThread(grpChild,"In Child ThreadGroup");

   // Start the threads...
   t.start();
   t2.start();

   // ... Do something...

   // Suspend all the threads...
   grpParent.suspend();

   // ... Do more work...

   // Resume all the threads...
   grpParent.resume();
```

TOSTRING

Class Name	ThreadGroup
Description	This method is used to return information about a ThreadGroup in a formatted String. The information includes the name of the ThreadGroup and its priority.
Syntax	public String **toString()**
Parameters	None.
Returns	A String with the name and priority of the ThreadGroup.
Exceptions	None.
See Also	String
Example	This code creates a ThreadGroup and displays its String representation.

```
// Create the ThreadGroup
ThreadGroup MyThreadGroup = new ThreadGroup("My ThreadGroup");
// Print out its String representation.
System.out.println(MyThreadGroup.toString());
```

UNCAUGHTEXCEPTION

Class Name	ThreadGroup
Description	This method is called when a Thread in a group has entered an uncaught exception state. This gives the ThreadGroup a chance to clean up the situation.
Syntax	public void **uncaughtException** (Thread *t*, Throwable *o*)
Parameters	
Thread *t*	The Thread that has the exception
Throwable *o*	The exception object.
Returns	None.
Exceptions	None.
See Also	Throwable
Example	In this example, the MyThreadGroup class is structured to handle uncaughtException().

```
class MyThreadGroup extends ThreadGroup {
    public void uncaughtException(Thread t, Throwable e) {
        // ... do something...
    }
}
```

The java.lang.ThreadDeath Class

THREADDEATH

Description	When the user calls the stop() method to end a Thread, an instance of the ThreadDeath class is thrown at the Thread to be terminated. ThreadDeath is a subclass of Error, which is derived from the Throwable class. ThreadDeath is not an Exception, because these are caught as part of normal programming practice. The ThreadDeath Error is a Thread specific way of saying that the user has issued the stop() method. Programmers usually do not need to deal with catching ThreadDeath, unless some special cleanup process needs to occur. If ThreadDeath is caught by the Thread, then it needs to be rethrown so that the Thread will die. No error will be passed to a top-level error handler if this is not handled properly.
Syntax	public class **ThreadDeath** extends Error
Package	java.lang
Import	java.lang.ThreadDeath
Constructors	public class **ThreadDeath()**
Parameters	None.
See Also	Error, Thread.stop()
Example	The standard version of stop() for the Thread class takes no parameter. However, this method calls the version of the stop() method that takes a Throwable object as a parameter. Technically, t.stop(new ThreadDeath(); is the same as t.stop();.

The Thread and ThreadGroup Project: Calculations in Background

The project for this chapter takes requests for numeric calculations and performs these calculations as separate Threads. The user submits the calculations in a series of batches. The program uses a subclass of ThreadGroup to manage these batch submissions. The status of the batches can be requested at any time, even while the calculations are still going on. Some features of the Threads and ThreadGroups can be altered, such as their priority.

This program is an applet. It presents itself through a series of simple text menus, which are executed with simple numeric inputs.

The first option lets the user create a batch request set. The user can submit up to three calculations in a batch. When the batch is assembled, the user executes it. He or she is then returned to the main menu.

Option 2 shows the status of a batch. If a calculation (or Thread) in the batch is running, it is said to be "active." If the calculation is complete, the user is presented with the result. When an entire batch is complete and the results are presented via the status menu, the program deletes the batch request.

The third option lets the user change the priority maximum of a batch (executed as a ThreadGroup method) or alter the priority of an individual calculation. The batch as a whole can also be stopped here.

Since the program is written as an applet, it can be run from any browser that supports Java.

This project is written mostly to illustrate the methods of this chapter. To find out about synchronization and threads, see the chapter overview and the synchronization example on the CD.

Project Classes

There are five classes in this project:

- **PrimeTest**   This is a subclass of Thread and performs the actual calculations in this program. Its function is to count the number of primes up to a certain value.

- **BatchRequestItem**   A simple class used for holding parameter information for executing a single item in a batch.

- **BatchRequest**   A class that uses an array of BatchRequestItem objects to build a composite batch request.

- **BatchExecute**   A subclass of ThreadGroup that takes a BatchRequest object and creates the Threads that execute the desired calculations.

- **BatchCalc**   The class that guides the user through a series of menus that execute and interact with the batch calculations.

Building the Project

1. Enter the following code into a file named PrimeTest.java.

```java
import java.lang.*;

// Thread to test count the number of primes up to a certain value
public class PrimeTest extends Thread {
    int data;        // The maximum value in which to calculate
    int count;      // The output

    // Constructor to add Thread to ThreadGroup.
    public PrimeTest(ThreadGroup tg, String thread_name,int test_num) {
        super(tg,thread_name);
        data = test_num;    // The value to calculate
        count = 0;  // Initialize the counter
    }

    // Simple constructor.  Only input is the maximum value in which to calculate
    public PrimeTest(int test_num) {
        super();
        data = test_num; // The maximum value in which to calculate
        count = 0;  // Initialize the counter
    }

    // Return the result of the calculations...
    public int GetCount() {
        return count;
    }

    // Calculate the number of primes up to a certain number
    // using the slow, brute force, algorithm
    public void run() {
        int i;
        // Count up to the maximum value
        for (i = 2; i <= data; ++i ) {
            if (IsPrime(i) == true)
                ++count;
        }
    }

    // Checks to see if a number is prime...
    public boolean IsPrime(int test_num) {
        int i;
        int stop = (test_num / 2) + 1;
        boolean is_prime = true;
        for (i = 2; i < stop; ++i) {
            if ((test_num % i) == 0) {
                    is_prime = false;
                    i = stop;
            }
        }
        return is_prime;
    }
}
```

This class calculates the total number of prime numbers up to a certain integer maximum. It is derived from the Thread class so the calculations can be performed in the background. The algorithm is intentionally not optimal, because it is useful to have a long-running calculation to illustrate the batch processing of this program. (The Eratosthenes' sieve algorithm is much more efficient.) Something should be said in regard to the input to PrimeTest (the integer maximum in which to calculate). While small numbers (a couple of thousand and less) will be calculated fairly quickly, very large numbers (over a million) may take quite a while. If you are writing code to enhance this program, you may want to find a value that is not calculated in a split second, but does not take hours either. Values over 10,000 are generally pretty good.

Note that there are two constructors. The one with three parameters is used to run the Thread as part of a ThreadGroup, the option that is exercised in this program. The one-parameter constructor is used only for development purposes and is not called as part of the application.

The GetCount() method is executed after the thread is stopped (has left the run() method). Recall that a Thread object is not destroyed, despite the fact that it has "died" (stopped running). Consequently, methods can be executed after the Thread has stopped, such as returning information about the calculations performed.

The prime number algorithm is intentionally left as the only calculation provided with this program. A good way to experiment with Threads and the menu system of this program is to write a new calculation Thread class and add it to the menu and the batch classes.

2. Build the file BatchRequestItem.java.

```
import java.lang.*;

// This class stores the information necessary to execute a single batch item
public class BatchRequestItem {
    int command;
    int param1;
    int param2;
    // Construct the object with the three item components
    public BatchRequestItem(int cmd,int p1,int p2) {
        command = cmd;
        param1 = p1;
        param2 = p2;
    }
    // Return the command of the batch request
    public int GetCommand() {
        return command;
    }
```

continued on next page

continued from previous page

```
    // Return the first parameter of the item
    public int GetParam1() {
        return param1;
    }
    // Return the second parameter of the item
    public int GetParam2() {
        return param2;
    }
}
```

The BatchRequestItem class is an accessor class that contains parameter information for executing a batch. The command variable is a number that is used by the batch executor to indicate which calculation is to be performed. The command value 1 is used to indicate the prime number calculation (corresponding to the menu option the user sees). BatchRequestItem provides room for two parameters to be used in a calculation, although the prime number class only needs one parameter (the value maximum to calculate).

3. Build the file BatchRequest.java.

```
// This class has an array of BatchRequestItems that describe the individual items
// to be calculated ...
class BatchRequest {
    int max_batch_items = 3;   // Maximum # of items in the batch
    int count;   // # of items in the request
    BatchRequestItem br[];   // The items to be calculated
    // Initialize the batch request array...
    public BatchRequest() {
        count = 0;
        br = new BatchRequestItem[max_batch_items];
    }
    // Get the maximum # of items allowed in the array...
    public int GetMaxItems() {
        return max_batch_items;
    }
    // Count the number of items added to the request array...
    public int GetCount() {
        return count;
    }
    // Add an BatchRequestItem to the array...
    public int Add(int cmd,int p1,int p2) {
        // Return error if maximum of batch items added to array...
        if (count >= max_batch_items) {
            System.out.println("Max batch request items exceeded.");
            return -1;
        }
        br[count++] = new BatchRequestItem(cmd,p1,p2);
        return 0;
    }
}
```

```
    // Get a reference to a BatchReqeustItem in the batch...
    public BatchRequestItem GetItem(int index) {
        return br[index];
    }
}
```

The BatchRequest class uses an array of BatchRequestItems to build a composite batch request. An item is added to the BatchRequest class through the Add() method.

4. Build the file BatchExecute.java.

```
import java.lang.*;

// The actual group responsible for executing a batch request...
class BatchExecute extends ThreadGroup{
    BatchRequest br;
    Thread th[];
    public BatchExecute(int index,BatchRequest batch_req) {
        // Initialize the thread group...
        super("Batch" + index);
        int cmd;
        br = batch_req;
        th = new Thread[br.GetCount()];
        // Load the requests into a thread group...
        for (int i = 0; i < br.GetCount(); ++i) {
            cmd = br.GetItem(i).GetCommand();
            System.out.println("Execute item " + i + " cmd " + cmd
                    + ":Param " + br.GetItem(i).GetParam1());
            // Execute the thread!
            switch(cmd) {
                case 0:
                default:
                    PrimeTest p;
                    p = new PrimeTest(this,"B" + index + "I" + i,
                        br.GetItem(i).GetParam1());
                    th[i] = (Thread) p;
                    p.start();
                    break;
            } // end switch
        } // end for
    }


    // Show the status of the batch in String array
    // Return # of active tasks in length of string array...
    public String[] ShowStatus() {
        int cmd;
 String s[] = new String[br.GetCount()];
        // Print out the thread statuses..
        for (int i = 0; i < br.GetCount(); ++i) {
```

continued on next page

continued from previous page

```
            // See if it is active...
            if (th[i].isAlive() ) {
                s[i] = "Thread " + i + " active";
            } // end if
            else {
                    cmd = br.GetItem(i).GetCommand();
                    switch(cmd) {
                        case 0:
                        default:
                        PrimeTest p = (PrimeTest) th[i];
                        // Show the results of the prime number test...
                        s[i] = "Prime number count up to "
                                + br.GetItem(i).GetParam1() +
                    " is: " + p.GetCount();
                        break;
                    } // end switch
            } // end else
        } // end for
        return s;
    }

    // Get the number of requests
    public int GetCount() {
        return br.GetCount();
    }
    // Get the priority of a thread...
    public int GetPriority(int index) {
        if (index >= br.GetCount())
                return 0;
        return th[index].getPriority();
    }

    // Set priority: trap error...
    // If priority is no good, throw exception...
    void SetPriority(int index,int pty) throws Exception {
        if (index >= br.GetCount())
                return;
th[index].setPriority(pty);
    }

    // Stop and wait for all Threads in the group to die...
    public void join() {
        // Loop through each Thread...
        for (int i = 0; i < br.GetCount(); ++i) {
            // Wait for each indivindual Thread to die..
            try {
                th[i].join();
            }
            catch (InterruptedException e) { }
        } // end for
    }

}
```

The BatchExecute class is derived from ThreadGroup. Its constructor takes a BatchRequest object that indicates the individual Thread calculations to be performed. These Thread classes are based on the value found in the command parameter for each request item. The only valid command at this time is the PrimeTest class. If you want to add new calculations to the application, you will need to modify the constructor switch statement to execute your class.

Since BatchExecute is a subclass of ThreadGroup, methods such as stop() and setMaxPriority() can be executed without additional code. However, the two priority methods, GetPriority() and SetPriority(), are added so that individual threads can be altered. Note that SetPriority throws exceptions if the priority is not within the range of the MIN_PRIORITY or MAX_PRIORITY constant values or the thread is no longer running.

The ShowStatus() method returns a String array indicating the status of a Thread or its calculated value. The switch statement code here will need to be modified if any new calculation classes are added.

5. Review BatchCalc.java on the CD. Look at the following code highlights.

The class BatchCalc based on the Applet class guides the user through a series of menus that execute and interact with the batch calculations. The applet code is kept simple so that you can focus on what is going on with the Threads and ThreadGroups. Much of this code is just going through the menus and managing the Applet interface. Therefore, the user is referred to the CD for most of this class. However, a few of the highlights will be discussed.

A couple of applet variables are worth noting for their use in the discussion that follows. The BatchRequest variable *br* is used to build a batch request. A new BatchRequest object is made whenever you select option number 1 from the main menu, which is used to create a new batch. When you decide to execute that batch, the batch_execute() method is called:

```
// Execute a batch request...
void execute_batch(BatchRequest br) {
    int index = -1;
  // Find a batch id to use...
    for (int i = 0; i < max_be; ++i) {
        if (be_active[i] == false) {
            index = i;
            break;
        } // end if
    } // end for
    // Return if full
    if (index == -1) {
getAppletContext().showStatus("No room left for requests. Check batch status.");
    return;
    } // end if
```

continued on next page

continued from previous page

```
        // Add the batch!
        getAppletContext().showStatus("Executing Batch id " + index);
        be_active[index] = true;
        be[index] = new BatchExecute(index,br);
    }
```

The main variable in all of this is an array of BatchExecute objects called *be*. Each element of this array is a BatchExecute object that is a subclass of ThreadGroup. Therefore, normal ThreadGroup methods such as setMaxPriority() and stop() can be called on this object. This in fact happens under option 3 of the main menu, which is used to change the batch state. The be_active array is a boolean array that keeps track of whether the batch has finished and has its results reported, or has been killed.

The method change_batch_state() modifies the state of the ThreadGroup class BatchExecute. The code in the change_batch_state() method that stops a batch is interesting. The first step is to call the BatchExecute method stop(), which terminates all threads in the group. The BatchExecute join() method is then called to wait for all the Threads to be terminated. The BatchExecute object is then freed simply by setting its link to the BatchLoop object (an index in the array *be*) to null. Recall that Java has automatic garbage collection—there is no delete clause in Java. When the BatchExecute object is no longer linked to any active object, it will be deleted automatically by the garbage collector. Any objects it refers to (which are not referenced elsewhere) will also be deleted. This code is also called when the user leaves the page the applet is running on. This results in the BatchCalc stop() method being called, which in turns executes the batch termination code just discussed.

The code that changes the priority of an individual thread in a batch is also worth listing.

```
// Change a thread's priority
   void change_thread_priority(int priority) {
       // Change the priority...
       try {
           be[current_batch_index].SetPriority(current_thread_index,priority);
           // Update the status bar
           getAppletContext().showStatus("New priority for thread " +
               current_thread_index + " set to " +
               be[current_batch_index].GetPriority(current_thread_index));
       }
       // May be an exception. Print message...
       catch (Exception e) {
           getAppletContext().showStatus("Change priority exception: " +
               e.getMessage());
       }
       // Redisplay the state menu...
       display_change_batch_state(current_batch_index);
   }
```

In this case, change_thread_priority ()_ tries to change the priority of a Thread through the BatchExecute SetPriority() method. This throws an exception if the Thread's priority value is not within the range of the MIN_PRIORITY or MAX_PRIORITY constant values or the thread is no longer running. If there is an exception, the detailed exception message is shown on the browser's status bar. If the call succeeds, the new priority is shown on the status bar. The applet frequently updates the browser's status bar when something notable occurs in the program.

9

EXCEPTIONS

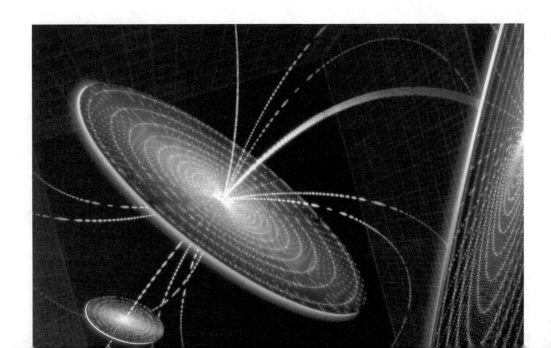

9

EXCEPTIONS

A key feature of a well-written, robust program is its ability to handle any unusual condition or error that can occur while the program is running. The designers of Java provided support for such an ability by adding exception constructs to indicate that a disruptive condition has occurred in the program. When a problem occurs within a method, it indicates the difficulty by "throwing" an exception. Like everything else in Java, the exception itself is an object. Because there are many types of problems that can occur when a program runs, the Java API classifies exceptions into an extensive class hierarchy, organizing the classes by both severity and type of problem. The fundamental class exception hierarchy, found in the java.lang package, is the focus of this chapter. Other exception classes, however, do exist and are located throughout the packages of the Java API. Furthermore, as will be shown, developers can create their own exception classes and position them in the correct place in the exception class hierarchy.

Exception Handling

Java programs use the *try-catch-finally* construct to handle exceptions. Code that is structured to use this construct is called an exception handler. Here is an exception handler that catches a divide-by-zero error:

```
try {
    int x = 3;
    int y = 0;
     // Throws divide by zero exception!
    int answer = x / y;
}
catch (Exception e) {
     System.out.println("Divide by zero error");
}
// This will be called no matter what happens above...
finally {
System.out.println("Done.");
}
```

The *try* block of an exception handler is the code that should be executed normally. If an exception is generated by any of the commands in the *try* block, Java tries to find an appropriate *catch* clause to handle the exception that was thrown. Recall that in Java, exceptions are objects and there is a hierarchy of exceptions. Java tries to resolve an error by finding an appropriate *catch* block to handle the exception. It first looks in the method where the problem occurred. It searches the *catch* clauses in order, looking for the first clause that either matches exactly the type of object that is thrown or is a superclass of the exception thrown. If there is no matching *catch* clause in the current method, Java will travel up the runtime stack looking for a method with an appropriate handler. It looks at each corresponding method in the stack, seeing if there is a *catch* clause that matches the class or superclass of the error. If the top of the stack is reached and no appropriate exception handler is found, Java will dump the stack trace of the exception, and the program may terminate abnormally.

As the example shows, a *finally* block can be added to the end of an exception handler after the last *catch* clause. Code in the *finally* clause is called no matter what happens in the *try* block—regardless of whether the code runs fine or if an exception is thrown. The *finally* block can be used for general cleanup operations.

To illustrate how Java tries to find an appropriate exception handler, the previous divide-by-zero example is modified to have multiple *catch* clauses.

```
try {
    int x = 3;
    int y = 0;
// Throws divide by zero exception!
    int answer = x / y;
}
// Try to catch an array exception ?? This is not used
catch (ArrayIndexOutOfBoundsException e) {
System.out.println("Invalid array index");
}
// This matches the exception that is thrown and so is used!
catch (ArithmeticException e) {
System.out.println("Divide by zero error");
}
// This is a superclass of ArithmeticException,
// but since an appropriate
// catch clause is found above, this clause is not used
catch (Exception e) {
System.out.println("Exception");
}
// A finally clause will be called no
// matter what happens above...
finally {
System.out.println("This will be called no matter what
happens...");
}
```

In this case, the ArithmeticException *catch* clause matches the exception that is thrown and is used.

Throwing Exceptions

A method can declare that it throws a certain class of exception with the *throws* clause. For example, here is the declaration of the read() method of the FileInputStream class.

```
public int read() throws IOException
```

This means that within the body of this method there probably exists some code that corresponds to

```
throw new IOException();
```

This line indicates that an instance of class IOException is to be created and then thrown. Alternately, the read() method could be passing along any IOException generated by some method that it calls. In this case, the method may simply "rethrow" the exception.

Java has very strict rules regarding the handling of exceptions. If a method is called that declares that it throws a certain class of exception, then it must either catch that exception using a *try-catch* block, or declare that exception and rethrow it. An important case where this does not hold is runtime exceptions, which will be discussed later.

The Throwable Class: Superclass of Exceptions

The Throwable class is the superclass of all objects that can be thrown. All of the exception classes that have been thrown or caught in the previous examples are subclasses of Throwable. All throwable objects must be either directly derived from the Throwable class or be from a subclass of Throwable.

The Throwable class (and hence all the exception subclasses) contains information about the runtime stack when the error occurred. The top of the stack is the method where the error occurred. This runtime stack information can be used for debugging purposes.

A detailed message also is provided with the Throwable class. This message is usually system generated, although an alternative Throwable constructor is provided for creating a custom detail message. The getMessage() method is used for retrieving the detail message.

As stated earlier, Throwable classes (and thus exceptions in general) are organized into a classification hierarchy to reflect both the type and severity of an error. Figure 9-1 reflects the significant classes of the Throwable hierarchy.

From the Throwable superclass, the classification breaks into two branches: the Exception and Error classes. Conditions that are appropriate for Exception classes are those that result from normal programming situations, such as divide by zero, or not being able to open a file. More extreme or "hard" errors, such as a runtime stack overflow, are reserved for the Error class. In most programming situations, the developer will be handling thrown objects that are subclasses of Exception. When a programmer creates a new set of classes of throwable objects, these are likely to be derived (directly or indirectly) from Exception.

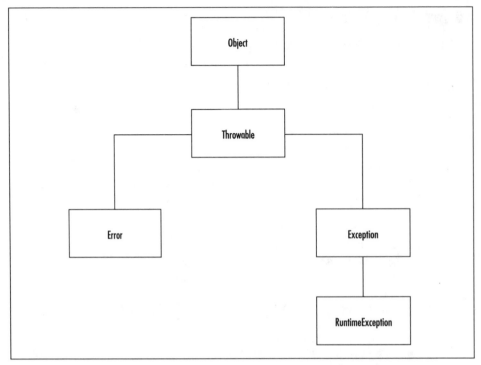

Figure 9-1 The significant classes of the Throwable hierarchy

The other notable branch of the Figure 9-1 hierarchy is the RuntimeException classes. These classes have an interesting place in the Java exception methodology. RuntimeException classes are used for objects that do not have to be caught when they are thrown. In general, RuntimeException classes represent runtime problems that occur in the Java virtual machine. Classic examples of this are null pointer exceptions and array accesses that are out of bounds. The main reason that these are RuntimeException classes is that it would be too cumbersome to have to catch these exceptions every time they could occur. Imagine code with an exception handler around every array access! Such code would be unreadable (and slow!).

While programmers can derive their own new Exception classes from RuntimeException, this practice is discouraged. The reason is obvious: overuse of RuntimeException would undermine some of the main goals of Java exception handling—the use of safe programming practices and explicit declaration of the behaviors of a method.

Writing Custom Exception Classes

It is easy to create a custom exception class. The following code declares such a class:

```
public class MyException extends Exception { }
```

That is all there is to it! Since MyException is indirectly derived from the Throwable class, it has access to all the features of that class. No other methods will probably be needed, although you may want to define a default constructor that defines an appropriate message.

The main trick in writing a custom Exception class is figuring out where it should be put in the exception hierarchy. Because Error classes are reserved for serious system problems, a custom class probably should not be placed here. It probably should not be of class RuntimeException, either, for reasons previously discussed. The best place is most likely under Exception.

There are some good techniques for classifying exceptions. For example, if a hash table class is going to be created, it might be good to create a HashTableException superclass. A specific problem, such as a full hash table, might be represented by a HashTableFullException, a subclass of HashTableException. Look at the figures throughout this chapter to see how the Java API organizes its own exceptions. These can be used as good guidelines for how to classify custom exceptions.

About the Project

The chapter project illustrates how to use exception handlers to validate array usage and number conversion. It shows how to throw and catch exceptions. The project also uses a custom Exception class. After completing this project, you should have a pretty good feel for when and how to use exceptions, and also how to write your own Throwable classes.

Exception Classes Summary

Table 9-1 is a listing of the exception classes discussed in this chapter. Significant classes are marked in bold.

Table 9-1 The Exception classes

Class	Extends
Throwable	Object
Exception	Throwable
ClassNotFoundException	Exception
CloneNotSupported	Exception
IllegalAccessException	Exception
InstantiationException	Exception
InterruptedException	Exception
NoSuchMethodException	Exception
RuntimeException	Exception
ArithmeticException	RuntimeException

continued on next page

continued from previous page

Class	Extends
ArrayIndexOutOfBoundsException	IndexOutOfBoundsException
ArrayStoreException	RuntimeException
ClassCastException	RuntimeException
IllegalArgumentException	RuntimeException
IllegalMonitorStateException	RuntimeException
IllegalThreadStateException	IllegalArgumentException
IndexOutOfBoundsException	RuntimeException
NegativeArraySizeException	RuntimeException
NullPointerException	RuntimeException
NumberFormatException	IllegalArgumentException
SecurityException	RuntimeException
StringIndexOutOfBoundsException	IndexOutOfBoundsException
Error	Throwable
AbstractMethodError	IncompatibleClassChangeError
ClassCircularityError	LinkageError
ClassFormatError	LinkageError
IllegalAccessError	IncompatibleClassChangeError
IncompatibleClassChangeError	LinkageError
InstantiationError	IncompatibleClassChangeError
InternalError	VirtualMachineError
LinkageError	Error
NoClassDefFoundError	LinkageError
NoSuchFieldError	IncompatibleClassChangeError
NoSuchMethodError	IncompatibleClassChangeError
OutOfMemoryError	VirtualMachineError
StackOverflowError	VirtualMachineError
ThreadDeath	Error
UnknownError	VirtualMachineError
UnsatisfiedLinkError	LinkageError
VerifyError	LinkageError
VirtualMachineError	Error

The java.lang.Throwable Class

The only objects that can be thrown when an exception occurs are those that are derived from the Throwable class. This means that thrown objects must either be directly derived from the Throwable class or be created from subclasses of Throwable. When these objects are caught, Throwable methods can be invoked to provide details about the error that occurred and the state of the runtime stack. Any classes derived from Throwable also will have these features.

Thrown Throwable objects are caught in the *catch* section of an exception handler. When an exception occurs, the Java runtime environment looks for a method to catch the object. It does this by propagating the object up the call stack, starting from the method where the error occurred. This propagation terminates when an appropriate exception handler is found. Such a handler is one that catches the class of object that is thrown. If no appropriate exception handler is found, the program is terminated.

Throwable objects are created with a detailed message in the form of a String object. This String can be retrieved through the getMessage() method. If the constructor with no parameters is used, a system-generated detailed message is provided with the object. A custom detail message can also be established with an alternate constructor.

Information about the runtime stack when the error occurred is also provided with Throwable objects. When an exception is not handled, it is this runtime stack information that is displayed to standard error when a program terminates abnormally. Several methods are provided with the Throwable class to get this stack information in a nonfatal manner. The methods of the Throwable class (and all of its subclasses) are described in Table 9-2.

Table 9-2 Summary of Throwable methods

Method	Description
Throwable	Constructs a Throwable object with no special message
Throwable(String *msg*)	Constructs a Throwable object with custom detail message
fillInStackTrace	Fills in stack trace of Throwable object with the current runtime stack information
getMessage	Returns the detail message of a Throwable object
printStackTrace	Prints the Throwable object description and its stack to the standard error stream
toString	Returns the String representation of a Throwable object

THROWABLE

Description	The ancestor of all throwable classes, this class signals the occurrence of an exceptional condition. Throwable also carries information about the runtime stack.
Syntax	public class **Throwable** extends Object
Package	*java.lang*
Import	*java.lang.Throwable*
Constructors	public **Throwable**()
	public **Throwable**(String *msg*)

Parameters

String *msg*	The detailed Message to be displayed.
See Also	Object, Exception, Error
Example	The following code details a method called MyDivider() that tries to divide two figures and throws an exception with a custom message if there is an error (probably divide by zero).

```
    // This method divides two numbers,
// catching any divide by zero error
    // Since the method throws an object,
     // the caller must catch any errors...
    int MyDivider(int numerator, int denominator)
       throws Throwable {
       int answer;
       // Try to come up with an answer...
       try {
           answer = numerator / denominator;
       }
           // Catch divide by zero error with
           // custom error message...
       catch (Throwable t) {
           // Create detail message using
// Throwable message plus
           // parameter information...
           String err = " Caught Error: "
+ t.getMessage()
                 + ". Numerator = " + numerator
+ " Denominator = " + denominator;
           // Create Throwable object that
// uses custom message...
           Throwable newT = new Throwable(err);
           // Throw the error!
           throw newT;
       }
       // If all goes well, return answer...
       return answer;
    }
```

This method has a couple of interesting points. First, note the *throws* clause in the method declaration. This indicates that a Throwable object is thrown when there is an error. Any code that uses MyDivider() must catch this object in its exception handler. When the divide-by-zero error occurs, a String is created with the message generated from the system-generated throwable object (it says "/ by zero") plus the values of the numerator and denominator. This String is passed to a new Throwable object, where it becomes the object's detail message. The new object is then thrown to indicate an exception to be passed to the calling routine.

This code provides an example of how to call MyDivider():

```
    int numerator = 10;
    int denominator = 0;
    // Print out result of calculation
// while catching any error...
    try {
```

```
        System.out.println("The answer = " +
            MyDivider(numerator, denominator) );
    }
    catch (Throwable t) {
// If error, simply print out
// its message...
        System.out.println(t.getMessage());
    }
```

The message that is displayed in the *catch* section of the exception clause is

```
Error / by zero. Numerator = 10 Denominator = 0
```

Methods

FILLINSTACKTRACE

Class Name	Throwable
Description	Throwable objects are created with the stack trace of the runtime environment when the exception occurred. If the thrown object is caught by another method and then rethrown, it may be desirable to set the stack trace to the method that caught the object and not where the exception originally occurred. The fillInStackTrace() method will update the Throwable object's stack information to that of the current runtime stack trace.
Syntax	public Throwable fillInStackTrace()
Parameters	None
Returns	This Throwable object
Exceptions	None
See Also	printStackTrace()
Example	This example illustrates the kind of case where it might be desirable to use the fillInStackTrace() method. First, a method that returns the value at an index in an integer array is described.

```
    // Return the value at an index in an array.
// An exception will occur
    // if the index is out of array bounds
    int getArrayIndexValue(int array[],int index)
  throws Throwable  {
        try { // If the index is good, return the value
            return array[index];
        }
        // Probably index out of bounds
        catch (Throwable t) {
            throw t;  // Throw the error up the stack
        }
    }
```

This method simply rethrows the Throwable object if an array out of bounds exception occurs. At this point, the getArrayIndexValue() method is at the top of the stack trace.

Next, the method testCalculation(), which invoked getArrayIndexValue(), traps the exception.

```
// This method gets the index in an array
// and gets its value by calling
// the getArrayIndexValue() method.  If an
// exception is thrown (and it  will!), it
// sets itself to the top
// of the stack trace and rethrows the object.
void testCalculation() throws Throwable {
// Values initialized at 0
        int intArray[] = new int[4];
        int index = 5;
        // Print out result of calculation
// while catching any error...
        try {
System.out.println("Value at index " + index + " = " + getArrayIndexValue(intArray,
index));
        }
        catch (Throwable t) {
            // If error, set testCalculation()
// to the top of the trace
            // and rethrow
            throw t.fillInStackTrace();
        }
}
```

Since it wants to take responsibility for the error, testCalculation() calls fillInStackTrace() to make it the top of the stack trace and then rethrows the object. If the object is caught and the printStackTrace() method is invoked, the method testCalculation() will appear at the top of the stack.

GETMESSAGE

Class Name	Throwable
Description	This method returns the detail message of a Throwable object. This message is automatically generated by the runtime system when the default constructor (no parameters) is used to create the object. If the other constructor is used, a custom detail message can be assembled.
Syntax	public String getMessage()
Parameters	None.
Returns	The detail message String.
Exceptions	None.
See Also	Throwable(), Throwable(String *msg*)
Example	This example causes and catches a divide-by-zero error. The default message displayed is "/ by zero".

```
        // Stupid programming.  Try to divide by zero!
        try {
            int denominator = 0;
            int numerator = 10;
System.out.println("Answer = " +
 numerator / denominator);
        }
        // Good programming.  Catch the error!
        catch (Throwable t) {
// Print the detail message
            System.out.println(t.getMessage());
        }
```

PRINTSTACKTRACE

Class Name	Throwable
Description	Throwable objects are created with the stack trace of the runtime environment when the exception occurred. This trace backtracks from the method where the error occurred to the main method that runs the application (the initial Thread object). The printStackTrace() method prints the String representation of the Throwable object followed by the stack trace.
Syntax	public void printStackTrace()
	public void printStackTrace(PrintStream s)
Parameters	
PrintStream *s*	The PrintStream that should receive the stack trace.
Returns	None.
Exceptions	None.
See Also	Throwable(),
Example	This example illustrates an applet that causes a Throwable object to be thrown when the user clicks on the mouse. The class of the object is ArrayIndexOutOfBoundsException. The following code shows the output from printStackTrace() when this applet is run in the Windows 95 environment.

```
public class TestApp extends java.applet.Applet  {
    public boolean mouseDown(Event e, int x, int y) {
        // Try to index out of the bounds of an array
        try {
            int intArray[] = new int[4];
            intArray[5] = 3;  // Bad assignment...
        }
        // Catch the error and print the stack trace
        catch (Throwable t) {
            t.printStackTrace();
        }
        return true;
    };
}
```

This extra example causes a Throwable object to be thrown because of some illegal casting to an array. The class of the thrown object is ClassCastException. The resulting stack trace is sent to the standard error PrintStream.

```
        try {    // Try to cast an
// incorrect type of Object into a
//   StringBuffer array
            StringBuffer strArray[] =
new StringBuffer[4];
            String s = "My String";
            Object q = (Object)s;
            // The next line will cause
// a ClassCastException
            strArray[0] = (StringBuffer)q;
        }
        catch (Throwable t) {    // Print to the
// System error PrintStream
            t.printStackTrace(System.err);
        }
java.lang.ArrayIndexOutOfBoundsException: 5
        at TestApp.mouseDown(TestApp.java:16)
        at java.awt.Component.handleEvent(Component.java:883)
        at java.awt.Component.postEvent(Component.java:838)
        at sun.awt.win32.MComponentPeer.handleMouseDown(MComponentPeer.java:246)
        at sun.awt.win32.MToolkit.run(MToolkit.java:57)
        at java.lang.Thread.run(Thread.java:289)

java.lang.ArrayIndexOutOfBoundsException:    5
    at TestApp.mouseDown(TestApp.java:    16
    at java.awt.Component.handleEvent(Component.java: 883)
    at java.awt.Component.postEvent(Component.java: 838)
    at sun.awt.win32.MComponentPeer.handleMouseDown
                    (MComponentPeer.java: 246)
    at sun.awt.win32.MToolkit.run(MToolkit.java: 57)
    at java.lang.Thread.run(Thread.java: 289)
```

TOSTRING

Class Name	Throwable
Description	This method returns the String representation of a Throwable object. This representation is the name of the package and class of the Throwable object (such as ArithmeticException or NullPointerException).
Syntax	public String **toString**()
Parameters	None.
Returns	The String representation of the Throwable object.
Exceptions	None.
See Also	Throwable(), Throwable(String *msg*), getMessage()
Example	This example causes a Throwable object to be thrown because of a null pointer error. The output string representation is "java.lang.NullPointerException".

```
        // Try to do some arithmetic
// with a null pointer
        try {
            int x = 5;
            Integer y = new Integer(5);
            y = null;  // Set Integer object to null
            // This next line will now cause an
// error to be Thrown
            int z = x * y.intValue();
        }
        catch (Throwable t) {
            System.out.println(t.toString());
        }
```

Exception Classes

Throwable classes used for handling exceptions are organized in a classification hierarchy for ease of use. Figure 9-1 shows the significant classes that are used for this classification. From the Throwable class, which is the ancestor of all classes that can be thrown, the classification breaks into two branches: the Exception and Error classes. Conditions that are appropriate for Exception classes are those that result from normal programming situations, such as divide by zero, or not being able to open a file. More extreme or "hard" errors, such as a runtime stack overflow, is reserved for the Error class. In most programming situations, the developer will be handling thrown objects that are subclasses of Exception. When a programmer creates a new throwable class, it is likely to be derived (directly or indirectly) from Exception. Since Exception classes are derived from the Throwable class, information about the runtime stack is part of the standard behavior. Methods for using this information are described in the Methods section of the Throwable class.

With one important exclusion, any time an Exception object is thrown, it must be caught. The Exceptions that have to be caught will be located in the *throws* clause of a method declaration. Any code that uses a method with this clause must have an exception handler to catch these classes of thrown objects.

RuntimeException classes represent a subclassification of thrown objects that do not have to be caught when they are thrown. In general, RuntimeException classes represent runtime problems that occur in the Java virtual machine. Classic examples of this are null pointer exceptions and array accesses that are out of bounds (NullPointerException and ArrayIndexOutOfBoundsException, respectively). The main reason that these are RuntimeException classes is that it would be too cumbersome to have to catch methods that throw these exceptions every time they are used. Imagine code with an exception handler around every array access!

While programmers can derive their own new Exception classes from RuntimeException, this practice is discouraged. The reason is obvious. Overuse of RuntimeException would undermine some of the main goals of Java exception handling—safe programming practices and explicit declaration of the behaviors of a method.

The Exception class adds no new behavior to the Throwable class. It does little more than override the two constructors of Throwable: one constructor creates a system-generated detail message; the other uses a custom detail message String supplied by the programmer. All Exception classes follow the same pattern. In the name of space and efficiency, the description of the Exception subclasses that follow will have only one example each using the default constructor of no special detailed message. The reader is referred to the description of the Exception methods that follow for how to use custom detail messages. For ease of reading, the discussion will be divided into non-RuntimeException classes and RuntimeException classes.

EXCEPTION

Description	This class marks the top of a classification hierarchy of Throwable classes that are used to indicate exceptional conditions that are not of a systematic nature.
Syntax	public class **Exception** extends Throwable
Package	java.lang
Import	java.lang.Exception
Constructors	public **Exception**()
	public **Exception**(String *msg*)
Parameters	
String *msg*	The detailed Message to be displayed.
See Also	Throwable
Example	This example shows an exception handler that catches a divide-by-zero error. It displays the message to standard output. The output from the getMessage() method is "/ by zero".

```
int numerator = 10;
int denominator = 0;
// Try to divide these.  There will be
// a divide by zero error thrown!
try {
int answer = numerator/denominator;
System.out.println("Answer is: " + answer);
}
// Catch the error and print out the
// Exception's detail message.
catch (Exception e) {
System.out.println("Error in Calculation.
Caught Throwable with message: "
+  e.getMessage());
}
```

Non-RuntimeException Classes

The following classes are not derived from RuntimeException. Code that uses methods that throw these classes of Exceptions must have an exception handler.

ClassNotFoundException

Description   This Exception is thrown by a couple of classes. The class Class is used to get runtime descriptions of classes. This information includes such things as the class's superclass and whether or not it implements an interface. When the forName() method of this class is used to dynamically get information about a class, a ClassNotFoundException will be thrown if the class could not be located. The ClassLoader class is used to determine a policy of how to locate and load classes. A couple of its methods throw a ClassNotFoundException when the class (specified by a String name) could not be found.

Syntax   public class **ClassNotFoundException** extends Exception

Package   java.lang

Import   java.lang.ClassNotFoundException

Constructors   public **ClassNotFoundException**()

                     public **ClassNotFoundException**(String *msg*)

Parameters

String *msg*   The detailed Message to be displayed.

See Also   Exception, Class, ClassLoader

Example   The following code tries to dynamically load a reference to the class descriptor of a class. A ClassNotFoundException is thrown if the class could not be located.

```
      try {
            // Use Class to get reference to
// a class descriptor
            // The parameter is the String
// name of the class
            Class c = Class.forName(className);
            // Print out the name and superclass
// name of the class...
            System.out.println("The superclass of " +
c.getName() + " is " + c.getSuperclass().getName() );
      }
      catch (ClassNotFoundException e) {
// Handle cases where class could
// not be found!
            System.out.println("Class not found!");
      }
```

CloneNotSupported

Description   This Exception is thrown when the clone() operation is called on an Object that does not support cloning. Any Object that supports cloning must implement the Cloneable interface. Otherwise, the CloneNotSupported exception will be thrown.

Syntax	public class CloneNotSupportedException extends Exception
Package	java.lang
Import	java.lang.CloneNotSupportedException
Constructors	public CloneNotSupportedException()
	public CloneNotSupportedException(String *msg*)

Parameters

String *msg*	The detailed Message to be displayed.
See Also	Exception, Object, Cloneable
Example	The following code has a method, dup(), that should support cloning. However, it does not implement the Cloneable interface, so a CloneNotSupported exception will be thrown.

```
// This is a simple subclass of Object which
// does not support cloning
class MyClass {
    // This object cannot be clone so throw an exception
    public Object dup() throws CloneNotSupportedException {
        try {   // This will not succeed!
                return clone();
        }
        // This Exception occurs instead. Rethrow it.
        catch (CloneNotSupportedException e) {
                throw e;
        }
    }
}
```

ILLEGALACCESSEXCEPTION

Description	This Exception is thrown by the class Class, which is used to get runtime descriptions of classes. An instance of a class can be done through Class via its newInstance() method. The newInstance() method throws an IllegalAccessException when the class does not support this method.
Syntax	public class IllegalAccessException extends Exception
Package	java.lang
Import	java.lang.IllegalAccessException
Constructors	public IllegalAccessException()
	public IllegalAccessException(String *msg*)

Parameters

String *msg*	The detailed Message to be displayed.
See Also	Exception, Class, InstantiationException
Example	The following code tries to dynamically load a reference to a custom class, MyObject. The newInstance() method is then called on the class to create an instance of MyObject. Since the newInstance() method throws both an

IllegalAccessException and an InstantiationException, both cases must be caught. The code below illustrates both nested exception handling and a handler that has multiple *catch* statements:

```
MyObject mob;
// First use get reference to a class descriptor
try {
Class c = Class.forName("MyClass");
    // Now try to create an instance of MyObject
    try {
        mob = (MyObject) c.newInstance();
    }
    catch (IllegalAccessException iae) {
// The method is not found!
        System.out.println("IllegalAccessException -
no instance created.");
    }
    catch (InstantiationException ie) {
// Instantiation failed because
        // class is abstract or an interface
        System.out.println("InstantiationException -
no instance created.");
    }
    catch (Exception o) {  // Handle any other error
        System.out.println("Exception -
no instance created.");
    }
}
catch (ClassNotFoundException e) {
// Handle cases where class could not be found!
System.out.println("Class not found!");
}
```

INSTANTIATIONEXCEPTION

Description	This Exception is thrown by the class Class, which is used to get runtime descriptions of classes. An instance of a class can be done through Class via its newInstance() method. The newInstance() method throws an InstantiationException when the class to be instantiated is an abstract class or an interface.
Syntax	public class InstantiationException extends Exception
Package	java.lang
Import	java.lang.InstantiationException
Constructors	public InstantiationException()
	public InstantiationException(String *msg*)
Parameters	
String *msg*	The detailed Message to be displayed.
See Also	Exception, Class, IllegalAccessException
Example	See example with IllegalAccessException.

INTERRUPTEDEXCEPTION

Description	This Exception is thrown by a variety of Thread methods. An InterruptedException object is thrown when another Thread has interrupted the Thread whose method is invoked.
Syntax	public class InterruptedException extends Exception
Package	java.lang
Import	java.lang.InterruptedException
Constructors	public InterruptedException()
	public InterruptedException(String *msg*)
Parameters	
String *msg*	The detailed Message to be displayed.
See Also	Exception, Thread
Comments	As of the time of this writing, the Java API had not built in support for interrupting Threads. Therefore, the InterruptedException may not occur.
Example	The following code traps the InterruptedException after a Thread is stopped and the program waits for the Thread to die via the join() method:

```
// Create and start a custom Thread
MyThread th = new MyThread();
th.start();
//
// Stop the Thread
th.stop();
// Wait for the Thread to die
try {
    th.join();
}
// Catch the exception
catch (InterruptedException e) {
//
}
```

NOSUCHMETHODEXCEPTION

Description	This Exception is thrown when Java cannot locate a particular method. It also can be thrown to indicate that a method has not yet been implemented.
Syntax	public class NoSuchMethodException extends Exception
Package	java.lang
Import	java.lang.NoSuchMethodException
Constructors	public NoSuchMethodException()
	public NoSuchMethodException(String *msg*)

Parameters

String *msg*   The detailed Message to be displayed.

See Also   Exception

Example   This example first starts with a class that has a method that is not yet implemented. Consequently, it throws a NoSuchMethodException object. This must be caught by any object that uses this method.

```
// Create a class with an unimplemented method
class MyClass {
    // Declare the unimplemented method
    public void MyMethod() throws NoSuchMethodException {
        // Throw the exception with
// a custom detail message.
        throw new NoSuchMethodException("Method
not yet implemented");
    }
};
```

The following code creates the class, calls the unimplemented method, and catches the NoSuchMethodException object.

```
// Create the custom class
MyClass m = new MyClass();
try {  // Call the unimplemented method
    m.MyMethod();
}
catch (NoSuchMethodException e) {
    // And catch the exception...
System.out.println(e.getMessage());
}
```

RuntimeException Classes

This section describes classes based on the RuntimeException class. Code that uses methods that throw RuntimeException objects is not required to have an exception handler.

RUNTIMEEXCEPTION

Description   RuntimeException classes are used for handling exception conditions that arise from normal programming practice. However, the classes and constructs that throw RuntimeException objects (such as arrays) are used frequently, and so having an exception handler everywhere would result in cumbersome and slower code.

Syntax   public class RuntimeException extends Exception

Package   java.lang

Import   java.lang.RuntimeException

Constructors   public RuntimeException()

          public RuntimeException(String *msg*)

Parameters

String *msg*   The detailed Message to be displayed.

See Also   Throwable, Exception

Example   The following code shows two cases where a RuntimeException could occur. In the first case, the RuntimeException is not handled. The object is of class ArrayIndexOutOfBoundsException.

```
    // Initialize the array
    int intArray[] = new int[4];
    // Good programming - use native
// definition of array length
    for (int i = 0; i < intArray.length; ++i)
            intArray[i] = i;
    // ...
    // Access the array.  Out of bounds
// error that is not caught
    int index = 5;
System.out.println("Val = " + intArray[index]);
```

This code handles the exception:

```
    // Initialize the array
    int intArray[] = new int[4];
    // Good programming - use native definition
// of array length
    for (int i = 0; i < intArray.length; ++i)
            intArray[i] = i;
    // ...
    // Access the array.  Handle the exception
    int index = 5;
    try {
        System.out.println("Val = " +
intArray[index]);
    }
    catch (RuntimeException e) {
// Handle the exception and print out the // detailed message...
System.out.println("RuntimeException: "
+ e.getMessage());
    }
```

RuntimeException classes represent a classification of objects that do not have to be caught when thrown. In general, RuntimeException classes represent runtime problems that occur in the Java virtual machine. Classic examples of this are null pointer exceptions and array accesses that are out of bounds (NullPointerException and ArrayIndexOutOfBoundsException, respectively). The main reasons that these are RuntimeException classes is that it would be too cumbersome to have to catch methods that throw these exceptions every time they are used. Imagine how cumbersome code with an exception handler around every array access would be. Furthermore, a NullPointerException could be thrown any time an object is used. Code that handles all of these conditions would be unreadable (and slow!). Figure 9-2 shows the significant classes of the RuntimeException hierarchy.

While programmers can derive their own new Exception classes from RuntimeException, this practice is discouraged. The reason is obvious: overuse of

RuntimeException would undermine some of the main goals of Java exception handling—safe programming and explicit declaration of the behaviors of a method. Since RuntimeException objects do not have to be caught, the program will continue to run even if they occur. However, they may signal a deeper problem in the program that will ultimately result in abnormal termination. Consequently, RuntimeException objects often will be more difficult to track down than those that require exception handlers.

ARITHMETICEXCEPTION

Description   This Exception is thrown when an exception arithmetic condition occurs. In most cases, this will be a divide-by-zero operation. Taking a modulus by zero also will throw an ArithmeticException.

Syntax   public class ArithmeticException extends RuntimeException

Package   java.lang

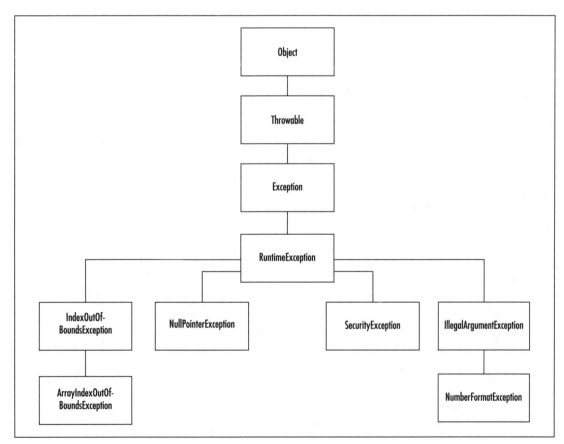

Figure 9-2   Significant classes of the RuntimeException hierarchy

Import	java.lang.ArithmeticException
Constructors	public ArithmeticException()
	public ArithmeticException(String *msg*)
Parameters	
String *msg*	The detailed Message to be displayed.
See Also	Exception, RuntimeException
Example	The following code tries to perform a modulus by zero operation. The ArithmeticException that is thrown is caught by the exception handler.

```
      int a = 25;
      int b = 0;
      // Try modulus operation that results
// in Arithmetic error...
      try {
          System.out.println("Answer = " + a % b);
      }
      // Catch errors...
      catch (ArithmeticException e) {
          // Print the detailed message...
          System.out.println("Arithmetic Exception:"
+ e.getMessage());
      }
```

ARRAYINDEXOUTOFBOUNDSEXCEPTION

Description	An ArrayIndexOutOfBoundsException is thrown when the user attempts to access an invalid index into an array. This will be either negative indexes or an index greater than the length of the array. This RuntimeException class is directly derived from IndexOutOfBoundsException, which is an extension of RuntimeException.
Syntax	public class ArrayIndexOutOfBoundsException extends IndexOutOfBoundsException
Package	java.lang
Import	java.lang.ArrayIndexOutOfBoundsException
Constructors	public ArrayIndexOutOfBoundsException()
	public ArrayIndexOutOfBoundsException(String *msg*)
Parameters	
String *msg*	The detailed Message to be displayed.
See Also	Exception, RuntimeException, IndexOutOfBoundsException
Example	This example creates an array and attempts to access it with a negative index. An ArrayIndexOutOfBoundsException is thrown.

```
      // Initialize the array
      int intArray[] = new int[4];
      for (int i = 0; i < intArray.length; ++i)
          intArray[i] = i;
```

```
        // ...
        // Access the array.  Handle the exception
// so we will live!
        int index = -1; // Try a negative index!?!
        try {
System.out.println("Val = " +
intArray[index]);
        }
        catch (ArrayIndexOutOfBoundsException e) {
            // Handle the exception and print out
// the detailed message...
    System.out.println(
"ArrayIndexOutOfBoundsException: "
+ e.getMessage());
        }
```

ARRAYSTOREEXCEPTION

Description	Arrays are first class Objects that are used to provide a list of objects. This means that objects assigned to an array must be of the class of object that the array was created to support. For example, if a StringBuffer array is created, an integer cannot be assigned to that array. Certain operations, such as arraycopy() of the System class, will throw an ArrayStoreException when an invalid assignment is attempted. This is not caught at compile time because the arraycopy() method takes Objects as its parameters (recall arrays are first class Objects); the actual assignments, however, cannot be type checked until runtime.
Syntax	public class ArrayStoreException extends RuntimeException
Package	java.lang
Import	java.lang.ArrayStoreException
Constructors	public ArrayStoreException()
	public ArrayStoreException(String *msg*)
Parameters	
String *msg*	The detailed Message to be displayed.
See Also	Exception, RuntimeException
Example	This example creates two arrays of different types. When the arraycopy() method attempts to assign elements of the StringBuffer array into the integer array, an ArrayStoreException object is thrown.

```
        // Create two arrays...
        int intArray[] = new int[4];
        StringBuffer sbArray[] = new StringBuffer[4];
        try {
            // Use System class to
// copy entire arrays...
        System.arraycopy(sbArray,0,intArray,0,4);
        }
```

continued on next page

continued from previous page
```
        catch (ArrayStoreException e) { // Catch
//   error resulting from arraycopy
System.out.println("Array copy results in
ArrayStoreException: "
                 + e.getMessage());
        }
```

CLASSCASTEXCEPTION

Description	Suppose there is an Object A of class X and an Object B of class Y. Class Y is a subclass of X. Therefore, it is valid to make Object B a reference to Object A (a class of X):
	X A = new X();
	Y B = (Y) A;
	However, there will be a problem when Object B attempts to utilize a method of class Y, since its reference actually points to class X. When this is attempted, a ClassCastException object is thrown. The example that follows explains this problem in more concrete terms.
Syntax	public class **ClassCastException** extends RuntimeException
Package	java.lang
Import	java.lang.ClassCastException
Constructors	public **ClassCastException**()
	public **ClassCastException**(String *msg*)
Parameters	
String *msg*	The detailed Message to be displayed.
See Also	Exception, RuntimeException
Example	This example attempts to coerce an Object into a StringBuffer by casting. However, the attempt to use a method of StringBuffer results in a ClassCastException object being thrown, since the StringBuffer is properly an Object.

```
        // Create an Object
        Object o = new Object();
        try {
            // Cast the Object into a StringBuffer
            StringBuffer s = (StringBuffer)o;
            // Using a StringBuffer method will fail,
            // however, since s is really an Object
        System.out.println("Length of StringBuffer
= " + s.length());
        }
        // Catch the casting exception .
        catch (ClassCastException e) {
            System.out.println("Invalid cast: "
+ e.getMessage() );
        }
```

ILLEGALARGUMENTEXCEPTION

Description	This Exception is thrown when an invoked method has been passed a parameter with an illegal value. An example of this is a method that requires an integer that must be within a specified range. The setPriority() method of the Thread class is an example of this. In this case, the priority needs to be within a minimum and maximum range (typically 1 to 10). If the integer argument is not within this range, an IllegalArgumentException is thrown.
Syntax	public class IllegalArgumentException extends RuntimeException
Package	java.lang
Import	java.lang.IllegalArgumentException
Constructors	public IllegalArgumentException()
	public IllegalArgumentException(String *msg*)
Parameters	
String *msg*	The detailed Message to be displayed.
See Also	Exception, RuntimeException, Thread.setPriority()
Example	This example tries to set the priority of a Thread subclass (called MyThread) to an illegal value. Typically, the allowable range to setPriority() is 1 to 10. In this case, however, a value that is too large is passed. This causes an IllegalArgumentException object to be thrown.

```
MyThread th;   // A subclass of Thread
// Try to set the priority to a ridiculous value
try {
    th.setPriority(100);
}
    // Indicate that an exception has been thrown
    catch (IllegalArgumentException e) {
        System.out.println(
"Illegal priority value.");
    }
```

ILLEGALMONITORSTATEEXCEPTION

Description	Multithreaded Java applications usually need a way to synchronize their behavior. One way threads can synchronize is through the use of monitors. Every object with a synchronized method has a unique monitor. Threads that use a monitor can be made to wait while another thread is using that monitor. When the thread is finished, it uses the notify() method to indicate that it has concluded using the monitor. The notify() method can only be called from the Object that owns the monitor. If it is called from anywhere else, an IllegalMonitorStateException is thrown.
Syntax	public class IllegalMonitorStateException extends RuntimeException

Package	java.lang
Import	java.lang.IllegalMonitorStateException
Constructors	public IllegalMonitorStateException()
	public IllegalMonitorStateException(String *msg*)
Parameters	
String *msg*	The detailed Message to be displayed.
See Also	Exception, RuntimeException, Object.notify(), Thread
Example	This example shows how the notify() method can be misused to cause an IllegalMonitorStateException to be thrown. First, a simple class is defined with nothing more than a Boolean, which will be used as a monitor.

```
// Declare a class that has a Boolean
// that will be used as a monitor
class MyClass {
    public Boolean myMonitor;
    public MyClass() {
        myMonitor = new Boolean(false);
    }
};
```

The following code uses the synchronized modifier to control access to the MyClass Boolean. This works fine. However, when it tries to use the notify() method to indicate that it is finished with the monitor, an IllegalMonitorStateException is thrown. This is because the thread does not own the monitor. Properly, notify() should be invoked within MyClass.

```
// Instantiate a MyClass object
MyClass m = new MyClass();
// Wait for synchronized access to the
// Boolean monitor
synchronized (m.myMonitor) {
    // Change its value.  This is fine.
    m.myMonitor = new Boolean(true);
    // Big mistake! Try to notify a
// monitor that
    // this thread does not own!
    try {
        notify();
    }
    catch(IllegalMonitorStateException e) {
    // Good move!
// Catch the exception!
System.out.println(e.getMessage());
}
```

IllegalThreadStateException

Description	Certain operations on Threads can only be performed when the Thread is in a certain state. For example, if the start() method is called after the Thread has been started, an IllegalThreadStateException is thrown. The

setDaemon() method throws the same object if it is called after the Thread has been started. Fortunately, when an IllegalThreadStateException object is thrown, the running of the Thread is usually not affected. The IllegalThreadStateException is a subclass of IllegalArgumentException.

Syntax	public class IllegalThreadStateException extends IllegalArgumentException
Package	java.lang
Import	java.lang.IllegalThreadStateException
Constructors	public IllegalThreadStateException()
	public IllegalThreadStateException(String *msg*)
Parameters	
String *msg*	The detailed Message to be displayed.
See Also	Exception, RuntimeException, Thread
Example	The following example tries to set the daemon state of a custom Thread (called MyThread) after it has been started. This is illegal, so an exception is thrown. If setDaemon() had been called before the start() method, however, all would have been fine.

```
MyThread t = new MyThread();
t.start();
try {
   t.setDaemon(true);
   }
catch (IllegalThreadStateException e) {
      System.out.println("Cannot set daemon!"
+ e.getMessage());
      }
```

INDEXOUTOFBOUNDSEXCEPTION

Description	The IndexOutOfBoundsException is used to classify RuntimeException classes that occur due to an index being out of an acceptable range of values. A subclass of IndexOutOfBoundsException is ArrayIndexOutOfBoundsException, which occurs when an index into an array is negative or too large.
Syntax	public class IndexOutOfBoundsException extends RuntimeException
Package	java.lang
Import	java.lang.IndexOutOfBoundsException
Constructors	public IndexOutOfBoundsException()
	public IndexOutOfBoundsException(String *msg*)
Parameters	
String *msg*	The detailed Message to be displayed.

See Also   Exception, RuntimeException, ArrayIndexOutOfBoundsException

Example   This example creates an array and attempts to access it with a large index.
An IndexOutOfBoundsException is thrown.

```
// Initialize the array
int intArray[] = new int[4];
for (int i = 0; i < intArray.length; ++i)
    intArray[i] = i;
// ...
    // Access the array.  Handle the
// exception so we will live!
    int index = 100;  // What kind of index
// is this?
    try {
        System.out.println("Val = " +
intArray[index]);
    }
    catch (IndexOutOfBoundsException e) {
        // Handle the exception and print out
// the detailed message...
    System.out.println(
"ArrayIndexOutOfBoundsException: "
+ e.getMessage());
    }
```

NEGATIVEARRAYSIZEEXCEPTION

Description   A NegativeArraySizeException object is thrown when an operation is performed on an array of negative size.

Syntax   public class **NegativeArraySizeException** extends RuntimeException

Package   java.lang

Import   java.lang.NegativeArraySizeException

Constructors   public **NegativeArraySizeException**()

public **NegativeArraySizeException**(String *msg*)

Parameters

String *msg*   The detailed Message to be displayed.

See Also   Exception, RuntimeException

Comments   As of the Java Developer's Kit 1.0, a NegativeArraySizeException object is *not* thrown when an array of negative size is *created*. However, it does occur when there is an attempt to access the array.

Example   The following code creates an array of negative size. When an attempt to assign a value to an element in it is made, a NegativeArraySizeException object is thrown.

```
        int sizeArray = -1; // What a bizarre size
// for an array!
        try {
            // Initialize the array with a bad size
            int intArray[] = new int[sizeArray];
intArray[0] = 6;
        }
        catch (NegativeArraySizeException e) {
            // Handle the exception and
// print out the detailed message...
            System.out.println("Bad array size = "
+ sizeArray + ". Msg = "
+ e.getMessage());
        }
```

NullPointerException

Description	This Exception is thrown whenever there is an attempt to use a variable or method of a null object, or when there is an access to a null array. Since, hypothetically, this could occur any time an object is used, it is not practical to trap for NullPointerException objects on a regular basis. Noting the exception, however, does aid in debugging.
Syntax	public class NullPointerException extends RuntimeException
Package	java.lang
Import	java.lang.NullPointerException
Constructors	public NullPointerException()
	public NullPointerException(String *msg*)
Parameters	
String *msg*	The detailed Message to be displayed.
See Also	Exception, RuntimeException
Example	This example causes a NullPointerException object to be thrown because an Object involved in the multiplication is set to null. The output string representation is "java.lang.NullPointerException".

```
        // Try to do some arithmetic
// with a null pointer
        try {
            int x = 5;
            Integer y = new Integer(5);
            y = null;  // Trick the compiler!
// Set Integer object to null
            // This next line will now cause
// an NullPointerException to be Thrown
            int z = x * y.intValue();
        }
        catch (NullPointerException e) {
            System.out.println(e.toString());
        }
```

NumberFormatException

Description   Java provides a variety of type wrappers for numeric objects. This allows numbers to be treated as objects, which is necessary for pure object-oriented programming. One of the constructors for subclasses of the Number type wrapper class takes a String and parses it to the appropriate numeric value. For example, the String constructor for the Integer class must be convertible to an integer value. Any time such a conversion fails, a NumberFormatException object is thrown. This is a potential problem for all String conversion methods of Number subclasses (such as Integer or Double).

Syntax   public class NumberFormatException extends IllegalArgumentException

Package   java.lang

Import   java.lang.NumberFormatException

Constructors   public NumberFormatException()

public NumberFormatException(String *msg*)

Parameters

String *msg*   The detailed Message to be displayed.

See Also   Exception, RuntimeException,

IllegalArgumentException,

any subclass of Number

Example   This example tries to create a Double object with a String that cannot be converted to a double. Consequently, a NumberFormatException object is thrown.

```
Double d;
String s = "Can You Parse this?";
// Try to construct a new Double object with
// this non-numeric String
try {
    d = new Double(s);
}
catch (NumberFormatException e) {
    // This will fail, so catch the exception
    System.out.println("Cannot convert " + s +
" to a number. Msg = " +
e.getMessage());
    }
```

SecurityException

Description   One of the key features of Java is the attention the language pays to security issues. Security is generally related to rules of access. There are tight regulations regarding I/O operations, network access, and Object modification. For example, Threads and ThreadGroups have access to each other restricted depending on their parent-child relationships. If a ThreadGroup attempts to access a ThreadGroup it does not have proper access to, a SecurityException object is thrown.

Syntax	public class SecurityException extends RuntimeException
Package	java.lang
Import	java.lang.SecurityException
Constructors	public SecurityException()
	public SecurityException(String *msg*)

Parameters

String *msg*	The detailed Message to be displayed.
See Also	Exception, RuntimeException,
	System. SecurityManager,
	Thread, ThreadGroup,
	java.net.*
Example	The following code checks to see if the current Thread has access to another custom Thread (MyThread) by catching SecurityException objects:

```
MyThread th = new MyThread();
//
// Print if if we have access to it...
String access;
try {
  th.checkAccess();
    access = new String("allowed");
}
// A SecurityException will be thrown if
// access is forbidden
catch (SecurityException se) {
    access = new String("forbidden");
}
// Print out the resulting access string
System.out.println("Access is " + access);
```

STRINGINDEXOUTOFBOUNDSEXCEPTION

Description	The charAt() method allows access to a character at a specific index into a String or StringBuffer object. If the index is negative or greater than or equal to its length, a StringIndexOutOfBoundsException object is thrown.
Syntax	public class StringIndexOutOfBoundsException extends IndexOutOfBoundsException
Package	java.lang
Import	java.lang.StringIndexOutOfBoundsException
Constructors	public StringIndexOutOfBoundsException()
	public StringIndexOutOfBoundsException(String *msg*)

Parameters

String *msg*   The detailed Message to be displayed.

See Also   Exception, RuntimeException,

        String, StringBuffer

Example   This example reflects a classic programming mistake. An attempt is made to access a String at the index corresponding to its length. However, Java is a zero-based system (like C), so the last valid index is at length -1. A StringIndexOutOfBoundsException object is thrown because of this mistake.

```
    // Create a string and try to access
// its last character
    String s = "MyString";
    try {
        System.out.println("Last char is "
+ s.charAt(s.length()));
    }
    // However the last valid index
// is s.length() - 1
    // And so an exception is thrown
    catch (StringIndexOutOfBoundsException e) {
System.out.println(e.getMessage());
    }
```

Error Classes

Since Error classes usually involve problems that are abnormal in nature or should not be caught because they are difficult to manage, the class descriptions that follow will only present examples where they are easily produced. However, these examples are only supplied for the purposes of illustration, and should not be used as a guide to how to write code for efficient handling of thrown Error objects. They also will not have their constructors defined, since you should never create them. For completion's sake, however, it should be pointed out that the Error subclasses have the same constructors as Error.

ERROR

Description   This class marks the top of a classification hierarchy of Throwable classes that are used to indicate abnormal conditions that are of a systematic nature that probably should not occur. Error classes are used for conditions that should not be caught or occur. Error objects are typically more extreme or "hard" errors, such as a runtime stack overflow.

Syntax   public class Error extends Throwable

Package   java.lang

Import   java.lang.Error

Constructors	public Error()
	public Error(String *msg*)
Parameters	
String *msg*	The detailed Message to be displayed.
See Also	Throwable
Example	A class is declared with a native method, MyNativeMethod(). Native methods are those written in a programming language other than Java, such as C. They are linked dynamically to the Java program at runtime.

```
// Declare a class that has a native method
class MyClass  {
public native void MyNativeMethod();
};
```

The following code instantiates MyClass and tries to call the native method. However, it does not exist, and an Error is thrown. It is caught and the detail message is displayed.

```
// Create the class and call its native method
MyClass m = new MyClass();
try {
    m.MyNativeMethod();
}
catch (Error e) {   // Catch the error
    // and print out its detail message
        System.out.println("Error: "
+ e.getMessage());
    }
```

Error classes are a subclass of the Throwable class, and are used to classify conditions that are abnormal. Typically these classes are for severe system conditions such as a runtime stack overflow, an internal error, or a problem with the Java virtual machine. Figure 9-3 shows the significant classes of the Error hierarchy. Other errors can be caused by inaccurate class definition caused by incorrectly compiled conditions, resulting in problems that are not caught until runtime.

Errors should not be caught, because they are difficult to manage and they will usually occur in unpredictable circumstances. In general, Java programs should not throw objects of class Error; in most cases, Exception classes should be used to indicate problems.

ABSTRACTMETHODERROR

Description	An abstract method is one that is not defined in a class, but needs to be defined in any subclass of the class. A class with an abstract method is itself abstract and so cannot be instantiated. An AbstractMethodError could occur if an abstract class and its subclasses are compiled in such a way that the fact that a method is abstract is not caught until runtime. For example, Class A is originally not abstract, and B is subclassed from it.

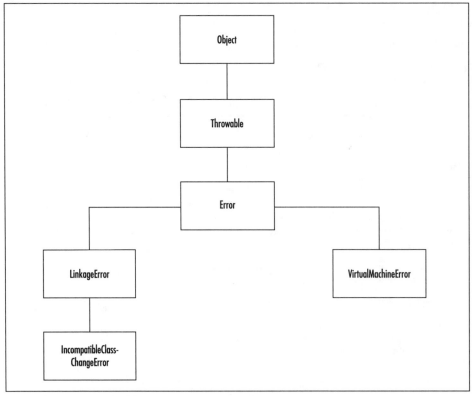

Figure 9-3 Class hierarchy of significant Error classes

	Then Class A is changed to abstract and compiled, but B is not. In this case, an abstract method in A called by B would not be caught until runtime.
Syntax	public class AbstractMethodError extends IncompatibleClassChangeError
Package	java.lang
Import	java.lang.AbstractMethodError
See Also	Throwable, Error, IncompatibleClassChangeError

CLASSCIRCULARITYERROR

Description	This error could occur if the Class A is declared as a subclass of B and vice versa. If these classes are not compiled correctly, the error would not be caught until runtime, resulting in a ClassCircularityError object being thrown.
Syntax	public class ClassCircularityError extends LinkageError

Package	java.lang
Import	java.lang.ClassCircularityError
See Also	Throwable, Error, LinkageError

ClassFormatError

Description	A ClassFormatError is thrown when the class that is used has an invalid file format. This problem could be caused by a variety of reasons, either hardware or software related.
Syntax	public class ClassFormatError extends LinkageError
Package	java.lang
Import	java.lang.ClassFormatError
See Also	Throwable, Error, LinkageError

IllegalAccessError

Description	Java methods have different levels of access control. On the extremes, public methods are available to any class, whereas private methods are only available to the class in which the method is declared. The compiler should catch any attempt to access a method that is private or unavailable to the class in question. However, an incomplete set of compilations could keep a class A that calls a private method in class B from being caught until runtime. In this case, an IllegalAccessError object is thrown.
Syntax	public class IllegalAccessError extends IncompatibleClassChangeError
Package	java.lang
Import	java.lang.IllegalAccessError
See Also	Throwable, Error, IncompatibleClassChangeError

IncompatibleClassChangeError

Description	Java provides very strong checking of a class definition at compile time. Class method access, use of abstract methods, and class inheritance relationships are inspected very thoroughly at compile time for any problematic conditions. However, incomplete compiles or problems related to this could cause such problems to go unnoticed until runtime. In these cases, an IncompatibleClassChangeError is thrown. Table 9-3 displays all subclasses of IncompatibleClassChangeError.
Syntax	public class IncompatibleClassChangeError extends LinkageError
Package	java.lang
Import	java.lang.IncompatibleClassChangeError
See Also	Throwable, Error, LinkageError

Table 9-3 IncompatibleClassChangeError subclasses

AbstractMethodError
IllegalAccessError
InstantiationError
NoSuchFieldError
NoSuchMethodError

INSTANTIATIONERROR

Description	Abstract classes and interfaces are constructs that need to be further defined by subclasses to create classes that can be instantiated at runtime. Attempts to instantiate abstract classes and interfaces usually will be caught by the compiler. However, unusual compilation conditions could result in these abnormalities not being caught until runtime. In these cases, an InstantiationError object may be thrown.
Syntax	public class InstantiationError extends IncompatibleClassChangeError
Package	java.lang
Import	java.lang.InstantiationError
See Also	Throwable, Error, IncompatibleClassChangeError

INTERNALERROR

Description	The Java virtual machine does not work in a vacuum. It will make certain demands on the native system's resources. Like any other program, it also may have internal difficulties. If any of these occur, an InternalError may be thrown. Such an error probably will be fatal.
Syntax	public class InternalError extends VirtualMachineError
Package	java.lang
Import	java.lang.InternalError
See Also	Throwable, Error, VirtualMachineError

LINKAGEERROR

Description	Because Java is an object-oriented environment, classes are very dependent in their relationships to each other. Access rules and inheritance relationships indicate some of the most important dependencies between classes. Java provides strict checking for these dependencies at compile time. However, a problem can occur due to unusual compilation conditions.

Suppose a class B depends on a definition of class A. After B is compiled, A is redefined to be no longer compatible with B. A is recompiled, but B is not. This will cause a problem that will not be caught until runtime. In these cases, an object of class LinkageError or a subclass of it will be thrown.

Syntax	public class LinkageError extends Error
Package	java.lang
Import	java.lang.LinkageError
See Also	Throwable, Error

NoClassDefFoundError

Description Java checks for the definition of all classes involved in the use of a class at compile time. If a class B uses a class A in any way, then the class definition of A, file A.class, must exist at compile time. However, if the class file cannot be found at runtime, a NoClassDefFoundError object will be thrown.

Syntax	public class NoClassDefFoundError extends LinkageError
Package	java.lang
Import	java.lang.NoClassDefFoundError
See Also	Throwable, Error, LinkageError

NoSuchFieldError

Description All references to a field in Java classes are usually resolved at compile time. If a class B refers to a field in class A, this field must exist in the definition of class B at the time B is compiled. However, if class A removes that field after B is compiled, then a problem will occur that will not be caught until runtime. In this case, an object of class NoSuchFieldError will be thrown.

Syntax	public class NoSuchFieldError extends IncompatibleClassChangeError
Package	java.lang
Import	java.lang.NoSuchFieldError
See Also	Throwable, Error, IncompatibleClassChangeError

NoSuchMethodError

Description All references to a method in Java classes are usually resolved at compile time. If a class B refers to a method in class A, this method must exist in the definition of class B at the time B is compiled. However, if class A removes that method after B is compiled, then a problem will occur that will not be caught until runtime. In this case, an object of class

NoSuchMethodError will be thrown. The NoSuchMethodError also may be thrown in cases where a method has not yet been implemented.

Syntax   public class NoSuchMethodError extends IncompatibleClassChangeError

Package   java.lang

Import   java.lang.NoSuchMethodError

See Also   Throwable, Error, IncompatibleClassChangeError, Thread

Example   At the time of this writing, the destroy() method of the class Thread had not yet been implemented. It throws a NoSuchMethodError object when it is called. The following code catches this object:

```
// Create an object of a custom Thread class
MyThread t;
//
// Call a method that has not
// yet been implemented
try {
    t.destroy();
}
catch (NoSuchMethodError e) {
    System.out.println(e.getMessage());
}
```

OutOfMemoryError

Description   Typically, Java will be implemented in environments with virtual memory. Consequently, it will be rare for an OutOfMemoryError object to be thrown. However, this could occur depending on the circumstances. When Java is implemented in embedded environments, this problem may occur more frequently. It will be difficult to trap for such errors, although some educated guesses could be made on where they could occur.

Syntax   public class OutOfMemoryError extends VirtualMachineError

Package   java.lang

Import   java.lang.OutOfMemoryError

See Also   Throwable, Error, VirtualMachineError

StackOverflowError

Description   This error will occur when a nested set of calls is made that results in too many variables and Object references being placed on Java's runtime stack. This will not occur frequently in most environments in which Java is implemented. If it does happen, however, a StackOverflowError object will be thrown.

Syntax   public class StackOverflowError extends VirtualMachineError

Package   java.lang

Import	java.lang.StackOverflowError
See Also	Throwable, Error

ThreadDeath

Description	A ThreadDeath object is thrown at a Thread when its stop() method is called. In general, it is not necessary to catch ThreadDeath unless some special cleanup process needs to occur. If ThreadDeath is caught by the Thread, then it needs to be rethrown so that the Thread will die. No error will be passed to a top-level error handler if this is not handled properly.
Syntax	public class ThreadDeath extends Error
Package	java.lang
Import	java.lang.ThreadDeath
See Also	Throwable, Error, Thread
Example	This example shows a Thread that catches ThreadDeath. It performs some cleanup, and then rethrows the ThreadDeath object.

```
// A custom Thread that custom catches ThreadDeath errors
class DeathCatcherThread extends Thread {
    // Threaded processing continues until ThreadDeath
    public void run() {
        try {
            // Loop forever
            while (true) {
// Do something
}
        }
// Catch ThreadDeath
        catch (ThreadDeath death) {
        //   Do some extraordinary cleanup here
            throw death;   // Rethrow ThreadDeath object
        }
    }
}
```

UnknownError

Description	This Error indicates that a serious problem of an unknown nature has occurred in the Java virtual machine. The throwing of an UnknownError probably indicates that the Java environment is in an unstable state and will probably soon terminate abnormally.
Syntax	public class UnknownError extends VirtualMachineError
Package	java.lang
Import	java.lang.UnknownError
See Also	Throwable, Error, VirtualMachineError

UNSATISFIEDLINKERROR

Description   Native methods are those written in a programming language other than Java, such as C. They are linked dynamically to the Java program at runtime. If the binary that contains the native method cannot be found, an UnsatisfiedLinkError object is thrown.

Syntax   public class UnsatisfiedLinkError extends LinkageError

Package   java.lang

Import   java.lang.UnsatisfiedLinkError

See Also   Throwable, Error, LinkageError

Example   A class is declared with a native method, MyNativeMethod().

```
// Declare a class that has a native method
class MyClass {
public native void MyNativeMethod();
};
```

The following code instantiates MyClass and tries to call the native method. However, it does not exist and an UnsatisfiedLinkError is thrown. It is caught and the detail message is displayed.

```
// Create the class and call its native method
MyClass m = new MyClass();
try {
    m.MyNativeMethod();
}
catch (UnsatisfiedLinkError e) {
// Catch the error
    // and print out its detail message
    System.out.println("Cannot link
native method");
}
```

VERIFYERROR

Description   One of the most important features of Java is its runtime verification of all classes that are used. The Java byte code verifier is used to ascertain whether the code being loaded is proper Java code or, possibly, some kind of virus or a corrupt file. If the verifier rejects the incoming code, the class will not be loaded. In this case, a VerifyError object is thrown.

Syntax   public class VerifyError extends LinkageError

Package   java.lang

Import   java.lang.VerifyError

See Also   Throwable, Error, LinkageError

VIRTUALMACHINEERROR

Description	The Java virtual machine is the heart of the runtime environment used for executing Java code. Like any other program, the Java virtual machine is dependent on system resources. It also may enter an internal state that prevents it from functioning properly. If any of these conditions occur, a VirtualMachineError object is thrown. Table 9-4 enumerates the VirtualMachineError subclasses.
Syntax	public class VirtualMachineError extends Error
Package	java.lang
Import	java.lang.VirtualMachineError
See Also	Throwable, Error

Table 9-4 VirtualMachineError subclasses

InternalError

OutOfMemoryError

StackOverflowError

UnknownError

The Exceptions Project: Validation Using Exception Handlers

Project Overview

The following project illustrates how to use exception handlers to validate array usage and number conversion. It shows how to both throw and catch exceptions. The project also uses a custom Exception class. After completing this project, you should have a pretty good feel for when and how to use exceptions, and also how to write your own Throwable classes.

Building the Project

1. Create a file called ExceptionApp and add the following code. This code imports the classes the application needs. The code also includes the menu options for creating an array, inserting an element into it, and listing its contents. The latter two trap for exceptions caused by bad array elements.

```
// Import the classes this program needs
import java.lang.*;
```

continued on next page

continued from previous page

```java
import java.io.DataInputStream;
import java.io.IOException;

// This standalone app is used for creating
// and adding elements to
// an integer array.   The program particularly illustrates
// exception that result from misusing an array.
public class ExceptionApp {
    // The actual array data...
    int dataArray[];  // The data array...

    // Constructor of ExceptionApp. Do nothing...
    public ExceptionApp() {
      // Initialize the array...
      setNewArrayDisplay(10);
    }

    // Start the application...
    public static void main(String args[]) {
        ExceptionApp a = new ExceptionApp();
        // Start at the main menu...
        a.gotoMainMenu();
    }

    // Start going through the menus...
    public void gotoMainMenu() {
      handleMainMenuSelection();
    }

    // Handle main menu selection
    void handleMainMenuSelection() {
     // Loop until user makes good choice...
     while (true) {
      displayMainMenu();
      int choice = getIntegerInput();
      switch (choice) {
       case 0: // Exit program...
         System.out.println("Exiting...");
         System.exit(0);
         break;
       case 1:
         createArrayMenu();
         break;
       case 2:
         insertElement();
         break;
       case 3:
         listElements();
         break;
       default:
         break;
      }
     } // end while...
    }

    // Display the main menu choices...
```

```java
    void displayMainMenu() {
      System.out.println("\n0. Quit");
      System.out.println("1. Create array");
System.out.println("2. Insert Element into the    array");
      System.out.println("3. List array contents");
      System.out.println("Enter choice:");
    }

    // Get input to create an array...
    void createArrayMenu() {
      System.out.println("Create size of new array:");
      int choice = getIntegerInput();
      setNewArrayDisplay(choice);
    }


    // Insert an element into the array...
    void insertElement() {
      System.out.println("Enter index to insert at:");
      int index = getIntegerInput();
      System.out.println("Enter value to insert:");
      int value = getIntegerInput();
      try {
        setElement(index,value);
        System.out.println("Index set!");
      }
      catch (DataArrayException e) {
        System.out.println("Error setting element: " +
          e.getMessage());
      }
    }

  // List elements in an array...
  void listElements() {
    try {
      for (int i = 0; i < dataArray.length; ++i) {
System.out.println(i + ": " + dataArray[i]);
          // Pause if a lot of lines...
if ((i > 0) && ((i % 20) == 0)) {
            System.out.println("Hit enter to
continue...");
            System.in.read();
          }
      }
    }
    catch (ArrayIndexOutOfBoundsException e) {
      System.out.println("Array out of bounds: " +
        e.getMessage());
    }
    catch (IOException e) {
      System.out.println("IOException: " +
        e.getMessage());
    }
    catch (Exception e) {
      System.out.println("Exception: " +
        e.getMessage());
    }
  }
```

2. Add the following code that creates an array and inserts elements into it. Exception handlers are used to both validate any changes to the array and verify the validity of any indexes into that array.

```
// Setup new display array...
void setNewArrayDisplay(int newSize)
{
 // Create the array of the specified size...
 try {
        createArray(newSize);
        // Initialize the array...
        for (int i = 0; i < dataArray.length; ++i)
                dataArray[i] = 0;
        System.out.println("Array created...");
 }
 // Handle any array size exceptions and
 // display message...
 catch (DataArrayException e) {
        invalidateArray(e.getMessage());
 }
 catch (Exception e) {
        invalidateArray(e.getMessage());
 }
 }

    // Invalidate the array...
   void invalidateArray(String msg) {
      System.out.println("Current Array is invalid");
      dataArray = null;  // Invalidate the array...
   }

   // Create an array of a certain size....
   // Throw a custom Exception to indicate an error...
void createArray(int newSize) throws
 DataArrayException {
        try {
            // Create the data array...
            dataArray = new int[newSize];
            // Initialize it with zeros.
                // Throws an exception if bad...
            for (int i = 0; i < dataArray.length; ++i)
                dataArray[i] = 0;
        }
        // Catch bad size exceptions...
        catch (ArrayIndexOutOfBoundsException e) {
            // Create detail message...
            String msg = "Array Out of Bounds: "
                + e.getMessage();
            throw new DataArrayException(msg);
        }
        // Catch bad size exceptions...
        catch (IllegalArgumentException e) {
            // Create detail message...
            String msg = "Illegal Argument: "
                + e.getMessage();
            throw new DataArrayException(msg);
        }
```

```
        // Catch any other exceptions...
        catch (Exception e) {
            // Create detail message...
            throw new DataArrayException("Exception: "
                    + e.getMessage() );
        }
    }

    // Set an element in the array...
    void setElement(int index, int val) throws
        DataArrayException {
        // See if we have a good index...
        try {
            dataArray[index] = val;
        }
        // Catch bad size exceptions...
        catch (ArrayIndexOutOfBoundsException e) {
            // Create detail message...
            String msg = "Array Out of Bounds: "
                + e.getMessage();
            throw new DataArrayException(msg);
        }
        // Catch any other exceptions...
        catch (Exception e) {
            // Create detail message...
            throw new DataArrayException("Exception: "
                    + e.getMessage() );
        }
    }
}
```

3. Finish by adding the code that gets an integer value from input. Note how NumberFormatException is used to trap input that is not numeric.

```
// Wait for an input string from the user
int getIntegerInput() {
    int choice;
    String in;
    DataInputStream dis = new DataInputStream(System.in);
    while (true) {
        try {
            in = dis.readLine();
            choice = Integer.valueOf(in).intValue();
            break;
        }
        catch (NumberFormatException e) {
            System.out.println("Invalid value.
Enter number");
        }
        // Catch any other exceptions...
        catch (IOException e) {
            System.out.println("Invalid value.
Enter number");
        }
    }
    return choice;
}
}
```

4. Add the definition of the custom Exception class for this project.

```
// This is a custom Exception handler to be thrown
// when an array error occurs...
class DataArrayException extends IllegalArgumentException {
  // Support the default constructor...
  public DataArrayException() {
    super();
  }
  // Construct a detail message...
  public DataArrayException(String s) {
    super(s);
  }
}
```

How It Works

This project illustrates exception handling by enabling you to freely change values that are used to create an array or modify the value of an index into the array. The program is a stand-alone Java application and presents you with text menus for creating an array of a specific size, changing an element, or listing the contents of the array. These are contained within the main class, ExceptionApp, which controls your interaction with the program. The class DataArrayException is a custom Exception class written specifically for this application.

The array that is created is called dataArray, and its size can be set dynamically by you. Whenever a new array is created, the old one is destroyed. An array of default size 10 is created when the frame is started.

The method used to create the array, createArray(), throws the custom exception DataArrayException when there is a problem with the size of the array. Java does not throw an error when an array of a bad size is created, but when it is accessed. Consequently, createArray() sets the initial values of the array to force an Exception to be thrown if there is a problem. The method traps a variety of potential problems. If any occur, the custom exception is thrown. The method that calls createArray() is called setNewArrayDisplay() and looks to see if there is any problem creating the array and setting its default current index. If there is an Exception here, the array is invalidated (set to null).

A couple of text prompts enable you to change the value of an element of the array at a specific index. After you pick the index and the new value, the program tries to update the current index via the setElement() method. This method throws a DataArrayException if the index is invalid. The current index is invalidated if this occurs.

The method getIntegerInput() is used to get an integer value from you. It uses a special type of InputStream object, called DataInputStream, to get a line of input. The method tries to convert the input String into a number using the Integer type wrapper class's valueOf() method. If it is not a numeric value, a NumberFormatException is thrown.

The listElements() method shows the current contents of the array. It traps for array index errors (which should not happen unless the array is bad). After a certain number of index elements is shown, it pauses and asks for you to press [ENTER] to continue. The read() method can throw an IOException, and so this exception is trapped here.

CLASSLOADER AND SECURITYMANAGER

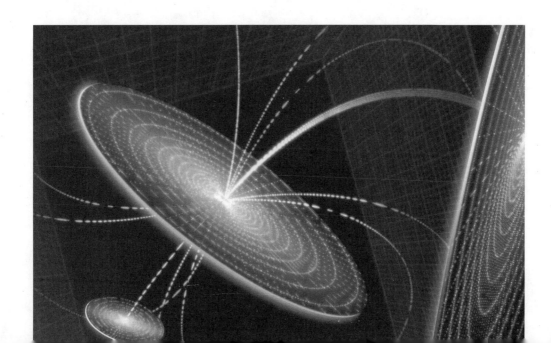

10

CLASSLOADER AND SECURITYMANAGER

One of Java's most notable features is its security mechanism, which is layered throughout its environment. On the lowest level, the language and the compiler provide the front line of security by removing dangerous constructs (such as pointers) from the language, and ensuring controlled access to objects. At the highest levels, the Java class loader ensures that classes come from authorized areas such as the local file system, a designated network host, or the applet server. At the next level, a runtime security manager has the job of enforcing a security policy regarding access to the local file system, network nodes, and other runtime components such as threads and system properties. The runtime class loader and security manager are implemented through two classes, ClassLoader and SecurityManager, which are the topics of this chapter.

Java Security

As just mentioned, Java has a multilayered security system. The role of security is to protect the computer that runs a Java application from any damage that can be wrought by the program intentionally or unintentionally. In the case of the latter, it is desirable that a poorly written program not cause the host computer to crash because of such things as mismanaged pointers or memory. In the worst case, a malicious program can attack the local file system or operate inside a network firewall. Looking at the big picture, both of these are very bad, since they compromise the user's faith in Java and loading code over the World Wide Web. Without strong security measures, one of the Web's greatest potentials may go unexploited because of the element of fear.

Java attacks the security problem at four different levels, two of which are now discussed briefly. The other two are addressed afterward at greater length.

Security at the Language and Compiler Level

The architects of Java have designed the language so that dangerous constructs that appear in operating-system-level languages such as C and C++ are removed. The worst of these are pointers. First of all, their misuse is the frequent cause of the most annoying and difficult to find bugs in a program. Even worse, pointers can be used in some operating environments to get access to system memory, compromising the stability of the host computer. For example, it is not hard to write a program that causes a Windows or Macintosh program to crash using C or C++! Consequently, Java has removed the memory pointer construct completely from its language. The result is not only a language that is more secure, but more graceful in its error recovery. For example, C programmers often deal with arrays using pointers. In Java, the array is a first class object. This means that, as objects, arrays support exception handling such as what occurs when an invalid index is accessed. In this case, an ArrayIndexOutOfBoundsException object may be thrown. The C language would just let your program corrupt memory.

Another element that is built into the lanaguage for security reasons is object access. Java has four access modifiers that address different levels of access to Java classes and methods: public, protected, private, and default. The compiler checks for any access that violates the declared access modifier of a class or method. If a violation is found, the compiler quits with an error.

Strong type checking also prevents an Object from casting itself into an Object from which it is not inherited. For example, a Hashtable object cannot cast itself into a Thread. Illegal casting is caught at both compile time and runtime.

Verifying Byte Codes

The Java compiler produces byte coded machine-independent instructions that are interpreted at runtime. This byte code instruction set effectively forms the foundation of the Java virtual machine. However, like any computerized machine, instructions can be mismanaged or misused to cause serious problems. The Java verifier ensures this does not happen by inspecting code as it is loaded into the Java environment. The verifier is a complex and powerful element of Java; it is perhaps its greatest line of defense against the intrusion of dangerous code. It functions as a sort of theorem prover, with code properties being established at the end of verification. The most important of these is that the code does not perform illegal conversions, which could let it be tricked into performing pointer operations. However, the verifier also validates that the code does not have stack problems (such as overflows), violate object access rules, or cause some violations of the type system.

The ClassLoader

The ClassLoader class implements the next level of Java security. The ClassLoader's role is to ensure a series of policies that define how a class is loaded and its interrelationship with the loading of another class. The key element of this is that classes are kept in a different namespace based on where they came from. There is a namespace for classes loaded from the local file system, which represents the default loader; classes loaded locally are called "built-ins." Classes can also be loaded from over a local network inside a firewall, or over the Web. In either case, the classes are partitioned into separate namespaces. The main thing about namespaces is that classes cannot illegally access classes from another namespace. How this works is now explained.

The built-in class namespace has the highest priority of the namespaces. Whenever a class is referenced, the runtime environment checks to see if the class appears in the built-in namespace. If it is not found there, then the namespace of the referencing class is searched. The crux of the class loader security is that a class from a network namespace cannot be loaded ahead of its counterpart in the built-in namespace. Otherwise, a network class can replace a high-priority class like the System class, thereby compromising security.

The namespace concept underlies the ClassLoader class that enforces a namespace policy. By default, a ClassLoader is not used. Instead, a mechanism for reading classes from the local file system is implemented. This is based on searching for classes in directories defined by the CLASSPATH environment variable. However, most browsers, such as Netscape Navigator, complement this default loading with a ClassLoader that is responsible for loading network classes. Some browsers, such as HotJava, may have loaders that differentiate classes loaded from within a firewall from those brought in over the Web. One way or another, an instantiated ClassLoader that is hooked into the runtime environment is called automatically by the virtual machine according to the namespace policy discussed in the previous paragraph.

The ClassLoader is an abstract class, with one method that needs to be defined in order to create a fully implemented subclass. This method is the loadClass() method, which loads a class from the file corresponding to its class name and converts it into a usable Class descriptor object. The loading of the class from a file is usually fairly simple, involving the standard reading of a file via input stream objects. The next step is to convert this data (in the form of a byte array) into a Class. This is done through the defineClass() method. This method, however, may cause a recursive call to loadClass() if the class being defined is a subclass of anything; in these cases, the superclass will need to be brought in before the subclass can be defined. If this superclass is not part of the loader's namespace, then the loader needs to define a policy for getting the class from a default namespace. Once defineClass() produces a Class descriptor object, the last step is to resolve the class with the resolveClass() method. This resolves any references the class makes to other classes and may also result in recursive calls to loadClass().

An example shows how to explicitly load a class from a specific class loader. In this case, the loader is the LocalClassLoader class discussed in the chapter project. To call this class and the loadClass() method, code like the following could be used:

```
// Get a reference to the loader
LocalClassLoader l = LocalClassLoader.getLocalClassLoader();
// Load the class from the local class loader
Class c = l.loadClass("MyClass",true);
// Instantiate the object
Object o = c.newInstance();
```

The newInstance() method of the Class class is used to create an instance of the loaded class.

The SecurityManager

The SecurityManager defines a set of policies for protecting the environment of the host as the instantiated classes are executed at runtime. It is an abstract class that has methods that must be defined to handle potentially dangerous actions. These SecurityManager methods throw a SecurityException object if the action in question is not permitted.

Foremost of these potentially dangerous actions is access to the local file system. Several methods, such as checkRead(), checkWrite(), and checkDelete() are used to see if an action can be performed on the local file system. If not, a SecurityException object is thrown. In some browsers, such as Netscape Navigator, network-loaded applets cannot perform *any* file operations; consequently, these check methods will always result in a security exception. Other browsers, such as HotJava, can be configured to have less rigid security based on whether or not the applet was loaded locally or originated from within a firewall. Applets loaded over the Web will almost never be granted access to the local file system.

Another area of concern is network security. By default, applets cannot open a network connection to any computer except the host that downloaded the applet. Furthermore, applets are generally prevented from running as network servers; Java servers are usually stand-alone applications. Methods such as checkConnect(), checkAccept(), and checkListen() are used to enforce network security policies.

The SecurityManager handles a variety of other runtime security concerns. The checkExec() method restricts the use of the Runtime to launch another process; this can be potentially risky, since the process may not be written in Java but in a system language such as C. Similarly, the checkLink() method restricts the invocation of native method libraries that can compromise security in a similar manner. The checkPropertiesAccess() and checkPropertyAccess() methods are used to verify access to System properties such as the Java class path. Changing these properties illegally can also compromise security.

The last area of concern ties in with the ClassLoader class. This involves checking the namespace in which a class originated, thus helping to prevent a class from an external source (such as network) from pretending that it is a built-in class. A variety of methods such as classLoaderDepth() and currentClassLoader() are used to manage this security concern. These methods bring in an important point. Unlike other classes, such as String, which a programmer "uses," the SecurityManager class is really meant for handling the internal state of the runtime environment. Its class loader and stack probing methods are protected and so must be implemented by a subclass to have any real use. Consequently, it is difficult to demonstrate how these methods are used except in the context of a full SecurityManager. On the other hand, the classes prefixed by "check" are usually public and can be called by your software to see if an operation (like file write) is allowed to be performed.

Related Classes

The System class can be used to get a reference to the current SecurityManager. This is done through the getSecurityManager() method. The code that follows shows how this reference can be used to see if a file can be deleted.

```
try {
        String filename = "myFile";
    // Get security manager and see if
        // delete operation is permitted...
        SecurityManager sm = System.getSecurityManager();
        sm.checkDelete(filename);
        File f = new File(filename);
        f.delete();
}
catch (SecurityException e) {
        System.out.println("Security Exception: " + e.toString());
}
catch (Exception e) {
        System.out.println("Exception: " + e.toString());
}
```

The System setSecurityManager() method is used to set the runtime SecurityManager. However, once the manager is set it cannot be replaced. For browsers, this occurs at initialization, and so a call to setSecurityManager() in an applet will result in a SecurityException object being thrown.

Finally, a quick note about the Compiler class. This was meant to be addressed in this section of the book. However, it was found to be designed mainly for implementation by companies that design products for Java development. Otherwise, the class does not do very much. Consequently, it is not of much interest to most developers.

About the Project

This chapter's project walks you through the steps that are necessary to create a custom subclass of ClassLoader. The particular ClassLoader in the example is a stand-alone application and reads in classes directly from the local file directory. On the surface this may not seem too difficult, but creating a ClassLoader can be a very involved process. The greatest challenge is how to deal with classes that have been brought in by the local file loader and reference classes brought in from another loader. This is related to security issues, since each class loader has a different namespace in which it maintains classes. If a class loaded in one namespace is superseded by one loaded in from another, the integrity of the runtime system can be compromised.

ClassLoader and SecurityManager Class and Method Summaries

Table 10-1 summarizes the system classes discussed in this chapter. Table 10-2 provides an overview of the methods of these classes.

Table 10-1 The ClassLoader and SecurityManager classes

Class	Description
ClassLoader	Enforces a policy regarding the loading of classes from various sources
SecurityManager	Enforces policies related to the runtime execution of instantiated classes

Table 10-2 ClassLoader and SecurityManager methods, by category

Class	Category	Methods
ClassLoader	Loading classes	loadClass
	Class definition	defineClass
	Class resolution	resolveClass, findSystemClass
SecurityManager	File security	checkDelete, checkRead, checkWrite
Network security		checkAccept, checkConnect, checkListen, checkSetFactory
Thread security		checkAccess
Runtime security		checkExec, checkExit, checkLink
Properties access		checkPropertiesAccess, checkPropertyAccess
Other security		checkPackageAccess, checkPackageDefinition, checkTopLevelWindow
Class loader actions	checkCreateClass Loader,	classLoaderDepth, currentClassLoader, inClassLoader,
Probes		classDepth, getClassContext, getInCheck, getSecurityContext, inClass

The java.lang.ClassLoader Class

Table 10-3 summarizes the methods of the ClassLoader class.

Table 10-3 Summary of ClassLoader methods

Method	Description
defineClass	Converts byte array into Class descriptor object
findSystemClass	Loads system class with base ClassLoader
loadClass	Takes class name and creates Class descriptor object
resolveClass	Resolves class references within a class

CLASSLOADER

Description   This abstract class is subclassed in order to implement a policy that controls how Java classes are loaded at runtime. One layer of Java security provides different levels of protection for the Java classes themselves. Classes can be loaded from different locations: typically they will come from either the local file system or the network. It is important to protect classes based on where they originated; otherwise, a class from over the Network can, for example, replace the System class and thus compromise security. The ClassLoader has a series of policies for how to load a class and how it should deal with classes that come from a different loader. The loader may maintain a cache or other structures for better performance.

Syntax   public abstract class **ClassLoader** extends Object

Package   java.lang

Import   java.lang.ClassLoader

Constructors   protected **ClassLoader()**

Parameters   None.

See Also   Object, Class, SecurityManager

Example   This code is from the chapter project and shows how to use static methods to construct a ClassLoader that loads classes from a local file directory. The LocalClassLoader cannot be instantiated by an external class. However, an outside class can get a reference to it through the public getLocalClassLoader() method.

```
// Loads classes from the current directory...
public class LocalClassLoader extends ClassLoader {
   // The loader is static and so can be created only once
   private static LocalClassLoader loader=new LocalClassLoader();

   // Private constructor
   private LocalClassLoader() {
    //    create cache and other stuff here .
   }
```

continued on next page

continued from previous page

```
   // Return reference to this LocalClassLoader object
   public static synchronized LocalClassLoader
    getLocalClassLoader() {
return loader;
   }
```

To get a reference to an instance of this class, use the following code:

```
LocalClassLoader l = LocalClassLoader.getLocalClassLoader();
```

Methods

DEFINECLASS

Class Name	ClassLoader
Description	This method takes a byte array and returns its class runtime representation as an instance of Class. A class loader will need to read in a class from some kind of storage mechanism. This could be a file storage system or network sockets. One way or another the information will arrive as an array of bytes. The defineClass() method takes these bytes and converts them to an instance of Class. The resulting Class will then be ready for the next step of being resolved.
Syntax	protected final Class defineClass(byte *data[]*, int *offset*, int *len*)
Parameters	
byte *data[]*	The byte array to be converted into a class.
int *offset*	Where to start loading from the byte array to begin Class definition.
int *len*	How many bytes from offset to use in Class definition.
Returns	An instance of Class representing the newly defined class.
Exceptions	A ClassFormatError is thrown if the byte array is not a valid class representation.
See Also	Object, Class, SecurityManager, loadClass(), resolveClass()
Example	This example tries to take a previously created byte array and convert it into a class.

```
try {
    // Get Class Loader from a previously created class
    ClassLoader l = c.getClassLoader();
    // Define new class from a byte stream
    Class c = l.defineClass(bytes,0,bytes.length);
}
catch (ClassFormatError e) {
System.out.println(e.getMessage());
}
```

FINDSYSTEMCLASS

Description	This method is used to load a system class that has the base ClassLoader. The Java runtime has a null default loader and reads in classes from a directory defined by the CLASSPATH environment variable.
Syntax	protected final Class findSystemClass(String *name*)
Parameters	
String *name*	The name of the System class.
Returns	A Class description of the system class with the base class loader.
Exceptions	A NoClassDefFoundError or ClassNotFoundException is thrown if the class is not defined or found.
See Also	Object, Class, SecurityManager
Example	Try to find the system class and handle any exception that may be thrown as a result of the call.

```
try {
   findSystemClass(name);
}
catch (ClassNotFoundException e) {
   //   handle not found system class
}
```

LOADCLASS

Class Name	ClassLoader
Description	This method takes the name of a class and returns a Class descriptor object. The loadClass() method is the only method that needs to be defined by an implementation of ClassLoader. This is the key class of the loader—it brings in the data corresponding to the class name and converts it into a usable Class descriptor object. The data could be brought in a variety of ways defined by the specific implementation of the ClassLoader: it could be loaded from local file storage, over the Internet, or from a host internal to a firewall. A loadClass() method will use the defineClass() method to convert this data into a Class descriptor. If the boolean value is set to true, the method should also resolve the class by calling resolveClass(). The loadClass() method is called by the underlying virtual machine as part of the general workings of the runtime environment.
Syntax	protected final Class loadClass(String *name*, boolean *resolve*)
Parameters	
String *name*	The name of the class to load.
boolean *resolve*	Whether the resulting class should be resolved.

continued on next page

continued from previous page

Returns	A Class descriptor of the loaded class.
Exceptions	A ClassNotFoundException is thrown if the class could not be located or defined.
See Also	Object, Class, SecurityManager, defineClass(), resolveClass()

Example

```
try {
    // Use an internally created class loader
    ClassLoader l = LocalFileLoader.getLocalFileLoader();
    // Load in the new class and resolve it
    Class c = l.loadClass("MyClass",true);
    // Instantiate the class
    MyClass m = (MyClass) c.newInstance();
    // Call a method of the new object
    m.myMethod();
}
catch (ClassNotFoundException e) {
}
```

RESOLVECLASS

Class Name	ClassLoader
Description	After a class is loaded by the ClassLoader (via the loadClass() method), it needs to be resolved before it is used. The resolveClass() method does this resolution by resolving the references to the classes used by this class. This may result in recursive calls to loadClass() so that the referenced classes may be loaded and resolved.
Syntax	protected final void **resolveClass**(Class *c*)
Parameters	
Class *c*	The class to be resolved.
Returns	None.
Exceptions	None.
See Also	Object, Class, SecurityManager, loadClass(), defineClass()
Example	Here is a rough outline of how a ClassLoader may use resolveClass() after a loadClass() call.

```
try {
    // Define new class from a byte stream
    Class c = defineClass(bytes,0,bytes.length);
    // Resolve the class
    resolveClass(c);
}
catch (ClassFormatError e) {
System.out.println(e.getMessage());
}
```

The java.lang.SecurityManager Class

Table 10-4 summarizes the methods of the SecurityManager.

Table 10-4 Summary of SecurityManager methods

Method	Description
checkAccept	Checks to see whether server will accept connection
checkAccess	Checks to see if a Thread or ThreadGroup has access to this ThreadGroup
checkConnect	Checks to see whether a socket can connect to a host
checkCreateClassLoader	Checks to see if the system already has a ClassLoader
checkDelete	Checks to see if a file is allowed to be deleted
checkExec	Checks to see if is a system command can be executed
checkExit	Checks to see if the program is allowed to exit the virtual machine
checkLink	Checks to see if the program is allowed to link in the specified library
checkListen	Checks to see whether a server socket can listen to the specified port
checkPackageAccess	Checks to see if access to a package is permitted
checkPackageDefinition	Checks to see whether definition of new classes in a package is permitted
checkPropertiesAccess	Checks to see if current application has access to system properties
checkPropertyAccess	Checks to see if current application has access to a system property
checkRead	Checks to see if a specific file read is permitted
checkSetFactory	Checks to see if a network factory has already been established
checkTopLevelWindow)	Checks to see if a top-level window can be created
checkWrite	Checks to see if a specific file write is permitted
classDepth	Returns first occurrence of a class name on the runtime stack
classLoaderDepth	Returns first occurrence of current ClassLoader on the runtime stack
currentClassLoader	Returns reference to current ClassLoader on runtime stack
getClassContext	Returns class context information
getInCheck	Tells whether SecurityManager is currently performing a security check
getSecurityContext	Returns object with security related information about the current execution state
inClass	Checks to see if a class is found on runtime stack
inClassLoader	Tells whether a classLoader is currently being used

SECURITYMANAGER

Description	This abstract class is subclassed in order to implement a security policy. The SecurityManager is used to provide control over potentially dangerous actions that an application method can perform. Foremost of these problematic actions are I/O and network calls, which are the areas that are most susceptible to security violations. However, the SecurityManager class is also used to restrict: access to System Properties and the Runtime; modification of Thread and ThreadGroup objects; and probing class loaders on the runtime stack. The SecurityManager is an abstract class and so must be implemented to construct an actual policy.
Syntax	public abstract class SecurityManager extends Object
Package	java.lang
Import	java.lang.SecurityManager
Constructors	protected SecurityManager()
Parameters	None.
Exceptions	A SecurityException is thrown if object cannot be created.
See Also	Object, System, ClassLoader
Example	This code instantiates a SecurityManager subclass and makes it the system SecurityManager.

```
try {
      // Try to set a new security manager
      System.setSecurityManager(new MySecurityManager());
}
catch (SecurityException e) {
      System.out.println("Security Manager already installed!");
}
```

Variables

INCHECK

Class	SecurityManager
Description	Tracks whether or not there is a security inspection in progress. This boolean variable is set to true whenever a security check is currently being performed. This might be useful for threaded implementations of the SecurityManager.
Syntax	public boolean **inCheck()**
See Also	getInCheck()
Example	

```
    if (!inCheck)
        //   start security check
```

Methods

CHECKACCEPT

Class Name	SecurityManager
Description	This method verifies that a socket connection at the specified host and port will be accepted. One of the key areas of concern in Java security is that of network connectivity. Applets typically cannot open a network connection to any computer except for the host that downloaded the applet classes. Some browsers also prevent applets from functioning as a server. The checkAccept() method is used to see if a server will accept a socket connection from the given host and port.
Syntax	public void **checkAccept**(String *host*, int *port*)
	public void **checkAccess**(Thread *t*)
Parameters	
String *host*	The host name of the computer to connect.
int *port*	The protocol port of the connection.
Thread *t*	The Thread to be tested to see if it has access to this ThreadGroup.
Returns	None.
Exceptions	SecurityException thrown if server will not access the connection.
See Also	java.net.ServerSocket
Example	

```
try {
        SecurityManager sm = System.getSecurityManager();
   sm.checkAccept(inSocket.getInetAddress().getHostName(),
    inSocket.getPort());
}
catch (SecurityException e) {
   System.out.println("Security Exception: " +    e.toString());
}
```

This code creates a custom Thread, called myThread, and checks to see if it has access to the current ThreadGroup. In this case, it does have access.

```
try {
        SecurityManager sm = System.getSecurityManager();
      MyThread t = new MyThread();
        sm.checkAccess(t);
}
catch (SecurityException e) {
   System.out.println("Security Exception: " +    e.toString());
}
```

CHECKACCESS(THREADGROUP G)

Class Name SecurityManager

Description This method checks to see if the specified ThreadGroup object is allowed to modify elements of this ThreadGroup. ThreadGroups are containers of Threads and other ThreadGroups. They are used, among other things, to control access relations. For example, a ThreadGroup cannot change a Thread in a parent ThreadGroup. The checkAccess() method is used to check to see if the specified ThreadGroup is allowed to modify elements of the ThreadGroup where the method was invoked.

Syntax public void **checkAccess**(ThreadGroup g)

Parameters

ThreadGroup g The ThreadGroup to be tested to see if it can modify this ThreadGroup.

Returns None.

Exceptions A SecurityException is thrown if the ThreadGroup cannot access the ThreadGroup.

See Also Thread, ThreadGroup

Example This code creates a ThreadGroup and checks to see if it has access to the current ThreadGroup. In this case, it does have access.

```
try {
   SecurityManager sm = System.getSecurityManager();
   // Create thread group where the current
       // ThreadGroup is the parent...
       ThreadGroup g = new ThreadGroup("My Group");
       // See if it has access to this ThreadGroup...
       sm.checkAccess(g);
       System.out.println("Access granted.");
   }
   catch (SecurityException e) {
   System.out.println("Security Exception: " +    e.toString());
   }
```

CHECKCONNECT

Class Name SecurityManager

Description This method checks to see whether or not a socket can connect to the specified host and port. One of the key areas of concern in Java security is that of network connectivity. Applets typically cannot open a network connection to any computer except for the host that downloaded the applet classes. The checkConnect() method is used to see if a connection to a specific host and port is allowed. In a browser environment, if the host is not the same as the host that originated the applet, a SecurityException object will probably be thrown.

Syntax	public void **checkConnect**(String *host*, int *port*)
	public void **checkConnect**(String *host*, int *port*, Object *context*)
Parameters	
String *host*	The host name of the computer to connect.
int *port*	The protocol port of the connection.
Object *context*	The additional context information.
Returns	None.
Exceptions	A SecurityException is thrown if the operation is not permitted.
See Also	java.net.SocketImpl
Example	

```
try {
        SecurityManager sm = System.getSecurityManager();
    sm.checkConnect("http://www.waite.com/",80);
    //   if success then connect
}
catch (SecurityException e) {
    System.out.println("Security Exception: " +    e.toString());
}
```

CHECKCREATECLASSLOADER

Class Name	SecurityManager
Description	This method checks to see if the system has been assigned a ClassLoader. A ClassLoader object is used to implement a policy for loading Java classes. For example, classes could be loaded off the network or a certain local disk directory. By default, the runtime environment does not have a ClassLoader, but loads files from the directory defined by the CLASSPATH environment variable. The checkCreateClassLoader() method can be used to check to see if a ClassLoader has already been loaded if there is a request to load a new one.
Syntax	public void **checkCreateClassLoader**()
Parameters	None.
Returns	None.
Exceptions	A SecurityException is thrown if the operation is not permitted.
See Also	ClassLoader

Example

```
try {
   SecurityManager sm = System.getSecurityManager();
   // Check to see if we are permitted to load a new
   // ClassLoader
   sm.checkCreateClassLoader(g);
         // If no exception, then create the new loader
      //    Load new class loader
   }
   catch (SecurityException e) {
   System.out.println("Security Exception: " +    e.toString());
   }
```

CHECKDELETE

Class Name	SecurityManager
Description	This method checks to see if the SecurityManager will allow a file to be deleted. A SecurityManager of a browser severely restricts file operations that an applet can perform. The checkDelete() method checks to see if a delete operation can be performed on a file. Note that the file name provided as the parameter is a String and so may be platform dependent. Thus, the String needs to be constructed carefully if portability is not to be compromised. See java.io.File for how this can be accomplished.
Syntax	public void **checkDelete**(String *filename*)
Parameters	
String *filename*	The file that is being considered for deletion.
Returns	None.
Exceptions	A SecurityException is thrown if the operation is not permitted.
See Also	File
Example	The following code checks to see if a file can be deleted. If the SecurityManager allows it, the file is removed.

```
try {
        String filename = "myFile";
   // Get security manager and see if
        // delete operation is permitted...
        SecurityManager sm = System.getSecurityManager();
        sm.checkDelete(filename);
        File f = new File(filename);
        f.delete();
}
catch (SecurityException e) {
        System.out.println("Security Exception: " + e.toString());
}
catch (Exception e) {
        System.out.println("Exception: " + e.toString());
}
```

CHECKEXEC

Class Name	SecurityManager
Description	This method checks to see if a system command can be executed. The exec() method of the Runtime class executes a system command. The command to be executed can be a Java application or another program. Since the Runtime represents the direct runtime environment of Java, access to it is restricted by many browsers. Furthermore, the exec() method can cause a serious compromise of basic security, since the command program could be written in another language (such as C) that has no restrictions. It would thus get access to a wide range of system resources, including disk files. Consequently, browser applets will usually be denied this operation. The checkExec() method can be used to see if the resident SecurityManager will allow a specific command to be executed.
Syntax	public void **checkExec**(String *cmd*)
Parameters	
String *cmd*	The command to be executed.
Returns	None.
Exceptions	A SecurityException is thrown if the operation is not permitted.
See Also	Runtime
Example	The following call checks to see if the Java compiler can be launched from the current program. If so, it then starts the Java compiler, which builds the class contained in the file ExecTest.java.

```
try {
        // Check to see if the command can be executed
    SecurityManager sm = System.getSecurityManager();
        sm.checkExec("javac");
        // Get a reference to the Runtime environment and
        // then launch the command to compile a file
        Runtime.getRuntime().exec("javac ExecTest.java");
}
catch (SecurityException e) {
        System.out.println("Security Exception: " + e.toString());
}
catch (IOException e) {
        System.out.println("Exec error " + e.getMessage() );
}
```

CHECKEXIT

Class Name	SecurityManager
Description	This method checks to see if the program is allowed to exit the virtual machine with the specified exit code. The exit() method of the Runtime class exits the virtual machine with the specified exit code. The exit() method shuts down the virtual machine and so, in a browser environment, would prevent any other applets from running. Furthermore, since the Runtime represents the direct runtime environment of Java, access to it is restricted by many browsers. The checkExit() method verifies that an exit() is allowed in the current environment.
Syntax	public void **checkExit**(int *status*)
Parameters	
int *status*	The exit status.
Returns	None.
Exceptions	A SecurityException is thrown if the operation is not permitted.
See Also	Runtime
Example	This code checks to see if there is an exit from the virtual machine. If so, the code exits.

```
try {
   SecurityManager sm = System.getSecurityManager();
         sm.checkExit(0);
         Runtime.getRuntime().exit(0);
}
catch (SecurityException e) {
         System.out.println("Security Exception: " + e.toString());
}
```

CHECKLINK

Class Name	SecurityManager
Description	This method checks to see if the applet is allowed to link to the specified library. If the library uses native methods, the link may be prohibited, since native methods can pose security problems. In particular, native methods can be written in a language other than Java and so may not be subjected to the same set of security restrictions. For example, if a native method is written in C, it will have access to all kinds of system resources that a Java program cannot use. Consequently, browsers will typically prevent applets from linking in native method libraries. The checkLink() method is used to verify whether or not this is actually the case.
Syntax	public void **checkLink**(String *lib*)

Parameters

String *lib*   The library to be linked to.

Returns   None.

Exceptions   A SecurityException is thrown if the operation is not permitted.

See Also   Runtime

Example

```
try {
   SecurityManager sm = System.getSecurityManager();
        sm.checkLink(MyLibrary);
        //   if success then link to library
}
catch (SecurityException e) {
        System.out.println("Security Exception: " + e.toString());
}
```

CHECKLISTEN

Class Name   SecurityManager

Description   This method checks to see if a server socket can listen to the specified
                         local port. One of the key areas of concern in Java security is that of net-
                         work connectivity. Applets typically cannot open a network connection to
                         any computer except to the host that downloaded the applet classes. Some
                         browsers also prevent applets from functioning as a server. The
                         checkListen() method is used to see if a socket server can listen to the
                         specified port.

Syntax   public void **checkListen**(int *port*)

Parameters

int *port*   The port to listen to.

Returns   None.

Exceptions   A SecurityException is thrown if the operation is not permitted.

See Also   java.net.SocketImpl

Example

```
try {
        SecurityManager sm = System.getSecurityManager();
   sm.checkListen(port);
   //   if success then listen
}
catch (SecurityException e) {
   System.out.println("Security Exception: " +    e.toString());
}
```

CHECKPACKAGEACCESS

Class Name	SecurityManager
Description	The checkPackageAccess() method is used to see whether the current applet is allowed to access the package specified in the String parameter.
Syntax	public void **checkPackageAccess**(String *pkg*)
Parameters	
String *pkg*	The name of the package to access.
Returns	None.
Exceptions	A SecurityException is thrown if the operation is not permitted.
See Also	Object
Example	

```
System.getSecurityManager().checkPackageAccess("java.net");
```

CHECKPACKAGEDEFINITION

Class Name	SecurityManager
Description	The checkPackageDefinition() method is used to see if the current application is allowed to define new classes in the package specified by the String parameter.
Syntax	public void checkPackageDefinition(String *pkg*)
Parameters	
String *pkg*	The name of the package to add definitions to.
Returns	None.
Exceptions	A SecurityException is thrown if the operation is not permitted.
See Also	Object
Example	

```
System.getSecurityManager().checkPackageDefinition("java.net");
```

CHECKPROPERTIESACCESS

Class Name	SecurityManager
Description	This method checks to see if the current application has access to the System properties. The System Properties object represents the environment in which a Java program is running. The Properties class is a hash table of String keys and String values and replaces the traditional getenv() and setenv() techniques that C programmers use to get the program's

environment. Since these properties are global to the System, their unfettered use may pose some security issues. Consequently, there may be some security restrictions regarding access to System properties. The checkPropertiesAccess() method is used to verify that an application has access to this data.

Syntax	public void checkPropertiesAccess()
Parameters	None.
Returns	None.
Exceptions	A SecurityException is thrown if access to System properties is denied.
See Also	System
Example	The following code checks to see if the application has access to the System properties. If so, then it retrieves a reference to the table and prints its contents to standard output.

```
try {
        System.out.println("Try method");
        // See if the program has access to the
        // System properties...
        System.getSecurityManager().checkPropertiesAccess();
        // If so get the properties and list to
        // standard out...
        Properties p = System.getProperties();
        p.list(System.out);
}
catch (SecurityException e) {
        System.out.println("Security Exception: " + e.toString());
}
```

CHECKPROPERTYACCESS

Class Name	SecurityManager
Description	This method checks to see if the current application has access to the System property matching the specified key. The System Properties object represents the environment in which a Java program is running. The Properties class is a hash table of String keys and String values and replaces the traditional getenv() and setenv() techniques that C programmers use to get the program's environment. Since these properties are global to the System, their unfettered use may pose some security issues. Consequently, there may be some security restrictions regarding access to System properties. The checkPropertyAccess() method is used to verify that an application has access to the property matching the specified key.
Syntax	public void **checkPropertyAccess**(String *key*)
	public void **checkPropertyAccess**(String *key*, String *def*)

Parameters

String *key*	The key of the property to check.
String *def*	The default value of the property.

Returns None.

Exceptions A SecurityException is thrown if access to System Properties object with the specified key is denied.

See Also System

Example The following code checks to see if the application has access to the System property matching the specified key. If so, then it retrieves the property and prints its contents to standard output.

```
try {
        System.out.println("Try method");
        // See if the program has access to the
        // System properties...
 SecurityManager sm = System.getSecurityManager();
 sm.checkPropertyAccess("java.version");
        // If so get the properties and list to
        // standard out...
        System.out.println(
System.getProperty("java.version"));
}
catch (SecurityException e) {
        System.out.println("Security Exception: " + e.toString());
}
```

CHECKREAD

Class Name	SecurityManager
Description	This method checks to see if an input stream with the specified FileDescriptor object can be created. File input operations pose a particular security concern. In particular, it is not desirable to let applets read files at random. These files may have secure information that is not meant to be released to the public at large. Consequently, a role of the SecurityManager is to prevent creation of illegal file input streams. This particular checkRead() method verifies that a file input operation can be initiated with the given FileDescriptor object.
Syntax	public void **checkRead**(FileDescriptor *fd*)

Parameters

FileDescriptor *fd*	The file descriptor that is to be used in the creation of an input stream.

Returns None.

Exceptions A SecurityException is thrown if the operation is not permitted.

See Also InputStream

Example   The following code creates an input stream, gets its file descriptor, and
then checks to see if can be used to create another input stream. If this is
allowed, then it proceeds with the operation.

```
try {
    // Open an input stream...
        FileInputStream in = new FileInputStream("MyFile");
        // Get its file descriptor and check
        // if a read operation can be performed with it...
        FileDescriptor fd = in.getFD();
        System.getSecurityManager().checkRead(fd);
        // If success, create another stream from it...
        FileInputStream in2 = new FileInputStream(fd);
}
catch (SecurityException e) {
        System.out.println("Security Exception: " + e.toString());
}
catch (IOException e) {
        System.out.println("IO Exception: " + e.toString());
}
catch (Exception e) {
        System.out.println("Exception: " + e.toString());
}
```

CHECKREAD(STRING NAME)

Class Name	SecurityManager
Description	This method checks to see if an input stream with the specified file name can be created. File input operations pose a special security concern. In particular, it is not desirable to let applets read files at random. These files may have secure information that is not meant to be released to the public at large. Consequently, a role of the SecurityManager is to prevent creation of illegal file input streams. This particular checkRead() method verifies that an input stream for the specified file can be initiated.
Syntax	public void **checkRead**(String *name*)
	public void **checkRead**(String *name*, Object *o*)
Parameters	
String *name*	The file to be opened.
Object *o*	The other context information to be inspected.
Returns	None.
Exceptions	A SecurityException is thrown if the operation is not permitted.
See Also	InputStream
Example	The following code checks to see if an input stream for the specified file can be created. If this is allowed, then it proceeds with the operation.

```
try {
      // Check to see if we can open the file
   System.getSecurityManager().checkRead("MyFile");
         // If success, create another stream from it...
         FileInputStream in = new FileInputStream("MyFile");
}
catch (SecurityException e) {
         System.out.println("Security Exception: " + e.toString());
}
catch (IOException e) {
         System.out.println("IO Exception: " + e.toString());
}
catch (Exception e) {
         System.out.println("Exception: " + e.toString());
}
```

CHECKSETFACTORY

Class Name	SecurityManager
Description	This method checks to see if a factory for network operations has already been established. The java.net package provides a series of interfaces for implementing "factories" that are used to manage network streams and related policies. These factories should be established once at initialization and not be allowed to be replaced afterwards. The checkSetFactory() method is used to see if a factory for network operations has already been established.
Syntax	public void **checkSetFactory()**
Parameters	None.
Returns	None.
Exceptions	A SecurityException is thrown if the operation is not permitted.
See Also	java.net
Example	

```
try {
        SecurityManager sm = System.getSecurityManager();
   sm.checkSetFactory();
   //   if success then set the factory
}
catch (SecurityException e) {
   System.out.println("Security Exception: " +    e.toString());
}
```

CHECKTOPLEVELWINDOW

Class Name	SecurityManager
Description	This method checks to see if a top-level window can be created. The Window class of the awt package is used to create pop-up windows. In some circumstances, it may be desirable to restrict the creation of such windows. The checkTopLevelWindow() method is used to find out when such circumstances apply.
Syntax	public boolean **checkTopLevelWindow**(Object *window*)
Parameters	
Object *window*	The top-level window that is going to be created.
Returns	True if top-level windows can be created, otherwise there should be a warning.
Exceptions	A SecurityException is thrown if the top-level window cannot be created.
See Also	java.awt.Window
Example	This example creates a Frame window and displays it if the checkTopLevelWindow() method indicates that this is the thing to do.

```
        // Create a Window frame
        SecurityManager sm = System.getSecurityManager();
        Frame fr = new Frame("My Frame");
        fr.resize(200,200);
        // See if we can or should display it
     try {
         if (sm.checkTopLevelWindow(fr) )
         fr.show();
    else
      System.out.println("Top level restrictions apply");
  }
  catch (SecurityException e) {
      System.out.println("Cannot create top
level window");
        }
```

CHECKWRITE

Class Name	SecurityManager
Description	This method checks to see if an output stream with the specified FileDescriptor object can be created. File output operations pose a special security concern. In particular, it is not desirable to let applets write files at random. These files could cause damage directly or indirectly (via executables) to the local system. Consequently, a role of the SecurityManager is to prevent creation of illegal file output streams. This particular checkWrite() method verifies that a file output operation can be initiated with the given FileDescriptor object.

Syntax	public void **checkWrite**(FileDescriptor *fd*)
	public void **checkWrite**(String *filename*)
Parameters	
FileDescriptor *fd*	The file descriptor that is to be used in the creation of an output stream.
String filename	The filename of the desired file to write.
Returns	None.
Exceptions	A SecurityException is thrown if the operation is not permitted.
See Also	OutputStream
Example	The following code creates an output stream, gets its file descriptor, and then checks to see if it can be used to create another output stream. If this is allowed, then it proceeds with the operation.

```
try {
        // Open an output stream...
        FileOutputStream out = new FileOutputStream("AFile");
        // Get its file descriptor and check
        // if a write operation can be performed with it...
        FileDescriptor fd = out.getFD();
        System.getSecurityManager().checkWrite(fd);
        // If success, create another stream from it...
        FileOutputStream out2 = new FileOutputStream(fd);
}
catch (SecurityException e) {
        System.out.println("Security Exception: " + e.toString());
}
catch (IOException e) {
        System.out.println("IO Exception: " + e.toString());
}
catch (Exception e) {
        System.out.println("Exception: " + e.toString());
}
```

The following code checks to see if an output stream for the specified file can be created. If this is allowed, then it proceeds with the operation.

```
try {
        // See if the output stream can be created for
        // the specifed file
        System.getSecurityManager().checkWrite("Afile");
    // Open an output stream...
        FileOutputStream out = new FileOutputStream("AFile");
}
catch (SecurityException e) {
        System.out.println("Security Exception: " + e.toString());
}
catch (IOException e) {
        System.out.println("IO Exception: " + e.toString());
}
catch (Exception e) {
        System.out.println("Exception: " + e.toString());
}
```

CLASSDEPTH

Class Name	SecurityManager
Description	This method returns the position of the first occurrence of a class name in the runtime stack. It is often necessary for the SecurityManager to inspect the runtime stack to make security decisions. In particular, it may check the stack to see which ClassLoader was used to load a class. Java uses separate namespaces for classes loaded over a local file system (called "built-ins") and those loaded from over a network (imported classes). When a class refers to another class, Java checks to see if the referencing class is a built-in or is imported. This is important for security reasons to prevent an imported class from taking over the behavior of a built-in. For example, an imported System class cannot take over the behavior of the built-in System class. Furthermore, an imported class needs to verify which host it came from—this further aids in the development of a security policy. The classDepth() method is an internal method that can be used to make decisions about built-in versus imported classes.
Syntax	protected int **classDepth**(String *classname*)
Parameters	
String *classname*	The class to be inspected.
Returns	The first occurrence of the class in the runtime stack.
Exceptions	None.
See Also	ClassLoader
Example	

```
int depth = classDepth("System");
```

CLASSLOADERDEPTH

Class Name	SecurityManager
Description	This method returns the position of the first occurrence of the current class loader in the runtime stack. It is often necessary for the SecurityManager to inspect the runtime stack to make security decisions. In particular, it may check the stack to see which ClassLoader was involved in loading a class. Java uses separate namespaces for classes loaded over a local file system (called "built-ins") and those loaded from over a network (imported classes). When a class refers to another class, Java checks to see if the referencing class is a built-in or is imported. This is important for security reasons to prevent an imported class from taking over the behavior of a built-in. For example, an imported System class cannot take over the behavior of the built-in System class. The classLoaderDepth() method is an internal method that can be used to make decisions about built-in versus imported classes.

Syntax	protected int **classLoaderDepth()**
Parameters	None.
Returns	The first occurrence of the current class loader in the runtime stack.
Exceptions	None.
See Also	ClassLoader
Example	

```
int depth = classLoaderDepth();
```

CURRENTCLASSLOADER

Class Name	SecurityManager
Description	This method returns the current class loader on the runtime stack. It is often necessary for the SecurityManager to inspect the runtime stack to make security decisions. In particular, it may check the stack to see which ClassLoader was involved in loading a class. Java uses separate namespaces for classes loaded over a local file system (called "built-ins") and those loaded from over a network (imported classes). When a class refers to another class, Java checks to see if the referencing class is a built-in or is imported. This is important for security reasons to prevent an imported class from taking over the behavior of a built-in. The currentClassLoader() method returns a reference to the current ClassLoader object on the runtime stack.
Syntax	protected ClassLoader **currentClassLoader()**
Parameters	None.
Returns	The current class loader on the runtime stack.
Exceptions	None.
See Also	ClassLoader
Example	

```
ClassLoader c = currentClassLoader();
```

GETCLASSCONTEXT

Class Name	SecurityManager
Description	Returns a Class array that provides context information about this SecurityManager.
Syntax	protected Class[] **getClassContext()**;
Parameters	None.

Returns	A Class array representing context information about this class.
Exceptions	None.
See Also	Class
Example	

```
Class context[] = getClassContext();
```

GETINCHECK

Class Name	SecurityManager
Description	The getInCheck() method is used to see if there is currently a security check in progress. It returns the value of the protected inCheck variable.
Syntax	public boolean **getInCheck**();
Parameters	None.
Returns	True if there is a security check in progress, false if not.
Exceptions	None.
See Also	Object
Example	This code prints out whether a security check is currently occurring.

```
System.out.println("A Security Check in progress is " +
        System.getSecurityManager().getInCheck());
```

GETSECURITYCONTEXT

Class Name	SecurityManager
Description	The getSecurityContext() method returns information about the current state of the execution environment. Sometimes it may be desirable to postpone a security check until a better time in the life of an applet. This information is encapsulated in an Object returned by getSecurityContext(), which may be queried at a later time to perform additional security checks.
Syntax	public Object **getSecurityContext**()
Parameters	None.
Returns	An Object encapsulating information about the current execution environment.
Exceptions	None.
See Also	Object
Example	

```
Object o = getSecurityContext();
```

inClass

Class Name	SecurityManager
Description	The inClass() method returns information as to whether the class specified in the String parameter is currently on the runtime stack. It does this by invoking the classDepth() method with the class as its parameter.
Syntax	public boolean **inClass**(String *name*)
Parameters	
String *name*	The class to inspect.
Returns	True if the class is on the stack, false if it is not.
Exceptions	None.
See Also	Object, classDepth()
Example	

```
boolean onStack = inClass("MyClass");
```

inClassLoader

Class Name	SecurityManager
Description	This method checks to see whether a ClassLoader is currently being used. The SecurityManager may often need to check the stack to see which ClassLoader was involved in loading a class. Java uses separate namespaces for classes loaded over a local file system (called "built-ins") and those loaded from over a network (imported classes). When a class refers to another class, Java checks to see if the referencing class is a built-in or is imported. This is important for security reasons to prevent an imported class from taking over the behavior of a built-in. The inClassLoader() method is used to see if a ClassLoader is currently being used. If false is returned, then the default built-in ClassLoader is probably being run.
Syntax	protected boolean **inClassLoader**()
Parameters	None.
Returns	A boolean indicating whether ClassLoader is null.
Exceptions	None.
See Also	ClassLoader, currentClassLoader()
Example	

```
boolean inLoader = inClassLoader();
```

The ClassLoader and SecurityManager Project: A Local File ClassLoader

Project Overview

This chapter's project walks through the steps that are necessary to create a custom subclass of ClassLoader. The particular ClassLoader in the example is a stand-alone application and reads in classes directly from the local file directory. While on the surface this may not seem to difficult, creating a ClassLoader can be very involved. The greatest challenge is how to deal with classes that have been brought in by the local file loader, but that reference classes brought in from another loader. This is related to security issues, since each class loader has a different namespace in which it maintains classes. If a class loaded in one namespace is superseded by one loaded in from another, the integrity of the runtime system can be compromised.

Building the Project

1. The custom ClassLoader used in this section is called LocalClassLoader. The first step in creating the loader is to define the variables and constructors of the class. This is done in Listing 10-1. The class uses static methods so that its internal data can persist across instantiations. A Hashtable object (defined in java.util) will be used to store any previously loaded Classes. This will function as a cache so there will not be any unnecessary file reads. The getLocalClassLoader() method allows external classes to get a reference to the LocalClassLoader so that the loadClass() method can be invoked.

Listing 10-1 First part of LocalClassLoader definition

```
import java.lang.*;
import java.io.*;
import java.util.Hashtable;

// Loads classes from the current directory...
public class LocalClassLoader extends ClassLoader {
   // A cache will be used to keep loaded classes around
   // so the aren't repeatedly reloaded...
   static Hashtable classCache = new Hashtable();

   // The loader is static and so can be created only once
   private static LocalClassLoader loader =
 new LocalClassLoader();

   // Constructor, just call default constructor
   private LocalClassLoader() {
    super();
   }
```

continued on next page

continued from previous page

```
// Return reference to this LocalClassLoader object
public static synchronized LocalClassLoader
  getLocalClassLoader() {
    return loader;
}
// ...
```

2. Before defining the loadClass() method, the readClassData() method is described. Its contents are posted in Listing 10-2. The readClassData() method is private to LocalClassLoader and is used for reading in a class from a local file. It reads the file from a BufferedInputStream and writes the incoming data into a ByteArrayOutputStream. When the method is done reading the file, it returns the OutputStream data converted to a byte array. It uses the toByteArray() method for this.

Listing 10-2 Reading class data from a local file directory

```
// Read data from file and return as byte array...
    private byte[] readClassData(String name) throws IOException {
        // Open stream for reading in data from file...
        // Look for file with .class appended to it...
        BufferedInputStream in =  new BufferedInputStream(
            new FileInputStream(name + ".class"));
        // Open stream for writing out data...
ByteArrayOutputStream out =
new ByteArrayOutputStream(10000);
        int b;
        // Read in the stream...
        while ((b = in.read()) != -1)
            out.write(b);    // Write to byte array
in.close();
        // Finally convert output stream into byte array...
        return out.toByteArray();
    }
```

3. Listing 10-3 displays the stub code for loadClass(). The first step is to see if the class has already been loaded by looking in its Hashtable cache with the get() method. If it is there, then it returns the class. Otherwise, the file has to be read in from the local directory with the readClassData() method. If the file read is successful, the class is defined by defineClass() and resolved by resolveClass(). At this point the class may be ready for use.

The problems begin if the class is a subclass. This will be the case if the class is anything but Object. The defineClass() and resolveClass() may then recurse and try to find the superclass. If it is not found in the local file directory, an IOException object is thrown. At this point, the program gets the class from the default loader by calling the forName() method of the Class class. The code then resolves the class manually. The code on the CD has print statements placed throughout the code so you can see what happens at every step of this process.

To call this class and the loadClass() method, code like the following could be used:

```
// Get a reference to the loader
LocalClassLoader l = LocalClassLoader.getLocalClassLoader();
// Load the class from the local class loader
Class c = l.loadClass("MyClass",true);
// Instantiate the object
Object o = c.newInstance();
```

Listing 10-3 Code for loadClass()

```
// Implement abstract ClassLoader method
   // Loads a class and resolves
   // Uses cache to avoid repreated file loads...
   public synchronized Class loadClass(String name,
     boolean resolve) throws ClassNotFoundException {
       Class c = null;
try {
       // See if class is in cache...
       if ((c = (Class) classCache.get(name)) == null) {
   // Read the data from the file...
          byte rawClass[] = readClassData(name);
          // Convert byte arrayinto a class...
       c = defineClass(rawClass,0,rawClass.length);
       // Place into cache...
          classCache.put(name,c);
       } // end if
       // Finally resolve class if desired...
       if (resolve) {
resolveClass(c);
       }
       // Return the class...
   return c;
     }
     // File is not found.  Try to get class from
   //   default (probably local) loader
       catch (IOException ioe) {
c = Class.forName(name);
       if (resolve) {
resolveClass(c);
       }
     classCache.put(name,c);
     return c;
}
   // Handle general problems...
     catch (Exception e) {
       throw new ClassNotFoundException("Error reading file");
     }
     // Handle case where class has bad format...
     catch (ClassFormatError e) {
throw new ClassNotFoundException(
"Class is invalid format");
     }
   }
```

PART IV

JAVA I/O

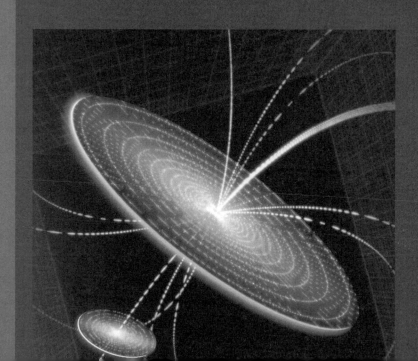

11

BASIC I/O

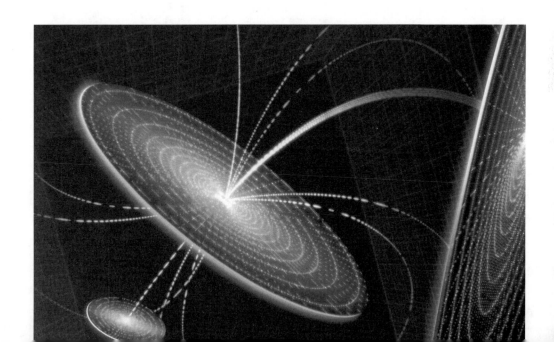

11

BASIC I/O

Input and output are the names given to the information that goes into and comes out of a computer program. Input and output are also the names given to the processes in a program that handle that information. Figure 11-1 illustrates the relationship between a program and its input and output processes. The simplicity of this illustration hides the true complexity of handling input and output. This chapter describes how the stream-based model of input and output overcomes some of that complexity.

Table 11-1, which appears later in the chapter under Basic I/O Classes and Interfaces Summaries, contains a brief description of the classes and interfaces covered in this chapter. Subsequent sections describe each class in more detail. Figure 11-2 depicts the inheritance relationship between the classes covered in this chapter and class Object.

Stream-Based Input and Output

Input and output comes from and goes to many different physical devices. Input to a program can come from the keyboard, the mouse, a file on disk, the network, or perhaps (though rarely) punched cards. Output from a program can go to the screen, a file on disk, the network, or a printer. At the level of the hardware, each of these devices looks very different. If a programmer had to write code to interact with every input and output device at this level, programming would become much more difficult. Luckily, most of these devices have several characteristics in common:

- Data moves in only one direction (a device, like a modem, that allows data to flow in two directions, can often be thought of as two independent devices, each moving data in only one direction).

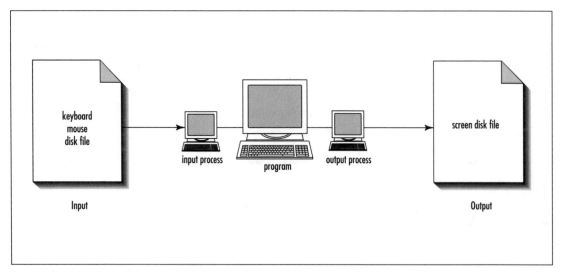

Figure 11-1 Input and output

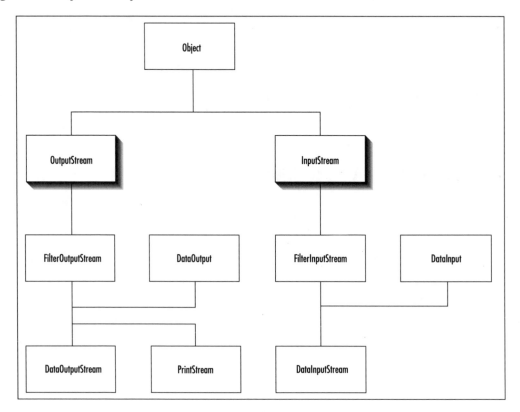

Figure 11-2 The inheritance diagram

■ The native data format can be transformed to and from a sequence of bytes—a byte becomes the common element of data exchange.

■ The device supports sequential access to the data (some devices also support random access to the data—however, for the model presented below, sequential access is all that is necessary).

The Java language uses the notion of a stream to model these common characteristics. The stream model takes advantage of the characteristics mentioned above and presents a uniform, easy to use, object-oriented interface to and from a variety of input and output devices.

Figure 11-3 depicts a stream. Streams are paths along which data flows. A stream has a source of data and a destination for that data. Both the source and the destination

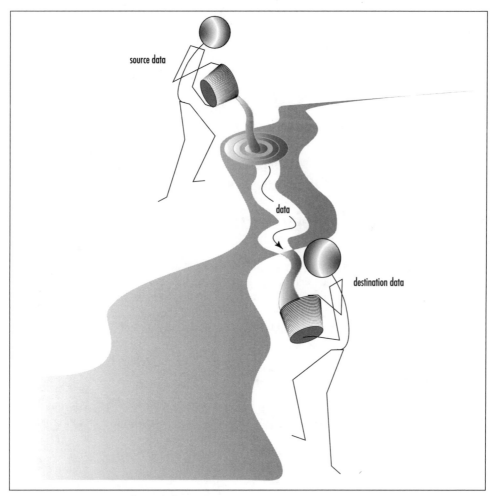

Figure 11-3 Conceptual view of a stream

may be physical devices or they may be other streams. The latter characteristic makes streams a very powerful information processing tool because complex processing operations can be built from a series of simple pieces.

The authors of the Java programming language were not the first people to implement stream-based input and output. In fact, they were very likely inspired by the work of others. The C++ programming language is one of several programming languages that also provide stream-based input and output.

Stream classes in the Java class library are designed to handle either input or output, although in theory, this distinction is not necessary. A stream class is an input stream class if it is used to extract data from the path (by reading from it). It is assumed that the data being read must have come from an outside source (but the program need not concern itself with where). A stream class is an output stream class if it is used to insert data into the path (by writing to it). It is assumed that the data being written is going to an outside destination (but, once again, the program need not concern itself with where).

The stream model provides the following benefits:

- The program is provided with a uniform method of accessing input and output devices—the program can free itself of device specific code and interact with all physical devices through the stream abstraction.

- The program doesn't need to know where the data is coming from or where it is going to.

- The stream model captures well the sequential nature of much real-world information.

Streams Are Naturally Object-Oriented

The stream model lends itself to an object-oriented implementation. Figure 11-4 illustrates a typical inheritance hierarchy. A generic input or output stream class sits at the top of the hierarchy. This class defines the set of operations common to either input streams or output streams of any type. Classes that redefine or extend this basic set of operations derive from this common base class. A useful specialization is a filter stream class. Filter stream objects are created from other stream objects and filter the data coming from or going to the original object.

Output Streams

Output streams, as they are implemented in the Java class library, are derived from the base class OutputStream. This class defines the portion of the output stream interface

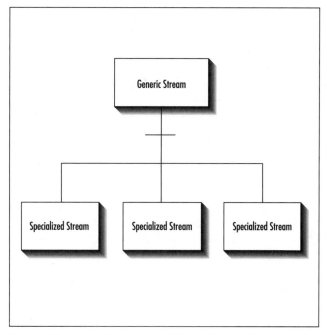

Figure 11-4 A typical stream hierarchy

common to all output streams. All derived classes must implement this common interface and may extend it as necessary. This interface includes methods for

- Writing bytes
- Closing the stream
- Flushing the stream

Classes derived from class OutputStream fall into two broad categories: terminal output streams and filters. Terminal output streams send their output to any destination other than another output stream. They are derived directly from class OutputStream. Filters are derived from class FilterOutputStream (which is derived from class OutputStream). Filters always pass their filtered output along to another output stream.

The Basics

Assume a program must write data to an output stream. The type of output stream is not important—the data could ultimately go to a disk file, a block of computer memory, or a network connection. How will the data be written?

By Byte

All classes derived from class OutputStream must define a method of the form void write(int). This method takes a single byte, which is passed as a parameter, and writes it to the stream destination. Using only this method, data in any format can be written to an output stream—by first breaking it into bytes and then writing it, one byte at a time, with calls to the method void write(int).

While this technique works, it is often inconvenient, especially when the data to be written resides in a large block of memory, such as a byte array. In addition, some output devices write blocks of bytes just as efficiently as they write single bytes. It would be good to take advantage of such a capability.

By Byte Array

Class OutputStream defines two methods that take a byte array as a parameter. These two methods, as implemented by class OutputStream, do nothing more than loop over the byte array and call the method void write(int) for each byte. However, classes derived from OutputStream may redefine these methods in order to provide a more efficient implementation. For example, the method void write(byte [], int, int) provided by the class ByteArrayOutputStream uses the method arraycopy(byte [], int, byte [], int, int) provided by the class System to write the whole byte array at one time.

However, even breaking data up into bytes is sometimes undesirable. In anticipation of this problem, the Java class library provides two output stream filter classes that allow a program to write all of the language's primitive data types and a few of its classes directly. The filter classes take care of the details of conversion.

DataOutputStream

The DataOutputStream class was designed to allow data to be written to a stream without building in any dependence on the machine architecture, the underlying operating system, or the specific Java implementation.

The DataOutputStream class implements the DataOutput interface. This interface includes methods for writing all of the primitive Java data types (boolean, char, byte, short, int, long, float, and double) as well as a class (String) and two arrays (byte array and char array). The DataOutputStream methods transform each of these types into a sequence of bytes, and do so in a well-defined, portable manner. The transformed data is then written to the output stream byte by byte. A companion class, DataInputStream, can then reconstruct the original data from the transformed representation.

PrintStream

The class PrintStream solves a similar problem. This class was designed to allow the textual representation of data to be printed to an output stream.

The PrintStream class defines methods for printing several of the primitive Java data types (boolean, char, int, long, float, and double) as well as a class (String) and an array (char array). It also defines a method for printing the textual representation of any class via a call to that class's toString() method. The PrintStream methods transform each of the types above into a sequence of characters. The transformed data is then written to the output stream byte by byte. Be warned—the PrintStream class is only useful for printing a portion of the entire Unicode character set. Its methods strip the high-order byte from each character before it is printed. It does this as a concession to the operating systems on which Java must run, which are still all ASCII based.

The PrintStream class methods are used for the same purposes as are the printf(), sprinf(), and fprintf() functions provided by C language standard I/O library.

Figure 11-5 illustrates how the integer value 1123 is actually output when written by methods from both classes.

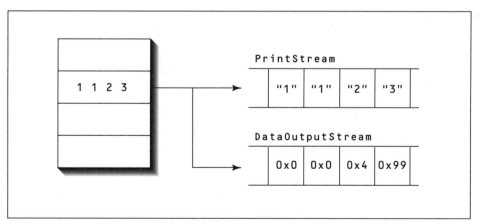

Figure 11-5 PrintStream and DataOutputStream output

Input Streams

Input streams, as they are implemented in the Java class library, are derived from the base class InputStream. This class defines the portion of the input stream interface common to all input streams. All derived classes must implement this common interface and may extend it as necessary. This interface includes methods for

- Reading bytes
- Closing the stream
- Marking positions in the stream
- Skipping forward in the stream
- Returning the number of bytes available in the stream

Classes derived from class InputStream fall into two broad categories: source input streams and filters. Source input streams receive their input from any source other than another input stream. They are derived directly from class InputStream. Filters are derived from class FilterInputStream (which is derived from class InputStream). Filters always receive their input from another input stream.

The Basics

Assume a program must read data from an input stream. The type of input stream is not important—the data could originally come from a disk file, a block of computer memory, or a network connection. How will the data be read?

By Byte

All classes derived from class InputStream must define a method of the form int read(). This method returns a single byte that has been read from the stream source. Using only this method, data in any format can be recovered from an input stream—by first reading it, one byte at a time, with calls to the method int read(), and then assembling it into the proper program structures.

While this technique works, it is often inconvenient, especially when the program needs to read the data into a large block of memory, such as a byte array. In addition, some input devices read blocks of bytes just as efficiently as they read single bytes. It would be good to take advantage of such a capability.

By Byte Array

Class InputStream defines two methods that take a byte array as a parameter. These two methods, as implemented by class InputStream, do nothing more than loop over the byte array and call the method int read() for each byte. However, classes derived from InputStream may redefine these methods in order to provide a more efficient implementation. For example, the method void read(byte [], int, int) provided by the class ByteArrayInputStream uses the method arraycopy(byte [], int, byte [], int, int) provided by the class System to read the whole byte array at one time.

However, even reconstructing data from bytes is sometimes undesirable. In anticipation of this problem, the Java class library provides an input stream filter class that allows a program to read all of the language's primitive data types and a few of its classes directly. The filter class takes care of the details of conversion.

DataInputStream

The DataInputStream class was designed to allow data to be read from a stream without regard to any particular machine architecture, underlying operating system, or specific Java implementation.

The DataInputStream class implements the DataInput interface. This interface includes methods for reading all of the primitive Java data types (boolean, char, byte, short, int, long, float, and double) as well as a class (String) and an array (byte array). The DataInputStream methods transform each of these types from a sequence of bytes into their Java language representation, and do so in a well-defined, portable manner.

Miscellaneous Topics

This section covers three topics of general relevance to both input and output streams.

Blocking

Many of the methods provided by the Java I/O class library are said to block. That is, they don't return until their function has been successfully carried out or an error occurs (in which case they typically throw exception IOException). If the input or output device can't perform the action immediately, the method waits until it can. The calling program is said to "blocked" from proceeding. When the input or output device is ready, the action is performed, and the method call returns.

Blocking is best understood by considering the example of writing to a slow output device like a printer. A printer is far slower than the computer sending data to it. While the printer is printing a character, the process writing the characters must wait, lest too many characters be written and some characters be lost. While it is waiting, the process is blocked. The process is only allowed to continue when the printer tells the computer it is ready for more characters. If the process wrote a block of data, the write operation won't return until the printer has printed all of the characters in the block successfully.

It is possible to create classes that do nonblocking I/O. A nonblocking I/O write method would store the data to be written and return immediately. The program could do something else, and check on the status of the write operation later.

IOException

The exception IOException is the general indicator that something has gone wrong. It is most often thrown when the input or output stream has been closed and an application tries to read from or write to the stream anyway. It is not a runtime error, so it must be caught or passed to the calling method.

UTF Encoding

The UCS Tranformation Form 8-bit format (UTF-8) encoding used by several of the classes in the Java class library allows 16-bit Unicode characters to be written as a sequence of one or more 8-bit bytes. The UTF-8 implementation used in the Java class library follows the Unicode standard except in one area: the character at position zero in the Unicode character set is represented as the sequence of bytes 0xC0 0x80 rather than the single byte 0x00.

About the Project

This chapter's project implements a collection of classes that know how to read their internal state from and write their internal state to a stream. Frames store instances of these classes and associate them with symbolic names. Frames (and the associations stored therein) also know how to write their internal state to and read their internal state from a stream, thereby allowing an entire collection of instances to be saved to and retrieved from a stream.

Basic I/O Classes and Interfaces Summaries

The classes and interfaces described in this chapter provides the basis for I/O processing in the Java programming language. Table 11-1 contains a brief description of each class and interface. Each will be described in detail in subsequent sections.

Table 11-1 The basic I/O classes/interfaces

Class/Interface	Description
InputStream	The class of objects used to represent input streams
OutputStream	The class of objects used to represent output streams
DataInput	The interface used to define input operations on basic data types
DataOutput	The interface used to define output operations on basic data types
FilterInputStream	The class of objects used to represent input stream filters
FilterOutputStream	The class of objects used to represent output stream filters
DataInputStream	The class of objects used to read data in a portable manner
DataOutputStream	The class of objects used to write data in a portable manner
PrintStream	The class of objects used to represent streams to which to print

The java.io.InputStream Class

The InputStream class is the class from which all input streams are derived. It is abstract, so it cannot be instantiated directly. Table 11-2 lists and provides a description of all of the methods provided by class InputStream.

Table 11-2 Summary of InputStream methods

Method	Description
available	Returns the number of bytes available
close	Closes the input stream
mark	Marks the current position
markSupported	Indicates whether or not this stream supports marks
read	Reads data from the input stream
reset	Repositions the stream to the last marked position
skip	Skips ahead in the input stream

INPUTSTREAM

Description	The abstract InputStream class defines the elements common to all input streams.
Syntax	public class **InputStream** extends Object
Package	java.io
Import	java.io.InputStream
Constructors	public **InputStream**()
Parameters	None.
Comments	Because the InputStream class is abstract, its constructor cannot be called directly. Instead, it is called as part of the constructor call sequence for newly created input stream objects (see the example below).
Example	The following example demonstrates how to call the InputStream constructor inside the constructor of a derived input stream class.

```
class DerivedInputStream extends InputStream
{
   DerivedInputStream()
   {
      super(); // call InputStream()

      // perform additional processing
   }
}
```

Methods

AVAILABLE

Class Name	InputStream
Description	This method returns the number of bytes that can be read from this stream before blocking will occur.

Syntax	public int **available**()
Parameters	None.
Returns	An integer containing the number of available bytes.
Exceptions	If the number of bytes available cannot be determined, this method will throw an IOException.
Comments	If an input stream is empty, a read operation on that stream will block until data becomes available. Often this is undesirable. In a loop in which the processing of data read from the input stream must be interspersed with other processing, blocking must be avoided. This method allows the program to determine whether data is available before attempting to read it.
Example	The following example demonstrates how to use this method to determine the number of bytes available in an input stream.

```
void ProcessLoop(InputStream [] rgis) throws IOException
{
    while (true)
    {
        for (int i = 0; i < rgis.length; i++)
        {
            if (rgis[i].available() > 0)
            {
                // read and process the available bytes

                int nNext = rgis[i].read();
                        .
                        .
                        .
            }
        }
    }
}
```

CLOSE

Class Name	InputStream
Description	This method closes the InputStream object. This action releases any associated resources. The method provided by the InputStream class does nothing, and should be redefined in any derived classes where such an operation has meaning.
Syntax	public void **close**()
Parameters	None.
Returns	None.
Exceptions	If the input stream cannot be closed, this method will throw an IOException.

Comments	Operating systems often allocate memory buffers and similar resources when input streams are created. These resources are typically beyond the reach of the cleanup facilities (such as the automatic garbage collector) provided by the Java runtime system. These resources must therefore be explicitly returned to the operating system when they are no longer needed. If they are not, the operating system will eventually run out of them. An example of a limited resource is the file descriptors (not to be confused with instances of the FileDescriptor class) that are assigned by the operating system to each open file. After the last file descriptor is allocated, no more files can be opened by that process. Closing an input stream returns the file descriptor to the operating system so that it may be reused.
Example	The following example demonstrates how to close a stream.

```
void ProcessData(InputStream is) throws IOException
{
    int n = is.read();

    for (int i = 0; i < n; i++)
    {
        int b = is.read();

        // process byte
    }

    is.close(); // close stream
}
```

MARK

Class Name	InputStream
Description	This method marks the current position in the input stream. Subsequent calls to reset() will reposition the stream to this position.
Syntax	public synchronized void **mark**(int *nLimit*)
Parameters	
int *nLimit*	This parameter specifies the number of bytes that may be read past this mark before the mark becomes invalid.
Returns	None.
Exceptions	None.
See Also	markSupported(), reset()
Comments	The mark() and reset() methods together provide a convenient mechanism for looking ahead at the data in an input stream. In a typical application, a program first sets a mark and then reads from the input stream. If the program cannot use the information in that portion of the input stream, the program repositions the stream at the mark and then passes the input stream to the proper handler. The amount of look ahead is limited and must be specified when the mark is set.

Example   The following example demonstrates how to mark a position in an input
stream and later reset the stream to that position.

```
void MarkAndReset(InputStream is) throws IOException
{
   is.mark(100); // mark the current position

   // read data from the stream

   is.reset(); // reposition the stream
}
```

MARKSUPPORTED

Class Name	InputStream
Description	This method indicates whether or not this stream type supports the mark and reset operations.
Syntax	public boolean **markSupported**()
Parameters	None.
Returns	The boolean value true if marks are supported and false otherwise. Input streams, by default, do not support marks.
Exceptions	None.
See Also	mark(), reset()
Comments	Attempting the reset operation on an input stream that does not support marks will result in an IOException. A program should therefore determine whether or not a stream supports marks before using reset().
Example	The following example demonstrates how to determine whether or not an input stream supports marks.

```
void Process(InputStream is) throws IOException
{
   if (!is.markSupported())
   {
      // if this stream does not support marks,
      // create a new stream that does

      is = new BufferedInputStream(is);
   }

   is.mark(50);

   // continue processing
}
```

READ

Class Name	InputStream
Description	These methods read a byte or series of bytes from the input stream.

Syntax	public abstract int **read**()
	public int **read**(byte [] *rgb*)
	public int **read**(byte [] *rgb*, int *nOffset*, int *nLength*)

Parameters

byte [] *rgb*	The byte array to read bytes into.
int *nOffset*	The offset from the beginning of the byte array.
int *nLength*	The number of bytes to read.

Returns   An int. The first of these three methods returns the value read from the input stream. Even though the result is returned as an int rather than as a byte, only values in the range 0 to 256 are permissible. It is possible to write a method that does return the full range of int values, but that would certainly cause incompatibility with the other classes in the Java language I/O class library. The other two methods return the number of bytes read into the byte array. All return a value of -1 if no more data is available from the input stream.

Exceptions   If data cannot be read from the input stream, these methods will throw an IOException.

Comments   The first of these three methods is abstract and must be redefined in all classes derived from this class. The other two methods may also be redefined. By default, they use the first method to read bytes into the byte array.

Example   The following example demonstrates how to read from an input stream.

```
void ReadAndProcess(InputStream is) throws IOException
{
    while (true)
    {
        int b = is.read();

        // process byte

        byte [] rgb = new byte [100];

        is.read(rgb);

        // process byte array

        is.read(rgb, 10, rgb.length);

        // process byte array
    }
}
```

RESET

Class Name	InputStream
Description	This method repositions the stream to the last marked position.

Syntax	public synchronized void **reset**()
Parameters	None.
Returns	None.
Exceptions	If the input stream has not been marked or if the mark is invalid, this method will throw an IOException.
See Also	mark(), markSupported()
Comments	The mark() and reset() methods together provide a convenient mechanism for looking ahead at the data in an input stream. In a typical application, a program first sets a mark and then reads from the input stream. If the program cannot use the information in that portion of the input stream, the program repositions the stream at the mark and then passes the input stream to the proper handler. The amount of look ahead is limited and must be specified when the mark is set.
Example	The following example demonstrates how to mark a position in the input stream and later reset the stream to that position.

```
void MarkAndReset(InputStream is) throws IOException
{
    is.mark(100); // mark the current position

    // read data from the stream

    is.reset(); // reposition the stream
}
```

SKIP

Class Name	InputStream
Description	This method skips up to *n* bytes ahead in the input stream. It will skip fewer than *n* bytes ahead if a full skip would cause the call to block.
Syntax	public long **skip**(long *n*)
Parameters	
long *n*	The number of bytes to skip.
Returns	The number of bytes skipped. This method returns a value of -1 if no more data is available from the stream.
Exceptions	If an error occurs while skipping ahead in the input stream, this method will throw an IOException.
Example	The following example demonstrates how to skip over a portion of the input stream.

```
boolean SkipAhead(InputStream is) throws IOException
{
    int i = is.read();  // determine how far to skip ahead
```

```
    int n = is.skip(i); // skip ahead

    return n < i;
}
```

The java.io.OutputStream Class

The OutputStream class is the class from which all output streams are derived. It is abstract, so it cannot be instantiated directly. Table 11-3 lists and provides a description of all of the methods provided by class OutputStream.

Table 11-3 Summary of OutputStream methods

Method	Description
close	Closes the output stream
flush	Flushes the output stream
write	Writes data to the output stream

OUTPUTSTREAM

Description	The abstract OutputStream class defines the elements common to all output streams.
Syntax	public class **OutputStream** extends Object
Package	java.io
Import	java.io.OutputStream
Constructors	public **OutputStream()**
Parameters	None.
Comments	Because the OutputStream class is abstract, its constructor cannot be called directly. Instead, it is called as part of the constructor call sequence for newly created output stream objects (see the example below).
Example	The following example demonstrates how to call the OutputStream constructor inside the constructor of a derived output stream class.

```
class DerivedOutputStream extends OutputStream
{
    DerivedOutputStream()
    {
        super(); // call OutputStream()

        // perform additional processing
    }
}
```

Methods

CLOSE

Class Name	OutputStream
Description	This method closes the OutputStream object. This action releases any associated resources. The method provided by the OutputStream class does nothing, and should be redefined in any derived classes where such an operation has meaning.
Syntax	public void **close**()
Parameters	None.
Returns	None.
Exceptions	If the output stream cannot be closed, this method will throw an IOException.
Comments	Operating systems often allocate memory buffers and similar resources when output streams are created. These resources are typically beyond the reach of the cleanup facilities (such as the automatic garbage collector) provided by the Java runtime system. These resources must therefore be explicitly returned to the operating system when they are no longer needed. If they are not, the operating system will eventually run out of them. An example of a limited resource is the file descriptors (not to be confused with instances of the FileDescriptor class) that are assigned by the operating system to each open file. After the last file descriptor is allocated, no more files can be opened by that process. Closing an output stream returns the file descriptor to the operating system so that it may be reused.
Example	The following example demonstrates how to close a stream.

```
void ProcessData(OutputStream os) throws IOException
{
   for (int i = 0; i < 100; i++)
   {
      int n = getValueAtPoint(i);

      os.write(n);
   }

   os.close(); // close stream
}
```

FLUSH

Class Name	OutputStream
Description	This method flushes the OutputStream object. Flushing immediately writes any buffered data. The method provided by class OutputStream

does nothing, and should be redefined in any derived classes where such an operation has meaning.

Syntax	public void **flush**()
Parameters	None.
Returns	None.
Exceptions	If the output stream cannot be flushed, this method will throw an IOException.
Comments	Output streams are usually buffered for performance reasons. Output devices such as hard disks can write a block of data just as fast as they can write a single byte of data. It therefore makes sense to write data in blocks if possible. By storing up sequential bytes of data and then writing them all at one time, buffered output streams take advantage of the fact that computer memory is typically many orders of magnitude faster than most output devices.
Example	The following example demonstrates how to flush an output stream.

```
void ProcessData(OutputStream os) throws IOException
{
    for (int i = 0; i < 100; i++)
    {
        int n = getValueAtPoint(i);

        os.write(n);
    }

    os.flush(); // flush stream
}
```

WRITE

Class Name	OutputStream
Description	These methods write a byte or series of bytes to the output stream.
Syntax	public abstract void **write**(int *n*)
	public void **write**(byte [] *rgb*)
	public void **write**(byte [] *rgb*, int *nOffset*, int *nLength*)
Parameters	
int *n*	The byte to write. Even though this parameter is passed to this method as an int rather than a byte, only values in the range -128 to 127 should be used. It is possible to write a method that does accept the full range of integer values, but that would certainly cause incompatibility with the other classes in the Java language I/O class library.
byte [] *rgb*	The byte array to write.
int *nOffset*	The offset from the beginning of the byte array.
int *nLength*	The number of bytes to write, beginning at the offset.

Returns	None.
Exceptions	If data cannot be written to the output stream, these methods will throw an IOException.
Comments	The first of these three methods is abstract and must be redefined in all classes derived from this class. The other two methods may also be redefined. By default, they use the first method to write bytes from the byte array.
Example	The following example demonstrates how to write to an output stream.

```
void GenerateAndWrite(OutputStream os) throws IOException
{
   while (true)
   {
      int b;

      // generate byte

      os.write(b);

      byte [] rgb;

      // generate byte array

      os.write(rgb);

      // generate byte array

      os.write(rgb, 10, rgb.length);
   }
}
```

The java.io.DataInput Interface

The DataInput interface defines the interface for classes that are used to read data in a machine independent fashion. Methods are provided for reading Java data types and classes from a source such as an input stream. Table 11-4 lists and briefly describes all of the methods defined by interface DataInput.

Table 11-4 Summary of DataInput methods

Method	Description
readBoolean	Reads a boolean from the source
readByte	Reads a byte from the source
readChar	Reads a char from the source
readDouble	Reads a double from the source
readFloat	Reads a float from the source
readFully	Reads a sequence of bytes from the source
readInt	Reads an int from the source

Method	Description
readLine	Reads a string from the source
readLong	Reads a long from the source
readShort	Reads a short from the source
readUnsignedByte	Reads an unsigned byte from the source
readUnsignedShort	Reads an unsigned short from the source
readUTF	Reads a string from the source
skipBytes	Skips ahead in the source

DataInput

Description	The DataInput interface defines input operations on basic data types.
Syntax	public interface DataInput extends Object
Package	java.io
Import	java.io.DataInput
Parameters	None.
Comments	The DataInput interface is provided to ensure that classes that operate on basic Java data types do so in a consistent manner.
Example	The following example demonstrates how the DataInput interface could be used in a method to prevent the method from having to know anything about the source of the data.

```
void ReadAndProcess(DataInput di) throws IOException
{
   while (true)
   {
      boolean bool = di.readBoolean();
      int i = di.readInt();
      float f = di.readFloat();

      // process values
   }
}
```

Methods

READBOOLEAN

Interface Name	DataInput
Description	This method reads a boolean value from the source.

Syntax	public abstract boolean **readBoolean**()
Parameters	None.
Returns	A boolean value.
Exceptions	If data cannot be read from the source, this method will throw an IOException. If the end-of-file condition is encountered while reading from the source, this method will throw an EOFException.
Example	The following example demonstrates how to read a boolean value from the source.

```
void ReadAndProcess(DataInput di) throws IOException
{
   while (true)
   {
      boolean bool = di.readBoolean();

      // process boolean value
   }
}
```

READBYTE

Interface Name	DataInput
Description	This method reads a byte (an 8-bit integer value) from the source.
Syntax	public abstract byte **readByte**()
Parameters	None.
Returns	A byte.
Exceptions	If data cannot be read from the source, this method will throw an IOException. If the end-of-file condition is encountered while reading from the source, this method will throw an EOFException.
Example	The following example demonstrates how to read a byte from the source.

```
void ReadAndProcess(DataInput di) throws IOException
{
   while (true)
   {
      byte b = di.readByte();

      // process byte
   }
}
```

READCHAR

Interface Name	DataInput
Description	This method reads a character from the source.
Syntax	public abstract char **readChar**()

Parameters	None.
Returns	A character.
Exceptions	If data cannot be read from the source, this method will throw an IOException. If the end-of-file condition is encountered while reading from the source, this method will throw an EOFException.
Example	The following example demonstrates how to read a character from the source.

```
void ReadAndProcess(DataInput di) throws IOException
{
   while (true)
   {
      char c = di.readChar();

      // process character
   }
}
```

READDOUBLE

Interface Name	DataInput
Description	This method reads a double (a 64-bit floating-point value) from the source.
Syntax	public abstract double **readDouble**()
Parameters	None.
Returns	A double.
Exceptions	If data cannot be read from the source, this method will throw an IOException. If the end-of-file condition is encountered while reading from the source, this method will throw an EOFException.
Example	The following example demonstrates how to read a double from the source.

```
void ReadAndProcess(DataInput di) throws IOException
{
   while (true)
   {
      double d = di.readDouble();

      // process double
   }
}
```

READFLOAT

Interface Name	DataInput
Description	This method reads a float (a 32-bit floating-point value) from the source.

Syntax	public abstract float **readFloat**()
Parameters	None.
Returns	A float.
Exceptions	If data cannot be read from the source, this method will throw an IOException. If the end-of-file condition is encountered while reading from the source, this method will throw an EOFException.
Example	The following example demonstrates how to read a float from the source.

```
void ReadAndProcess(DataInput di) throws IOException
{
   while (true)
   {
      float f = di.readFloat();

      // process float
   }
}
```

READFULLY

Interface Name	DataInput
Description	These methods read bytes from the source and place them in the byte array specified in the parameter list. They block until enough bytes are read to fill the byte array.
Syntax	public abstract void **readFully**(byte [] *rgb*)
	public abstract void **readFully**(byte [] *rgb*, int *nOffset*, int *nLength*)
Parameters	
byte [] *rgb*	The byte array to read bytes into.
int *nOffset*	The offset from the beginning of the byte array.
int *nLength*	The number of bytes to read.
Returns	None.
Exceptions	If data cannot be read from the source, these methods will throw an IOException. If the end-of-file condition is encountered while reading from the source, they will throw an EOFException.
Example	The following example demonstrates how to read a block of bytes from the source.

```
void ReadAndProcess(DataInput di) throws IOException
{
   while (true)
   {
      byte [] rgb = new byte [100];

      di.readFully(rgb);
```

```
      // process byte array

      di.readFully(rgb, 10, rgb.length);

      // process byte array
   }
}
```

READINT

Interface Name	DataInput
Description	This method reads an int (a 32-bit integer value) from the source.
Syntax	public abstract int **readInt**()
Parameters	None.
Returns	An int.
Exceptions	If data cannot be read from the source, this method will throw an IOException. If the end-of-file condition is encountered while reading from the source, this method will throw an EOFException.
Example	The following example demonstrates how to read an int from the source.

```
void ReadAndProcess(DataInput di) throws IOException
{
   while (true)
   {
      int i = di.readInt();

      // process int
   }
}
```

READLINE

Interface Name	DataInput
Description	This method reads a line of characters from the source and places them in a String object. A line is delimited by a carriage return, a newline, a carriage return/newline combination, or the end-o-file condition.
Syntax	public abstract String **readLine**()
Parameters	None.
Returns	A String object.
Exceptions	If data cannot be read from the source, this method will throw an IOException. If the end-of-file condition is encountered while reading from the source, this method will throw an EOFException.
Example	The following example demonstrates how to read a line of characters from the source.

```
void ReadAndProcess(DataInput di) throws IOException
{
   while (true)
   {
      String str = di.readLine();

      // process String object
   }
}
```

READLONG

Interface Name	DataInput
Description	This method reads a long (a 64-bit integer value) from the source.
Syntax	public abstract long **readLong**()
Parameters	None.
Returns	A long.
Exceptions	If data cannot be read from the source, this method will throw an IOException. If the end-of-file condition is encountered while reading from the source, this method will throw an EOFException.
Example	The following example demonstrates how to read a long from the source.

```
void ReadAndProcess(DataInput di) throws IOException
{
   while (true)
   {
      long l = di.readLong();

      // process long
   }
}
```

READSHORT

Interface Name	DataInput
Description	This method reads a short (a 16-bit integer value) from the source.
Syntax	public abstract short **readShort**()
Parameters	None.
Returns	A short.
Exceptions	If data cannot be read from the source, this method will throw an IOException. If the end-of-file condition is encountered while reading from the source, this method will throw an EOFException.
Example	The following example demonstrates how to read a short from the source.

```
void ReadAndProcess(DataInput di) throws IOException
{
   while (true)
```

```
    {
        short s = di.readShort();

        // process short
    }
}
```

READUNSIGNEDBYTE

Interface Name	DataInput
Description	This method reads an unsigned byte (an 8-bit integer value) from the source.
Syntax	public abstract int **readUnsignedByte**()
Parameters	None.
Returns	An unsigned byte (an integer in the range 0 to 255).
Exceptions	If data cannot be read from the source, this method will throw an IOException. If the end-of-file condition is encountered while reading from the source, this method will throw an EOFException.
Example	The following example demonstrates how to read an unsigned byte from the source.

```
void ReadAndProcess(DataInput di) throws IOException
{
    while (true)
    {
        int ub = di.readUnsignedByte();

        // process unsigned byte
    }
}
```

READUNSIGNEDSHORT

Interface Name	DataInput
Description	This method reads an unsigned short (a 16-bit integer value) from the source.
Syntax	public abstract int **readUnsignedShort**()
Parameters	None.
Returns	An unsigned short (an integer in the range 0 to 65535).
Exceptions	If data cannot be read from the source, this method will throw an IOException. If the end-of-file condition is encountered while reading from the source, this method will throw an EOFException.
Example	The following example demonstrates how to read an unsigned short from the source.

```
void ReadAndProcess(DataInput di) throws IOException
{
   while (true)
   {
      int us = di.readUnsignedShort();

      // process unsigned short
   }
}
```

READUTF

Interface Name	DataInput
Description	This method reads a String object that has been formatted as a UTF-8 encoded sequence of bytes from the source.
Syntax	public abstract String **readUTF**()
Parameters	None.
Returns	A String object.
Exceptions	If data cannot be read from the source, this method will throw an IOException. If the end-of-file condition is encountered while reading from the source, this method will throw an EOFException.
Example	The following example demonstrates how to read a UTF-8 encoded string from the source.

```
void ReadAndProcess(DataInput di) throws IOException
{
   while (true)
   {
      String str = di.readUTF();

      // process String object
   }
}
```

SKIPBYTES

Interface Name	DataInput
Description	This method skips *n* bytes ahead in the source. It is guaranteed to skip *n* bytes even if it must block to do so.
Syntax	public abstract int **skipBytes**(int *n*)
Parameters	
int *n*	The number of bytes to skip.
Returns	The number of bytes skipped. This will always be equal to the specified number of bytes to skip.

Exceptions   If an error occurs while skipping ahead in the source, this method will throw an IOException. If the end-of-file condition is encountered while skipping ahead in the source, this method will throw an EOFException.

Example   The following example demonstrates how to skip over a portion of the source.

```
void SkipAhead(DataInput di) throws IOException
{
    int i = di.readByte(); // determine how far to skip ahead

    di.skipBytes(i);       // skip ahead
}
```

The java.io.DataOutput Interface

The DataOutput interface defines the interface for classes that are used to write data in a machine independent fashion. Methods are provided for writing Java data types and classes to a destination such as an output stream. Table 11-5 lists and briefly describes all of the methods defined by interface DataOutput.

Table 11-5 Summary of DataOutput methods

Method	Description
write	Writes data to the destination
writeBoolean	Writes a boolean to the destination
writeByte	Writes a byte to the destination
writeBytes	Writes a sequence of bytes to the destination
writeChar	Writes a char to the destination
writeChars	Writes a sequence of chars to the destination
writeDouble	Writes a double to the destination
writeFloat	Writes a float to the destination
writeInt	Writes an int to the destination
writeLong	Writes a long to the destination
writeShort	Writes a short to the destination
writeUTF	Writes a string to the destination

DATAOUTPUT

Description   The DataOutput interface defines output operations on basic data types.

Syntax   public interface DataOutput extends Object

Package   java.io

Import   java.io.DataOutput

Constructors	None.
Parameters	None.
Comments	The DataOutput interface is provided to ensure that classes that operate on basic Java data types do so in a consistent manner.
Example	The following example demonstrates how the DataOutput interface could be used in a method to prevent the method from having to know anything about the destination of the data.

```
void GenerateAndWrite(DataOutput do) throws IOException
{
   while (true)
   {
      boolean bool;
      int i;
      float f;

      // generate values

      do.writeBoolean(bool);
      do.writeInt(i);
      do.writeFloat(f)
   }
}
```

Methods

WRITE

Interface Name	DataOutput
Description	These methods write a byte or series of bytes to the destination.
Syntax	public abstract void **write**(int *n*)
	public abstract void **write**(byte [] *rgb*)
	public abstract void **write**(byte [] *rgb*, int *nOffset*, int *nLength*)
Parameters	
int *n*	The byte to write. Even though this parameter is passed to this method as an int rather than a byte, only values in the range -128 to 127 should be used. It is possible to write a method that does accept the full range of integer values, but that would certainly cause incompatibility with the other classes in the Java language I/O class library.
byte [] *rgb*	The byte array to write.
int *nOffset*	The offset from the beginning of the byte array.
int *nLength*	The number of bytes to write, beginning at the offset.
Returns	None.
Exceptions	If data cannot be written to the destination, these methods will throw an IOException.

Example   The following example demonstrates how to write a byte to the destination.

```
void GenerateAndWrite(DataOutput do) throws IOException
{
   while (true)
   {
      int b;

      // generate byte

      do.write(b);

      byte [] rgb;

      // generate byte array

      do.write(rgb);

      // generate byte array

      do.write(rgb, 10, rgb.length);
   }
}
```

WRITEBOOLEAN

Interface Name	DataOutput
Description	This method writes a boolean value to the destination.
Syntax	public abstract void **writeBoolean**(boolean *bool*)
Parameters	
boolean *bool*	The boolean value to write.
Returns	None.
Exceptions	If data cannot be written to the destination, this method will throw an IOException.
Example	The following example demonstrates how to write a boolean value to the destination.

```
void GenerateAndWrite(DataOutput do) throws IOException
{
   while (true)
   {
      boolean bool;

      // generate boolean value

      do.writeBoolean(bool);
   }
}
```

WRITEBYTE

Interface Name	DataOutput
Description	This method writes a byte (an 8-bit integer value) to the destination.
Syntax	public abstract void **writeByte**(int *n*)
Parameters	
int *n*	The byte to write. Even though this parameter is passed to this method as an int rather than a byte, only values in the range -128 to 127 should be used. It is possible to write a method that does accept the full range of integer values, but that would certainly cause incompatibility with the other classes in the Java language I/O class library.
Returns	None.
Exceptions	If data cannot be written to the destination, this method will throw an IOException.
Example	The following example demonstrates how to write a byte to the destination.

```
void GenerateAndWrite(DataOutput do) throws IOException
{
   while (true)
   {
      byte b;

      // generate byte

      do.writeByte(b);
   }
}
```

WRITEBYTES

Interface Name	DataOutput
Description	This method writes a String object to the destination as a series of bytes.
Syntax	public abstract void **writeBytes**(String *str*)
Parameters	
String *str*	The String object to write.
Returns	None.
Exceptions	If data cannot be written to the destination, this method will throw an IOException.
Example	The following example demonstrates how to write a String object to the destination as a series of bytes.

```
void GenerateAndWrite(DataOutput do) throws IOException
{
   while (true)
```

```
    {
        String str;

        // generate a String object

        do.writeBytes(str);
    }
}
```

WRITECHAR

Interface Name	DataOutput
Description	This method writes a character to the destination.
Syntax	public abstract void **writeChar**(int *n*)
Parameters	
int *n*	The character to write. Even though this parameter is passed to this method as an int rather than a char, only values representing valid Unicode characters should be used. It is possible to write a method that does accept the full range of integer values, but that would certainly cause incompatibility with the other classes in the Java language I/O class library.
Returns	None.
Exceptions	If data cannot be written to the destination, this method will throw an IOException.
Example	The following example demonstrates how to write a character to the destination.

```
void GenerateAndWrite(DataOutput do) throws IOException
{
    while (true)
    {
        int c;

        // generate character

        do.writeChar(c);
    }
}
```

WRITECHARS

Interface Name	DataOutput
Description	This method writes a String object to the destination as a series of characters.
Syntax	public abstract void **writeChars**(String *str*)

Parameters

String *str*   The String object to write.

Returns   None.

Exceptions   If data cannot be written to the destination, this method will throw an IOException.

Example   The following example demonstrates how to write a String object to the destination as a series of characters.

```
void GenerateAndWrite(DataOutput do) throws IOException
{
   while (true)
   {
      String str;

      // generate a String object

      do.writeChars(str);
   }
}
```

WRITEDOUBLE

Interface Name	DataOutput
Description	This method writes a double (a 64-bit floating-point value) to the destination.
Syntax	public abstract void **writeDouble**(double *d*)

Parameters

double *d*   The double to write.

Returns   None.

Exceptions   If data cannot be written to the destination, this method will throw an IOException.

Example   The following example demonstrates how to write a double to the destination.

```
void GenerateAndWrite(DataOutput do) throws IOException
{
   while (true)
   {
      double d;

      // generate double

      do.writeDouble(d);
   }
}
```

WRITEFLOAT

Interface Name	DataOutput
Description	This method writes a float (a 32-bit floating-point value) to the destination.
Syntax	public abstract void **writeFloat**(float *f*)
Parameters	
float *f*	The float to write.
Returns	None.
Exceptions	If data cannot be written to the destination, this method will throw an IOException.
Example	The following example demonstrates how to write a float to the destination.

```
void GenerateAndWrite(DataOutput do) throws IOException
{
   while (true)
   {
      float f;

      // generate float

      do.writeFloat(f);
   }
}
```

WRITEINT

Interface Name	DataOutput
Description	This method writes an int (a 32-bit integer value) to the destination.
Syntax	public abstract void **writeInt**(int *n*)
Parameters	
int *n*	The int to write.
Returns	None.
Exceptions	If data cannot be written to the destination, this method will throw an IOException.
Example	The following example demonstrates how to write an int to the destination.

```
void GenerateAndWrite(DataOutput do) throws IOException
{
   while (true)
   {
```

continued on next page

continued from previous page

```
      int i;

      // generate int

      do.writeInt(i);
   }
}
```

WRITELONG

Interface Name	DataOutput
Description	This method writes a long (a 64-bit integer value) to the destination.
Syntax	public abstract void **writeLong**(long *l*)
Parameters	
long *l*	The long to write.
Returns	None.
Exceptions	If data cannot be written to the destination, this method will throw an IOException.
Example	The following example demonstrates how to write a long to the destination.

```
void GenerateAndWrite(DataOutput do) throws IOException
{
   while (true)
   {
      long l;

      // generate long

      do.writeLong(l);
   }
}
```

WRITESHORT

Interface Name	DataOutput
Description	This method writes a short (a 16-bit integer value) to the destination.
Syntax	public abstract void **writeShort**(int *n*)
Parameters	
int *n*	The short to write. Even though this parameter is passed to this method as an int rather than a short, only values in the range $-32768 \leq n \leq 32767$ should be used. It is possible to write a method that does accept the full range of integer values, but that would certainly cause incompatibility with the other classes in the Java language I/O class library.

Returns	None.
Exceptions	If data cannot be written to the destination, this method will throw an IOException.
Example	The following example demonstrates how to write a short to the destination.

```
void GenerateAndWrite(DataOutput do) throws IOException
{
   while (true)
   {
      int s;

      // generate short

      do.writeShort(s);
   }
}
```

write**UTF**

Interface Name	DataOutput
Description	This method writes a String object to the destination as a series of bytes in UTF-8 format.
Syntax	public abstract void **writeUTF**(String *str*)
Parameters	
String *str*	The String object to write.
Returns	None.
Exceptions	If data cannot be written to the destination, this method will throw an IOException.
Example	The following example demonstrates how to write a UTF-8 encoded string to the destination.

```
void GenerateAndWrite(DataOutput do) throws IOException
{
   while (true)
   {
      String str;

      // generate a String object

      do.writeUTF(str);
   }
}
```

The java.io.FilterInputStream Class

The FilterInputStream class is the class from which all filtering input streams are derived. It is not meant to be instantiated directly (although doing so is possible).

Tables 11-6 and 11-7 list and briefly describe all of the variables and methods provided by class FilterInputStream.

Table 11-6 Summary of FilterInputStream variables

Variable	Description
in	A reference to the input stream from which to read

Table 11-7 Summary of FilterInputStream methods

Method	Description
available	Returns the number of bytes available
close	Closes the input stream
mark	Marks the current position
markSupported	Indicates whether or not this stream supports marks
read	Reads data from the input stream
reset	Repositions the stream to the last marked position
skip	Skips ahead in the input stream

FILTERINPUTSTREAM

Description	The FilterInputStream class defines the elements common to all filtering input streams.
Syntax	public class **FilterInputStream** extends InputStream
Package	java.io
Import	java.io.FilterInputStream
Constructors	protected **FilterInputStream**(InputStream *in*)
Parameters	
InputStream *in*	The InputStream object from which to read the data to be filtered.
Comments	The constructor creates a FilterInputStream object from the InputStream object specified in the parameter list. This constructor is usually not called directly. Instead, it is called as part of the constructor call sequence for newly created input stream objects (see the example below).
Example	The following example demonstrates how to call the FilterInputStream constructor inside the constructor of a derived input stream class.

```
class DerivedFilterInputStream extends FilterInputStream
{
    DerivedFilterInputStream(InputStream is)
    {
```

```
      super(is); // call FilterInputStream()

      // perform additional processing
   }
}
```

Variables

IN

Class Name	FilterInputStream
Description	This variable contains a reference to the input stream from which to read the data to be filtered. It provides derived classes direct access to the source input stream.
Syntax	protected InputStream **in**
Example	The following example illustrates how a derived class can use its access to the source input stream to pass along a close operation.

```
class DerivedFilterInputStream extends FilterInputStream
{
   DerivedFilterInputStream(InputStream is)
   {
      super(is); // call FilterInputStream()

      // perform additional processing
   }

   void close()
   {
      in.close();
   }
}
```

Methods

AVAILABLE

Class Name	FilterInputStream
Description	This method returns the number of bytes that can be read from this stream before blocking will occur.
Syntax	public int **available**()
Parameters	None.
Returns	An integer containing the number of available bytes.

Exceptions   If the number of bytes available cannot be determined, this method will throw an IOException. This might occur, for instance, if the input stream had previously been closed.

Comments   If an input stream is empty, a read operation on that stream will block until data becomes available. Often this is undesirable. In a loop in which the processing of data read from the input stream must be interspersed with other processing, blocking must be avoided. This method allows the program to determine whether data is available before attempting to read it.

Example   The following example demonstrates how to use this method to determine the number of bytes available in an input stream.

```
void ProcessLoop(FilterInputStream [] rgfis) throws IOException
{
    while (true)
    {
        for (int i = 0; i < rgfis.length; i++)
        {
            if (rgfis[i].available() > 0)
            {
                // read and process the available bytes

                int nNext = rgfis[i].read();
                    .
                    .
                    .
            }
        }
    }
}
```

CLOSE

Class Name   FilterInputStream

Description   This method flushes the FilterInputStream object and then closes it. This action releases any associated resources.

Syntax   public void **close**()

Parameters   None.

Returns   None.

Exceptions   If the input stream cannot be closed, this method will throw an IOException.

Comments   Operating systems often allocate memory buffers and similar resources when input streams are created. These resources are typically beyond the reach of the cleanup facilities (such as the automatic garbage collector) provided by the Java runtime system. These resources must therefore be explicitly returned to the operating system when they are no longer need-ed. If they are not, the operating system will eventually run out of them. An example of a limited resource is the file descriptors (not to be confused with instances of the FileDescriptor class) that are assigned by the operating system to each open file. After the last file descriptor is allocated, no more files can be opened by that process. Closing an input stream returns the file descriptor to the operating system so that it may be reused.

Example   The following example demonstrates how to close a stream.

```
void ProcessData(FilterInputStream fis) throws IOException
{
   int n = fis.read();

   for (int i = 0; i < n; i++)
   {
      int b = fis.read();

      // process byte
   }

   fis.close(); // close stream
}
```

MARK

Class Name	FilterInputStream
Description	This method marks the current position in the input stream. Subsequent calls to reset() will reposition the stream to this position.
Syntax	public synchronized void **mark**(int *nLimit*)
Parameters	
int *nLimit*	This parameter specifies the number of bytes that may be read past this mark before the mark becomes invalid.
Returns	None.
Exceptions	None.
See Also	markSupported(), reset()
Comments	The mark() and reset() methods together provide a convenient mechanism for looking ahead at the data in an input stream. In a typical application, a program first sets a mark and then reads from the input stream. If the program cannot use the information in that portion of the input stream, the program repositions the stream at the mark and then passes the input stream to the proper handler. The amount of look ahead is limited and must be specified when the mark is set.
Example	The following example demonstrates how to mark a position in the input stream and later reset the stream to that position.

```
void MarkAndReset(FilterInputStream fis) throws IOException
{
   fis.mark(100); // mark the current position

   // read data from the stream

   fis.reset(); // reposition the stream
}
```

MARKSUPPORTED

Class Name	FilterInputStream
Description	This method indicates whether or not this stream type supports the mark and reset operations.
Syntax	public boolean **markSupported**()
Parameters	None.
Returns	The boolean value true if marks are supported and false otherwise.
Exceptions	None.
See Also	mark(), reset()
Comments	Attempting the reset operation on an input stream that does not support marks will result in an IOException. A program should therefore determine whether or not a stream supports marks before using reset().
Example	The following example demonstrates how to determine whether or not an input stream supports marks.

```
void Process(FilterInputStream fis) throws IOException
{
   if (!fis.markSupported())
   {
      // if this stream does not support marks,
      // create a new stream that does

      fis = new BufferedInputStream(fis);
   }

   fis.mark(50);

   // continue processing
}
```

READ

Class Name	FilterInputStream
Description	These methods read a byte or series of bytes from the input stream.
Syntax	public int **read**()
	public int **read**(byte [] *rgb*)
	public int **read**(byte [] *rgb*, int *nOffset*, int *nLength*)

Parameters

byte [] *rgb*	The byte array to read bytes into.
int *nOffset*	The offset from the beginning of the byte array.
int *nLength*	The number of bytes to read.

Returns   An int. The first of these three methods returns the value read from the input stream. Even though the result is returned as an int rather than as a byte, only values in the range 0 to 256 are permissible. It is possible to write a method that does return the full range of int values, but that would certainly cause incompatibility with the other classes in the Java language I/O class library. The other two methods return the number of bytes read into the byte array. All return a value of -1 if no more data is available from the input stream.

Exceptions   If data cannot be read from the input stream, these methods will throw an IOException.

Comments   All three of these methods may be redefined. By default, the last two methods use the first method to read bytes into the byte array.

Example   The following example demonstrates how to read from an input stream.

```
void ReadAndProcess(FilterInputStream fis) throws IOException
{
    while (true)
    {
        int b = fis.read();

        // process byte

        byte [] rgb = new byte [100];

        fis.read(rgb);

        // process byte array

        fis.read(rgb, 10, rgb.length);

        // process byte array
    }
}
```

RESET

Class Name	FilterInputStream
Description	This method repositions the stream to the last marked position.
Syntax	public synchronized void **reset**()
Parameters	None.
Returns	None.

Exceptions	If the input stream has not been marked or if the mark is invalid, this method will throw an IOException.
See Also	mark(), markSupported()
Comments	The mark() and reset() methods together provide a convenient mechanism for looking ahead at the data in an input stream. In a typical application, a program first sets a mark and then reads from the input stream. If the program cannot use the information in that portion of the input stream, the program repositions the stream at the mark and then passes the input stream to the proper handler. The amount of look ahead is limited and must be specified when the mark is set.
Example	The following example demonstrates how to mark a position in the input stream and later reset the stream to that position.

```
void MarkAndReset(FilterInputStream fis) throws IOException
{
    fis.mark(100); // mark the current position

    // read data from the stream

    fis.reset(); // reposition the stream
}
```

SKIP

Class Name	FilterInputStream
Description	This method skips up to *n* bytes ahead in the input stream. It will skip fewer than *n* bytes ahead if a full skip would cause the call to block.
Syntax	public long **skip**(long *n*)
Parameters	
long *n*	The number of bytes to skip.
Returns	The number of bytes skipped. This method returns a value of -1 if no more data is available from the stream.
Exceptions	If an error occurs while skipping ahead in the input stream, this method will throw an IOException.
Example	The following example demonstrates how to skip over a portion of the input stream.

```
boolean SkipAhead(FilterInputStream fis) throws IOException
{
    int i = fis.read();  // determine how far to skip ahead

    int n = fis.skip(i); // skip ahead

    return n < i;
}
```

The java.io.FilterOutputStream Class

The FilterOutputStream class is the class from which all filtering output streams are derived. It is not meant to be instantiated directly (although doing so is possible). Tables 11-8 and 11-9 list and briefly describe all of the variables and methods provided by class FilterOutputStream.

Table 11-8 Summary of FilterOutputStream variables

Variable	Description
out	A reference to the output stream to which to write

Table 11-9 Summary of FilterOutputStream methods

Method	Description
close	Closes the output stream
flush	Flushes the output stream
write	Writes data to the output stream

FILTEROUTPUTSTREAM

Description	The FilterOutputStream class defines the elements common to all filtering output streams.
Syntax	public class **FilterOutputStream** extends OutputStream
Package	java.io
Import	java.io.FilterOutputStream
Constructors	public **FilterOutputStream**(OutputStream *out*)
Parameters	
OutputStream *out*	The OutputStream object to which to write the filtered data.
Comments	This constructor creates a FilterOutputStream object from the OutputStream object specified in the parameter list. This constructor is usually not called directly. Instead, it is called as part of the constructor call sequence for newly created output stream objects (see the example below).
Example	The following example demonstrates how to call the FilterOutputStream constructor inside the constructor of a derived output stream class.

```
class DerivedFilterOutputStream extends FilterOutputStream
{
   DerivedFilterOutputStream(OutputStream os)
   {
      super(os); // call FilterOutputStream()

      // perform additional processing
   }
}
```

Variables

OUT

Class Name	FilterOutputStream
Description	This variable contains a reference to the output stream to which to write the filtered data. It provides derived classes direct access to the destination output stream.
Syntax	protected OutputStream **out**
Example	The following example illustrates how a derived class can use its access to the source output stream to pass along a close operation.

```
class DerivedFilterOutputStream extends FilterOutputStream
{
   DerivedFilterOutputStream(OutputStream os)
   {
      super(os); // call FilterOutputStream()

      // perform additional processing
   }

   void close()
   {
      out.close();
   }
}
```

Methods

CLOSE

Class Name	FilterOutputStream
Description	This method flushes the FilterOutputStream object and then closes it. This action releases any associated resources.
Syntax	public void **close**()
Parameters	None.

Returns	None.
Exceptions	If the output stream cannot be closed, this method will throw an IOException.
Comments	Operating systems often allocate memory buffers and similar resources when output streams are created. These resources are typically beyond the reach of the cleanup facilities (such as the automatic garbage collector) provided by the Java runtime system. These resources must therefore be explicitly returned to the operating system when they are no longer needed. If they are not, the operating system will eventually run out of them. An example of a limited resource is the file descriptors (not to be confused with instances of the FileDescriptor class) that are assigned by the operating system to each open file. After the last file descriptor is allocated, no more files can be opened by that process. Closing an output stream returns the file descriptor to the operating system so that it may be reused.
Example	The following example demonstrates how to close a stream.

```
void ProcessData(FilterOutputStream fos) throws IOException
{
   for (int i = 0; i < 100; i++)
   {
      int n = getValueAtPoint(i);

      fos.write(n);
   }

   fos.close(); // close stream
}
```

FLUSH

Class Name	FilterOutputStream
Description	This method flushes the FilterOutputStream object. Flushing immediately writes any buffered data.
Syntax	public void **flush**()
Parameters	None.
Returns	None.
Exceptions	If the output stream cannot be flushed, this method will throw an IOException.
Comments	Output streams are usually buffered for performance reasons. Output devices such as hard disks can write a block of data just as fast as they can write a single byte of data. It therefore makes sense to write data in blocks if possible. By storing up sequential bytes of data and then writing them all at one time, buffered output streams take advantage of the fact that computer memory is typically many orders of magnitude faster than most output devices.

Example   The following example demonstrates how to flush an output stream.

```
void ProcessData(FilterOutputStream fos) throws IOException
{
   for (int i = 0; i < 100; i++)
   {
      int n = getValueAtPoint(i);

      fos.write(n);
   }

   fos.flush(); // flush stream
}
```

WRITE

Class Name	FilterOutputStream
Description	These methods write a byte or series of bytes to the output stream.
Syntax	public void **write**(int *n*)
	public void **write**(byte [] *rgb*)
	public void **write**(byte [] *rgb*, int *nOffset*, int *nLength*)
Parameters	
int *n*	The byte to write. Even though this parameter is passed to this method as an int rather than a byte, only values in the range -128 to $\leq$ 127 should be used. It is possible to write a method that does accept the full range of integer values, but that would certainly cause incompatibility with the other classes in the Java language I/O class library.
byte [] *rgb*	The byte array to write.
int *nOffset*	The offset from the beginning of the byte array.
int *nLength*	The number of bytes to write, beginning at the offset.
Returns	None.
Exceptions	If data cannot be written to the output stream, these methods will throw an IOException.
Comments	All three of these methods may be redefined. By default, the last two methods use the first method to write bytes from the byte array.
Example	The following example demonstrates how to write to an output stream.

```
void GenerateAndWrite(FilterOutputStream fos) throws IOException
{
   while (true)
   {
      int b;

      // generate byte

      fos.write(b);
```

```
    byte [] rgb;

    // generate byte array

    fos.write(rgb);

    // generate byte array

    fos.write(rgb, 10, rgb.length);
  }
}
```

The java.io.DataInputStream Class

The DataInputStream class provides the programmer with methods for reading Java data types and classes from an input stream in a machine independent fashion. Table 11-10 lists and briefly describes all of the methods defined by class DataInputStream.

Table 11-10 Summary of DataInputStream methods

Method	Description
read	Reads a sequence of bytes from the input stream
readBoolean	Reads a boolean from the input stream
readByte	Reads a byte from the input stream
readChar	Reads a char from the input stream
readDouble	Reads a double from the input stream
readFloat	Reads a float from the input stream
readFully	Reads a sequence of bytes from the input stream
readInt	Reads an int from the input stream
readLine	Reads a string from the input stream
readLong	Reads a long from the input stream
readShort	Reads a short from the input stream
readUnsignedByte	Reads an unsigned byte from the input stream
readUnsignedShort	Reads an unsigned short from the input stream
readUTF	Reads a string from the input stream
skipBytes	Skips ahead in the input stream

DATAINPUTSTREAM

Description	The DataInputStream class provides methods for reading Java data types and classes from an input stream in a machine independent fashion.
Syntax	public class **DataInputStream** extends FilterInputStream implements DataInput

Package	java.io
Import	java.io.DataInputStream
Constructors	public **DataInputStream**(InputStream *in*)
Parameters	
InputStream *in*	The InputStream object from which to read the data.
Comments	Instances of the class DataInputStream are used in conjunction with instances of the class DataOutputStream to provide platform independent exchange of data.
Example	This example demonstrates how to create a DataInputStream object from an InputStream object.

```
void Create(InputStream is)
{
    DataInputStream dis = new DataInputStream(is);

    // process
}
```

Methods

READ

Class Name	DataInputStream
Description	These methods read a series of bytes from the input stream.
Syntax	public final int **read**(byte [] *rgb*)
	public final int **read**(byte [] *rgb*, int *nOffset*, int *nLength*)
Parameters	
byte [] *rgb*	The byte array to read bytes into.
int *nOffset*	The offset from the beginning of the byte array.
int *nLength*	The number of bytes to read.
Returns	An int. These two methods return the number of bytes read into the byte array. They return a value of -1 if no more data is available from the stream.
Exceptions	If data cannot be read from the input stream, these methods will throw an IOException.
Example	The following example demonstrates how to read from an input stream.

```
void ReadAndProcess(DataInputStream dis) throws IOException
{
    while (true)
    {
        byte [] rgb = new byte [100];

        dis.read(rgb);
```

```
        // process byte array

        dis.read(rgb, 10, rgb.length);

        // process byte array
    }
}
```

READBOOLEAN

Class Name	DataInputStream
Description	This method reads a boolean value from the input stream.
Syntax	public final boolean **readBoolean**()
Parameters	None.
Returns	A boolean value.
Exceptions	If data cannot be read from the input stream, this method will throw an IOException.
Example	The following example demonstrates how to read a boolean value from an input stream.

```
void ReadAndProcess(DataInputStream dis) throws IOException
{
    while (true)
    {
        boolean bool = dis.readBoolean();

        // process boolean value
    }
}
```

READBYTE

Class Name	DataInputStream
Description	This method reads a byte (an 8-bit integer value) from the input stream.
Syntax	public final byte **readByte**()
Parameters	None.
Returns	A byte.
Exceptions	If data cannot be read from the input stream, this method will throw an IOException.
Example	The following example demonstrates how to read a byte from an input stream.

```
void ReadAndProcess(DataInputStream dis) throws IOException
{
    while (true)
    {
```

continued on next page

continued from previous page
```
      byte b = dis.readByte();

      // process byte
   }
}
```

READCHAR

Class Name	DataInputStream
Description	This method reads a character from the input stream.
Syntax	public final char **readChar**()
Parameters	None.
Returns	A character.
Exceptions	If data cannot be read from the input stream, this method will throw an IOException.
Example	The following example demonstrates how to read a character from an input stream.

```
void ReadAndProcess(DataInputStream dis) throws IOException
{
   while (true)
   {
      char c = dis.readChar();

      // process character
   }
}
```

READDOUBLE

Class Name	DataInputStream
Description	This method reads a double (a 64-bit floating-point value) from the input stream.
Syntax	public final double **readDouble**()
Parameters	None.
Returns	A double.
Exceptions	If data cannot be read from the input stream, this method will throw an IOException.
Example	The following example demonstrates how to read a double from an input stream.

```
void ReadAndProcess(DataInputStream dis) throws IOException
{
   while (true)
   {
```

```
        double d = dis.readDouble();

        // process double
    }
}
```

READ FLOAT

Class Name	DataInputStream
Description	This method reads a float (a 32-bit floating-point value) from the input stream.
Syntax	public final float **readFloat**()
Parameters	None.
Returns	A float.
Exceptions	If data cannot be read from the input stream, this method will throw an IOException.
Example	The following example demonstrates how to read a float from an input stream.

```
void ReadAndProcess(DataInputStream dis) throws IOException
{
    while (true)
    {
        float f = dis.readFloat();

        // process float
    }
}
```

READ FULLY

Class Name	DataInputStream
Description	These methods read bytes from the input stream and place them in the byte array specified in the parameter list. They block until enough bytes are read to fill the byte array.
Syntax	public final void **readFully**(byte [] *rgb*)
	public final void **readFully**(byte [] *rgb*, int *nOffset*, int *nLength*)
Parameters	
byte [] *rgb*	The byte array to read bytes into.
int *nOffset*	The offset from the beginning of the byte array.
int *nLength*	The number of bytes to read.
Returns	None.

Exceptions If data cannot be read from the input stream, these methods will throw an IOException. If the end-of-file condition is encountered while reading from the input stream, this method will throw an EOFException.

Example The following example demonstrates how to read from an input stream.

```
void ReadAndProcess(DataInputStream dis) throws IOException
{
   while (true)
   {
      byte [] rgb = new byte [100];

      dis.readFully(rgb);

      // process byte array

      dis.readFully(rgb, 10, rgb.length);

      // process byte array
   }
}
```

READINT

Class Name	DataInputStream
Description	This method reads an int (a 32-bit integer value) from the input stream.
Syntax	public final int **readInt**()
Parameters	None.
Returns	An int.
Exceptions	If data cannot be read from the input stream, this method will throw an IOException.
Example	The following example demonstrates how to read an int from an input stream.

```
void ReadAndProcess(DataInputStream dis) throws IOException
{
   while (true)
   {
      int i = dis.readInt();

      // process int
   }
}
```

READLINE

Class Name	DataInputStream
Description	This method reads a line of characters from the input stream and places them in a String object. A line is delimited by a carriage return, a newline, a carriage return/newline combination, or the end-of-file condition.

Syntax	public final String **readLine**()
Parameters	None.
Returns	A String object.
Exceptions	If data cannot be read from the input stream, this method will throw an IOException.
Example	The following example demonstrates how to read a line of characters from an input stream.

```
void ReadAndProcess(DataInputStream dis) throws IOException
{
   while (true)
   {
      String str = dis.readLine();

      // process String object
   }
}
```

READLONG

Class Name	DataInputStream
Description	This method reads a long (a 64-bit integer value) from the input stream.
Syntax	public final long **readLong**()
Parameters	None.
Returns	A long.
Exceptions	If data cannot be read from the input stream, this method will throw an IOException.
Example	The following example demonstrates how to read a long from an input stream.

```
void ReadAndProcess(DataInputStream dis) throws IOException
{
   while (true)
   {
      long l = dis.readLong();

      // process long
   }
}
```

READSHORT

Class Name	DataInputStream
Description	This method reads a short (a 16-bit integer value) from the input stream.
Syntax	public final short **readShort**()
Parameters	None.

Returns	A short.
Exceptions	If data cannot be read from the input stream, this method will throw an IOException.
Example	The following example demonstrates how to read a short from an input stream.

```
void ReadAndProcess(DataInputStream dis) throws IOException
{
   while (true)
   {
      short s = dis.readShort();

      // process short
   }
}
```

READUNSIGNEDBYTE

Class Name	DataInputStream
Description	This method reads an unsigned byte (an 8-bit integer value) from the input stream.
Syntax	public final int **readUnsignedByte**()
Parameters	None.
Returns	An unsigned byte.
Exceptions	If data cannot be read from the input stream, this method will throw an IOException.
Example	The following example demonstrates how to read an unsigned byte from an input stream.

```
void ReadAndProcess(DataInputStream dis) throws IOException
{
   while (true)
   {
      int ub = dis.readUnsignedByte();

      // process unsigned byte
   }
}
```

READUNSIGNEDSHORT

Class Name	DataInputStream
Description	This method reads an unsigned short (a 16-bit integer value) from the input stream.
Syntax	public final int **readUnsignedShort**()
Parameters	None.

Returns   An unsigned short.

Exceptions   If data cannot be read from the input stream, this method will throw an IOException.

Example   The following example demonstrates how to read an unsigned short from an input stream.

```
void ReadAndProcess(DataInputStream dis) throws IOException
{
   while (true)
   {
      int us = dis.readUnsignedShort();

      // process unsigned short
   }
}
```

READ**UTF**

Class Name   DataInputStream

Description   This method reads a String object that has been formatted as a UTF-8 encoded sequence of bytes from the input stream.

Syntax   public final String **readUTF**()

public final static String **readUTF**(DataInput *in*)

Parameters

InputStream *in*   The DataInput object from which to read the UTF-8 encoded string.

Returns   A String object.

Exceptions   If data cannot be read from the input stream, these methods will throw an IOException.

Comments   The second method operates on the input stream specified in the parameter list.

Example   The following example demonstrates two ways to read a UTF-8 encoded string from an input stream.

```
void ReadAndProcess(DataInputStream dis) throws IOException
{
   while (true)
   {
      String str;

      str = dis.readUTF();

      // process String object

      str = DataInputStream.readUTF(dis);

      // process String object
   }
}
```

SkipBytes

Class Name	DataInputStream
Description	This method skips *n* bytes ahead in the input stream. It is guaranteed to skip *n* bytes even if it must block to do so.
Syntax	public final int **skipBytes**(int *n*)
Parameters	
int *n*	The number of bytes to skip.
Returns	The number of bytes skipped. This will always be equal to the specified number of bytes to skip.
Exceptions	If an error occurs while skipping ahead in the input stream, this method will throw an IOException.
Example	The following example demonstrates how to skip over a portion of the input stream.

```
void SkipAhead(DataInputStream dis) throws IOException
{
   int i = dis.readByte(); // determine how far to skip ahead

   dis.skipBytes(i);       // skip ahead
}
```

The java.io.DataOutputStream Class

The DataOutputStream class provides the programmer with methods for writing Java data types and classes to an output stream in a machine independent fashion. Tables 11-11 and 11-12 list and briefly describe all of the methods defined by class DataOutputStream.

Table 11-11 Summary of DataOutputStream variables

Variable	Description
written	The number of bytes written to the output stream

Table 11-12 Summary of DataOutputStream methods

Method	Description
flush	Flushes the output stream
size	Returns the number of bytes written to the output stream
write	Writes data to the output stream
writeBoolean	Writes a boolean to the output stream
writeByte	Writes a byte to the output stream

Method	Description
writeBytes	Writes a sequence of bytes to the output stream
writeChar	Writes a char to the output stream
writeChars	Writes a sequence of chars to the output stream
writeDouble	Writes a double to the output stream
writeFloat	Writes a float to the output stream
writeInt	Writes an int to the output stream
writeLong	Writes a long to the output stream
writeShort	Writes a short to the output stream
writeUTF	Writes a string to the output stream

DATAOUTPUTSTREAM

Description	The DataOutputStream class provides methods for writing Java data types and classes to an output stream in a machine independent fashion.
Syntax	public class **DataOutputStream** extends FilterOutputStream implements DataOutput
Package	java.io
Import	java.io.DataOutputStream
Constructors	public **DataOutputStream**(OutputStream *out*)
Parameters	
OutputStream *out*	The OutputStream object to which to write the data.
Comments	Instances of the class DataOutputStream are used in conjunction with instances of the class DataInputStream to provide platform independent exchange of data.
Example	This example demonstrates how to create a DataOutputStream object from an OutputStream object.

```
void Create(OutputStream os)
{
   DataOutputStream dos = new DataOutputStream(os);

   // process
}
```

Variables

WRITTEN

Class Name	DataOutputStream
Description	This variable contains the number of bytes written to the output stream.
Syntax	protected int **written**
Example	The following example demonstrates how a derived class might access the number of bytes written to the output stream.

```
class DerivedDataOutputStream extends DataOutputStream
{
   DerivedDataOutputStream(OutputStream os)
   {
      super(os); // call DataOutputStream()

      // read and/or write the internal state of
      // the DataOutputStream

      int n = written;

      // process
   }
}
```

Methods

FLUSH

Class Name	DataOutputStream
Description	This method flushes the DataOutputStream object. Flushing immediately writes any buffered data
Syntax	public void **flush**()
Parameters	None.
Returns	None.
Exceptions	If the output stream cannot be flushed, this method will throw an IOException.
Comments	Output streams are usually buffered for performance reasons. Output devices such as hard disks can write a block of data just as fast as they can write a single byte of data. It therefore makes sense to write data in blocks if possible. By storing up sequential bytes of data and then writing them all at one time, buffered output streams take advantage of the fact that computer memory is typically many orders of magnitude faster than most output devices.

Example   The following example demonstrates how to flush an output stream.

```
void ProcessData(DataOutputStream dos) throws IOException
{
   for (int i = 0; i < 100; i++)
   {
      int n = getValueAtPoint(i);

      dos.write(n);
   }

   dos.flush(); // flush stream
}
```

SIZE

Class Name	DataOutputStream
Description	This method returns the number of bytes written to the stream since it was created.
Syntax	public final int **size**()
Parameters	None.
Returns	An integer.
Exceptions	None.
Example	The following example demonstrates how to get the size of an output stream.

```
void Process(DataOutputStream dos)
{
   int n = dos.size();

   for (int i = 0; i < n; i++)
   {
      // process
   }
}
```

WRITE

Class Name	DataOutputStream
Description	These methods write a byte or series of bytes to the output stream.
Syntax	public synchronized void **write**(int *n*)
	public synchronized void **write**(byte [] *rgb*, int *nOffset*, int *nLength*)
Parameters	
int *n*	The byte to write. Even though this parameter is passed to this method as an int rather than a byte, only values in the range -128 to 127 should be used. It is possible to write a method that does accept the full range of

integer values, but that would certainly cause incompatibility with the other classes in the Java language I/O class library.

byte [] *rgb*	The byte array to write.
int *nOffset*	The offset from the beginning of the byte array.
int *nLength*	The number of bytes to write, beginning at the offset.
Returns	None.
Exceptions	If data cannot be written to the output stream, these methods will throw an IOException.
Example	The following example demonstrates how to write to an output stream.

```
void GenerateAndWrite(DataOutputStream dos) throws IOException
{
   while (true)
   {
      int b;

      // generate byte

      dos.write(b);

      byte [] rgb;

      // generate byte array

      dos.write(rgb, 10, rgb.length);
   }
}
```

WRITEBOOLEAN

Class Name	DataOutputStream
Description	This method writes a boolean value to the output stream.
Syntax	public final void **writeBoolean**(boolean *bool*)
Parameters	
boolean *bool*	The boolean value to write.
Returns	None.
Exceptions	If data cannot be written to the output stream, this method will throw an IOException.
Example	The following example demonstrates how to write a boolean value to an output stream.

```
void GenerateAndWrite(DataOutputStream dos) throws IOException
{
   while (true)
   {
      boolean bool;
```

```
    // generate boolean value

    dos.writeBoolean(bool);
  }
}
```

WRITEBYTE

Class Name	DataOutputStream
Description	This method writes a byte (an 8-bit integer value) to the output stream.
Syntax	public final void **writeByte**(int *n*)
Parameters	
int *n*	The byte to write. Even though this parameter is passed to this method as an int rather than a byte, only values in the range -128 to 127 should be used. It is possible to write a method that does accept the full range of integer values, but that would certainly cause incompatibility with the other classes in the Java language I/O class library.
Returns	None.
Exceptions	If data cannot be written to the output stream, this method will throw an IOException.
Example	The following example demonstrates how to write a byte to an output stream.

```
void GenerateAndWrite(DataOutput do) throws IOException
{
    while (true)
    {
        byte b;

        // generate byte

        do.writeByte(b);
    }
}
```

WRITEBYTES

Class Name	DataOutputStream
Description	This method writes a String object to the output stream as a series of bytes.
Syntax	public final void **writeBytes**(String *str*)
Parameters	
String *str*	The String object to write. The high-order byte of each 2-byte Unicode character is discarded.

Returns	None.
Exceptions	If data cannot be written to the output stream, this method will throw an IOException.
Example	The following example demonstrates how to write a String object to an output stream as a series of bytes.

```
void GenerateAndWrite(DataOutputStream dos) throws IOException
{
   while (true)
   {
      String str;

      // generate a String object

      dos.writeBytes(str);
   }
}
```

WRITECHAR

Class Name	DataOutputStream
Description	This method writes a character to the output stream.
Syntax	public final void **writeChar**(int *n*)
Parameters	
int *n*	The character to write. Even though this parameter is passed to this method as an int rather than a char, only values representing valid Unicode characters should be used. It is possible to write a method that does accept the full range of integer values, but that would certainly cause incompatibility with the other classes in the Java language I/O class library.
Returns	None.
Exceptions	If data cannot be written to the output stream, this method will throw an IOException.
Example	The following example demonstrates how to write a character to an output stream.

```
void GenerateAndWrite(DataOutputStream dos) throws IOException
{
   while (true)
   {
      char c;

      // generate character

      dos.writeChar(c);
   }
}
```

WRITECHARS

Class Name	DataOutputStream
Description	This method writes a String object to the output stream as a series of characters.
Syntax	public final void **writeChars**(String *str*)
Parameters	
String *str*	The String object to write.
Returns	None.
Exceptions	If data cannot be written to the output stream, this method will throw an IOException.
Example	The following example demonstrates how to write a String object to an output stream as a series of characters.

```
void GenerateAndWrite(DataOutputStream dos) throws IOException
{
   while (true)
   {
      String str;

      // generate a String object

      dos.writeChars(str);
   }
}
```

WRITEDOUBLE

Class Name	DataOutputStream
Description	This method writes a double (a 64-bit floating-point value) to the output stream.
Syntax	public final void **writeDouble**(double *d*)
Parameters	
double *d*	The double to write.
Returns	None.
Exceptions	If data cannot be written to the output stream, this method will throw an IOException.
Example	The following example demonstrates how to write a double to an output stream.

```
void GenerateAndWrite(DataOutputStream dos) throws IOException
{
   while (true)
   {
```

continued on next page

continued from previous page

```
    double d;

    // generate double

    dos.writeDouble(d);
  }
}
```

WRITEFLOAT

Class Name	DataOutputStream
Description	This method writes a float (a 32-bit floating-point value) to the output stream.
Syntax	public final void **writeFloat**(float *f*)
Parameters	
float *f*	The float to write.
Returns	None.
Exceptions	If data cannot be written to the output stream, this method will throw an IOException.
Example	The following example demonstrates how to write a float to an output stream.

```
void GenerateAndWrite(DataOutputStream dos) throws IOException
{
   while (true)
   {
      float f;

      // generate float

      dos.writeFloat(f);
   }
}
```

WRITEINT

Class Name	DataOutputStream
Description	This method writes an int (a 32-bit integer value) to the output stream.
Syntax	public final void **writeInt**(int *n*)
Parameters	
int *n*	The int to write.
Returns	None.
Exceptions	If data cannot be written to the output stream, this method will throw an IOException.

Example   The following example demonstrates how to write an int to an output stream.

```
void GenerateAndWrite(DataOutputStream dos) throws IOException
{
   while (true)
   {
      int i;

      // generate int

      dos.writeInt(i);
   }
}
```

WRITELONG

Class Name	DataOutputStream
Description	This method writes a long (a 64-bit integer value) to the output stream.
Syntax	public final void **writeLong**(long *l*)
Parameters	
long *l*	The long to write.
Returns	None.
Exceptions	If data cannot be written to the output stream, this method will throw an IOException.
Example	The following example demonstrates how to write a long to an output stream.

```
void GenerateAndWrite(DataOutputStream dos) throws IOException
{
   while (true)
   {
      long l;

      // generate long

      dos.writeLong(l);
   }
}
```

WRITESHORT

Class Name	DataOutputStream
Description	This method writes a short (a 16-bit integer value) to the output stream.
Syntax	public final void **writeShort**(int *n*)

Parameters

int *n*   The short to write. Even though this parameter is passed to this method as an int rather than a short, only values in the range $-32768 \le n \le 32767$ should be used. It is possible to write a method that does accept the full range of integer values, but that would certainly cause incompatibility with the other classes in the Java language I/O class library.

Returns   None.

Exceptions   If data cannot be written to the output stream, this method will throw an IOException.

Example   The following example demonstrates how to write a short to an output stream.

```
void GenerateAndWrite(DataOutputStream dos) throws IOException
{
   while (true)
   {
      int s;

      // generate short

      dos.writeShort(s);
   }
}
```

WRITEUTF

Class Name   DataOutputStream

Description   This method writes a String object to the output stream as a series of bytes in UTF-8 format.

Syntax   public final void **writeUTF**(String *str*)

Parameters

String *str*   The String object to write.

Returns   None.

Exceptions   If data cannot be written to the output stream, this method will throw an IOException.

Example   The following example demonstrates how to write a UTF-8 encoded string to an output stream.

```
void GenerateAndWrite(DataOutputStream dos) throws IOException
{
   while (true)
   {
      String str;

      // generate a String object

      dos.writeUTF(str);
   }
}
```

The java.io.PrintStream Class

The PrintStream class provides the programmer with methods for printing the textual representation of Java data types and classes to an output stream. Table 11-13 lists and briefly describes all of the methods defined by class PrintStream.

Table 11-13 Summary of PrintStream methods

Method	Description
checkError	Checks the state of the stream for errors
close	Closes the output stream
flush	Flushes the output stream
print	Prints the textual representation of data to the output stream
println	Prints the textual representation of data to the output stream followed by a newline
write	Writes data to the output stream

PrintStream

Description	The PrintStream class provides methods for printing the textual representation of Java data types to an output stream.
Syntax	public class **PrintStream** extends FilterOutputStream
Package	java.io
Import	java.io.PrintStream
Constructors	public **PrintStream**(OutputStream *out*)
	public **PrintStream**(OutputStream *out*, boolean *boolFlush*)
Parameters	
OutputStream *out*	The OutputStream object to which to print the data.
boolean *boolFlush*	If true, the output stream is automatically flushed whenever a newline character is written.
Comments	These constructors create a PrintStream object from the OutputStream object specified in the parameter list. If a PrintStream object is to be used for output in an interactive setting, the *boolFlush* flag should be set to true upon creation. If this flag is set to true, output meant for the console appears immediately rather than being buffered.
Example	This example demonstrates how to create a PrintStream object from an OutputStream object.

```
void Create(OutputStream os)
{
    PrintStream ps = new PrintStream(os, true);

    // process
}
```

Methods

CHECKERROR

Class Name	PrintStream
Description	This method indicates whether or not an error has occurred during any previous write to the output stream. The internal error indicator is never reset. Once the stream encounters an error, this method will thereafter always return true. This method flushes the output stream before returning.
Syntax	public boolean **checkError**()
Parameters	None.
Returns	The boolean value true if an error has occurred since the stream was created, and false otherwise.
Exceptions	None.
Comments	The PrintStream methods do not throw exceptions. If an error occurs, it is noted internally and can be retrieved via this method.
Example	The following example demonstrates how to check the error state of the PrintStream object.

```
void CheckState(PrintStream ps)
{
    // print

    if (ps.checkError())
    {
        System.out.println("an error occurred");
    }
}
```

CLOSE

Class Name	PrintStream
Description	This method closes the PrintStream object.
Syntax	public void **close**()
Parameters	None.
Returns	None.

Exceptions	None.
Comments	Operating systems often allocate memory buffers and similar resources when output streams are created. These resources are typically beyond the reach of the cleanup facilities (such as the automatic garbage collector) provided by the Java runtime system. These resources must therefore be explicitly returned to the operating system when they are no longer needed. If they are not, the operating system will eventually run out of them. An example of a limited resource is the file descriptors (not to be confused with instances of the FileDescriptor class) that are assigned by the operating system to each open file. After the last file descriptor is allocated, no more files can be opened by that process. Closing an output stream returns the file descriptor to the operating system so that it may be reused.
Example	The following example demonstrates how to close a stream.

```
void ProcessData(PrintStream ps)
{
   for (int i = 0; i < 100; i++)
   {
      int n = getValueAtPoint(i);

      ps.println(n);
   }

   ps.close(); // close stream
}
```

FLUSH

Class Name	PrintStream
Description	This method flushes the PrintStream object.
Syntax	public void **flush**()
Parameters	None.
Returns	None.
Exceptions	None.
Comments	Output streams are usually buffered for performance reasons. Output devices such as hard disks can write a block of data just as fast as they can write a single byte of data. It therefore makes sense to write data in blocks if possible. By storing up sequential bytes of data and then writing them all at one time, buffered output streams take advantage of the fact that computer memory is typically many orders of magnitude faster than most output devices.
Example	The following example demonstrates how to flush an output stream.

```
void ProcessData(PrintStream ps)
{
```

continued on next page

continued from previous page

```
for (int i = 0; i < 100; i++)
{
    int n = getValueAtPoint(i);

    ps.println(n);
}

ps.flush(); // flush stream
}
```

PRINT

Class Name	PrintStream
Description	These methods print the textual representation of the parameter specified in the parameter list to the output stream.
Syntax	public void **print**(Object *obj*)
	public synchronized void **print**(String *str*)
	public synchronized void **print**(char [] *rgc*)
	public void **print**(boolean *bool*)
	public void **print**(char *c*)
	public void **print**(int *n*)
	public void **print**(long *l*)
	public void **print**(float *f*)
	public void **print**(double *d*)
Parameters	
Object *obj*	The object to print.
String *str*	This String object to print.
char [] *rgc*	The character array to print
boolean *bool*	The bool value to print.
char *c*	The char to print.
int *n*	The int to print.
long *l*	The long to print.
float *f*	The float to print.
double *d*	The double to print.
Returns	None.
Exceptions	None.
See Also	println()
Example	The following example demonstrates how to use these methods to print to the output stream.

```
void GenerateAndPrint(PrintStream ps)
{
    while (true)
    {
        Object obj;

        // generate an object

        ps.print(obj);

        String str;

        // generate a String object

        ps.print(str);

        char [] rgc;

        // generate a char array

        ps.print(rgc);

        int i;

        // generate an integer

        ps.print(i);
    }
}
```

PRINTLN

Class Name	PrintStream
Description	These methods print the textual representation of the parameter specified in the parameter list to the output stream, followed by a newline.
Syntax	public void **println**()
	public synchronized void **println**(Object *obj*)
	public synchronized void **println**(String *str*)
	public synchronized void **println**(char [] *rgc*)
	public synchronized void **println**(boolean *bool*)
	public synchronized void **println**(char *c*)
	public synchronized void **println**(int *n*)
	public synchronized void **println**(long *l*)
	public synchronized void **println**(float *f*)
	public synchronized void **println**(double *d*)
Parameters	
Object *obj*	The object to print.
String *str*	This String object to print.

char [] *rgc*	The character array to print.
boolean *bool*	The bool to print.
char *c*	The char to print.
int *n*	The int to print.
long *l*	The long to print.
float *f*	The float to print.
double *d*	The double to print.
Returns	None.
Exceptions	None.
See Also	print()
Example	The following example demonstrates how to use these methods to print to the output stream.

```
void GenerateAndPrint(PrintStream ps)
{
   while (true)
   {
      Object obj;

      // generate an object

      ps.println(obj);

      String str;

      // generate a String object

      ps.println(str);

      char [] rgc;

      // generate a char array

      ps.println(rgc);

      int i;

      // generate an integer

      ps.println(i);
   }
}
```

WRITE

Class Name	PrintStream
Description	These methods write a byte or series of bytes to the output stream.
Syntax	public void **write**(int *n*)
	public void **write**(byte [] *rgb*, int *nOffset*, int *nLength*)

Parameters

int *n*	The byte to write. Even though this parameter is passed to this method as an int rather than a byte, only values in the range -128 to ≤ 127 should be used. It is possible to write a method that does accept the full range of integer values, but that would certainly cause incompatibility with the other classes in the Java language I/O class library.
byte [] *rgb*	The byte array to write.
int *nOffset*	The offset from the beginning of the byte array.
int *nLength*	The number of bytes to write, beginning at the offset.
Returns	None.
Exceptions	None.
Example	The following example demonstrates how to write to an output stream.

```
void GenerateAndWrite(PrintStream ps)
{
    while (true)
    {
        int b;

        // generate byte

        ps.write(b);

        byte [] rgb;

        // generate byte array

        ps.write(rgb, 10, rgb.length);
    }
}
```

The Basic I/O Project: Persistent Elements and Frames

Project Overview

This chapter's project implements a collection of classes that know how to read their internal state from and write their internal state to a stream. Instances of these classes are called elements. Frames store elements and associate them with symbolic names. Frames (and the associations stored therein) also know how to write their internal state to and read their internal state from a stream, thereby allowing an entire collection of elements to be saved to and retrieved from a stream. Both elements and frames also know how to print a textual representation of themselves to a stream. In providing all of this functionality, these classes make heavy use of the DataInputStream, DataOutputStream, and PrintStream classes.

The Project Internals

Elements are represented as instances of a subtype of class Element. Four types of elements have been defined. They are the StringValue and IntegerValue classes (which represent strings and integers, respectively), the SymbolicValue class (which is used by frames to associate names with the elements stored in the frame), and the ConsCell class (which is used to build data structures such as lists from collections of other elements).

In addition to reading themselves from and writing themselves to streams, elements know how to copy and to evaluate themselves. An element's copy() method creates a perfect duplicate of the element. The operation of an element's eval() method depends on the element type. All eval() methods require that an instance of the Frame class be specified when the method is called. Typically, an element evaluates to itself. That is, the evaluation of an element returns a copy of the element. However, when an instance of class SymbolicValue is evaluated, the eval() method returns the instance of class Element that has been associated with the instance of class SymbolicValue in the specified instance of class Frame. In that respect, instances of SymbolicValue operate something like variables do in a programming language. They refer to other elements.

An instance of the Frame class represents a frame. The Frame class uses the Hashtable class to hold the mapping between instances of class SymbolicValue and instances of class Element and its subtypes.

Building the Project

1. The file Element.java contains the definition of the abstract class Element as well as the four classes derived from it—classes StringValue, IntegerValue, SymbolicValue, and ConsCell. The classes defined in this file require the services of several classes from the Java language class library.

```
import java.io.InputStream;
import java.io.DataInputStream;

import java.io.OutputStream;
import java.io.DataOutputStream;

import java.io.PrintStream;

import java.io.IOException;

import java.util.Vector;
```

2. The abstract class Element specifies the methods that all classes derived from class Element must provide definitions for. An instance of Element (or its subtypes) must be able to write itself to and read itself from a stream. It must also be able to print a textual representation of itself to a stream. An instance of Element (or its subtypes) may be copied—this creates an exact duplicate of the original instance. An instance may also be evaluated. This operation returns an instance of Element.

```
abstract class Element
{
   abstract public void writeTo(OutputStream os) throws IOException;
   abstract public void readFrom(InputStream is) throws IOException;
   abstract public void printTo(OutputStream os);

   abstract public Element eval(Frame fr) throws
      UndefinedSymbolException;

   abstract public Element copy();
}
```

3. The class StringValue implements an element that represents a string. The sequence of character data is contained within the variable *str*. The class may be constructed from a String object.

```
class StringValue extends Element
{
   private String str;

   public StringValue()
   {
      this.str = "";
   }

   public StringValue(String str)
   {
      this.str = str;
   }

   public void setValue(String str)
   {
      this.str = str;
   }
```

4. The following methods write the state of a StringValue object to, read the state of a StringValue object from, and print the textual representation of the state of a StringValue object to a stream.

```
public void writeTo(OutputStream os) throws IOException
{
   DataOutputStream dos = new DataOutputStream(os);
   dos.writeUTF(str);
}

public void readFrom(InputStream is) throws IOException
{
   DataInputStream dis = new DataInputStream(is);
   str = dis.readUTF();
}

public void printTo(OutputStream os)
{
   PrintStream ps = new PrintStream(os);
   ps.print("\"" + str + "\"");
}
```

5. The evaluation of a StringValue instance results in a copy of the original instance.

```
public Element eval(Frame fr) throws UndefinedSymbolException
{
    return copy();
}

public Element copy()
{
    return new StringValue(str);
}
}
```

6. The class IntegerValue implements an element that represents an integer. The integer value is contained within the variable *n*. The class may be constructed from an int.

```
class IntegerValue extends Element
{
    private int n;

    public IntegerValue()
    {
        this.n = 0;
    }

    public IntegerValue(int n)
    {
        this.n = n;
    }

    public void setValue(int n)
    {
        this.n = n;
    }
```

7. The following methods write the state of an IntegerValue object to, read the state of an IntegerValue object from, and print the textual representation of the state of an IntegerValue object to a stream.

```
public void writeTo(OutputStream os) throws IOException
{
    DataOutputStream dos = new DataOutputStream(os);
    dos.writeInt(n);
}

public void readFrom(InputStream is) throws IOException
{
    DataInputStream dis = new DataInputStream(is);
    n = dis.readInt();
}

public void printTo(OutputStream os)
{
    PrintStream ps = new PrintStream(os);
    ps.print(n);
}
```

8. The evaluation of an IntegerValue instance results in a copy of the original instance.

```
public Element eval(Frame fr) throws UndefinedSymbolException
{
    return copy();
}

public Element copy()
{
    return new IntegerValue(n);
}
}
```

9. The class SymbolicValue implements a symbolic value. Much like a variable, a symbolic value is a sequence of characters that evaluates to some value other than itself. The sequence of characters that name the SymbolicValue is stored in the variable *str*. An instance of SymbolicValue can be created with or without a name.

```
class SymbolicValue extends Element
{
    private String str;

    public SymbolicValue()
    {
        this.str = null;
    }

    public SymbolicValue(String str)
    {
        this.str = str;
    }

    public void setValue(String str)
    {
        this.str = str;
    }
```

10. The following methods write the state of a SymbolicValue object to, read the state of a SymbolicValue object from, and print the textual representation of the state of a SymbolicValue object to a stream.

```
public void writeTo(OutputStream os) throws IOException
{
    DataOutputStream dos = new DataOutputStream(os);
    dos.writeUTF(str);
}

public void readFrom(InputStream is) throws IOException
{
    DataInputStream dis = new DataInputStream(is);
    str = dis.readUTF();
}

public void printTo(OutputStream os)
```

continued on next page

continued from previous page

```
{
    PrintStream ps = new PrintStream(os);
    ps.print(str);
}
```

11. The mapping between a symbolic value and the element it evaluates to is stored within a frame. The eval() method queries the frame specified in its parameter list in order to find the element to be returned. This class redefines the methods hashcode() and equals() so that they will work with the Frame class.

```
public Element eval(Frame fr) throws UndefinedSymbolException
{
    return fr.get(this);
}

public Element copy()
{
    return new SymbolicValue(str);
}

public int hashCode()
{
    return str.hashCode();
}

public boolean equals(Object obj)
{
    if (obj instanceof SymbolicValue)
        return str.equals(((SymbolicValue)obj).str);

    return false;
}

public String getChars()
{
    return str;
}
}
```

12. The class ConsCell implements a cons cell. A cons cell consists of two references to other elements—one called the *car* (stored in the variable *elemCar*) and the other called the *cdr* (stored in the variable *elemCdr*). Figure 11-6 contains a figurative representation of a cons cell. Both the *car* and the *cdr* may reference other cons cells. If a collection of cons cells is strung together, such that the *cdr* of one cell refers to the next cons cell in the sequence, and the *cdr* of the last cell is null, the collection of cons cells forms a *list*. Figure 11-7 illustrates a list. A cons cell can be created by specifying both the *car* and the *cdr*, by specifying neither the *car* nor the *cdr*, or by specifying only the *car*. In our system, cons cells can be used to create complicated data structures.

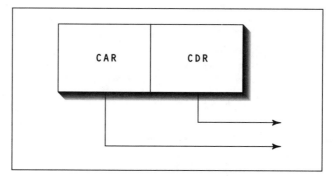

Figure 11-6 A cons cell

```
class ConsCell extends Element
{
    private Element elemCar;
    private Element elemCdr;

    public ConsCell()
    {
        this(null, null);
    }

    public ConsCell(Element elemCar)
    {
        this(elemCar, null);
    }

    public ConsCell(Element elemCar, Element elemCdr)
    {
        this.elemCar = elemCar;
        this.elemCdr = elemCdr;
    }

    public void setValue(Element elemCar, Element elemCdr)
    {
        this.elemCar = elemCar;
        this.elemCdr = elemCdr;
    }
```

13. The following methods write the state of a ConsCell object to and read the state
of a ConsCell object from a stream. They do so by instructing each of the elements that make up the cons cell to write itself to or read itself from the stream.

```
public void writeTo(OutputStream os) throws IOException
{
```

continued on next page

continued from previous page

```
    DataOutputStream dos = new DataOutputStream(os);

    dos.writeByte(Mapper.map(elemCar));
    if (elemCar != null) elemCar.writeTo(dos);

    dos.writeByte(Mapper.map(elemCdr));
    if (elemCdr != null) elemCdr.writeTo(dos);
}

public void readFrom(InputStream is) throws IOException
{
    DataInputStream dis = new DataInputStream(is);

    elemCar = (Element)Mapper.map(dis.readByte());
    if (elemCar != null) elemCar.readFrom(dis);

    elemCdr = (Element)Mapper.map(dis.readByte());
    if (elemCdr != null) elemCdr.readFrom(dis);
}
```

14. The following method prints the textual representation of the state of a ConsCell object to a stream. It does so by instructing each of the elements that make up the cons cell to write itself to or read itself from the stream. A cons cell may be printed in one of two ways, depending on whether or not it is at the head of a list. If it is at the head of a list, the *car* of each cons cell making up the list is printed sequentially (recall that the *cdr* of each cons cell points to the next cons cell in the list). If the cons cell is not at the head of a list, both the *car* and the *cdr* are printed, separated by a period.

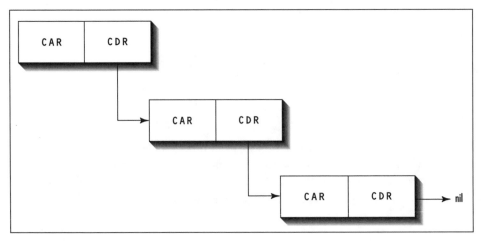

Figure 11-7 A list

```
public void printTo(OutputStream os)
{
    PrintStream ps = new PrintStream(os);

    if (listp())
    {
        ps.print("(");

        if (elemCar == null) ps.print("nil");
        else elemCar.printTo(ps);

        ConsCell cc = (ConsCell)elemCdr;

        while (cc != null)
        {
            ps.print(" ");

            cc.elemCar.printTo(ps);
            cc = (ConsCell)cc.elemCdr;
        }

        ps.print(")");
    }

    else
    {
        ps.print("(");

        if (elemCar == null) ps.print("nil");
        else elemCar.printTo(ps);

        ps.print(" . ");

        if (elemCdr == null) ps.print("nil");
        else elemCdr.printTo(ps);

        ps.print(")");
    }
}
```

15. The evaluation of a ConsCell instance results in a copy of the original instance.

```
public Element eval(Frame fr) throws UndefinedSymbolException
{
    return copy();
}

public Element copy()
{
    return new ConsCell(elemCar.copy(), elemCdr.copy());
}
```

16. The following two methods return information about a ConsCell instance. The first method indicates whether or not a ConsCell instance is at the head of a list. The second method returns the number of elements in the list that this ConsCell instance is at the head of.

```
public boolean listp()
{
   if (elemCdr == null)
   {
      return true;
   }
   else if (elemCdr instanceof ConsCell)
   {
      return ((ConsCell)elemCdr).listp();
   }
   return false;
}

public int listlen()
{
   if (listp())
   {
      int i = 1;

      ConsCell cc = (ConsCell)elemCdr;

      while (cc != null)
      {
         cc = (ConsCell)cc.elemCdr;
         i++;
      }
   }

   return -1;
}
}
```

17. The file Frame.java contains the definition of the class Frame and the class UndefinedSymbolException. A frame is a collection of elements, each associated with a symbolic value (that "names" the element). The Frame class requires the services of several classes from the Java language class library.

```
import java.io.InputStream;
import java.io.DataInputStream;

import java.io.OutputStream;
import java.io.DataOutputStream;

import java.io.PrintStream;

import java.io.IOException;

import java.util.Enumeration;
import java.util.Hashtable;
```

18. An instance of UndefinedSymbolException is created and thrown whenever an instance of the Frame class is unable to find the element that goes along with a symbolic value.

```
class UndefinedSymbolException extends Exception
```

```
{
   UndefinedSymbolException() { super(); }
   UndefinedSymbolException(String str) { super(str); }
}
```

19. The class Frame implements a frame. The Frame class defines two variables. The variable *htSymbols* is a reference to the hash table that holds the mapping between symbolic name and element. The variable *frParent* is a reference to the parent frame. Frame objects form a linked list. If a symbolic value cannot be resolved to an element in the current frame, resolution is then attempted for each parent frame. An instance of class Frame is created by specifying the parent Frame object (or null, if a parent frame does not exist).

```
public class Frame
{
   Hashtable htSymbols;

   Frame frParent;

   public Frame(Frame frParent)
   {
      this.htSymbols = new Hashtable();
      this.frParent = frParent;
   }
```

20. The following three methods add a symbolic value and its associated element to the frame, delete a symbolic value and its associated element from the frame, and get the element associated with a particular symbolic value from the frame. The method get() throws a UndefinedSymbolException if the symbolic value cannot be resolved to an element.

```
public void add(SymbolicValue sym, Element elem)
{
   htSymbols.put(sym, elem);
}

public void remove(SymbolicValue sym)
{
   htSymbols.remove(sym);
}

public Element get(SymbolicValue sym) throws UndefinedSymbolException
{
   Element elem = null;

   if ((elem = (Element)htSymbols.get(sym)) == null)
   {
      if (frParent == null) throw new UndefinedSymbolException();
      elem = frParent.get(sym);
   }

   if (elem == null) throw new UndefinedSymbolException();

   return elem;
}
```

21. The following method writes the contents of this frame (all of the symbolic value-element pairs) to the specified output stream. It does so by first obtaining an enumeration of all of the keys (the symbolic values) in the hash table and then looping over them. Inside of the loop, the corresponding element is obtained and both the symbolic value and the element are written to the output stream.

```
public void writeTo(OutputStream os) throws IOException,
    UndefinedSymbolException
{
    DataOutputStream dos = new DataOutputStream(os);

    dos.writeInt(htSymbols.size());

    Enumeration enum = htSymbols.keys();

    while(enum.hasMoreElements())
    {
        SymbolicValue sym = (SymbolicValue)enum.nextElement();

        sym.writeTo(dos);

        Element el = get(sym);

        dos.writeByte(Mapper.map(el));

        el.writeTo(dos);
    }
}
```

22. The following method reads the contents of this frame (all of the symbolic value-element pairs) from the specified input stream.

```
public void readFrom(InputStream is) throws IOException,
    UndefinedSymbolException
{
    DataInputStream dis = new DataInputStream(is);

    int n = dis.readInt();

    for (int i = 0; i < n; i++)
    {
        SymbolicValue sym = new SymbolicValue();

        sym.readFrom(dis);

        Element el = (Element)Mapper.map(dis.readByte());

        el.readFrom(dis);

        add(sym, el);
    }
}
```

23. The following method prints the textual representation of the contents of this frame (all of the symbolic value-element pairs) to the specified output stream.

```
public void printTo(OutputStream os) throws IOException,
   UndefinedSymbolException
{
   PrintStream ps = new PrintStream(os);

   Enumeration enum = htSymbols.keys();

   while(enum.hasMoreElements())
   {
      SymbolicValue sym = (SymbolicValue)enum.nextElement();

      Element el = get(sym);

      sym.printTo(ps);
      ps.print(" = ");
      el.printTo(ps);
      ps.println();
   }
}
}
```

24. The file Mapper.java defines the Mapper class. The Mapper class methods map objects to values and values to objects. The values are used as markers in the input and output streams to indicate the meaning of the bytes that are about to be written to or read from the stream.

```
public class Mapper
{
   public static final byte Null = 0;
   public static final byte String = 1;
   public static final byte Integer = 2;
   public static final byte Symbol = 3;
   public static final byte Cons = 4;

   static byte map(Object obj)
   {
      if (obj instanceof StringValue) return Mapper.String;
      else if (obj instanceof IntegerValue) return Mapper.Integer;
      else if (obj instanceof SymbolicValue) return Mapper.Symbol;
      else if (obj instanceof ConsCell) return Mapper.Cons;
      else return Mapper.Null;
   }

   static Object map(byte n)
   {
      if (n == Mapper.String) return new StringValue();
      else if (n == Mapper.Integer) return new IntegerValue();
      else if (n == Mapper.Symbol) return new SymbolicValue();
      else if (n == Mapper.Cons) return new ConsCell();
      else return null;
   }
}
```

25. The file Reader.java defines the Reader class. The main() method of the Reader class loops over each String in the String array and opens the file with the specified name. After opening the file, it creates an empty frame and reads in the contents of the frame from the file input stream. Finally, it prints the contents of the frame to the console.

```java
import java.io.FileInputStream;

public class Reader
{
   public static void main(String [] args)
   {
      for (int i = 0; i < args.length; i++)
      {
         try
         {
            FileInputStream fis = new FileInputStream(args[i]);

            Frame fr = new Frame(null);

            fr.readFrom(fis);

            fr.printTo(System.out);
         }
         catch (Exception e)
         {
            e.printStackTrace();
         }
      }
   }
}
```

26. The file Writer.java defines the Writer class. The main() method of the Writer class loops over each String in the String array and opens the file with the specified name. After opening the file, it creates an empty frame and fills the frame with information. It then writes the contents of the frame to the output stream. Finally, it prints the contents of the frame to the console.

```java
import java.io.FileOutputStream;

public class Writer
{
   public static void main(String [] args)
   {
      for (int i = 0; i < args.length; i++)
      {
         try
         {
            FileOutputStream fos = new FileOutputStream(args[i]);

            Frame fr = new Frame(null);

            Element el;

            el = new ConsCell(new StringValue("ten"),
                              new SymbolicValue("eleven"));

            fr.add(new SymbolicValue("one"), el);

            el = new ConsCell(new SymbolicValue("seven"));
```

```
        el = new ConsCell(new IntegerValue(123), el);
        el = new ConsCell(new StringValue("one-two-three"), el);

        fr.add(new SymbolicValue("two"), el);

        el = new ConsCell(new ConsCell(new SymbolicValue("one"),
                                       new SymbolicValue("two")),
                          new ConsCell(new IntegerValue(123)));

        fr.add(new SymbolicValue("three"), el);

        el = new IntegerValue(100);

        fr.add(new SymbolicValue("four"), el);

        fr.writeTo(fos);

        fr.printTo(System.out);
      }
      catch (Exception e)
      {
        e.printStackTrace();
      }
    }
  }
}
```

27. The Java language source files comprising the project can be compiled as follows:

```
javac Element.java Frame.java Mapper.java Reader.java Writer.java
```

28. The Writer class must be run first in order to create a data file. From the command line, run it as follows:

```
java Writer out
```

29. The Reader class can read and display data files created by the Writer class. From the command line, type

```
java Reader out
```

12

FILE I/O

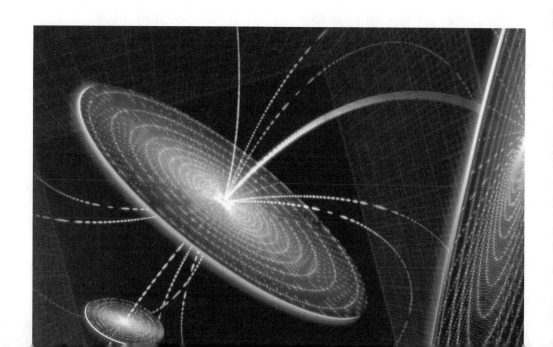

12

FILE I/O

All operating systems have their own unique way of treating and manipulating files. Different operating systems use different terminology, access control methods, and file organization on the disk. Java provides a set of API classes that provide methods to manipulate and modify files in a platform independent manner. These APIs hide the details of the idiosyncrasies of different operating systems in handling files. You can extend these classes to organize information stored in the files without bothering about the actual implementation of files on different operating systems. Using the file stream APIs it is very easy to implement persistent Java classes and objects in your applications.

Most of the functionality of files in Java is derived from the Java's input and output streams. One consequence of deriving the functionality of files from streams is that the same model that performs I/O for the keyboard and terminal works just fine with disk files. The file input and output is treated in exactly the same manner as terminal input and output. This approach greatly simplifies the programming task. Just like C and C++, Java opens three streams as soon as the Java interpreter starts executing a Java program. These files are usually referred to as System.in, System.out, and System.err. They are used for reading input data from the terminal, writing output data, and writing error to the terminal, respectively.

In this chapter you are introduced to the basic concepts of files that are common to all the operating systems. Then you are introduced to the different types of files supported by Java, followed by the class APIs used to manipulate them. Detailed explanation of all the classes, interfaces, and methods are also presented to assist you in using these classes effectively. A list of classes with a brief description is shown in Table 12-1. A summary of methods by category is shown in Table 12-2. The hierarchical relationship between these classes is shown in Figure 12-1.

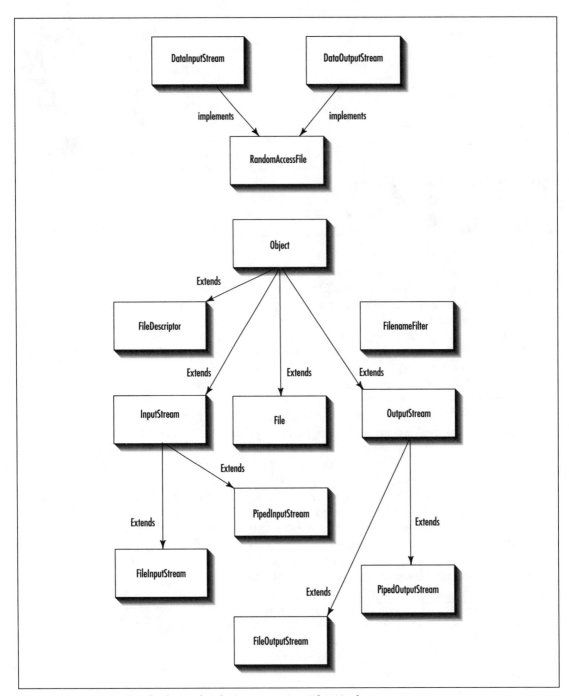

Figure 12-1 Hierarchical relationship between various File I/O classes

Basic Concepts

The class File in Java is an abstraction layer over different system implementations of the files. There are three types of files supported in Java. They are

- Ordinary files
- Directory files
- Special files

Ordinary files contain bytes of data that are organized into a linear array and stored on a disk. A directory, on the other hand, just contains the information about the files contained within it. A directory also stores the information about the access permissions and location of the files on the disk. Using a combination of directory files and ordinary files, you can organize your information into a hierarchical structure on the hard drive. Every Java file (ordinary or directory), has the following properties:

- **File name**

  Every file has a file name. A file name is a unique string that helps identify a file on the disk. The length of a file name and the characters allowed in a file name are dependent on the operating system on which the Java program is being executed. For example, the UNIX operating system allows all characters except '/' in the file name, and MS-DOS imposes a 15-character length restriction on the file name.

- **Path name**

  A path name is a Java String that is generated from one or more directory names. The directory names in a path name are separated using a special character. On UNIX, this character is '/'. On MS-DOS, this character is '\'. A path name can either be relative or absolute.

- **Relative path name**

  A relative path name is the path name of the file that starts with the current directory. For example, lib/X11/bin/xeyes is a relative path for a file on the UNIX operating system. On MS-DOS, msapps\msword is a relative path for a file.

- **Absolute path name**

  An absolute path name is the path name of the file starting from the root directory or device. For example, /usr/lib/X11/bin is an absolute path on the UNIX operating system. On MS-DOS, c:\windows\msapps\msword is an absolute path for a file.

- **Access permissions**

  On some operating systems, like UNIX and Windows NT, access permissions are associated with every file. Access permissions selectively allow the owner, the group, or everybody to read, write, or execute the files.

You can perform the following operations on ordinary files (provided you have the access permissions):

- Create a file
- Open a file
- Read data from the file
- Write data to a file
- Close a file
- Delete a file

In the case of a directory file, you can perform the following operations (provided you have the access permissions):

- Create a directory
- Get a list of all the files in the directory
- Remove a directory

File Properties

Java provides modular classes to deal with system-specific file features such as the file separator character, the date modified, etc. Using these classes, you can query the properties of the file on the host machine. Let's begin the discussion on the file properties by developing a simple Java program that determines if a file exists in the current directory. If it does, it prints a few properties of the file. The program listing is shown in Listing 12-1.

The files properties in Java are encapsulated in the class File that is defined in the package java.io. This class provides a common denominator of the basic file properties. Most methods in the class File can potentially compromise the security of the system on which the Java program is executing. For example, an applet could be developed that reads files on your system and deletes them without your knowledge. To close this potential security hole, Java does not allow the following operations when the Java program is running as an applet:

- Check to see if a file exists on the host system
- Check to see if a file is an ordinary file or a directory
- Check to see if a file has read permissions
- Check to see if a file has write permissions
- Check the time when the file was last modified
- Check the size of the file

■ Create a new directory

■ Rename a file

■ Delete a file

■ List the files in the directory

In the program shown in Listing 12-1, a class FilePropertiesTest is defined, which contains just one public static method, main(). The method main() creates an instance of the class File. In the program shown in Listing 12-1, an instance of the class File is created by passing the file name to the constructor. The code segment that creates a new instance of the class File is shown here.

```
File aFile = new File(args[0]);
```

The file is then checked to see if it is a valid one. This is done by calling the method exists(). If the file is not valid, an error message is printed on the System.out. Otherwise, a few properties of the file are printed. The separator character is printed on the System.out. The separator character printed on the System.out would vary depending upon the host system on which you are executing the Java program. The method getName() returns the name of the file. The method getPath() returns the path name of the file. The method getAbsolutePath() returns the absolute path name of the file. The method isFile() returns a boolean value indicating whether or not a file is an ordinary file. The method isDirectory() returns a boolean value indicating whether or not the file is a directory file. In case the file is neither an ordinary file nor a directory, an error message is printed on the System.out. Tables 12-3 and 12-4 provide a comprehensive list of all the variables and methods in the class File.

Listing 12-1 A new instance of the class File

```
import java.io.*;
import java.lang.*;

// This class prints the properties of the file.

class FilePropertiesTest
{

    public static void main(String[] args)
    {
      // Create a new instance of the class File.
        File aFile = new File(args[0]);
      // Check if the file exists.
        if(! aFile.exists())
        {
            // Missing file ?
            System.out.println("File " + args[0] + " is missing or invalid.");
        }
        else
        {
```

continued on next page

continued from previous page

```
            // Print the file separator character.

            System.out.println("File Separator = " + File.separator);

            // Print the name of the file.

            System.out.println("File Name: " + aFile.getName());

            // Print the path name of the file

            System.out.println("Path Name: " + aFile.getPath());

            // Print the Absolute name of the file

            System.out.println("Absolute Path Name: " +
aFile.getAbsolutePath());

            // check if aFile  is an ordinary file

            if(aFile.isFile())
            {
    System.out.println("The file is a Ordinary File.");
            }
            // check if aFile is directory
            else if(aFile.isDirectory())
            {
                System.out.println("The file is a Directory.");
                System.out.println("Parent Directory Name: " +
                aFile.getParent());
            }
             // neither a file nor a directory ? -- Special file.
            else
            {
                System.out.println("Unknown file type");
            }
        }
    }
}
```

Execute

```
java FilePropertiesTest xyz.txt
```

Output

```
File xyz.txt is missing or invalid.
```

Execute

```
java FilePropertiesTest abc.txt
```

Output

```
File Separator = /
File Name: abc.txt
Path Name: abc.txt
Absolute Path Name: /home/javauser/example/abc.txt
The file is a Ordinary File.
```

Execute

```
java FilePropertiesTest ./abc.txt
```

Output

```
File Separator = /
File Name: abc.txt
Path Name: ./abc.txt
Absolute Path Name: /home/javauser/example/./abc.txt
The file is a Ordinary File.
```

Execute

java FilePropertiesTest /home/javauser/example

Output
```
File Separator = /
File Name:
Path Name: /home/javauser/example
Absolute Path Name: /home/javauser/example
The file is a Directory.
 Parent Directory Name: /home/javauser
```

File Descriptors

Whenever a file is opened for I/O, the operating system allocates the necessary data structures and returns a handle to the structure. This handle is generally called the file descriptor. The allowable values for the file descriptor are from zero up to a maximum, depending on the operating system. The class FileDescriptor encapsulates the system dependent features of the file descriptors. This class is final, so no other class can inherit and modify its properties. This class does not have a public constructor, so you cannot instantiate this class. You can obtain an instance of the class java.io.FileDescriptor when you call the method getFD() on instances of class FileInputStream, FileOutputStream, or RandomAccessFile. A summary of variables and methods of the class FileDescriptor is shown in Tables 12-5 and 12-6, respectively. Java opens three files as soon as the program starts executing. These files generally handle the input, the output, and the error of the program. The file descriptors for the files are

- java.io.FileDescriptor.in
- java.io.FileDescriptor.out
- java.io.FileDescriptor.err

File Name Filter

The Java API class library provides an interface to selectively filter file names. The interface FilenameFilter can be used to filter out unwanted files from the list() method of the class File. Listing 12-2 gives an example of an implementation of the filter class that filters out all files except those with the suffix ".java". The class FileSuffixFilter implements the interface FilenameFilter. The constructor of FileSuffixFilter takes a file suffix as an argument and stores the suffix in the instance variable. The method accept() returns true if the file name ends with the suffix, and returns false otherwise. The class method main() creates a new instance of the class File and a new instance of the class FileSuffixFilter with the suffix ".java". You get a list of files that end with ".java" by calling the method list() of the instance of the class File with the instance of the FileSuffixFilter as an argument. If the file list returned by the method list() is non-null, then the list of all the files in the file list is printed out. The *try-catch* statements handle the IOException raised by the method list(). Table 12-7 provides a comprehensive list of all the methods in the interface FilenameFilter.

Listing 12-2 An example of an implementation of FilenameFilter

```java
import java.io.*;
import java.lang.*;

// This class implements the interface FilenameFilter.

class FileSuffixFilter implements FilenameFilter
{
    String suffix;

    // Constructor

    public FileSuffixFilter(String fileSuffix)
    {
        suffix = fileSuffix; // Store the suffix
    }

    // accept only the filename that ends with  suffix
    // Returns true if the filename ends with the suffix. false otherwise.


    public boolean accept(File dir, String name)
    {
        return name.endsWith(suffix);
    }


    public static void main(String args[])
    {
        // Create a new Instance of the File.
        File aFile = new File("/home/javauser/example");

        // Filter out the files that don't end with ".java"
        FileSuffixFilter javaFiles = new FileSuffixFilter(".java");


        // Get a list of all the files that end with ".java"
        // by using the FileSuffixFilter.

        String[] fileList = aFile.list(javaFiles);
```

```
    if(fileList != null) // If the filelist is not null.
    {
        for(int i=0; i < fileList.length; ++i)
        {
            // Print the files from the list.
            System.out.println(fileList[i]);
                                                }
    }

}

}
```

Compile the program:

```
javac FileSuffixFilter.java
```

Execute the program:

```
java FileSuffixFilter
```

Output
```
FileSuffixFilter.java
FilePropertiesTest.java
```

Sequential Access File I/O

Java programming language, like C++, treats all the I/O as a character string operation. Java treats disk files as streams even when they include binary (nontext) values. Like C++, Java uses the file as a basic model for all input and output even if the I/O goes to the display terminal rather than the disk. In fact, Java automatically opens the standard input, output, and error files called System.in, System.out, and System.err, respectively. These streams become the interface between the program and the user. The file System.in handles all the inputs from the terminal keyboard. In contrast, the file System.out handles all the standard output. The file System.err generally is used for handling the standard error output to the terminal. The file I/O in Java is managed by three classes. They are

■ **FileInputStream**

This class is used for handling the file input. This class inherits from the class InputStream. The inheritance relationship is depicted in Figure 12-1.

■ **FileOutputStream**

This class is used for handling the file output. This class inherits from the class OutputStream. The inheritance relationship is shown in Figure 12-1.

■ **RandomAccessFile**

This class is used for handling both file input and output. This class implements the interfaces DataInput and DataOutput. The inheritance relationship is shown in Figure 12-1.

The code in Listing 12-3 shows how to use the classes FileInputStream and FileOutputStream. This program reads one line of input at a time from the input file and writes it to the output file. The class CopyFile has only the method main(). The method main() takes command line arguments as the input. If the number of command line arguments is less than two, then the usage information is printed on the System.err. The command line arguments *args[0]* and *args[1]* are the input file name and output file name, respectively. New instances of the input file stream (*fin*) and the output file stream (*fout*) are created. A new instance of the input file stream is created by the following statement:

```
fin = new FileInputStream(inputFile);
```

A new instance of the output file stream is created by the following statement:

```
fout = new FileOutputStream(outputFile);
```

To read from file input stream, you can either use the low-level methods like read(), etc., or create a new instance of DataInputStream. A new instance of DataInputStream is created by the following statement:

```
DataInputStream din = new DataInputStream(fin);
```

To read from the file inputFile, you can now use the methods defined in the class DataInputStream. (The details of the class DataInputStream are described in Chapter 11, Basic I/O.) Similarly, a new instance of DataOutputStream is created by the statement

```
DataOutputStream dout = new DataOutputStream(dout);
```

To write data to the outputFile, you can now use the methods defined in the class DataOutputStream. (The details of the class DataOutputStream are described in Chapter 11, Basic I/O.) One line at a time from DataInputStream (din) is read until there is no more data in the input stream. After one line is read from *din*, it is written to the output stream, and the output stream is flushed. Exceptions are handled by the *try-catch* block of the code. The final block closes any open files. Table 12-8 provides a comprehensive list of all the methods in the class FileInputStream. Table 12-9 provides a comprehensive list of all the methods in the class FileOutputStream.

Listing 12-3 An example of file stream APIs

```java
import java.io.*;
import java.lang.*;

// This class reads one line of input from a file at a time and writes it the output file.

class CopyFile
{

    public static void main(String args[])
    {
        // Check the number of command line arguments passed.
```

```java
if(args.length < 2 )
{
    System.err.println("Usage: CopyFile input-file output-file");
    return;
}

String inputFile = args[0]; // First argument is the input-file
String outputFile = args[1]; // Second argument is the output-file

FileInputStream fin = null; // Input file
FileOutputStream fout = null; // Output file

try
{
    //Create a new instance of the Input file stream
    fin = new FileInputStream(inputFile);

    //Create a new instance of the output file stream
    fout = new FileOutputStream(outputFile);


    // Create an instance of the class DataInputStream
    DataInputStream din = new DataInputStream(fin);

    // Create an instance of the class DataOutputStream
    DataOutputStream dout = new DataOutputStream(fout);

    // a reference to a String to store one line of input at a time
    String aLine;

    // Read one line from the din -The instance of DataInputStream
    // Till there are no more lines in the input stream
    while( (aLine = din.readLine()) != null)
    {
        // Write the line to the dout - DataOutputStream
        dout.writeBytes(aLine);
        // Write a newline character to the dout
        dout.writeByte('\n');
        // Flush the dout - DataOutputStream
        dout.flush();
    }
}
catch (FileNotFoundException e)
{
    System.err.println("Error " + e);
}
catch (IOException e)
{
    System.err.println("Error " + e);
}
finally
{
    try
    {
        // close the open files
        if(fin != null)
            fin.close();
```

continued on next page

continued from previous page

```
                if(fout != null)
                    fout.close();
            }
            catch (IOException e)
            {
                System.err.println("Error " + e);
                return;
            }
        }
    }
}
```

Random Access File I/O

Until this point you have dealt with files in which the input and output are handled in a sequential manner. You could open a file, read, or write sequentially through the end of the file, and finally close the file. You can write several useful programs despite this restriction, but if you want to move back and forth in a file to perform reads and writes on the same file, you need to use the class RandomAccessFile. The random access file is very useful in updating and changing the values already in the file. Random access files provide a method to access data in the file without having to read all of the data before it. The class RandomAccessFile provides methods to move to the exact location within the file where I/O needs to be performed. The class RandomAccessFile implements the interfaces DataInput and DataOutput. The API for the class RandomAccessFile has methods for reading and writing all the primitive data types like byte, char, short, int, long, float, and double. It also has methods to position the file pointer to the exact location within the file for reading and writing. The following code segment creates a new instance of the random access file.

```
RandomAccessFile rfile = new RandomAccessFile("randomfile.txt", "rw");
```

The above code creates an instance of the class RandomAccessFile called *rfile* and opens the file randomfile.txt in both read and write mode. You can get the current file pointer position by calling the method getFilePointer(). You can set the file position by calling the method seek(). Most of the functionality is similar to the formatted file I/O streams. Methods in the DataInput and DataOutput are described in greater detail in Chapter 11, Basic I/O. Table 12-10 gives a comprehensive list of all the methods in the class RandomAccessFile.

Special Files

The only special file type supported in Java is Pipes. Pipes are first-in first-out (FIFO) files. Typically, a reader thread creates a pipe in output mode, and a writer thread opens the pipe in the input mode. If the reader of the pipe reads ahead of the writer, then the reader just waits for the data. If the writer writes too far ahead of the reader, it sleeps until the reader has a chance to catch up, so the kernel doesn't have too much data queued. Pipes are typically used to communicate between two different threads.

Figure 12-2 shows two threads, a write thread and a read thread, using pipes for communication. The read calls in the pipe are destructive, i.e., once a byte is read, it is gone forever. This is done so that the running processes connected via pipes do not fill up the file system of the host machine.

The code shown in Listing 12-4 clarifies some basic concepts of piped I/O. The program comprises three classes, namely ReaderClass, WriterClass, and PipeTest. The ReaderClass extends the class Object, implements the interface Runnable, and has just one method, run(). The constructor of the ReaderClass takes an instance of the PipedInputStream as an argument and uses the reference to instantiate the class DataInputStream—*din*. The method run() basically reads one line of input from *din*, and prints it out on the standard output. When either the data has been completely read or when there has been an error, the *finally* section of the *try-catch* block is executed. In the *finally* block the data input stream is closed.

The WriterClass extends the class Object and implements the interface Runnable. The constructor of the class WriterClass takes an instance of the PipedOutput stream as an argument and creates an instance of the DataOutputStream—*dout*. The method run() of the WriterClass writes a String to *dout* and sleeps for a random interval. After writing 10 such strings or when an error occurs, the *finally* block is executed. In the *finally* block, the data output stream is closed.

The class PipeTest just contains the method main(). The method main() creates a pair of pipe streams—*pinp* and *pout*. Now, *pinp* can be used for reading data from a pipe in a FIFO manner, and *pout* can be used for writing to a pipe. An instance of the class ReaderClass is then created—*rdr*, as well as an instance of the class WriterClass— *wtr*. Since ReaderClass and WriterClass implement the interface Runnable, they can be run in two separate threads.

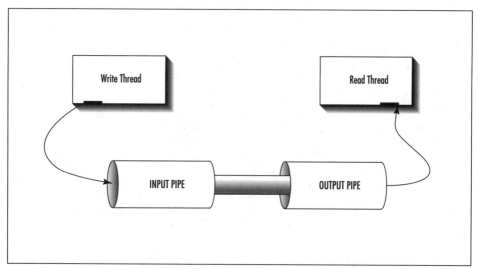

Figure 12-2　Read thread and write thread using pipes to communicate

Two threads, *thr1* and *thr2*, are created with arguments *rdr* and *wtr*, respectively. When the method start() is called for the threads *thr1* and *thr2*, it in turn calls the method run() of *rdr* and *wtr*. When both the threads are done with their task, the input and output pipe streams are finally closed. The output of the program is also shown in the Listing 12-4. The exact output on your system may vary. Summaries of the methods in the class PipedInputStream and the class PipedOutputStream are shown in the Tables 12-11 and 12-12, respectively.

Listing 12-4 An example of the classes PipeInputStream and PipeOutputStream

```
import java.lang.*;
import java.io.*;


// Reader Class Reads data from an open PipeInputStream.

class ReaderClass extends Object implements Runnable
{
    DataInputStream din = null; // Input Stream.

    public ReaderClass(PipedInputStream inp)
    {
        din = new DataInputStream(inp); // We create a new instance.
    }

    // The main body  of the Class ReaderClass
    public void run()
    {
        String str = null; // The string read

        System.out.println("Starting Reader Thread");

        try
        {
            // Read one line of input at a time
            while( (str = din.readLine()) != null)
            {
                // Print it out on the output stream.
                System.out.println("Received: " + str);
            }
            System.out.println("Done Reading data.....");
        }
        // In case of a error while reading
        catch(IOException e)
        {
            System.out.println("Unable to read data.");
        }
        finally
        {
            // Perform  a cleanup
            try
            {
                // close the data input stream.
```

```
                    din.close();
                    System.out.println("Closing the Read Pipe");
                }
                catch(IOException e1)
                {
                }
                return;
            }
        }
    }


// Writer Class Writes data to an open PipeOutputStream.

class WriterClass extends Object implements Runnable
{
    DataOutputStream dout = null; // Output Stream

    public WriterClass(PipedOutputStream out)
    {
        // Create a new instance of Data OutputStream.
        dout = new DataOutputStream(out);

    }

    public void run()
    {
        String str = null;

        System.out.println("Starting Writer Thread");

        try
        {
            // Write 10 Strings to dout

            for(int i=0; i < 10; i++)
            {
                System.out.println("Sent Data: ");

                // Write a String to the DataOutputStream dout

                dout.writeBytes("Hello World " + i + "\n");

                // Sleep for a random interval

                Thread.sleep( (long) (1000 * Math.random()));
            }

            System.out.println("Done Writing data.....");
        }
        // In case of error while writing to pipe
        catch(IOException e)
        {
            System.out.println("Unable to write data.");
        }
        finally
        {
```

continued on next page

continued from previous page

```
            // Perform a cleanup

            try
            {
                // close the data output stream.
                dout.close();
                System.out.println("Closing the Write Pipe");
            }
            catch(IOException e1)
            {
            }
            return;
        }
    }
}

class PipeTest
{
    public static void main(String[] args)
    {
        PipedInputStream pinp = null; // input pipe
        PipedOutputStream pout = null; // output pipe

        try
        {
            /*
                Steps to create a new pipe Input-Output pair.
                1. Create a new instance of PipedInputStream.
                2. Create a new instance of PipedOutputStream using
                   the instance of the PipedInputStream as an argument
                3. Connect the the instance of the PipedInputStream
                   to the instance of PipedOutputStream.
            */

            pinp = new PipedInputStream();
            pout = new PipedOutputStream(pinp);
            pinp.connect(pout);

            // Create a new instance of the ReaderClass.
            ReaderClass rdr = new ReaderClass(pinp);

            // Create a new instance of the WriterClass.
            WriterClass wtr = new WriterClass(pout);

            // Create two thread thr1 and thr2 using the arguments
            // rdr and wtr respectively.

            Thread thr1 = new Thread(rdr);
            Thread thr2 = new Thread(wtr);


            // Starts the two threads.

            thr1.start();
```

```
        thr2.start();

        // Wait till both of them are done.

        thr1.join();
        thr2.join();
    }
    // In case of an error in during the creation of PipedInputStream or
    // PipedOutputStream,
    catch(Exception e)
    {
        System.out.println("Error " + e);
    }
    finally
    {
        // Perform a cleanup.
        try
        {
            // Close input and the output pipes.
            pinp.close();
            pout.close();
        }
        catch(IOException e)
        {
            System.out.println("Error " + e);
        }
    }
}
}
```

Execute

```
java PipeTest
```

Output

```
Starting Reader Thread
Starting Writer Thread
Sent Data:
Sent Data:
Received: Hello World 0
Received: Hello World 1
Sent Data:
Sent Data:
Sent Data:
Received: Hello World 2
Received: Hello World 3
Received: Hello World 4
Sent Data:
Sent Data:
Sent Data:
Received: Hello World 5
Received: Hello World 6
Received: Hello World 7
Sent Data:
Sent Data:
```

continued on next page

continued from previous page

```
Done Writing data.....
Closing the Write Pipe
Received: Hello World 8
Received: Hello World 9
Done Reading data.....
Closing the Read Pipe
```

Exceptions

The following exceptions are thrown by the file I/O classes:

- **IOException**

    This exception signals that an exception condition has occurred while performing input or output. This class has several subclasses to handle more specific exception types.

- **InterruptedIOException**

    This exception signals that an I/O operation was interrupted.

- **UTFDataFormatException**

    This exception signals that a malformed UTF string has been encountered by a class that implements the DataInput interface.

- **EOFException**

    This is an IOException that signals that end-of-file has been reached.

- **FileNotFoundException**

    This IOException signals that a specified file was not found.

About the Project

In this chapter's project, a Java database program is developed to manage customer records. The program allows the user to add a new customer record, display an existing customer record, and delete an existing customer record using the customer name as the key. The project demonstrates how to use the File I/O classes to store/modify/retrieve information in files using Java.

File I/O Method Summaries

Table 12-1 The File I/O classes/interfaces

Class/Interface	Description
File	A class encapsulating the system dependent file properties
FileDescriptor	A class encapsulating the system dependent features of the file descriptors

Class/Interface	Description
FilenameFilter	An interface to selectively filter file names
FileInputStream	A class for handling the file input
FileOutputStream	A class for handling the file output
RandomAccessFile	A class for handling input and output in a random order
PipedInputStream	A class for handling first-in first-out (FIFO) files for input
PipedOutputStream	A class for handling first-in first-out (FIFO) files for output

Table 12-2 File I/O methods, by category

Class/Interface	Category	Methods
File	Accessor	getAbsolutePath, getName, getParent, getPath, list, length
	Verifier	canRead, canWrite, equals, exists, isAbsolute, isDirectory, isFile, lastModified,
	Modifier	delete, mkdir, mkdirs, renameTo,
	Converter	hashCode, toString
FileDescriptor	Verifier	isValid
FilenameFilter	Verifier	accept
FileInputStream	Accessor	getFD
	Verifier	available
	Modifier	close, skip
	Others	read
FileOutputStream	Accessor	getFD
	Modifier	close
	Others	write
RandomAccessFile	Accessor	getFD, getFilePointer, length
	Modifier	close, seek, skipBytes
	Reading	read, readBoolean, readByte, readChar, readDouble, readFloat, readFully, readInt, readLine, eadLong, readShort, readUnsignedByte, readUnsignedShort, readUTF
	Writing	write, writeBoolean, writeByte, writeBytes, writeChar, writeChars, writeDouble, writeFloat, writeInt, writeLine, writeLong, writeShort, writeUTF
PipedInputStream	Modifier	close, connect
	Others	read
PipedOutputStream	Modifier	close, connect
	Others	write

The java.io.File Class

This class provides a machine independent definition of file and directory information. It provides methods to verify the existence of files, get modification dates, and rename and modify files and directories. In addition to these, the java.io.File class inherits methods from Object. The File object overrides equals(), hashCode(), and toString() inherited from the Object. Tables 12-3 and 12-4 provide a comprehensive list of all the public variables and methods in the class File.

Table 12-3 Summary of File variables

Variable	Type	Description
pathSeparator	String	The system dependent path separator string
pathSeparatorChar	char	The system dependent path separator character
separator	String	The system dependent file separator String
separatorChar	char	The system dependent file separator character

Table 12-4 Summary of File methods

Method	Description
canRead	Returns a boolean value indicating whether or not a file is readable.
canWrite	Returns a boolean value indicating whether or not a file is writable.
delete	Deletes the file and returns a boolean indicating whether or not the operation was successful.
equals	Returns a boolean as a result of comparison against the specified object.
exists	Returns a boolean value indicating whether or not a file exists.
getAbsolutePath	Returns the absolute path name of the file.
getName	Returns the name of the file.
getParent	Returns the parent directory name or null if none is found.
getPath	Returns the path name of the file.
hashCode	Returns the hash code for the file.
isAbsolute	Returns a boolean value indicating whether or not the file name is absolute.
isDirectory	Returns a boolean value indicating whether or not it is directory file.
isFile	Returns a boolean value indicating whether or not it is an ordinary file.
lastModified	Returns the last modification time. The return value can only be used for comparison.
length	Returns the size of the file in bytes.
list	Returns a list of all the files in the directory. This method only works on the directories.
mkdir	Creates the directory and returns a boolean indicating whether or not the operation was successful.
mkdirs	Creates all the directories in the path and returns a boolean indicating whether or not the operation was successful.
renameTo	Renames the file and indicates whether or not the operation was successful.
toString	Returns the string representation of the file path.

FILE

Description	The class File represents a file name of a file on the host system. This class provides an abstraction layer over most of the system dependent features of files and directories.
Syntax	public class **File** extends Object
Package	java.io
Import	java.io.File
Constructors	**File**(String *path*)
	File(String *dirPath*, String *fileName*)
	File(File *dir*, String *fileName*)
Parameters	
String *path*	A fully qualified name of the file (relative or absolute).
String *dirPath*	The path of the directory (relative or absolute).
String *fileName*	The name of the file.
File *dir*	The name of the directory where the file resides.
Exceptions	A NullPointerException is thrown if the path is equal to null.
See Also	String
Comments	The file name or path must comply with the host machine's file name conventions.
Example	The following example shows different ways you can create a new instance of the class File. This example works fine on a UNIX machine. The paths and the file name(s) must be modified depending upon the host system you are running on.

```java
import java.lang.*;
import java.io.*;

class  FileTest
{

    public static void main(String[] args)
    {
        File aFile = new File("/home/javauser/example/abc.txt");
        File bFile = new File("/home/javauser/example","abc.txt");
        File cFile = new File("/home/javauser/example");
        File dFile = new File(cFile, "abc.txt");
    }
}
```

Variables

pathSeparator

Class Name	File
Description	This class variable contains a system dependent file path separator string.
Syntax	public static final String **pathSeparator**
See Also	pathSeparatorChar

pathSeparatorChar

Class Name	File
Description	This class variable contains a system dependent file path separator character.
Syntax	public static final char **pathSeparatorChar**
See Also	pathSeparator

separator

Class Name	File
Description	This class variable contains a system dependent file separator string.
Syntax	public static final String separator
See Also	separatorChar

separatorChar

Class Name	File
Description	This class variable contains a system dependent file separator character.
Syntax	public static final char separatorChar
See Also	separator

Methods

canRead

Class Name	File
Description	This method returns a boolean value indicating whether or not a file is readable.

Syntax	public boolean **canRead**()
Parameters	None.
Returns	A boolean value indicating whether or not a file is readable.
Exceptions	None.
Example	

```
import java.lang.*;
import java.io.*;

class ReadTest
{

    public static void main(String[] args)
    {
        File aFile = new File("abc.txt");
        File bFile = new File("/home/root/mbox");

        System.out.println(aFile.canRead());
        System.out.println(bFile.canRead());
    }
}
```

Execute
```
cd /home/javauser/example
java ReadTest
```

Output
```
true
false
```

canWrite

Class Name	File
Description	This method returns a boolean value indicating whether or not a file is writable.
Syntax	public boolean **canWrite**()
Parameters	None.
Returns	A boolean value indicating whether or not a file is writable.
Exceptions	None.
Example	

```
import java.lang.*;
import java.io.*;

class WriteTest
{

    public static void main(String[] args)
```

continued on next page

continued from previous page

```
    {
        File aFile = new File("abc.txt");
        File bFile = new File("/");

        System.out.println(aFile.canWrite());
        System.out.println(bFile.canWrite());
    }
}
```

Execute

```
cd /home/javauser/example
java WriteTest
```

Output

```
true
false
```

DELETE

Class Name	File
Description	This method deletes the file. The method returns true if the file was successfully deleted, and returns false otherwise.
Syntax	public boolean **delete**()
Parameters	None.
Returns	A boolean value true if the delete operation was successful, and false if it was unsuccessful.
Exceptions	None.
Example	

```
import java.lang.*;
import java.io.*;

class DeleteTest
{
    public static void main(String[] args)
    {
        File aFile = new File("abc.txt");

        if(aFile.delete(bFile) )
        {
            System.out.println("abc.txt sucessfully deleted.");
        }
        else
        {
            System.out.println("Could not delete abc.txt.");
        }
    }
}
```

Execute

```
java DeleteTest
```

Output

```
abc.txt successfully deleted.
```

EQUALS

Class Name	File
Description	This method compares the current File with the specified object and returns true or false based on the comparison.
Syntax	public boolean **equals**(Object *obj*)
Parameters	
Object *obj*	The object to be compared.
Returns	A boolean value true or false based on the result of the comparison.
Exceptions	None.
Example	

```
import java.lang.*;
import java.io.*;

class EqualTest
{
    public static void main(String[] args)
    {
        File aFile = new File("abc.txt");
        File bFile = new File("foo.txt");
        File cFile = new File("foo.txt");

        if(aFile.equals(bFile) )
        {
            System.out.println("aFile and bFile are equal");
        }
        else if( bFile.equals(cFile) )
        {
            System.out.println("bFile and cFile are equal");
        }
        else
        {
            System.out.println("They are all different");
        }
    }
}
```

Execute

```
java EqualTest
```

Output

```
bFile and cFile are equal
```

EXISTS

Class Name	File
Description	This method returns a boolean value indicating whether or not a file exists in the current directory.
Syntax	public boolean **exists**()
Parameters	None.
Returns	A boolean value indicating the existence of the file.
Exceptions	None.
Example	

```
import java.lang.*;
import java.io.*;

class ExistsTest
{

    public static void main(String[] args)
    {
        File aFile = new File("abc.txt");
        File bFile = new File("foo.txt");
        File cFile = new File("/");

        System.out.println(aFile.exists());
        System.out.println(bFile.exists());
        System.out.println(cFile.exists());
    }
}
```

     Execute
```
cd /home/javauser/example
java ExistsTest
```

     Output
```
true
false
true
```

GETABSOLUTEPATH

Class Name	File
Description	This method gets the absolute path name of the file.
Syntax	public String **getAbsolutePath**()
Parameters	None.
Returns	A string containing the absolute path of the file.
Exceptions	None.
See Also	String

Example

```
import java.lang.*;
import java.io.*;

class AbsolutePathTest
{

    public static void main(String[] args)
    {
        File aFile = new File("abc.txt");
        File bFile = new File("/home/javauser/example/abc.txt");

        System.out.println(aFile.getAbsolutePath());
        System.out.println(bFile.getAbsolutePath());
    }
}
```

Execute

```
cd /home/javauser/example
java PathTest
```

Output

```
/home/javauser/example/abc.txt
/home/javauser/example/abc.txt
```

GETNAME

Class Name	File
Description	This method gets the name of the file. The string returned does not include the name or path name of the directory.
Syntax	public String **getName**()
Parameters	None.
Returns	A string that represents the name of the file. The file name returned does not include the path name of the directory in which the file is present.
Exceptions	None.
See Also	String

Example

```
import java.lang.*;
import java.io.*;

class FileNameTest
{

    public static void main(String[] args)
    {
        File aFile = new File("abc.txt");
        File bFile = new File("/home/javauser/example/abc.txt");
```

continued on next page

continued from previous page

```
        System.out.println(aFile.getName());
        System.out.println(bFile.getName());
    }
}
```

Execute

```
cd /home/javauser/example
java FileNameTest
```

Output

```
abc.txt
abc.txt
```

GETPARENT

Class Name	File
Description	This method gets the name of the parent directory of the current file.
Syntax	public String **getParent**()
Parameters	None.
Returns	A string containing the path of the parent directory or null if it is not found.
Exceptions	None.
See Also	String
Example	

```
import java.lang.*;
import java.io.*;

class ParentTest
{

    public static void main(String[] args)
    {
        File aFile = new File("abc.txt");
        File bFile = new File("/home/javauser/example");
        File cFile = new File("/");

        System.out.println(aFile.getParent());
        System.out.println(bFile.getParent());
        System.out.println(cFile.getParent());
    }
}
```

Execute

```
cd /home/javauser/example
java ParentTest
```

Output

```
null
/home/javauser/
null
```

GETPATH

Class Name	File
Description	This method gets the path name of the file.
Syntax	public String **getPath**()
Parameters	None.
Returns	A string containing a fully qualified path name of the file.
Exceptions	None.
See Also	String

Example

```
import java.lang.*;
import java.io.*;

class PathTest
{
    public static void main(String[] args)
    {
        File aFile = new File("abc.txt");
        File bFile = new File("/home/javauser/example/abc.txt");

        System.out.println(aFile.getPath());
        System.out.println(bFile.getPath());
    }
}
```

Execute

```
cd /home/javauser/example
java PathTest
```

Output

```
abc.txt
/home/javauser/example/abc.txt
```

HASHCODE

Class Name	File
Description	This method returns a hash code for the file name.
Syntax	public int **hashCode**()
Parameters	None.
Returns	An int value that is a hash code for the file.

Exceptions   None.

See Also   String, FilenameFilter

Example

```
import java.lang.*;
import java.io.*;

class HashTest
{
    public static void main(String[] args)
    {
        File bFile = new File("/home/javauser/example/abc.txt");

        System.out.println("Hash code for the file is " + bFile.hashCode() );
    }
}
```

Execute

```
java HashTest
```

Output

```
Hash code for the file is -462776175
```

ISABSOLUTE

Class Name	File
Description	This method returns a boolean value indicating whether or not a file name is an absolute file name.
Syntax	public boolean **isAbsolute**()
Parameters	None.
Returns	A boolean value indicating whether the file name is an absolute file name.
Exceptions	None.
Example	

```
import java.lang.*;
import java.io.*;

class AbsoluteTest
{

    public static void main(String[] args)
    {
        File aFile = new File("abc.txt");
        File bFile = new File("/home/harish/book/chap10/abc.txt");
        File cFile = new File("/");

        System.out.println(aFile.isAbsolute());
        System.out.println(bFile.isAbsolute());
        System.out.println(cFile.isAbsolute());
    }
}
```

Execute

```
cd /home/javauser/example
java AbsoluteTest
```

Output

```
false
true
true
```

isDirectory

Class Name	File
Description	This method returns a boolean value indicating whether or not a file is a directory file.
Syntax	public boolean **isDirectory**()
Parameters	None.
Returns	A boolean value indicating whether the file is a directory.
Exceptions	None.
Example	

```
import java.lang.*;
import java.io.*;

class DirectoryTest
{

    public static void main(String[] args)
    {
        File aFile = new File("abc.txt");
        File bFile = new File("/home/root");

        System.out.println(aFile.isDirectory());
        System.out.println(bFile.isDirectory());
    }
}
```

Execute

```
cd /home/javauser/example
java DirectoryTest
```

Output

```
false
true
```

isFile

Class Name	File
Description	This method returns a boolean value indicating whether or not a file is an ordinary file.

Syntax	public boolean **isFile**()
Parameters	None.
Returns	A boolean value indicating whether the file is an ordinary file.
Exceptions	None.
Example	

```
import java.lang.*;
import java.io.*;

class FileTest
{

    public static void main(String[] args)
    {
        File aFile = new File("abc.txt");
        File bFile = new File("/home/root");

        System.out.println(aFile.isFile());
        System.out.println(bFile.isFile());
    }
}
```

Execute

```
cd /home/javauser/example
java FileTest
```

Output

```
true
false
```

LASTMODIFIED

Class Name	File
Description	This method returns the time when the current file was last modified. The return value should only be used to compare modification dates.
Syntax	public long **lastModified**()
Parameters	None.
Returns	A long integer that is the number of seconds since 00:00:00 GMT, January 1, 1970, measured in seconds.
Exceptions	None.
Comments	In some systems the value returned may not make any sense as an absolute time, so the result must only be used for comparison.
Example	

```
import java.lang.*;
import java.io.*;

class TimeTest
{
```

```
    public static void main(String[] args)
    {
        File aFile = new File("abc.txt");
        File bFile = new File("foo.txt");

        if(aFile.lastModified() > bFile.lastModified() )
        {
            System.out.println(aFile.getName() +
                " has been modified more  recently than " +
                    bFile.getName());
        }
        else
        {
            System.out.println(aFile.getName() +
                " has been modified more  recently than " +
                    bFile.getName());
        }
    }
}
```

Execute

```
cd /home/javauser/example
java TimeTest
```

Output

```
abc.txt has been modified more  recently than foo.txt
```

LENGTH

Class Name	File
Description	This method returns the length of the file in number of bytes.
Syntax	public long **length**()
Parameters	None.
Returns	The length of the file expressed in bytes.
Exceptions	None.

Example

```
import java.lang.*;
import java.io.*;

class LengthTest
{
    public static void main(String[] args)
    {
        File aFile = new File("abc.txt");

        System.out.println("The length of the file is " + aFile.length()
                    + " bytes");
    }
}
```

Execute

```
cd /home/javauser/example
java LengthTest
```

Output

```
The length of the file is 234 bytes
```

LIST

Class Name	File
Description	This method is used to get a list of all the files in a directory. This method works only on directories. It returns all the files in the directory except the equivalents of . and .. (current directory and the parent directory).
Syntax	public String[] **list**()
	public String[] **list**(FilenameFilter *filt*)
Parameters	
FilenameFilter	The file name filter used *filt*.
Returns	A list of all the files in the directory as an array of String objects.
Exceptions	None.
See Also	String, FilenameFilter
Example	This program lists all the files in the directory /home/javauser/example.

```
import java.lang.*;
import java.io.*;
class ListTest
{
    public static void main(String[] args)
    {
        File bFile = new File("/home/javauser/example");

        String[] fList = bFile.list();

        System.out.println("All the files are : \n");

        for(int i=0; i < fList.length; ++i)
        {
            System.out.println(fList[i]);
        }
    }
}
```

Execute

```
java ListTest
```

Output

```
All the files are :

ListTest.class
abc.txt
xyz.java
test.java
AbsoluteTest.class
FilePropertiesTest.class
PathTest.class
foo
boo.txt
```

Example   The following example lists all the ".class" files in the current directory:

```
import java.lang.*;
import java.io.*;

class ClassFilter implements FilenameFilter
{
    public boolean accept(File file, String filename)
    {
        return filename.endsWith(".class");
    }
}

class ListTest
{
    public static void main(String[] args)
    {
        File bFile = new File("/home/javauser/example");
        ClassFilter cfilt = new ClassFilter();

        String[] fList = bFile.list(cfilt);

        System.out.println("The .class files are : \n");

        for(int i=0; i < fList.length; ++i)
        {
            System.out.println(fList[i]);
        }
    }
}
```

Execute

```
java ListTest
```

Output

```
The .class files are :

ListTest.class
ClassFilter.class
AbsoluteTest.class
FilePropertiesTest.class
PathTest.class
```

MKDIR

Class Name	File
Description	This method creates a directory with the given name.
Syntax	public boolean **mkdir**()
Parameters	None.
Returns	A true boolean value if the directory was created, and false if the creation of the directory was unsuccessful.
Exceptions	None.
Comments	The directory creation can fail because the process does not have the access permissions to write to the directory, or because a directory or a file with that name already exists.

Example

```
import java.lang.*;
import java.io.*;

class MkDirTest
{
    public static void main(String[] args)
    {
        File aFile = new File("foo");

        if(aFile.mkdir())
        {
            System.out.println("The directory was successfully created.");
        }
        else
            System.out.println("The directory creation was unsuccessful.");
    }
}
```

Execute

```
cd /home/javauser/example
java MkDirTest
```

Output

```
The directory was successfully created.
```

MKDIRS

Class Name	File
Description	This method creates all the directories in the path of the current file name.
Syntax	public boolean **mkdirs**()
Parameters	None.
Returns	A true boolean value if all the directories were successfully created, and false if the creation of the directories was unsuccessful.

Exceptions	None.
Comments	The directory creation can fail because the process does not have the access permissions to write to the directory, or because a directory or a file with that name already exists.

Example

```
import java.lang.*;
import java.io.*;

class MkDirsTest
{
    public static void main(String[] args)
    {
        File aFile = new File("boo/foo/boo/foobar");

        if(aFile.mkdir())
        {
            System.out.println("The directory was successfully created.");
        }
        else
            System.out.println("The directory creation was unsuccessful.");
    }
}
```

Execute

```
cd /home/javauser/example
java MkDirsTest
```

Output

```
The directory was successfully created.
```

RENAMETO

Class Name	File
Description	This method is used to rename files. This method returns a boolean value indicating whether or not renaming of the file was successful.
Syntax	public boolean **renameTo**(File *dest*)
Parameters	
File *dest*	The destination File.
Returns	A true boolean value if the file was successfully renamed, and false otherwise.
Exceptions	None.
Example	

```
import java.lang.*;
import java.io.*;

class RenameTest
```

continued on next page

continued from previous page

```
{
    public static void main(String[] args)
    {
        File srcFile = new File("foo.txt");
        File destFile = new File("boo.txt");

        if(srcFile.renameTo(destFile) )
        {
            System.out.println(srcFile.getName() + " was renamed to " +
destFile.getName());
        }
    }
}
```

Execute

```
cd /home/javauser/example
java RenameTest
```

Output

```
foo.txt was renamed to boo.txt
```

TOSTRING

Class Name	File
Description	This method returns a string object representation of this file. This method is used by the printing routines to print out the string form of the object. This method behaves just like the method getPath().
Syntax	public String **toString**()
Parameters	None.
Returns	A String representing the object.
Exceptions	None.

The java.io.FileDescriptor Class

This class encapsulates the operating system dependent features of file descriptor—the data structures needed for handling files. This class is final, so there can be no subclass of this class. This class does not have a public constructor, and it inherits all the public methods defined in the Object. The class variable and method summary is shown in the Tables 12-5 and 12-6.

Table 12-5 Summary of FileDescriptor variables

Variable	Type	Description
err	FileDescriptor	A file descriptor to handle error output of the program
in	FileDescriptor	A file descriptor to handle input to the program
out	FileDescriptor	A file descriptor to handle output of the program

Table 12-6 Summary of FileDescriptor methods

Method	Description
valid	This method returns true if the file descriptor is a valid one, and returns false if it is not.

FILEDESCRIPTOR

Description	This class encapsulates the operating system dependent detail of data structures needed to manipulate files.
Syntax	public final class **FileDescriptor** extends Object
Package	java.io
Import	java.io.FileDescriptor
Constructors	None.
Parameters	None.
Comments	This class provides an abstraction layer over the system dependent details of the file descriptors. You can get a handle to the FileDescriptor object by calling the method getFD() on the instances of the file stream classes.

Variables

ERR

Class Name	FileDescriptor
Description	An instance of the class FileDescriptor for standard error stream.
Syntax	public static final FileDescriptor **err**
See Also	FileDescriptor.in, FileDescriptor.out, FileDescriptor.err
Example	

```
class InTest
{

    static void main(String[] args)
    {
        int x = 5;
        errStream = new BufferedOutputStream( new
FileOutputStream(FileDescriptor.err), 256);
        errStream.write(x); // writes 5 to the standard error
    }
}
```

IN

Class Name	FileDescriptor
Description	An instance of the class FileDescriptor for standard input stream.
Syntax	public static final FileDescriptor **in**
See Also	out, err
Example	

```
class InTest
{

    static void main(String[] args)
    {
        int x = 0;
        inpStream = new BufferedInputStream( new
FileInputStream(FileDescriptor.in), 256);
        x = inpStream.read(); // reads an integer from the standard input
    }
}
```

OUT

Class Name	FileDescriptor
Description	An instance of the class FileDescriptor for standard output stream.
Syntax	public static final FileDescriptor **out**
See Also	in, err
Example	

```
class InTest
{

    static void main(String[] args)
    {
        int x = 5;
        outStream = new BufferedOutputStream( new
FileOutputStream(FileDescriptor.out), 256);
        outStream.write(x); // writes 5 to the standard output
    }
}
```

Methods

VALID

Class Name	FileDescriptor
Description	This method returns a boolean value indicating if the file descriptor object is a valid one.

Syntax	public native boolean **valid**()
Parameters	None.
Returns	A boolean value true if this file descriptor is a valid one, and false otherwise.
Exceptions	None.
Example	The following example program prints out information as to whether the file descriptors in, out, and err are valid.

```
class ValidTest
{

    static void main(String[] args)
    {
        System.out.println("Is file FileDescriptor.in valid ? "+
FileDescriptor.in.valid());
        System.out.println("Is file FileDescriptor.out valid ? "+
FileDescriptor.out.valid());
        System.out.println("Is file FileDescriptor.err valid ? "+
FileDescriptor.err.valid());
    }
}
```

Execute

```
java ValidTest
```

Output

```
Is file FileDescriptor.in valid ? true
Is file FileDescriptor.out valid ? true
Is file FileDescriptor.err valid ? true
```

The java.io.FilenameFilter Interface

This interface declares a method accept() that must be implemented by any object that filters a subset of file names from a list of file names. There are no default implementations of the interface FilenameFilter. Anyone who wishes to filter file names must implement this interface. Table 12-7 gives a list of methods in the interface FilenameFilter.

Table 12-7 Summary of FilenameFilter methods

Method	Description
accept	Returns a boolean value indicating whether the file should be included in file list

Methods

ACCEPT

Interface Name	FilenameFilter
Description	This method determines whether a file name should be included in the file list.
Syntax	public boolean **accept**(File *dir*, String *name*)
Parameters	
File *dir*	The directory in which the file was found.
String *name*	The name of the file.
Returns	A boolean true if the file should be included in the file list; false otherwise
Exceptions	None.

The java.io.FileInputStream Class

This class is a subclass of the class InputStream that reads bytes of data from a specified file. The class FileInputStream provides a low-level interface to reading bytes of data from a specified file. For reading basic data types other than byte, you would typically use the class DataInputStream. This class overrides the following methods defined in the abstract class InputStream: read(), skip(), available(), close(). This class inherits the following methods from the class InputStream: mark(), reset(), and markSupported(). Comprehensive list of the public methods in the class FileInputStream is shown in the Table 12-8.

Table 12-8 Summary of FileInputStream methods

Method	Description
available	Returns the number of bytes of data that can be read without blocking.
close	Closes the input stream.
getFD	Returns the file descriptor associated with this stream.
read	Returns one or more bytes of data. This method will block if no input is available.
skip	Skips specified number of bytes of input.

FILEINPUTSTREAM

Description	This class abstracts a file input stream in a system independent manner.
Syntax	public class **FileInputStream** extends InputStream
Package	java.io

Import	java.io.FileInputStream
Constructors	**FileInputStream**(String *filename*)
	FileInputStream(File *file*)
	FileInputStream(FileDescriptor *fdes*)

Parameters

String *filename*	The name of the file.
File *file*	A reference to the instance of the class File.
FileDescriptor *fdes*	A reference to the file descriptor.
See Also	String, FileDescription, File
Comments	The file name must comply with the host machine's file name conventions.
Example	This example shows the different ways to create a new instance of the class FileInputStream.

```
import java.lang.*;
import java.io.*;

class FileInputTest
{
    public static void main(String[] args)
    {
        try
        {
            FileInputStream aFin = new FileInputStream("abc.txt");

            File    bFile = new File("foo.txt");
            FileInputStream bFin = new FileInputStream(bFile);

            FileDescriptor  fd = bFin.getFD();
            FileInputStream cFile = new FileInputStream(fd);
        }
        catch(Exception e)
        {
            e.printStackTrace();
        }
    }
}
```

Methods

AVAILABLE

Class Name	FileInputStream
Description	This method is used to find the number of bytes that can be read without blocking.
Syntax	public native int **available**()
Parameters	None.

Returns	Actual number of bytes that can be read without blocking.
Exceptions	This method throws IOException whenever an I/O error occurs.
Example	

```java
import java.lang.*;
import java.io.*;

class AvailableTest
{
    public static void main(String[] args)
    {
        try
        {
            char i;
            FileInputStream aFin = new FileInputStream("abc.txt");

            System.out.println("Total number of bytes that can read = " +
                        aFin.available());
            aFin.close();

        }
        catch(Exception e)
        {
            e.printStackTrace();
        }
    }
}
```

Execute

```
java AvailableTest
```

Output

```
Total number of bytes that can read = 18
```

CLOSE

Class Name	FileInputStream
Description	This method closes the input stream. This method must be called to release any resources associated with the stream.
Syntax	public native void **close**()
Parameters	None.
Returns	None.
Exceptions	This method throws an IOException if an I/O error occurs.

GETFD

Class Name	FileInputStream
Description	This method is used to get the file descriptor associated with the current file input stream.

Syntax	public final FileDescriptor **getFD**()
Parameters	None.
Returns	The file descriptor associated with this file stream.
Exceptions	This method throws an IOException if an I/O error occurs.
See Also	FileDescriptor

READ

Class Name	FileInputStream
Description	This method is used to read one or more bytes of data. This method will block if no input is available.
Syntax	public native int **read**()
	public native int **read**(byte[] *barr*)
	public native int **read**(byte[] *barr*, int *off*, int *len*)
Parameters	
byte[] *barr*	The name of the byte array.
int *off*	The offset of the data in the byte array.
int *len*	The maximum number of bytes to read.
Returns	The actual number of bytes read. It returns -1 when the end of the stream is reached.
Exceptions	An IOException will be thrown if an I/O error occurs.
Example	

```java
import java.lang.*;
import java.io.*;

class ReadTest
{
    public static void main(String[] args)
    {
        try
        {
            char i;
            FileInputStream aFin = new FileInputStream("abc.txt");

            while( (i = aFin.read()) >= 0)
            {
                System.out.print((char) i);
            }
        }
        catch(Exception e)
        {
            e.printStackTrace();
        }
    }
}
```

SKIP

Class Name	FileInputStream
Description	This method is used to skip *n* bytes of input from the current file.
Syntax	public native long **skip**(long *nbytes*)
Parameters	
long *nbytes*	Number of bytes to be skipped.
Returns	Actual number of bytes skipped.
Exceptions	An IOException will be thrown if an I/O error occurs.
Example	

```java
import java.lang.*;
import java.io.*;

class SkipTest
{
    public static void main(String[] args)
    {
        try
        {
            char i;
            FileInputStream aFin = new FileInputStream("abc.txt");

            aFin.skip(6);
            while( (i = aFin.read()) >= 0)
            {
                System.out.print((char) i);
            }

            aFin.close();
        }
        catch(Exception e)
        {
            e.printStackTrace();
        }
    }
}
```

Execute

```
java SkipTest
```

Output

```
hello world
```

The java.io.FileOutputStream Class

This class is a subclass of the class OutputStream that writes bytes of data to a specified file. The class FileOutputStream provides a low-level interface to write bytes of data to a specified file. For writing basic data types other than byte, you would typically use the class DataOutputStream. This class overrides the following methods defined in the abstract class OutputStream: write(), flush(), close(). Table 12-9 gives a summary of the methods in the class FileOutputStream.

Table 12-9 Summary of FileOutputStream methods

Method	Description
close	Closes the output stream.
getFD	Returns the file descriptor associated with this stream.
write	Writes a byte of data. This method blocks until the data is actually written.

FILEOUTPUTSTREAM

Description	This class abstracts an output file stream in a system independent manner.
Syntax	public class **FileOutputStream** extends OutputStream
Package	java.io
Import	java.io.FileOutputStream
Constructors	**FileOutputStream**(String *filename*)
	FileOutputStream(File *file*)
	FileOutputStream(FileDescriptor *fdes*)
Parameters	
String *filename*	The name of the file.
File *file*	A reference to the instance of the class File.
FileDescriptor *fdes*	A reference to a file descriptor.
See Also	String, File, FileDescriptor
Comments	The file name must comply with the host machine's file name conventions.
Example	

```
import java.lang.*;
import java.io.*;

class FileOutputTest
{
    public static void main(String[] args)
    {
        try
        {
            FileOutputStream aFout = new FileOutputStream("foo.txt");

            File    bFout = new File("foo.txt");
            FileOutputStream bFout = new FileOutputStream(bFile);

            FileDescriptor  fd = bFout.getFD();
```

continued on next page

continued from previous page

```
            FileOutputStream cFout = new FileOutputStream(fd);
        }
        catch(Exception e)
        {
            e.printStackTrace();
        }
    }
}
```

Methods

CLOSE

Class Name	FileOutputStream
Description	This method closes the output stream. This method must be called to release any resources associated with the stream.
Syntax	public native void **close**()
Parameters	None.
Returns	None.
Exceptions	An IOException will be thrown if an I/O error occurs.

GETFD

Class Name	FileOutputStream
Description	This method is used to get the file descriptor associated with the file.
Syntax	public final FileDescriptor **getFD**()
Parameters	None.
Returns	The file descriptor associated with this file output stream.
Exceptions	An IOException will be thrown if an I/O error occurs.
See Also	FileDescriptor

WRITE

Class Name	FileOutputStream
Description	These methods are used to write one or more bytes of data to the current file output stream. This method will block if the output could not be written.

Syntax	public native void **write**(int *b*)
	public native void **write**(byte[] *barr*)
	public native void **write**(byte[] *barr*, int *off*, int *len*)

Parameters

int *b*	The byte to be written.
byte[] *barr*	The name of the byte array.
int *off*	The offset of the data in the byte array.
int *len*	The maximum number of bytes to write.

Returns None.

Exceptions An IOException will be thrown if an I/O error occurs.

Example

```
import java.lang.*;
import java.io.*;

class WriteTest
{
    public static void main(String[] args)
    {
        try
        {
            FileOutputStream aFout = new FileOuputStream("foo.txt");
            String aString = "Hello World\n";
            byte[] byteArray = new byte[aString.length()];
            aString.getBytes(0, aString.length(), byteArray, 0);
            aFout.write(byteArray);

            aFout.close();
        }
        catch(Exception e)
        {
            e.printStackTrace();
        }
    }
}
```

An IOException will be thrown if an I/O error occurs.

The java.io.RandomAccessFile Class

This class enables reading and writing of arbitrary bytes and other basic Java language data types. It also implements two interfaces, DataInputStream and DataOutputStream. This class enables the file access in a random order by using the method seek(). The method seek() allows positioning of the file pointer for both reading and writing at any given location within the file. A comprehensive list of all the methods in the class RandomAccessFile is shown in the Table 12-10.

Table 12-10 Summary of RandomAccessFile methods

Method	Description
close	Closes the file stream.
getFD	Returns an instance of the class FileDescriptor for the current file.
getFilePointer	Returns the current location of the file pointer.
length	Returns the length of the file in bytes.
read	Returns a byte of data. This method will block if no input is available.
readBoolean	Reads a boolean value from the current file position.
readByte	Reads a byte value from the current file position.
readChar	Reads a char value from the current file position.
readDouble	Reads a double value from the current file position.
readFloat	Reads a float value from the current file position.
readFully	Reads bytes, blocking until all bytes are read.
readInt	Reads an int value from the current file position.
readLine	Reads a line terminated by a '\n' from the current file position.
readLong	Reads a long value from the current file position.
readShort	Reads a short value from the current file position.
readUnsignedByte	Reads an unsigned byte value from the current file position.
readUnsignedShort	Reads an unsigned short value from the current file position.
readUTF	Reads a UTF formatted string from the current file position.
seek	Sets the file pointer to the specified position.
skipBytes	Skips a specified number of bytes in the file.
write	Writes a byte of data. This method blocks until the data is actually written.
writeBoolean	Writes a boolean value starting at the current file position.
writeByte	Writes a byte value starting at the current file position.
writeBytes	Writes a string as a sequence of bytes starting at the current file position.
writeChar	Writes a char value starting at the current file position.
writeChars	Writes a string as a sequence of chars starting at the current file position.
writeDouble	Writes a double value starting at the current file position.
writeFloat	Writes a float value starting at the current file position.
writeInt	Writes an int value starting at the current file position.
writeLine	Writes a line terminated by a '\n' starting at the current file position.
writeLong	Writes a long value starting at the current file position.
writeShort	Writes a short value starting at the current file position.
writeUTF	Writes a UTF formatted string starting at the current file position.

RANDOMACCESSFILE

Description	This class abstracts random access files for both reading and writing in a system independent manner.
Syntax	public class **RandomAccessFile** implements DataInputStream, DataOutputStream
Package	java.io
Import	java.io.RandomAccessFile
Constructors	**RandomAccessFile**(String *name*, String *mode*)
	RandomAccessFile(File *file*, String *mode*)
Parameters	
String *name*	Name of the file.
String *mode*	The mode of the file access. Can only be one of "r" or "rw".
String *file*	Reference to the File object.
See Also	File, String
Comments	The constructor of the class throws an IOException if the mode string is anything other than an "r" or "rw".
Example	The following example shows how to create instances of the class RandomAccessFile.

```
import java.lang.*;
import java.io.*;

class RandomTest
{
        public static void main(String[] args)
        {
        try
        {
            RandomAccessFile ra = new RandomAccessFile("abc.txt", "rw");
            File afile = new File("foo.txt");
            RandomAccessFile rb = new RandomAccessFile(afile, "r");

            ra.close();
            rb.close();
        }
        catch(IOException e)
        {
            System.out.println("Error " + e);
        }
        }
}
```

Methods

CLOSE

Class Name	RandomAccessFile
Description	This method closes the file stream. This method must be called to release any resources associated with the stream.
Syntax	public native void **close**()
Parameters	None.
Returns	None.
Exceptions	An IOException will be thrown if an I/O error occurs.

GETFD

Class Name	RandomAccessFile
Description	This method used to get the file descriptor associated with the current file.
Syntax	public final FileDescriptor **getFD**()
Parameters	None.
Returns	The file descriptor associated with this file stream.
Exceptions	An IOException will be thrown if an I/O error occurs.
See Also	FileDescriptor

GETFILEPOINTER

Class Name	RandomAccessFile
Description	This method returns the current location of the file pointer.
Syntax	public native long **getFilePointer**()
Parameters	None.
Returns	A long value that represents the current location of the file pointer.
Exceptions	An IOException will be thrown if an I/O error occurs.

LENGTH

Class Name	RandomAccessFile
Description	This method returns the length of the file.
Syntax	public native long **length**()
Parameters	None.
Returns	The length of the file in the number of bytes as a long value.
Exceptions	An IOException will be thrown if an I/O error occurs.

READ

Class Name	RandomAccessFile
Description	This method is used to read one or more bytes of data. This method will block if no input is available.
Syntax	public native int **read**()
	public int **read**(byte[] *barr*)
	public int **read**(byte[] *barr*, int *off*, int *len*)

Parameters

byte[] *barr*	The name of the byte array.
int *off*	The offset of the data in the byte array.
int *len*	The maximum number of bytes to read.
Returns	The actual number of bytes read. This method returns -1 when the end of the stream is reached.
Exceptions	An IOException will be thrown if an I/O error occurs.

Example

```
import java.lang.*;
import java.io.*;

class ReadTest
{
    public static void main(String[] args)
    {
        try
        {
            char i;
            RandomAccessFile aFile = new RandomAccessFile("abc.txt", "r");

            while( (i = aFile.read()) != -1)
            {
                System.out.print((char) i);
            }
        }
        catch(Exception e)
        {
            System.out.println("Error " + e);
        }
    }
}
```

Execute

```
java ReadTest
```

Output

```
hello hello world
```

READBOOLEAN, READBYTE, READCHAR, READDOUBLE, READFLOAT, READINT, READLINE, READLONG, READSHORT, READUNSIGNEDBYTE, READUNSIGNEDSHORT, READUTF

Class Name	RandomAccessFile
Description	These methods generally are used for reading primitive data types in Java from a RandomAccessFile.
Syntax	public final boolean **readBoolean**()
	public final byte **readByte**()
	public final char **readChar**()
	public final double **readDouble**()
	public final float **readFloat**()
	public final int **readInt**()
	public final String **readLine**()
	public final long **readLong**()
	public final short **readShort**()
	public final int **readUnsignedByte**()
	public final int **readUnsignedShort**()
	public final String **readUTF**()
Parameters	None.
Returns	The corresponding data type.
Exceptions	An IOException will be thrown if an I/O error occurs.
See Also	DataInputStream
Comments	The above methods are very similar to the methods in the class DataInputStream. These calls block until the data is read from the stream.

READFULLY

Class Name	RandomAccessFile
Description	This method is used for reading all the bytes in the file. This method blocks until all the bytes are read.
Syntax	public final void **readFully**(byte[] *barr*)
	public final void **readFully**(byte[] *barr*, int *off*, int *len*)
Parameters	
byte[] *barr*	The byte array into which the data is read.
int *off*	The offset of the data in the byte array.
int *len*	The maximum number of bytes to read.

Returns	The actual number of bytes read; -1 is returned when the end of the stream is reached.
Exceptions	An IOException will be thrown if an I/O error occurs.
Example	

```
import java.lang.*;
import java.io.*;

class ReadFullyTest
{
    public static void main(String[] args)
    {
        try
        {
            char i;
            RandomAccessFile aFile = new RandomAccessFile("abc.txt", "r");
            byte    barr[] = new byte[(int) aFile.length()];

            aFile.readFully(barr);

            String aString = new String(barr, 0);

            System.out.println("The data read was : " + aString);
        }
        catch(Exception e)
        {
            System.out.println("Error " + e);
        }
    }
}
```

Execute

```
java ReadFullyTest
```

Output

```
The data read was : hello hello world
```

SEEK

Class Name	RandomAccessFile
Description	This method sets the current file pointer to the specified absolute position.
Syntax	public native void **seek**(long *pos*)
Parameters	
long *pos*	A long value specifying the absolute position of the file pointer.
Returns	None.
Exceptions	An IOException will be thrown if an I/O error occurs.

SKIPBYTES

Class Name	RandomAccessFile
Description	This method is used for skipping from the current input stream. The file pointer is positioned at the specified offset from the current position.
Syntax	public int **skipBytes**(int *nbytes*)
Parameters	
int *nbytes*	The number of bytes of data that should be skipped.
Returns	The actual number of bytes skipped.
Exceptions	An IOException will be thrown if an I/O error occurs.

WRITE

Class Name	RandomAccessFile
Description	These methods are used to write one or more bytes of data. This method will block until the output is actually written.
Syntax	public native void **write**(int *b*)
	public void **write**(byte[] *barr*)
	public void **write**(byte[] *barr*, int *off*, int *len*)
Parameters	
int *b*	The byte to be written.
byte[] *barr*	The name of the byte array.
int *off*	The offset of the data in the byte array.
int *len*	The maximum number of bytes to write.
Returns	None.
Exceptions	An IOException will be thrown if an I/O error occurs.
Example	

```
import java.lang.*;
import java.io.*;

class WriteTest
{
        public static void main(String[] args)
        {
        try
        {
            RandomAccessFile aFout = new RandomAccessFile("foo.txt", "rw");
                String aString = "Hello World\n";

                byte[] byteArray = new byte[aString.length()];

                aString.getBytes(0, aString.length(), byteArray, 0);
                aFout.write(byteArray);
```

```
                    aFout.close();
        }
        catch(IOException e)
        {
            System.out.println("Error: " + e);
        }
        }
}
```

WRITEBOOLEAN, WRITEBYTE,WRITEBYTES, WRITECHAR, WRITECHARS, WRITEDOUBLE, WRITEFLOAT, WRITEINT, WRITELONG, WRITESHORT, WRITEUTF

Class Name	RandomAccessFile
Description	These methods generally are used for writing primitive data types in Java to a RandomAccessFile.
Syntax	public final void **writeBoolean**(boolean *data*)
	public final void **writeByte**(byte *data*)
	public final void **writeBytes**(String *data*)
	public final void **writeChar**(char *data*)
	public final void **writeBytes**(String *data*)
	public final void **writeDouble**(double *data*)
	public final void **writeFloat**(float *data*)
	public final void **writeInt**(int *data*)
	public final void **writeLong**(long *data*)
	public final void **writeShort**(short *data*)
	public final void **writeUTF**(String *data*)
Parameters	
data	An appropriate data type.
Returns	None.
Exceptions	An IOException will be thrown if an I/O error occurs.
See Also	DataOutputStream
Comments	The above methods are very similar to the methods in the class DataOutputStream. These calls block until the data is written to the output stream.

The java.io.PipedInputStream Class

The class PipedInputStream serves as the input half of a FIFO input mechanism. FIFO file streams can be used very effectively as a method of communication between two threads. An instance of the PipedInputStream must be connected to an instance of the PipedOutputStream to serve as a complete FIFO stream. A summary of the methods in the class PipedInputStream is shown in Table 12-11.

Table 12-11 Summary of PipedInputStream methods

Method	Description
close	Closes the input stream.
connect	Connects the input stream to the sender.
read	Reads a byte of data. This method will block if no input is available.

PIPEDINPUTSTREAM

Description	The class PipedInputStream implements the input half of first-in first-out file streams. An instance of a PipedInputStream must be connected to a piped output stream to be useful. A thread reading data from an instance of a PipedInputStream receives data from a thread writing to an instance of a PipedOutputStream it is connected to.
Syntax	public class **PipedInputStream** extends InputStream
Package	java.io
Import	java.io.PipedInputStream
Constructors	**PipedInputStream**()
	PipedInputStream(PipedOutputStream *pout*)
Parameters	
PipedOutputStream pout	A reference to an instance of the PipedOutputStream that acts as a source of the data.
See Also	PipedOutputStream
Example	

```
import java.lang.*;
import java.io.*;

class PipeTest
{
    public static void main(String[] args)
        {
                try
                {
                        PipedOutputStream pout = new PipedOutputStream();
                        PipedInputStream apipe = new PipedInputStream();

                // bpipe is connected to pout
                        PipedInputStream bpipe = new PipedInputStream(pout);

                        pout.close();
                        apipe.close();
                        bpipe.close();
```

```
          }
          catch(IOException e)
          {
      System.out.println("Error: " + e);
          }
      }
}
```

Methods

CLOSE

Class Name	PipedInputStream
Description	This method closes the open pipe stream. This method must be called to release any resources associated with the stream.
Syntax	public void **close**()
Parameters	None.
Returns	None.
Exceptions	An IOException will be thrown if an I/O error occurs.

CONNECT

Class Name	PipedInputStream
Description	This method is used to connect this pipe to an instance of PipedOutputStream.
Syntax	public void **connect**(PipedOutputStream *pout*)
Parameters	
PipedOutputStream *pout*	A reference to an instance of the PipedOutputStream that acts as a source of the data.
Returns	None.
Exceptions	An IOException will be thrown if an I/O error occurs.
See Also	PipedOutputStream
Example	

```
import java.lang.*;
import java.io.*;

class PipeTest
{
    public static void main(String[] args)
        {
                try
                {
                        PipedOutputStream oPipe = new PipedOutputStream();
```

continued on next page

continued from previous page

```
                    PipedInputStream iPipe = new PipedInputStream();

        // They need to be connected to one another to
        // be of any use.

            iPipe.connect(oPipe);
            oPipe.connect(iPipe);

                oPipe.close();
                iPipe.close();
        }
        catch(IOException e)
        {
        System.out.println("Error: " + e);
        }
    }
}
```

READ

Class Name	PipedInputStream
Description	This method reads one or more bytes of data from the open pipe. This method blocks if no input is available.
Syntax	public synchronized int **read**()
	public synchronized int **read**(byte *barr[]*, int *off*, int *len*)
Parameters	
byte *barr[]*	The name of the byte array into which data is read.
int *off*	The offset of the data in the byte array.
int *len*	The maximum number of bytes read.
Returns	This method returns -1 if the end of stream is reached, otherwise it returns the actual number of bytes read.
Exceptions	An IOException will be thrown if an I/O error occurs.
Example	

```
import java.lang.*;
import java.io.*;

class PipeTest
{
    public static void main(String[] args)
        {
                try
                {
                    PipedOutputStream oPipe = new PipedOutputStream();
                    PipedInputStream iPipe = new PipedInputStream();

                //      They need to be connected to one another to
```

```
//      be of any use.

iPipe.connect(oPipe);
oPipe.connect(iPipe);

oPipe.write('a');

byte readChar = iPipe.read();

System.out.println("The char read was : " + readChar);

    oPipe.close();
    iPipe.close();
}
catch(IOException e)
{
System.out.println("Error: " + e);
}
  }
}
```

Execute

```
java PipeTest
```

Output

```
The char read was : 97
```

The PipedOutputStream Class

The class PipedOutputStream serves as the output half of an FIFO stream mechanism. FIFO file streams can be used very effectively as a method of communication between two threads. An instance of the PipedOutputStream must be connected to an instance of the PipedInputStream to serve as a complete FIFO stream. A summary of the methods in the class PipedOutputStream is shown in Table 12-12.

Table 12-12 Summary of PipedOutputStream methods

Method	Description
close	Closes the input stream.
connect	Connects the input stream to the sender.
write	Writes a byte of data to the stream. This method will block until the data is actually written.

PipedOutputStream

Description
The class PipedInputStream implements the input half of first-in first-out file streams. An instance of a PipedInputStream must be connected to an

instance of PipedOutputStream to be useful. A thread reading data from an instance of a PipedInputStream receives data from a thread writing to an instance of a PipedOutputStream it is connected to.

Syntax	public class **PipedOutputStream** extends OutputStream
Package	java.io
Import	java.io.PipedOutputStream
Constructors	**PipedOutputStream**()
	PipedOutputStream(PipedInputStream *pinp*)

Parameters

PipedInputStream *pinp*	A reference to an instance of the PipedInputStream that acts as a source of the data.
See Also	PipedInputStream

Example

```
import java.lang.*;
import java.io.*;

class PipeTest
{
    public static void main(String[] args)
        {
                try
                {
                    PipedInputStream apipe = new PipedInputStream();
                    PipedOutputStream apout = new PipedOutputStream();
                    PipedOutputStream bpout = new PipedOutputStream(apipe);

                apipe.close();
                apout.close();
                bpout.close();
                }
                catch(IOException e)
                {
                System.out.println("Error: " + e);
                }
        }
}
```

Methods

CLOSE

Class Name	PipedInputStream
Description	This method closes the open pipe stream. This method must be called to release any resources associated with the stream.

Syntax	public void **close**()
Parameters	None.
Returns	None.
Exceptions	An IOException will be thrown if an I/O error occurs.

CONNECT

Class Name	PipedOutputStream
Description	This method is used to connect this pipe to an instance of a PipedInputStream.
Syntax	public void **connect**(PipedInputStream *pinp*)
Parameters	
PipedInputStream *pinp*	A reference to an instance of the PipedInputStream that acts as a sink for the data.
Returns	None.
Exceptions	An IOException will be thrown if an I/O error occurs.
See Also	PipedInputStream
Example	

```java
import java.lang.*;
import java.io.*;

class PipeTest
{
    public static void main(String[] args)
        {
                try
                {
                        PipedOutputStream oPipe = new PipedOutputStream();
                        PipedInputStream iPipe = new PipedInputStream();

                // They need to be connected to one another
                // to be of any use.

                iPipe.connect(oPipe);
                oPipe.connect(iPipe);

                        oPipe.close();
                        iPipe.close();
                }
                catch(IOException e)
                {
                System.out.println("Error: " + e);
                }
        }
}
```

WRITE

Class Name	PipedInputStream
Description	This method writes one or more bytes of data to the open output pipe. This method blocks until data is written to the pipe.
Syntax	public void **write**()
	public void **write**(byte *barr[]*, int *off*, int *len*)
Parameters	
byte *barr[]*	The name of the byte array from which data is written.
int *off*	The offset of the data in the byte array.
int *len*	The maximum number of bytes written.
Returns	None.
Exceptions	An IOException will be thrown if an I/O error occurs.
Example	

```java
import java.lang.*;
import java.io.*;

class PipeTest
{
    public static void main(String[] args)
        {
                try
                {
                        PipedOutputStream oPipe = new PipedOutputStream();
                        PipedInputStream iPipe = new PipedInputStream();

                // They need to be connected to one another to
                // be of any use.

                iPipe.connect(oPipe);
                oPipe.connect(iPipe);

                oPipe.write('a');

                byte readChar = iPipe.read();

                System.out.println("The char read was : " + readChar);

                        oPipe.close();
                        iPipe.close();
                }
                catch(IOException e)
                {
                System.out.println("Error: " + e);
                }
        }
}
```

Execute

```
java PipeTest
```

Output

```
The char read was : 97
```

The File I/O Project: A Simple Customer Record Database

Project Overview

This project uses the APIs explained earlier in the chapter to develop a simple Java program to manage a customer record database. The code for the program is shown in Listing 12-5. This program allows the user to add a new customer record comprising customer name, customer phone number, and customer address to the customer record database. It also allows the user to display and delete the customer record in the customer record database using the customer name as the key. This project demonstrates the following techniques:

- Use of sequential files for input and output
- Use of random access files for storing and accessing records
- Use of an index file to access the records in the database files randomly

The program uses two different kinds of files to store the customer record information. The file structure used in the database is shown in Figure 12-3. The files have been organized to expedite the access to a particular record in the database. If you know the exact location of the record in the customer record database, you can randomly access the record in the file without reading the data sequentially. The first file, called the customer record database file, stores the customer records. The second file, called the index file, stores the key of the customer record and the location of the customer record in the customer record database file. The database program supports the following operations:

- Add   By choosing this option, a user can add a customer record to the customer record database and create an index for the above record in the index file.

- Delete   By choosing this option, a user will be able to delete an entry in the index file, thereby making the record in the customer record database file inaccessible. Note that the record is not physically deleted from the customer record database file.

- Display   By choosing this option, a user can display any record from the customer record database. The location of the record in the customer record database is obtained from the index file, and the customer record is randomly accessed from the customer record database file.

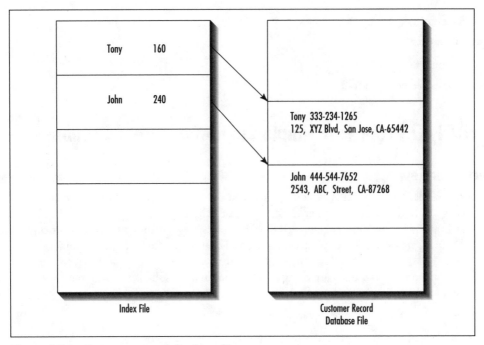

Figure 12-3   Customer record database file structure

Building the Project

The following project has been implemented using seven Java classes. Detailed description of each of these classes is given here.

1. The first class in Listing 12-5 is the class IndexRecord. This class extends the class Object. The class IndexRecord has just two instance variables, key and position. The instance variable key is the key of the class CustomerRecord (described later). The instance variable position stores the starting position of the record in the customer record database. The constructor of the class initializes the instance variable with its parameters. The methods getKey() and getPosition() return the key of the IndexRecord and the position of the CustomerRecord in the customer record database. The method equals() that is defined in the class Object is overridden. The method equals() takes a reference to another Object as an argument and figures out if the instance variable key of the two objects is the same. If they are similar, the method equals() returns true, otherwise it returns false.

2. The class IndexRecordManager manages the reading and writing of the IndexRecords into the index file. The constructor of this class creates a new vector in which the IndexRecords are stored. The index file is opened for both reading and writing. The method readIndexFile() reads all the IndexRecord records in the database index file and adds them to a vector. The method writeIndexFile() writes the contents of the vector into the index file. The methods

readIndexRecord() and writeIndexRecord() are private methods of the class that are used to read and write a single IndexRecord from the database. The method getIndexRecord() returns an IndexRecord from the vector of IndexRecords that matches the specified key. The method addIndexRecord() adds an IndexRecord to the vector. The method deleteIndexRecord() deletes the IndexRecord from the vector.

3. The class CustomerRecord extends the class Object. This method has three instance variables: name, phone, and address. The instance variables of the class CustomerRecord store the customer name, customer phone, and the customer address. The constructor of the class initializes the instance variables. The methods getName(), getPhone(), and getAddress() get the customer name, phone, and address, respectively.

4. The class RecordReader is used to read a CustomerRecord from the customer record database. The constructor of the class takes a reference to an instance of RandomAccessFile as an argument and stores the reference in the instance variable. The method readRecord() basically reads 80 bytes of data from the customer record database at a specified position. It converts the 80 bytes of data into the strings representing name, phone, and address. Using these strings, the method creates and returns a new CustomerRecord database.

5. The class RecordWriter is used to write a CustomerRecord to the customer record database. The constructor of the class takes a reference to a RandomAccessFile as an argument and stores it in the instance variable. The method writeRecord() writes 80 bytes of data from the customer record database at a specified position. It converts customer name, phone, and address into 80 bytes of data. This method writes the data at the specified position.

6. The class CustomerRecordManager is the main class that manages the customer record database and the index file. The constructor for the class CustomerRecordManager takes two arguments, the database file name and the index file name. The constructor of the class creates new instances of RandomAccessFile and initializes the instance variables. It creates new instances of the class RecordReader and RecordWriter. It creates an instance of the IndexRecordManager and reads all the IndexRecords into the main memory. The method readRecord() prompts the user for customer name, telephone number, and address, and returns a new instance of CustomerRecord. The method PrintRecord() prints the name, phone number, and address in the specified CustomerRecord on the terminal. The method option() reads a byte of input and skips all the bytes until the end of stream is reached and returns the first byte. The method printMainMenu() displays the menu options available for manipulating the customer database. The method performAddRecord() reads customer name, phone number, and the address from the user, and adds an IndexRecord to the index file and a CustomerRecord to the customer record database file. The method performCleanup() writes all the IndexRecords in the memory to the index file and closes the customer record database file and the index file. The

method performDelete() reads the name of the user and uses it as a key to delete the IndexRecord in the vector. The method performDisplay() displays an existing record in the CustomerRecord database. If the record does not exist, then the method displays an error message. The method run() loops forever, waiting for the user to enter 1, 2, q, or x. Specific actions are performed by the method run() depending upon the option selected by the user.

7. The class RecordTest has just one method, main(), that simply instantiates the class CustomerRecordManager and calls the method run().

Listing 12-5 An example of the program that manages a customer record database

```java
import java.lang.*;
import java.io.*;
import java.util.*;

/*      CustomerRecord
            28 bytes for the name;
            12 bytes for the telephone number;
            40 bytes for the address;

        IndexRecord
            28 bytes for the name;
            4  bytes for the position;
*/


/* IndexRecord - This class stores the index of the CustomerRecord in the
   RandomAccess File
*/

class IndexRecord
{
    String  key; // The key of the CustomerRecord.
    Long    position; // The position of the Record in the
                      // CustomerRecord file.

    public IndexRecord(String name, long pos) // The constructor
    {
        key = name;
        position = pos;
    }

    public String getKey()
    {
        return key; // Return the key value of the current record.
    }

    public long getPosition()
    {
        return position; // Return the position of the current record.
    }

    // Check if the key of the obj is the same as this object's key.
```

```
        // Return true if they are equal ---- false otherwise.

    public boolean equals(Object obj)
    {
        IndexRecord otherKey = (IndexRecord) obj;

        // We need to trim the keys for some leading & trailing spaces
        int retval = (key.trim()).compareTo((otherKey.getKey()).trim());

        // if retval == 0 then the keys are the same ;
        // otherwise the keys are different.

        if(retval == 0)
            return true;
        else
            return false;
    }
}

/* IndexRecordManager - This class manages a Vector of  IndexRecords.
*/

class IndexRecordManager
{
    Vector indexRecordVect; // Reference to the IndexRecord vector.
    RandomAccessFile    rfile; // The file in which the vector of
                       // IndexRecords are stored in.

    public IndexRecordManager(String indexFileName ) // Constructor
    {
        indexRecordVect = new Vector(); // Create a new Vector
        try
        {
            // open the file in which the vector of IndexRecords
            // are stored.
            // The file is opened in the Read-Write mode

            rfile = new RandomAccessFile(indexFileName, "rw");
        }
        // Problems opening the RandomAccessFile
        catch(IOException e)
        {
            System.out.println("Error : " + e);
        }
    }

    public void readIndexFile() // Reads the file into the memory.
    {
        while(true)
        {
            try
            {
                // read one record at a time
                IndexRecord rec = readIndexRecord();

                // add the record to the vector
                indexRecordVect.addElement(rec);
```

continued on next page

continued from previous page

```
            }
            // Reached the EOF ?
            catch(IOException e)
            {
                // Done reading ? So, exit the function.
                return;
            }
        }
    }

    // Write the contents of the vector into the file.
    public void writeIndexFile()
    {
        int size = indexRecordVect.size(); // The size contains the number of
                        // elements in the vector.
        try
        {
            rfile.seek((long) 0); // Get to the beginning of the file

            // Do; for all the elements in the vector.

            for(int i=0; i < size; ++i)
            {
                // Get the element at the index "i"

                IndexRecord elem = (IndexRecord)
                        indexRecordVect.elementAt(i);
                // Write element to the file.
                writeIndexRecord(elem);
            }
        }
        //  Could not write to the file -- An IO Error ? Exit the method
        catch(IOException e)
        {
            return;
        }
    }

    // Write an IndexRecord to the file.
    private void writeIndexRecord(IndexRecord rcd) throws IOException
    {
        String key = rcd.getKey(); // get the key of the IndexRecord
        byte[] bkey = new byte[28]; // Create a byte Array of the size 28

        // Now for some sanity check.

        if(key.length() > 28) // Just copy the first 28 bytes of the string to
                        //   the byte array.
            key.getBytes(0, 27, bkey, 0);
        else
                // otherwise Copy  as many there are.
            key.getBytes(0, key.length(), bkey, 0);

        // Write the key to the file
        rfile.write(bkey, 0, 28);

        // Write the position of the key to the file
        rfile.writeLong(rcd.getPosition());
```

```
    }

    // Read an IndexRecord from the file.
    private IndexRecord readIndexRecord() throws IOException
    {
        byte[] bname = new byte[28];

        rfile.read(bname, 0, 28); // Read the 28 bytes
        String name = new String(bname, 0); // convert the byte array
                                    // to a String

        return (new IndexRecord(name, rfile.readLong())); // Create a new
                                    // IndexRecord
    }

    // Get the IndexRecord from the indexRecordVector
    // Returns null if not found.
    public IndexRecord getIndexRecord(String key)
    {
        IndexRecord temp = new IndexRecord(key, (long) 0); // Create a new
                                    // IndexRecord
        int index = indexRecordVect.indexOf(temp);  // Check if this record
                                        // is present.

        if(index < 0) // A Bad Index
            return null;
        else
            return (IndexRecord) indexRecordVect.elementAt(index); // Get
                            // the element in the vector
    }

    // Adds the specified IndexRecord to the indexRecordVector
    public void addIndexRecord(IndexRecord irecord)
    {
        indexRecordVect.addElement(irecord);
    }

    // Creates and Adds IndexRecordVector
    public void addIndexRecord(String name, long pos)
    {
        IndexRecord irec = new IndexRecord(name, pos);
        addIndexRecord(irec);
    }

    // Delete the IndexVector in the indexRecordVector with the specified
    // Key.
    public boolean deleteIndexRecord(String aKey)
    {
        IndexRecord irec = new IndexRecord(aKey, (long) 0); // create a new
                                    // IndexRecord

        return indexRecordVect.removeElement(irec);
    }
}

// A Customer Record class.
class CustomerRecord
```

continued on next page

continued from previous page

```
{
    String name;
    String phone;
    String address;

    public CustomerRecord(String custName, String custPhone, String custAddr)
    {
        // Set the values passed to the constructor.
        name = custName;
        phone = custPhone;
        address = custAddr;
    }

    public String getName()
    {
        // Return the name
        return name;
    }

    public String getPhone()
    {
        // Return the phone
        return phone;
    }

    public String getAddress()
    {
        // Return the address
        return address;
    }
}

// This class reads a customer record.

class RecordReader
{
    RandomAccessFile rfile;

    public RecordReader(RandomAccessFile raccessFile)
    {
        rfile = raccessFile; // A reference to a Random Access File.
    }

    public CustomerRecord readRecord(long position) throws IOException
    {
        // Go to the correct position in the File.
        rfile.seek(position);

        // Allocate space for the byte array.
        byte[] bname = new byte[28];
        byte[] bphone = new byte[12];
        byte[] baddr = new byte[40];

        // Read 28 bytes from the file.
        rfile.read(bname, 0, 28);
        String name = new String(bname, 0); // Convert the byte array
                                             // to a String
```

```
        // Read 12 bytes from the file.
        rfile.read(bphone, 0, 12);
        String phone = new String(bphone, 0); // Convert the byte array
                                    // to a String

        // Read 40 bytes from the file.
        rfile.read(baddr, 0, 40);
        String addr = new String(baddr, 0); // Convert the byte array
                                    // to a String

        return (new CustomerRecord(name, phone, addr)); // Return a new
                                                // CustomerRecord
    }
}

// This class writes a customer record.

class RecordWriter
{
    RandomAccessFile rfile;

    public RecordWriter(RandomAccessFile raccessFile)
    {
        rfile = raccessFile; // create a reference to the RandomAccess File
    }

    public void writeRecord(CustomerRecord rcd, long position) throws IOException
    {
        rfile.seek(position); // Seek to the specified position.

        String name = rcd.getName(); // Get the Name
        String phone = rcd.getPhone(); // Get the Phone
        String addr = rcd.getAddress(); // Get the Address

        // Allocate the space for the byte array.
        byte[] bname = new byte[28];
        byte[] bphone = new byte[12];
        byte[] baddr = new byte[40];

        // If the name is greater than 28 bytes copy 28 bytes into the array
        // otherwise copy 28 bytes into the file into the array

        if(name.length() > 28)
            name.getBytes(0, 27, bname, 0);
        else
            name.getBytes(0, name.length(), bname, 0);

        // If the name is greater than 12 bytes copy 12 bytes into the array
        // otherwise copy 12 bytes into the file into the array

        if(phone.length() > 12)
            phone.getBytes(0, 11, bphone, 0);
        else
            phone.getBytes(0, phone.length(), bphone, 0);

        // If the name is greater than 40 bytes copy 40 bytes into the array
        // otherwise copy 40 bytes into the file into the array
```

continued on next page

continued from previous page

```
        if(addr.length() > 40)
            addr.getBytes(0, 39, baddr, 0);
        else
            addr.getBytes(0, addr.length(), baddr, 0);

        // Write the data into the file.

        rfile.write(bname, 0, 28);
        rfile.write(bphone, 0, 12);
        rfile.write(baddr, 0, 40);
    }
}

class CustomerRecordManager
{
    RandomAccessFile dbsFile; // The file where the Customer Records are stored.
    RandomAccessFile inxFile; // The file where the indexes to the
                      // Customer Record are  stored.

    RecordReader rdr; // Reads CustomerRecords from the CustomerRecord file
    RecordWriter wtr; // Writes CustomerRecods into the CustomerRecord file

    IndexRecordManager indxMgr; // Manages all the IndexRecords in the System
    DataInputStream din; // Input stream to read formatted input from  the
                      // Standard Input.

    CustomerRecordManager(String dataBaseFile, String indexFile) throws IOException
    {
        dbsFile = new RandomAccessFile(dataBaseFile , "rw"); //Open the file
        inxFile = new RandomAccessFile(indexFile , "rw");//in Read-Write mode.

        rdr = new RecordReader(dbsFile); // Creates a Reader for the
                                    // CustomerRecord File.
        wtr = new RecordWriter(dbsFile); // Creates a Writer for the
                                    // CustomerRecord File.

        indxMgr = new IndexRecordManager(indexFile); // Creates an index file
                                            // manager for the IndexFile.
        indxMgr.readIndexFile(); // Creates the indexes.

        din = new DataInputStream(System.in); // Initializes the formatted
                                        // input stream.
    }

    // This method prompts the user on the terminal and creates a
    // new CustomerRecord.
    private CustomerRecord readRecord() throws IOException
    {
        System.out.print("Name: ");
        System.out.flush(); // Needed because it's a buffered output stream.
        String aName = din.readLine(); // Read in the name.
        System.out.print("Phone #: ");
        System.out.flush(); // Needed because it's a buffered output stream.
        String aPhone = din.readLine(); // Read in the phone number.
        System.out.print("Address: ");
        System.out.flush(); // Needed because it's a buffered output stream.
        String aAddr = din.readLine(); // Read in the address.
```

```
        return ( new CustomerRecord(aName, aPhone, aAddr) ); // Create a new
                                    // CustomerRecord.
}

// This method prints the CustomerRecord on the terminal
private void PrintRecord(CustomerRecord rec)
{
    System.out.println("\nName   : " + rec.getName());
    System.out.println("Phone  : " + rec.getPhone());
    System.out.println("Address: " + rec.getAddress());
    System.out.println("\n");
}

// This method reads in a byte of input from the standard input
// It skips all the bytes till the end of the stream.
private byte option() throws IOException
{
    byte opt = din.readByte(); // Read the first byte

    while (true)
    {
        try
        {
            din.skipBytes(1); // Skip one byte at a time
        }
        // Till you get an End of Stream Exception.
        catch(Exception e)
        {
            // Break out of the While
            break;
        }
    }

    // Return the first byte.
    return opt;
}

// This method prints out the main menu on the terminal output.
private void printMainMenu()
{
    System.out.println("\nSelect one of the following options:");
    System.out.println("1. Add a Record");
    System.out.println("2. Delete a Record");
    System.out.println("3. Display a Record");
    System.out.println("\nType 'q' or 'x'  to EXIT \n");
    System.out.print("OPTION: ");
    System.out.flush();
}

// This method Adds Record both into the index file and
// CustomerRecord.

private void performAddRecord() throws IOException
{
    CustomerRecord rec = readRecord(); // Reads the Inputs from the User
    dbsFile.seek(dbsFile.length()); // Seek to the End of the
                                    // Database file
```

continued on next page

continued from previous page

```
        long position = dbsFile.getFilePointer(); // set the current
                                         // file pointer offset.

        if(indxMgr.getIndexRecord(rec.getName()) == null) // Get an Index
                                    // Record corresponding to the Name.
                                    // If the record was not found add it.
        {
            // Add the record.
            indxMgr.addIndexRecord(rec.getName(), position);

            // Write the record at the determined  position.
            wtr.writeRecord(rec, position);
        }
        // If the record with the same key already exists in the database.
        else
        {
            // Flag off an error.
            System.out.println("\nDuplicate Record. Insertion Failed !!");
        }
    }


    // Writes the indexes back to the IndexFile.
    // close the files.
    private void performCleanup() throws IOException
    {
        indxMgr.writeIndexFile();
        dbsFile.close();
        inxFile.close();
    }


    // This method deletes an existing record from the CustomerRecord database.
    private void performDelete() throws IOException
    {
        System.out.print("Name: ");
        System.out.flush();

        String aKey = din.readLine(); // get the Name of the Customer
                                    // (The CustomerRecord key)

        if(!indxMgr.deleteIndexRecord(aKey)) // If the delete was unsuccessful
        {
            System.out.println("The Record was not found.Deletion failed!!");
        }
    }


    // This method displays an existing record from the
    // CustomerRecord database.
    private void performDisplay() throws IOException
    {
        System.out.print("Name: ");
        System.out.flush();

        String aKey = din.readLine();     // get the Name of the Customer
                                    // (The CustomerRecord key)
        IndexRecord irec = indxMgr.getIndexRecord(aKey); // Check if the
                                         // index Record exists

        CustomerRecord rec = null;
```

```
        if(irec != null) // If the indexRecord exists
        {
            // read a record from the CustomerRecord database,
            rec = rdr.readRecord(irec.getPosition());
        }
        else // If the indexRecord was not present.
        {
            // flag an error
            System.out.println("The Record was not found.!!");
            return;
        }

        // If the record was found
        if(rec != null)
        {
            // print the record.
            PrintRecord(rec);
        }
        // Should never reach here; - Just a sanity check.
        else
        {
            // If in here; somebody has tampered with the files.
            System.out.println("The Record was not found.!!");
        }
    }


// This method is the main method that interacts with the user.
public void run() throws IOException
{
    while(true) // forever.
    {
        printMainMenu(); // Display the main menu

        switch( option() ) // get the user response.
        {
            case '1':
                    performAddRecord();
                    break;

            case '2':
                    performDelete();
                    break;

            case '3':
                    performDisplay();
                    break;

            case 'x':
            case 'q':
                performCleanup();
                return; // Exit the function.
            default:
                continue;
        }
    }
}
}
```

continued on next page

continued from previous page

```
class RecordTest
{
    // The main function.
    public static void main(String[] args)
    {
        try
        {
            // Create an instance of a CustomerRecordManager
            CustomerRecordManager cm = new
                CustomerRecordManager("custom.dbs", "custom.inx");

            // Just run it.
            cm.run();
        }
        // If an exception arises.
        catch(IOException e)
        {
            System.out.println("Error : " + e);
        }
    }
}
```

13

ADDITIONAL I/O

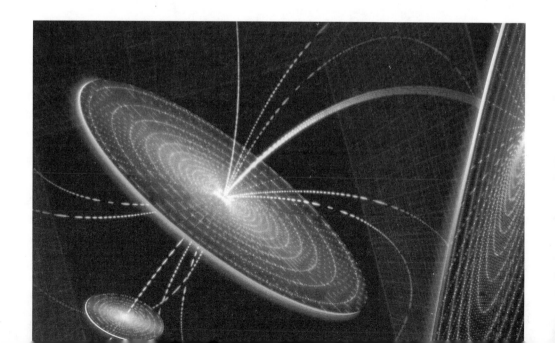

13

ADDITIONAL I/O

Chapter 13 begins where Chapter 11 ends. Chapter 11, Basic I/O, introduced stream based input and output, and the classes introduced there handled basic input and output processing tasks. The classes introduced in this chapter are intended to be used to solve advanced input and output problems. Also included are instructions explaining how to create your own specialized input and output stream classes.

Table 13-1, which appears later in the chapter under the section "Additional I/O Classes Summaries," briefly describes the classes included in this chapter. Figure 13-1 illustrates the relationship between these classes and the input and output stream foundation classes presented in Chapter 11.

The Design of Custom Stream Classes

Properly used, the input and output stream classes described in this and the preceding two chapters help solve a broad spectrum of problems. However, no prepackaged set of classes can solve every problem. This section of the chapter describes the steps a programmer must take to define a new input or output stream class.

Derivation Steps

New input and output stream classes should be derived from either class InputStream or class OutputStream or one of their descendants. They may then be used wherever InputStream objects or OutputStream objects are acceptable.

There are three different derivation scenarios:

1. An existing stream class needs only slight modifications (perhaps the addition of a new constructor). In this case, simply extend the existing class.

2. The new class is sufficiently different from any existing class. If the new class primarily acts by modifying information going to or coming from another stream class, then extend either class FilterInputStream or class FilterOutputStream.

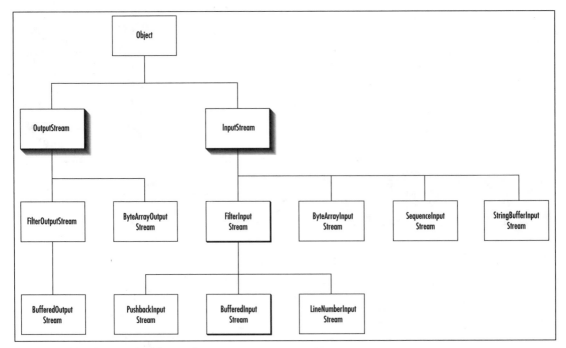

Figure 13-1 The I/O class hierarchy

3. The new class is sufficiently different from any existing class and case two does not apply. In this case, extend either class InputStream or class OutputStream to implement the necessary functionality (if the class must talk to some novel hardware device, this step may require the use of native methods).

When deriving a class from class InputStream, the abstract method read() must be redefined in order for instances of the class to read data from the desired stream source. When deriving a class from class FilterInputStream, redefine this method only if the input stream is being transformed at the byte level. Otherwise, the default implementation of the read() method (which simply reads from the underlying input stream) is probably adequate.

When deriving a class from class OutputStream, the abstract method write() must be redefined in order for instances of the class to write data to the desired stream destination. When deriving a class from class FilterOutputStream, redefine this method if the output stream is being transformed at the byte level. Otherwise, the default implementation of the write() method (which simply writes to the underlying output stream) is probably adequate.

It is not absolutely necessary to redefine the read() and write() methods that operate on byte arrays, because they, by default, make use of the single-byte read() and write() methods (which were redefined above) to read or write the byte arrays. However, these two methods can be redefined if redefinition would result in better performance.

The InputStream and FilterInputStream classes define default behaviors for the methods available(), close(), mark(), markSupported(), reset(), and skip(). The OutputStream and FilterOutputStream classes define default behaviors for the methods close() and flush(). If, in either case, the default behaviors aren't correct, these methods, too, can be redefined.

Each derived stream class may require additional methods specific to the problem it is designed to solve.

An Example

The example code in Listing 13-1 defines a filter output stream that run-length encodes data written to it. This class should extend class FilterOutputStream rather than class OutputStream, since it transforms, at the byte level, data destined for another output stream. The flush() method emits the byte and a count for the last byte in the latch, and resets the byte latch. The close() method simply calls flush().

Listing 13-1 Class RunLengthEncodedOutputStream

```java
import java.io.*;

public class RunLengthEncodedOutputStream extends FilterOutputStream
{
    private byte byteLatch;
    private int nCount;

    public RunLengthEncodedOutputStream(OutputStream out)
    {
        super(out);
        byteLatch = '\0';
        nCount = 0;
    }

    public void write(int nByte) throws IOException
    {
        if (byteLatch != nByte || nCount >= 255)
            flush()

        byteLatch = (byte)nByte;
        nCount++;
    }

    public void flush() throws IOException
    {
        out.write(nCount);
        out.write(byteLatch);
        byteLatch = '\0';
        nCount = 0;
    }

    public void close() throws IOException
    {
        flush();
        out.close();
    }
}
```

About the Project

Java's growing popularity notwithstanding, HTML (HyperText Markup Language) is the principal language of the World Wide Web. A Web browser reads raw HTML and converts it into a nicely formatted page. At the heart of every Web browser is a piece of code, called a parser, that understands the layout of an HTML document and can successfully navigate its way between tag and text. The project in this chapter describes the steps necessary to construct such a parser—one capable of differentiating between the text of an HTML document and the markup that accompanies it.

Additional I/O Classes' Summaries

The classes described in this chapter expand the range of I/O processing a Java program can perform. Table 13-1 contains a brief description of each class. Each will be described in detail in subsequent sections.

Table 13-1 The additional I/O classes

Class	Description
ByteArrayInputStream	The class of objects that use a byte array as an input stream
ByteArrayOutputStream	The class of objects that use a byte array as an output stream
BufferedInputStream	The class of objects that buffer the data going to an input stream
BufferedOutputStream	The class of objects that buffer the data going to an output stream
SequenceInputStream	The class of objects that group multiple input streams into one
StringBufferInputStream	The class of objects that use a String object as an input stream
LineNumberInputStream	The class of objects that track the line number of the input stream
PushbackInputStream	The class of objects that allow one character pushback of read data
StreamTokenizer	The class of objects that tokenize a stream

The java.io.ByteArrayInputStream Class

The ByteArrayInputStream class allows data to be read from a byte array as if it were an input stream. Tables 13-2 and 13-3 list and briefly describe all of the variables and methods defined by class ByteArrayInputStream.

Table 13-2 Summary of ByteArrayInputStream variables

Variable	Description
buf	A reference to the internal byte array
count	The last position to use from the internal byte array
pos	The current position in the internal byte array

ByteArrayInputStream

Description	The ByteArrayInputStream class allows data to be read from a byte array as if it were an input stream.
Syntax	public class **ByteArrayInputStream** extends InputStream
Package	java.io
Import	java.io.ByteArrayInputStream
Constructors	public **ByteArrayInputStream**(byte []*rgb*)
	public **ByteArrayInputStream**(byte [] *rgb*, int *nOffset*, int *nLength*)
Parameters	
byte [] *rgb*	The byte array to read bytes from.
int *nOffset*	The offset from the beginning of the byte array.
int *nLength*	The number of bytes to read.
Comments	The constructors create a ByteArrayInputStream object from the byte array specified in the parameter list.
Example	This example demonstrates how to create a ByteArrayInputStream object from a byte array.

```
void Create(byte [] rgb)
{
   ByteArrayInputStream bais =
      new ByteArrayInputStream(rgb, 0, rgb.length);

   // process
}
```

Variables

BUF

Class Name	ByteArrayInputStream
Description	This variable contains a reference to the internal byte array. It provides derived classes direct access to the internal byte array.

Syntax	protected byte [] **buf**
Example	The following example demonstrates how a derived class might access the bytes in the internal byte array:

```
class DerivedByteArrayInputStream extends ByteArrayInputStream
{
   DerivedByteArrayInputStream(byte [] rgb)
   {
      super(rgb); // call ByteArrayInputStream()

      // read and/or write the internal state of
      // the ByteArrayInputStream

      byte [] rgbBuf = buf;

      // process
   }
}
```

COUNT

Class Name	ByteArrayInputStream
Description	This variable contains the last position to use from the internal byte array.
Syntax	protected int **count**
Example	The following example demonstrates how a derived class might access the last position to use in the internal byte array:

```
class DerivedByteArrayInputStream extends ByteArrayInputStream
{
   DerivedByteArrayInputStream(byte [] rgb)
   {
      super(rgb); // call ByteArrayInputStream()

      // read and/or write the internal state of
      // the ByteArrayInputStream

      int n = count;

      // process
   }
}
```

POS

Class Name	ByteArrayInputStream
Description	This variable contains the current position in the internal byte array.
Syntax	protected int **pos**
Example	The following example demonstrates how a derived class might access the current position in the internal byte array:

```
class DerivedByteArrayInputStream extends ByteArrayInputStream
{
    DerivedByteArrayInputStream(byte [] rgb)
    {
        super(rgb); // call ByteArrayInputStream()

        // read and/or write the internal state of
        // the ByteArrayInputStream

        int n = pos;

        // process
    }
}
```

Methods

AVAILABLE

Class Name	ByteArrayInputStream
Description	This method returns the number of bytes that can be read from this stream before blocking will occur.
Syntax	public synchronized int **available**()
Parameters	None.
Returns	An integer containing the number of available bytes.
Exceptions	None.
Comments	If an input stream is empty, a read operation on that stream will block until data becomes available. Often this is undesirable. In a loop in which the processing of data read from the input stream must be interspersed with other processing, blocking must be avoided. This method allows the program to determine whether data is available before attempting to read it.
Example	The following example demonstrates how to use this method to determine the number of bytes available in an input stream:

```
void ProcessLoop(ByteArrayInputStream [] rgbais)
{
    while (true)
    {
        for (int i = 0; i < rgbais.length; i++)
        {
            if (rgbais[i].available() > 0)
            {
```

continued on next page

continued from previous page

```
        // read and process the available bytes

        int nNext = rgbais[i].read();
                    .
                    .
                    .
        }
      }
    }
  }
}
```

READ

Class Name	ByteArrayInputStream
Description	These methods read a byte or series of bytes from the input stream.
Syntax	public synchronized int **read**()
	public synchronized int **read**(byte [] *rgb*, int *nOffset*, int *nLength*)
Parameters	
byte [] *rgb*	The byte array to read bytes into.
int *nOffset*	The offset from the beginning of the byte array.
int *nLength*	The number of bytes to read.
Returns	An int. The first of these two methods returns the value read from the input stream. Even though the result is returned as an int rather than as a byte, only values in the range 0 to 256 are permissible. It is possible to write a method that does return the full range of int values, but that would certainly cause incompatibility with the other classes in the Java language I/O class library. The other method returns the number of bytes read into the byte array. Both return a value of -1 if no more data is available from the input stream.
Exceptions	None.
Example	The following example demonstrates how to read from an input stream:

```
void ReadAndProcess(ByteArrayInputStream bais)
{
    while (true)
    {
        int b = bais.read();

        // process byte

        byte [] rgb = new byte [100];

        bais.read(rgb, 10, rgb.length);

        // process byte array
    }
}
```

RESET

Class Name	ByteArrayInputStream
Description	This method repositions the stream to the beginning of the byte array. It is not used in conjunction with the mark() method.
Syntax	public synchronized void **reset**()
Parameters	None.
Returns	None.
Exceptions	None.
Comments	By resetting a ByteArrayInputStream object, the data in the object can be reused.
Example	The following example demonstrates how to reset a ByteArrayInputStream object:

```
void Process(ByteArrayInputStream bais)
{
    // process bytes in stream

    bais.reset();

    // process bytes again
}
```

SKIP

Class Name	ByteArrayInputStream
Description	This method skips up to *n* bytes ahead in the input stream. It will skip fewer than *n* bytes ahead if a full skip would cause the call to block.
Syntax	public synchronized long **skip**(long *n*)
Parameters	
long *n*	The number of bytes to skip.
Returns	The number of bytes skipped. This method returns a value of -1 if no more data is available from the stream.
Exceptions	None.
Example	The following example demonstrates how to skip over a portion of the input stream:

```
boolean SkipAhead(ByteArrayInputStream bais)
{
    int i = bais.read();  // determine how far to skip ahead

    int n = bais.skip(i); // skip ahead

    return n < i;
}
```

The java.io.ByteArrayOutputStream Class

The ByteArrayOutputStream class allows data to be written to a byte array as if it were an output stream. Tables 13-4 and 13-5 list and briefly describe all of the variables and methods defined by class ByteArrayOutputStream.

Table 13-4 Summary of ByteArrayOutputStream variables

Variable	Description
buf	A reference to the internal byte array
count	The number of bytes in the internal byte array

Table 13-5 Summary of ByteArrayOutputStream methods

Method	Description
reset	Resets the output stream
size	Returns the number of bytes written to the internal buffer
toByteArray	Returns a copy of the bytes in the internal buffer
toString	Returns a copy of the bytes in the internal buffer converted to a string
write	Writes data to the output stream
writeTo	Writes the bytes in the internal buffer to an output stream

BYTEARRAYOUTPUTSTREAM

Description	The ByteArrayOutputStream class allows data to be written to a byte array as if it were an output stream.
Syntax	public class **ByteArrayOutputStream** extends OutputStream
Package	java.io
Import	java.io.ByteArrayOutputStream
Constructors	public **ByteArrayOutputStream**()
	public **ByteArrayOutputStream**(int *nSize*)
Parameters	
int *nSize*	The initial size of the internal buffer.
Comments	These constructors create a ByteArrayOutputStream object. The initial size of the internal byte array may be specified in the parameter list. If the total number of characters that will be written or the upper bound on the total number of characters that will be written is known, it is better,

performancewise, to specify the initial size of the internal buffer. This prevents the time-consuming allocate and copy operations that occur if the internal buffer has to be resized.

Example   This example demonstrates how to create a ByteArrayOutputStream object.

```
void Create(int nSize)
{
   ByteArrayOutputStream baos = new ByteArrayOutputStream(nSize);

   // process
}
```

Variables

BUF

Class Name	ByteArrayOutputStream
Description	This variable contains a reference to the internal byte array. It provides derived classes direct access to the internal byte array:
Syntax	protected byte [] **buf**
Example	The following example demonstrates how a derived class might access the bytes in the internal byte array:

```
class DerivedByteArrayOutputStream extends ByteArrayOutputStream
{
   DerivedByteArrayOutputStream()
   {
      super(); // call ByteArrayOutputStream()

      // read and/or write the internal state of
      // the ByteArrayOutputStream

      byte [] rgb = buf;

      // process
   }
}
```

COUNT

Class Name	ByteArrayOutputStream
Description	This variable contains the number of bytes in the internal byte array.
Syntax	protected int **count**
Example	The following example demonstrates how a derived class might access the number of bytes in the internal byte array:

```
class DerivedByteArrayOutputStream extends ByteArrayOutputStream
{
   DerivedByteArrayOutputStream()
   {
      super(); // call ByteArrayOutputStream()

      // read and/or write the internal state of
      // the ByteArrayOutputStream

      int n = count;

      // process
   }
}
```

Methods

RESET

Class Name	ByteArrayOutputStream
Description	This method resets the state of the output stream.
Syntax	public synchronized void **reset**()
Parameters	None.
Returns	None.
Exceptions	None.
Comments	This method resets the state of the output stream without throwing away the internal buffer. The ByteArrayOutputStream object thus can be used again, as if it had been newly created.
Example	The following example demonstrates how to reset and reuse a ByteArrayOutputStream object:

```
void Process(ByteArrayOutputStream baos)
{
   // write bytes to stream and process

   baos.reset();

   // write bytes to stream and process bytes again
}
```

SIZE

Class Name	ByteArrayOutputStream
Description	This method returns the number of bytes written to the stream since it was created or last reset.

Syntax	public int **size**()
Parameters	None.
Returns	An integer.
Exceptions	None.
Example	The following example demonstrates how to determine the number of bytes that have been written to an output stream:

```
void Process(ByteArrayOutputStream baos)
{
   int n = baos.size();

   for (int i = 0; i < n; i++)
   {
      // process
   }
}
```

TOBYTEARRAY

Class Name	ByteArrayOutputStream
Description	This method returns a copy of the internal buffer.
Syntax	public synchronized byte [] **toByteArray**()
Parameters	None.
Returns	A byte array containing a copy of the data in the internal buffer.
Exceptions	None.
See Also	toString()
Example	The following example demonstrates how to retrieve the information that has been written to an output stream:

```
void Extract(ByteArrayOutputStream baos)
{
   byte [] rgb = baos.toByteArray();

   // process the resulting byte array
}
```

TOSTRING

Class Name	ByteArrayOutputStream
Description	This method returns a copy of the internal buffer converted to a String object. Each byte in the internal buffer becomes the low-order byte of a 2-byte Unicode character. The high-order byte may be specified. If it is not specified, it will default to zero.
Syntax	public String **toString**()
	public String **toString**(int *nHighByte*)

Parameters

int *nHighByte*   The value of the high-order byte of each 2-byte Unicode character. Even though it is passed as an int, it must be a valid unsigned 8-bit quantity ($0 \leq nHighByte \leq 256$).

Returns   A String object.

Exceptions   None.

See Also   toByteArray()

Example   The following example demonstrates how to retrieve the information that has been written to an output stream formatted as a String object:

```
void Extract(ByteArrayOutputStream baos)
{
   String str = baos.toString(0);

   // process the resulting String object
}
```

WRITE

Class Name   ByteArrayOutputStream

Description   These methods write a byte or series of bytes to the output stream.

Syntax   public synchronized void **write**(int *n*)

public synchronized void **write**(byte [] *rgb*, int *nOffset*, int *nLength*)

Parameters

int *n*   The byte to write. Even though this parameter is passed to this method as an int rather than a byte, only values in the range -128 to ≤127 should be used. It is possible to write a method that does accept the full range of integer values, but that would certainly cause incompatibility with the other classes in the Java language I/O class library.

byte [] *rgb*   The byte array to write.

int *nOffset*   The offset from the beginning of the byte array.

int *nLength*   The number of bytes to write, beginning at the offset.

Returns   None.

Exceptions   None.

See Also   writeTo()

Example   The following example demonstrates how to write to an output stream:

```
void GenerateAndWrite(ByteArrayOutputStream baos)
{
   while (true)
   {
```

```
        int b;

        // generate byte

        baos.write(b);

        byte [] rgb;

        // generate byte array

        baos.write(rgb, 10, rgb.length);
    }
}
```

WRITETO

Class Name	ByteArrayOutputStream
Description	This method writes the contents of the internal buffer to the OutputStream object specified in the parameter list.
Syntax	public synchronized void **writeTo**(OutputStream *out*)
Parameters	
OutputStream *out*	The OutputStream object to which to write.
Returns	None.
Exceptions	If data cannot be written to the output stream, this method will throw an IOException.
See Also	write()
Example	The following example demonstrates how to write the information that has been written to the ByteArrayOutputStream object to the standard output stream:

```
void Write(ByteArrayOutputStream baos) throws IOException
{
    baos.writeTo(System.out);
}
```

The java.io.BufferedInputStream Class

The BufferedInputStream class buffers the data coming from an input stream. A read from a BufferedInputStream object will not necessarily cause a read from the underlying input stream. Rather, the data will be read from an internal buffer. If the buffer is emptied, it will be refilled with data from the input stream. Buffering improves performance when reading from slow input devices by reading a large number of bytes at once, rather than by performing a series of smaller read operations. Tables 13-6 and 13-7 list and briefly describe all of the variables and methods defined by class BufferedInputStream.

Table 13-6 Summary of BufferedInputStream variables

Variable	Description
buf	A reference to the internal buffer
count	The number of bytes in the internal buffer
marklimit	The maximum number of bytes that may be read beyond a marked position before reset will fail to reposition the stream
markpos	The position of the mark in the internal buffer
pos	The current position in the internal buffer

Table 13-7 Summary of BufferedInputStream methods

Method	Description
available	Returns the number of bytes available
mark	Marks the current position
markSupported	Indicates whether or not this stream supports marks
read	Reads data from the input stream
reset	Repositions the stream to the last marked position
skip	Skips ahead in the input stream

BufferedInputStream

Description	The BufferedInputStream class buffers the data coming from an input stream.
Syntax	public class **BufferedInputStream** extends FilterInputStream
Package	java.io
Import	java.io.BufferedInputStream
Constructors	public **BufferedInputStream**(InputStream *in*)
	public **BufferedInputStream**(InputStream *in*, int *nSize*)
Parameters	
InputStream *in*	The InputStream object from which to read the data to be buffered.
int *nSize*	The initial size of the internal buffer.
Comments	The constructors create a BufferedInputStream object from the InputStream object specified in the parameter list. The size of the internal buffer may be specified in the parameter list. A read from a BufferedInputStream object will not necessarily cause a read from the underlying input stream. Rather, the data will be read from the internal buffer. If the buffer is emptied, it will be refilled with data from the input stream.

Example
This example demonstrates how to create a BufferedInputStream object with a buffer of a particular size.

```
void Create(InputStream is)
{
   BufferedInputStream bis = new BufferedInputStream(is, 1000);

   // process
}
```

Variables

BUF

Class Name	BufferedInputStream
Description	This variable contains a reference to the internal buffer. It provides derived classes direct access to the internal buffer.
Syntax	protected byte [] **buf**
Example	The following example demonstrates how a derived class might access the bytes in the internal buffer:

```
class DerivedBufferedInputStream extends BufferedInputStream
{
   DerivedBufferedInputStream(InputStream is)
   {
      super(is); // call BufferedInputStream()

      // read and/or write the internal state of
      // the BufferedInputStream

      byte [] rgb = buf;

      // process
   }
}
```

COUNT

Class Name	BufferedInputStream
Description	This variable contains the number of bytes in the internal buffer.
Syntax	protected int **count**
Example	The following example demonstrates how a derived class might access the number of bytes in the internal buffer:

```
class DerivedBufferedInputStream extends BufferedInputStream
{
```

continued on next page

continued from previous page

```
    DerivedBufferedInputStream(InputStream is)
    {
        super(is); // call BufferedInputStream()

        // read and/or write the internal state of
        // the BufferedInputStream

        int n = count;

        // process
    }
}
```

MARKLIMIT

Class Name	BufferedInputStream
Description	This variable contains the maximum number of bytes that may be read beyond a marked position before reset will fail to reposition the stream.
Syntax	protected int **marklimit**
See Also	markpos
Example	The following example demonstrates how a derived class might access the mark limit:

```
class DerivedBufferedInputStream extends BufferedInputStream
{
    DerivedBufferedInputStream(InputStream is)
    {
        super(is); // call BufferedInputStream()

        // read and/or write the internal state of
        // the BufferedInputStream

        int n = marklimit;

        // process
    }
}
```

MARKPOS

Class Name	BufferedInputStream
Description	This variable contains the position of the mark in the internal buffer.
Syntax	protected int **markpos**
See Also	marklimit
Example	The following example demonstrates how a derived class might access the mark position:

```
class DerivedBufferedInputStream extends BufferedInputStream
{
    DerivedBufferedInputStream(InputStream is)
    {
        super(is); // call BufferedInputStream()

        // read and/or write the internal state of
        // the BufferedInputStream

        int n = markpos;

        // process
    }
}
```

POS

Class Name	BufferedInputStream
Description	This variable contains the current position in the internal buffer.
Syntax	protected int **pos**
Example	The following example demonstrates how a derived class might access the current position in the internal buffer:

```
class DerivedBufferedInputStream extends BufferedInputStream
{
    DerivedBufferedInputStream(InputStream is)
    {
        super(is); // call BufferedInputStream()

        // read and/or write the internal state of
        // the BufferedInputStream

        int n = pos;

        // process
    }
}
```

Methods

AVAILABLE

Class Name	BufferedInputStream
Description	This method returns the number of bytes that can be read from this stream before blocking will occur.
Syntax	public synchronized int **available**()
Parameters	None.

Returns	An integer containing the number of available bytes.
Exceptions	If the number of bytes available cannot be determined, this method will throw an IOException. This might occur, for instance, if the input stream had previously been closed.
Comments	If an input stream is empty, a read operation on that stream will block until data becomes available. Often this is undesirable. In a loop in which the processing of data read from the input stream must be interspersed with other processing, blocking must be avoided. This method allows the program to determine whether data is available before attempting to read it.
Example	The following example demonstrates how to use this method to determine the number of bytes available in an input stream:

```
void ProcessLoop(BufferedInputStream [] rgbis) throws IOException
{
   while (true)
   {
      for (int i = 0; i < rgbis.length; i++)
      {
         if (rgbis[i].available() > 0)
         {
            // read and process the available bytes

            int nNext = rgbis[i].read();
              .
              .
              .
         }
      }
   }
}
```

MARK

Class Name	BufferedInputStream
Description	This method marks the current position in the input stream. Subsequent calls to reset() will reposition the stream to this position.
Syntax	public synchronized void **mark**(int *nLimit*)
Parameters	
int *nLimit*	This parameter specifies the number of bytes that may be read past this mark before the mark becomes invalid.
Returns	None.
Exceptions	None.
See Also	markSupported(), reset()
Comments	The mark() and reset() methods together provide a convenient mechanism for looking ahead at the data in an input stream. In a typical application, a program first sets a mark and then reads from the input stream. If the

program cannot use the information in that portion of the input stream, the program repositions the stream at the mark and then passes the input stream to the proper handler. The amount of look ahead is limited and must be specified when the mark is set.

Example   The following example demonstrates how to mark a position in the input stream and later reset the stream to that position:

```
void MarkAndReset(BufferedInputStream bis) throws IOException
{
   bis.mark(100); // mark the current position

   // read data from the stream

   bis.reset(); // reposition the stream
}
```

MARKSUPPORTED

Class Name	BufferedInputStream
Description	This method indicates whether or not this stream type supports the mark and reset operations. One of the functions of a BufferedInputStream object is to add mark and reset support to input streams that do not already provide such support.
Syntax	public boolean **markSupported**()
Parameters	None.
Returns	The boolean value true—marks are supported.
Exceptions	None.
See Also	mark(), reset()
Comments	Attempting the reset operation on an input stream that does not support marks will result in an IOException. A program should therefore determine whether or not a stream supports marks before using reset().
Example	The following example demonstrates how to determine whether or not an input stream supports marks:

```
void Process(InputStream is) throws IOException
{
   if (!is.markSupported())
   {
      // if this stream does not support marks,
      // create a new stream that does

      is = new BufferedInputStream(is);
   }

   is.mark(50);

   // continue processing
}
```

READ

Class Name	BufferedInputStream
Description	These methods read a byte or series of bytes from the input stream.
Syntax	public synchronized int **read**()
	public synchronized int **read**(byte [] *rgb*, int *nOffset*, int *nLength*)
Parameters	
byte [] *rgb*	The byte array to read bytes into.
int *nOffset*	The offset from the beginning of the byte array.
int *nLength*	The number of bytes to read.
Returns	An int. The first of these two methods returns the value read from the input stream. Even though the result is returned as an int rather than as a byte, only values in the range 0 to 256 are permissible. It is possible to write a method that does return the full range of int values, but that would certainly cause incompatibility with the other classes in the Java language I/O class library. The other method returns the number of bytes read into the byte array. Both return a value of -1 if no more data is available from the input stream.
Exceptions	If data cannot be read from the input stream, these methods will throw an IOException.
Example	The following example demonstrates how to read from an input stream:

```
void ReadAndProcess(BufferedInputStream bis) throws IOException
{
   while (true)
   {
      int b = bis.read();

      // process byte

      byte [] rgb = new byte [100];

      bis.read(rgb, 10, rgb.length);

      // process byte array
   }
}
```

RESET

Class Name	BufferedInputStream
Description	This method repositions the stream to the last marked position.
Syntax	public synchronized void **reset**()
Parameters	None.
Returns	None.

Exceptions	If the input stream has not been marked or if the mark is invalid, this method will throw an IOException.
See Also	mark(), markSupported()
Comments	The mark() and reset() methods together provide a convenient mechanism for looking ahead at the data in an input stream. In a typical application, a program first sets a mark and then reads from the input stream. If the program cannot use the information in that portion of the input stream, the program repositions the stream at the mark and then passes the input stream to the proper handler. The amount of look ahead is limited and must be specified when the mark is set.
Example	The following example demonstrates how to mark a position in the input stream and later reset the stream to that position:

```
void MarkAndReset(BufferedInputStream bis) throws IOException
{
   bis.mark(100); // mark the current position

   // read data from the stream

   bis.reset(); // reposition the stream
}
```

SKIP

Class Name	BufferedInputStream
Description	This method skips up to *n* bytes ahead in the input stream. It will skip fewer than *n* bytes ahead if a full skip would cause the call to block.
Syntax	public synchronized long **skip**(long *n*)
Parameters	
long *n*	The number of bytes to skip.
Returns	The number of bytes skipped. This method returns a value of -1 if no more data is available from the stream.
Exceptions	If an error occurs while skipping ahead in the input stream, this method will throw an IOException.
Example	The following example demonstrates how to skip over a portion of an input stream:

```
boolean SkipAhead(BufferedInputStream bis) throws IOException
{
   int i = bis.read(); // determine how far to skip ahead

   int n = bis.skip(i); // skip ahead

   return n < i;
}
```

The java.io.BufferedOutputStream Class

The BufferedOutputStream class buffers the data going to an output stream. A write to a BufferedOutputStream object will not necessarily cause a write to the underlying output stream. Rather, the data will be written to an internal buffer. When the buffer fills completely, the data it contains will be written to the output stream. Buffering improves performance when writing to slow output devices by writing a large number of bytes at once, rather than by performing a series of smaller write operations. Tables 13-8 and 13-9 list and briefly describe all of the variables and methods defined by class BufferedOutputStream.

Table 13-8 Summary of BufferedOutputStream variables

Variable	Description
buf	A reference to the internal buffer
count	The number of bytes in the buffer

Table 13-9 Summary of BufferedOutputStream methods

Method	Description
flush	Flushes the output stream
write	Writes data to the output stream

BUFFEREDOUTPUTSTREAM

Description	The BufferedOutputStream class buffers the data going to an output stream.
Syntax	public class **BufferedOutputStream** extends FilterOutputStream
Package	java.io
Import	java.io.BufferedOutputStream
Constructors	public **BufferedOutputStream**(OutputStream *out*)
	public **BufferedOutputStream**(OutputStream *out*, int *nSize*)
Parameters	
OutputStream *out*	The OutputStream object to which to write the buffered data.
int *nSize*	The initial size of the internal buffer.
Comments	The constructors create a BufferedOutputStream object from the OutputStream object specified in the parameter list. The size of the internal buffer may be specified in the parameter list. A write to a

BufferedOutputStream object will not necessarily cause a write to the underlying output stream. Rather, the data will be written to the internal buffer. When the buffer fills completely, the data it contains will be written to the output stream.

Example   This example demonstrates how to create a BufferedOutputStream object with a buffer of a specific size.

```
void Create(OutputStream os)
{
    BufferedOutputStream bos = new BufferedOutputStream(os, 1000);

    // process
}
```

Variables

BUF

Class Name	BufferedOutputStream
Description	This variable contains a reference to the internal buffer. It provides derived classes direct access to the internal buffer.
Syntax	protected byte [] **buf**
Example	The following example demonstrates how a derived class might access the bytes in the internal buffer:

```
class DerivedBufferedOutputStream extends BufferedOutputStream
{
    DerivedBufferedOutputStream(OutputStream os)
    {
        super(os); // call BufferedOutputStream()

        // read and/or write the internal state of
        // the BufferedOutputStream

        byte [] rgb = buf;

        // process
    }
}
```

COUNT

Class Name	BufferedOutputStream
Description	This variable contains the number of bytes in the buffer.
Syntax	protected int **count**

Example   The following example demonstrates how a derived class might access the number of bytes in the internal buffer:

```
class DerivedBufferedOutputStream extends BufferedOutputStream
{
    DerivedBufferedOutputStream(OutputStream os)
    {
        super(os); // call BufferedOutputStream()

        // read and/or write the internal state of
        // the BufferedOutputStream

        int n = count;

        // process
    }
}
```

Methods

FLUSH

Class Name	BufferedOutputStream
Description	This method flushes the BufferedOutputStream object. Flushing immediately writes any buffered data. The stream is automatically flushed whenever the internal buffer fills up with data.
Syntax	public synchronized void **flush**()
Parameters	None.
Returns	None.
Exceptions	If the output stream cannot be flushed, this method will throw an IOException.
Comments	Output streams are usually buffered for performance reasons. Output devices such as hard disks can write a block of data just as fast as they can write a single byte of data. It therefore makes sense to write data in blocks if possible. By storing up sequential bytes of data and then writing them all at one time, buffered output streams take advantage of the fact that computer memory is typically many orders of magnitude faster than most output devices.
Example	The following example demonstrates how to flush an output stream:

```
void ProcessData(BufferedOutputStream bos) throws IOException
{
    for (int i = 0; i < 100; i++)
    {
```

```
        int n = getValueAtPoint(i);

        bos.write(n);
    }

    bos.flush(); // flush stream
}
```

WRITE

Class Name	BufferedOutputStream
Description	These methods write a byte or series of bytes to the output stream.
Syntax	public synchronized void **write**(int *n*)
	public synchronized void **write**(byte [] *rgb*, int *nOffset*, int *nLength*)
Parameters	
int *n*	The byte to write. Even though this parameter is passed to this method as an int rather than a byte, only values in the range -128 to ≤127 should be used. It is possible to write a method that does accept the full range of integer values, but that would certainly cause incompatibility with the other classes in the Java language I/O class library.
byte [] *rgb*	The byte array to write.
int *nOffset*	The offset from the beginning of the byte array.
int *nLength*	The number of bytes to write, beginning at the offset.
Returns	None.
Exceptions	If data cannot be written to the output stream, these methods will throw an IOException.
Example	The following example demonstrates how to write to an output stream:

```
void GenerateAndWrite(BufferedOutputStream bos) throws IOException
{
    while (true)
    {
        int b;

        // generate byte

        bos.write(b);

        byte [] rgb;

        // generate byte array

        bos.write(rgb, 10, rgb.length);
    }
}
```

The java.io.SequenceInputStream Class

The SequenceInputStream class joins two or more input streams together as one without actually copying the contents of each stream. Table 13-10 lists and briefly describes all of the methods defined by class SequenceInputStream.

Table 13-10 Summary of SequenceInputStream methods

Method	Description
close	Closes the input stream
read	Reads data from the input stream

SEQUENCEINPUTSTREAM

Description	The SequenceInputStream class joins two or more input streams together as one.
Syntax	public class **SequenceInputStream** extends InputStream
Package	java.io
Import	java.io.SequenceInputStream
Constructors	public **SequenceInputStream**(Enumeration *e*)
	public **SequenceInputStream**(InputStream *inFirst*, InputStream *inNext*)
Parameters	
Enumeration *e*	An Enumeration—the elements of the Enumeration object must be InputStream objects.
InputStream	The first InputStream object from which to read data. *inFirst*
InputStream	The second InputStream object from which to read data. *inNext*
Comments	The constructors create a SequenceInputStream object from the set of InputStream objects specified in the parameter list. A SequenceInputStream object joins together two or more input streams without actually copying the contents of each stream. Data is read from an InputStream object until end of file. Data is then read from the next InputStream object in the set.
Example	This example demonstrates two ways to create a SequenceInputStream object from two InputStream objects.

```
void Create(InputStream isOne, InputStream isTwo)
{
    SequenceInputStream sis;

    sis = new SequenceInputStream(isOne, isTwo);
```

```
    // or

    Vector vec = new Vector();

    vec.addElement(isOne);
    vec.addElemtnt(isTwo);

    sis = new SequenceInputStream(vec.elements());
}
```

Methods

CLOSE

Class Name	SequenceInputStream
Description	This method closes the SequenceInputStream object. This action closes each of the input streams that make up this object.
Syntax	public void **close**()
Parameters	None.
Returns	None.
Exceptions	If the input stream cannot be closed, this method will throw an IOException.
Comments	Operating systems often allocate memory buffers and similar resources when input streams are created. These resources are typically beyond the reach of the cleanup facilities (such as the automatic garbage collector) provided by the Java runtime system. Therefore these resources must be explicitly returned to the operating system when they are no longer needed. If they are not, the operating system eventually will run out of them. An example of a limited resource is the file descriptors (not to be confused with instances of the FileDescriptor class) that are assigned by the operating system to each open file. After the last file descriptor is allocated, no more files can be opened by that process. Closing an input stream returns the file descriptor to the operating system so that it may be reused.
Example	The following example demonstrates how to close a stream:

```
void ProcessData(SequenceInputStream sis) throws IOException
{
    int n = sis.read();

    for (int i = 0; i < n; i++)
    {
```

continued on next page

continued from previous page

```
    int b = sis.read();

    // process byte
}

sis.close(); // close stream
}
```

READ

Class Name	SequenceInputStream
Description	These methods read a byte or series of bytes from the input stream. They switch input stream sources if they encounter the end-of-file condition in the current input stream source.
Syntax	public int **read**()
	public int **read**(byte [] *rgb*, int *nOffset*, int *nLength*)
Parameters	None.
Returns	An int. The first of these two methods returns the value read from the input stream. Even though the result is returned as an int rather than as a byte, only values in the range 0 to 256 are permissible. It is possible to write a method that does return the full range of int values, but that would certainly cause incompatibility with the other classes in the Java language I/O class library. The other method returns the number of bytes read into the byte array. Both return a value of -1 if no more data is available from the input stream.
Exceptions	If data cannot be read from the input stream, these methods will throw an IOException.
Example	The following example demonstrates how to read from an input stream:

```
void ReadAndProcess(SequenceInputStream sis) throws IOException
{
    while (true)
    {
        int b = sis.read();

        // process byte

        byte [] rgb = new byte [100];

        sis.read(rgb, 10, rgb.length);

        // process byte array
    }
}
```

The java.io.StringBufferInputStream Class

The StringBufferInputStream class allows data to be read from a String object as if it were an input stream. Tables 13-11 and 13-12 list and briefly describe all of the variables and methods defined by class StringBufferInputStream.

Table 13-11 Summary of StringBufferInputStream variables

Variable	Description
buffer	A reference to the internal buffer
count	The number of characters in the internal buffer
pos	The current position in the internal buffer

Table 13-12 Summary of StringBufferInputStream methods

Method	Description
available	Returns the number of bytes available
read	Reads data from the input stream
reset	Repositions the stream to the last marked position
skip	Skips ahead in the input stream

STRINGBUFFERINPUTSTREAM

Description	The StringBufferInputStream class allows data to be read from a String object as if it were an input stream.
Syntax	public class **StringBufferInputStream** extends InputStream
Package	java.io
Import	java.io.StringBufferInputStream
Constructors	public **StringBufferInputStream**(String *str*)
Parameters	
String *str*	The String object to read bytes from. The high-order byte of each Unicode character in the String object will be truncated.
Comments	The constructor creates a StringBufferInputStream object from the String object specified in the parameter list.
Example	This example demonstrates how to create a StringBufferInputStream object from a String object.

```
void Create(String str)
{
    StringBufferInputStream sbis = new StringBufferInputStream(str);

    // process
}
```

Variables

BUFFER

Class Name	StringBufferInputStream
Description	This variable contains a reference to the internal buffer. It provides derived classes direct access to the internal buffer.
Syntax	protected String **buffer**
Example	The following example demonstrates how a derived class might access the characters in the internal buffer:

```
class DerivedStringBufferInputStream extends StringBufferInputStream
{
    DerivedStringBufferInputStream(String str)
    {
        super(str); // call StringBufferInputStream()

        // read and/or write the internal state of
        // the StringBufferInputStream

        String str = buffer;

        // process
    }
}
```

COUNT

Class Name	StringBufferInputStream
Description	This variable contains the number of characters in the internal buffer.
Syntax	protected int **count**
Example	The following example demonstrates how a derived class might access the number of characters in the internal buffer:

```
class DerivedStringBufferInputStream extends StringBufferInputStream
{
    DerivedStringBufferInputStream(String str)
    {
        super(str); // call StringBufferInputStream()

        // read and/or write the internal state of
```

```
   // the StringBufferInputStream

   int n = count;

   // process
   }
}
```

POS

Class Name	StringBufferInputStream
Description	This variable contains the current position in the internal buffer.
Syntax	protected int **pos**
Example	The following example demonstrates how a derived class might access the current position in the internal buffer:

```
class DerivedStringBufferInputStream extends StringBufferInputStream
{
   DerivedStringBufferInputStream(String str)
   {
      super(str); // call StringBufferInputStream()

      // read and/or write the internal state of
      // the StringBufferInputStream

      int n = pos;

      // process
   }
}
```

Methods

AVAILABLE

Class Name	StringBufferInputStream
Description	This method returns the number of bytes that can be read from this stream before blocking will occur.
Syntax	public synchronized int **available**()
Parameters	None.
Returns	An integer containing the number of available bytes.
Exceptions	None.
Comments	If an input stream is empty, a read operation on that stream will block until data becomes available. Often this is undesirable. In a loop in which the processing of data read from the input stream must be interspersed

with other processing, blocking must be avoided. This method allows the program to determine whether data is available before attempting to read it.

Example   The following example demonstrates how to use this method to determine the number of bytes available in an input stream:

```
void ProcessLoop(StringBufferInputStream [] rgsbis)
{
   while (true)
   {
      for (int i = 0; i < rgsbis.length; i++)
      {
         if (rgsbis[i].available() > 0)
         {
            // read and process the available bytes

            int nNext = rgsbis[i].read();
               .
               .
               .
         }
      }
   }
}
```

READ

Class Name	StringBufferInputStream
Description	These methods read a byte or series of bytes from the input stream.
Syntax	public synchronized int **read**()
	public synchronized int **read**(byte [] *rgb*, int *nOffset*, int *nLength*)
Parameters	
byte [] *rgb*	The byte array to read bytes into.
int *nOffset*	The offset from the beginning of the byte array.
int *nLength*	The number of bytes to read.
Returns	An int. The first of these two methods returns the value read from the input stream. Even though the result is returned as an int rather than as a byte, only values in the range 0 to 256 are permissible. It is possible to write a method that does return the full range of int values, but that would certainly cause incompatibility with the other classes in the Java language I/O class library. The other method returns the number of bytes read into the byte array. Both return a value of -1 if no more data is available from the input stream.
Exceptions	None.
Example	The following example demonstrates how to read from an input stream:

```
void ReadAndProcess(StringBufferInputStream sbis)
{
   while (true)
   {
      int b = sbis.read();

      // process byte

      byte [] rgb = new byte [100];

      sbis.read(rgb, 10, rgb.length);

      // process byte array
   }
}
```

RESET

Class Name	StringBufferInputStream
Description	This method repositions the stream to the beginning of the String object. It is not used in conjunction with the mark() method.
Syntax	public synchronized void **reset**()
Parameters	None.
Returns	None.
Exceptions	None.
Comments	By resetting a StringBufferInputStream object, the data in the object can be reused.
Example	The following example demonstrates how to reset a StringBufferInputStream object:

```
void Process(StringBufferInputStream sbis)
{
   // process bytes in stream

   sbis.reset();

   // process bytes again
}
```

SKIP

Class Name	StringBufferInputStream
Description	This method skips up to *n* bytes ahead in the input stream. It will skip fewer than *n* bytes ahead if a full skip would cause the call to block.
Syntax	public synchronized long **skip**(long *n*)
Parameters	
long *n*	The number of bytes to skip.

Returns	The number of bytes skipped. This method returns a value of -1 if no more data is available from the stream.
Exceptions	None.
Example	The following example demonstrates how to skip over a portion of the input stream:

```
boolean SkipAhead(StringBufferInputStream sbis)
{
   int i = sbis.read();  // determine how far to skip ahead

   int n = sbis.skip(i); // skip ahead

   return n < i;
}
```

The java.io.LineNumberInputStream Class

The LineNumberInputStream class provides a mechanism for tracking the number of lines read from an input stream. Table 13-13 lists and briefly describes all of the methods defined by class LineNumberInputStream.

Table 13-13 Summary of LineNumberInputStream methods

Method	Description
available	Returns the number of bytes available
getLineNumber	Gets the current line number
mark	Marks the current position
read	Reads data from the input stream
reset	Repositions the stream to the last marked position
setLineNumber	Sets the current line number
skip	Skips ahead in the input stream

LINENUMBERINPUTSTREAM

Description	The LineNumberInputStream class provides a mechanism for tracking the number of lines read from an input stream.
Syntax	public class **LineNumberInputStream** extends FilterInputStream
Package	java.io
Import	java.io.LineNumberInputStream
Constructors	public **LineNumberInputStream**(InputStream *in*)

Parameters

InputStream *in*   The InputStream object from which to read the lines to be numbered.

Comments   The constructor creates a LineNumberInputStream object from the
                  InputStream object specified in the parameter list. A line is defined as a
                  sequence of characters terminated by a newline character.

Example   This example demonstrates how to create a LineNumberInputStream
                  object from the InputStream object specified in the parameter list.

```
void Create(InputStream is)
{
   LineNumberInputStream lnis = new LineNumberInputStream(is);

   // process
}
```

Methods

AVAILABLE

Class Name   LineNumberInputStream

Description   This method returns the number of bytes that can be read from this stream
                    before blocking will occur.

Syntax   public int **available**()

Parameters   None.

Returns   An integer containing the number of available bytes.

Exceptions   If the number of bytes available cannot be determined, this method will
                    throw an IOException. This might occur, for instance, if the input stream
                    had previously been closed.

Comments   If an input stream is empty, a read operation on that stream will block
                    until data becomes available. Often this is undesirable. In a loop in which
                    the processing of data read from the input stream must be interspersed
                    with other processing, blocking must be avoided. This method allows the
                    program to determine whether data is available before attempting to read
                    it.

Example   The following example demonstrates how to use this method to determine
                    the number of bytes available in an input stream:

```
void ProcessLoop(LineNumberInputStream [] rglnis) throws IOException
{
   while (true)
   {
      for (int i = 0; i < rglnis.length; i++)
```

continued on next page

continued from previous page

```
        {
            if (rglnis[i].available() > 0)
            {
                // read and process the available bytes

                int nNext = rglnis[i].read();
                    .
                    .
                    .
            }
        }
    }
}
```

GETLINENUMBER

Class Name	LineNumberInputStream
Description	This method gets the current line number.
Syntax	public int **getLineNumber**()
Parameters	None.
Returns	The current line number.
Exceptions	None.
See Also	setLineNumber()
Example	The following example demonstrates how to get the current line number of the input stream being processed.

```
void GetLineNumber(LineNumberInputStream lnis)
{
    int n = lnis.getLineNumber();

    // process
}
```

MARK

Class Name	LineNumberInputStream
Description	This method marks the current position in the input stream. Subsequent calls to reset() will reposition the stream to this position.
Syntax	public void **mark**(int *nLimit*)
Parameters	
int *nLimit*	This parameter specifies the number of bytes that may be read past this mark before the mark becomes invalid.
Returns	None.

Exceptions	None.
See Also	reset()
Comments	The mark() and reset() methods together provide a convenient mechanism for looking ahead at the data in an input stream. In a typical application, a program first sets a mark and then reads from the input stream. If the program cannot use the information in that portion of the input stream, the program repositions the stream at the mark and then passes the input stream to the proper handler. The amount of look ahead is limited and must be specified when the mark is set.
Example	The following example demonstrates how to mark a position in the input stream and later reset the stream to that position:

```
void MarkAndReset(LineNumberInputStream lnis) throws IOException
{
    lnis.mark(100); // mark the current position

    // read data from the stream

    lnis.reset(); // reposition the stream
}
```

READ

Class Name	LineNumberInputStream
Description	These methods read a byte or series of bytes from the input stream.
Syntax	public int **read**()
	public int **read**(byte [] *rgb*, int *nOffset*, int *nLength*)
Parameters	
byte [] *rgb*	The byte array to read bytes into.
int *nOffset*	The offset from the beginning of the byte array.
int *nLength*	The number of bytes to read.
Returns	An int. The first of these two methods returns the value read from the input stream. Even though the result is returned as an int rather than as a byte, only values in the range 0 to 256 are permissible. It is possible to write a method that does return the full range of int values, but that would certainly cause incompatibility with the other classes in the Java language I/O class library. The other method returns the number of bytes read into the byte array. Both return a value of -1 if no more data is available from the input stream.
Exceptions	If data cannot be read from the input stream, these methods will throw an IOException.
Example	The following example demonstrates how to read from an input stream:

```
void ReadAndProcess(LineNumberInputStream lnis) throws IOException
{
   while (true)
   {
      int b = lnis.read();

      // process byte

      byte [] rgb = new byte [100];

      lnis.read(rgb, 10, rgb.length);

      // process byte array
   }
}
```

RESET

Class Name	LineNumberInputStream
Description	This method repositions the stream to the last marked position.
Syntax	public void **reset**()
Parameters	None.
Returns	None.
Exceptions	If the input stream has not been marked or if the mark is invalid, this method will throw an IOException.
See Also	mark()
Comments	The mark() and reset() methods together provide a convenient mechanism for looking ahead at the data in an input stream. In a typical application, a program first sets a mark and then reads from the input stream. If the program cannot use the information in that portion of the input stream, the program repositions the stream at the mark and then passes the input stream to the proper handler. The amount of look ahead is limited and must be specified when the mark is set.
Example	The following example demonstrates how to mark a position in the input stream and later reset the stream to that position:

```
void MarkAndReset(LineNumberInputStream lnis) throws IOException
{
   lnis.mark(100); // mark the current position

   // read data from the stream

   lnis.reset(); // reposition the stream
}
```

SETLINENUMBER

Class Name	LineNumberInputStream
Description	This method sets the current line number.
Syntax	public void **setLineNumber**(int *nLineNumber*)
Parameters	
int *nLineNumber*	The new value of the current line number.
Returns	None.
Exceptions	None.
See Also	getLineNumber()
Example	The following example demonstrates how to set the current line number of the input stream being processed:

```
void SetLineNumber(LineNumberInputStream lnis)
{
    lnis.setLineNumber(0);

    // process
}
```

SKIP

Class Name	LineNumberInputStream
Description	This method skips up to *n* bytes ahead in the input stream. It will skip fewer than *n* bytes ahead if a full skip would cause the call to block.
Syntax	public long **skip**(long *n*)
Parameters	
long *n*	The number of bytes to skip.
Returns	The number of bytes skipped. This method returns a value of -1 if no more data is available from the stream.
Exceptions	If an error occurs while skipping ahead in the input stream, this method will throw an IOException.
Example	The following example demonstrates how to skip over a portion of the input stream:

```
boolean SkipAhead(LineNumberInputStream lnis) throws IOException
{
    int i = lnis.read();  // determine how far to skip ahead

    int n = lnis.skip(i); // skip ahead

    return n < i;
}
```

The java.io.PushbackInputStream Class

The PushbackInputStream class provides a mechanism for pushing a single character back into the input stream. Tables 13-14 and 13-15 list and briefly describe all of the variables and methods defined by class PushbackInputStream.

Table 13-14 Summary of PushbackInputStream variables

Variable	Description
pushback	The pushback storage location

Table 13-15 Summary of PushbackInputStream methods

Method	Description
available	Returns the number of bytes available
markSupported	Indicates whether or not this stream supports marks
read	Reads data from the input stream
unread	Writes data back to the input stream

PUSHBACKINPUTSTREAM

Description	The PushbackInputStream class allows a single character to be pushed back into the input stream. That character will be returned by the next read.
Syntax	public class **PushbackInputStream** extends FilterInputStream
Package	java.io
Import	java.io.PushbackInputStream
Constructors	public **PushbackInputStream**(InputStream *in*)
Parameters	
InputStream *in*	The InputStream object from which to read data.
Comments	The constructor creates a PushbackInputStream object from the InputStream object specified in the parameter list. It is common to write code that reads and processes characters from a stream until an unexpected character is encountered. When an unexpected character is encountered, that character is pushed back into the stream, and code that can handle that character is called and reading continues. Between reads, only one character may be pushed back into the input stream.

Example
This example demonstrates how to create a PushbackInputStream object from the InputStream object specified in the parameter list.

```
void Create(InputStream is)
{
   PushbackInputInputStream pbis = new PushbackInputStream(is);

   // process
}
```

Variables

PUSHBACK

Class Name
PushbackInputStream

Description
This variable contains the pushback storage location. It provides derived classes direct access to the pushback storage location.

Syntax
protected int **pushback**

Example
The following example demonstrates how to use this variable to get the value of the last character pushed back into the input stream:

```
class DerivedPushbackInputStream extends PushbackInputStream
{
   DerivedPushbackInputStream(InputStream is)
   {
      super(is); // call PushbackInputStream()

      // perform additional processing
   }

   // provide a look at the pushback character

   char peek()
   {
      return in.pushback;
   }
}
```

Methods

AVAILABLE

Class Name
PushbackInputStream

Description
This method returns the number of bytes that can be read from this stream before blocking will occur.

Syntax	public int **available**()
Parameters	None.
Returns	An integer containing the number of available bytes.
Exceptions	If the number of bytes available cannot be determined, this method will throw an IOException. This might occur, for instance, if the input stream had previously been closed.
Comments	If an input stream is empty, a read operation on that stream will block until data becomes available. Often this is undesirable. In a loop in which the processing of data read from the input stream must be interspersed with other processing, blocking must be avoided. This method allows the program to determine whether data is available before attempting to read it.
Example	The following example demonstrates how to use this method to determine the number of bytes available in an input stream:

```
void ProcessLoop(PushBackInputStream [] rgpbis) throws IOException
{
   while (true)
   {
      for (int i = 0; i < rgpbis.length; i++)
      {
         if (rgpbis[i].available() > 0)
         {
            // read and process the available bytes

            int nNext = rgpbis[i].read();
               .
               .
               .
         }
      }
   }
}
```

MARKSUPPORTED

Class Name	PushbackInputStream
Description	This method indicates whether or not this stream type supports the mark and reset operations.
Syntax	public boolean **markSupported**()
Parameters	None.
Returns	The boolean value false—marks are not supported.
Exceptions	None.
See Also	FilterInputStream.mark(), FilterInputStream.reset()

Comments	Attempting the reset operation on an input stream that does not support marks will result in an IOException. A program should therefore determine whether or not a stream supports marks before using reset().
Example	The following example demonstrates how to determine whether or not an input stream supports marks:

```
void Process(InputStream is) throws IOException
{
   if (!is.markSupported())
   {
      // if this stream does not support marks,
      // create a new stream that does

      is = new BufferedInputStream(is);
   }

   is.mark(50); // continue processing
}
```

READ

Class Name	PushbackInputStream
Description	These methods read a byte or series of bytes from the input stream.
Syntax	public int **read**()
	public int **read**(byte [] *rgb*, int *nOffset*, int *nLength*)
Parameters	
byte [] *rgb*	The byte array to read bytes into.
int *nOffset*	The offset from the beginning of the byte array.
int *nLength*	The number of bytes to read.
Returns	An int. The first of these two methods returns the value read from the input stream. Even though the result is returned as an int rather than as a byte, only values in the range 0 to 256 are permissible. It is possible to write a method that does return the full range of int values, but that would certainly cause incompatibility with the other classes in the Java language I/O class library. The other method returns the number of bytes read into the byte array. Both return a value of -1 if no more data is available from the input stream.
Exceptions	If data cannot be read from the input stream, these methods will throw an IOException.
See Also	unread()
Example	The following example demonstrates how to read from an input stream:

```
void ReadAndProcess(PushBackInputStream pbis) throws IOException
{
   while (true)
```

continued on next page

continued from previous page

```
    {
        int b = pbis.read();

        // process byte

        byte [] rgb = new byte [100];

        pbis.read(rgb, 10, rgb.length);

        // process byte array
    }
}
```

UNREAD

Class Name	PushbackInputStream
Description	This method pushes a byte back into the input stream. Only one byte may be so pushed between any two read operations.
Syntax	public void **unread**(int *n*)
Parameters	
int *n*	The byte to push back into the input stream. Even though this parameter is passed to this method as an int rather than a byte, only values in the range -128 to £ 127 should be used.
Returns	None.
Exceptions	If an attempt is made to push back more than one character between read operations, this method will throw an IOException.
See Also	read()
Example	The following example demonstrates how to push a character back into the input stream.

```
void Push(PushbackInputStream pbis) throws IOException
{
    int c;

    while ((c = pbis.read()) < 20)
    {
        // process character
    }

    pbis.unread(c); // push back the last character read

    // process
}
```

The java.io.StreamTokenizer Class

The StreamTokenizer class allows an input stream to be read as a series of tokens rather than characters. The StreamTokenizer class is not an input stream. It is, however, often used in conjunction with input streams. Tables 13-16, 13-17, and 13-18 list and briefly describe all of the constants, variables, and methods defined by class StreamTokenizer.

Table 13-16 Summary of StreamTokenizer constants

Constant	Description
TT_EOF	The token representing end of file
TT_EOL	The token representing end of line
TT_NUMBER	The token representing a number
TT_WORD	The token representing a string

Table 13-17 Summary of StreamTokenizer variables

Variable	Description
nval	The numeric value of the number token
sval	The textual value of the string token
ttype	The value of the current token

Table 13-18 Summary of StreamTokenizer methods

Method	Description
commentChar	Informs the tokenizer that this character begins a single line comment
eolIsSignificant	Informs the tokenizer that the end-of-line condition should be returned as a token
lineno	Returns the current line number
lowerCaseMode	Informs the tokenizer that string should be converted to lowercase before tokenization
nextToken	Scans the input stream for the next token
ordinaryChar	Informs the tokenizer that this character has no special meaning
ordinaryChars	Informs the tokenizer that characters in this range have no special meaning
parseNumbers	Informs the tokenizer that numbers should be parsed
pushBack	Pushes a token back into the tokenizer
quoteChar	Informs the tokenizer that this character is used to delimit quoted strings
resetSyntax	Resets the syntax table used for tokenization
slashSlashComments	Informs the tokenizer that it should recognize C++ style comments
slashStarComments	Informs the tokenizer that it should recognize C style comments
toString	Returns the string representation of the current token
whitespaceChars	Informs the tokenizer that characters in this range should be treated as whitespace
wordChars	Informs the tokenizer that characters in this range are part of words

STREAMTOKENIZER

Description	The StreamTokenizer class allows an input stream to be read as a series of tokens rather than characters. A token is a sequence of one or more characters with a well-defined internal arrangement.
Syntax	public class **StreamTokenizer** extends Object
Package	java.io
Import	java.io.StreamTokenizer
Constructors	public **StreamTokenizer**(InputStream *in*)
Parameters	
InputStream *in*	The InputStream object from which to read the data to be tokenized.
Comments	The constructor creates a StreamTokenizer object from the InputStream object specified in the parameter list. A new StreamTokenizer object must be created for each input stream to be tokenized. By default, a newly created StreamTokenizer object recognizes the sequences of characters that represent numbers (in decimal notation), words (composed of the letters in the English alphabet, the digits from zero to nine, the period, and the dash), quotes (characters between single or double quotation marks), and comments (which begin with a single slash and continue to the end of the line).
Example	The following example demonstrates how to create and use a StreamTokenizer object.

```
void Create(InputStream is)
{
   StreamTokenizer st = new StreamTokenizer(is);

   // modify the default syntax tables

   while (st.nextToken() != st.TT_EOF)
   {
      switch (st.ttype)
      {
         case st.TT_WORD:
            .
            .
            .

   }
}
```

Constants

TT_EOF

Class Name	StreamTokenizer
Description	This constant contains the token representing end of file.

Syntax	public final static int **TT_EOF**
See Also	TT_EOL, TT_NUMBER, TT_WORD
Example	The following example demonstrates how to use this constant when processing the tokens returned during scanning:

```
void Process(InputStream is)
{
   boolean boolEndOfFileFlag = false;

   StreamTokenizer st = new StreamTokenizer(is);

   st.nextToken();

   switch (st.ttype)
   {
      case TT_EOF:
         boolEndOfFileFlag = true;
            .
            .
            .

}
```

TT_EOL

Class Name	StreamTokenizer
Description	This constant contains the token representing end of line.
Syntax	public final static int **TT_EOL**
See Also	TT_EOF, TT_NUMBER, TT_WORD
Example	The following example demonstrates how to use this constant when processing the tokens returned during scanning:

```
void Process(InputStream is)
{
   boolean boolEndOfLineFlag = false;

   StreamTokenizer st = new StreamTokenizer(is);

   st.nextToken();

   switch (st.ttype)
   {
      case TT_EOL:
         boolEndOfLineFlag = true;
            .
            .
            .

}
```

TT_NUMBER

Class Name	StreamTokenizer
Description	This constant contains the token representing a number.
Syntax	public final static int **TT_NUMBER**
See Also	TT_EOF, TT_EOL, TT_WORD
Example	The following example demonstrates how to use this constant when processing the tokens returned during scanning:

```java
void Process(InputStream is)
{
    StreamTokenizer st = new StreamTokenizer(is);

    st.nextToken();

    switch (st.ttype)
    {
        case TT_NUMBER:
            System.out.println(st.nval);
                .
                .
                .
}
```

TT_WORD

Class Name	StreamTokenizer
Description	This constant contains the token representing a string.
Syntax	public final static int **TT_WORD**
See Also	TT_EOF, TT_EOL, TT_NUMBER
Example	The following example demonstrates how to use this constant when processing the tokens returned during scanning:

```java
void Process(InputStream is)
{
    StreamTokenizer st = new StreamTokenizer(is);

    st.nextToken();

    switch (st.ttype)
    {
        case TT_WORD:
            System.out.println(st.sval);
                .
                .
                .
}
```

Variables

NVAL

Class Name	StreamTokenizer
Description	This variable contains the numeric value of the corresponding number token.
Syntax	public double **nval**
See Also	sval
Example	The following example demonstrates how to use this variable to get the numeric value of the last token:

```
void Process(InputStream is)
{
    StreamTokenizer st = new StreamTokenizer(is);

    st.nextToken();

    switch (st.ttype)
    {
       case TT_NUMBER:
          System.out.println(st.nval);
             .
             .
             .
}
```

SVAL

Class Name	StreamTokenizer
Description	This variable contains the textual value of the corresponding string token.
Syntax	public String **sval**
See Also	nval
Example	The following example demonstrates how to use this variable to get the textual value of the last token:

```
void Process(InputStream is)
{
    StreamTokenizer st = new StreamTokenizer(is);

    st.nextToken();

    switch (st.ttype)
    {
       case TT_WORD:
```

continued on next page

continued from previous page

```
        System.out.println(st.sval);
            .
            .
            .
}
```

TTYPE

Class Name	StreamTokenizer
Description	This variable contains the type of the current token.
Syntax	public int **ttype**
Example	The following example demonstrates how to use this variable to get the type of the last token:

```
void Process(InputStream is)
{
    StreamTokenizer st = new StreamTokenizer(is);

    st.nextToken();

    switch (st.ttype)
    {
        .
        .
        .
}
```

Methods

COMMENTCHAR

Class Name	StreamTokenizer
Description	This method is used to inform the tokenizer that the character specified in the parameter list begins a single-line comment.
Syntax	public void **commentChar**(int *nChar*)
Parameters	
int *nChar*	A character.
Returns	None.
Exceptions	None.
See Also	slashSlashComments(), slashStarComments()

Comments	Characters in a line of input, from the comment character to the end of the line, are completely ignored by the tokenizer. More than one character can be specified by multiple calls to this method.
Example	The following example demonstrates how to inform the tokenizer that a character indicates the beginning of a single-line comment:

```
void Process(InputStream is)
{
   StreamTokenizer st = new StreamTokenizer(is);

   // modify the default syntax tables

   st.commentChar('#');

   // process
}
```

EOLISSIGNIFICANT

Class Name	StreamTokenizer
Description	This method is used to inform the tokenizer that the end-of-line condition should be returned as a token instead of ignored.
Syntax	public void **eolIsSignificant**(boolean *bool*)
Parameters	
boolean *bool*	A boolean value that should be set to true if the end-of-line condition should be returned as a token and set to false otherwise.
Returns	None.
Exceptions	None.
Comments	Typically, the end of a line is not syntactically important for parsing. The newline character at the end of a line is considered to be whitespace. In the Java programming language, for example, a statement or expression can span several lines. However, in some languages, the end of a line indicates the end of a statement or expression, and is syntactically very important.
Example	The following example demonstrates how to use this method to indicate that the end-of-line condition is syntactically important for scanning:

```
void Process(InputStream is)
{
   StreamTokenizer st = new StreamTokenizer(is);

   // modify the default syntax tables

   st.eolIsSignificant(true);

   // process
}
```

LINENO

Class Name	StreamTokenizer
Description	This method returns the current line number.
Syntax	public int **lineno**()
Parameters	None.
Returns	The current line number.
Exceptions	None.
Example	The following example demonstrates how to determine the current line number of an input stream being scanned:

```
void GetLineNumber(StreamTokenizer st)
{
    int n = st.lineno();

    // process
}
```

LOWERCASEMODE

Class Name	StreamTokenizer
Description	This method is used to inform the tokenizer that strings should be automatically converted to lowercase before tokenization.
Syntax	public void **lowerCaseMode**(boolean *bool*)
Parameters	
boolean *bool*	A boolean value that should be set to true if string tokens should be converted to lowercase and set to false otherwise.
Returns	None.
Exceptions	None.
Comments	The distinction between upper- and lowercase is sometimes of no importance to an application. In such cases, program logic can be simplified if case information is removed from the returned tokens. This method performs such pruning by instructing the tokenizer to convert all strings to lowercase before returning the appropriate token.
Example	The following example demonstrates how to use this method to indicate that string tokens should be converted to lowercase before being returned:

```
void Process(InputStream is)
{
    StreamTokenizer st = new StreamTokenizer(is);

    // modify the default syntax tables

    st.lowerCaseMode(true);
```

```
   // process
}
```

NEXTTOKEN

Class Name	StreamTokenizer
Description	This method is used to cause the tokenizer to scan the input stream for another token.
Syntax	public int **nextToken**()
Parameters	None.
Returns	The new token. This value is also placed in the member variable *ttype*.
Exceptions	If an error occurs while scanning for the next token, this method will throw an IOException.
Comments	A StreamTokenizer object is typically used in the following fashion: First, a new StreamTokenizer is created. Second, the default syntax tables are modified if necessary. Third, the program enters a loop in which a token is fetched (via a call to the nextToken() method) and processed. The program continues to loop as long as the tokenizer finds tokens to return.
Example	The following example demonstrates how to use this method to return successive tokens from the input stream:

```
void Process(InputStream is) throws IOException
{
   StreamTokenizer st = new StreamTokenizer(is);

   // modify the default syntax tables

   while (st.nextToken() != st.TT_EOF)
   {
      switch (st.ttype)
      {
         case st.TT_WORD:
            .
            .
            .
   }
}
```

ORDINARYCHAR

Class Name	StreamTokenizer
Description	This method is used to inform the tokenizer that the character specified in the parameter list has no special meaning.
Syntax	public void **ordinaryChar**(int *n*)
Parameters	
int *n*	A character.

Returns	None.
Exceptions	None.
See Also	ordinaryChars()
Comments	An ordinary character has no special meaning. It is not part of a word, a string, or a number. An ordinary character is itself a token and is returned as such from a call to the nextToken() method.
Example	The following example demonstrates how to inform the tokenizer that a character has no special meaning:

```
void Process(InputStream is)
{
    StreamTokenizer st = new StreamTokenizer(is);

    // modify the default syntax tables

    st.ordinaryChar('+');

    // process
}
```

ORDINARYCHARS

Class Name	StreamTokenizer
Description	This method is used to inform the tokenizer that characters in the range *nLow* to *nHigh* have no special meaning.
Syntax	public void **ordinaryChars**(int *nLow*, int *nHigh*)
Parameters	
int *nLow*	The low end of the character range.
int *nHigh*	The high end of the character range.
Returns	None.
Exceptions	None.
See Also	ordinaryChar()
Comments	An ordinary character has no special meaning. It is not part of a word, a string, or a number. An ordinary character is itself a token and is returned as such from a call to the nextToken() method.
Example	The following example demonstrates how to inform the tokenizer that a range of characters has no special meaning:

```
void Process(InputStream is)
{
    StreamTokenizer st = new StreamTokenizer(is);

    // modify the default syntax tables
```

```
   st.ordinaryChar('0', '9');

   // process
}
```

PARSE**N**UMBERS

Class Name	StreamTokenizer
Description	This method is used to inform the tokenizer that numbers should be parsed and returned as tokens. The parsing of numbers can be turned off by resetting the syntax table or by making all of the digit characters as well as the characters "." and "-" ordinary.
Syntax	public void **parseNumbers**()
Parameters	None.
Returns	None.
Exceptions	None.
Example	The following example demonstrates how to inform the tokenizer that numbers should be parsed:

```
void Process(InputStream is)
{
   StreamTokenizer st = new StreamTokenizer(is);

   // modify the default syntax tables

   st.parseNumbers();

   // process
}
```

PUSH**B**ACK

Class Name	StreamTokenizer
Description	This method pushes the current token back into the StreamTokenizer object.
Syntax	public void **pushBack**()
Parameters	None.
Returns	None.
Exceptions	None.
Comments	It is common practice to write code that reads and processes tokens from a stream until an unexpected token is encountered in the stream. The code then pushes that token back into the stream and returns. Alternate code is then evoked and reading continues.

Example   The following example demonstrates how to use this method to push the
                     current token back into the tokenizer:

```
void Process(InputStream is)
{
   StreamTokenizer st = new StreamTokenizer(is);

   // modify the default syntax tables

   while (st.nextToken() != st.TT_EOF)
   {
      if (st.ttype == '<')
      {
         st.pushBack();
         break;
      }

      // process
   }

   // process
}
```

QUOTECHAR

Class Name	StreamTokenizer
Description	This method is used to inform the tokenizer that the character specified in the parameter list is used to delimit quoted strings.
Syntax	public void **quoteChar**(int *nChar*)
Parameters	
int *nChar*	A character.
Returns	None.
Exceptions	None.
Comments	When a quoted string is encountered, the nextToken() method will return the quote delimiter character, and the string itself will be placed in the variable *nval*.
Example	The following example demonstrates how to inform the tokenizer that a character delimits a quoted string:

```
void Process(InputStream is)
{
   StreamTokenizer st = new StreamTokenizer(is);

   // modify the default syntax tables

   st.quoteChar('"');

   // process
}
```

RESETSYNTAX

Class Name	StreamTokenizer
Description	This method resets the syntax table used by the tokenizer. As a consequence, none of the characters from the input stream has special meaning.
Syntax	public void **resetSyntax**()
Parameters	None.
Returns	None.
Exceptions	None.
Comments	A StreamTokenizer object is created with a default syntax table that may be totally inappropriate for the problem to which it is being applied. In such a situation, it may be easier to reset and then re-create the syntax table rather than fix it.
Example	The following example demonstrates how to use this method to reset the internal syntax table:

```
void Process(InputStream is)
{
    StreamTokenizer st = new StreamTokenizer(is);

    st.resetSyntax();

    // modify the default syntax tables
}
```

SLASHSLASHCOMMENTS

Class Name	StreamTokenizer
Description	This method is used to inform the tokenizer that it should recognize C++ style comments. C++ style comments begin with two slashes ("//") and continue to the end of the line. Manipulation of the syntax table alone will not allow the tokenizer to properly distinguish C++ style comments.
Syntax	public void **slashSlashComments**(boolean *bool*)
Parameters	
boolean *bool*	A boolean value that should be set to true if the tokenizer should recognize C++ style comments and set to false otherwise.
Returns	None.
Exceptions	None.
See Also	commentChar(), slashStarComments()
Example	The following example demonstrates how to inform the tokenizer that it should recognize C++ style comments:

```
void Process(InputStream is)
{
   StreamTokenizer st = new StreamTokenizer(is);

   // modify the default syntax tables

   st.slashSlashComments(true);

   // process
}
```

SLASHSTARCOMMENTS

Class Name	StreamTokenizer
Description	This method is used to inform the tokenizer that it should recognize C style comments. C style comments begin with a slash-asterisk pair ("/*") and continue until an asterisk-slash pair ("*/") is encountered. Manipulation of the syntax table alone will not allow the tokenizer to properly distinguish C style comments.
Syntax	public void **slashStarComments**(boolean *bool*)
Parameters	
boolean *bool*	A boolean value that should be set to true if the tokenizer should recognize C style comments and set to false otherwise.
Returns	None.
Exceptions	None.
See Also	commentChar(), slashSlashComments()
Example	The following example demonstrates how to inform the tokenizer that it should recognize C style comments:

```
void Process(InputStream is)
{
   StreamTokenizer st = new StreamTokenizer(is);

   // modify the default syntax tables

   st.slashStarComments(true);

   // process
}
```

TOSTRING

Class Name	StreamTokenizer
Description	This method returns the string representation of the current token.

Syntax	public String **toString**()
Parameters	None.
Returns	A String object.
Exceptions	None.
Example	The following example demonstrates how to use this method to return the string representation of the current token:

```
void Process(InputStream is)
{
    StreamTokenizer st = new StreamTokenizer(is);

    // modify the default syntax tables

    while (st.nextToken() != st.TT_EOF)
    {
        System.out.println(st.toString());
    }
}
```

WHITESPACE**C**HARS

Class Name	StreamTokenizer
Description	This method is used to inform the tokenizer that characters in the range *nLow* to *nHigh* are whitespace characters:
Syntax	public void **whitespaceChars**(int *nLow*, int *nHigh*)
Parameters	
int *nLow*	The low end of the character range.
int *nHigh*	The high end of the character range.
Returns	None.
Exceptions	None.
Comments	Whitespace separates tokens but is otherwise ignored by the tokenizer.
Example	The following example demonstrates how to inform the tokenizer that a range of characters are whitespace characters:

```
void Process(InputStream is)
{
    StreamTokenizer st = new StreamTokenizer(is);

    // modify the default syntax tables

    st.whitespaceChars(0, ' ');

    // process
}
```

WORDCHARS

Class Name	StreamTokenizer
Description	This method is used to inform the tokenizer that characters in the range *nLow* to *nHigh* are part of words. Sequential word characters are grouped together and returned as a single token.
Syntax	public void **wordChars**(int *nLow*, int *nHigh*)
Parameters	
int *nLow*	The low end of the character range.
int *nHigh*	The high end of the character range.
Returns	None.
Exceptions	None.
Comments	In a programming language like Java, words typically represent keywords (*if*, *then*, *else*, *try*…) or identifiers (variable names, function names, class names…).
Example	The following example demonstrates how to inform the tokenizer that a range of characters are word characters:

```
void Process(InputStream is)
{
   StreamTokenizer st = new StreamTokenizer(is);

   // modify the default syntax tables

   st.wordChars('a', 'z');
   st.wordChars('A', 'Z');

   // process
}
```

The Additional I/O Project: An HTML Parser

Project Overview

An HTML document consists of two types of information: data characters and markup. The data characters of the document define the text of the document, the markup controls how that text is displayed. Consider the HTML in Listing 13-2. The text of the document consists of the phrases "Sample Document", "This is an example of a simple sample document.", and "By Dr. Seuss". Everything else is markup. The first step in parsing HTML is distinguishing between the text and the markup.

Listing 13-2 Sample.html

```
<title>Sample Document</title>

<body>
```

```
<h1>Sample Document</h1>
This is an example of a simple sample document. <br>
By Dr. Seuss <br>
</body>
```

The HTML parser implemented in this project is somewhat limited. It contains only enough features to demonstrate the functionality of the classes in this chapter. Its most noticeable limitations are

■ It doesn't recognize entity character references (such as &lt, &gt, &amp, or &quot).

■ It doesn't recognize numeric character references (such as &#60).

■ It doesn't recognize document type declarations.

■ It doesn't recognize comment declarations.

Aside from these limitations, the parser is capable of separating data characters from HTML tags, and of parsing the information contained within the tags.

Building the Project

1. The file Parser.java contains the definition of the Parser class. The parse() method provided by the Parser class consists of two sections. The code in the first section scans the input stream and looks for the '<' character, which signifies the beginning of a tag. Once it has been found, the parser pushes that character back into the input stream and calls the tag parser (which expects to read the '<' character itself). An instance of class LineNumberInputStream is used to count the input lines. An instance of class PushbackInputStream allows the parser to push the character it has read back into the input stream.

```java
import java.io.InputStream;
import java.io.LineNumberInputStream;
import java.io.PushbackInputStream;
import java.io.IOException;

class Parser
{
    static void parse(InputStream is) throws IOException
    {
        LineNumberInputStream lnis = new LineNumberInputStream(is);
        PushbackInputStream pbis = new PushbackInputStream(lnis);

        int c;

        while (true)
        {
            while ((c = pbis.read()) > -1)
            {
                if (c == '<')
```

continued on next page

continued from previous page

```
            {
                pbis.unread(c);
                break;
            }
        }

        if (c < 0) break;

        System.out.println("tag at line " + Lnis.getLineNumber());

        try
        {
            TagParser.parse(pbis);
        }
        catch (SyntaxError se)
        {
            System.out.println(se);
        }
        }
    }
}
```

2. The file TagParser.java contains the definition of the TagParser class. It requires several classes from the Java language class library.

```
import java.io.InputStream;
import java.io.StreamTokenizer;
import java.io.IOException;
```

3. An instance of class SyntaxError is created and thrown if the tag parser fails to parse the input stream. This class extends the definitions of the basic Exception class.

```
class SyntaxError extends Exception
{
    SyntaxError() { super(); }
    SyntaxError(String str) { super(str); }
}
```

4. The tag parser requires the services of the StreamTokenizer class. It first creates an instance of StreamTokenizer and resets the syntax table, thus deleting the default configuration. The tag parser then defines a syntax table configuration suitable for parsing HTML.

```
class TagParser
{
    static void parse(InputStream is) throws IOException, SyntaxError
    {
        boolean boolEndTag = false;

        StreamTokenizer st = new StreamTokenizer(is);

        st.resetSyntax();
```

```
st.lowerCaseMode(true);
st.wordChars('a', 'z');
st.wordChars('A', 'Z');
st.wordChars('_', '_');
st.whitespaceChars(' ', ' ');
st.whitespaceChars('\n', '\n');
st.whitespaceChars('\t', '\t');
st.quoteChar('\'');
st.quoteChar('"');
st.parseNumbers();
```

5. The nextToken() method returns successive tokens from the input stream. If an unexpected token is encountered, a SyntaxError exception is generated and thrown. The tag parser first checks for the presence of the '<' character. The '<' character signifies the beginning of a tag.

```
st.nextToken();
if (st.ttype != '<')
{
    throw new SyntaxError("'<' expected");
}
```

6. The tag parser then determines whether or not the tag name begins with the slash ('/') character. Such tags are called *end tags*. In HTML, tags often (but not always) come in pairs. The first tag, called the *start tag*, indicates that the text that follows has a particular property or is of a particular type. The corresponding end tag has the same name as the start tag, except that its name is preceded by a slash character. The presence of an end tag indicates the end of the region. If any character other than the '/' character is encountered, it is pushed back into the tokenizer.

```
st.nextToken();
if (st.ttype == '/')
{
    boolEndTag = true;
}
else
{
    st.pushBack();
}
```

7. The tag parser now expects to find a word. In step 4, a word was defined to be any sequence of characters consisting of the uppercase letters, the lowercase letters, the digits, the period, the dash, and the underscore. The word is the tag name.

```
st.nextToken();
if (st.ttype != st.TT_WORD)
{
    throw new SyntaxError("invalid tag name");
}
if (boolEndTag)
```

continued on next page

continued from previous page

```
{
    System.out.println("end-tag: " + st.sval);
}
else
{
    System.out.println("start-tag: " + st.sval);
}
```

8. A tag may have zero or more attribute specifications. An attribute specification typically consists of a word, followed by the equal sign, followed by the attribute value. An attribute specification may simply be, however, just a name. The attribute value may be a string (enclosed in either single or double quotation marks), a word, or a number. This section of code loops until the '>' character, signifying the end of the tag, occurs and identifies the attribute specifications.

```
while(true)
{
    st.nextToken();
    if (st.ttype == '>') return;

    if (st.ttype != st.TT_WORD)
    {
        throw new SyntaxError("invalid attribute name");
    }
    String str = st.sval;

    st.nextToken();
    if (st.ttype == '=')
    {
        st.nextToken();
        if (st.ttype == '"' || st.ttype == '\'')
        {
            System.out.println(" value: " + str + " = " + st.sval);
        }
        else if (st.ttype == st.TT_WORD)
        {
            System.out.println(" value: " + str + " = " + st.sval);
        }
        else if (st.ttype == st.TT_NUMBER)
        {
            System.out.println(" value: " + str + " = " + st.nval);
        }
        else
        {
            throw new SyntaxError("invalid attribute value");
        }
    }
    else
    {
        st.pushBack();
    }
}
}
```

```
}
```

9. The file Main.java contains the code that initializes the system. The parser accepts input from three different sources: the argument list, standard input (the keyboard), or files. Each input source is handled by a different input stream type. Input from the argument list is transformed into an input stream by an instance of the StringBufferInputStream class. Input from standard input is transformed into an input stream by reading from standard input and writing to an instance of class ByteArrayOutputStream. The byte array is then extracted and a ByteArrayInputStream is created. This multistep process is necessary so that more than one input record can be read from standard input (each separated by end-of-file markers). File input is retrieved by opening the file named on the command line with an instance of FileInputStream. Each of these input streams is combined into one by using a SequenceInputStream object. Finally, the parser itself is called on the resulting instance of SequenceInputStream.

```java
import java.util.Vector;
import java.io.*;

class Main
{
   public static void main(String [] args)
   {
      try
      {
         Vector vec = new Vector();

         // Parse the command line arguments.  This program supports
         // command line arguments that start with both - (for UNIX)
         // and / (for MS-DOS).

         for (int i = 0; i < args.length; i++)
         {
            if (args[i].equals("-") || args[i].equals("/"))
            {
               int c;
               byte [] rgb = new byte [1000];

               ByteArrayOutputStream baos = new ByteArrayOutputStream();

               while ((c = System.in.read(rgb)) > -1)
                  baos.write(rgb, 0, c);

               vec.addElement(new
                  ByteArrayInputStream(baos.toByteArray()));
            }
            else if (args[i].equals("-e") || args[i].equals("/e"))
            {
               vec.addElement(new
                  StringBufferInputStream(args[++i] + "\n"));
            }
            else
```

continued on next page

continued from previous page

```
            {
                vec.addElement(new FileInputStream(args[i]));
            }
        }

        SequenceInputStream sis = new
            SequenceInputStream(vec.elements());

        Parser.parse(sis);
    }
    catch (Exception e) e.printStackTrace();
    }
}
```

10. The Java language source files comprising the project can be compiled as follows:

```
javac Main.java Parser.java TagParser.java
```

11. Class Main understands three different types of command line arguments when run from the shell. An argument not preceded by a dash ('-') or slash ('/') is considered to be the name of a file. The named file is opened and its contents used as input. An argument consisting of only a dash or slash causes the program to get its input from standard input (the keyboard). The argument "-e" or "/e" causes the program to read the next argument from the command line and use that as input. All three of these methods may be combined in one invocation of the program. The following examples indicate how the program may be run:

```
java Main -
java Main foo.html bar.html
java Main -e "<BODY>" - -e "</BODY>"
java Main foo.html - bar.html
```

PART V

JAVA DEBUGGING TOOLS

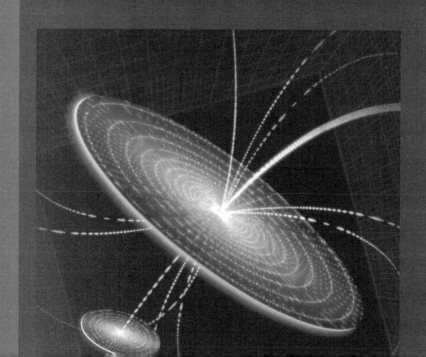

14

JAVA DEBUGGING MODEL

14

JAVA DEBUGGING MODEL

As a programmer you are probably well aware of the joy and pain associated with debugging any program. The simplest form of debugging, of course, is sprinkling your code with print statements and analyzing the trace output to uncover and fix the bugs. This approach is very simple, but extremely time-consuming, and makes debugging large programs in Java extremely difficult. In addition, this approach is rendered utterly useless if you attempt to debug an applet running remotely on the Internet. To debug applets remotely, designers of Java have included classes that enable a user to debug a remote Java applet interactively. These debugging classes can be used by a Java programmer to write a debugging utility without having to worry about security and other issues.

In this chapter you are introduced to the Java debugging model and the Java debugger jdb. You are also introduced to various debugging classes that are provided in the Java Developer's Kit (JDK) that can help you write a debugging utility. A list of all the classes and interfaces in the package sun.tools.debug is shown in Table 14-1. The hierarchical relationship between these classes is shown in Figure 14-1. A list of all the remote debugging methods classified by category is shown in Table 14-2. By the end of this chapter you will able to develop your own debugger written completely in Java.

Debugging in Java

Debuggers for programming languages like Java, C, and C++ allow the user to trace through the program in steps that enable him or her to uncover bugs in the code. A debugger performs the following functions:

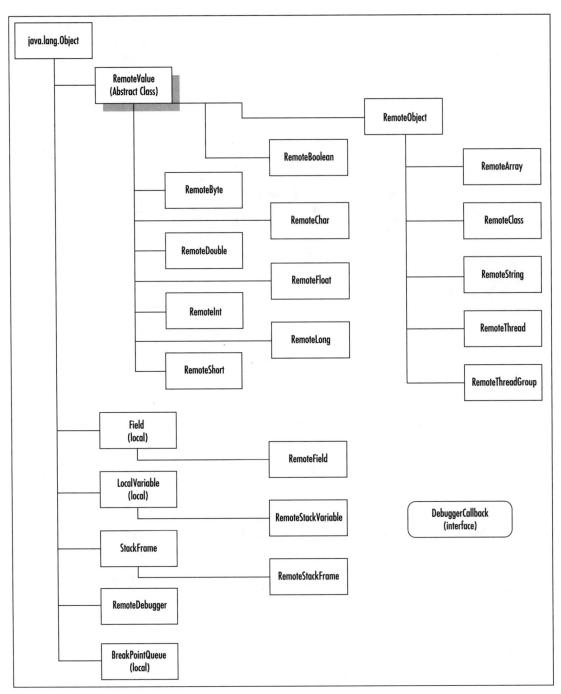

Figure 14-1 Hierarchical relationship between remote debugging classes

■ Maintains source code line number information so that the user can execute the program as he or she steps through the source code, and stops execution at a particular source line or language construct such as a method in a class, and so on.

■ Allows a user to inspect a variable within the current scope.

■ Allows a user to inspect a particular thread of execution and suspend other threads of execution.

■ Allows a user to set and unset break points within the source code.

■ Retrieves some operating parameters, like the exceptions that the execution will terminate on, memory left in the system, and so on.

■ Provides a stack trace of the execution of any thread at any given point.

In addition, a Java debugger must have the following four features:

■ The interface to the debugger should be object-oriented, just like the Java language.

■ The Java runtime features like threads and monitors must be fully supported.

■ Remote debugging of Java programs and applets should be possible.

■ Security should not be compromised at any cost.

To fulfill these requirements, the Java debugger API was included in the JDK. This API supports the model of a remote viewer to a running Java interpreter with proxy support for the objects under observation. The JDK has a class RemoteDebugger that acts as a front end to the remote agent running on the Java interpreter. This class communicates to the agent using an application-level protocol. The RemoteDebugger class acts as a remote viewer for debugging activities like setting and unsetting break points. Whenever a user calls a method of a Remote data type, the agent executes a command on the user's behalf, and sends the results back to the client side using the proprietary protocol. Java's debugging model is clearly demonstrated in a debugging tool called jdb, included in the JDK. jdb serves as a primitive debugger that supports basic object browsing and debugging. The debugger communicates with the Java interpreter via a TCP/IP-based network socket–based proprietary protocol. Figure 14-2 shows the relationship between the Java interpreter and the Java debugger.

There are two ways to use jdb for debugging your Java program. The first way is to have jdb start the Java interpreter with the class to be debugged. This is done by substituting jdb for Java in the command line. For example, to debug the class xyz in the source file xyz.java, jdb is invoked using the command line

```
jdb xyz
```

When jdb is started in this manner, it invokes a Java interpreter in the background with the specified parameters, loads the specified class, and stops executing before that class's first instruction. After the loading is complete, a > prompt is displayed indicating

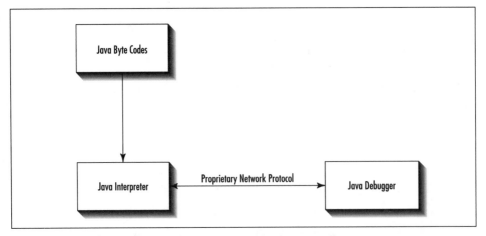

Figure 14-2   Relationship between the Java interpreter and the Java debugger

that there is currently no default thread. Now you can try to execute the following commands:

- Type *help* or *?* to show a list of commands available in jdb.

- Type *threadgroups* to show a list of thread groups that are running. The *system* and *main* thread groups should be present.

- To see all the threads in the thread group *main*, type *threads main* on the command line.

- Try dumping the *main* thread using the dump command. To refer to a currently executing thread, you can use a shorthand notation for threads: *t@<thread_number>*; in this case, type the command *dump t@1*.

- Object variables can also be printed using the shorthand thread notation. Type the command *print t@1.group* to print the *main* thread group. You can also print the number of threads in that thread group by the command *print t@1.group.nthreads*.

- The command *print* is also used to browse Java objects. The print command calls the object's toString() method, so it will be formatted differently depending on its class. Objects are specified by their object ID (a hexadecimal integer). To print out a dump of all the object's instance variables, use the command *dump 234a4f*.

- Classes are specified by either their object ID or by name. If a class is already loaded, then a substring of the class name can be used. For example, Thread can be used in place of java.lang.Thread. If a class is not loaded, its full name must be specified, and the class will be loaded as a side effect. A class must be loaded before you can set a break point. You can set a break point in one of two ways. For example, if you want to stop at source line 25 in the class TestClass, you can execute the command *stop at TestClass:25*, or if you want to set a break point at the method init() in the class TestClass, you can execute the command *stop at TestClass.init().*

■ The command *clear* removes break points using a syntax very similar to setting the break points.

■ You can print a list of all the classes that are currently loaded by the command *classes.*

■ The local (stack) variables can be browsed only if the class has been compiled with the -g option.

■ You can dump the main thread's stack by specifying *where t@1*. Each line is a separate stack frame that displays the full method name and the signature.

■ The commands *up* and *down* let you select the stack frame that you are interested in.

■ When an exception occurs for which there is not a *catch* statement anywhere in the Java program stack, the Java runtime normally dumps an exception trace and exits. When running in the jdb, an exception is treated as an unrecoverable break point, and jdb stops at the instruction that threw the exception. To ignore the exception, you can use the command *ignore <exception name>*. The *ignore* command does not cause the Java interpreter to ignore the specific exception; only jdb ignores it.

■ When you are done playing with the debugger, you can exit the jdb command line environment by typing *quit*.

The second way to use jdb is by attaching it to the Java interpreter that is already running. For security reasons, Java interpreters can only be debugged if started with the *-debug* flag. When a Java interpreter is started this way, the interpreter prints out a password to be used by the debugger, and begins listening on a dynamically allocated port. To attach jdb to a running Java interpreter after the password for the session is known, invoke it by the following command line:

```
jdb -host <hostname> -password <password>
```

The debugger must specify the correct host and password when creating an instance of the class RemoteDebugger. If you are running on the local machine, then you can execute the following command to invoke jdb:

```
jdb -host localhost  -password <password>
```

Once you are connected to jdb, you can execute all the commands described earlier. You can now debug any program across the Internet, provided it has been started with the *-debug* option and you know the password and the host name of the machine on which the Java interpreter is executing. Once the password authentication is done by the Java interpreter, the debugger starts talking to an agent residing within the Java interpreter. The debugger creates a new instance of the class RemoteDebugger to talk to the agent. Now you can send commands to the agent and it replies to the commands though the network socket back to the instance of the class RemoteDebugger. When a request for the value of a particular variable is received by the agent, it copies the result into a subclass of the class RemoteValue. If the type of the requested value is a primitive data type such as an Integer, then the agent copies the value of the Integer into the instance of the class RemoteInteger. If the data type requested by the instance of the RemoteDebugger is not a primitive type, then an instance of a RemoteObject is returned. Only one instance of the debugger can be connected to the agent on the Java interpreter in the debug mode. Figure 14-3 shows the debugging model in Java. The agent runs on the Java interpreter, executes commands on the behalf of the Java debugger client, and returns the results in the form of remote data types back to the client.

Example Debugging Session

Here is an example of a debugging session involving the program shown later in the chapter in Listing 14-2. Compile this program using the following command:

```
D> javac -g urlTest.java
```

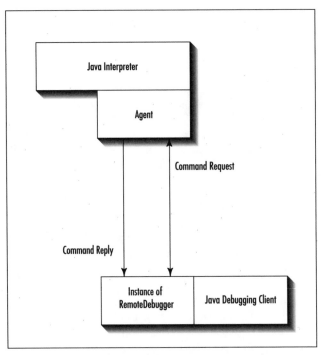

Figure 14-3 Logical depiction of the debugging model in Java

Once the program has been successfully compiled, run it under the Java debugger jdb. The bold font represents the keyboard inputs that must be entered, and the normal font indicates the responses of the jdb.

```
D:> jdb urlTest http://www.finex.com/test.html
Initializing jdb...
0x104f650:class(urlTest)
> help
> ** command list **
threads [threadgroup]      -- list threads
thread <thread id>         -- set default thread
suspend [thread id(s)]     -- suspend threads (default: all)
resume [thread id(s)]      -- resume threads (default: all)
where [thread id] | all    -- dump a thread's stack
threadgroups               -- list threadgroups
threadgroup <name>         -- set current threadgroup

print <id> [id(s)]         -- print object or field
dump <id> [id(s)]          -- print all object information

locals                     -- print all local variables in current stack frame

classes                    -- list currently known classes
methods <class id>         -- list a class's methods

stop in <class id>.<method> -- set a breakpoint in a method
stop at <class id>:<line>  -- set a breakpoint at a line
up [n frames]              -- move up a thread's stack
down [n frames]            -- move down a thread's stack
clear <class id>:<line>    -- clear a breakpoint
step                       -- execute current line
cont                       -- continue execution from breakpoint

catch <class id>           -- break for the specified exception
ignore <class id>          -- ignore when the specified exception

list [line number]         -- print source code
use [source file path]     -- display or change the source path

memory                     -- report memory usage
gc                         -- free unused objects

load classname             -- load Java class to be debugged
run <class> [args]         -- start execution of a loaded Java class
!!                         -- repeat last command
help (or ?)                -- list commands
exit (or quit)             -- exit debugger
> ignore java.lang.Exception
>
> threadgroups
1. (java.lang.ThreadGroup)0x10430b8 system
2. (java.lang.ThreadGroup)0x1043b58 main
> dump t@1
> t@1 = (java.lang.Thread)0x10431f8 {
    private char name[] = "Finalizer thread"
```

continued on next page

continued from previous page

```
    private int priority = 1
    private Thread threadQ = null
    private int PrivateInfo = 3138700
    private int eetop = 74841916
    private boolean single_step = false
    private boolean daemon = true
    private boolean stillborn = false
    private Runnable target = null
    private ThreadGroup group = (java.lang.ThreadGroup)0x10430b8
}
> dump t@2
> t@2 = (java.lang.Thread)0x1043ad0 {
    private char name[] = "Debugger agent"
    private int priority = 10
    private Thread threadQ = null
    private int PrivateInfo = 3236036
    private int eetop = 76087100
    private boolean single_step = false
    private boolean daemon = true
    private boolean stillborn = false
    private Runnable target = (sun.tools.debug.Agent)0x1043758
    private ThreadGroup group = (java.lang.ThreadGroup)0x10430b8
}
> print t@1.group
> t@1.group = java.lang.ThreadGroup[name=system,maxpri=10]
> stop in urlTest:main
> Breakpoint set in urlTest.main
> run
> run urlTest http://www.finex.com/test.html
running ...
main[1]
Breakpoint hit: urlTest.main (urlTest:11)
> where t@1
main[1]    [1] urlTest.main (urlTest:11)
main[1] list
7              static URL url = null;
8
9              public static void main(String[] args)
10             {
11     =>          InputStream inp = null;
12
13                 if( args.length < 1)
14                 {
15                     System.out.println("usage urlTest URL");
main[1] next
Breakpoint hit: urlTest.main (urlTest:13)
main[1] list
9              public static void main(String[] args)
10             {
11                 InputStream inp = null;
12
13     =>          if( args.length < 1)
14                 {
15                     System.out.println("usage urlTest URL");
16                     return;
17                 }
```

```
main[1] cont
main[1] quit
D:>
```

Exceptions Thrown by the Remote Debugging Classes

The following exceptions are thrown by the remote debugging classes.

■ **Exception**

This exception signals that some generic type of exception has occurred. Sometimes more specific exceptions are thrown by the remote debugging classes.

■ **ArrayIndexOutOfBoundsException**

This exception is thrown by the remote debugging classes whenever the array index that is referenced by it goes out of the range.

■ **ClassCastException**

This exception is thrown whenever an illegal cast operation is performed by the remote debugging classes.

■ **IllegalAccessError**

This exception is thrown by the remote debugging classes whenever a class or its initializer is not accessible.

Details of these exception classes can be found in Chapter 9, Exceptions.

About the Project

In this chapter a Java program is developed that can be used to profile other Java programs. The profiler will print information regarding

■ Memory

■ Threads and thread groups

■ Exceptions

■ Names of classes, interfaces, and their instance variables

This project demonstrates how to use the remote debugging classes in Java to control and obtain information regarding the execution of the Java program on the Java interpreter.

The Debugging Classes Method Summaries

In this section you are also introduced to various debugging classes that are provided in package sun.tools.debug. A list of all the classes and interfaces in this package is shown in Table 14-1. A list of all the remote debugging methods classified by category is shown in Table 14-2.

Table 14-1 The debugging classes/interfaces

Class/Interface	Category	Description
RemoteArray	Primitive type	This class allows remote debugging of arrays.
RemoteBoolean	Primitive type	This class allows remote debugging of booleans.
RemoteByte	Primitive type	This class allows remote debugging of bytes.
RemoteChar	Primitive type	This class allows remote debugging of chars.
RemoteDouble	Primitive type	This class allows remote debugging of double.
RemoteFloat	Primitive type	This class allows remote debugging of floats.
RemoteInt	Primitive type	This class allows remote debugging of ints.
RemoteLong	Primitive type	This class allows remote debugging of long integers.
RemoteShort	Primitive type	This class allows remote debugging of short integers.
RemoteString	Primitive type	This class allows remote debugging of Strings.
RemoteClass	Complex type	This class allows access to classes and interfaces in the remote Java interpreter.
RemoteField	Method/Variable	This class allows access to a variable or a method of an object or a class in the remote debugger.
RemoteObject	Base class	A generic base class for nonprimitive data objects.
RemoteValue	Value	This class allows access to a copy of a value in the Java interpreter.
StackFrame	Stack trace	This class represents the stack frame of a suspended thread.
RemoteStackFrame	Stack trace	This class provides access to a stack frame of a suspended thread.
RemoteStackVariable	Stack trace	This class provides an access to the variable on the stack frame.
RemoteThreadGroup	Stack trace	This class allows access to a thread group in the Java interpreter.
RemoteThread	Thread	This class allows access to a thread in the Java interpreter.
RemoteDebugger	Client interface	This class defines a client interface to the Java debugging classes. It is used to instantiate a connection to the Java interpreter.
DebuggerCallback	Asynchronous Communication	This interface is used to communicate the information from the debugger to the client asynchronously.

Table 14-2 Remote debugging methods, by category

Class/Interface	Category	Methods
RemoteArray	Accessor	arrayTypeName, getElement, getElements, getElementType, getSize, typeName
	Converter	description, toString
RemoteBoolean	Accessor	get, typeName
	Converter	toString
RemoteByte	Accessor	get, typeName
	Converter	toString
RemoteChar	Accessor	get, typeName
	Converter	toString
RemoteDouble	Accessor	get, typeName
	Converter	toString

Class/Interface	Category	Methods
RemoteFloat	Accessor	get, typeName
	Converter	toString
RemoteInt	Accessor	get, typeName
	Converter	toString
RemoteLong	Accessor	get, typeName
	Converter	toString
RemoteShort	Accessor	get, typeName
	Converter	toString
RemoteString	Accessor	typeName
	Converter	description, toString
RemoteClass	Accessor	getClassLoader, getField, getFields, getFieldValue, getInstanceField, getInstanceFields, getInterfaces, getMethod, getMethodNames, getMethods, getName, getSourceFile, getSourceFileName, getStaticFields, getSuperclass, typeName
	Modifier	catchExceptions, clearBreakpoint, clearBreakpointLine, clearBreakpointMethod, ignoreExceptions, setBreakpointLine, setBreakpointMethod
	Verifier	isInterface
	Converter	description, toString
RemoteField	Accessor	getModifiers, getName, getType
	Verifier	isStatic
	Converter	toString
RemoteObject	Accessor	getClazz, getField, getFields, getFieldValue, getId, typeName
	Converter	description, toString
RemoteValue	Accessor	getType, typeName
	Verifier	isObject
	Converter	description, fromHex, toHex
StackFrame	Converter	toString
RemoteStackFrame	Accessor	getLineNumber, getLocalVariable, getLocalVariables, getMethodName, getPC, getRemoteClass
RemoteStackVariable	Accessor	getName, getValue
	Verifier	isScope
RemoteThreadGroup	Accessor	getName
	Modifier	stop
	Others	listThreads
RemoteThread	Accessor	getCurrentFrame, getCurrentFrameIndex, getName, getStackVariable, getStackVariables, getStatus
	Modifier	resetCurrentFrameIndex, resume, setCurrentFrameIndex, suspend
	Verifier	isSuspended
	Others	cont, down, dumpStack, next, step, stop, up

continued on next page

continued from previous page

Class/Interface	Category	Methods
RemoteDebugger	Accessor	findClass, get, getExceptionCatchList, getSourcePath, totalMemory
	Modifier	close, freeMemory, gc, run, setSourcePath
	Others	itrace, listBreakpoints, listClasses, listThreadGroups, trace
DebuggerCallback	Others	breakpointEvent, exceptionEvent, printToConsole, quitEvent, threadDeathEvent

The sun.tools.debug.RemoteArray Class

The class RemoteArray provides methods for debugging remote arrays in a Java program executing on the Java interpreter. This class has methods to access the size of the array, the element type, and the elements in the remote array. A method summary for this class is shown in the Table 14-3. The class RemoteArray inherits from the class RemoteObject and overrides the following methods: description(), typeName(), toString().

Table 14-3 Summary of RemoteArray methods

Method	Description
arrayTypeName	Returns the element type as a String
description	Returns the description of the array
getElement	Returns an array element at the given index
getElements	Returns a copy of the array as instances of RemoteValue
getElementType	Returns the element type, such as TC_CHAR (a system-defined integer)
getSize	Returns the number of elements in the array
toString	Returns the string representation of the array
typeName	Returns the type of the array as a String ("array")

REMOTEARRAY

Description	The class RemoteArray is used to obtain information regarding the remote array objects in the Java interpreter. This class provides methods to access the elements and their types.
Syntax	public class **RemoteArray** extends RemoteObject
Package	sun.tools.debug
Import	sun.tools.debug.RemoteArray
Constructors	Does not have a public constructor (only created by other classes in the package).

Parameters	None.
See Also	RemoteObject

Methods

ARRAYTYPENAME

Class Name	RemoteArray
Description	This method returns a string with the type name given the specified type int.
Syntax	public String arrayTypeName(int *type*)
Parameters	
int *type*	Returns the element type as a string.
Returns	A String object with the element type.
Exceptions	None.
See Also	String
Example	This segment of code shows how to access the type information from the RemoteArray object.

```
RemoteArray  rarr;
.
.
.
String firstType  = rarr.arrayTypeName(rarr.getElementType());
```

DESCRIPTION

Class Name	RemoteArray
Description	This method returns a verbose description of the RemoteArray. This method can be used for providing detailed information about the RemoteArray.
Syntax	public String **description**()
Parameters	None.
Returns	A String describing the RemoteArray.
Exceptions	None.
Example	This segment of code shows how to access the description information from the RemoteArray object.

```
RemoteArray  rarr;
.
.
.
String  fullDescription  = rarr.description();
```

GetElement

Class Name	RemoteArray
Description	This method returns an element at the specified index from RemoteArray.
Syntax	public final RemoteValue **getElement**(int *index*)
Parameters	
int *index*	Index of the element in the RemoteArray.
Returns	The RemoteValue object at the given index.
Exceptions	This method throws an ArrayIndexOutOfBoundsException if the index crosses the bounds of the array.
Example	This segment of code shows how to access the first element from the RemoteArray.

```
RemoteArray  rarr;
.
.
RemoteValue  elem  = rarr.getElement(0);
```

GetElements

Class Name	RemoteArray
Description	This method returns an array of RemoteValues of all or a portion of the elements in the RemoteArray.
Syntax	public final RemoteValue[] **getElements**()
	public final RemoteValue[] **getElements**(int *beginIndex*, int *endIndex*)
Parameters	
int *beginIndex*	Beginning index of the element in the RemoteArray.
int *endIndex*	Ending index of the element in the RemoteArray.
Returns	An array of RemoteValue objects.
Exceptions	This method throws an ArrayIndexOutOfBoundsException if the index crosses the bounds of the array.
Example	This segment of code shows how to access the type information from the RemoteArray object.

```
RemoteArray  rarr;
.
.
RemoteValue[]  fullElemArr  = rarr.getElements();
RemoteValue[]  partElemArr  = rarr.getElements(2, 5);
```

GETELEMENTTYPE

Class Name	RemoteArray
Description	This method returns a constant integer indicating the element type in the RemoteArray.
Syntax	public int **getElementType()**
Parameters	None.
Returns	A constant integer like TC_CHAR, etc., indicating the element type in the RemoteArray.
Exceptions	If an error occurs, this method throws the exception Exception.
Example	This segment of code shows how to access the type information from the RemoteArray object.

```
RemoteArray  rarr;
.
.
int  etype  = rarr.getElementType();
```

GETSIZE

Class Name	RemoteArray
Description	This method returns the number of elements in the RemoteArray object.
Syntax	public final int **getSize()**
Parameters	None.
Returns	The number of elements in the RemoteArray.
Exceptions	None.
Example	This segment of code shows how to get the number of elements from the RemoteArray object.

```
RemoteArray  rarr;
.
.
int nelements = rarr.getSize();
```

TOSTRING

Class Name	RemoteArray
Description	This method returns a string version of the RemoteArray. This method is called whenever a print method is called on this object.
Syntax	public String **toString()**
Parameters	None.

Returns	A String representation of the RemoteArray.
Exceptions	None.
Example	This segment of code shows how to access the string representation of the RemoteArray object.

```
RemoteArray  rarr;
.
.
String  fullDescription  = rarr.toString();
```

TYPENAME

Class Name	RemoteArray
Description	This method returns a string with the type name of the RemoteArray object.
Syntax	public String **typeName()**
Parameters	None.
Returns	A String object with the string "array."
Exceptions	None.
See Also	String
Example	This segment of code shows how to access the type information from the RemoteArray object.

```
RemoteArray  rarr;
.
.
String rtype  = rarr.typeName();
```

The sun.tools.debug.RemoteBoolean, sun.tools.debug.RemoteByte, sun.tools.debug.RemoteChar, sun.tools.debug.RemoteDouble, sun.tools.debug.RemoteFloat, sun.tools.debug.RemoteInt, sun.tools.debug.RemoteLong, and sun.tools.debug.RemoteShort Classes

The classes RemoteBoolean, RemoteByte, RemoteChar, RemoteDouble, RemoteFloat, RemoteInt, RemoteLong, and RemoteShort provide methods for accessing the values of the remote objects in a Java program executing on the Java interpreter. These classes have methods to access the value of the remote object and the type name of the object. A method summary for these classes is shown in Table 14-4. All these classes inherit from the class RemoteValue and override the methods typeName() and toString().

Table 14-4 Summary of RemoteBoolean, RemoteByte, RemoteChar, RemoteDouble, RemoteFloat, RemoteInt, RemoteLong, and RemoteShort methods

Class	Method	Description
RemoteBoolean	get	Returns the boolean value
	toString	Returns the boolean value as a String
	typeName	Returns the type of this object as a String("boolean")
RemoteByte	get	Returns the byte value
	toString	Returns the byte value as a String
	typeName	Returns the type of this object as a String("byte")
RemoteChar	get	Returns the char value
	toString	Returns the char value as a String
	typeName	Returns the type of this object as a String("char")
RemoteDouble	get	Returns the double value
	toString	Returns the double value as a String
	typeName	Returns the type of this object as a String("double")
RemoteFloat	get	Returns the float value
	toString	Returns the float value as a String
	typeName	Returns the type of this object as a String("float")
RemoteInt	get	Returns the int value
	toString	Returns the int value as a String
	typeName	Returns the type of this object as a String("int")
RemoteLong	get	Returns the long value
	toString	Returns the long value as a String
	typeName	Returns the type of this object as a String("long")
RemoteShort	get	Returns the short value
	toString	Returns the short value as a String
	typeName	Returns the type of this object as a String("short")

REMOTEBOOLEAN, REMOTEBYTE, REMOTECHAR, REMOTEDOUBLE, REMOTEFLOAT, REMOTEINT, REMOTELONG, REMOTESHORT

Description   These classes are used to obtain the values associated with remote objects in the Java interpreter. This class provides methods to access the values and their types.

Syntax	public class **RemoteBoolean** extends RemoteValue
	public class **RemoteByte** extends RemoteValue
	public class **RemoteChar** extends RemoteValue
	public class **RemoteDouble** extends RemoteValue
	public class **RemoteFloat** extends RemoteValue
	public class **RemoteInt** extends RemoteValue
	public class **RemoteLong** extends RemoteValue
	public class **RemoteShort** extends RemoteValue
Package	sun.tools.debug
Import	sun.tools.debug.RemoteBoolean
	sun.tools.debug.RemoteByte
	sun.tools.debug.RemoteChar
	sun.tools.debug.RemoteDouble
	sun.tools.debug.RemoteFloat
	sun.tools.debug.RemoteInt
	sun.tools.debug.RemoteLong
	sun.tools.debug.RemoteShort
Constructors	Does not have a public constructor (only created by other classes in the package).
Parameters	None.
See Also	RemoteValue

Methods

GET

Class Name	RemoteBoolean, RemoteByte, RemoteChar, RemoteDouble, RemoteFloat, RemoteInt, RemoteLong, RemoteShort.
Description	This method is used for retrieving the remote object's value.
Syntax	public boolean **get**()
	public byte **get**()
	public char **get**()
	public double **get**()
	public float **get**()
	public int **get**()
	public long **get**()
	public short **get**()
Parameters	None.
Returns	The value of the remote object.

Exceptions	None.
Example	This segment of code shows how to access the value of the RemoteBoolean object. Other remote objects' values are retrieved in a similar manner.

```
RemoteBoolean  rbool;
.
.
boolean  value  = rbool.get();
```

TOSTRING

Class Name	RemoteBoolean, RemoteByte, RemoteChar, RemoteDouble, RemoteFloat, RemoteInt, RemoteLong, RemoteShort
Description	This method returns a string version of the remote object. This method is called whenever a print method is called on this object.
Syntax	public String **toString**()
Parameters	None.
Returns	A String representation of the remote object.
Exceptions	None.
Example	This segment of code shows how to access the string representation of the RemoteBoolean object. Other remote objects' string representations are retrieved in a similar manner.

```
RemoteBoolean  rbool;
.
.
String  fullDescription  = rbool.toString();
```

TYPENAME

Class Name	RemoteBoolean, RemoteByte, RemoteChar, RemoteDouble, RemoteFloat, RemoteInt, RemoteLong, RemoteShort
Description	This method returns a string with the type name of the remote object.
Syntax	public String **typeName**()
Parameters	None.
Returns	A String object containing the type name of the remote object, like "boolean", "byte", "int", etc.
Exceptions	None.
See Also	String
Example	This segment of code shows how to access the type information from the RemoteBoolean object. Other remote objects' type names are retrieved in a similar manner.

```
RemoteBoolean  rbool;
.
.
String rtype  = rbool.typeName();
```

The sun.tools.debug.RemoteString Class

The class RemoteString provides methods for debugging remote string objects in a Java program executing on the Java interpreter. A method summary for this class is shown in Table 14-5. The class RemoteArray inherits from the class RemoteObject and overrides all three methods.

Table 14-5 Summary of RemoteString methods

Method	Description
description	Returns the String value or "null"
toString	Returns the value of the String or "null"
typeName	Returns the type of this object as a String("String")

REMOTESTRING

Description	The class RemoteString is used to obtain information regarding the remote string objects in the Java interpreter.
Syntax	public class **RemoteString** extends RemoteObject
Package	sun.tools.debug
Import	sun.tools.debug.RemoteString
Constructors	Does not have a public constructor (only created by other classes in the package).
Parameters	None.
See Also	RemoteObject

Methods

DESCRIPTION

Class Name	RemoteString
Description	This method is used for retrieving the RemoteString object's value.
Syntax	public String **description**()
Parameters	None.
Returns	A verbose description of the RemoteString object.

Exceptions	None.
Example	This segment of code shows how to access the description of the RemoteString object.

```
RemoteString  rstring;
.
.
.
String  value  = rstring.description();
```

TOSTRING

Class Name	RemoteString
Description	This method returns a string version of the RemoteString. This method is called whenever a print method is called on this object.
Syntax	public String **toString**()
Parameters	None.
Returns	A String representation of the RemoteString.
Exceptions	None.
Example	This segment of code shows how to access the string representation of the RemoteString object.

```
RemoteString  rstring;
.
.
.
String  fullDescription  = rstring.toString();
```

TYPENAME

Class Name	RemoteString
Description	This method returns a string with the type name of the RemoteString object.
Syntax	public String **typeName**()
Parameters	None.
Returns	A String object with the string "string".
Exceptions	None.
Example	This segment of code shows how to access the type information from the RemoteString object.

```
RemoteString  rstring;
.
.
.
String rtype  = rstring.typeName();
```

The sun.tools.debug.RemoteClass Class

The class RemoteClass provides methods for debugging remote classes in a Java program executing on the Java interpreter. This class has methods to access information regarding the interfaces, methods, instance variables, source file, break points, etc. A method summary for this class is shown in Table 14-6. The class RemoteClass inherits from the class RemoteObject and overrides the following methods: typeName(), getFields(), getField(), getFieldValue(), description(), and toString().

Table 14-6 Summary of RemoteClass methods

Method	Description
catchExceptions	Enters the debugger when an instance of this class is thrown
clearBreakpoint	Clears a break point at a specified address in a class
clearBreakpointLine	Clears a break point at a specified line
clearBreakpointMethod	Clears a break point at a specified method
description	Returns a string with a verbose description of the class
getClassLoader	Returns a class loader for this class
getField	Returns the static field specified by the index or name
getFields	Returns an array of all the static fields in the class
getFieldValue	Returns the value of the static field specified by the index or name
getInstanceField	Returns the instance field specified by the index
getInstanceFields	Returns the instance fields for this class
getInterfaces	Returns the interfaces for this class
getMethod	Returns the method specified by name
getMethodNames	Returns the names of all the methods supported by this class in an array
getMethods	Returns an array of all the methods for this class
getName	Returns the name of the class
getSourceFile	Returns the source file referenced by this stack frame
getSourceFileName	Returns the source file name referenced by this stack frame
getStaticFields	Returns an array containing all the static fields for this class
getSuperclass	Returns the superclass for this class
ignoreExceptions	Does not enter the debugger when an instance of this class is thrown
isInterface	Returns a boolean value true or false if the instance of the RemoteClass is an interface
setBreakpointLine	Sets the break point at the specified source line number in the class
setBreakpointMethod	Sets the break point at the first line of the specified method
toString	Returns a verbose description of the RemoteClass object
typeName	Returns the name of the class as the type

REMOTECLASS

Description	The class RemoteClass is used to obtain information regarding the objects that hold the information regarding a class in the Java interpreter.
Syntax	public class **RemoteClass** extends RemoteObject
Package	sun.tools.debug
Import	sun.tools.debug.RemoteClass
Constructors	Does not have a public constructor (only created by other classes in the package).
Parameters	None.
See Also	RemoteObject

Methods

CATCHEXCEPTIONS

Class Name	RemoteClass
Description	This method enters the debugger when an instance of the RemoteClass is thrown.
Syntax	public void **catchExceptions**()
Parameters	None.
Returns	None.
Exceptions	If an error occurs, this method throws the exception ClassCastException.
Example	This example shows how to invoke the method catchExceptions() in your program.

```
RemoteClass rmt;
 .
 .
 .
rmt.catchExceptions();
```

CLEARBREAKPOINT

Class Name	RemoteClass
Description	This method is used to clear break points set in the class.
Syntax	public String **clearBreakpoint**(int *pc*)
Parameters	
int *pc*	The address of the break point that should be cleared.
Returns	This method returns an empty string if the break point was successfully cleared; otherwise, it returns a string containing a description of the error message.

Exceptions	If an error occurs, this method throws the exception ClassCastException.
Example	This example shows how to clear the break points in a class.

```
RemoteClass rmt;
 .
 .
 .
int  brkPt = 0xff2c;
String msg = rmt.clearBreakpoint(brkPt);

System.out.println(msg + "\n");
```

CLEARBREAKPOINTLINE

Class Name	RemoteClass
Description	This method is used to clear a break point at a specified line.
Syntax	public String **clearBreakpointLine**(int *lineNum*)
Parameters	
int *lineNum*	The line number where the break point should be cleared.
Returns	This method returns an empty string if the break point was successfully cleared; otherwise, it returns a string containing a description of the error message.
Exceptions	If an error occurs, this method throws the exception Exception.
See Also	String
Example	

```
RemoteClass rmt;
 .
 .
 .
int line = 34;
String msg = rmt.clearBreakpointLine(line);

System.out.println(msg + "\n");
```

CLEARBREAKPOINTMETHOD

Class Name	RemoteClass
Description	This method is used to clear a break point at a specified method.
Syntax	public String **clearBreakpointMethod**(RemoteField *method*)
Parameters	
RemoteField *method*	A reference to an instance of the class RemoteMethod where the break point should be cleared.
Returns	This method returns an empty string if the break point was successfully cleared; otherwise, it returns a string containing a description of the error message.

Exceptions   If an error occurs, this method throws the exception Exception.

See Also   String

Example

```
RemoteClass rmt;
.
.
.
RemoteField mName; // Method Name..
.
.
.
String msg = rmt.clearBreakpointLine(mName);

System.out.println(msg + "\n");
```

DESCRIPTION

Class Name	RemoteClass
Description	This method is used for retrieving the RemoteClass object's description.
Syntax	public String **description**()
Parameters	None.
Returns	A string containing a verbose description the RemoteClass.
Exceptions	None.
See Also	String
Example	This segment of code shows how to access the verbose description of the RemoteClass object.

```
RemoteClass  rclss;
.
.
String  value  = rclss.description();
```

GetClassLoader

Class Name	RemoteClass
Description	This method is used for retrieving the class loader for this instance of the RemoteClass.
Syntax	public RemoteObject **getClassLoader**()
Parameters	None.
Returns	An instance of the RemoteObject containing the class loader for this object.
Exceptions	If an error occurs, this method throws the exception Exception.
See Also	RemoteObject

Example

```
RemoteClass rclss;
    .
    .
RemoteObject robj = rclss.getClassLoader();
```

GETFIELD

Class Name	RemoteClass
Description	This method returns a static field (variable) for this class specified by the index or name.
Syntax	public RemoteField **getField**(int *ndx*)
	public RemoteField **getField**(String *name*)
Parameters	
int *ndx*	Index of the static field in the current class.
String *name*	Name of the current class.
Returns	An instance of the class RemoteField containing information about the field.
Exceptions	If an error occurs, this method throws the exception Exception.
See Also	RemoteField
Example	

```
RemoteClass rmt;
    .
    .
RemoteField fld1 = rmt.getField(2);
RemoteField fld2 = rmt.getField("dataInputStream");
    ..
```

GETFIELDS

Class Name	RemoteClass
Description	This method returns all the static fields (variables) for this class. This class basically overrides the getFields() class in the RemoteObject class.
Syntax	public RemoteField[] **getFields**()
Parameters	None.
Returns	An array of the class RemoteField containing all the static fields for this class.
Exceptions	If an error occurs, this method throws the exception Exception.
See Also	RemoteField

Example

```
RemoteClass rmt;
.
.
RemoteField fldArr[] = rmt.getFields();
..
```

GETFIELDVALUE

Class Name	RemoteClass
Description	This method returns the value of the static field specified by the index or the name.
Syntax	public RemoteValue **getFieldValue**(int *ndx*)
	public RemoteValue **getFieldValue**(String *name*)
Parameters	
int *ndx*	Index of the static field in the current class.
String *name*	Name of the current class.
Returns	An instance of the class RemoteValue containing value of the field.
Exceptions	If an error occurs, this method throws the exception Exception.
See Also	RemoteValue
Example	

```
RemoteClass rmt;
.
.
RemoteValue fld1 = rmt.getFieldValue(2);
RemoteValue fld2 = rmt.getFieldValue("dataInputStream");
..
```

GETINSTANCEFIELD

Class Name	RemoteClass
Description	This method returns instance fields (variables) for the specified index.
Syntax	public RemoteField **getInstanceField**(int *ndx*)
Parameters	
int *ndx*	Index of the instance field in the current class.
Returns	An instance of the RemoteField object at the specified index.
Exceptions	This method throws an ArrayIndexOutOfBoundsException if the index is greater than the number of instance variables.
See Also	RemoteField
Comments	Since the return value is RemoteClass, only the type and the name information are valid. The data is not valid in the returned RemoteField object.

Example

```
RemoteClass rmt;
    .
    .
    .
RemoteField fld = rmt.getInstanceField(0);
    .
    .
```

GETINSTANCEFIELDS

Class Name	RemoteClass
Description	This method returns an array of all the instance fields (variables) for this class.
Syntax	public RemoteField[] **getInstanceFields**()
Parameters	None.
Returns	An array of the RemoteField objects, each containing the instance field information.
Exceptions	If an error occurs, this method throws the exception Exception.
See Also	RemoteField
Comments	Only the type and the name information is valid for the instances of the RemoteField.

Example

```
RemoteClass rmt;
    .
    .
RemoteField fldArr[] = rmt.getInstanceFields();
```

GETINTERFACES

Class Name	RemoteClass
Description	This method gets a list of Interfaces that this class implements.
Syntax	RemoteClass[] **getInterfaces**()
Parameters	None.
Returns	A array of RemoteClass objects that are interfaces implemented by this class.
Exceptions	If an error occurs, this method throws the exception Exception.
See Also	RemoteClass

Example

```
RemoteClass rmt;
    .
```

```
  .
  .
RemoteClass intArr[] = rmt.getInterfaces();

System.out.println("Interfaces implemented by the class " +
 rmt.getName() + " are:\n");
for(int i=0; i < intArr.length; ++i)
{
     System.out.println(i + ". " + intArr[i].getName());
}
  .
```

GETMETHOD

Class Name	RemoteClass
Description	This method returns an instance of the class RemoteField that contains all the information about the method.
Syntax	public RemoteField **getMethod**(String *name*)
Parameters	
String *name*	Name of the method.
Returns	An instance of the RemoteField containing the information about the method.
Exceptions	If an error occurs, this method throws the exception Exception.
See Also	RemoteField
Example	

```
RemoteClass rmt;
  .
  .
RemoteField mthd = rmt.getMethod("toString");
```

GETMETHODNAMES

Class Name	RemoteClass
Description	This method returns an array of all the method names supported by this class.
Syntax	public String[] **getMethodNames**()
Parameters	None.
Returns	An array of String containing the names of the methods supported by the class.
Exceptions	None.
See Also	String

Example

```
RemoteClass rmt;
 .
 .
String strArr[] = rmt.getMethodNames();
```

GETMETHODS

Class Name	RemoteClass
Description	This method returns an array of the RemoteField objects that contain all the information about the method.
Syntax	public RemoteField[] **getMethod**()
Parameters	None.
Returns	An array of the RemoteField objects, each containing the information about the method.
Exceptions	If an error occurs, this method throws the exception Exception.
See Also	RemoteField

Example

```
RemoteClass rmt;
 .
 .
RemoteField mthdArr[] = rmt.getMethods();
```

GETNAME

Class Name	RemoteClass
Description	This method returns the name of the class.
Syntax	public String **getName**()
Parameters	None.
Returns	A String containing name of the class.
Exceptions	If an error occurs, this method throws the exception Exception.
See Also	String

Example

```
RemoteClass rmt;
 .
 .
String clssName = rmt.getName();
```

GETSOURCEFILE

Class Name	RemoteClass
Description	This method gets a reference to the source file of the currently executing stack frame.
Syntax	public InputStream **getSourceFile**()
Parameters	None.
Returns	An instance of the FileInputStream of the currently executing stack frame.
Exceptions	If an error occurs, this method throws the exception Exception.
See Also	InputStream
Example	

```
RemoteClass rmt;
.
.
InputStream istrm = rmt.getSourceFile();
..
```

GETSOURCEFILENAME

Class Name	RemoteClass
Description	This method gets the name of the source file of the currently executing stack frame.
Syntax	public String **getSourceFileName**()
Parameters	None.
Returns	A string containing the file name of the current stack frame.
Exceptions	None.
See Also	String
Example	

```
RemoteClass rmt;
.
.
    .
System.out.println("Currently executing stack frame is " +
rmt.getSourceFileName());
..
```

GETSTATICFIELDS

Class Name	RemoteClass
Description	This method returns all the static fields (variables) for this class. This class basically overrides the getFields() class in the RemoteObject class.

Syntax	public RemoteField[] **getStaticFields**()
Parameters	None.
Returns	An array of the class RemoteField containing all the static fields for this class.
Exceptions	If an error occurs, this method throws the exception Exception.
See Also	RemoteField
Example	

```
RemoteClass rmt;
.
.
RemoteField fldArr[] = rmt.getStaticFields();
..
```

GETSUPERCLASS

Class Name	RemoteClass
Description	This method returns the superclass for this class.
Syntax	public RemoteClass **getSuperclass**()
Parameters	None.
Returns	An instance of the RemoteClass containing information about the super-class of the current class.
Exceptions	If an error occurs, this method throws the exception Exception.
Example	

```
RemoteClass rmt;
.
.
RemoteClass superClass = rmt.getSuperclass();
```

IGNOREEXCEPTIONS

Class Name	RemoteClass
Description	This method ensures that it does not enter the debugger when an instance of the RemoteClass is thrown.
Syntax	public void **ignoreExceptions**()
Parameters	None.
Returns	None.
Exceptions	If an error occurs, this method throws the exception ClassCastException.
Example	

```
RemoteClass rmt;
.
.
```

```
  .
rmt.ignoreExceptions();
```

ISINTERFACE

Class Name	RemoteClass
Description	This method returns a boolean true if the RemoteClass object is an interface, and a false if it is not.
Syntax	public boolean **isInterface**()
Parameters	None.
Returns	A true or false boolean value indicating whether the instance of the RemoteClass object is an interface or not.
Exceptions	If an error occurs, this method throws the exception Exception.
Example	

```
RemoteClass rmt;
.
.
if( rmt.isInterface())
System.out.println("interface");
else
System.out.println("class");
..
```

SETBREAKPOINTLINE

Class Name	RemoteClass
Description	This method is used for setting the break point at a specified line in the source text.
Syntax	public String **setBreakpointLine**(int *lineno*)
Parameters	
int *lineno*	The line number where the break point is set.
Returns	An empty string if the break point was successfully set and a description of the error message otherwise.
Exceptions	If an error occurs, this method throws the exception Exception.
Example	

```
RemoteClass rmt;
.
.
rmt.setBreakpointLine(20);
```

SETBREAKPOINTMETHOD

Class Name	RemoteClass
Description	This method is used for setting the break point at a specified method in a class.
Syntax	public String **setBreakpointMethod**(RemoteField *method*)
Parameters	
RemoteField *method*	The method where the break point is set to.
Returns	An empty string if the break point was successfully set and a description of the error message otherwise.
Exceptions	If an error occurs, this method throws the exception Exception.
Example	

```
RemoteClass rmt;
    .
    .
RemoteField rfld;
    .
    .
rmt.setBreakpointLine(rfld);
```

TOSTRING

Class Name	RemoteClass
Description	This method returns a string version of the RemoteClass. This method is called whenever a print method is called on this object.
Syntax	public String **toString**()
Parameters	None.
Returns	A String representation of the RemoteClass.
Exceptions	None.
Example	This segment of code shows how to access the string representation of the RemoteClass object.

```
RemoteClass rclss;
    .
    .
String  fullDescription = rclss.toString();
```

TYPENAME

Class Name	RemoteClass
Description	This method returns a string with the type name of the RemoteClass object.

Syntax	public String **typeName**()
Parameters	None.
Returns	A String object with the name of the class.
Exceptions	None.
See Also	String
Example	This segment of code shows how to access the type information from the RemoteClass object.

```
RemoteClass  rclss;
.
.
String rtype  = rclss.typeName();
```

The sun.tools.debug.RemoteField Class

The class RemoteField provides methods for debugging remote fields within the objects in a Java program executing on the Java interpreter. This class has methods to access information regarding the name, type, and other modifiers of the field. A method summary for this class is shown in Table 14-7. The class RemoteField inherits from the class Field and implements the interface AgentConstants. Both the class Field and the interface AgentConstants are local to the package sun.tools.debug.

Table 14-7 Summary of RemoteField methods

Method	Description
getModifiers	Returns the string with the field's modifiers, such as "static", "public", etc.
getName	Returns the name of the field
getType	Returns the type string describing the field
isStatic	Returns a boolean specifying whether the field is static
toString	Returns a string that represents the value of this object

REMOTEFIELD

Description	The class RemoteField is used to obtain information regarding the fields within the objects in the Java interpreter.
Syntax	public class **RemoteField** extends Field implements AgentConstants
Package	sun.tools.debug
Import	sun.tools.debug.RemoteField
Constructors	Does not have a public constructor (only created by other classes in the package).
Parameters	None.

Methods

GETMODIFIERS

Class Name	RemoteField
Description	This method returns all the modifiers, including the type modifiers, such as public, private, static, etc., for this field.
Syntax	public String **getModifiers**()
Parameters	None.
Returns	A String containing a list of access and type modifiers for this field separated by blank spaces. If the field has no modifiers, an empty String is returned.
Exceptions	None.
See Also	String
Example	

```
RemoteField rmt;
    .
    .
String modString = rmt.getModifiers();
```

GETNAME

Class Name	RemoteField
Description	This method returns the name of the remote field.
Syntax	public String **getName**()
Parameters	None.
Returns	A String containing the name of the RemoteField object.
Exceptions	None.
See Also	String
Example	

```
RemoteField rmt;
    .
    .
String fldName = rmt.getName();
```

GETTYPE

Class Name	RemoteField
Description	This method returns the type information of this remote field.
Syntax	public String **getType**()

Parameters	None.
Returns	A String containing the type information of this RemoteField object.
Exceptions	None.
See Also	String
Example	

```
RemoteField rmt;
.
.
String fldType = rmt.getType();
```

isStatic

Class Name	RemoteField
Description	This method returns a boolean value indicating whether this field is a class field or an instance field.
Syntax	public boolean **isStatic**()
Parameters	None.
Returns	A boolean value true if the field is static, false otherwise.
Exceptions	None.
Example	

```
RemoteField rmt;
.
.
if(rmt.isStatic())
{
    // Class field ...
}
else
{
    // instance field ...
}
```

toString

Class Name	RemoteField
Description	This method returns a string version of the RemoteField. This method is called whenever a print method is called on this object.
Syntax	public String **toString**()
Parameters	None.
Returns	A String representation of the RemoteField.
Exceptions	None.
Example	This segment of code shows how to access the string representation of the RemoteField object.

```
RemoteField  rfld;
.
.
String  fullDescription  = rfld.toString();
```

The sun.tools.debug.RemoteObject Class

The RemoteObject class allows access to an object in a remote Java interpreter. Remote debugging objects are not created by the local debugger, but are returned by the remote debugging agent when queried for the values of the instance or class variables or the stack (local) variables. Each remote object has a reference cached by the remote Java interpreter, so that object will not be garbage collected during examination. An instance of the RemoteObject is created when the value returned is not of a primitive type. A method summary for this class is shown in Table 14-8.

Table 14-8 Summary of RemoteObject methods

Method	Description
description	Returns a string with a verbose description of the object
getClazz	Returns the object's class (The name of the method is getClazz(), not getClass(), so that it does not conflict with (override) the method getClass() of the Object.)
getField	Returns an instance variable specified by the slot number or name
getFields	Returns an array of the instance fields of an object
getFieldValue	Returns the value of an instance variable specified by the slot number or name
getId	Returns the ID of the object
toString	Returns a string that represents the value of this object
typeName	Returns the RemoteValue's type name String("Object")

REMOTEOBJECT

Description	The class allows access to information about the objects in the Java interpreter.
Syntax	public class **RemoteObject** extends RemoteValue
Package	sun.tools.debug
Import	sun.tools.debug.RemoteObject
Constructors	Does not have a public constructor (only created by other classes in the package).
Parameters	None.
See Also	RemoteValue

Methods

DESCRIPTION

Class Name	RemoteObject
Description	This method is used for retrieving the description information about the instance of RemoteObject.
Syntax	public String **description**()
Parameters	None.
Returns	A string containing a verbose description the RemoteObject.
Exceptions	None.
See Also	String
Example	This segment of code shows how to access the verbose description of the instance of RemoteObject.

```
RemoteObject  robj;
.
.
String  value  = robj.description();
```

GETCLAZZ

Class Name	RemoteObject
Description	This method returns the name of the class of this object.
Syntax	public String **getClazz**()
Parameters	None.
Returns	A String containing the class name of this RemoteObject.
Exceptions	None.
See Also	String
Example	This segment of code shows how to access the class name from an instance of the RemoteObject.

```
RemoteObject robj;
.
.
String cname = robj.getClazz();
```

GETFIELD

Class Name	RemoteObject
Description	This method returns a specified instance variable from an instance of this object.

Syntax	public String **getField**(String *fldName*)
	public String **getField**(int *slotNum*)
Parameters	
String *fldName*	The name of the instance field.
int *slotNum*	The slot number (offset) of the instance variable in the object.
Returns	This method returns an instance of the RemoteField if it is found in this RemoteObject; otherwise, it returns a null.
Exceptions	If an error occurs, this method throws the exception Exception.
See Also	RemoteObject
Example	This segment of code shows how to access the instance fields from an instance of the RemoteObject.

```
RemoteObject robj;
 .
 .
RemoteField rfld = robj.getField("descrip");
RemoteField rfld1 = robj.getField(1);
```

GETFIELDS

Class Name	RemoteObject
Description	This method returns all the instance fields (variables) for this RemoteObject.
Syntax	public RemoteField[] **getFields**()
Parameters	None.
Returns	An array of the instances of the class RemoteField in this RemoteObject.
Exceptions	If an error occurs, this method throws the exception Exception.
See Also	RemoteField
Example	

```
RemoteObject robj;
 .
 .
RemoteField fldArr[] = robj.getFields();
 ..
```

GETFIELDVALUE

Class Name	RemoteObject
Description	This method returns the value of the specified instance variable from this RemoteObject.
Syntax	public String **getFieldValue**(String *fldName*)
	public String **getFieldValue**(int *slotNum*)

Parameters

String *fldName*	The name of the instance field.
int *slotNum*	The slot number (offset) of the instance variable in the object.
Returns	This method returns the value of an instance field if it is found in this RemoteObject; otherwise, it returns a null.
Exceptions	If an error occurs, this method throws the exception Exception.
See Also	RemoteValue
Example	This segment of code shows how to access the value of the instance fields from an instance of the RemoteObject.

```
RemoteObject robj;
.
.
RemoteValue rval1 = robj.getField("descrip");
RemoteValue rval2 = robj.getField(1);
```

GETID

Class Name	RemoteObject
Description	This method returns a unique ID for the object.
Syntax	public final int **getId**()
Parameters	None.
Returns	An integer value representing the ID of the object.
Exceptions	None.
Example	

```
RemoteObject robj;
.
.
int rid = robj.getId();
..
```

TOSTRING

Class Name	RemoteObject
Description	This method returns a string version of the RemoteObject. This method is called whenever a print method is called on this object.
Syntax	public String **toString**()
Parameters	None.
Returns	A String representation of the RemoteObject.
Exceptions	None.
Example	This segment of code shows how to access the string representation of the RemoteObject object.

```
RemoteObject  robj;
.
.
String  fullDescription  = robj.toString();
```

TYPENAME

Class Name	RemoteObject
Description	This method returns a string with the type name of this RemoteObject.
Syntax	public String **typeName**()
Parameters	None.
Returns	A String object with the type name of this RemoteObject, i.e., String("Object").
Exceptions	None.
See Also	String
Example	This segment of code shows how to access the type information from the RemoteObject object.

```
RemoteObject  robj;
.
.
String rtype  = robj.typeName();
```

The sun.tools.debug.RemoteValue Class

The RemoteValue class allows access to a copy of the value in the remote Java interpreter. This value may be of a primitive type, such as boolean, float or an object, class or an array, and so on. Remote values are not created by the local debugger but are returned by the remote debugging agent when queried for the instance or class variable or local variable. A method summary for this class is shown in Table 14-9.

Table 14-9 Summary of RemoteValue methods

Method	Description
description	Returns a string with a verbose description of this object
fromHex	Converts hexadecimal strings into ints
getType	Returns the type of the RemoteValue
isObject	Returns a boolean specifying whether the RemoteValue is an Object (as opposed to a primitive type such as int, char, etc.)
toHex	Converts an int to a hexadecimal String
typeName	Returns the RemoteValue's type as a String

RemoteValue

Description	The class allows access to information about the objects in the Java interpreter.
Syntax	public class **RemoteValue** extends Object
Package	sun.tools.debug
Import	sun.tools.debug.RemoteValue
Constructors	Does not have a public constructor (only created by other classes in the package).
Parameters	None.
See Also	Object

Methods

DESCRIPTION

Class Name	RemoteValue
Description	This method is used for retrieving the description information about the instance of RemoteValue.
Syntax	public String **description**()
Parameters	None.
Returns	A string containing a verbose description the RemoteValue object.
Exceptions	None.
See Also	String
Example	This segment of code shows how to access the verbose description of the instance of RemoteValue.

```
RemoteValue  rval;
  .
  .
String  descrip  = rval.description();
```

FROMHEX

Class Name	RemoteValue
Description	This method is used to convert hexadecimal strings into integers with the base 10.
Syntax	public static int **fromHex**(String *hexStr*)
Parameters	
String *hexStr*	A hexadecimal string that needs to be converted to a decimal integer value.

Returns	An integer value representation of the hexadecimal string.
Exceptions	None.
See Also	String
Example	This segment of code shows how to convert the hexadecimal string representation to integers.

```
int value = RemoteValue.fromHex("0xff3452");
```

GETTYPE

Class Name	RemoteValue
Description	This method returns the type information of this RemoteValue.
Syntax	public final int **getType**()
Parameters	None.
Returns	An integer representing the type information of this RemoteValue object.
Exceptions	None.
Example	

```
RemoteValue rval;
 .
 .
int fldType = rval.getType();
```

ISOBJECT

Class Name	RemoteValue
Description	This method is used to query this RemoteValue to figure out if it is of primitive type or not.
Syntax	public boolean **isObject**()
Parameters	None.
Returns	This method returns a boolean value true if the object is of a nonprimitive type; otherwise, it returns false.
Exceptions	None.
See Also	String
Example	This segment of code shows how to query the value of a RemoteValue object.

```
RemoteValue  rval;
 .
 .
if(rval.isObject())
{
   // A non-primitive type
}
```

```
else
{
   // A primitive type.
}
```

toHEX

Class Name	RemoteValue
Description	This method is used to convert an integer into a hexadecimal string.
Syntax	public String **toHex**(int *val*)
Parameters	
int *val*	A integer value.
Returns	A String representation of the hexadecimal string.
Exceptions	None.
See Also	String
Example	This segment of code shows how to convert integer values to hexadecimal strings.

```
String sval = RemoteValue.toHex(267373);
```

TYPENAME

Class Name	RemoteValue
Description	This method returns a string with the type name of this RemoteValue.
Syntax	public String **typeName**()
Parameters	None.
Returns	A String object with the type name of this RemoteValue.
Exceptions	None.
See Also	String
Example	This segment of code shows how to access the type information from the RemoteValue object.

```
RemoteValue  rval;
.
.
String rtype  = rval.typeName();
```

The sun.tools.debug.StackFrame Class

This class represents the stack frame of the suspended thread. The class StackFrame provides methods for debugging the stack frame of a Java program executing on the Java interpreter. A method summary for this class is shown in Table 14-10.

Method	Description
toString	Returns a string that represents the value of this object

StackFrame

Description	This class allows access to information about the StackFrame.
Syntax	public class **StackFrame** extends Object
Package	sun.tools.debug
Import	sun.tools.debug.StackFrame
Constructors	public **StackFrame**()
Parameters	None.
See Also	Object

Methods

toString

Class Name	StackFrame
Description	This method returns a string version of this StackFrame. This method is called whenever a print method is called on this object to display the stack frame.
Syntax	public String **toString**()
Parameters	None.
Returns	A String representation of the StackFrame.
Exceptions	None.
Example	This segment of code shows how to access the string representation of the StackFrame object.

```
StackFrame  rstack;
  .
  .
String  fullDescription  = rstack.toString();
```

The sun.tools.debug.RemoteStackFrame Class

This class provides an access to a stack frame of the suspended thread. The class RemoteStackFrame provides methods for accessing the stack frame of a Java program executing on the Java interpreter. A method summary for this class is shown in Table 14-11.

Table 14-11 Summary of RemoteStackFrame methods

Method	Description
getLineNumber	Returns the source file line number
getLocalVariable	Returns a specific stack variable
getLocalVariables	Returns an array of all valid variables and method arguments for this stack frame
getMethodName	Gets the method name referenced by this stack frame
getPC	Gets the program counter referenced by this stack frame
getRemoteClass	Gets the class this stack frame references

REMOTESTACKFRAME

Description	This class allows access to information about the RemoteStackFrame.
Syntax	public class **RemoteStackFrame** extends StackFrame
Package	sun.tools.debug
Import	sun.tools.debug.RemoteStackFrame
Constructors	Does not have a public constructor (only created by other classes in the package).
Parameters	None.
See Also	StackFrame

Methods

GETLINENUMBER

Class Name	RemoteStackFrame
Description	This method returns the source line where the current thread has been suspended.
Syntax	public int **getLineNumber**()
Parameters	None.
Returns	The line number of the source file as an integer value.
Exceptions	None.
Example	This segment of code shows how to get line number information of the current stack frame.

```
RemoteStackFrame sframe;
 .
 .
int lineNumber = sframe.getLineNumber();
```

GETLOCALVARIABLE

Class Name	RemoteStackFrame
Description	This method returns a specified stack variable.
Syntax	public RemoteStackVariable **getLocalVariable**(String *name*)
Parameters	
String *name*	The name of the stack variable.
Returns	An instance of a RemoteStackVariable.
Exceptions	If an error occurs, this method throws the exception Exception.
See Also	String, RemoteStackVariable
Example	The following code segment shows how to access a stack variable from a stack frame.

```
RemoteStackFrame sframe;
.
.
RemoteStackVariable rvar = sframe.getLocalVariable("i");
```

GETLOCALVARIABLES

Class Name	RemoteStackFrame
Description	This method returns an array containing all the stack variables. The stack variables include all the arguments to the method.
Syntax	public RemoteStackVariable[] **getLocalVariables**()
Parameters	None.
Returns	An array of instances of RemoteStackVariable.
Exceptions	If an error occurs, this method throws the exception Exception.
See Also	RemoteStackVariable
Example	The following code segment shows how to access a stack variable from a stack frame.

```
RemoteStackFrame sframe;
.
.
RemoteStackVariable rvar[] = sframe.getLocalVariables("i");
```

GETMETHODNAME

Class Name	RemoteStackFrame
Description	This method returns the name of the method where the current thread has been suspended.

Syntax	public String **getMethodName**()
Parameters	None.
Returns	The name of the method where the current thread has been suspended.
Exceptions	None.
Example	This segment of code shows how to get the name of the method referenced by the current stack frame.

```
RemoteStackFrame sframe;
.
.
String  mname = sframe.getMethodName();
```

GETPC

Class Name	RemoteStackFrame
Description	This method returns the program counter referenced by the current stack frame.
Syntax	public int **getPC**()
Parameters	None.
Returns	An integer value representing the program counter location in this thread of execution.
Exceptions	None.
Example	This code segment retrieves the program counter from the current stack frame.

```
RemoteStackFrame sframe;
.
.
int  pc = sframe.getPC();
```

GETREMOTECLASS

Class Name	RemoteStackFrame
Description	This method returns the remote class where the current thread has been suspended.
Syntax	public RemoteClass **getRemoteClass**()
Parameters	None.
Returns	The instance of the RemoteClass.
Exceptions	None.
See Also	RemoteClass
Example	This segment of code shows how to get the remote class referenced by the current stack frame.

```
RemoteStackFrame sframe;
.
.
RemoteClass rclass = sframe.getRemoteClass();
```

The sun.tools.debug.RemoteStackVariable Class

This class provides an access to a variable on the stack frame of the suspended thread. The class RemoteStackVariable provides methods for accessing the variable on the stack frame of a Java program executing on the Java interpreter. A method summary for this class is shown in Table 14-12.

Table 14-12 Summary of RemoteStackVariable methods

Method	Description
getName	Returns the name of a stack variable or argument
getValue	Returns the value of a stack variable or argument
isScope	Returns information as to whether variable is in scope

REMOTESTACKVARIABLE

Description	This class allows access to information about the RemoteStackVariable.
Syntax	public class **RemoteStackVariable** extends LocalVariable
Package	sun.tools.debug
Import	sun.tools.debug.RemoteStackVariable
Constructors	Does not have a public constructor (only created by other classes in the package).
Parameters	None.

Methods

GETNAME

Class Name	RemoteStackVariable
Description	This method returns the name of the remote stack variable.
Syntax	public String **getName**()
Parameters	None.
Returns	A String containing the name of the remote stack variable.
Exceptions	None.
See Also	String

Example   This example shows how to get the name of the stack variable.

```
RemoteStackVariable rmtvar;
  .
  .
String varName = rmtvar.getName();
```

GETVALUE

Class Name	RemoteStackVariable
Description	This method returns the value of the remote stack variable.
Syntax	public RemoteValue **getValue**()
Parameters	None.
Returns	An instance of a RemoteValue object representing the value of the remote stack variable.
Exceptions	None.
See Also	RemoteValue
Example	This segment of code shows how to retrieve the value from an instance of the RemoteStackVariable object.

```
RemoteStackVariable rmtvar;
  .
  .
RemoteValue varValue = rmtvar.getValue();
```

ISSCOPE

Class Name	RemoteStackVariable
Description	This method returns a boolean value indicating whether this local variable is in scope or not.
Syntax	public boolean **isScope**()
Parameters	None.
Returns	A boolean value true if this local variable is in scope; false otherwise.
Exceptions	None.
Example	This segment of code shows how to retrieve scope information from an instance of the RemoteStackVariable object.

```
RemoteStackVariable rmtvar;
  .
  .
if(rmtvar.isScope())
{
    // variable in scope...
```

continued on next page

continued from previous page
```
        // do something...
    }
    else
    {
        // Flag off an error.
    }
```

The sun.tools.debug.RemoteThreadGroup Class

This class allows access to the thread groups in a remote Java interpreter. The class RemoteThreadGroup provides methods for accessing the information about the thread groups within a Java program executing on the Java interpreter. A method summary for this class is shown in Table 14-13.

Table 14-13 Summary of RemoteThreadGroup methods

Method	Description
getName	Returns the name of the thread group
listThreads	Returns a list of threads that are currently running on the Java interpreter
stop	Stops the remote thread group

REMOTETHREADGROUP

Description	This class allows access to information about the remote thread groups in the Java interpreter.
Syntax	public class **RemoteThreadGroup** extends RemoteObject
Package	sun.tools.debug
Import	sun.tools.debug.RemoteThreadGroup
Constructors	Does not have a public constructor (only created by other classes in the package).
Parameters	None.
See Also	RemoteObject

Methods

GETNAME

Class Name	RemoteThreadGroup
Description	This method returns the name of this remote thread group.

Syntax	public String **getName**()
Parameters	None.
Returns	A String containing the name of the remote thread group.
Exceptions	If an error occurs, this method throws the exception Exception.
See Also	String
Example	This example shows how to get the name of the remote thread group.

```
RemoteThreadGroup rmtThr;
    .
    .
String varName = rmtThr.getName();
```

LISTTHREADS

Class Name	RemoteThreadGroup
Description	This method returns all the threads running in this remote thread group.
Syntax	public RemoteThread[] **listThreads**(boolean *recurs*)
Parameters	
boolean *recurs*	A true value would recursively fetch all the threads and their children, while a false value would fetch only the threads running directly under the thread group.
Returns	An array containing references to the remote thread.
Exceptions	If an error occurs, this method throws the exception Exception.
See Also	RemoteThread
Example	This example shows how to get the list of all the threads in a thread group.

```
RemoteThreadGroup rmtThr;
    .
    .
RemoteThread thrList[] = rmtThr.listThreads();
```

STOP

Class Name	RemoteThreadGroup
Description	This method returns all the threads running in this remote thread group.
Syntax	public void **stop**()
Parameters	None.
Exceptions	If an error occurs, this method throws the exception Exception.
Example	This example shows how to stop all the threads in a thread group.

```
RemoteThreadGroup rmtThr;
    .
    .
rmtThr.stop();
```

The sun.tools.debug.RemoteThread Class

The RemoteThread class allows access to a thread of execution in a remote Java interpreter. The class RemoteThread provides methods for accessing the information about the thread within a Java program executing on the Java interpreter. This class provides methods for accessing setting/unsetting the break point, getting the variables on the stack, getting the status of the thread, etc. A method summary for this class is shown in Table 14-14.

Table 14-14 Summary of RemoteThread methods

Method	Description
cont	Resumes a nonsuspended thread from the current break point
down	Changes the position of the current stack frame to be one or more frames lower toward the current program counter
dumpStack	Dumps the stack frame
getCurrentFrame	Gets the current stack frame
getCurrentFrameIndex	Gets the index of the current stack frame—depth of the stack frame
getName	Returns the name of the thread
getStackVariable	Gets the stack variable from the current stack frame
getStackVariables	Gets the stack variables (including the argument list) from the current stack frame
getStatus	Returns the thread status description
isSuspended	Returns a boolean value indicating whether this thread is suspended
next	Continues execution of this thread to the next line, but doesn't step into the method call
resetCurrentFrameIndex	Resets the stack frame index
resume	Resumes execution of this thread
setCurrentFrameIndex	Sets the stack frame index to the specified value
step	Continues execution of this thread to the next instruction
stop	Stops the execution of the remote thread
suspend	Suspends the execution of the thread
up	Changes the position of the current stack frame to be one or more frames higher or against the current program counter

REMOTETHREAD

Description	This class allows access to information about the remote thread in the Java interpreter.
Syntax	public class **RemoteThread** extends RemoteObject
Package	sun.tools.debug
Import	sun.tools.debug.RemoteThread

Constructors	Does not have a public constructor (only created by other classes in the package).
Parameters	None.
See Also	RemoteObject

Methods

CONT

Class Name	RemoteThread
Description	This method resumes the execution of a nonsuspended thread from the current break point.
Syntax	public void **cont**()
Parameters	None.
Returns	None.
Exceptions	If an error occurs, this method throws the exception Exception.
Example	This example shows how to continue the execution of the thread.

```
RemoteThread rmtThr;
.
.
rmtThr.cont();
// Resume execution from the current break point.
```

DOWN

Class Name	RemoteThread
Description	This method changes the current stack frame to be one or more frames lower toward the program counter.
Syntax	public void **down**(int *numFrames*)
Parameters	
int *numFrames*	The number of stack frames to move down.
Returns	None.
Exceptions	This method throws IllegalAccessError exception when the thread is not suspended or waiting at the break point. This method also throws ArrayIndexOutOfBoundsException exception when the requested stack frame is beyond the stack boundary. In case of any other exception this method throws Exception.

Example

```
RemoteThread rmtThr;
.
.
rmtThr.down(1);
```

DUMPSTACK

Class Name	RemoteThread
Description	This method is used to get a stack dump at a given point.
Syntax	public RemoteStackFrame[] **dumpStack**()
Parameters	None.
Returns	An array containing instances of the class RemoteStackFrame.
Exceptions	If an error occurs, this method throws the exception Exception.
See Also	RemoteStackFrame
Example	

```
RemoteThread rmtThr;
.
.
RemoteStackFrame sframe[] = rmtThr.dumpStack();
```

GETCURRENTFRAME

Class Name	RemoteThread
Description	This method is used to get the current stack frame.
Syntax	public RemoteStackFrame **getCurrentFrame**()
Parameters	None.
Returns	An instance of the class RemoteStackFrame.
Exceptions	This method throws an IllegalAccessError exception when the thread is not suspended or waiting at the break point.
See Also	RemoteStackFrame
Example	

```
RemoteThread rmtThr;
.
.
RemoteStackFrame rframe = rmtThr.getCurrentFrame();
```

GETCURRENTFRAMEINDEX

Class Name	RemoteThread
Description	This method is used to get the index of the current stack frame.
Syntax	public int **getCurrentFrameIndex**()
Parameters	None.
Returns	An integer that is an index in the stack frame.

Exceptions	None.
Example	

```
RemoteThread rmtThr;
    .
    .
int indx = rmtThr.getCurrentFrameIndex();
```

GETNAME

Class Name	RemoteThread
Description	This method returns the name of this remote thread.
Syntax	public String **getName**()
Parameters	None.
Returns	A String containing the name of the remote thread.
Exceptions	If an error occurs, this method throws the exception Exception.
See Also	String
Example	This example shows how to get the name of the remote thread.

```
RemoteThread rmtThr;
    .
    .
String thrName = rmtThr.getName();
```

GETSTACKVARIABLE

Class Name	RemoteThread
Description	This method returns a specified stack variable from the current stack frame.
Syntax	public RemoteStackVariable **getStackVariable**(String *name*)
Parameters	
String *name*	The name of the stack variable.
Returns	An instance of a RemoteStackVariable.
Exceptions	If an error occurs, this method throws the exception Exception.
See Also	String, RemoteStackVariable
Example	The following code segment shows how to access a stack variable from a stack frame.

```
RemoteThread rmtThr;
    .
    .
RemoteStackVariable rvar = rmtThr.getStackVariable("i");
```

GETSTACKVARIABLES

Class Name	RemoteThread
Description	This method returns an array containing all the stack variables including the arguments to the methods.
Syntax	public RemoteStackVariable[] **getStackVariables**()
Parameters	None.
Returns	An array of instances of RemoteStackVariable.
Exceptions	If an error occurs, this method throws the exception Exception.
See Also	RemoteStackVariable
Example	The following code segment shows how to access a stack variable from the current stack frame.

```
RemoteThread rmtThr;
  .
  .
RemoteStackVariable rvar[] = rmtThr.getStackVariables();
```

GETSTATUS

Class Name	RemoteThread
Description	This method returns a String containing the status information.
Syntax	public String **getStatus**()
Parameters	None.
Returns	A String with the status information about this thread.
Exceptions	If an error occurs, this method throws the exception Exception.
See Also	String
Example	The following code segment accesses the status information of the current thread.

```
RemoteThread rmtThr;
  .
  .
String statusInfo = rmtThr.getStatus();
```

ISSUSPENDED

Class Name	RemoteThread
Description	This method is used to find if the thread is suspended or not.
Syntax	public boolean **isSuspended**()

Parameters	None.
Returns	A boolean value true if the thread is suspended, and false otherwise.
Exceptions	None.
Example	The following segment of code shows how the method can be used.

```
RemoteThread rmtThr;
.
.
.
if(rmtThr.isSuspended())
{
    // A suspended thread....
}
else
{
    // A running thread...
}
```

NEXT

Class Name	RemoteThread
Description	This method continues the execution of the program to the next line. If the next source line happens to be a method call, this method does not step into that method. If no line number information is available, the call to this method is equivalent to the method step().
Syntax	public void **next**()
Parameters	None.
Returns	None.
Exceptions	This method throws an IllegalAccessError when the thread is not suspended or waiting at a break point.
Example	The following code segment show how to use this method.

```
RemoteThread rmtThr;
.
.
.
rmtThr.next();
```

RESETCURRENTFRAMEINDEX

Class Name	RemoteThread
Description	This method resets the current stack frame to the currently active one.
Syntax	public void **resetCurrentFrameIndex**()
Parameters	None.
Returns	None.

Exceptions	This method throws an IllegalAccessError when the thread is not suspended or waiting at a break point. This method also throws ArrayIndexOutOfBoundsException exception when the requested stack frame is beyond the stack boundary. In case of any other error, this method throws the exception Exception.
Example	The following segment of code demonstrates how to reset the stack frame.

```
RemoteThread rmtThr;
.
.
rmtThe.resetCurrentFrameIndex();
```

RESUME

Class Name	RemoteThread
Description	This method resumes the execution of the suspended thread.
Syntax	public void **resume**()
Parameters	None.
Returns	
Exceptions	In case of any error, this method throws the exception Exception.
Example	The following code shows how to use the method resume() to resume the current thread.

```
RemoteThread rmtThr;
.
.
  // Suspend the current thread..
.
rmtThr.resume(); // Thread starts
```

SETCURRENTFRAMEINDEX

Class Name	RemoteThread
Description	This method is used to get the index of the current stack frame.
Syntax	public void **setCurrentFrameIndex**(int *indx*)
Parameters	
int *indx*	Index of the stack frame.
Returns	None.
Exceptions	None.
Example	

```
RemoteThread rmtThr;
.
.
rmtThr.setCurrentFrame(4);
```

STEP

Class Name	RemoteThread
Description	This method continues the execution of the program to the next line. If the next source line happens to be a method call, this method steps into that method.
Syntax	public void **step**(boolean *skipLine*)
Parameters	
boolean *skipLine*	If the *skipLine* is set to true, the interpreter executes all the instructions up to the next source line; otherwise, it steps to the next instruction.
Returns	None.
Exceptions	This method throws an IllegalAccessError when the thread is not suspended or waiting at a break point.
Example	The following code segment shows how to use this method.

```
RemoteThread rmtThr;
 .
 .
rmtThr.step();
```

STOP

Class Name	RemoteThread
Description	This method stops the execution of the current thread.
Syntax	public void **stop**()
Parameters	None.
Returns	None.
Exceptions	In case of any error, this method throws the exception Exception
Example	This example shows how to stop the currently running threads.

```
RemoteThread rmtThr;
 .
 .
rmtThr.stop();
```

SUSPEND

Class Name	RemoteThread
Description	This method suspends the execution of the suspended thread.
Syntax	public void **suspend**()
Parameters	None.
Returns	None.

Exceptions	In case of any error, this method throws the exception Exception.
Example	The following code shows how to use the method suspend() to suspend the current thread.

```
RemoteThread rmtThr;
.
.
.
rmtThr.suspend(); // Thread stops
```

UP

Class Name	RemoteThread
Description	This method changes the current stack frame to be one or more frames higher.
Syntax	public void **up**(int *numFrames*)
Parameters	
int *numFrames*	The number of stack frames to move up.
Returns	None.
Exceptions	This method throws an IllegalAccessError exception when the thread is not suspended or waiting at the break point. This method also throws an ArrayIndexOutOfBoundsException exception when the requested stack frame is beyond the stack boundary. In all other cases this method throws Exception.
Example	

```
RemoteThread rmtThr;
.
.
rmtThr.up(1);
```

The sun.tools.debug.RemoteDebugger Class

This class defines a client interface to the Java debugging classes. It is used to instantiate a connection with the agent on the Java interpreter. The class RemoteDebugger provides methods for establishing a connection to the agent on the Java interpreter. This class provides methods for getting the threads and thread groups on the Java interpreter, lists of all the classes and break points, and methods to query the memory availability on the Java interpreter. A method summary for this class is shown in Table 14-15.

Table 14-15 Summary of RemoteDebugger methods

Method	Description
close	Closes the connection to the debugging agent
findClass	Finds a specified class
freeMemory	Reports the free memory available in the Java interpreter
gc	Initiates a garbage collection
get	Retrieves an object from the remote object cache
getExceptionCatchList	Returns a list of exceptions the debugger will stop on
getSourcePath	Returns the source file path the agent is currently using
itrace	Turns off/on the instruction tracing
listBreakpoints	Returns a list of break points that are currently set
listClasses	Returns a list of currently known classes
listThreadGroups	Lists all the thread groups that are currently running in the Java interpreter
run	Loads and runs a Java class
setSourcePath	Specifies a list of paths to use when searching for files
totalMemory	Reports the total memory usage of the Java interpreter
trace	Turns on/off method call tracing

REMOTEDEBUGGER

Description	This class makes a connection to the agent on the Java interpreter and provides access to the execution context of the Java program on the interpreter. This class is the entry point to access the remote debugging classes.
Syntax	public class **RemoteDebugger** extends Object
Package	sun.tools.debug
Import	sun.tools.debug.RemoteDebugger
Constructors	Public **RemoteDebugger**(String *javaArgs*, DebuggerCallback *client*, boolean *verbose*)
	public **RemoteDebugger**(String *host*, String *password*, DebuggerCallback *client*, boolean *verbose*)
Parameters	
String *javaArgs*	Optional Java command-line options like -*classpath*, etc.
DebuggerCallback *client*	The object to which the notifications are sent (the object must implement the DebuggerCallback interface).
boolean *verbose*	Turns on/off the internal debugging messages.

String *host*	The name of the system where the Java interpreter is running (default is the *localhost*).
String *password*	The password reported by the debuggable Java instance.
Exceptions	In case of any error, this method throws the exception Exception.
Example	This example shows how to create a new instance of RemoteDebugger to debug a local Java program.

```
RemoteDebugger dbgr;
DebuggerCallback clnt;
.
.   // create an instance of the DebuggerCallback
.
dbgr = new RemoteDebugger("", clnt, true);
.
```

This example shows how to create an instance of RemoteDebugger to debug a remote Java program.

```
RemoteDebugger dbgr;
DebuggerCallback clnt;
.
.   // create an instance of the DebuggerCallback
.
dbgr = new RemoteDebugger("abc.xyz.com","3afccd", clnt, true);
.
```

Methods

CLOSE

Class Name	RemoteDebugger
Description	This method is used to close the connection to the remote debugging agent.
Syntax	public void **close**()
Parameters	None.
Returns	None.
Exceptions	None.
Example	

```
RemoteDebugger dbgr;
.
.
dbgr.close();
```

FINDCLASS

Class Name	RemoteDebugger
Description	This method is used to find a specified class.
Syntax	public RemoteClass **findClass**(String *name*)
Parameters	
String *name*	The name of the class that needs to be searched. If a substring such as "String" is used in place of "java.lang.String", a first found match is returned.
Returns	An instance of the RemoteClass or null if not found.
Exceptions	In case of any error, this method throws the exception Exception.
Comments	A cache of all the known classes is maintained by the RemoteDebugger client; if a class name requested is not found in that cache, the request is passed on to the agent.

Example

```
RemoteDebugger dbgr;
.
.
RemoteClass rclss = dbgr.findClass("MyClass");

if(rclss != null)
{
    // The class has been found.!!
}
else
{
    // The class was not found???
}
```

FREEMEMORY

Class Name	RemoteDebugger
Description	This method is used to find out the amount of free memory available to the Java interpreter being debugged.
Syntax	public int **freeMemory**()
Parameters	None.
Returns	An integer value indicating the amount of free memory available to the Java interpreter.
Exceptions	None.
Example	

```
RemoteDebugger dbgr;
.
.
int freeMem = dbgr.freeMemory();
```

GC

Class Name	RemoteDebugger
Description	This method frees all the objects referenced by the debugger except the ones specified.
Syntax	public void **gc**(RemoteObject *saveList[]*)
Parameters	
RemoteObject *saveList[]*	An array of objects that should be left untouched by the garbage collector.
Returns	None.
Exceptions	Exception
See Also	RemoteObject
Comments	The remote debugger maintains a copy of each object it has examined, so that references won't become invalidated by the garbage collector of the Java interpreter being debugged.
Example	The following example illustrates the use of the garbage collection method.

```
RemoteDebugger dbgr;
.
.
RemoteObject objArr[] = new RemoteObject[10];
.
dbgr.gc(objArr);
```

GET

Class Name	RemoteDebugger
Description	This method is used to get an object from the remote object cache.
Syntax	public RemoteObject **get**(Integer *id*)
Parameters	
Integer *id*	The remote object's ID.
Returns	The specified RemoteObject, or null if the object has not been cached.
Exceptions	None.
See Also	RemoteObject
Example	The following example shows how to get a remote object from remote object cache.

```
RemoteDebugger dbgr;
.
.
RemoteObject obj = dbgr.get(Integer(0x254fac));
```

GETEXCEPTIONCATCHLIST

Class Name	RemoteDebugger
Description	This method is used to get the list of the exceptions the debugger will stop on.
Syntax	public String[] **getExceptionCatchList**()
Parameters	None.
Returns	An array of exception class names that the debugger stops on.
Exceptions	In case of any error, this method throws the exception Exception.
See Also	String
Example	The following example shows how to get a list of exceptions currently trapped by the debugger.

```
RemoteDebugger dbgr;
 .
 .
 .
String execpList[] = dbgr.getExceptionCatchList();
```

GETSOURCEPATH

Class Name	RemoteDebugger
Description	This method is used to get the source file path the agent is currently using.
Syntax	public String **getSourcePath**()
Parameters	None.
Returns	A string consisting of a list of colon-delineated paths.
Exceptions	In case of any error, this method throws the exception Exception.
See Also	String
Example	The following example shows how to get a source path the agent is currently using.

```
RemoteDebugger dbgr;
 .
 .
 .
String srcPath = dbgr.getSourcePath();
```

ITRACE

Class Name	RemoteDebugger
Description	This method is used to toggle instruction tracing. When turned on, each Java instruction is reported to the *stdout* of the Java interpreter being debugged. This output is not captured in any way by the remote debugger.
Syntax	public void **itrace**(boolean *traceFlag*)

Parameters

boolean *traceFlag*   A boolean value to toggle instructions on/off.

Returns   None.

Exceptions   In case of any error, this method throws the exception Exception.

Example   The following example illustrates the usage of the method itrace().

```
RemoteDebugger dbgr;
  .
  .
dbgr.itrace();
```

LISTBREAKPOINTS

Class Name	RemoteDebugger
Description	This method is used to get the list of the break points the debugger will stop on.
Syntax	public String[] **listBreakpoints**()
Parameters	None.
Returns	An array of break points in the form className:lineNumber that the debugger stops on.
Exceptions	In case of any error, this method throws the exception Exception.
See Also	String
Example	The following example shows how to get a list of break points currently trapped by the debugger.

```
RemoteDebugger dbgr;
  .
  .
String bpList[] = dbgr.listBreakpoints();
```

LISTCLASSES

Class Name	RemoteDebugger
Description	This method lists the currently known classes.
Syntax	public RemoteClass[] **listClasses**()
Parameters	None.
Returns	An array of RemoteClass objects that are currently known to the client.
Exceptions	In case of any error, this method throws the exception Exception.
See Also	RemoteClass
Example	The following example shows how to get a list of classes currently known to the debugger.

```
RemoteDebugger dbgr;
.
.
RemoteClass rlist[] = dbgr.listClasses();
```

LISTTHREADGROUPS

Class Names	RemoteDebugger
Description	This method lists the currently known thread groups.
Syntax	public RemoteThreadGroup[] **listThreadGroups**(RemoteThreadGroup *rgrp*)
Parameters	
RemoteThreadGroup *rgrp*he	The thread group that holds the groups to be listed, or null for all thread groups.
Returns	An array of RemoteThreadGroup objects that are currently known to the client.
Exceptions	In case of any error, this method throws the exception Exception.
See Also	RemoteThreadGroup
Example	The following example shows how to get a list of all the thread groups currently known to the debugger.

```
RemoteDebugger dbgr;
.
.
RemoteThreadGroup rlist[] = dbgr.listThreadGroups();
```

RUN

Class Name	RemoteDebugger
Description	This method is used to load and run a runnable Java class, with any optional parameters. The class is started inside a new thread group in the Java interpreter being debugged.
Syntax	public RemoteThreadGroup **run**(int *argc*, String *argv[]*)
Parameters	
int *argc*	The number of parameters.
String *argv[]*	The array of parameters. The class to be run is first, followed by any optional parameters used by that class.
Returns	A reference to the new ThreadGroup the class is running in, or null on error.
Exceptions	In case of any error, this method throws the exception Exception.
See Also	RemoteThreadGroup

Example The following example shows how to run a runnable Java class within an instance of the RemoteDebugger class.

```
RemoteDebugger dbgr;
.
.
.
String argv[] = {"MyClass"};
.
.
.
RemoteThreadGroup ngrp = dbgr.run(1, argv);
```

SETSOURCEPATH

Class Name	RemoteDebugger
Description	This method is used to specify the list of paths to use when searching for a source file.
Syntax	public void **setSourcePath**(String *spath*)
Parameters	
String *spath*	A string consisting of a list of colon-delineated paths.
Returns	None.
Exceptions	In case of any error, this method throws the exception Exception.
See Also	String
Example	The following example shows how to set the source path.

```
RemoteDebugger dbgr;
.
.
.
dbgr.setSourcePath(
"C:\java\mylib\classes:c:\thirdparty\classes");
```

TOTALMEMORY

Class Name	RemoteDebugger
Description	This method is used to find out the total amount of memory used by the Java interpreter being debugged.
Syntax	public int **totalMemory**()
Parameters	None.
Returns	An integer value indicating the amount of memory used by the Java interpreter.
Exceptions	In case of any error, this method throws the exception Exception.
Example	

```
RemoteDebugger dbgr;
.
.
.
int tMem = dbgr.totalMemory();
```

TRACE

Class Name	RemoteDebugger
Description	This method is used to toggle method call tracing. When turned on, each Java method call is reported to the *stdout* of the Java interpreter being debugged. This output is not captured in any way by the remote debugger.
Syntax	public void **trace**(boolean *traceFlag*)
Parameters	
boolean *traceFlag*	A boolean value to toggle tracing on/off.
Returns	None.
Exceptions	In case of any error, this method throws the exception Exception.
Example	The following example illustrates the usage of the method trace().

```
RemoteDebugger dbgr;
.
.
dbgr.trace();
```

The sun.tools.debug.DebuggerCallback Interface

The DebuggerCallback interface is used to asynchronously communicate information from the agent to the debugger. A method summary for this interface is shown in Table 14-16.

Table 14-16 Summary of DebuggerCallback methods

Method	Description
breakpointEvent	A break point has been hit in the specified thread.
exceptionEvent	An exception has occurred.
printToConsole	Prints information to the debugger's console window.
quitEvent	The Java interpreter has exited.
threadDeathEvent	A thread has died.

DEBUGGERCALLBACK

Description	This interface is used by the agent to communicate to the debugger.
Syntax	public interface **DebuggerCallback**
Package	sun.tools.debug
Import	sun.tools.debug.DebuggerCallback
Constructors	None.
Parameters	None.

Methods

BREAKPOINTEVENT

Interface Name	DebuggerCallback
Description	This method is called when a break point has been hit in the specified thread.
Syntax	public abstract void **breakpointEvent**(RemoteThread *t*)
Parameters	
RemoteThread *t*	The thread in which the break point has been encountered.
Returns	None.
Exceptions	Exception

EXCEPTIONEVENT

Interface Name	DebuggerCallback
Description	This method is called when an exception has occurred in the specified thread.
Syntax	public abstract void **exceptionEvent**(RemoteThread *t*, String *errText*)
Parameters	
RemoteThread *t*	The thread in which the break point has been encountered.
String *errText*	Text description about the event.
Returns	None.
Exceptions	Exception

PRINTTOCONSOLE

Interface Name	DebuggerCallback
Description	This method is called whenever text needs to be printed to the debugger's console window.
Syntax	public abstract void **printToConsole**(String text)
Parameters	
String *text*	The text to be printed on the debugger's console window.
Returns	None.
Exceptions	Exception

QUITEVENT

Interface Name	DebuggerCallback
Description	This method is called when the client interpreter has exited, either by returning from its main thread, or by calling System.exit().
Syntax	public abstract void **quitEvent**()
Parameters	None.
Returns	None.
Exceptions	None.

THREADDEATHEVENT

Interface Name	DebuggerCallback
Description	This method is called when the thread has died.
Syntax	public abstract void **threadDeathEvent**(RemoteThread *t*)
Parameters	
RemoteThread *t*	The thread in which the break point has been encountered.
Returns	None.
Exceptions	Exception

The Java Debugging Model Project: A Simple Execution Profiler

Project Overview

This project uses the APIs explained in this chapter to develop a simple Java program to profile a Java program executing in the Java interpreter. The profiler will print the following profile information on the console:

- Memory available on the client
- The thread groups and the threads that are currently running on the Java interpreter
- List of exceptions that the agent recognizes
- List of all the classes that have been loaded by the agent
- Details of the class (that contains main()) that is being executed, like the class and instance variables and methods

The complete listing of the program is shown in Listing 14-1.

The program does not print out the result of the execution because all that's needed is a profile of execution, such as the classes it loads, names of the classes, etc. The program comprises just one class—ExecutionProfiler, which implements the interface DebuggerCallback. So the class ExecutionProfiler implements the following methods:

- breakpointEvent()

- exceptionEvent()

- printToConsole()

- quitEvent()

- threadDeathEvent()

Building the Project

1. To instantiate the class RemoteDebugger, you need a class that implements the interface DebuggerCallback. Since the class ExecutionProfiler implements the interface DebuggerCallback, you can use the this reference to instantiate the class RemoteDebugger. The constructor of the class ExecutionProfiler takes three arguments—an array of Strings, a reference to a print stream, and a boolean value. In the constructor, the instance variables are initialized and a new instance of the class RemoteDebugger is created. The program is then executed within the instance of the RemoteDebugger. This is done by passing *argc* and *argv* to the method run(). Then a global profile (memory usage, etc.), thread profile (names of threads and thread groups), exception profile (exceptions being trapped by the agent), and class profile (a list of classes that are loaded) are printed. Next, the garbage collector is run on the remote debugger to free any unused references and again print the global profile. Before exiting the constructor, the connection to the agent is closed.

2. The method printFields() checks to see if the array of RemoteField is empty. If the array returned has at least one element, then the details about the field, like the access modifiers for the field and type information, are printed. The method printClassProfile() takes either one argument that is a name of a class, or no argument. If the method printClassProfile() is called with no arguments, the remote debugger is queried to get a list of all the classes loaded by the agent. It prints out the names of all the classes and the interfaces that are loaded by the agent. If the method printClassProfile() is called with one argument, then a reference is first retrieved to the instance of RemoteClass from the remote debugger. If the class is present, the following information is printed on the console:

- Type information like "class" or "interface"

- Superclass of the current class

- Source file name where this class can be found

- List of the instance variables
- List of the class variables
- List of the class/instance methods

3. The method printExceptionProfile() prints out a list of all the exceptions that the debugger stops on. The method printGlobalProfile() queries the remote debugger and prints out the total memory and the free memory in bytes. The method printThreadProfile() gets a list of all the thread groups running in the Java interpreter. The code iterates over all the thread groups, looks recursively for threads, and prints them on the console.

4. The method breakpointEvent() is called whenever a break point is encountered by the remote debugger. Since no break points are being set, this handler is unnecessary. Similarly, there is no need to do anything in the method exceptionEvent(). You don't want to print the output of program you are executing under the remote debugger, so the method printToConsole() does nothing. In the event of program termination or a thread death, the methods quitEvent() and threadDeathEvent() are called. In the methods quitEvent() and threadDeathEvent(), the connection of the remote debugger to the agent is closed and the system is exited.

5. The main program creates a new instance of the class ExecutionProfiler and sends the output of the profiler to the System.out. The verbose flag is set to true and all the command-line arguments are passed to the constructor. Any exceptions that are generated are caught in the *catch* block, and an appropriate error message and the usage information is printed out on the console.

Now, let's run this program on a very simple program called urlTest. The urlTest program takes an HTTP URL in the command line, and prints the HTML file on the standard output. The program can be used to find out if such a URL exists on the network. The program listing is shown in Listing 14-2. This program can be run on the command line using the following commands:

compile

```
javac urlTest.java
```

execute

```
java urlTest http://www.finex.com/
```

The above command will print the uninterpreted HTML file on your terminal. To see the execution profiler report, try the following on the command line:

compile

```
javac ExecutionProfiler.java
```

execute

```
java ExecutionProfiler urlTest http://www.finex.com/
```

output

```
[debugger: starting child: C:\JAVA\BIN\..\bin\java_g -debug  sun.tools.debug.EmptyApp]
[debugger: password returned: 4iccss]


Total Memory: 3145720 bytes
Free Memory : 2773416 bytes


Thread Groups:
ThreadGroup Name: system
     Thread Name: Finalizer thread
     Thread Name: Debugger agent
     Thread Name: Breakpoint handler
     Thread Name: main
     Thread Name: main
ThreadGroup Name: main
     Thread Name: main
ThreadGroup Name: urlTest.main
     Thread Name: main


Exception Groups:
(none)


Loaded Classes/Interfaces :
Class:         java.lang.Thread
Class:         java.lang.Object
Class:         java.lang.Class
Class:         java.lang.String
Class:         java.lang.ThreadDeath
Class:         java.lang.Error
Class:         java.lang.Throwable
Class:         java.lang.Exception
Class:         java.lang.RuntimeException
Interface:     java.lang.Cloneable
Class:         java.lang.ThreadGroup
Class:         java.lang.System
Class:         java.io.BufferedInputStream
Class:         java.io.FilterInputStream
Class:         java.io.InputStream
Class:         java.io.FileInputStream
Class:         java.io.FileDescriptor
Class:         java.io.PrintStream
Class:         java.io.FilterOutputStream
Class:         java.io.OutputStream
Class:         java.io.BufferedOutputStream
Class:         java.io.FileOutputStream
Class:         java.lang.StringBuffer
Class:         java.lang.Integer
Class:         java.lang.Number
Class:         java.lang.NoClassDefFoundError
Class:         java.lang.LinkageError
Class:         java.lang.OutOfMemoryError
Class:         java.lang.VirtualMachineError
Class:         sun.tools.debug.EmptyApp
Class:         sun.tools.debug.Agent
```

```
Class:        java.lang.Runtime
Class:        java.util.Properties
Class:        java.util.Hashtable
Class:        java.util.Dictionary
Class:        java.util.HashtableEntry
Class:        java.net.ServerSocket
Class:        java.net.PlainSocketImpl
Class:        java.net.SocketImpl
Class:        java.net.InetAddress
Class:        java.lang.Character
Class:        java.net.InetAddress;
Class:        java.lang.Math
Class:        java.util.Random
Class:        java.lang.Compiler
Class:        sun.tools.java.ClassPath
Class:        java.io.File
Class:        sun.tools.java.ClassPathEntry
Class:        sun.tools.zip.ZipFile
Class:        java.io.RandomAccessFile
Interface:    sun.tools.zip.ZipConstants
Class:        sun.tools.zip.ZipEntry
Class:        sun.tools.debug.BreakpointHandler
Class:        sun.tools.debug.BreakpointQueue
Class:        java.util.Vector
Class:        java.net.Socket
Class:        java.io.DataInputStream
Class:        java.net.SocketInputStream
Class:        sun.tools.debug.ResponseStream
Class:        java.net.SocketOutputStream
Class:        java.io.DataOutputStream
Class:        sun.tools.debug.AgentOutputStream
Class:        java.util.HashtableEnumerator
Class:        java.util.VectorEnumerator
Class:        urlTest
Class:        sun.tools.debug.MainThread


Class Details:
Name: urlTest
Super Class: java.lang.Object
Source File Name: urlTest.java

Instance Variable List:
(none)

Class Variable List:
static  URL url

Class/Instance Methods:
public static  void main(String[])
public  void <init>()
static  void <clinit>()


After Garbage Collection
Total Memory: 3145720 bytes
Free Memory : 2870416 bytes
```

Listing 14-1 Program ExecutionProfiler.java

```java
import java.lang.*;
import java.io.*;
import java.net.*;
import sun.tools.debug.*;

//
// This class prints out all the thread/attributes/methods of the program
// that is being executed by the agent in the java interpreter.
//


class ExecutionProfiler implements DebuggerCallback
{
    RemoteDebugger          rmtDebugger; // reference to the instance of the
                                         // RemoteDebugger
    PrintStream           console; // Where the output is printed.
                                   // You could Add a GUI interface to this
                                   // program, with minimum changes.

    // Constructor.

    ExecutionProfiler(String[] args, PrintStream consl, boolean verbose)
                                throws Exception
    {
        String argLine = "";
                // Let's create an instance of the rmtDebugger with no
                // command line arguments.
        console = consl;        // A reference to the PrintStream.
        rmtDebugger = new RemoteDebugger(argLine, this, verbose);
                // Create a new instance of the class
                // RemoteDebugger
        rmtDebugger.run(args.length, args);
                    // Now lets start the debugger with the
                    // specified command line arguments.
        console.print("\n\n");
        printGlobalProfile();
                    // Print global profile information like the memory
                    // Total memory & free memory in the client.
        printThreadProfile(); // Thread related information.
        printExceptionProfile();
                // A list of exceptions that the client/RemoteDebugger
                // will stop on.
        printClassProfile();
                // Print all the classes that have been loaded into the
                // system.
        printClassProfile(args[0]);
                // print details of the class that we are executing.
        RemoteObject[] robj = new RemoteObject[0];
                // Create an array containing no elements.
        rmtDebugger.gc(robj); // Run the garbage collector
        console.println("After Garbage Collection");
        printGlobalProfile(); // Check the memory usage etc.
        rmtDebugger.close();  // Close the debugger.
    }

    private void printFields(RemoteField[] rfield) throws Exception
```

```
{
    if(rfield.length == 0) //If the remote field array is empty
    {
        console.println("(none)");
        return;
    }

    // If the array has some elements.

    for(int i=0; i < rfield.length; ++i)
    {
        // Print the details about this field.
        console.println(rfield[i].getModifiers() +
                        " " + rfield[i].getType());
    }
}

private void printClassProfile(String clssName) throws Exception
{
    // Retrieve the class from the rmtDebugger
    RemoteClass rclss = rmtDebugger.findClass(clssName);

    if(rclss == null)
        return;

    if(rclss.isInterface()) //Check if the RemoteClass is an interface
    {
        console.print("Interface ");
    }
    else
    {
        console.print("Class ");
    }

    console.println("Details: ");
    console.println("Name: " + rclss.getName());
                        // print the name of the class
                        // and the name of the super class.
    console.println("Super Class: " + (rclss.getSuperclass()).getName());

    console.println("Source File Name: " +
                rclss.getSourceFileName()); // Name of the file.
    console.println("\nInstance Variable List:");
    RemoteField[] ifield = rclss.getInstanceFields();
    // Get a list of all the instance variables
    printFields(ifield);
    console.println("\nClass Variable List:");
    RemoteField[] sfield = rclss.getStaticFields();
    // Get a list of all class varibles.
    printFields(sfield); // Print them.
    console.println("\nClass/Instance Methods:");
    RemoteField[] mfield = rclss.getMethods();
    // Get a list of all methods
    printFields(mfield); // print them.
    console.print("\n\n");
}
```

continued on next page

continued from previous page

```java
    private void printClassProfile() throws Exception
    {
        RemoteClass[] rmtClass = rmtDebugger.listClasses();
                                // Get a list of all the
                                // classes loaded by the agent.
        console.println("Loaded Classes/Interfaces : ");
        for(int i=0; i < rmtClass.length; ++i)
        {
            if(rmtClass[i].isInterface())
                console.print("Interface:\t");
            else
                console.print("Class:\t\t");

            console.println(rmtClass[i].getName());
                                // print the class/interface.
        }

        console.print("\n\n");
    }

    private void printExceptionProfile() throws Exception
    {
        String[] exceptList = rmtDebugger.getExceptionCatchList();
            // Get a list of all exceptions caught by the client.
        console.println("Exception Groups: ");

        if(exceptList.length == 0)
        {
            console.println("(none)");
        }

        for(int i=0; i < exceptList.length; ++i)
        {
            console.println("\t" + exceptList[i]);
            // Print a list of all the Exceptions.
        }

        console.print("\n\n");
    }

    private void printGlobalProfile() throws Exception
    {
        console.println("Total Memory: " + rmtDebugger.totalMemory()
                                + " bytes");
        console.println("Free Memory : " + rmtDebugger.freeMemory()
                                + " bytes");
        console.print("\n\n");
    }

    private void printThreadProfile() throws Exception
    {
        console.println("Thread Groups: ");
        RemoteThreadGroup[] thrGrp = rmtDebugger.listThreadGroups(null);
                // Get a list of all ThreadGroup in the java interpreter.

        for(int i=0; i < thrGrp.length; ++i)
        {
```

```
            console.println("ThreadGroup Name: " + thrGrp[i].getName());
                            // get ThreadGroup
            RemoteThread[] thrList = thrGrp[i].listThreads(true);
                            // List all the threads recursively.
            for(int j=0; j < thrList.length; ++j)
            {
                console.println("\t" + "Thread Name: " +
                                thrList[j].getName());
                // print the name of the thread.
            }
        }

        console.print("\n\n");
}

public void breakpointEvent(RemoteThread rThr)
{
    // This method is used to Handle the breakpoint exception.
    // We don't need this handler.
}

public void exceptionEvent(RemoteThread rThr, String msg)
{
    // This Method is called when an exception is encountered.
    // We don't need this at all.
}

public void printToConsole(String txt)
{
    // We don't want the output of the program to clutter the profile
    // information, so we do nothing.
}

public void quitEvent()
{
    rmtDebugger.close(); // close the connection to the agent.
    System.exit(1); // Exit the program.
}

public void threadDeathEvent(RemoteThread t)
{
    rmtDebugger.close(); // close the connection to the agent.
    System.exit(1); // Exit the program.
}

public static void main(String arg[])
{
    ExecutionProfiler rpf;     // A refrence to the profiler.
    boolean verbose = true; // We choose verbose mode.

    try
    {
        // Create a new instance of the Execution profiler.
        // Send in all the arguments that are passed to the program
        // Send the output of the profiler to the System.out.
        rpf = new ExecutionProfiler(arg, System.out, verbose);
    }
```

continued on next page

continued from previous page

```
        catch(Exception e)
        {
            // In case of an exception............

            System.out.println("Execution Profiler Error: " + e);
            System.out.print("\nUsage: ");
            System.out.println("java ExecutionProfiler <JavaProgram> \
            <arg1> <arg2>      ...");
            System.out.flush();
            System.exit(1);
        }
    }
}
```

Listing 14-2 Program urlTest.java

```
import java.io.*;
import java.net.*;


public class urlTest
{
    static URL url = null;

    public static void main(String[] args)
    {
        InputStream inp = null;

        if( args.length < 1)
        {
            System.out.println("usage urlTest URL");
            return;
        }

        try
        {
            url = new URL(args[0]);
        }
        catch (MalformedURLException e)
        {
            System.out.println("Malformed URL Exception");
            return;
        }

        try
        {
            inp = url.openStream();

        } catch (IOException e)
        {
            System.out.println("IO Exception");
            return;
        }
```

```
    //   System.out.println("The value == " + inp);

DataInputStream din = new DataInputStream(inp);

while(true)
{
    try
    {
        System.out.print( (char) din.readByte());
    }
    catch(EOFException e)
    {
        break;
    }
    catch(IOException e)
    {
        break;
    }
}
}
}
```

APPENDIX A

CLASS AND INTERFACE INHERITANCE DIAGRAMS

The Java Developer's Kit (JDK) has classes organized into logical units called *packages*. A package is a logical collection of one or more classes with similar functionality. For example, all the classes related to networking are logically grouped together in a package called java.net. Grouping classes together in the form of packages makes it easier for the programmer to browse a given class in the toolkit, and it also helps in hiding classes and interfaces across different applications. In this appendix, all the classes and interfaces in the JDK are shown in the form of inheritance diagrams. Inheritance diagrams show the relationship between various classes and interfaces in the JDK. These diagrams can be an excellent reference for basic information about a class or an interface. Inheritance diagrams in this appendix are organized according to the packages in the JDK. The list of packages in the JDK and their brief description is shown in Table A-1. Inheritance diagrams can be helpful in developing Java applets and programs. Figure A-1 shows the conventions used in the inheritance diagrams. Figures A-2 to A-9 show the inheritance diagrams organized according to the packages in the JDK.

Table A-1 Packages in the Java Developer's Kit

Package	Description
java.applet	This package contains classes and interfaces needed to create Java applets.
java.awt	This package contains classes for simple graphics and user interface component objects.
java.awt.image	This package contains classes that help in manipulating image data.
java.io	This package contains classes to handle buffered and file input and output.
java.net	This package contains classes to establish a network connection using sockets. It also contains classes to manipulate URLs and the IP addresses.
java.util	This package contains the Java implementation of a few core data structures like vector, stack, dictionary, etc.
sun.tools.debug	This package contains classes needed for debugging a Java program.

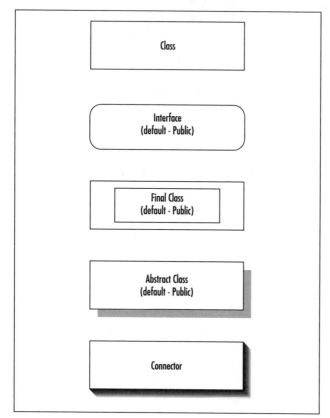

Figure A-1 Conventions used in the class inheritance diagrams

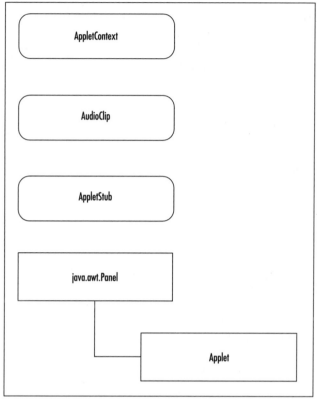

Figure A-2 Package java.applet

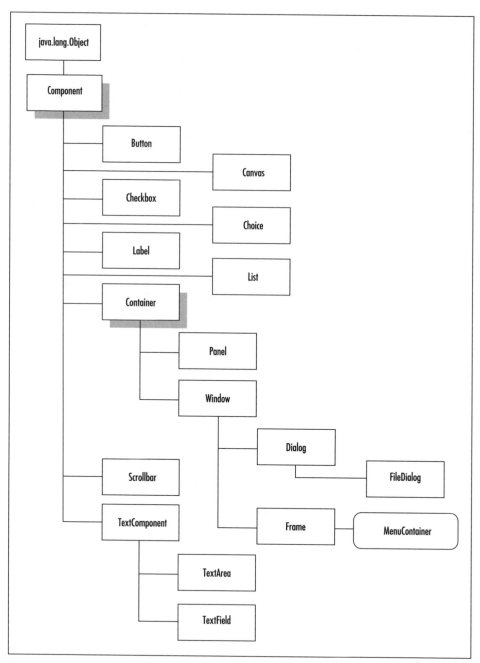

Figure A-3 Package java.awt

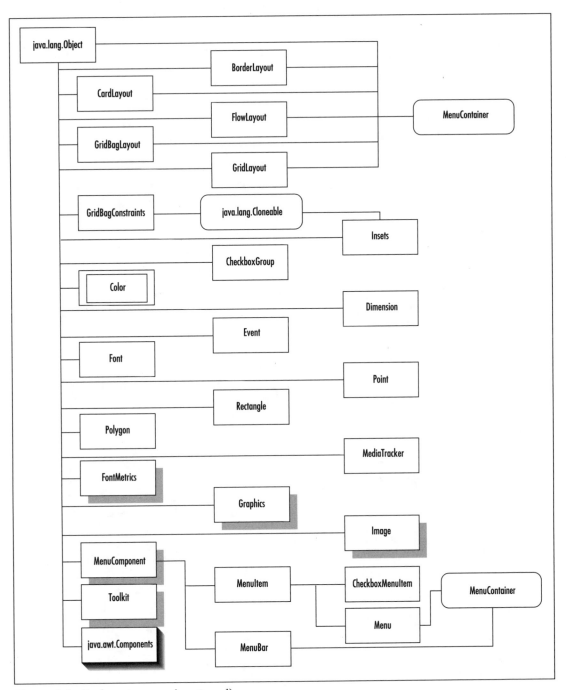

Figure A-3 Package java.awt (continued)

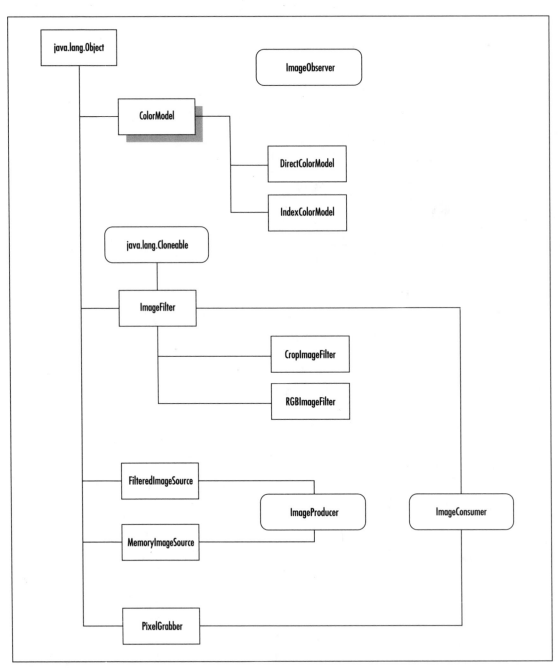

Figure A-4 Package java.awt image

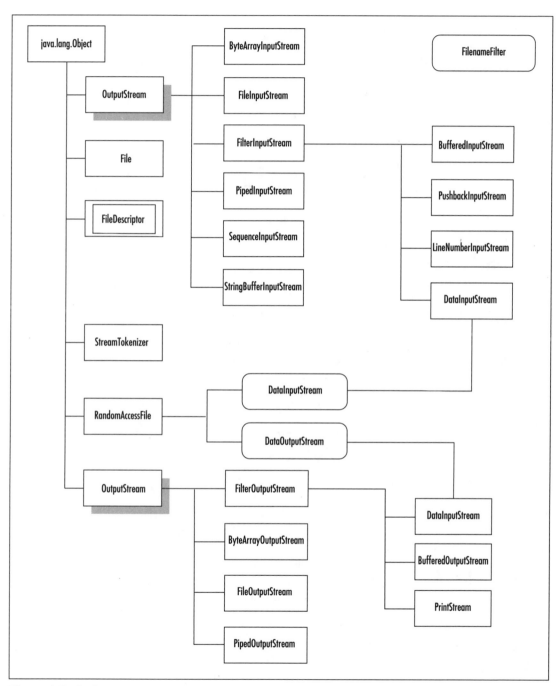

Figure A-5 Package java.io

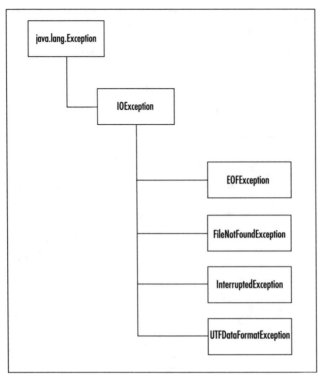

Figure A-5   Package java.io (continued)

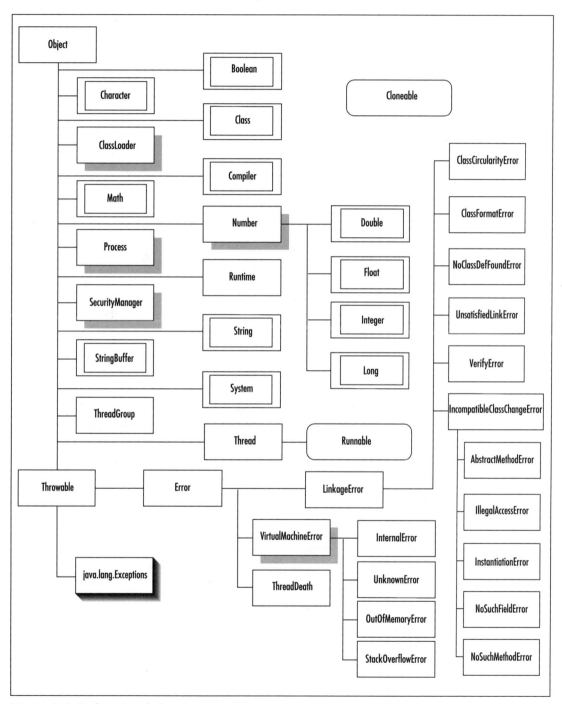

Figure A-6 Package java.lang

Figure A-6 Package java.lang

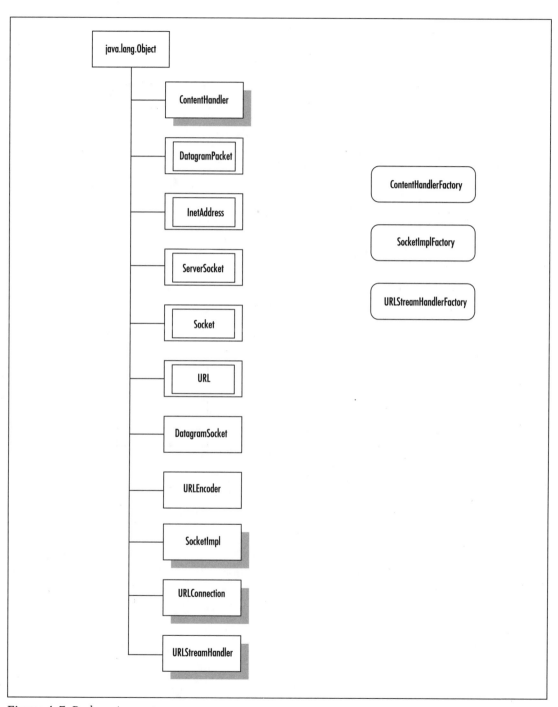

Figure A-7 Package java.net

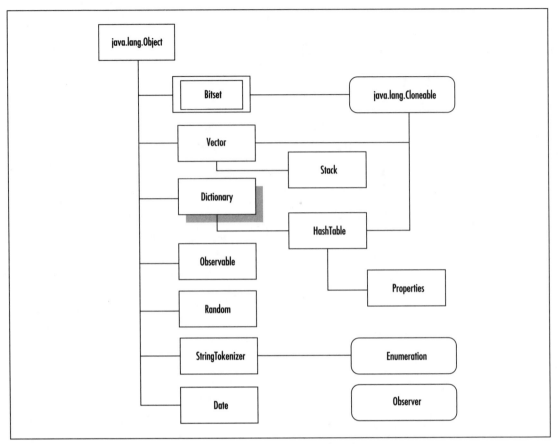

Figure A-8 Package java.util

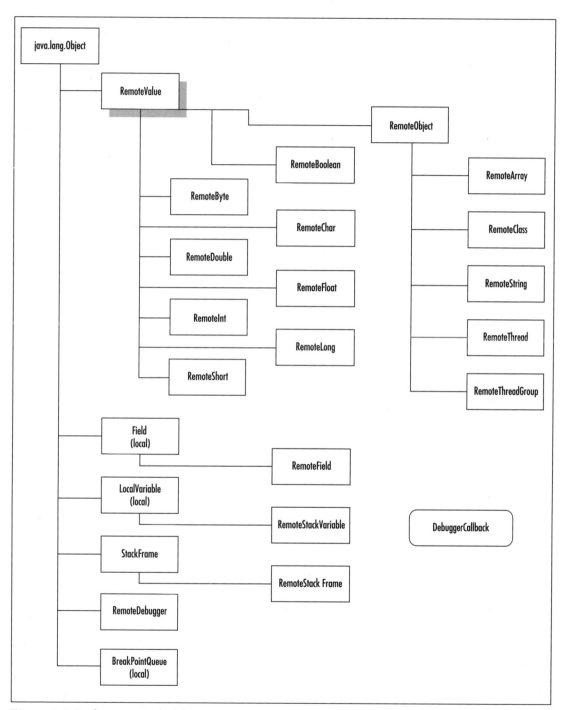

Figure A-9 Package sun.tools.debug

EXCEPTION CROSS-REFERENCE

This appendix provides a cross-reference between exceptions found in the Java Developer's Kit and the classes that *explicitly* declare or are documented to throw such exceptions. Note that the RuntimeException subclasses are somewhat deceiving in terms of this cross-reference. RuntimeException objects do not have to be caught, so it is possible that a method may throw such an exception without explicitly declaring that it does.

Table B-1 lists the exceptions and the packages they belong to. Table B-2 lists the exceptions and the classes or interfaces that throw them. For each exception, a list of the classes/interfaces in which these exceptions are thrown is shown in the table. Because of the special status of runtime exceptions (which can occur anywhere) the tag <Runtime> appears next to subclasses of the RuntimeException class in Table B-2. Note that Error classes do not appear in any of these tables, since they represent unusual conditions that are not meant to be caught.

Table B-1 Exceptions and the packages they belong to

Exception	Package
ArithmeticException	java.lang
ArrayIndexOutOfBoundsException	java.lang
ArrayStoreException	java.lang
AwtException	java.awt
ClassCastException	java.lang
ClassNotFoundException	java.lang
CloneNotSupportedException	java.lang
EmptyStackException	java.util
EOFException	java.io
FileNotFoundException	java.io
IllegalAccessException	java.lang

continued on next page

continued from previous page

IllegalArgumentException	java.lang
IllegalMonitorStateException	java.lang
IllegalThreadStateException	java.lang
IndexOutOfBoundsException	java.lang
InstantiationException	java.lang
InterruptedException	java.lang
InterruptedIOException	java.io
IOException	java.io
MalformedURLException	java.net
NegativeArraySizeException	java.lang
NoSuchElementException	java.util
NoSuchMethodException	java.lang
NullPointerException	java.lang
NumberFormatException	java.lang
ProtocolException	java.net
RuntimeException	java.lang
SecurityException	java.lang
SocketException	java.net
StringIndexOutOfBoundsException	java.lang
UnknownHostException	java.net
UnknownServiceException	java.net
UTFDataFormatException	java.net

Table B-2 Exceptions and the classes/interfaces that throw these exceptions

Exception	Class(es)/Interface(s) that generate(s) this exception
ArithmeticException	<Runtime>, java.lang.Math
ArrayIndexOutOfBoundsException	<Runtime>, java.awt.Container, java.awt.image.IndexColorModel, java.lang.System, java.util.Vector
ArrayStoreException	<Runtime>, java.lang.System,
ClassCastException	<Runtime>
ClassNotFoundException	java.lang.Class, java.lang.ClassLoader
CloneNotSupportedException	java.lang.Object
EmptyStackException	<Runtime>, java.util.Stack
EOFException	java.io.DataInput, java.io.DataInputStream java.io.RandomAccessFile
FileNotFoundException	java.io.FileInputStream, java.io.FileOutputStream
IllegalAccessException	java.lang.Class
IllegalArgumentException	<Runtime>, java.awt.Choice, java.awt.GridLayout, java.awt.Label, java.awtScrollbar, java.lang.Thread, java.util.Date, java.util.Hashtable

Exception	Class(es)/Interface(s) that generate(s) this exception
IllegalMonitorStateException	<Runtime>, java.lang.Object
IllegalThreadStateException	<Runtime>, java.lang.Process, java.lang.Thread, java.lang.ThreadGroup
InstantiationException	java.lang.Class
InterruptedException	java.lang.Object, java.lang.Process, java.lang.Thread
IOException	java.io.BufferedInputStream, java.io.BufferedOutputStream, java.io.ByteArrayOutputStream, java.io.DataInput, java.io.DataInputStream, java.io.DataOutput, java.io.DataOutputStream, java.io.FileInputStream, java.io.FilterInputStream, java.io.FilterOutputStream, java.io.InputStream, java.io.LineNumberInputStream, java.io.OutputStream, java.io.PipedInputStream, java.io.PipedOutputStream, java.io.PrintStream, java.io.PushbackInputStream, java.io.RandomAccessFile, java.io.SequenceInputStream, java.io.StreamTokenizer, java.lang.Runtime, java.net.ContentHandler, java.net.DatagramSocket, java.net.ServerSocket, java.net.Socket, java.net.SocketImpl, java.net.URL, java.net.URLConnection, java.net.URLStreamHandler, java.util.Properties
MalformedURLException	java.net.URL
NegativeArraySizeException	<Runtime>
NoSuchElementException	<Runtime>, java.util.Enumeration, java.util.Hashtable, java.util.StringTokenizer, java.util.Vector
NoSuchMethod	<Runtime>
NullPointerException	<Runtime>, java.awt.Choice, java.io.File, java.lang.ThreadGroup, java.util.Dictionary, java.util.Hashtable
NumberFormatException	<Runtime>, java.lang.Double, java.lang.Float, java.lang.Integer, java.lang.Long
SecurityException	<Runtime>, java.lang.SecurityManager, java.lang.System, java.lang.Thread, java.lang.ThreadGroup
SocketException	java.net.DatagramSocket, java.net.ServerSocket, java.net.Socket
StringIndexOutOfBoundsException	<Runtime>, java.lang.String, java.lang.StringBuffer
UnknownHostException	java.net.InetAddress, java.net.PlainSocketImpl, java.net.Socket, java.net.URL
UnknownServiceException	java.net.URLConnection
UTFDataFormatException	java.io.DataInputStream

APPENDIX C

WRITING NATIVE METHODS IN C/C++

This appendix shows you how to integrate code you have written in other languages, such as C, with Java programs. The steps are illustrated with a working example written in C language.

The Java program you will develop in this appendix is for verifying that a given string is a palindrome (a string that reads the same backward or forward). You will implement a class named Palindrome. It will have a method called findPalindrome(), which is a native method. A C function is written to implement this native method. The details of this native code implementation and integration are discussed step-by-step here.

Writing the Java Code

First you'll create a Java class, named Palindrome, that contains a constructor and two methods, one of which is native. The code (in a file named Palindrome.java) is as follows:

```java
class Palindrome {

    String str;
    public Palindrome(String s) {
        str = s;
    }

    public native boolean findPalindrome(int length);

    public void testNative() {
        boolean b = findPalindrome(str.length());
        if (b)
         System.out.println(" The string " + str + " is a palindrome");
        else
         System.out.println(" The string " + str + " is not a palindrome");
    }

    static {
        System.loadLibrary("palindrome");
    }
}
```

The constructor takes a string argument, which initializes the String member of the class. The method findPalindrome() takes the length of the member string as input and checks to see if the string is a palindrome. This method is the native method in your program. A test driver method, testNative() , calls the native method. It is important to note that the method findPalindrome() is declared as a *public native* method. The keyword *native* communicates to the compiler that the method is defined as a native method. To get the method definition, the static block in the code contains a statement *System.loadLibrary("palindrome");*. The C code that implements the findPalindrome() method has to be compiled and dynamically loaded into the Java program. The dynamic library that you will build is named palindrome. This library is loaded by the call to the System.loadLibrary() method.

Having written the Java code for the Palindrome class, let's write a driver class to instantiate an object of type palindrome and test the methods of the class. This class will be called Main, because the main() is its only method. In the main() method, the Palindrome object is instantiated with the string "malayalam" (a language in the Indian subcontinent), itself a palindrome. Spell it in either direction and verify. Here's the code as it appears in the file named Main.java:

```
class Main {
    public static void main(String args[]) {
        Palindrome p = new Palindrome("malayalam");
        p.testNative();
    }
}
```

Compiling the Java Code

You can now compile the Palindrome.java and Main.java programs using the Java compiler, javac. The result will be two files: Palindrome.class and Main.class.

Generating Headers

To make the Java program effectively "communicate" with the native C code, you need to generate header files and stubs. These header files will contain the necessary definitions and declarations of structures and methods, providing the mapping between Java and C code.

Writing these complicated headers and stubs is tedious, but the *javah* utility provided with the Java Development Kit makes it easier. Run the javah utility on the Palindrome by typing *javah Palindrome*. This will generate the Palindrome.h file shown here:

```
/* DO NOT EDIT THIS FILE - it is machine generated */
#include <native.h>
/* Header for class Palindrome */

#ifndef _Included_Palindrome
#define _Included_Palindrome
struct Hjava_lang_String;
```

```
typedef struct ClassPalindrome {
    struct Hjava_lang_String *str;
} ClassPalindrome;
HandleTo(Palindrome);

extern /*boolean*/ long Palindrome_findPalindrome(struct HPalindrome *,long);
#endif
```

This header file should be included (using *#include*) when you build your native library. It defines a struct ClassPalindrome that contains a struct member of type Hjava_lang_String. The naming convention, as you might have guessed, is package name followed by the class name (each package/class separated by an underscore character). This is the C equivalent to the Palindrome class with a String member. The native method in a Java program is declared extern, in the header, again following the naming convention, package name followed by class name, which is finally followed by the method name. In this case it is the default package, so only the class name and method name are written as the extern C function:

```
extern /*boolean*/ long Palindrome_findPalindrome(struct HPalindrome *,long);
```

You might notice that though you had specified a single parameter of type int in your program, this definition contains your arguments. The first one is the pointer to the class structure itself. It is provided by default, even if there is no argument for the native code method. You can make use of this parameter for accessing the members of the class, in your native C code. The next argument is the C equivalent for your Java argument type. In this case, for the int type specified in the Java program, it has generated the type as long in C. Also the return type is changed from boolean to the type long in C. The main detail you should be concerned about here is that the extern declaration is the C function signature that binds Java and C. So the C function you will write should adhere to this signature.

Writing the C Code

Now comes the task of writing the C code for the native method. You can write it in any file you want. In this case, the file is named myPalindrome.c. Here is the code listing:

```
#include <StubPreamble.h>
#include <java_lang_String.h>
#include "Palindrome.h"
#include <stdio.h>

long Palindrome_findPalindrome(struct HPalindrome *this, long length) {

    char buffer1[256], buffer2[256];
    int i;
    long yes=1;

    javaString2CString(unhand(this)->str, buffer1, sizeof(buffer1));

    buffer2[length]='\0';
```

continued on next page

continued from previous page

```
for (i=0; i <length; i++) {
  buffer2[length-i-1] = buffer1[i];
}

for (i=0; i<length; i++) {
  if (buffer1[i] != buffer2[i]) {
    yes=0;
    break;
  }
}

return yes;

}
```

As you can see, there are four header files included in this code. The file StubPreamble.h is included in every native code you write. It provides the details the C code needs to interact with the Java runtime. The java_lang_String.h header is included in this example because String is used in the Java program (again, note the naming convention). Palindrome.h is the header file generated using the javah utility.

When you write native methods, to work with Java classes you get a reference to the class as a structure. This reference is the first parameter in the C stub generated for any native method, and the variable is named *this*. You can access the values of the members of the class by using the variable *this*. In the above code, *struct HPalindrome *this* is the first parameter for the native method call. It is passed as C construct, in this case struct HPalindrome. You can dereference the structure and then use the reference to the members. Here, to access the String variable named *str*, you can use *unhand(this)->str* and thus obtain a handle to the string member. Note that Java treats strings differently from C. So converting the Java string (which is an object) to a C string (which is an array of characters) is made possible by the use of the library method provided in the Java Developer's Kit (JDK) environment, namely, javaString2CString(string-member-reference, local-string-variable, string-length). In the example listing, the string member is copied into a local variable (*buffer1*, a character array). Then after reversing the string, it is compared against the original character array. The result of the comparison, which is stored in the variable *yes* is returned by the method.

Generating Stubs

You generate the stubs file for the Java program using the javah utility, which contains the information needed to bind the Java class and its equivalent C structure together. Run the javah utility with the *-stubs* option. So when you execute *javah -stubs Palindrome*, it generates a file named Palindrome.c as shown here:

```
/* DO NOT EDIT THIS FILE - it is machine generated */
#include <StubPreamble.h>

/* Stubs for class Palindrome */
/* SYMBOL: "Palindrome/findPalindrome(I)Z", Java_Palindrome_findPalindrome_stub */
stack_item *Java_Palindrome_findPalindrome_stub
```

```
(stack_item *_P_,struct execenv *_EE_) {
    extern long Palindrome_findPalindrome(void *,long);
    _P_[0].i = (Palindrome_findPalindrome(_P_[0].p,((_P_[1].i))) ? TRUE : FALSE);
    return _P_ + 1;
}
```

By default, this file is placed in the directory from which you execute the javah command. Use the -d option if you want to place it in another directory.

Creating the Dynamically Loadable Library

Now two C files are available. One is the stub-generated Palindrome.c. Compile the C file without linking. So when the command *cc -c -o Palindrome.o Palindrome.c* is executed, the object file Palindrome.o is created. Similarly create the object file for myPalindrome.c by executing the command *cc -c -o myPalindrome.o myPalindrome.c*.

You might have to include the directories in which the files you have included (such as StubPreamble.h) exist. So when you compile the above C files, use the -I option (in Solaris) to the C compiler to include the path to find the required header files to be included (in the JDK package, these files are in the directory named "include" under the root directory of JDK). For example, in case the machine in which you are compiling is a Solaris host, and if the JDK is installed in a directory /home, then you must give the command

```
cc -c -I /home/jdk/include -I /home/jdk/include/solaris -o myPalindrome.o myPalindrome.c
```

Having generated the two object files, you're ready to create a dynamically loadable library. Remember that you have declared the library name to be palindrome in your Java program. On a UNIX system this library file will be named libpalindrome.so, and in an NT-based system it will be named palindrome.dll. On a UNIX system, you can create the library using the *ld* command. The command that you issue for UNIX system is similar to

```
ld -G Palindrome.o myPalindrome.o -o libpalindrome.so
```

whereas in NT you might issue a command similar to

```
ld -G Palindrome.o myPalindrome.o -o palindrome.dll
```

Having created the library file needed, the last step is to execute the Java program using the Java interpreter.

Executing the Java Program

You have now generated the dynamically loadable library "palindrome" required in Palindrome.java. To execute this method, run the main() method inside the Main class that you have implemented as a driver code to test your Palindrome program. Using the Java interpreter, execute the Main.class file by issuing the following command at the shell prompt:

```
java Main
```

It will print the message, "The string malayalam is a palindrome." Try changing the word that is passed as parameter to the Palindrome class initialization. You should make the changes inside the Main.java file. Of course, you can also change the program such that the string can be given as a command line argument.

In this appendix, you have been introduced to the steps involved in integrating native code written in C/C++ with Java. By integrating existing applications written in C/C++ with Java, it is fairly easy to make those applications Web based. You can now exploit this capability to integrate code written in other languages. In this limited space, only the basics of native code integration have been covered. If you need more information, see Waite Group Press's *Java Primer Plus* by Paul Tyma, Gabriel Torok, and Troy Downing. Have fun!

APPENDIX D

GLOSSARY

abstract class: A class that has one or more methods that are not implemented. It is typically used as the superclass for one or more inheriting classes.

Applet: A Java component that can be dynamically loaded into World Wide Web (WWW) pages by Java-aware WWW browsers. Similar in concept to an X-Windows widget, or a Windows custom control (VBX, OCX, or ActiveX Control).

application: A Java program that can be run without the help of a browser.

AWT: The Abstract Windowing Toolkit (AWT) is a set of classes that abstract windowed operating systems such as X-Windows, Macintosh System 7, and Microsoft Windows. The characteristics common to all of these windowing systems have been included in the java.awt package. Through the objects and methods of the classes in the java.awt package you can create windowed user interfaces to your applications and applets.

boolean: A primitive Java type that can have the values of true or false.

browser: An application that can display HTML pages from the World Wide Web. A Java-aware browser that can display applets is called an "applet browser." For example, Netscape's Navigator 2.0 and Microsoft's Internet Explorer 3.0 are both capable applet browsers.

byte: A primitive Java type that represents the smallest range of numbers (-255 to 255).

byte code: Java's platform independent way of specifying virtual machine instructions.

catch: A keyword used in handling exceptions, which specifies what types of exceptions are handled by a particular block.

char: A primitive Java type for storing characters.

class: A definition of data (variables) and/or operations (methods).

class loader: Defines a series of policies that define how a class is loaded into the run-time environment. Maintains and separates a different namespace for classes loaded from different systems. For example, the local file system has the highest priority namespace. Classes loaded from a remote system cannot override a class loaded from the local system.

class member: A variable or method of a class.

compiler: A program that converts Java language into Java byte code.

component: The element of an array.

concatenation: The joining of two strings.

constructor: A method that creates an instance of a given class.

DataInputStream: A Java class that provides methods to read primitive Java language data types.

DebuggerCallback: An interface that is used as a callback communication mechanism between the debugger and its client, so that the client is called whenever specific events occur.

double: A Java primitive for floating-point numbers that has more precision and range than a Java float.

Exception: A class or subclass of Throwable that is instantiated when a particular type of error occurs at runtime.

exception handler: A series of statements, built out of *try-catch-finally* (the last is optional) clauses, written to handle any exception objects that may be thrown.

File: A Java class that encapsulates file properties like path name, access permissions, etc.

FileNameFilter: A Java interface, whose implementers are responsible for filtering out file names.

final: A Java keyword indicating that a method can't be overridden, or that a variable's value can't be changed.

float: A Java primitive representing floating-point numbers.

garbage collection: A low-priority thread that removes any unreferenced objects from memory. This frees the programmer from having to worry about explicitly removing (deleting) objects from memory, hence making the Java runtime environment more reliable.

hash code: An integer code used for indexing into a collection of items.

HotJava: Sun's World Wide Web browser written entirely in the Java programming language.

HTTP: HyperText Transfer Protocol, the protocol by which HTML is transported across the World Wide Web.

implements: A Java keyword indicating that a class supports the methods of a particular interface.

import: Java allows classes to be collected into packages; a particular package can be imported in order to use abbreviated class names.

inheritance: A characteristic of object-oriented systems, in which a class acquires some or all of the behavior of another class.

instance: A particular occurrence of a class.

instantiate: The creation of an object.

int: A Java primitive for storing integer values.

interface: A definition (but not implementation) of methods and/or variables, which classes may elect to implement.

Java interpreter: Java virtual machine upon which the byte codes are interpreted.

javadoc: A program in the JDK that generates HTML documentation from source code.

javah: A program in the JDK used for generating C header files to be used in conjunction with native methods.

JDK: The Java Developer's Kit, a collection of Java tools for building, running, debugging, and documenting Java applications and applets.

long: The largest Java primitive for storing integers.

main() method: A required method for a Java application, which unlike C and C++, is contained in a class.

method: A function defined as part of a class.

multithreading: The capability to have a program executing more than one thread of execution at a time.

NaN: "Not a Number," a special value that results from invalid numerical operations.

native method: A Java class method declared with the *native* keyword. Native method implementations are written as platform specific, dynamically loadable libraries.

native resources: Any system resource allocated by native methods. For example, if a native method allocates memory, this memory is considered a "native resource."

null: A special value indicating that a reference type (object or array) does not refer to anything.

Oak: The original name given to the Java programming language.

object: An instance of a class.

Object: The class that all other Java classes extend, directly or indirectly.

overloading: The feature allowing a single method name within a class to have several variations distinguished by different signatures.

overriding: The redefinition of a method by a subclass.

package: A collection of Java classes.

parent class: A class that provides behavior to classes that extend it.

PipedInputStream: A Java class that implements the input half of a first-in first-out (FIFO) file.

PipedOutputStream: A Java class that implements the output half of a first-in first-out (FIFO) file.

primitive type: A Java type that is not a class or array, such as int and float.

radian: A way to measure angles, using the numeric constant pi for 180 degrees.

random number: A number generated by a pseudo-random method, often used for simulations or games.

RandomAccessFile: A Java class that allows both reading and writing to be performed on a file in a nonsequential manner.

reference type: Any class or array, so named because variables of these types refer to memory containing the data.

remote agent: The part of the Java interpreter that communicates with an instance of the class RemoteDebugger.

remote debugger: This class initiates a connection to a Java agent and retrieves information regarding the Java program executing on the Java interpreter.

remote debugging client: A program that contains an instance of the class RemoteDebugger.

RemoteValue: A data type sent by the remote agent whenever a command requesting a variable is received.

SecurityManager: Defines a set of policies for protecting the runtime environment of the client from potentially dangerous actions carried out by objects. Such problematic activities include reading and writing to the hard disk, and unauthorized network activity.

set-top box: A system that turns a home television set into an interactive device. Similar to, but more powerful than, the current generation of cable television boxes, a set-top box provides the user with access to services such as on-demand television programming, online shopping, and even the Internet.

short: A Java primitive for representing small integer values.

signature: The ordered list of types of a method's parameters.

static method: A method that is not associated with any particular class instance.

static variable: A variable of which there is one per class.

String: A class for representing an immutable sequence of characters. Java does not follow C's convention of using a null-terminated array of characters.

StringBuffer: The class representing a mutable (changeable) sequence of characters.

subclass: A class that extends another class.

super: A special variable that refers to the superclass's instance for the current object.

superclass: The class that a subclass extends.

synchronized: A modifier that is used to lock an object so that only one thread may execute synchronized code at a single point in time. This is used to ensure that an object worked upon by concurrent threads will function reliably.

this: A special variable that refers to the current instance of an object.

thread: A single sequential flow of execution within a process. A process consists of one or more threads.

thread group: Construct that contains multiple threads and thread groups. A thread group action, such as stopping a thread, may be iteratively applied to all items in a thread group.

throw: The keyword that allows program flow to be interrupted in the event of an exceptional condition.

try block: A set of statements that have an associated set of *catch* blocks for handling exceptions.

Unicode: A multilingual, 16-bit standard for representing characters.

URL: URL stands for Uniform Resource Locator. It is a structured address that uniquely identifies a resource (e.g., document or image) on the World Wide Web.

verifier: Inspects code as it is loaded into the Java environment to ensure that the code meets a set of properties that guarantee a certain degree of security as an object is executed in the runtime environment.

World Wide Web: The name given to a loose collection of servers and clients (or browsers) whose preferred method of communication is via the underlying Internet. Servers that understand HTTP (HyperText Transfer Protocol) serve up HTML (HyperText Markup Language) documents to browsers across the Web.

APPENDIX E

USING THE ENCLOSED CD-ROM

The CD-ROM enclosed in this book contains Java code that is in the preceding chapters, as well as additional information and tools. This appendix gives you an overview of what is on the CD, and how its directories are arranged. Instructions for installing the files are found in the About the CD-ROM section in the front of the book.

The files in the CD-ROM fall into these groups:

■ Source code for the projects given in each chapter

■ Listings taken from each chapter's narrative and reference sections

■ The Java Developer's Kit (JDK) tools from Sun Microsystems, including versions for Solaris (Sparc), 32-bit Windows (95 and NT), and Macintosh

■ Selected chapters from the *Java Networking and AWT API SuperBible*, in Acrobat format

■ An acrobat reader for viewing the extra chapters

Organization

The files are organized along the categories described above. The directory structure is illustrated in Figure E-1. Directories with names like chapX (X is from 1 to 14) contain the Java code from the respective chapter. Each chapter is further subdivided into the subdirectories: examples, listings, and project. The "examples" directory contains the longer examples from the chapter's reference section. These are named with the class and method, plus an extension of .java if it can be compiled, or .txt if not. The "listing" directory contains the longer listings from the chapter's text. Not all chapters have a listings or examples subdirectory. The "project" directory contains the files that comprise the chapter's project.

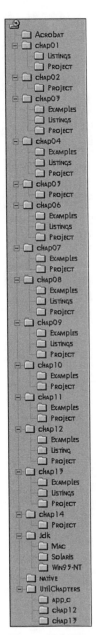

Figure E-1 Directory structure on the CD-ROM

The directory named "Native" contains code from Appendix C, which details calling non-Java functions from a Java program.

The UtilChapters directory contains two chapters from this book's companion volume, *Java Networking and AWT API SuperBible*. These chapters provide reference information on the Java utility package classes. Chapter 12 is Data Structures and Random Number Generation, and Chapter 13 is Date and Advanced Classes. These chapters are in Acrobat format; to view them, you must have an acrobat reader. One is provided in the CD directory called Acrobat.

Sun Microsystems, Inc., provides the JDK for compiling and running Java programs (including the project code from this book). These are available for Solaris (Sparc), Windows 95, Windows NT, and Macintosh. These JDK tools are provided to save you the trouble of downloading them, if you haven't already done so. They are under the subdirectory JDK, which is partitioned by platform into Solaris, Win95-NT, and Mac subdirectories.

The files and tools provided on the CD are intended to help get you up and running quickly with Java. So drink up!

INDEX

Q-R

W-Z

Books have a substantial influence on the destruction of the forests of the Earth. For example, it takes 17 trees to produce one ton of paper. A first printing of 30,000 copies of a typical 480-page book consumes 108,000 pounds of paper, which will require 918 trees!

Waite Group Press™ is against the clear-cutting of forests and supports reforestation of the Pacific Northwest of the United States and Canada, where most of this paper comes from. As a publisher with several hundred thousand books sold each year, we feel an obligation to give back to the planet. We will therefore support organizations that seek to preserve the forests of planet Earth.

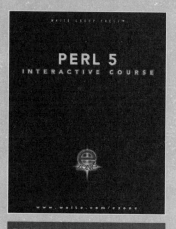

This is a legal agreement between you, the end user and purchaser, and The Waite Group®, Inc., and the authors of the programs contained in the disk. By opening the sealed disk package, you are agreeing to be bound by the terms of this Agreement. If you do not agree with the terms of this Agreement, promptly return the unopened disk package and the accompanying items (including the related book and other written material) to the place you obtained them for a refund.

SOFTWARE LICENSE

1. The Waite Group, Inc. grants you the right to use one copy of the enclosed software programs (the programs) on a single computer system (whether a single CPU, part of a licensed network, or a terminal connected to a single CPU). Each concurrent user of the program must have exclusive use of the related Waite Group, Inc. written materials.

2. The program, including the copyrights in each program, is owned by the respective author and the copyright in the entire work is owned by The Waite Group, Inc. and they are therefore protected under the copyright laws of the United States and other nations, under international treaties. You may make only one copy of the disk containing the programs exclusively for backup or archival purposes, or you may transfer the programs to one hard disk drive, using the original for backup or archival purposes. You may make no other copies of the programs, and you may make no copies of all or any part of the related Waite Group, Inc. written materials.

3. You may not rent or lease the programs, but you may transfer ownership of the programs and related written materials (including any and all updates and earlier versions) if you keep no copies of either, and if you make sure the transferee agrees to the terms of this license.

4. You may not decompile, reverse engineer, disassemble, copy, create a derivative work, or otherwise use the programs except as stated in this Agreement.

GOVERNING LAW

This Agreement is governed by the laws of the State of California.

LIMITED WARRANTY

The following warranties shall be effective for 90 days from the date of purchase: (i) The Waite Group, Inc. warrants the enclosed disk to be free of defects in materials and workmanship under normal use; and (ii) The Waite Group, Inc. warrants that the programs, unless modified by the purchaser, will substantially perform the functions described in the documentation provided by The Waite Group, Inc. when operated on the designated hardware and operating system. The Waite Group, Inc. does not warrant that the programs will meet purchaser's requirements or that operation of a program will be uninterrupted or error-free. The program warranty does not cover any program that has been altered or changed in any way by anyone other than The Waite Group, Inc. The Waite Group, Inc. is not responsible for problems caused by changes in the operating characteristics of computer hardware or computer operating systems that are made after the release of the programs, nor for problems in the interaction of the programs with each other or other software.

THESE WARRANTIES ARE EXCLUSIVE AND IN LIEU OF ALL OTHER WARRANTIES OF MERCHANTABILITY OR FITNESS FOR A PARTICULAR PURPOSE OR OF ANY OTHER WARRANTY, WHETHER EXPRESS OR IMPLIED.

EXCLUSIVE REMEDY

The Waite Group, Inc. will replace any defective disk without charge if the defective disk is returned to The Waite Group, Inc. within 90 days from date of purchase.

This is Purchaser's sole and exclusive remedy for any breach of warranty or claim for contract, tort, or damages.

LIMITATION OF LIABILITY

THE WAITE GROUP, INC. AND THE AUTHORS OF THE PROGRAMS SHALL NOT IN ANY CASE BE LIABLE FOR SPECIAL, INCIDENTAL, CONSEQUENTIAL, INDIRECT, OR OTHER SIMILAR DAMAGES ARISING FROM ANY BREACH OF THESE WARRANTIES EVEN IF THE WAITE GROUP, INC. OR ITS AGENT HAS BEEN ADVISED OF THE POSSIBILITY OF SUCH DAMAGES.

THE LIABILITY FOR DAMAGES OF THE WAITE GROUP, INC. AND THE AUTHORS OF THE PROGRAMS UNDER THIS AGREEMENT SHALL IN NO EVENT EXCEED THE PURCHASE PRICE PAID.

COMPLETE AGREEMENT

This Agreement constitutes the complete agreement between The Waite Group, Inc. and the authors of the programs, and you, the purchaser.

Some states do not allow the exclusion or limitation of implied warranties or liability for incidental or consequential damages, so the above exclusions or limitations may not apply to you. This limited warranty gives you specific legal rights; you may have others, which vary from state to state.

SATISFACTION REPORT CARD

Please fill out this card if you wish to know of future updates to *Java Language API SuperBible*, or to receive our catalog.

First Name: _____ **Last Name:** _____

Street Address: _____

City: _____ **State:** _____ **Zip:** _____

E-mail Address _____

Daytime Telephone: (   ) _____

Date product was acquired: Month _____ **Day** _____ **Year** _____ **Your Occupation:** _____

Overall, how would you rate *Java Language API SuperBible*?

☐ Excellent ☐ Very Good ☐ Good
☐ Fair ☐ Below Average ☐ Poor

What did you like MOST about this book? _____

_____

_____

What did you like LEAST about this book? _____

_____

_____

Please describe any problems you may have encountered with installing or using the disk: _____

_____

How did you use this book (problem-solver, tutorial, reference...)?

_____

What is your level of computer expertise?

☐ New ☐ Dabbler ☐ Hacker
☐ Power User ☐ Programmer ☐ Experienced Professional

What computer languages are you familiar with? _____

_____

Please describe your computer hardware:

Computer _____ Hard disk _____

5.25" disk drives _____ 3.5" disk drives _____

Video card _____ Monitor _____

Printer _____ Peripherals _____

Sound Board _____ CD ROM _____

Where did you buy this book?

☐ Bookstore (name): _____
☐ Discount store (name): _____
☐ Computer store (name): _____
☐ Catalog (name): _____
☐ Direct from WGP ☐ Other _____

What price did you pay for this book? _____

What influenced your purchase of this book?

☐ Recommendation ☐ Advertisement
☐ Magazine review ☐ Store display
☐ Mailing ☐ Book's format
☐ Reputation of Waite Group Press ☐ Other

How many computer books do you buy each year? _____

How many other Waite Group books do you own? _____

What is your favorite Waite Group book? _____

_____

Is there any program or subject you would like to see Waite Group Press cover in a similar approach? _____

_____

Additional comments? _____

_____

_____

Please send to: **Waite Group Press**
200 Tamal Plaza
Corte Madera, CA 94925

☐ **Check here for a free Waite Group catalog**

DATE DUE

AUG 4 1998		
8/24/98		
MAY 2 0 2001		
JUN 2 8 2000		
JUL 3 1 2000		
NOV 1 6 2000		
MAR 1 3 2001		
8-30-01		
APR 2 5 2005		
12/4/14 KR		
3/16/17 EL		

HIGHSMITH 45-220

STOP!

BEFORE YOU OPEN THE DISK OR CD-ROM PACKAGE ON THE FACING PAGE, CAREFULLY READ THE LICENSE AGREEMENT.

Opening this package indicates that you agree to abide by the license agreement found in the back of this book. If you do not agree with it, promptly return the unopened disk package (including the related book) to the place you obtained them for a refund.